CATALOGUE

OF THE

MERCANTILE LIBRARY

OF

BOSTON.

BOSTON:

PRINTED BY JOHN WILSON AND SON,

22, School Street.

1854.

Commonwealth of Massachusetts.

IN THE YEAR ONE THOUSAND EIGHT HUNDRED AND FORTY-FIVE.

AN ACT TO INCORPORATE THE MERCANTILE LIBRARY ASSOCIATION.

Be it enacted by the Senate and House of Representatives in General Court assembled, and by the authority of the same, as follows:

SECT. 1. — Alexander L. Stimson, Nathaniel B. Kemp, Elliot C. Cowdin, M. A. Herrick, Alonzo C. Haskell, G. Francis Thayer, their associates and successors, are hereby made a Corporation, by the name of the MERCANTILE LIBRARY ASSOCIATION, OF BOSTON, for the purpose of diffusing and promoting knowledge among young men now engaged in, or destined for, the mercantile profession, with all the powers and privileges, and subject to all the duties, restrictions, and liabilities set forth in the forty-fourth chapter of the Revised Statutes.

SECT. 2. — The said Corporation may hold real and personal estate, to be used for the purposes aforesaid, not exceeding in all the value of fifty thousand dollars, the legal title of which shall be in five Trustees, to be appointed by a majority of the members of the Corporation; and all of the said Trustees shall be of adult age, but subject, in the care and management and disposal thereof, to the control and direction of a majority of a Joint Board, consisting of the said Trustees and of the Board of Directors for the time being, which Board of Directors shall not consist of more than thirteen members.

SECT. 3. — Persons engaged in mercantile pursuits, or preparing themselves therefor, and above the age of fourteen years, shall be eligible as members of the Corporation, and entitled to vote and act as officers thereof; excepting that no person under twenty-one years of age shall be a Trustee.

Passed to be enacted. House of Representatives, March 17, 1845.
SAMUEL H. WALLEY, JUN., *Speaker.*

Passed to be enacted. In Senate, March 17, 1845.
LEVI LINCOLN, *President.*

March 18, 1845. Approved:
GEO. N. BRIGGS.

A true copy. March 19, 1845.
Attest: JOHN G. PALFREY,
Secretary of the Commonwealth.

OFFICERS

OF THE

MERCANTILE LIBRARY ASSOCIATION,

1854–55.

SEYMOUR LYMAN	PRESIDENT.
AUGUSTUS HAMMOND	VICE-PRESIDENT.
JOHN B. NORRIS	CORRESPONDING SECRETARY.
EDWIN J. SWETT	RECORDING SECRETARY.
JACOB H. BROWN	TREASURER.
WILLIAM F. POOLE	LIBRARIAN.

Directors.

NATHANIEL APPLETON.
HORACE A. WHITE.
A. G. WYMAN, JUN.
JAMES D. WYMAN.
WARREN F. GILBERT.
GEORGE NOYES.
WM. H. WITHINGTON.
WM. J. SEAVER, JUN.

Trustees.

CHARLES G. CHASE.
JOHN STETSON.
CHARLES H. ALLEN.
GEORGE S. BLANCHARD.
JAMES A. WOOLSON.

PREFACE.

SINCE 1848, the date of our last printed Catalogue, the Library has increased from six thousand to sixteen thousand volumes; and, although a hastily prepared Supplement was printed in 1851, the titles of nearly six thousand volumes, the latest and most valuable additions to the Library, were not to be found on any printed Catalogue. For more than a year, the Catalogue of 1848 has been out of print; and, for several months, the entire edition of the Supplement of 1851 has been exhausted. Hence the preparation of a new and complete Catalogue seemed to be an imperative necessity; and this measure was strongly recommended in the Annual Report of the last Board of Government.

At the monthly meeting of the present Board of Government in April last, a Committee was appointed with full powers to make the necessary arrangements for the preparation and printing of a new Catalogue. A plan proposed to the Committee by the Librarian was accepted, and to him was committed its execution.

The plan of the work will be best understood by an examination of the Catalogue itself. It will be seen that short titles have been adopted; that each work has been catalogued under its *author* and under its *subject*, and works of fiction have been placed under their *titles* as well as authors. The whole being arranged in one alphabetical series, a work can be easily found, if either its author, subject, or title is known.

Whatever advantages other systems of cataloguing may have in particular instances, no other system appears to combine so many advantages for a popular circulating library like ours.

The titles of such works as have been added to the Library since the printing of the Catalogue was commenced, and too late to admit of their appearing in the alphabetical series, have been placed in the ADDENDA.

MERCANTILE LIBRARY ROOMS,
BOSTON, Nov. 1854.

HISTORICAL SKETCH.

The Mercantile Library Association originated at a meeting of merchants' clerks, and others, held at the Commercial Coffee House, corner of Batterymarch and Milk Streets, March 11, 1820. The meeting was numerously attended; and Mr. Theodore Lyman, jun. (afterwards mayor of Boston), was called upon to preside.

The better intellectual and moral condition of young men engaged as merchants' clerks, was the object which had called together these persons; and for this end a Committee, consisting of Messrs. John G. Gibson, Samuel A. Otis, Nathl. A. Barrett, Thomas Gorham, James T. Blanchard, Lynde M. Walter, Charles J. Johnson, Edward Codman, Henry A. Davis, and Samuel W. Pomeroy, jun., was appointed who subsequently reported a list of Rules and Regulations for an Institution to be named the Mercantile Library.* The government was vested in a Board of seven Directors, a Secretary, and a Treasurer.

The original Rules required that "one of the Directors should be in the employment of a dry-goods' merchant;" and, at a later date, a vote authorizing the appointment of a Committee was passed with a similar proviso.

The terms of subscription were two dollars annually; and each subscriber, on becoming such, was required to present to the Library "one or more volumes, either in biography, history, voyages, travels,

* This name was retained until the adoption of a new Constitution in 1830.

or works relative to mercantile subjects;" a condition which was afterwards abolished, the books given being generally of a worthless character.

A room was soon after procured in Merchants' Hall, corner of Congress and Water Streets, where, on the 24th of April following, the Library was formally opened.

Active exertions were now made to increase its available resources; and, before the close of a year, two hundred and twenty members were enrolled, many of the leading newspapers and magazines of the day were received, and the library numbered eleven hundred volumes.

But these flattering prospects were of short duration. The history of the Institution for the next fifteen years is, with but few exceptions, a history of uninterrupted reverses.

A Report, made in 1829, stated that there were then but eighty-one members; that the funds were exhausted, and there were many unsettled demands. The Investigating Committee also stated that the financial aspect of the Treasurer's Report seemed "an emphatic earnest of a process of ejectment, and a writ of attachment on books and chattels." The following year, owing in part to donations of money from its friends among the merchants, but chiefly to an arrangement which had been entered into with the Society for the Diffusion of Useful Knowledge, whereby the members were privileged to attend the lectures of that society at one-half the usual price, affairs wore a more cheerful aspect, and the Directors reported the Association out of debt, and with two hundred and thirty members.

During the next two years, however, the number of members fell off slightly; and, in 1832, but one hundred and seventy retained their membership. Again, in 1834, there occurred a critical era; for, during that year, the number of subscribers had diminished to eighty-eight, and so small was the income that only $20 had been appropriated during the year for the purchase of books.

Truly, this was an unpromising state of affairs; but even more disheartening reports than these were yet to be submitted. In September of the same year, a Committee, appointed to investigate the affairs of the Institution, reported that the whole number of members was but seventy-six; and they presented an estimated statement of the finances, by which it appeared that there would be a deficit, on the first of October, 1835, of $246.

Yet, during this period, the Institution was not wholly without assistance. Shortly after its formation, Messrs. Theodore Lyman, jun., Charles Williams, Israel Thorndike, Peter C. Brooks, and Andrew Brimmer, contributed to it $160; later in the year, Mr. Wm. Sturgis gave $30; and, in 1826, a period when but for timely pecuniary assistance the Institution must have been dissolved, about $400 were, upon the earnest solicitation of a Committee, subscribed, and added to the treasury. This sum, procured through the exertions of three active members, was given by "seventy-seven prominent individuals and firms, and in no one case exceeded the sum of $10."

In 1832, an Address to the merchants of Boston for a second time was prepared and published, setting forth the objects of the Institution, its then reduced circumstances, and soliciting aid. As the result of this measure, small sums were given to the amount of about $150, though by far the most important was the generous donation of Mr. Amos Lawrence, from whom the Directors received, in June, a friendly letter enclosing $100.

Encouraged by Mr. Lawrence's kindness, the Directors addressed him a lengthy letter of thanks in reply, in which they complained that the Society had suffered great neglect from the mercantile community. They stated, that, on the opening of their new Rooms, at No. 93, Washington Street (whither they had removed in December previous), invitations, personal and through the newspapers, were extended to the merchants to visit them on three evenings set apart for the purpose, but not a merchant appeared.

Mr. Lawrence soon afterwards presented to the Library thirty-nine volumes of valuable works, one of which, "Chalmers's Discourses on Christianity applied to the Commercial and Ordinary Affairs of Life," he especially recommended.

Nor does the Association seem to have been without its drawbacks and annoyances from the members themselves. Instances were not of unfrequent occurrence where resolutions of censure upon individual members were read, adopted, and placed upon the Records; and, in many cases, fines of small amount imposed. A case occurred in January, 1832, where two members were fined one dollar each for "improper conduct in the Library-Room, dishonorable to the Institution, and in violation of its By-Laws," which were afterwards reduced to twenty-five cents; "order, and not money," the minutes of the meeting say, "being the object of the fine." Indeed, these frequent fines formed no inconsiderable part of the income.

In 1831, the number of Directors was increased to thirteen;* and, in 1834, the office of President was created. A Vice-President was first chosen in 1835, and a Corresponding Secretary in 1844.

In October, 1833, the Association removed to 53, Washington Street; where, in 1836, the calamity of fire did great damage to the books and other property. Fortunately, however, insurance was recovered to the amount of $800; which sum was immediately applied to the replenishing of the Library. A removal was soon after made to more convenient rooms in Harding's Building, School Street.

But the leading members, in these dark days, were zealous, efficient, and self-sacrificing. They signed pledges binding themselves to procure new members, or, from their own resources, pay into the treasury the amount of subscription; they made loans to the Association; they subscribed money for books; they made personal application for aid; and they not unfrequently made donations themselves.

Where so many have labored, it were difficult certainly, and perhaps invidious, to particularize; yet Sampson and McCandish — both of whom have died beloved and respected — and Coates and Stearns and Atkins and Mather and Whipple and Cowdin and Haskell and Allen are names so inseparably connected with the very existence of the Society, that no historical account of it can be complete without them.

In the year 1835, the affairs of the Institution assumed a more favorable aspect. The establishment of the nucleus of a reserved fund in July of that year, and the introduction of the weekly Literary Exercises in 1836, seem to have infused into it new life and spirit.

* By the present Constitution, the number is eight.

The fund was started by a subscription from the Hon. Abbott Lawrence of $100, and amounted to $676. Small additions were made to it from year to year until 1845, when, immediately following the Act of Incorporation, Hon. Thomas H. Perkins made the Association the handsome donation of five shares in the Merchants' Exchange Company, equal to $2,500; and, in January following, Messrs. Abbott Lawrence, William Sturgis, Nathan Appleton, John Bryant, William Appleton, Amos Lawrence, John P. Cushing, and Samuel Appleton, gave $1,000 each, to be applied, at some future period, to the erection of a suitable building. These sums, together with other donations made at different times, and the excess of receipts over expenses, have been added to the fund, and the Association now holds certificates of stock to the amount of about $20,000.

The subject of connecting Literary Exercises with the Institution was first brought forward in October, 1830; but they were not permanently established until January, 1836. It was proposed, when the matter was first agitated, to set apart the second and fourth Wednesdays of each month for this purpose; but the subject met with little favor. Many regarded them as an innovation upon the objects of the Library, and urged that if undertaken they would not succeed. In 1836, however, their foundation was laid by the embodiment into the Constitution of provisions for an Elocution Class. Such a class had been formed some time previous as a distinct organization; and, at its weekly meetings during the winter months, questions were discussed, original compositions read, and selections recited for improvement in declamation. Occasionally, the exercises were varied by the delivery, by some one of the members, of a written lecture. In the next year, they took the general form, which is embodied in the present By-Laws, consisting alternately of debate, composition, and declamation.

Whatever may have been the misgivings of our predecessors a generation ago, the weight of evidence now proves conclusively, that no more judicious variation from the original plan has ever been adopted; and the Literary Exercises are justly regarded as a most interesting and valuable means of improvement.

In August, 1835, a Committee was appointed to inquire into the expediency of celebrating the Fifteenth Anniversary by an Address and a supper. They subsequently reported, that they deemed it expedient and proper that an Address should be delivered, but discountenanced the supper. One of their resolutions cannot but be commended for its good sense, and just views of the objects of the Institution: "Resolved, That to celebrate our annual meetings by public entertainments is contrary to the intention of the founders of the Association, and, aside from the bad effects which it may have on its individual members, — and more especially the younger portion, — will strike a blow on its future prosperity in the minds of the mercantile community (to whose assistance we look in hours of adversity), from which it may never recover." The recommendations of the Committee were approved of; but no member could be found willing to deliver the Address. The next year, however, Mr. G. W. Tyler, an honorary member, delivered an Address; and the Anniversaries have since been regularly celebrated.

They have often been occasions of much interest. That in 1838 — when the Hon. Edward Everett, then Governor of Massachusetts, delivered a felicitous and appropriate Address; and Mr. James T. Fields, then an active and prominent member, a spirited Poem — was particularly brilliant. It was celebrated in the Odeon, which was filled with an intelligent and fashionable audience, the members occupying the body of the house.

Among the distinguished orators who have at different times delivered these Anniversary Addresses, are Hon. Daniel Webster, Hon. Robert C. Winthrop, Hon. Rufus Choate, Hon. Geo. S. Hillard, Hon. Horace Mann, and others of eminence in letters and statesmanship; while the wit and pathos of Holmes and Saxe and Fields have never shone more brilliantly than as poets before the Mercantile Library Association.

In 1835, also, the practicability of establishing a course of public lectures was first discussed, but decided to be inexpedient. In 1838, an arrangement was entered into with J. Silk Buckingham, Esq., of England, to deliver a course of eight Lectures on Egypt.

These proved quite successful, and were the means of adding one hundred and twenty-four new members; though, as Lectures, they were of no pecuniary income to the Association. In 1843, the present plan was adopted; and, in October of the same year, a course was delivered at the Odeon, which resulted in a profit of $325.83. The Annual Report of the Directors, prepared by Mr. Elliott C. Cowdin, the chief originator of the scheme, stated that "the enterprise had succeeded beyond the expectation of its most zealous advocates." These courses of Lectures have been continued from year to year, and have conduced, in an eminent degree, to the prosperity of the Institution. In 1851, their popularity had so increased, the number of members being about twenty-two hundred, that it was found necessary to establish a second course; an expedient which met with success, and has since been continued.

In September, 1841, a fourth removal was made, — this time to the Amory Hall Building, corner of West and Washington Streets; and in January, 1848, the Rooms at present occupied were dedicated. On both these occasions, an Address was delivered by Mr. Daniel N. Haskell; and, on the latter one, a Poem was also pronounced by Mr. S. A. Dix. An incident from Mr. Haskell's interesting Address of 1848 illustrates the strength and beauty of many of the social ties here formed: "Ten years ago last October, one of our most active and beloved members died, leaving an interesting family of sisters, with their mother, in destitute circumstances. One hundred and eight of our members came forward and raised a fund, by contributing one or two dollars each year, till the sum of five hundred dollars was paid the mother of their friend Torrey, in quarterly payments of twenty-five dollars each, for the term of five years."

The Association was incorporated in 1845. An attempt to procure a charter was first made in 1837, but was not then pressed forward with much zeal; and the petitioners had leave to withdraw. In 1845, by the advice of the Hon. William Sturgis, the subject was again taken up; and an Act of Incorporation, drafted by Chas. G. Loring, Esq., and presented by the venerable Edmund Dwight, received the signature of the Governor. The good offices, in this connection, of the Hon. Peleg W. Chandler, then Chairman of the Committee on Education, received a grateful acknowledgment.

Ten years after its formation, the Library contained eighteen hundred and forty-six volumes; and, in 1833, the number was twenty-three hundred and seventy-eight. In 1844, the Association became again indebted to its generous and wise patrons, Messrs. Wm. Sturgis, Abbott Lawrence, Nathan Appleton, William Appleton, John P. Cushing, John Bryant, David Sears, William Lawrence, Robert G. Shaw, and Amos Lawrence, who each subscribed $100, to be expended in the purchase of books. This was followed by the munificent donation of $500, from the late Hon. Daniel Webster, in behalf of the Society for the Diffusion of Useful Knowledge, of which he was President, to be invested in the same manner. These sums were judiciously expended, and in 1848 the Library contained about six thousand volumes. Since that time, by means of increased resources, the income from the fund, and the profits of the lectures, large additions have been made. The Library now contains sixteen thousand volumes; and the Association has about two thousand members. The circulation of books, especially within the last few years, has been larger probably than that of any similar library in the country. In 1853, it reached eighty-one thousand volumes.

The design of making the Reading-Room an attractive place of resort, has been steadily kept in view. At its very commencement, it received, gratis, the leading Boston newspapers; and these generous contributions have been continued to the present time. Now the principal Reviews and Periodicals, and more than a hundred Newspapers, daily invite the perusal of its members.

In December, 1850, the Rooms were opened from one to ten o'clock, P.M., instead of during the evening only, as had hitherto been the practice; and the services of a permanent Librarian were secured. In July, 1852, the Reading-Room was made accessible during the entire day and evening.

The subject of a new building, owned by and devoted to the purposes of the Association, with ample accommodations for its various requirements, has for many years engaged the attention of its members.

Annual Reports, so far back as 1830, with scarce an exception, have not failed to allude to this growing necessity. The burden of complaint has been, and *is*, inconvenient and insufficient rooms.

As already stated, in 1846 Hon. Thomas H. Perkins gave $2500, and eight other generous men gave $8000, for this purpose. In 1851, it was made the subject of a special meeting. The result was the appointment of a Committee, to solicit further aid for this object. They reported, in March, 1853, that the sum of $9,050 had been subscribed through their solicitation, upon the condition, on the part of several of the donors, that $15,000 be raised; this sum, in addition to the already invested funds, being considered a necessary building capital. By the Annual Report for the year ending in April last, it appeared that the whole amount subscribed reached the sum of $9,600. The names of the gentlemen who have subscribed so liberally in aid of this project may be found by reference to the Annual Reports. The Committee acknowledged their indebtedness to Hon. Nathan Appleton, Hon. William Appleton, and Hon. Abbott Lawrence, "who are not only among the largest contributors of money, but have made personal application to gentlemen of their acquaintance in aid of the object."

From the important influence which this Association is exerting on the future commercial character of our city, and from the proverbial liberality of Boston merchants, when they come to appreciate the merits of a noble object, it cannot be that the want of proper accommodations should much longer circumscribe the usefulness of our Institution.

B Y - L A W S.

Art. I. — Members.

Sect. 1. — Any person eligible by the Charter can become a member of the Association by signing these By-Laws, and paying into the Treasury the sum of two dollars, payable in advance, which shall constitute his first year's assessment.

Sect. 2. — Every member shall be subject to an annual assessment of two dollars, payable in advance.

Art. II. — Directors.

The Board of Directors of the Association shall consist of a President, Vice-President, Corresponding Secretary, Recording Secretary, Treasurer, and eight Directors. They shall be elected with written ballot, by general ticket.

Art. III. — President.

Sect. 1. — The President, when present, shall preside at all meetings both of the Association and Board of Directors, and, in case of an equal division of the members on any question, shall give the casting vote.

Sect. 2. — The President shall have power to call special meetings of the Board of Directors and Trustees, whenever he may deem it expedient.

Art. IV. — Vice-President.

The Vice-President shall preside in the absence of the President, and perform all the duties of that office.

Art. V. — Secretaries.

Sect. 1. — The Corresponding Secretary shall be the organ of the Association, in its conference with other societies and the public. He shall retain copies of all letters written by him, and record the same in a book kept for that purpose.

Sect. 2. — The Recording Secretary shall affix his name to all the advertisements and notices emanating from the Board of Directors, or from the Association (if not otherwise ordered); he shall attend all meetings, and, in the absence of the President and Vice-President, shall call the same to order; and shall, accurately and at large, record the proceedings in the Journal of the Institution, which shall be deposited in the rooms, subject to the inspection of the members.

Art. VI. — Treasurer.

Sect. 1. — The Treasurer shall hold all the funds of the Association, except the property invested in the name of the Trustees, subject to the order of a majority of the Joint Board of Trustees and Directors.

Sect. 2. — The Treasurer shall pay no bill unless sanctioned by the Board of Directors and signed by the Chairman; he shall make a report semi-annually of all his receipts and disbursements; and, for the better security of these trusts, he shall assure to the *Trustees* the sum of two thousand dollars.

Sect. 3. — The above sections shall not be construed to prevent Committees appointed for special purposes from holding funds accruing to them during the performance of their duties; they being at all times responsible for such funds.

Sect. 4. — Notice shall be given to the members, by the Treasurer, of their assessments becoming due, at least one week before the expiration thereof.

Art. VII. — Directors.

Sect. 1. — The Board of Directors shall meet on the first Monday of every month for the transaction of business; they shall have control of the general affairs of the Association; they shall have power to make such regulations as may be found necessary for the better government of the Association, which shall be submitted to the members for their approval. They shall examine the Library, and make an annual report to the members on the state of the Association.

Sect. 2. — At all meetings of the Board of Directors, seven members must be present to proceed to business.

Art. VIII. — Trustees.

Sect. 1. — The Board of Trustees shall be chosen for the term of three years, and may continue to hold office until their successors are elected.

Sect. 2. — Should any vacancy occur in the Board, it shall be filled for the unexpired portion of the term.

Sect. 3. — The Joint Board of Trustees and Directors shall meet on the first Mondays of January, May, and September.

Sect. 4. — At all meetings of the Joint Board, three Trustees and seven Directors shall constitute a quorum.

Art. IX. — Meetings.

Sect. 1. — At all meetings of the Association, twenty members must be present for the transaction of business, except when it is proposed to alter or amend these By-Laws, when fifty members must be present.

Sect. 2. — The Annual Meeting for the Election of Officers shall be holden on the third Wednesday in April.

Sect. 3. — There shall be a meeting of the Association on the Friday evening succeeding the first Monday in every month, at such hour as the Directors may appoint, for the transaction of any business that may come before it.

Sect. 4. — The Recording Secretary shall call meetings of the Association when deemed expedient by the Board of Directors, or whenever requested in writing by fifteen of the members; and he shall cause notices to be conspicuously placed in the room, at least one week previous, expressing the hour and probable business of such meeting.

Sect. 5. — If, at any meeting of the Association, a member doubts the decision of a vote, he may call for a division; and the members voting on each side shall then be counted by tellers, appointed by the Chairman, and the result declared by him.

Sect. 6. — When a motion has been made and seconded, it shall be put in writing if desired, and read by the Chairman before the same be open for discussion.

Sect. 7. — When a motion is under discussion, no other shall be received, except to adjourn, to lie on the table, to postpone indefinitely, or the call for the previous question; which several motions shall have precedence in the order in which they stand arranged.

Sect. 8. — No member who did not vote with the majority on any question shall move the reconsideration of the vote.

Sect. 9. — Voting by proxy shall not be allowed.

Sect. 10. — If, at any meeting of the Association, questions should arise which are not treated upon in the before-mentioned By-Laws, they shall be decided by an appeal to "Jefferson's Manual."

Art. X. — Literary Exercises.

Sect. 1. — Regular meetings shall be held for improvement in Declamation, Debate, and Composition, on such evenings as the Directors may appoint, during the months of October, November, December, January, February, and March.

Sect. 2. — Committees on Debate, Declamation, and Composition, shall be chosen, to consist of three each; the Chairman of each Committee to be chosen from the Board of Directors.

Sect. 3. — It shall be the duty of the Committee on Debate to furnish questions for discussion, and to provide suitable persons to open and carry on the same.

Sect. 4. — It shall be the duty of the Committee on Declamation to engage persons to declaim on evenings set apart for that purpose.

Sect. 5. — The Committee on Compositions shall receive all pieces, and read such as meet their approval.

Sect. 6. — Any member, whose compositions shall be rejected by the Committee, can appeal from their decision; and the matter shall be referred to a Committee consisting of the Chairmen of the Committees on Debate and Declamation, and the President, *ex officio*, who are empowered to take such action as they may deem expedient.

SECT. 7. — At any meeting of the Association held for the purpose of Declamation, there shall be but one exercise on the same evening. On the evening appropriated to Debate, there shall be but one exercise; provided, however, that this By-Law shall not be so construed as to preclude the discussion of more than one subject on that evening. At the meetings for Composition, there may be a debate on such subjects as the members shall decide. These exercises shall take place in the following order, viz.: Declamation, Debate, Composition.

ART. XI. — BOOKS.

SECT. 1. — A member, upon application to the Librarian, may take out one volume from the rooms, or he may remove both volumes of any work comprised in two volumes of duodecimo or smaller size, and retain the same two weeks (except those works specified in Section 2); at the expiration of which time, an extension of one week shall be given if desired; after which time, there shall be no extension, nor shall the same person retake either of the same volumes until they shall have remained upon the shelves of the Library one entire evening.

SECT. 2. — The Directors shall have power to limit the time of retention for new books during the first six months after their purchase, which time shall be conspicuously marked on their covers; and they shall also have power to withhold from circulation such volumes and periodicals as may be injured thereby.

SECT. 3. — If, at the expiration of the time specified in Sects. 1 and 2 for the retention of any book or books, the same are not returned, the sum of ten cents shall be imposed and demanded for every week so retained, and a retention of one day over the stipulated time shall incur the same penalty.

SECT. 4. — If any member shall refuse to pay the amount of any fine or fines which may be assessed him, his right to remove books from the Library shall be suspended until he complies with the requirements.

SECT. 5. — If any proprietor shall lose or deface a volume, he shall replace the same, or present an equivalent in money. If it be one of a set, he shall receive the odd volumes at a fair appraisal, or make an ample recompense.

SECT. 6. — All books shall be returned one week previous to the annual examination.

SECT. 7. — Members shall not take out books on another's page without a written order; and, if any books so taken are lost, the Librarian shall be held accountable therefor.

SECT. 8. — No member shall have the liberty to transfer his right to take out books to a person not a member of the Association.

ART. XII.

If the Trustees or Directors, in their several official capacities, shall neglect the performance of their duties, or shall not administer the laws of the Association efficiently and equitably, on written complaint of fifteen members a meeting shall be called, and a Committee appointed, consisting of two members and one Director, who shall report and refer the subject to the members of the Association; and they shall censure the accused, remove from office, or fully exonerate, as the circumstances of the case may warrant.

Art. XIII.

The distinction of Honorary Member shall be conferred on any person, by a vote of a majority of the members present at any regular meeting.

Art. XIV. — Expulsion of Members.

If any member shall wantonly create a disturbance at any meeting of the Association, or misrepresent its character abroad, or devise or take part in any measure, designedly to injure the Association, or shall purposely deface the books, the room, or its appurtenances, on written complaint of fifteen members a meeting shall be called, and the matter referred to a Committee of two Directors and one member, who shall investigate the charges and report at a future meeting, when, if the same be made apparent, he shall be reproved, or deprived of his privileges of membership; always allowing the accused ample opportunity to excuse or extenuate his conduct.

Art. XV.

These By-Laws shall not be altered or amended, unless by the written votes of three-fourths of the members present at a meeting called exclusively for the purpose.

REGULATIONS.

Art. I.

The Library shall be open every day (except Sunday) from one to ten o'clock, P.M., and the Reading-Room during the entire day and evening.

Art. II. — Librarian.

Sect. 1. — A Librarian shall be appointed by the Board of Directors, whose duty it shall be to attend to the Rooms every day on which they are opened.

Sect. 2. — He shall keep a record of all books, magazines, maps, charts, papers, and all other property belonging to the Association, arrange them in proper order, and keep an accurate account of all books delivered to members.

Sect. 3. — He shall keep a full and accurate catalogue of all books belonging to the Association, which shall be open to the inspection of members.

Sect. 4. — He shall ascertain, once in two months, by an examination of the account of each member, all books not returned in due season, and shall cause the same *to be procured of the members in default.*

Sect. 5. — He shall collect all fines and assessments, and pay the same over to the Treasurer; and shall submit to the Board of Directors a monthly report of the same, together with the names of all persons who have become members of the Association during the month.

Sect. 6. — For the faithful discharge of his duties, he shall give bonds in the sum of five hundred dollars.

Art. III.

The Board of Directors shall, from time to time, appoint one of their number, who shall be styled the "Director for the Week," and whose duty shall be to have the general supervision of the internal affairs of the Association, to receive strangers who may visit the Rooms, and to repress any disorderly conduct on the part of the members.

Art. IV.

Members shall not remain covered in the Rooms.

Art. V.

No loud conversation shall be permitted in the Reading-Room.

Art. VI.

A member shall not assume the liberty of arranging the books or periodicals, or of performing any of the minor duties which devolve upon the Librarian.

Art. VII.

Sect. 1. — No member or officer of the Association shall enter the Rooms at unseasonable hours (except on business), to remove books, pamphlets, newspapers, or any other property belonging to the Association.

Sect. 2. — No member shall take from the Rooms any book belonging to the Institution, unless the same be recorded; or remove a newspaper from the file.

Sect. 3. — Any member who shall deface any book belonging to the Association, by marking upon it with a pencil, or otherwise, shall be considered amenable to Article XIV. of By-Laws.

Art. VIII. — Meetings.

If different opinions shall be expressed regarding questions of order, or mode of debate, upon subjects before a meeting of the Association, such opinions shall be governed by the decision of the Presiding Officer, and, if such is objected to, then by an appeal to the members present; and, if any individual persists in opposition to such decision, his right of membership shall be suspended.

Art. IX.

A member shall not be permitted to interrupt another, unless it be to call him to order, or correct a mistake, nor be permitted to pass unnecessarily between the Presiding Officer and the person speaking.

Art. X.

Members shall have the liberty of introducing a friend, not a resident of the city, to the privileges of the Rooms, except that of removing books from the Library, for the term of one month.

Art. XI.

Should a member transgress any Article of these Regulations, he shall be reported to the Board of Directors, who may take such measures thereon as they may deem proper.

CATALOGUE.

A star (*) prefixed to a title denotes that the work may be found in the cases of Reference and Illustrated Works in the ante-room, and is not to be taken from the Library.

When more than one number is annexed to a title, the first is the general number of an entire set; and the remaining numbers designate particular volumes of the set.

A.

Abauzit, F. Essays on Theology. Boston, 1823. 12°. 368, 1
Abbot. Sir W. Scott. Boston, 1848. 2 v. 12°. 999, 19, 20
The same. Edinburgh, 1849. 2 v. 12°. . . 4100, 20, 21
The same. Edinburgh, 1850. roy. 8°. . . . 4531, 5
Abbot, A. Letters from the Interior of Cuba. Boston, 1829. 8°. . . 1309
Abbot, A. & E. Genealogical Register of the Abbots. Boston, 1847. 8°. 2846
Abbot, E., jun. Catalogue of Cambridge High School Lib. Camb. 1853. 8°. 5986
Abbott, C. Law of Merchant Ships and Seamen. Philadelphia, 1802. 8°. 1365
Abbott, J. Corner Stone. New York, 1851. 12°. 6205
Franconia Stories. Malleville. New York, 1850. 12°. . . 4033
Wallace. New York, 1850. 12°. 3813
Mary Erskine. New York, 1850. 12°. 3814
Mary Bell. New York, 1850. 12°. 4154
Beechnut. New York, 1850. 12°. 4155
Rodolphus. New York, 1852. 12°. 5294
Stuyvesant. New York, 1854. 12°. 5295
Ellen Linn. New York, 1852. 12°. 5296
Caroline. New York, 1855. 12°. 5297
Agnes. New York, 1855. 12°. 5298
History of Alexander the Great. New York, 1848. 12°. . . . 2465
History of Alfred the Great. New York, 1849. 12°. . . . 3451
History of Julius Cæsar. New York, 1849. 12°. 3381
History of Charles I. New York, 1848. 12°. 2463
History of Charles II. New York, 1849. 12°. 3767
History of Cleopatra. New York, 1851. 12°. 4212
History of Cyrus. New York, 1852. 12°. 6208
History of Darius. New York, 1850. 12°. 3765
History of Queen Elizabeth. New York, 1849. 12°. . . . 3766

Abbott, J. History of Hannibal. New York, 1849. 12°. 2467
History of Mary, Queen of Scots. New York, 1848. 12°. . . 2461
History of Nero. New York, 1853. 12°. 5267
History of Pyrrhus. New York, 1854. 12°. 6171
History of Romulus. New York, 1852. 12°. 5023
History of William the Conqueror. New York, 1850. 12°. . . 3575
History of Xerxes. New York, 1850. 12°. 4490
Rollo on the Atlantic. Boston, 1854. 12°. 5622
Rollo in Paris. Boston, 1854. 12°. 5782
Rollo in Switzerland. Boston, 1854. 12°. 6207
Summer in Scotland. New York, 1848. 12°. 3110
Way to do Good. New York, 1852. 12°. 6206
Young Christian. New York, 1851. 12°. 633
Abbott, J. S. C. History of Marie Antoinette. New York, 1850. 12°. . 3380
History of Josephine. New York, 1851. 12°. 4402
History of Madame Roland. New York, 1850. 12°. . . . 4418
Kings and Queens. New York, 1848. 12°. 3146
Abel Allnut. J. Morier. Philadelphia, 1837. 2 v. 12°. . . . 984
Abel, F. A., & C. L. Bloxam. Handbook of Chemistry. Phil. 1854. 18°. 5934
Abell, Mrs. E. Recollections of Napoleon at St. Helena. Lond. 1844. 12°. 3074
Abell, Mrs. L. G. Gems by the Wayside. New York, 1850. 12°. . 4088
Abercrombie, J. Intellectual Powers. Boston, 1839. 12°. . . . 1572
The same. (H. F. L.) New York, 1846. 12°. . . 3683, 37
Philosophy of the Moral Feelings. Boston, 1843. 12°. . . 1570
Abelard and Heloïse, Romance of. O. W. Wight. N.Y. 1853. 12°. . 5367
Abolitionist; a Record of the N. E. Anti-Slavery Soc. Boston, 1833. 8°. 1442
Abrantes, Duchess d'. Memoirs of Napoleon. New York, 1832. 8°. . 5150
Abyssinia, Life in. M. Parkyns. New York, 1854. 2 v. 12°. . . 5859
Travels in Southern. C. Johnston. London, 1844. 2 v. 8°. . 4691
Travels into. J. Bruce. Boston, 1798. 12°. 319
Academical Speaker. B. D. Emerson. Philadelphia, 1835. 12°. . . 1807
Achillé, G. Dealings with the Inquisition. New York, 1851. 12°. . 4175
Acton; or, the Circle of Life. New York, 1849. 12°. 3254
Actor and Manager, Life of an. F. C. Wemyss. N.Y. 1847. 2 v. 12°. . 2968
Acts of the Apostles, Commentary on. H. B. Hackett. Boston, 1852. 8°. 4724
Notes on. A. Barnes. New York, 1851. 12°. 4731
Acts passed at the First Session of Congress, 1791. Philadelphia, n. d. 8°. 760
Adalbert, Prince. Travels in Europe and Brazil. London, 1849. 2 v. 8°. 5131
Adam, A. Roman Antiquities. New York, 1819. 8°. 626
Adam Blair. J. Galt. Boston, 1822. 12°. 352
Adam Brown, the Merchant. Horace Smith. New York, 1843. 8°. . 2762
Adams, Abigail. Journal and Correspondence. New York, 1841. 2 v. 12°. 3045
Adams, C. Boys at Home. New York, 1854. 12°. 5778
Edgar Clifton; or, Right and Wrong. New York, 1853. 12°. . 5344
Adams, C. F. (Editor.) Works of John Adams. Boston, 1850–54. 10 v. 8°. 4012
Adams, G. Massachusetts Register, 1852–54. Boston. 3 v. 8°. . . 256
Adams, Hannah. History of the Jews. Boston, 1812. 2 v. 12°. . . 883
History of New England. Dedham, 1799. 8°. 585

Adams, John. Novanglus; a Political Essay. Boston, 1819. 8°. . . 781
Defence of the Const. and Govt. of U. S. London, 1787. 3 v. 8°. 701
Letters to his Wife. Ed. by C. F. Adams. Boston, 1841. 2 v. 12°. 1663
Works, with Life. Ed. by C. F. Adams. Boston, 1850–54. 10 v. 8°. 4012
Adams, Mrs. John. Letters, with Memoir. C. F. Adams. Bost. 1848. 12°. 1592
Adams, Rev. John. Flowers of Modern Travels. Boston, 1816. 2 v. 12°. 1652
Adams, J. Q., Discourses and Eulogies on. Boston, 1848. 8°. . . 3533
By D. Sharp, R. C. Waterston, W. P. Lunt, W. Hague, E. Everett.
Letters on the Masonic Institution. Boston, 1847. 8°. . . 2857
Lectures on Rhetoric and Oratory. Cambridge, 1810. 2 v. 8°. . 1945
Letters to his Son on the Study of the Bible. Boston, 1848. 12°. 1592
Life and Public Services. W. H. Seward. Auburn, 1849. 12°. . 2908
Lives of Madison and Monroe. Boston, 1850. 12°. . . . 3934
Lives of Madison, Lafayette, and Monroe. New York, 1846. 8°. . 2739
Report on Weights and Measures. Washington, 1821. 8°. . . 1254
Speech on the Right of Petition. Washington, 1838. 8°. . . 1441
Adams, N. Friends of Christ in the New Testament. Boston, 1853. 8°. 5118
Addison, C. G. Damascus and Palmyra. Philadelphia, 1838. 2 v. 12°. 835
Addison, J. Life. Lucy Aiken. Philadelphia, 1846. 12°. . . . 2936
Works. New York, 1842. 3 v. 8°. 792
Vols. 1, 2. Spectator.
3. Tatler; Guardian; Freeholder; Dialogues on Medals; Remarks on Italy; Evidences of Christianity; Miscellaneous Poems.

Works, edited by G. W. Greene. New York, 1853–54. 5 v. 12°. 5562
Vol. 1. Macaulay's Essay on the Life and Writings of Addison; Translations; Poems; Dramas, &c.
2. Dialogues on Medals; Travels; Essay on Virgil's Georgics; Ancient and Modern Learning; Christian Religion; Letters; Political Writings.
3. Freeholder; Plebeian and Old Whig; Tatler; Guardian; Lover.
4. Spectator. (Vol. 5 not published.)

and R. Steele. The Spectator. New York, 1854. 6 v. 8°. . . 5898
The Tatler and Guardian. New York, 1852. Roy. 8°. . 4840
The same. New York, 1853. 12°. 5562, 3
Addresses and Messages of the Presidents of the U. S. N.Y. 1842. 8°. . 1782
Adelaide Lindsay. Mrs. Marsh. New York, 1850. 8°. 3976
Adler, G. F. German and English Dictionary. New York, 1849. 8°. . 3525
Administrations of Washington and Adams. G. Gibbs. N.Y. 1846. 2 v. 8°. 2728
Adolphe Renouard. J. Ward. London, 1852. 12°. 5641
Adolphus, J. History of Reign of George III. London, 1802. 3 v. 8°. . 5908
Adopted Child, History of. G. E. Jewsbury. New York, 1853. 12°. . 5225
Adrian, or Clouds of the Mind. G. P. R. James & M. B. Field. N.Y. 1852. 12°. 4599
Adsonville; or, Marrying Out. Albany, 1824. 12°. 1577
Adventure, American. (H. F. L.) New York, 1848. 2 v. 12°. 3683, 174–5
Adventures of an Atom. T. Smollett. Philadelphia, 1851. 8°. . . 801–2
in Fairy Land. R. H. Stoddard. Boston, 1853. 12°. . . . 5234
of a French Sergeant. R. Guillemard. Philadelphia, 1826. 12°. . 1068
of a Gentleman in Search of a Horse. Philadelphia, 1836. 12°. . 3772
of a Medical Student. R. Douglas. New York, 1848. 2 v. 12°. . 3153
of Mr. Ledbury. Albert Smith. London, 1853. 12°. . . 5734
of the Rifle Brigade. J. Kincaid. Philadelphia, 1836. 8°. . 2228, 1

Adventures of a Younger Son. Capt. Trelawney. London, 1851. 12°. . 5664
Advice in the Pursuits of Literature. S. L. Knapp. New York, 1832. 12°. 326
Aeronautics, System of. J. Wise. Philadelphia, 1850. 8°. . . . 4148
Æschylus. Tragedies, translated by T. Buckley. London, 1848. post 8°. 4380
Tragedies, translated by R. Potter. New York, 1842. 12°. . 1854, 13
The same. New York, 1848. 12°. 3762
Æsop's Fables; a New Version, and Illustrated. T. James. Lond. 1848. 8°. 4536
Affinities of Foreigners; a Tale. London, 1850. 2 vols. 12°. . . 4612
Afloat and Ashore; or, Miles Wallingford. J. F. Cooper. Phil. 1844. 4 v. 12°. 1898
Africa, Adventures in. W. C. Harris. Philadelphia, 1850. 8°. . . 3946
and the American Flag. A. H. Foote. New York, 1854. 12°. . 5826
Central, Journey in. B. Taylor. New York, 1854. 12°. . . 6185
Discovery and Advent. in. H. Murray and others. N.Y. 1840. 12°. 107
The same. (H. F. L.) New York, 1843. 12°. . . 3683, 16
Second Expedition into. H. Clapperton. Philadelphia, 1829. 8°. 1335
South, Hunter's Life in. R. G. Cumming. N.Y. 1850. 2 v. 12°. 3933
South, Narrative of Residence in. T. Pringle. London, 1840. 8°. 2613
South, Travels in. J. Campbell. Andover, 1816. 8°. . . 756
Travels in. R. & J. Lander. (H. F. L.) N.Y. 1846. 2 v. 12°. 3683, 35, 36
Travels in Interior of. C. F. Damberger. Charlestown, 1801. 8°. 215
Voyage to the Coast of. J. Hawkins. Philadelphia, 1797. 12°. . 831
Voyage to the West Coast of. J. A. Carnes. Boston, 1852. 12°. 4798
Western Travels in, 1845–46. J. Duncan. London, 1847. 2 v. 12°. 4965
African Cruiser, Journal of. H. Bridge. New York, 1853. 12°. . . 2398
African History, Lights and Shadows of. S. G. Goodrich. Bost. 1849. 12°. 4900, 10
African Repository. Vol. 19. Washington, 1843. 8°. 2837
African Slave Trade. T. F. Buxton. Philadelphia, 1839. 12°. . . 1527
Africans, Appeal in Favor of. L. M. Child. New York, 1836. 12°. . 322
Agassiz, L. Physical Character, &c., of Lake Superior. Boston, 1850. 8°. 3604
and A. A. Gould, Principles of Zoölogy. Boston, 1848. 12°. . 3141
Agatha Beaufort; or, Family Pride. New York, 1854. 12°. . . . 6161
Agatha's Husband. Miss Muloch. New York, 1853. 8°. 5968
Age of Gold, and other Poems. G. Lunt. Boston, 1843. 12°. . . 1730
Agincourt; a Romance. G. P. R. James. New York, 1844. 8°. . . 2217
Agnes Grey; an Autobiography. Caroline Bronte. Philadelphia, 1850. 8°. 3523
Agnes Morris; or, Heroine of Domestic Life. New York, 1847. 12°. . 3353
Agnes Serle. Ellen Pickering. Philadelphia, 1846. 8°. 2709
Agnes Sorel. G. P. R. James. New York, 1853. 8°. 5173
Agricultural Engineering. G. H. Andrews. London, 1852. 12°. . 6078
Agricultural Societies of Massachusetts, 1850. Boston, 1851. 8°. . . 4360
1851. Boston, 1852. 8°. 5126
Agriculture, and Rural Economy, European. H. Colman. Bost. 1849. 2 v. 8°. 3268
Chemistry applied to. J. A. Chaptal. Boston, 1835. 12°. . . 665
Farmer's Encyclopædia. C. W. Johnson. Philadelphia, 1850. roy. 8°. 4358
Journal of. Edited by W. S. King. Vol. 1. Boston, 1851. 8°. . 257
of Massachusetts. G. L. Flint. Boston, 1853. 8°. 5955
Aguilar, Grace. Days of Bruce. New York, 1852. 2 v. 12°. . . 4790
Home Influence. New York, 1848. 12°. 3167

Aguilar, Grace. Home Scenes and Heart Studies. New York, 1853. 12°. 5066
Josephine; or, the Edict. Philadelphia, 1850. 12°. 4025
Mother's Recompense. New York, 1851. 12°. 4093
Vale of Cedars. New York, 1850. 12°. 3871
Women of Israel. New York, 1851. 2 v. 12°. 4029
Woman's Friendship. New York, 1851. 12°. 3650
Aids to Reflection. S. T. Coleridge. Burlington, 1840. 8°. . . . 1992
The same. New York, 1853. 12°. 5561, 1
Aiken, J. British Poets. Jonson to Beattie. Philadelphia, 1843. 3 v. 8°. 1962
and Mrs. Barbauld. Evenings at Home. New York, 1850. 12°. 3445
Aiken, Lucy. Life of Joseph Addison. Philadelphia, 1846. 12°. . . 2936
Memoirs of the Court of James I. Boston, 1822. 2 v. 8°. . . 1217
Aiken, S. Memoirs of Court of Queen Elizabeth. Philadelphia, 1823. 8°. 671
Aims and Obstacles; a Romance. G. P. R. James. New York, 1851. 8°. 4550
Ainsworth, N. Latin and English Dictionary. London, 1763. 2 v. 8°. . 1353
Ainsworth, W. H. Crichton. New York, 1846. 2 v. 12°. . . . 122
Guy Fawkes. Philadelphia, 1843. 8°. 2064
Lancashire Witches. New York, 1849. 8°. 3293
Rookwood. London, 1853. 12°. 5712
Star Chamber. New York, 1854. 8°. 5948
Tower of London. London, 1845. 8°. 1977
Airs of Palestine, and other Poems. J. Pierpont. Boston, 1840. 12°. . 1579
Akerman, J. Y. Spring-Tide; or, Angler, &c. London, 1850. 12°. . 4278
Akenside, M. Pleasures of the Imagination. Baltimore, 1804. 12°. . 144
Poetical Works. London, 1806. 24°. 1863
A l'Abri; or, The Tent Pitched. N. P. Willis. New York, 1839. 12°. . 987
Alban; a Tale of the New World. J. V. Huntington. N. Y. 1851. 12°. 4448
Alcohol, and the Constitution of Man. E. L. Youmans. N. Y. 1854. 12°. 6158
Alcoholic Drinks, Physiological Effects of. Boston, 1848. 12°. . . 2450
Alcoholic Liquors, Use and Abuse of. W. B. Carpenter. Bost. 1851. 12°. 4099
Alcoran of Mahomet. — See *Koran*.
Alcott, W. A. House I Live in. Boston, 1842. 12°. 1027
Lectures on Life and Health. Boston, 1853. 12°. 5256
(Editor.) Library of Health. Boston, 1837. 2 v. 12°. . . . 955
Young Wife. Boston, 1837. 12°. 912
Alderbrook. Emily Chubbuck. Boston, 1848. 2 v. 12°. 2941
Alexander A. Authenticity and Inspir. of Scriptures. Phil. 1850. 12°. 4744
History of the Israelitish Nation. Philadelphia, 1853. 8°. . . 5155
Life. J. W. Alexander. New York, 1854. 8°. 5947
Outlines of Moral Science. New York, 1852. 12°. 4987
Thoughts on Religious Experience. Philadelphia, 1851. 12°. . 4743
Alexander I., of Russia, Memoirs of. E. Gibbon. Baltimore, 1818. 12°. 478
Alexander the Great, History of. J. Abbott. New York, 1848. 12°. . 2465
History of his Successors. M. Rollin. Hartford, 1823. 2 v. 12°. . 454
Life. J. Williams. (H. F. L.) New York, 1843. 12°. . 3683, 7
Alexander, J. A. Isaiah, Translated and Explained. N. Y. 1851. 2 v. 12°. 4742
Psalms, Translated and Explained. New York, 1851. 3 v. 12°. . 1112
Alexander, J. H. Dictionary of Weights and Measures. Balt. 1850. 8°. 3978

Alexander, J. W. Life of Archibald Alexander. New York, 1854. 8°. . 5947
Alexander W. (Earl of Stirling). Life. W. A. Duer. N. Y. 1847. 8°. 2800
Alfieri, V. Autobiography, translated by C. E. Lester. N. Y. 1845. 12°. 2492
Alfred the Great, History of. J. Abbott. New York, 1849. 12°. . . 3451
Life. R. Pauli. London, 1853. Post 8°. 5364
Algebra, Treatise on. J. Haddon. London, 1850. 12°. 6097
Algic Researches. H. R. Schoolcraft. New York, 1839. 2 v. 12°. . . 240
Algiers, French in. C. Lamping and M. de France. N. Y. 1845. 12°. . 2365
Letters from. T. Campbell. Philadelphia, 1836. 12°. . . . 252
Alhambra. W. Irving. New York, 1851. 12°. 532
Ali Bey. Travels in Morocco, Tripoli, &c. 1803–7. Phil. 1816. 2 v. 8°. 1265
Alice (Sequel to Ernst Maltravers). E. L. Bulwer. New York, n. d. 8°. 932
Alice Paulet (Sequel to Sydenham). Philadelphia, 1833. 2 v. 12°. . 529
Alida; or, Town and Country. Mrs. Sedgwick. New York, 1844. 8°. 2086
Alison, Sir A. History of Europe. 1789–1815. N. Y. 1843. 4 v. 8°. . 1735
History of Europe from 1815 to 1852. New York, 1853. 8°. . 5156
Miscellaneous Essays. Philadelphia, 1848. 8°. . . . 3418, 2
All in the Wrong. T. E. Hook. London, 1852. 12°. 5679
Alldridge, W. J. Universal Merchant. Philadelphia, 1797. 8°. . . 597
Alleghany Mountains, Letters from. C. Lanman. N. Y. 1849. 12°. . 3405
Allen, C. B. Cottage Building. London, 1854. 12°. 6064
Allen, Ethan. Life. J. Sparks. Boston, 1838. 12°. . . . 1076, 1
Allen, John. Principles of Modern Riding for Ladies. Lond. 1825. 8°. 5956
Allen, John. Royal Prerogative Power in England. London, 1849. 8°. 5415
Allen, Jos. Battles of the British Navy. London, 1852. 2 v. post 8°. . 5015
Allen, Wilkes. History of Chelmsford. Haverhill, 1820. 8°. . . 667
Allen, Wm. Memoir of John Codman. Boston, 1853. 8°. 5449
Decade of Addresses at Bowdoin College. Concord, 1830. 12°. . 506
Allen, Wm., & T. R. H. Thomson. Niger Exped. London, 1848. 2 v. 8°. 4641
*Allen, Wm. Am. Biographical and Hist. Dictionary. Bost. 1832. 8°. 3995
The same. Cambridge, 1809. 8°. 723
Allen, Wm. Life, and Selections from Correspondence. Phil. 1847. 8°. 3637
Memoir. J. Sherman. London, 1851. 12°. 4284
Allen, Z. Philosophy of the Mechanics of Nature. N. York, 1852. 8°. 4538
Allen Prescott. Mrs. Sedgwick. New York, 1834. 2 v. 12°. . . 466
Alliott, R. Lectures on the Children of Israel. London, 1849. 12°. . 3395
*Allom, T. Character and Costume of Turkey and Italy. Lond. n. d. 4°. 2050
All's not Gold that Glitters. Alice B. Neal. New York, 1853. 12°. . 5541
Allston, W. Lectures on Art and Poems. New York, 1850. 12°. . 3669
Lectures on Works and Genius of. W. Ware. Boston, 1852. 12°. 4913
Monaldi; a Tale. Boston, 1841. 12°. 1655
Almacks. New York, 1827. 12°. 450
Almacks Revisited. New York, 1828. 2v. 12°. 556
Almanac, Banker's, 1851, 1852. Boston. 8°. 4141
Illustrated, London, 1845–50. London. 4°. 5102
Alnwick Castle, and other Poems. F. G. Halleck. N. York, 1845. 12°. 2324
Alone; a Tale. Virginia Hawes. Richmond, 1854. 12°. 5832
Alp, Jungfrau, Pilgrim in the Shadow of. G. B. Cheever. N.Y. 1846. 12°. 2533

Alps and the Rhine. J. T. Headley. New York, 1847. 12°. . . 2529
*Illustrations of the Passes of. W. Brockedon. Lond. 1838. 2 v. 4°. 4829
of Savoy. Travels in. J. D. Forbes. Edinburgh, 1845. Roy. 8°. 5470
Alton Locke, Tailor and Poet. C. Kingsley. New York, 1850. 12°. . 4065
Alton Riots, and Death of E. P. Lovejoy. E. Beecher. Alton, 1838. 12°. 1532
Trials for. W. S. Lincoln. New York, 1838. 12°. . . . 1545
Altowan; or, Adven. in Rocky Mount. J. W. Webb. N. Y. 1846. 2 v. 12°. 2924
Amabel; a Family History. Elizabeth Wormeley. N. Y. 1853. 12°. . 5240
Amari, M. War of the Sicilian Vespers. London, 1850, 3 v. 12°. . . 4587
Amaury. A. Dumas. New York, 1845. 8°. 2634
Amazon, Scenes and Adventures on. J. E. Warren. N. Y. 1851. 12°. 4258
Valley of. W. L. Herndon. Washington, 1854. 8°. . . . 5462
Voyage up. W. H. Edwards. New York, 1847. 12°. . . 3003
Amber Witch. W. Meinhold. New York, 1845. 12°. 2329
Amelia. H. Fielding. Philadelphia, 1843. 8°. 1232, 2
Amelia. [Amelia B. Welby.] Poems. New York, 1846. 12°. . . 2988
Amenities of Literature. I. D'Israeli. New York, 1841. 2 v. 12°. . 1878
America, and the American People. F. von Raumer. N. York, 1846. 8°. 2633
and the American Revolution, History of. Philadelphia, 1790. 12°. 437
and the Americans. A. Murat. New York, 1849. 12°. . . 2976
and the West Indies. London, 1845. 8°. 3198
Annals of. A. Holmes. Cambridge, 1829. 2 v. 8°. . . . 1403
as I Found it. Mrs. Duncan. New York, 1852. 12°. . . 916
British, Voyages and Trav. through. A. Mackenzie. Phil. 1802. 8°. 766
Democracy in. A. de Tocqueville. New York, 1839. 2 v. 8°. . 948
Diary in. F. Marryat. New York, 1839. 12°. 193
Discoveries of the North Coast of. T. Simpson. Lond. 1843. 8°. 4344
The same. P. F. Tytler. (H. F. L.) N. Y. 1848. 12°. 3683, 53
Discovery of, Indian Wars, &c. H. Trumbull. Boston, 1833. 8°. 1334
General Survey of. A. H. Everett. Philadelphia, 1827. 8°. . 1354
History of. W. Robertson. London, 1803. 4 v. 8°. . . . 1213
Men and Manners in. T. Hamilton. Philadelphia, 1833. 2 v. 12°. 1166
Parisian Pastor's Glance at. J. H. G. Pierre. Boston, 1854. 12°. 6159
Peter Schlemihl in. G. Wood. Philadelphia, 1848. 12°. . . 4928
Pictorial History of. S. G. Goodrich. Philadelphia, 1846. 12°. . 1362
*Progress of. J. Macgregor. London, 1847. 2 v. 8°. . . 4023
Recollections of. F. A. de Chateaubriand. Philadelphia, 1816. . 740
Rule and Misrule of English in. T. C. Haliburton. N. Y. 1851. 12°. 4467
Society and Manners in. New York, 1821. 8°. 1276
Society in. H. Martineau. New York, 1837. 2 v. 12°. . . 367
Spanish. R. H. Bonnycastle. Philadelphia, 1819. 8°. . . 764
Subaltern in. Philadelphia, 1833. 12°. 298
Travels in. Lord Morpeth. New York, 1851. 12°. . . . 4183
American Adventure. (H. F. L.) New York, 1848. 2 v. 12°. 3683, 174–5
American Almanac. Vols. 1–25 [continued]. Boston, 1830–54. 12°. . 3078
American Anecdotes, Original and Selected. Boston, 1830. 2 v. 12°. . 4075
American Annals. A. Holmes. Cambridge, 1805. 2 v. 8°. . . . 1618
American Annual Register. New York, 1827–35. 8 v. 8°. . . . 5108

American Antiquarian Soc. Trans. and Collec. Worces. 1820–36. 2 v. 8°. 1420
American Antiquities. J. Priest. Albany, 1833. 8°. 2121
American Asso. for the Adv. of Science. 4th Meeting. Wash. 1851. 8°. 4311
American Authors, Homes of. New York, 1853. 8°. 5452
American Academy of Arts & Sciences. Memoirs, vol. 1. Bost. 1785. 4°. 2006
American Bible Society, History of. W. B. Strickland. N. Y. 1849. 8°. 3388
*American Biograph. & Hist. Dictionary. W. Allen. Boston, 1832. 8°. 3995
The same. Cambridge, 1809. 8°. 723
American Biography. (No titlepage.) 1318
J. Belknap. Boston, 1794. 8°. 643
The same. (H. F. L.) New York, 1848. 3 v. 12°. 3683, 161–63
American Clerk's Magazine. S. Freeman. Boston, 1814. 12°. . . 327
American Coast Pilot. L. Furlong. Newburyport, 1798. 8°. . . 1221
American Colonies, Book of. J. Frost. New York, 1846. 12°. . . 2515
History of. J. Marshall. Philadelphia, 1824. 8°. . . . 1987
History of the Revolt of. G. Chalmers. Boston, 1845. 2 v. 8°. . 2264
American Common Place Book of Poetry. G. B. Cheever. Phil. 1843. 12°. 1775
of Prose. Boston, 1833. 12°. 104
American Criminal Trials. P. W. Chandler. Boston, 1841–44. 2 v. 12°. 1921
American Cruiser. G. Little. New York, 1851. 12°. 2949
American Democrat. J. F. Cooper. Cooperstown, 1838. 12°. . . 1009
American Elocutionist. W. Russell. Boston, 1844. 12°. . . . 2142
American Ethnological Society, Transactions of. N. York, 1845. 2 v. 8°. 3384
American Facts. G. P. Putnam. London, 1845. 12°. 2695
American Farmer. Vols. 5, 7, 8. Baltimore, 1823–26. 4°. . . . 2011
American Female Poets. Caroline May. Philadelphia, 1848. 8°. . . 3535
American First Class Book. J. Pierpont. Boston, 1834. 12°. . . 1564
American Fruit Culturist. J. J. Thomas. Auburn, 1852. 12°. . . 5078
American Gazetteer. J. Morse. Charlestown, 1844. 8°. . . . 628
*American Historical and Literary Curiosities. New York, 1850. 4°. . 2468
American History, Incidents in. J. W. Barber. New York, 1847. 12°. 2987
Lights and Shadows of. S. G. Goodrich. Boston, 1849. 12°. 4900, 7
American in England. A. S. Mackenzie. New York, 1835. 2 v. 12°. . 1108
American Institutions, & their Influence. A. de Tocqueville. N. Y. 1851. 12°. 3829
American Journal of Education, 1830. Boston. 8°. 666
of Science. Vols. 29–50; 2d s., 1–17. N. Haven, 1836–54. 8°. . 921
American Lady, Memoirs of. Mrs. Grant. New York, 1846. 12°. . 2500
American Liberties and Am. Slavery. S. B. Treadwell. N. Y. 1838. 12°. 1555
American Literature and Manners. P. Chasles. New York, 1852. 12°. 4905
American Loyalists. L. Sabine. Boston, 1847. 8°. 2789
American Magazine of Useful and Entertaining Knowl. Bost. 1839. 8°. 1436
American Mechanics, Memoirs of Eminent. H. Howe. N. Y. 1847. 12°. 2990
American Missionary Memorial. H. W. Pierson. New York, 1853. 8°. 5113
American Monthly Mag. (Ed. by N. P. Willis). Bost. 1829–30. 2 v. 8°. 600
and Critical Review. Vols. 1–4. New York, 1817–18. 8°. 1312
American Naval Biography. I. Bailey. Providence, 1815. 12°. . . 209
American Notes for General Circulation. C. Dickens. N. Y. 1842. 8°. 1689
American Orator. L. C. Munn. Boston, 1853. 12°. 5026

American Orator's Own Book. Philadelphia, 1840. 24°. 1669
American Oratory. Philadelphia, 1849. 8°. 4139
American Publications, Cat. of, 1820–52. O. A. Roorbach. N.Y. 1852. 8°. 5993
American Quarterly Reg. Vols. 2, 4–10. Andover & Bost. 1830–38. 9 v. 8°. 1421
Stryker's. Vols. 1–6 [continued]. Phil. 1848–51. 8°. . 3408
American Review of Hist. and Politics. (Walsh's.) Vols. 1, 2. Phil. 1811–12. 1262
American Revolution, Camp Fires of. H. C. Watson. Phil. 1850. 8°. . 3828
Border Wars of. W. L. Stone. (H. F. L.) N.Y. 1848. 2 v. 12°. 3683, 167–8
Correspondence of. Ed. by J. Sparks. Boston, 1853. 4 v. 8°. . 5389
Diplomatic Corres. of. Ed. by J. Sparks. Bost. 1829. 12 v. 8°. . 3613
Domestic History of. Mrs. E. F. Ellet. New York, 1850. 12°. . 3923
History of. G. Bancroft. Boston, 1852–54. 3 v. 8°. . . 954, 4–6
History of. C. Botta. Philadelphia, 1821. 3 v. 8°. . . . 776
History of. W. Gordon. London, 1788. 4 v. 8°. . . . 578
History of. R. Hildreth. Boston, 1852. 8°. . . . 2851, 3
History of. D. Ramsay. Philadelphia, 1789. 8°. . . . 675
History of. C. Stedman. Dublin, 1794. 2 v. 8°. . . . 1917
in the Southern Department. H. Lee. Washington, 1827. 8°. . 899
Lives of the Heroes of. Boston, 1847. 12°. 3010
Military Journal during. J. Thacher. Boston, 1823. 8°. . . 637
Military Journal during. J. G. Simcoe. New York, 1844. 8°. . 1983
Pictorial Field Book of. B. J. Lossing. N. Y. 1852. 2 v. roy. 8°. 4130
Principles and Acts of. H. Niles. Baltimore, 1822. Roy. 8°. . 4000
Public Men of. W. Sullivan. Philadelphia, 1847. 8°. . . 2809
Relic of. C. Herbert. Boston, 1847. 12°. 3049
1776; or, the War of. B. J. Lossing. New York, 1847. 8°. . 2818
Women of. Mrs. E. F. Ellet. New York, 1848. 2 v. 12°. . . 3170
Americanisms, Dictionary of. J. R. Bartlett. New York, 1848. 8°. . 4956
Americans, The. F. J. Grund. Boston, 1837. 12°. 445
Domestic Manners of. Mrs. Trollope. New York, 1832. 8°. . 2078
Notions of. J. F. Cooper. New York, 1850. 2 v. 12°. . . 3778
Ames, F. Works, with Life. Boston, 1809. 8°. 649
Works, Speeches, and Corres. Ed. by S. Ames. Bos. 1854. 2 v. 8°. 5994
Ames, N. Mariner's Sketches. Providence, 1830. 12°. . . . 590
American Slavery as it Is; Testimony of 1000 Witnesses. N. Y. 1839. 8°. 1443
American Society, Sketches of. F. & T. Pulszky. N. Y. 1853. 2 v. 12°. 5245
American Speaker. J. Frost. Philadelphia, 1844. 12°. 1806
American Theatre, History of. W. Dunlap. New York, 1832. 8°. . 1993
American Tract Society, Publications of. New York, n. d. 9 v. 12°. . 388
American Whig Review. Vols. 1–16. New York, 1845–52. 8°. . . 2732
Amos, A. Trial of the Earl of Somerset. London, 1846. 8°. . . 4644
Amusement, Endless; a Collection of 400 Experiments. Phil. 1847. 12°. 2440
Amusements, Plea for. F. W. Sawyer. New York, 1847. 12°. . . 3060
Amy Harrington; or, a Sister's Love. New York, 1850. 12°. . . 3882
Amy Herbert; a Tale. E. M. Sewell. New York, 1853. 12°. . . 6225
Amy Lawrence; or, The Freemason's Daughter. J. F. Smith. N.Y. 1852. 8°. 4695
Anacreon. Odes, translated by T. Bourne. New York, 1837. 12°. 1851, 36
Select Odes, translated by H. Younge. London, 1802. 12°. . 43

Analectic Magazine. Philadelphia, 1831–17. 10 v. 8°. 700
Analogy of Religion. J. Butler. New York, 1843. 12°. . . . 1779
Criticism on. D. Wilson. Boston, 1834. 12°. . . . 1479
Analytical Reader. S. Putnam. Dover, 1830. 12°. 362
Sequel to. S. Putnam. Dover, 1832. 12°. . . . 363
Analytical Review (vol. 3 wanting). London, 1788–93. 16 v. 8°. . . 1277
Anastasius; or, Memoirs of a Greek. T. Hope. Paris, 1831. 2 v. 8°. . 432
Anastasis; or, the Resurrection of the Body. G. Bush. N. Y. 1845. 12°. 2522
Anatomy and Physiology. T. S. Lambert. New York, 1850. 12°. . 3625
Comparative, Lectures on. W. Lawrence. London, 1848. Post 8°. 4395
Anatomy of Melancholy. R. Burton. Philadelphia, 1836. 2 v. 8°. . 1960
Ancient Britons; a Tale of Primeval Life. London, 1851. 12°. . . . 4610
Ancient Geography and Ancient History. R. Mayo. Philadelphia, 1813. 8°. 739
Compendium of. M. D'Anville. New York, 1814. 2 v. 8°. . 1344
Ancient History. C. Rollin. New York, 1845. 2 v. roy. 8°. . . 704
Ancient and Hon. Artillery Co., History of. Z. G. Whitman. Bost. 1820. 8°. 750
Ancient Moral Tales. New York, 1845. 12°. 2375
Ancient Mysteries and Miracle Plays described. W. Hone. Lond. 1823. 8°. 2694
Ancient Regime; a Tale. G. P. R. James. New York, 1841. 2 v. 12°. 1602
Ancient Spanish Ballads. J. G. Lockhart. New York, 1842. 8°. . . 2349
Ancient World; or, Sketches of Creation. D. T. Ansted. Phil. 1847. 12°. 3054
Andersen, H. C. Improvisatore. London, 1853. 12°. 5736
The same. New York, 1845. 8°. 2243
Only a Fiddler, and O. T. New York, 1846. 8°. . . . 2637
True Story of my Life. Boston, 1847. 12°. 3022
Anderson, A. Origin and History of Commerce. London, 1764. 2 v. folio. 2025
Anderson, C. Annals of the English Bible. New York, 1849. 8°. . 3406
Anderson, James. Ladies of the Covenant. New York, 1851. 12°. . 4471
Anderson, John. Course of Creation. Cincinnati, 1851. 12°. . . 4196
Anderson, Robert. Life of Samuel Johnson. London, 1795. 12°. . 513
Anderson, Rufus. Peloponnesus and Greek Islands. Boston, 1830. 12°. 544
Anderson, W. Popular Scottish Biography. Edinburgh, 1842. 12°. . 3601
Practical Mercantile Correspondence. New York, 1851. 12°. . 4032
Andrews, E. A. Latin-English Lexicon. New York, 1851. Roy. 8°. . 4350
Leisure Hours; Readings in Prose. Boston, 1844. 12°. . . 2303
Andrews, G. H. Agricultural Engineering. London, 1852. 12°. . . 6078
Andrews, I. D. Report on Colonial and Lake Trade. Wash. 1852. 8°. 2747
Anecdotes, American, Original and Selected. Boston, 1830. 2 v. 12°. . 4075
and Aphorisms, Kaleidoscope of. C. Sinclair. London, 1851. 12°. 4400
Biographical, Literary, and Political. London, 1797. 3 v. 8°. . 685
Book of. J. Frost. New York, 1847. 12°. 2939
Cyclopædia of. K. Arvine. Boston, 1851. Roy. 8°. 3379
Cyclopædia of Moral and Religious. K. Arvine. N. Y. 1850. 8°. 4551
for the Railroad and Steamboat. New York, 1853. 12°. . . 5288
London; Electric Telegraph. London, n. d. 24°. 5047
Pictures and Painters. London, n. d. 24°. 5048
of the Animal Kingdom. S. G. Goodrich. Boston, 1849. 12°. 4900, 15
of Distinguished Persons. London, 1796. 4 v. 12°. 1554

Anecdotes of Painters, Engravers, &c. S. Spooner. N.Y. 1853. 3 v. 12°. 5750
Percy; with American. New York, 1847. 2 v. 8°. . . . 1763
Angel World, and other Poems. P. J. Bailey. Boston, 1850. 12°. . 3898
Angela; a Novel. Mrs. Marsh. 1848. 12°. 3145
Angela Wildon. G. W. M. Reynolds. New York, 1852. 8°. . . 645
Angell, J. K. Law of Assignments. Boston, 1835. 12°. . . . 1164
Law of Carriers. Boston, 1849. 8°. 4022
Angelo, Michael. Life. London, 1833. 8°. 602
Anger; or, The Fire-brand. E. Sue. New York, 1849. . . . 3255
Angler, Complete. I. Walton and C. Cotton. London, 1835. 12°. . 1869
Angler and his Friends. J. Y. Akerman. London, 1850. 12°. . . 4278
Angler's Manual, British. T. C. Hofland. London, 1848. Post 8°. . 4972
Angling, Hints on. P. Hackle. London, 1846. 8°. 5098
Anglo-Saxon Chronicle. London, 1847. Post 8°. 4365
Anglo-Saxon Church, Antiquities of. J. Lingard. Philadelphia, n. d. 8°. 2084
Anglo-Saxons, History of. S. Turner. Philadelphia, 1841. 2 v. 8°. . 1953
Animal Chemistry. J. Liebig. Cambridge, 1843. 12°. 1752
Animal Kingdom. Baron Cuvier. New York, 1831. 4 v. 8°. . . 1990
Animal Magnetism. W. Newnham. New York, 1845. 12°. . . 2342
Animal Mechanism and Phys. J.H.Griscom. (H.F.L.) N.Y. 1846. 12°. 3683, 85
Animals, Domesticated, of British Islands. D. Low. London, 1853. 8°. 5453
History, Habits, Instincts, &c. of. W. Kirby. Phil. 1836. 8°. . 1422
Stories about. F. C. Woodworth. Boston, 1851. 12°. . . 3937
The same. New York, 1850. 12°. 3311
Anne of Geierstein. Sir W. Scott. Boston, 1848. 2 v. 12°. . . 999, 43, 44
The same. Edinburgh, 1849. 2 v. 12°. . . 4100, 44, 45
The same. Edinburgh, 1850. Roy. 8°. . . . 4531, 11
Anley, Charlotte. Earlswood. New York, 1853. 12°. 4999
Annie Grayson; or, Life at Wash. Mrs. N. P. Lasselle. N.Y. 1853. 12°. 5379
Annual Retrospect of English Public Affairs, 1831. Boston, 1831. 2 v. 12°. 1013
Annual Review and Hist. of Literature, 1802–8. Lond. 1803–9. 7 v. 8°. 1636
Annual of Scientific Discovery. Ed. by D. A. Wells. Bost. 1850–4. 5 v. 12°. 3570
Ansted, D. T. Ancient World; or, Sketches of Creation. Phil. 1847. 12°. 3054
Antediluvian Antiquities. Vol. 1. Boston, 1829. 12°. 1278
Anthon, C. Ancient and Mediæval Geography. New York, 1850. Roy. 8°. 3514
*Classical Dictionary. New York, 1850. Roy. 8°. . . . 2840
The same. New York, 1847. Roy. 8°. 1243
(Editor.) Smith's Classical Dictionary. New York, 1851. Roy. 8°. 4347
Anthon, J. American Precedents of Declarations. Brookfield, 1821. 8°. 1402
Law Student. New York, 1850. 8°. 4307
Antifanaticism; a Tale of the South. Martha H. Butt. Phil. 1853. 12°. 5338
Antiquarian Enthusiast. R. Bigsby. London, 1848. 3 v. 8°. . . 4820
Antiquary. Sir W. Scott. Boston, 1848. 2 v. 12°. . . . 999, 5, 6
The same. Edinburgh, 1849. 2 v. 12°. . . . 4100, 5, 6
The same. Edinburgh, 1850. roy. 8°. . . . 4531, 2
Antiquities, American. J. Priest. Albany, 1833. 8°. 2121
and Marbles in the British Museum. London, 1848. 18°. . . 4776
*Dictionary of Greek and Roman. W. Smith. London, 1849. 8°. 3958

Antiquities, Northern. M. Mallet. London, 1847. Post 8°. 3561
of the Anglo-Saxon Church. J. Lingard. Philadelphia, n. d. 8°. 2084
of Great Britain, Popular. J. Brand. London, 1848. 3 v. post 8°. 4369
Peruvian. M. E. Rivero & J. J. von Tschadi. N. York, 1853. 8°. 5440
Roman. A. Adam. New York, 1819. 8°. 626
Antisell, T. Handbook of Useful Arts. New York, 1852. 12°. . . 4603
Anti-Slavery and Colonization Schemes. W. Jay. N. York, 1838. 12°. 1526
Anti-Slavery Documents. 1837–39. 1444
Anti-Slavery Examiner. Vol. 1. New York, 1836. 8°. 785
Anti-Slavery Manual. La Roy Sunderland. New York, 1839. 16°. . 1506
Anti-Slavery Pamphlets, bound in 5 vols. 1639
Anti-Slavery Record. Vols. 1, 2, 3. New York, 1835–37. 12°. . . 1529
Anti-Slavery Riots. New York, 1835. 12°. 1535
Antonina; or, the Fall of Rome. W. W. Collins. New York, 1850. 8°. . 3988
Appleton, J. Lectures, and Occasional Sermons. Brunswick, 1822. 8°. 1386
*Appleton's Dictionary of Mechanics. New York, 1851. 2 v. roy. 8° . 4124
Appleton's Library Manual. New York, 1847. 8°. 2830
Appleton's Mechanics' Magazine. New York, 1851–52. 2 v. 8° & 4°. . 5395
Appleton's Northern and Eastern Traveller's Guide. N. Y. 1853. 12° . 5353
Apocalypse Revealed. E. Swedenborg. Boston, 1836. 3 v. 12°. . . 903
Apocalyptic Sketches. J. Cumming. Philadelphia, 1854. 2 v. 12°. . 5821
Apostolic Church. History of. P. Schaff. New York, 1853. 8°. . . 5448
Apuleius. Works, translated. London, 1853. Post 8°. 5746
Arabella Stuart; a Romance. G. P. R. James. New York, 1847. 8°. . 1761
Arabia, History of. A. Crichton. (H. F. L.) N. Y. 1848. 12°. 3683, 68, 69
Arabian Night's Entertainments. New York, 1848. 3 v. 12°. . . 3336
The same. Philadelphia, 1848. 8°. 24
Arabs in Spain. J. A. Condé. London, 1854–55. 3 v. post 8°. . . 5939
Ararat, Journey to. F. Parrot. Trans. by W. D. Cooley. N. Y. 1846. 12°. 2558
Arbell; a Tale. Jane W. Hooper. New York, 1853. 12°. . . . 5313
Arboretum et Fruticetum, Britannicum. — See *Loudon, J. C., Trees.*
Arbouville, Countess d'. Three Tales. New York, 1853. 12°. . . 5290
Archæological Journal. Vols. 1–5. London, 1846–48. 8°. . . . 3633
*Archer, J. W. Vestiges of Old London. London, 1851. 4°. . . 5429
Archer, Maj. Upper India and Himalaya Mountains. Phil. 1833. 8°. 1357, 1
Archery, Book of. G. A. Hansard. London, 1841. 8°. 4135
Archibald Cameron; or, Heart Trials. New York, 1852. 12°. . . 4932
Architecture, City. M. Field. New York, 1853. 8°. 5438
Designs for Cottages and Villas. Walter & Smith. Phil. 1847. 4°. 2980
*Designs for Shop Fronts and Door Cases. London, n. d. 4°. . 1580
Designs for Village. P. F. Robinson. London, 1837. 4°. . . 5977
Dictionary of Terms in. J. Weale. London, 1849. 12°. . . 6061
Encyclopædia of. J. Gwilt. London, 1851. 8°. 4528
Glossary of Terms in, with 1700 Woodcuts. Oxford, 1852. 2 v. 8°. 2052
Gothic, for Modern Residences. D. H. Arnot. N. Y. 1851. 4°. . 3748
History and Rudiments of. Ed. by J. Bullock. N. Y. 1853. 12°. 5507
of Country Houses. A. J. Downing. New York, 1850. 8°. . 3968
of the Heavens. J. P. Nichol. New York, 1842. 12°. . . 2309

Architecture, Orders of. W. H. Leeds. London, 1854. 12°. . . 6046
and Painting, Lectures on. J. Ruskin. Philadelphia, 1854. 12°. 6170
Principles of Design in. E. L. Garbett. London, 1850. 12°. . 6048
School. H. Barnard. New York, 1854. 8°. 5959
Sculpture and Painting. J. S. Memes. Boston, 1834. 12°. . 1003
Seven Lamps of. J. Ruskin. New York, 1849. 12° . . . 2910
Specimens of Gothic. A. Pugin. London, 1821. 2 v. 4°. . . 5101
Styles of. T. T. Bury. London, 1854. 12°. 6047
Archy Moore, Memoirs of. R. Hildreth. Boston, 1839. 2 v. 12°. . . 1194
Arctic Journal. S. Osborn. New York, 1852. 12°. 4886
*Arctic Regions, Second Voyage to. Sir J. Ross. London, 1835. 4°. . 5895
and Sir John Franklin. P. L. Simmons. Buffalo, 1852. 12°. . 968
T. Simpson's Travels in. A. Simpson. London, 1845. 8°. . . 4684
Arctic Sea Exploring Expedition. A. K. Kane. New York, 1854. 8°. 5892
Arctic Searching Expedition. Sir J. Richardson. New York, 1852. 12°. 318
Ardent Troughton. F. Marryat. New York, 1846. 8°. 2812
Arethusa; a Naval Story. F. Chamier. Philadelphia, 1837. 2 v. 12°. . 276
Argentine Republic, Twenty-four Years in. J. A. King. N.Y. 1846. 12°. 2597
Ariosto, L. Orlando Furioso. Trans. by J. Hoole. Phil. 1816. 6 v. 18°. 138
Aristotle. Rhetoric. Trans. by T. Buckley. London, 1850. Post 8°. . 4381
Ethics. Translated by R. W. Browne. London, 1850. Post 8°. . 4388
Aristocrat, The; an American Tale. Philadelphia, 1833. 2 v. 12°. . 168
Arithmetic, and Key. J. R. Young. London, 1854. 2 v. 12°. . . 6095
Equational. W. Hipsley. London, 1852. 12°. 6096
Arkansaw Doctor, Life and Adventures of. Philadelphia, 1851. 12°. . 4475
Armenians; a Tale of Constantinople. C. MacFarlane. Phil. 1830. 2 v. 12°. 1227
Arminius, J. Life. N. Bangs. New York, 1843. 12°. 2203
Armstrong, J. Art of Preserving Health. A Poem. Balt. 1804. 12°. 144
Armstrong, J. History of the Island of Minorca. London, 1756. 8°. . 2536
Armstrong, J. Life of Richard Montgomery. Boston, 1838. 12°. . 1076, 1
Life of Anthony Wayne. Boston, 1840. 12°. . . . 1076, 4
Armstrong, R. Treatise on Steam Boilers. London, 1850. 12°. . . 6075
Army, Book of the. J. Frost. New York, 1845. 12°. 2180
of U. S., Dictionary of. C. K. Gardner. New York, 1853. 12°. 5242
of the U. States, Organization of. F. Robinson. Phil. 1848. 2 v. 12°. 3087
Arnold, B. Life. J. Sparks. Boston, 1838. 12°. 1076, 3
Arnold, T. History of Rome. New York, 1851. 8°. 5115
Lectures on Modern History. London, 1845. 8°. 2615
Life and Correspondence. A. P. Stanley. New York, 1845. 12°. 2350
The same. New York, 1846. 8°. 3536
Miscellaneous Works. New York, 1845. 8°. 2624
Arnot, D. H. Gothic Architecture for Mod. Residences. N. Y. 1851. 4°. 3748
Arnot, N. Elements of Physic, or Nat. Philosophy. London, 1828. 8°. 1989
Arnot, W. Race for Riches. Six Lectures. Philadelphia, 1853. 12°. . 5339
Arrah Neil; or, Times of Old. G. P. R. James. New York, 1848. 8°. 2172
Art and Industry at Crystal Palace. Ed. by H. Greeley. N. Y. 1854. 12°. 5643
Art, Criticisms on. W. Hazlitt. London, 1844. 12°. 1870
Dictionary of Terms of. J. Weale. London, 1850. 12°. . . 6061

Art, Essays on. J. W. von Goethe. Boston, 1845. 12°. 2367
Lectures on, and Poems. W. Allston. New York, 1850. 12°. . 3669
Philosophy of. F. W. J. Schelling. London, 1845. 12°. . . 2394
Student at Munich. Anna M. Howitt. Boston, 1854. 12°. . 5805
Theory of Effect in. Philadelphia, 1851. 12°. 3816
Arthur Arundel; a Tale. H. Smith. New York, 1844. 12°. . . 2212
Arthur Conway; or, Scenes in the Tropics. E. H. Milman. N.Y. 1851. 8°. 4508
Arthur O'Leary. C. Lever. Philadelphia, 1846. 8°. 2215
Arthur, T. S. Advice to Young Ladies. Boston, 1848. 12°. . . 3059
Advice to Young Men. Boston, 1847. 16°. 2434
Banker's Wife. Philadelphia, 1851. 8°. 4126
Cecilia Howard. New York, 1844. 12°. 2138
The same. Philadelphia, 1851. 8°. 4537
Confessions of a Housekeeper. Philadelphia, 1851. 12°. . . 4460
Heart Histories and Life Pictures. New York, 1853. 12°. . . 5180
Keeping up Appearances. New York, 1847. 16°. . . . 2435
Old Man's Bride. New York, 1853. 12°. 5276
Prose Fictions. Philadelphia, 1844. 12°. 2138
Riches have Wings. New York, 1847. 12°. 2441
Sketches of Life and Character. Philadelphia, 1850. 8°. . . 3634
Sparing and to Spend. New York, 1853. 12°. 5539
Sweethearts and Wives. New York, 1844. 12°. 2195
Ten Nights in a Bar Room. Philadelphia, 1854. 12°. . . 6169
Two Brides. Philadelphia, 1850. 8°. 672
Two Wives; or, Lost and Won. Philadelphia, 1851. 16°. . . 4202
Young Artist; or, Dream of Italy. New York, 1850. 12°. . . 3768
and W. H. Carpenter. History of Kentucky. Phil. 1852. 12°. . 4864
History of Georgia. Philadelphia, 1852. 12°. 4866
History of Virginia. Philadelphia, 1852. 12°. 4865
Arthur, W. Successful Merchant. New York, 1852. 12°. . . . 1056
Artillery and Fortification, Treatise on. H. Straith. Lond. 1850. 2 v. 8°. 4823
and Infantry, Treatise on. C. P. Kingsbury. N. Y. 1849. 12°. . 3412
Artist Life; or, Sketches of Am. Painters. H. T. Tuckerman. N.Y. 1847. 12° 3057
Artist, Merchant, and Statesman. C. E. Lester. N. York, 1845. 2 v. 12°. 2501
Artist Wife; and other Tales. Mary Howitt. New York, 1853. 12°. . 5504
Artist's Chromatic Handbook. J. B. Ridner. New York, 1850. 12°. . 4059
Artist's Married Life. L. Schefer. Boston, 1849. 12°. 3333
Artisan; a Jour. of Operative Arts. Vols. 4, 5, 7–9. Lond. 1846–51. 4°. 5103
Arts and Manufactures, Chem. applied to. F. Knapp. Lond. 1848. 2 v. 8°. 4137
Fine. — See *Fine Arts*.
Handbook of Useful. T. Antisell. New York, 1852. 12°. . 4603
Manufactures, and Mines, Dictionary of. A. Ure. N. Y. 1849. 8°. 1687
*The same. New York, 1853. 2 v. 8°. 1687
*Pictorial Gallery of the Useful and Fine. London, 1847. 2 v. 4°. 4830
Register of. T. G. Fessenden. Philadelphia, 1808. 8°. . . 738
Useful; their Birth and Development. S. Martin. Lond. 1851. 12°. 4214
Useful, with Applications of Science. J. Bigelow. Bost. 1840. 12°. 2923
Arvine, K. Cyclopædia of Anecdotes. Boston, 1851. Roy. 8°. . . 3379

Arvine, K. Cyclopædia of Moral and Religious Anecdotes. N.Y. 1850. 8°. 4551
As Good as a Comedy; a Tennesseean's Story. Philadelphia, 1852. 12°. 3470
Ascanio; or, the Sculptor's Apprentices. A. Dumas. N. Y. 1846. 8°. . 2643
Ashton, W. T. Hatchie, the Guardian Slave. Boston, 1853. 12°. . 5228
Asia, Travels in South Eastern. H. Malcom. Boston, 1839. 2 v. 12° . 1250
Asia Minor, Egypt, &c., Sketches of. C. J. Monk. Lond. 1851. 2 v. 12°. 4233
Asiatic History, Lights & Shadows of. S. G. Goodrich. Bost. 1849. 12°. 4900, 9
Asiatic Researches. London, 1799. 5 v. 4°. 2001
Asmodeus; or, Devil on Two Sticks. A. R. Le Sage. London, 1845. 12°. 2426
Asmodeus at Large. E. L. Bulwer. Philadelphia, 1833. 12°. . . 1208
Aspects of Nature in Different Lands. A. von Humboldt. Phil. 1849. 12°. 3469
Assayer's Guide. O. M. Lieber. Philadelphia, 1852. 12°. . . . 5006
Assignments, Law of. J. K. Angell. Boston, 1835. 12°. . . . 1164
Association, and Organization of Labor. M. Briancourt. N. Y. 1847. 12°. 2439
and Re-organization of Industry. A. Brisbane. Phil. 1840. 12°. 2136
Astoria; or, Advent. beyond Rocky Mount. W. Irving. N. Y. 1849. 12°. 3361
The same. New York, 1851. 12°. 595
Astræa; a Poem. O. W. Holmes. Boston, 1850. 12°. 4040
Astronomer, Practical. T. Dick. New York, 1846. 12°. . . . 2532
Astronomy, Compendium of. D. Olmsted. New York, 1841. 12°. . 1695
Cycle of Celestial Objects. W. H. Smyth. London, 1844. 2 v. 8°. 5466
*Descriptive Atlas of. T. Milner. London, 1850. 4°. . . . 3965
Elements of. S. Vince. Philadelphia, 1811. 8°. . . . 616
Historical Account of. J. Narrien. London, 1850. 8°. . . 1157
Introduction to. J. Ferguson. Philadelphia, 1805. 12°. . . 337
Orbs of Heaven. O. M. Mitchel. London, 1851. 12°. . . 4274
Outlines of. J. F. W. Herschel. Philadelphia, 1849. 8°. . . 3471
Planetary and Stellar Worlds. O. M. Mitchel. N. Y. 1848. 12°. 3143
Practical. G. Jeans. London, n. d. 12°. 5050
Progress in United States. E. Loomis. New York, 1851. 12°. . 4027
Solar System. J. R. Hind. New York, 1852. 12°. . . . 4880
Solar System. J. P. Nichol. New York, 1843. 12°. . . . 2308
System of. J. Vose. Concord, 1827. 8°. 634
Treatise on. R. Main. London, 1852. 12°. 6104
Atheism among the People. A. de Lamartine. Boston, 1850. 12°. . 3877
Athenæum. Vols. 13, 14; 2d s., 4, 7, 8; 3d s., 3. Bost. 1823–30. 6 v. 8°. 688
Athenæus. Deipnosophists. Tr. by C. D. Yonge. Lond. 1854. 3 v. post 8°. 5943
Athenian Oracle. London, 1738. 4 v. 8°. 1561
Athens; its Rise and Fall. E. L. Bulwer. New York, 1852. 2 v. 12°. . 153
Atherton, and other Tales. Mary R. Mitford. Boston, 1854. 12°. . 5885
Atlantic and Transatlantic. Capt. Mackinnon. New York, 1852. 12°. . 5018
Atlantic Club-Book. Sketches in Prose and Verse. N. Y. 1847. 2 v. 12°. 2971
Atlas and Gazetteer of the Bible. W. Jenks. Boston, 1847. 4°. . . 3232
*Black's General. Edinburgh, 1851. 4°. 1702
*Comprehensive. T. G. Bradford. Boston, 1835. 4°. . . . 3741
*Morse's North American. New York, 1842. 4°. 2049
*of the World, Appleton's Complete. New York, n. d. 4°. . . 5450
*Tallis's Illustrated. Ed. by R. M. Martin. London, 1851. 4°. . 4948

Atlas to Walker's Geography. London, 1806. 8°. 689
Attila; a Romance. G. P. R. James. New York, 1837. 2 v. 12°. . 202
Attorney, Confessions of an. S. Warren. New York, 1852. 12°. . 4772
Attorneys and Solicitors, Moral Duties of. S. Warren. N.Y. 1849. 12°. 2464
Auber, P. Rise & Progress of British Power in India. Lond. 1837. 2 v. 8° 4660
Aubin, Mrs. Noble Slaves. Boston, 1821. 16°. 45
Aubrey. Mrs. Marsh. New York, 1854. 8°. 5966
Auchindrane; or, the Ayrshire Tragedy. W. Scott. N. Y. 1839. 12°. 860, 6
Aunt Kitty's Tales. Maria J. McIntosh. New York, 1849. 12°. . . 3932
Aunt Phillis's Cabin. Mary H. Eastman. Philadelphia, 1852. 12°. . 4853
Austen, Jane. Novels. Philadelphia, 1838. 2 v. 8°. 1585

Vol. 1. Pride and Prejudice; Mansfield Park; Persuasion.
2. Sense and Sensibility; Emma; Northanger Abbey.

Emma. London, 1853. 12°. 5692
Mansfield Park. London, 1853. 12°. 5693
Northanger Abbey. London, 1853. 12°. 5694
Pride and Prejudice. London, 1853. 12°. 5691
Sense and Sensibility. London, 1853. 12°. 5690
Persuasion. Philadelphia, 1832. 2 v. 12°. 531
Austin, J. M. Golden Steps for Youth. Auburn, 1850. 12°. . . 3860
Austin, J. T. Life of Elbridge Gerry. Boston, 1828. 3 v. 8°. . . 1311
Austin, W. Letters from London, 1802–3. Boston, 1804. 8°. . . 733
Australia, History of. R. M. Martin. London, n. d. Roy. 8°. . . 4941
Nine Years in. Mrs. C. Meredith. New York, 1853. 12°. . . 5275
Three Colonies of. S. Sidney. London, 1852. 8°. 5153
Australia Felix, Impressions of. R. Howitt. London, 1845. 12°. . . 2392
Austria and the Austrians. London, 1837, 2 v. 12°. 4440
During its Revolutionary Crisis. W. Peake. Lond. 1851. 2 v. 12°. 4617
History of House of. W. Coxe. London, 1847. 3 v. post 8°. . 3553
in 1848–49. W. H. Stiles. New York, 1852. 2 v. 8°. . . 4833
Vienna, and Prague. J. G. Kohl. Philadelphia, 1844. 8°. . 2684
Authors, Homes of American. New York, 1853. 8°. 5452
of England. Living. T. Powell. New York, 1849. 12°. . . 3439
Quarrels of. I. D'Israeli. New York, 1814. 2 v. 12°. . . 453
Autobiography of an Actress. Mrs. A. C. Mowatt. Boston, 1854. 12°. 5625
of a Dissenting Minister. Philadelphia, 1854. 12°. . . . 5827
of an English Soldier in the U. S. Army. New York, 1853. 12°. 5274
Ava, Embassy to Court of. J. Crawfurd. London, 1834. 2 v. 8°. . 4817
Ayrshire Legatees; or Prindle Family. J. Galt. New York, 1823. 12°. 1906
Ayton, R. Essays and Sketches of Character. London, 1825. 12°. . 2387
Aytoun, W. E. Firmilian; a Spasmodic Tragedy. New York, 1854. 12°. 6212
Lays of the Scottish Cavaliers. New York, 1853. 12°. . . 6227

B.

Babbage, C. Exposition of 1851. London, 1851. 8°. 4345
Bachelor of the Albany. M. W. Savage. New York, 1848. 12°. . . 2878
Bachelor of Salamanca. A. R. Le Sage. Philadelphia, 1854. 12°. . 6209
Back, G. Arctic Land Expedition, 1833-35. Philadelphia, 1836. 8°. . 1423
Backus, J. Church Hist. of New England, 1602-1804. Bost. 1804. 12°. 5560
Bacon, F. (Lord). Essays, Moral, Economical, &c. Boston, 1807. 12°. . 1041
The same. Philadelphia, 1818. 12°. 889
The same. (H. F. L.) New York, 1848. 12°. . . 3683, 171
Works, with Life. B. Montague. Philadelphia, 1844. 3 v. roy. 8°. 1996
Bacon, L. Life of Richard Baxter. New Haven, 1834. 8°. . . 2058, 1
Bacon, N. Life. W. Ware. Boston, 1844. 12°. 1076, 13
Bacon, W. T. Poems. Cambridge, 1848. 12°. 3331
Bailey, I. American Naval Biography. Providence, 1815. 12°. . . 209
Bailey, P. J. Angel World, and other Poems. Boston, 1850. 12°. . 3898
Festus, a Poem. Boston, 1849. 12°. 2396
Bailey, S. Essays. Boston, 1854. 12°. 5855

• On the Formation and Publication of Opinions; On the Pursuit of Truth; On the Progress of Knowledge.

Essays on the Formation and Pub. of Opinions. Phil. 1831. 12°. 2160
Essays on the Pursuit of Truth. Philadelphia, 1831. 12°. . . 2156
Baillie, Joanna. Complete Poetical Works. Philadelphia, 1832. 8°. . 2700
Dramas. Philadelphia, 1836. 8°. 2228, 2
Bainbridge, W. (Com.). Life and Services. T. Harris. Phil. 1837. 8°. 627
Baird, R. Christian Retrospect and Register. New York, 1851. 12°. . 4206
Impressions of West Indies and North America. Phil. 1850. 12°. 3873
Visit to Northern Europe. New York, 1841. 2 v. 12°. . . 2119
Baird, R. H. American Cotton Spinner. Philadelphia, 1851. 12°. . 4263
Baker, T. Land and Engineering Surveying. London, 1850. 12°. . 6076
Treatise on Mechanism. London, 1852. 12°. 6106
Treatise on Mensuration. London, 1850. 12°. 6102
Treatise on Statics and Dynamics. London, 1851. 12°. . . 6105
Baldwin, J. G. Flush Times of Alabama. New York, 1853. 12°. . 5602
Baldwin, T. Universal Pronouncing Gazetteer. Philadelphia, 1847. 12°. 2973
*and J. Thomas. Gazetteer of the United States. Phil. 1854. 8°. 5494
Ballads, Book of. Edited by "Bon Gaultier." New York, 1852. 12°. . 4399
Ballantyne, R. M. Hudson's Bay. Edinburgh, 1848. 12°. . . . 5550
Balloons, History of, and Experience with. J. Wise. Phil. 1850. 8°. . 4148
Ballou, M. M. Biography of Hosea Ballou. Boston, 1852. 12°. . . 4994
History of Cuba. Boston, 1854. 12°. 6165
Baltic, Letters from the Shores of. London, 1845. 12°. . . . 2393
Bancroft, E. Philosophy of Permanent Colors. Phil. 1814. 2 v. 8°. . 654
Bancroft, G. History of the United States. Boston, 1837-54. 6 v. 8°. . 954
Bangs, N. Life of James Arminius. New York, 1843. 12°. . . . 2203
Banim, J. Bit o' Writin', and other Tales. Philadelphia, 1838. 2 v. 12°. 1034

Banim, J. Croppy; a Tale. Philadelphia, 1829. 12°. 1153
Denounced. New York, 1830. 2 v. 12°. 543
Loaded Dice. New York, 1844. 8°. 2167, 3
Mayor of Wind-Gap. New York, 1835. 12°. 1146
Smuggler. London, 1851. 12°. 5656
The same. New York, 1832. 2 v. 12°. 403
Banker's Almanac, 1851–52. Boston. 8°. 4141
Banker's Common-Place Book. Boston, 1851. 12°. 3821
Banker's Magazine. Vols. 5–9 [continued]. Bost. & N. Y. 1850–54. 8°. 3733
Banker's Wife. T. S. Arthur. Philadelphia, 1851. 8°. . . . 4126
Banking, Free. C. Duncombe. Cleveland, 1841. 12°. 992
History of. W. J. Lawson. London, 1850. 8°. 4646
Practical Treatise on. J. W. Gilbart. London, 1849. 2 v. 8°. . 3802
Banks, History of, and Free Competition in Banking. Boston, 1837. 12°. 134
in Europe, Hist. of the Prominent. T. H. Goddard. N.Y. 1831. 8°. 749
Banner of the Constitution. Vols. 1–3. Wash. & Phil. 1830–33. 4°. . 2023
Banque du France, Législation relative à. Paris, 1830. 4°. . . . 2020
Banvard, J. Daniel Webster, the American Statesman. Bost. 1853. 12°. 5554
Novelties of the New World. Boston, 1852. 16°. 4632
Plymouth and the Pilgrims. Boston, 1851. 12°. 4272
Priscilla; or, Trials for the Truth. Boston, 1854. 12°. . . . 5644
Romance of American History. Boston, 1852. 12°. 4924
Baptist Missions, History of American. W. Gammell. Bost. 1849. 12°. 3504
Barba Tassi, the Greek Patriot; a Romance. London, 1850. 12°. . . 4226
Barbary States, History of. M. Russell. (H. F. L.) N. Y. 1846. 12°. 3683, 73
Lady's Diary in. London, 1850. 2 v. 12°. 4243
White Slavery in. C. Sumner. Boston, 1853. 12°. 5249
Barber, J. W. Hist. Collections of Connecticut. N. Haven, 1836. 8°. . 652
Historical Collections of Massachusetts. Worcester, 1848. 8°. . 1964
Historical Collections of New York. New York, 1851. 8°. . . 2718
Hist. & Antiq. of New Eng., N. Y., N. J., & Penn. Hart. 1846. 8°. 2721
Incidents in American History. New York, 1847. 12°. . . 2987
and H. Howe. Hist. Collections of New Jersey. N. Y. 1845. 8°. 2720
Barber, M. A. S. Du Bourg; or, The Mercuriale. London, 1851. 12°. 4608
Barclay, J. Complete English Dictionary. London, n. d. 4°. . . 2024
Barclay, R. Apology for Quakerism. Philadelphia, 1805. 8°. . . 1918
Barclays of Boston. Mrs. H. G. Otis. Boston, 1854. 12°. . . . 5777
Barham, R. H. D. Ingoldsby Legends, 1st series. New York, 1852. 12°. 4775
My Cousin Nicholas. London, 1852. 12°. 5681
Barker, W. B. Lares & Penates; or, Cilicia & its Governors. Lond. 1853. 8°. 5461
Barnaby Rudge. C. Dickens. Philadelphia, 1849. 8°. 1674
Barnard, H. National Education in Europe. New York, 1854. 8°. . 5960
School Architecture. New York, 1854. 8°. 5959
Barnes, A. Notes on Daniel. New York, 1853. 12°. 5538
Notes on Isaiah. New York, 1851. 2 v. 12°. 4739
Notes on Job. New York, 1850. 2 v. 12°. 4740
Notes on the Gospels. New York, 1851. 2 v. 12°. . . . 4730
Notes on the Acts. New York, 1851. 12°. 4731

Barnes, A. Notes on Romans. New York, 1851. 12°. 4732
Notes on 1st Corinthians. New York, 1851. 12°. . . . 4733
Notes on 2d Corinthians and Galatians. New York, 1851. 12°. . 4734
Notes on Ephesians, Philippians and Colossians. N. Y. 1851. 12°. 4735
Notes on Thes. Timothy, Titus, and Phil. New York, 1849. 12°. 4736
Notes on Hebrews. New York, 1851. 12°. 4737
Notes on Epistles of James, Peter, John, & Jude. N. Y. 1851. 12°. 4738
Practical Sermons. Philadelphia, 1851. 12°. 4741
Barnum, H. L. Spy Unmasked. New York, 1828. 8°. . . . 1363
Barnwell, R. G. (Editor.) New Orleans Book. New Orleans, 1851. 12°. 3928
Baron, J. Life of Edward Jenner. London, 1818. 2 v. 8°. . . . 4552
*Baronial Halls of England. London, n. d. 4°. 5451
Barony. Miss A. M. Porter. New York, 1830. 2 v. 12°. . . . 1192
Barrell, G., jun. Pedestrian in France and Switzerland. N. Y. 1853. 12°. 5376
Barrett, Elizabeth B. Drama of Exile, &c. N. Y. 1845. 2 v. 12° . . 2179
Seraphim, and other Poems. London, 1838. 12°. . . . 2475
See also *Browning, Mrs. E. B.*
Barrington, Sir J. Personal Sketches. New York, 1853. 12°. . . 5422
Barrister, Experiences of a. S. Warren. New York, 1852. 12°. . . 4771
Barrow, I. Works, with Life. A. Hill. New York, 1845. 3 v. 8°. . 4719
Barrow, J. Life & Corres. of Sir W. Sidney Smith. Lond. 1848. 2 v. 8°. 5146
Life of Peter the Great. (H. F. L.) New York, 1848. 12°. 3683, 65
Naval Worthies of Queen Elizabeth's Reign. London, 1845. 8°. 2666
Pitcairn's Island, &c. (H. F. L.) New York, 1848. 12°. . 3683, 31
Travels in China. Philadelphia, 1805. 8°. 763
Barrows, E. P., jun. American Slavery Question. N. York, 1836. 16°. 1505
Barry, J., J. Opie, & H. Fuseli. Lectures on Painting. Lond. 1848. Post 8°. 4361
Barry, J. S. Genealogical Sketch of the Family of Stetson. Bost. 1847. 8°. 3046
Barry, P. Fruit Garden. New York, 1851. 12°. 4164
Barry, W. History of Framingham, Mass. Boston, 1847. 8°. . . 2834
Barstow, G. History of New Hampshire. Concord, 1842. 8°. . . 1975
Bartlett, D. W. What I Saw in London. Auburn, 1852. 12°. . . 4782
Bartlett, J. R. Dictionary of Americanisms. New York, 1848. 8°. . 4956
Explorations in Texas and New Mexico. N. York, 1854. 2 v. 8°. 5950
Progress of Ethnology. New York, 1847. 8°. 2792
Bartlett, W. H. Nile Boat; or, Glimpses of Egypt. N. Y. 1851. Roy. 8°. 4516
*Ports and Harbors of Great Britain. London, 1842. 2 v. 4°. . 3742
*Switzerland Illustrated. London, 1834. 4°. 3744
Bartol, C. A. Discourses on Christian Body and Form. Bost. 1853. 12°. 5219
Discourses on Christian Spirit and Life. Boston, 1850. 12°. . 3844
Barton, B. Memoir, Letters, and Poems. Philadelphia, 1850. 12°. . 3649
Barton, K. Io; a Tale of Olden Fane. New York, 1851. 12°. . . 4437
Barton, Wm. Biography. Mrs. C. R. Williams. Prov. 1839. 12°. . 1571
Bartram, J., and H. Marshall. Memoir. W. Darlington. Phil. 1849. 8°. 2864
Basil; a Story of Modern Life. W. W. Collins. New York, 1853. 12°. 5058
Basire, I. Correspond., with Memoir. W. N. Darnell. Lond. 1831. 8°. 1490
Bass Rock, Geology of. H. Miller. New York, 1851. 12°. . . . 4269
Bastile, History of, and its Captives. R. A. Davenport. Phil. 1846. 12°. 2595

Batavian Anthology; or, Spec. of Dutch Poets. J.Bowring. Lond. 1824. 12° 2416
Battle of Lake Erie. T. Burges. Boston, 1839. 12°. 417
of Life; a Love Story. C. Dickens. New York, 1847. 12°. . 2958
of Niagara. A Poem. Baltimore, 1818. 18°. 135
of Waterloo, Story of. G. R. Gleig. New York, 1847. 12°. . 3023
Battle Summer. D. G. Mitchell. New York, 1850. 12°. . . . 3486
Battles of the British Navy. J. Allen. London, 1852. 2 v. post 8°. . 5015
of the World, Fifteen Decisive. E. S. Creasy. Lond. 1851. 2 v. 12°. 4442
Baucher, F. Method of Horsemanship. Philadelphia, 1852. 12°. . . 5834
Bayard, Chevalier. Life. W. G. Simms. New York, 1847. 12°. . 3098
Bayly, T. H. Songs and Ballads, with Mem. of Author. Phil. 1834. 12°. 2360
Baxter, R. Saints' Everlasting Rest. Boston, 1850. 12°. . . . 1017
Select Practical Writings, with Life. New Haven, 1835. 2 v. 8°. 2058
Beasley, H. Druggist's General Receipt Book. Philadelphia, 1853. 12°. 5063
The same. Philadelphia, 1850. 12°. 3672
Beatrice; or, the Influence of Words. S. S. Jones. London, 1850. 12°. 4229
Beatrice; or, Unknown Relatives. Cath. Sinclair. N. York, 1853. 12°. 5257
Beatson, R. Naval & Military Mem. of G. Britain. Lond. 1804. 6 v. 8°. 5905
Beattie, J. Minstrel; or, Progress of Genius. Baltimore, 1804. 12°. . 144
Poetical Works. New York, 1844. 12°. 12
Beattie, W. (Editor). Life & Letters of T. Campbell. N. Y. 1850. 2 v. 12°. 3895
*Ports of G. Britain. Illustrated by Bartlett. Lond. 1842. 2 v. 4°. 3742
*Switzerland. Illus. by W. H. Bartlett. London, 1834. 4°. . 3744
*Waldenses. Illus. by Bartlett and Brockedon. London, 1836. 4°. 3746
Beauchamp; or, the Error. G. P. R. James. New York, 1847. 8°. . 2766
Beauchampe; or, the Ky. Tragedy. W. G. Simms. Phil. 1842. 2 v. 12°. 1678
Beauclerk, Misses. Tales of Fashion and Reality. Phil. 1836. 12°. . 236
Beaumont, G. de, & A. de Tocqueville. Peni. Syst. in U. S. Phil. 1833. 8°. 1583
Beaumont, F., and J. Fletcher. Dramatic Works. Lond. 1840. 2 v. 8°. 1827
Beaumont, J. A. B. Travels in Buenos Ayres. London, 1828. 8°. . 5010
Beauties of the Court of Charles II. Mrs. A. Jameson. Boston, 1834. 8°. 2083
of Nature. C. Bucke. (H. F. L.) New York, 1848. 12°. . 3683, 145
of Shakspeare. Edited by W. Dodd. London, n. d. 12°. . . 2207
of the Spectator, Tatler, and Guardian. Boston, 1801. 2 v. 12°. . 863
and Wonders of Nature and Art. P. Wakefield. Phil. 1819. 12°. 435
and Wonders of Nat. & Science. Ed. by L. Gilbert. Lond. n.d. 8°. 2839
Beautiful Bertha. Mrs. L. C. Tuthill. New York, 1854. 16°. . . 6216
Beauty in Woman. A. Walker. Hartford, 1848. 12°. 1753
Beawes, W. Merchant's Directory. London, 1783. Folio. . . . 2036
Bechstein, J. M. Cage and Chamber Birds. London, 1853. Post 8°. . 5758
Becker, W. A. Charicles; or, Private Life of the Greeks. Lond. 1854. 12°. 5831
Gallus; or, Roman Scenes. London, 1849. 12°. 5646
Beckford, W. Italy, Spain, and Portugal. New York, 1845. 2 v. 12°. . 2913
Monasteries of Alcobaça and Batalha. Philadelphia, 1835. 12°. . 1081
Vathek; an Arabian Tale. London, 1853. 12°. 5702
Beckmann, J. History of Inventions, Discov. &c. Lond. 1846. 2 v. post 8°. 3090
Bede (The Venerable). Ecclesiastical Hist. of Eng. Lond. 1847. Post 8°. 4365
Beechen Tree; a Tale in Rhyme. F. W. Thomas. New York, 1844. 12°. 2097

Beecher, Cath. E. Remedy for the Wrongs of Woman. Bost. 1851. 12°. 4415
Slavery and Abolitionists. Philadelphia, 1837. 12°. . . . 1509
Truth Stranger than Fiction. New York, 1850. 12°. . . . 3881
Beecher, C. Incarnation; or, Pictures of the Virgin. N. Y. 1849. 12°. 3306
Beecher, E. Conflict of Ages. Boston, 1853. 12°. 5528
Riots at Alton, and Death of E. P. Lovejoy. Alton, 1838. 12°. . 1532
Beecher, H. W. Lectures to Young Men. Indianapolis, 1844. 12°. . 2181
Beecher, L. Works. Boston, 1852–53. 3 v. 12°. 4593
Vol. 1. Lectures on Political Atheism; Six Lectures on Intemperance.
2. Sermons on Various Occasions.
3. Views of Theology; Trial before Presbytery; Remarks on the Princeton Review.

Beechnut; a Franconia Story. J. Abbott. New York, 1850. 12°. . 4155
Bees, Management of. London, n. d. Roy. 8°. 3635, 2
Natural History of. — Dunbar. Edinburgh, 1843. 12°. . 4901, 34
Beetles, Natural History of. J. Duncan. Edinburgh, 1843. 12°. . 4901, 33
Before and Behind the Curtain. W. K. Northall. N. Y. 1851. 12°. . 4110
Begbie, P. I. Supernatural Illusions. London, 1851. 2 v. 12°. . . 4197
Behavior Book. Miss Leslie. Philadelphia, 1854. 12°. 5880
Behind the Curtain; a Tale of Elville. Dansville, 1853. 12°. . . 5283
Behind the Scenes. Lady Bulwer. New York, 1854. 12°. . . . 5849
Belcher, Sir E. Voyage round the World, 1836–42. Lond. 1843. 2 v. 8°. 2853
Belfast, Earl of. Two Generations; a Novel. London, 1851. 2 v. 12°. . 4237
Belford Regis. M. R. Mitford. Philadelphia, 1846. 8°. . . . 1637
Belfry of Bruges, & other Poems. H. W. Longfellow. Camb. 1846. 12°. 2535
Belgian Traveller in 1804–5. Middletown, 1807. 8°. 734
Belgium. J. E. Tennent. London, 1841. 2 v. 12°. 4572
Since the Revolution of 1830. W. Trollope. Lond. 1842. 12°. . 4629
Belisarius, Life of. Lord Mahon. Philadelphia, 1832. 12°. . . . 216
Belknap, J. American Biography. Boston, 1794. 8° 643
The same. (H. F. L.) New York, 1844. 3 v. 12°. 3683, 161–3
History of New Hampshire. Philadelphia, 1784–92. 3 v. 8°. . 583
The same. Dover, N. H. 1812. 3 v. 8°. 1303
Bell, Currer. — See *Bronte, Caroline.*
Bell, H. G. Life of Mary, Queen of Scots. New York, 1844. 2 v. 12°. . 2401
The same. (H. F. L.) New York, 1847. 2 v. 12°. 3683, 21, 22
Bell, J. Observations on Italy. Boston, 1826. 12°. 495
Bell, Mrs. M. Julia Howard; a Romance. London, 1850. 3 v. 12°. . 4273
Bell, R. Life of George Canning. New York, 1846. 12°. . . . 2904
Bellamy, J. Works. Boston, 1850. 2 v. 8°. 4718
Belshazzar, a Poem. H. H. Milman. Boston, 1822. 12°. . . . 837
Belzoni, G. Discoveries in Egypt and Nubia. London, 1822. 2 v. 8°. . 2655
Bemis, G. Report of Trial of J. W. Webster. Boston, 1850. 8°. . . 4315
Ben Brace. F. Chamier. London, 1852. 12°. 5671
Benecke, W. Indemnity in Marine Insurance, &c. Boston, 1833. 8°. . 2060
Benedictions; or, the Blessed Life. J. Cumming. Boston, 1854. 12°. . 5753
Bengalee; or, Sketches in India. Philadelphia, 1833. 8°. . . 1357, 3
Benger, Elizabeth O. Memoirs of Anne Boleyn. Phil. 1850. 12°. . 3918
Bennet, B. Memorial of the Reformation. Edinburgh, 1748. 8°. . . 476

Bennett, E. Pioneer's Daughter. New York, 1851. 8°. 4336
Bennett, G. J. Pedestrian's Guide through N. Wales. Lond. 1840. 8°. 4665
Bennett, J. Letters to a Young Lady. Philadelphia, 1793. 2 v. 12°. . 185
Bennett, J. C. Poultry Book. Boston, 1851. 12°. 3663
Bennett, W. C. Poems. London, 1850. 12°. 5299
Bensley, B. Henry VIII., and his Contemporaries. London, 1844. 12°. 2395
Bentham, J. Principles of Legislation. Boston, 1830. 8°. . . . 786

Bentley's Library of Standard Novels. London, 1850-54. 100 v. 12°.:—

Ainsworth, W. H. Rookwood. . . 5712
Andersen, H. C. Improvisatore. . . 5736
Austen, Jane. Emma. 5692
Mansfield Park. 5693
Northanger Abbey. . . . 5694
Pride and Prejudice. . . . 5691
Seuse and Sensibility. . . . 5690
Banim, J. Smuggler. 5656
Barham, R. H. D. My Cousin Nicholas. 5681
Beckford, W. Vathek. 5702
Brown, C. B. Edgar Huntley. . . 5699
Brunton, Mary. Discipline. . . . 5651
Self-Control. 5650
Bulwer, E. L. Eugene Aram. . . 5701
Last Days of Pompeii. . . . 5721
Paul Clifford. 5706
Chamier, F. Ben Brace. . . . 5671
Life of a Sailor. 5689
Cooper, J. F. Heidenmauer. . . . 5710
Costellow, L. S. Catharine de Medicis. . 5739
Dacre, Lady. Tales of the Peerage, &c. 5687
Recollections of a Chaperon. . 5685
Edgeworth, Maria. Helen. . . . 5669
Experiences of a Gaol Chaplain. . . 5686
Ferrier, Susan. Destiny. . . . 5676
Inheritance. 5725
Marriage. 5724
Galt, John. Lawrie Todd. . . . 5653
Gleig, G. R. Country Curate. . . 5703
Godwin, Wm. Caleb Williams. . . 5695
Fleetwood. 5654
St. Leon. 5647
Grattan, T. C. Heiress of Bruges. . 5661
Jacqueline of Holland. . . 5726
Legends of the Rhine. . . . 5738
Gore, Mrs. C. Hamiltons. . . . 5688
Mothers and Daughters. . . 5660
Soldier of Lyons. 5675
Hall, Mrs. S. C. Buccaneer. . . . 5723
Outlaw. 5682
Hood, T. Tylney Hall. 5673
Hook, T. E. All in the Wrong. . . 5679
Gilbert Gurney. 5677
Jack Brag. 5670
Maxwell. 5659
Parson's Daughter. . . . 5663
Widow and the Marquis. . . 5678
Howard, E. Ratlin the Reefer. . . 5667
Hugo, V. Hunchback of Notre Dame. . 5658
Hunt, L. Sir Ralph Esher. . . . 5737
Inchbald, Eliza. Simple Story. . . 5655
James, G. P. R. Darnley. . . . 5707
De l'Orme. 5709
Henry Masterton. . . . 5713
Man-at-Arms. 5727
Philip Augustus. 5711
Landon, Miss. Romance and Reality. . 5684
Lee, Misses. Canterbury Tales. . . 5649
Lewis, M. G. Bravo of Venice. . . 5702
Manzoni, A. Betrothed. . . . 5662
Marryat, F. Dog Fiend. . . . 5733
Jacob Faithful. 5715
Japhet in Search of a Father. . 5716
King's Own. 5717
Midshipman Easy. 5718
Newton Forster. 5719
Pacha of Many Tales. . . . 5720
Percival Keene. 5735
Peter Simple. 5714
Phantom Ship. 5732
Poacher. 5731
Marsh, Mrs. Two Old Men's Tales. . 5728
Maxwell, W. H. Bivouac. . . . 5722
Capt. Blake. 5668
Hector O'Halloran. . . . 5683
Stories of Waterloo. . . . 5657
Morier, J. Hajji Baba. 5704
Hajji Baba in England. . . 5705
Zorab. 5708
Murray, C. A. Prairie Bird. . . . 5730
Peacock, G. Headlong Hall. . . . 5665
Porter, Anna M. Hungarian Brothers. . 5648
Porter, Jane. Pastor's Fireside. 2 v. . 5652
Scottish Chiefs. 2 v. . . . 5697
Thaddeus of Warsaw. . . . 5696
Schiller, T. Ghost-Seer. . . 5698, 5699
Shelley, Mrs. Frankenstein. . . . 5698
Smith, A. Adventures of Mr. Ledbury. 5734
Marchioness of Brenvilliers. . 5680
Staël, Mad. de. Corinne. . . . 5700
Trelawney, Capt. Younger Son. . . 5664
Trevelyan. 5666
Trollope, Mrs. F. Vicar of Wrexhill. . 5672
Widow Barnaby. 5674
Walpole, H. Castle of Otranto. . . 5702
Whitehead, C. Richard Savage. . . 5729

Bentley's Miscellany. 7 imperfect vols. New York, 1839–42. 8°. . . 1611
Benton, T. H. Thirty Years' View of U. S. Government. N. Y. 1854. 8°. 5931
Béranger, P. J. de. Lyrical Poems. Trans. by W. Young. N.Y. 1850. 12°. 4057
Berber; a Tale of Morocco. W. S. Mayo. New York, 1850. 12°. . 3901
Berkeley E. World's Laconics. New York, 1853. 12°. . . . 5029
Berkeley, G. (Bishop). Works, with Life. London, 1837. 8°. . . 1979
Berkshire Jubilee, at Pittsfield, 1844. Albany, 1845. 8°. . . . 2220
Berlin, Ten Months' Residence in. Major Whittingham. Lond. 1846. 8°. 1129
Berlyn, P. and C. Fowler, jun. Crystal Palace. London, 1851. 8°. . 4310
Bernard, C. de. Lion's Skin and Lover Hunt. New York, 1853. 12°. . 5241
Bernhard (Duke of Saxe-Weimar). Travels in N. Am. Phil. 1828. 2 v. 8°. 1398
Berridge, J. Christian World Unmasked. Boston, 1854. 12°. . . 5606
Bertha and Lily. Elizabeth O. Smith. New York, 1854. 12°. . . 6172
Bertha; a Rom. of the Dark Ages. W. B. MacCabe. Lond. 1851. 3 v. 12°. 4246
Bethune, G. W. British Female Poets. Philadelphia, 1848. 8°. . . 3191
Orations and Occasional Discourses. New York, 1850. 12°. . 3449

Genius; True Glory; Leisure, its Uses and Abuses; Age of Pericles; Oration at University of Pennsylvania; Prospects of Art in the United States; Discourse on the Death of Wm. H. Harrison; Eloquence of the Pulpit; Duties of Educated Men; Duty of a Patriot; Plea for Study; Claims of our Country upon Literary Men.

Sermons. Philadelphia, 1846. 8°. 3607
Betrothed, The. A. Manzoni. New York, 1845. 2 v. 12°. . . . 2496
The same. London, 1851. 12°. 5662
Better Land; or, the Believer's Jour. A. C. Thompson. Bost. 1854. 12°. 6193
Betterton, T. History of the English Stage. Boston, 1814. 8°. . . 2074
Beverly, Mass., History of. E. M. Stone. Boston, 1843. 12°. . . 3072
Bewick, T. History of British Birds. Newcastle, 1847. 2 v. 8°. . . 4957
and J. Select Fables. Newcastle, 1820. 8°. 5899
Beza, T. Life of John Calvin. Philadelphia, 1836. 12°. . . . 1935
Bible, The; containing the Old and New Testaments. N. York, 1819. 8°. 1371
Annals of the English. C. Anderson. New York, 1849. 8°. . 3406
Atlas, and Scripture Gazetteer. W. Jenks. Boston, 1847. 4°. . 3232
Catholic History of. J. Reeve. Boston, 1849. 12°. . . . 3681
Dictionary of. A. Calmet. Boston, 1843. Roy. 8°. . . . 1439
Family Pictures from. Mrs. E. F. Ellet. New York, 1849. 12°. 3442
Four Gospels, with Dissertations. G. Campbell. And. 1837. 2 v. 8°. 4703
Historical Geography of. L. Coleman. Philadelphia, 1849. 12°. . 3428
History of. G. R. Gleig. (H. F. L.) N. Y. 1843. 2 v. 12°. 3683, 12, 13
Illustrations, Daily. J. Kitto. New York, 1850–53. 7 v. 12°. . 4296
in the Counting House. H. A. Boardman. Phil. 1853. 12°. . 5635
in the Family. H. A. Boardman. Philadelphia, 1851. 12°. . 4485
in our Public Schools. G. B. Cheever. New York, 1854. 12°. . 5749
in Spain. G. Borrow. Philadelphia, 1843. 8°. 1720
New Testament, and Psalms. New York, 1848. 8°. . . . 4077
Society. — See *American Bible Society.*

See also *Old Testament* and *New Testament.*

Biblical Archæology. J. Jahn. Trans. by T. C. Upham. N. Y. 1849. 8°. 3528
Biblical Criticism, Treatise on. S. Davidson. Boston, 1853. 2 v. 8°. . 5119

Biblical Literature, Cyclopædia of. J. Kitto. N. Y. 1850. 2 v. roy. 8°. 3526
The same, condensed. Boston, 1851. Roy. 8°. 4332
Biblical Researches in Palestine. E. Robinson. Boston, 1841. 3 v. 8°. . 1985
Bibliotheca Americana. London, 1789. 4°. 2759
American Publications, 1820–52. O. A. Roorbach. N.Y. 1852. 8°. 5993
Bibliotheca Sacra. Vols. 1–10 [continued]. N. Y. & And. 1844–53. 8°. 4839
Bickersteth's Treatise on the Lord's Supper. Phil. 1831. 16°. . . 822
Biddle, N. (Com.). Biography. S. P. Waldo. Hartford, 1823. 8°. . 651
Big Abel, and the Little Manhattan. C. Matthews. N. York, 1845. 12°. 2488
Bigelow, A. Rambles in N. Britain and Ireland, 1817. Bost. 1821. 12°. 444
Travels in Malta and Sicily, 1827. Boston, 1831. 8°. 787
Bigelow, Jacob. Plants of Boston and Vicinity. Boston, 1840. 12°. . 1842
Useful Arts, with Applications of Science. Boston, 1840. 2 v. 12°. 2923
Bigelow, John. Jamaica in 1850. New York, 1851. 12°. 4072
Bigland, J. History of England. Boston, 1815. 2 v. 8°. . . . 698
Letters on the Study and Use of History. Phil. 1806. 8°. . . 648
Biglow Papers. J. R. Lowell. Cambridge, 1848. 12°. 3183
Bigsby, R. Visions of the Times of Old. London, 1848. 3 v. 8°. . . 4820
Bills of Exchange & Prom. Notes, Law of. S. Kyd. Albany, 1800. 12°. 884
Bills of Exchange, Checks, Notes, &c. J. Chitty. Portland, 1807. 8°. . 1159
Law of. J. Story. Boston, 1847. 8°. 3594
Binney, C. J. F. Gen. of Prentice or Prentiss Family. Bost. 1852. 8°. 4813
Binney, T. Sketch of Sir T. F. Buxton. Boston, 1851. 12°. . . 3776
Biographia Americana. (No titlepage.) 1318
Biographia Literaria. S. T. Coleridge. New York, 1852. 12°. . . 1032
The same. New York, 1853. 12°. 5561, 3
Biographical Dictionary. New York, 1826. 12°. 1062
R. A. Davenport. Boston, 1832. 8°. 805
J. Gorton. London, 1847. 3 v. 8°. 3597
*H. J. Rose. London, 1850. 12 v. 8°. 5438
*American. W. Allen. Boston, 1832. 8°. 3995
The same. Cambridge, 1809. 8°. 723
of the First Settlers of New England. J. Eliot. Salem, 1809. 8°. 1313
Biographical, Literary, and Political Anecdotes. London, 1797. 3 v. 8°. 685
Biographical Sketches of Lawyers, Statesmen. S. L. Knapp. Bost. 1821. 8°. 659
Biographical Treasury. S. Maunder. London, 1851. 12°. 4470
Biographies of American Naval Heroes. S. P. Waldo. Hart. 1823. 8°. 651
of Distinguished New Eng. Men. A. Bradford. Bost. 1842. 12°. 1696
of Officers of the Am. Navy. B. Folsom. Newburyport, 1814. 8°. 758
Biography, American. J. Belknap. (H. F. L.) N.Y. 1848. 3 v. 12°. 3683, 161–3
The same. Boston, 1794. 2 v. 8°. 643
*and Mythology, Dict. of Ancient. W. Smith. Lond. 1849. 3 v. 8°. 3957
Chambers's Library of. Boston, 1849. 2 v. 12°. 3314
Female. S. L. Knapp. Philadelphia, 1836. 12°. 1840
Handbook of Universal. P. Godwin. New York, 1852. 12°. . 4489
of Self-taught Men. B. B. Edwards. Boston, 1832. 12°. . . 1803
Popular Scottish. W. Anderson. Edinburgh, 1842. 12°. . . 3601
Sacred. H. Hunter. Philadelphia, 1832. 8°. 1288

Birch, H., Memoirs of. H. L. Barnum. New York, 1828. 8°. . . . 1363
Bird, R. M. Adventures of Robin Day. Philadelphia, 1839. 2 v. 12°. . 990
Calavar; or, Knight of the Conquest. New York, 1854. 12°. . 6136
Hawks of Hawk-Hollow. Philadelphia, 1835. 2 v. 12°. . . 1096
Nick of the Woods. New York, 1853. 12°. 501
Peter Pilgrim. Philadelphia, 1838. 2 v. 12°. 105
Bird-keeper's Manual. J. Mann. Boston, 1848. 12°. 3308
Birds, British. Sir W. Jardine. Edinburgh, 1843. 4 v. 12°. . . 4901, 1-4
Cage and Chamber. J. M. Bechstein. London, 1853. Post 8°. . 5758
Fly-Catchers. W. Swainson. Edinburgh, 1843. 12°. . 4901, 13
Game. Sir W. Jardine. Edinburgh, 1843. 12°. . . . 4901, 8
History of British. T. Bewick. Newcastle, 1847. 2 v. 8°. . . 4957
History of British. W. Macgillivray. London, 1839. 2 v. 8°. . 3547
Humming. Sir W. Jardine. Edinburgh, 1843. 2 v. 12°. . 4901, 6, 7
Natural History of. J. Rennie. (H. F. L.) N. Y. 1846. 12°. 3683, 98
of British Islands. R. Mudie. London, 1854. 2 v. post 8°. . 5940
of Massachusetts. W. B. O. Peabody. Boston, 1839. 8°. . . 722
of Western Africa. W. Swainson. Edin. 1843. 2 v. 12°. 4901, 11, 12
Pigeons and Parrots. P. J. Selby. Edin. 1843. 2 v. 12°. 4901, 9, 10
Stories about. F. C. Woodworth. Boston, 1851. 12°. . . 3938
Sun. Sir W. Jardine. Edinburgh, 1843. 12°. . . . 4901, 5
Birthright, The. Emilie F. Carlen. London, 1851. 3 v. 12°. . . 4616
Births, Deaths, and Marriages. T. E. Hook. Phil. 1839. 2 v. 12°. . 989
Bisset, R. History of the Reign of George III. Albany, 1816. 2 v. 8°. 1264
Bit o' Writin', and other Tales. J. Banim. Phil. 1838. 2 v. 12°. . . 1034
Bivouac. W. H. Maxwell. London, 1853. 12°. 5722
Black Dwarf. Sir W. Scott. Boston, 1848. 2 v. 12°. . . . 999, 9
The same. Edinburgh, 1849. 2 v. 12°. . . . 4100, 9
The same. Edinburgh, 1850. Roy. 8°. . . . 4531, 2
*Black's General Atlas of the World. Edinburgh, 1851. 4°. . . 1702
Blackburne, F. Confessions of Faith. Boston, 1823. 12°. . . . 368, 1
Blackgown Papers. L. Mariotti. London, 1846. 2 v. 12°. . . . 4970
Blackstone, Sir W. Commentaries on the Laws of Eng. N. Y. 1844. 2 v. 8°. 2218
The same. New York, 1849. 2 v. 8°. 3592
Blackwater Chronicle. New York, 1853. 12°. 5564
Blackwell, Elizabeth. Laws of Life. New York, 1852. 12°. . . 4885
*Blackwood's Edin. Magazine. Vols. 1-74 [con.]. Edin. 1817-53. 8°. 1360
The same. Vols. 59-74. New York, 1846-53. 8°. . . 1360
Stories from. New York, 1852. 12°. 4929
Blair, D. Easy Grammar of Philosophy. Philadelphia, 1812. 12°. . 15
Blair, H. Lectures on Rhetoric and Belles Lettres. Phil. 1848. 8°. . 635
Blake, L. Constitutional Text Book. New York, 1854. 12°. . . 5780
Blake, J. L. Parlor Book; or, Family Encyclop. New York, 1837. 8°. . 1884
Blake, R. (Admiral). Life. London, 1833. 8°. 602
Blanc, H. le. Art of Tying the Cravat. New York, 1829. 16°. . . 64
Blanc, L. History of French Revolution of 1789. Phil. 1840. 2 v. 12°. 3623
History of Ten Years, 1830-40. Philadelphia, 1848. 2 v. 8°. . 2883
Blanc, Mont. — See *Mont Blanc.*

Blanchard, E. L. Heirs of Derwentwater. N. York, 1851. 8°. . . 4127
Blanchard, L. Life and Remains of L. E. Landon. Phil. 1841. 2 v. . 1623
Sketches from Life, with Memoir by Bulwer. N. York, 1846. 12°. 2548
Bland, W. Forms of Ships and Boats. London, 1853. 12°. 6094
Blasting and Quarrying Stone. Sir J. Burgoyne. London, 1852. 12°. . 6058
Bleak House. C. Dickens. Philadelphia, 1853. 8°. 5428
Blennerhassett, H. Life. W. H. Safford. Cincinnati, 1853. 12°. . . 5815
Blessington, Countess of. Idler in Italy. Philadelphia, 1839. 2 v. 12°. . 486
Confessions of an Elderly Lady and Gentleman. Phil. 1838. 2 v. . 456
Ella Strafford; or, the Orphan Child. Philadelphia, 1850. 8°. . 3460
Repealers. Philadelphia, 1833. 2 v. 12°. 534
Marmaduke Herbert. New York, 1849. 8°. 2820
Victims of Society. Philadelphia, 1846. 2 v. 12°. 360
Blewitt, O. Handbook for Central Italy. London, 1850, 12°. . . 74
Blind, Literature and Education of the. J. Gall. Edinburgh, 1834. 8°. 1156
Blithedale Romance. N. Hawthorne. Boston, 1852. 12°. 4881
Block House, Nights in. H. C. Watson. Philadelphia, 1852. 12°. . 1198
Bloodstone, The. D. MacLeod. New York, 1854. 12°. 5616
Bloomfield, R. Farmer's Boy; a Rural Poem. New York, 1803. 12°. . 2354
Poems. London, 1845. 12°. 2554
Bloomfield, S. T. Greek Testament, with Notes. Phil. 1848. 2 v. 8°. . 4705
Blunt, J. Shipmaster's Assistant. New York, 1848. 8°. 3242
Blunt, J. J. Coincidences of Old & New Testaments. N. Y. 1851. 8°. 4704
Blue-Stocking Hall. Mrs. Wilmot. New York, 1828. 2 v. 12°. . . 550
Boardman, H. A. Bible in the Counting House. Phil. 1853. 12°. . 5635
Bible in the Family. Philadelphia, 1851. 12°. 4485
Bodenstedt, F. Morning-Land; or, 1001 Days in the East. Lon. 1851. 2 v. 12°. 4444
Body, The, in relation to Mind. G. Moore. New York, 1847. 12°. . 2943
Bogart, W. H. Daniel Boone, and the Hunters of Ky. Aub. 1854. 12°. 6175
Bogen, F. W. German in America. Boston, 1851. 18°. 4403
Bogue, D. Divine Authority of the New Testament. N. Y. n. d. 12°. . 1022
Theological Lectures. New York, 1849. 8°. 4722
Bohn, H. G. (Editor.) Handbook of Games. London, 1850. Post 8°. . 4362
Boismont, A. B. de. Hallucinations, Apparitions, &c. Phil. 1853. 8°. 5423
Bokhara, Narrative of a Mission to. J. Wolff. New York, 1845. 8°. . 2626
Boleyn, Anne. Memoirs. Elizabeth O. Benger. Phil. 1850. 12°. . 3918
Bolingbroke, H. St. J. Study and Use of History. Paris, 1808. 8°. . 790
Bolivar, S., Memoirs of. H. L. V. D. Holstein. Boston, 1829. 8°. . 1390
Bombet, L. A. C. Lives of Haydn and Mozart. Boston, 1839. 12°. . 471
Bonaparte Family, History of. New York, 1852. 8°. 4846
Bonaparte, Lucien, Memoirs of. New York, 1836. 12°. 277
Charlemagne; or, the Church Delivered: a Poem. Phil. 1815. 2 v. 16°. 75
Bonaparte, Napoleon. — See *Napoleon.*
Bonar, A. A. Commentary on Leviticus. New York, 1851. 8°. . . 4715
Bond, J. W. Minnesota and its Resources. New York, 1853. 12°. . 5580
Bond, T. E. Practical Treatise on Dental Medicine. Phil. 1852. 8°. . 5106
Bonneville, Capt. Advent. in Rocky Moun. Ed. by W. Irving. N.Y. 1849. 12°. 3366
The same. Philadelphia, 1837. 2 v. 12°. 510

Bonnet, C. Views of Christianity. London, 1787. 12°. 187
Bonnycastle, Sir R. H. Newfoundland in 1842. London, 1842. 2 v. 8°. 4963
Spanish America. Philadelphia, 1819. 8°. 764
Boaden, J. Memoirs of Mrs. Eliza Inchbald. London, 1833. 2 v. 8°. . 2293
Book of Anecdotes. J. Frost. New York, 1847. 12°. 2939
of Archery. G. A. Hansard. London, 1841. 8°. . . . 4135
of the Army. J. Frost. New York, 1845. 12°. . . . 2180
of Ballads. Edited by "Bon Gaultier." New York, 1852. 12°. . 4399
of Beauty. L. E. Landon. Philadelphia, 1847. 8°. . . 1343, 2
of the Boudoir. Lady S. Morgan. New York, 1829. 2 v. 12°. . 530
of the Church. R. Southey. Flemington, N. J., 1844. 8°. . 2224
of Colonies comprising the United States. J. Frost. N. Y. 1846. 12°. 2515
of Commerce by Sea and Land. Philadelphia, 1836. 12°. . . 2113
of Common Prayer. New York, 1854. 12°. 2449
of Common Prayer, Illustration of. C. Wheatley. Lon. 1849. Post 8°. 4394
for a Corner. L. Hunt. New York, 1852. 2 v. 12°. 1088
of the Indians. J. Frost. New York, 1845. 12°. . . . 2210
of Nature. J. M. Good. Boston, 1826. 2 v. 8°. . . . 1263
of Nature; an Introd. to the Sciences. F. Schoedler. Phil. 1853. 8°. 5441
of the Navy. J. Frost. New York, 1845. 12°. . . . 2208
of Oratory. E. C. Marshall. New York, 1851. 12°. . . . 4198
of Snobs. W. M. Thackeray. New York, 1852. 12°. . . 4884
Bookkeeping by Double Entry. J. C. Colt. Cincinnati, 1838. Roy. 8°. 1995
G. N. Comer. Boston, 1850. 8°. 2731
J. Dando. Philadelphia, 1842. 4°. 3850
C. C. Marsh. Philadelphia, 1843. 8°. 1645
The same. New York, 1851. 8°. 4078
and Single Entry. B. W. Foster. Boston, 1844. 8°. . 1709
by Single Entry. C. C. Marsh. New York, 1843. 8°. . . 1614
Commercial. B. F. Foster. Boston, 1837. 12°. . . . 1350
System of Practical. N. Harris. Hartford, 1838. 8°. . . 1991
Treatise on. J. Haddon. London, 1851. 12°. 6091
Boone, D., and the Hunters of Kentucky. W. H. Bogart. Auburn, 1854. 12°. 6175
Life. J. M. Peck. Boston, 1848. 12°. 1076, 23
Booth, J. C., and C. Morfit. Improvements in Chem. Arts. Wash. 1852. 8°. 5163
Boots and Shoes, History of. J. S. Hall. New York, 1847. 12°. . 4420
Border Beagles; a Tale of Mississippi. W. G. Simms. Phil. 1840. 2 v. 12°. 1465
Border Warfare of New York. W. W. Campbell. New York, 1849. 12°. 3292
Border Wars of the Revolution. W. L. Stone. N.Y. 1848. 2 v. 12°. 3683, 167–8
Borneo, Residence at. H. Low. London, 1848. 8°. 4671
Borrow, G. Bible in Spain. Philadelphia, 1843. 8°. 1720
Gypsies of Spain. Philadelphia, 1844. 8°. 2124
Lavengro; the Scholar, Gipsy, and Priest. New York, 1851. 12°. 3785
Bosphorus and Ægean, Land and Sea in. W. Colton. N. Y. 1851. 12°. 4219
Bossu, M. Travels through Louisiana. London, 1771. 2 v. 8°. . . 1283
Boston Athenæum, Catalogue of the Books in. Boston, 1827. 8°. . 2907
History of. J. Quincy. Cambridge, 1851. 8°. 3803
Boston, Auditor's Report, 1847. Boston, 1847. 8°. 2881

Boston, Auditor's Reports, 1848–54. Boston, 1848–54. 8°. 3951
Book. Ed. by B. B. Thatcher. Boston, 1836, 1837, 1841. 3 v. 12°. 248
Book. Specimens of Metropolitan Literature. Boston, 1851. 12°. 3455
By-Laws and Town Orders, 1785–86. Boston, 1786. 12°. . . . 539
Census Report, 1845. L. Shattuck. Boston, 1846. 8°. . . . 2736
City Documents, 1852–53. Boston, 1852–53. 4 v. 8°. 5168
Directory, 1851–54. G. Adams. Boston, 1851–54. 8°. . . . 5401
Female Anti-Slavery Society's Reports. Boston, 1835–37. 3 v. 16°. 1513
History and Antiquities of. S. G. Drake. Boston, 1854. Roy. 8°. 5929
History of. C. H. Snow. Boston, 1825. 8° 1971
History of the Siege of. R. Frothingham, jun. Boston, 1851. 8°. 3518
Journal of Natural History. Vols. 1, 2. Boston, 1837–45. 8°. . 3619
List of Taxes, 1848. Boston, 1849. 8°. 3948
Local Loiterings in the Vicinity of. Boston, 1845. 12°. . . . 2539
Massacre, Narrative of. New York, 1849. 8°. 3274
Miscellany. Edited by N. Hale, jun. Vol. 1. Boston, 1842. 8°. 1829
Monthly Magazine. Vol. 1. Boston, 1825. 8°. 703
Municipal History of. J. Quincy. Boston, 1852. 8°. 567
Municipal Register, 1848. Boston 1848. 12°. 3169
1850. Boston, 1850. 12°. 3925
1851. Boston, 1851. 8°. 4142
Notions, 1630–1847. N. Dearborn. Boston, 1848. 16°. . . . 2453
Orations on the 5th March. Boston, 1785. 16°. 825
Orators, Hundred. J. S. Loring. Boston, 1852. 8°. . . . 4832
Pearl and Literary Gazette. Vol. 4 [imperfect]. Boston, 1830. 4°. 2022
Picture of. A. Bowen. Boston, 1838. 16°. 1512
Theatre. Prize Poems. Boston, 1824. 12°. 490
Railroad Jubilee, Sept. 1851. Boston, 1852. 8°. 778
Reminiscences of, and Guide through. N. Dearborn. Bos. 1851. 18°. 4209
Report on Cholera. Boston, 1849. 8°. 3953
Sketches of, Past and Present. J. S. Homans. Boston, 1851. 16°. 2725
Slave Riot, and Trial of Anthony Burns. Boston, 1854. 8°. . 5958
Stage, Record of. W. W. Clapp, jun. Boston, 1853. 12°. . 5523
Tea Party, &c. H. C. Watson. Philadelphia, 1852. 12°. . . 3256
Traits of. New York, 1835. 12°. 1471
Weekly Magazine. Vols. 1–4. Boston, 1802–5. 4°. 2017
Boswell, J. Life of Samuel Johnson. London, 1821. 5 v. 12°. . . 1154
The same. Ed. by J. W. Croker. London, 1847. Roy. 8°. 1139
The same. New York, 1841. 2 v. roy. 8°. . . 1253
Botanic Gardens, Cambridge (Eng.), Catalogue of. J. Donn. Lon. 1845. 8°. 3545
Botany, Manual of. A. Eaton. Albany, 1824. 12°. 458
Plants of Boston and Vicinity. J. Bigelow. Boston, 1840. 12°. . 1842
Popular Exposition of. M. J. Schleiden. Cincinnati, 1853. 12°. . 5316
Botta, C. History of the War of Independence of U. S. Phil. 1821. 3 v. 8°. 776
Bourdaloue in the Court of Louis XIV. L. Bungener. Boston, 1853. 12°. 5247
Bourne, B. F. Captive in Patagonia. Boston, 1853. 12°. 5215
Bourne, G. Picture of Slavery in the United States. Boston, 1838. 12°. 1524
Bourne, W. O. Gems from Fable Land. New York, 1853. 12°. . 5022

Bourne, W. O. Goldenlink; or, Tales and Poems. New York, 1854. 12°. 5572
Bourrienne, M. de. Life of Napoleon. Philadelphia, 1832. 8°. . . . 1373
Bouvier, J. Law Dictionary of the United States. Phil. 1848. 2 v. 8°. 3596
Bowditch, N., Discourse on. A. Young. Boston, 1838. 8°. . . . 2225
Memoir. N. I. Bowditch. Boston, 1839. 4°. 2018
Practical Navigator. New York, 1846. 8°. 2249
Bowditch, N. I. History of the Mass. General Hospital. Bos. 1851. 8°. 4535
Bowen, A. Picture of Boston. Boston, 1838. 16°. 1512
Bowen, E. United States Post Office Guide. New York, 1851. 8°. . 4507
Bowen, F. Critical Essays. Boston, 1842. 12°. 2093
Life of James Otis. Boston, 1844. 12°. 1076, 12
Life of Sir William Phipps. Boston, 1840. 12°. . . . 1076, 7
Life of Baron Steuben. Boston, 1844. 12°. 1076, 9
Bower of Taste. Edited by Mrs. K. A. Ware. Boston, 1829–30. 3 v. 8°. 658
Bowers, J., Sermons. Hallowell, 1820. 8°. 1266
Bowring, J. Poetry of the Magyars. London, 1830. 12°. . . . 3092
Specimens of the Russian Poets. Boston, 1822. 12°. . . . 1928
and H. S. Van Dyk. Batavian Anthology. London, 1824. 12°. 2416
Boyne Water; a Tale. New York, 1826. 2 v. 12°. 448
Boy Hunters. M. Reid. Boston, 1853. 12°. 5082
Boyhood of Great Men. New York, 1853. 12°. 5355
Boy's Treasury of Sports, Pastimes, &c. Philadelphia, 1847. 12°. . . 2442
Boys at Home. C. Adams. New York, 1854. 12°. 5778
Brace, C. L. Home Life in Germany. New York, 1853. 12°. . . 5308
Hungary in 1851. New York, 1852. 12°. 980
Brace, J. P. Fawn of the Pale Faces. New York, 1853. 12°. . . 5380
Bracebridge Hall. W. Irving. New York, 1851. 12°. 369
The same. New York, 1851. 12°. 3365
Brackenridge, H. H. Modern Chivalry. Pittsburgh, 1819. 2 v. 12°. . 1067
Brackenridge, H. M. Views of Louisiana. Pittsburgh, 1814. 8°. . 609
Bradford, A. Distinguished Men in New England. Boston, 1842. 12°. 1696
History of the Federal Government, 1789–1839. Boston, 1840. 8°. 1587
History of Massachusetts, 1620–1820. Boston, 1835. 8°. . . 767
History of Massachusetts, 1764–1775. Boston, 1822. 8°. . . 761
New England Chronology, 1497–1800. Boston, 1843. 12°. . . 1838
* Bradford, T. G. Comprehensive Atlas. Boston, 1835. 4°. . . . 3741
Bradford, W. J. A. Notes on the North-west. New York, 1846. 12°. . 2931
Bragelonne, the Son of Athos. A. Dumas. New York, 1850. 8°. . 3806
Brainard, J. G. C. Poems, with Memoir. Hartford, 1842. 12°. . . 1670
Brainerd, D. Life. J. Edwards. (Abridged.) Boston, 1821. 12°. . 205
Life. W. B. O. Peabody. Boston, 1844. 12°. 1076,8
Brande, W. T. Dictionary of Science, Literature, & Art. N. Y. 1848. 8°. 2641
Brand, J. Popular Antiquities of Great Britain. Lon. 1848. 3 v. post. 8°. 4369
Brant, J. Life. W. L. Stone. New York, 1838. 2 v. 8°. . . . 1946
Bravo, The. J. F. Cooper. Philadelphia, 1848. 2 v. 12°. . . . 332
Bravo of Venice. M. G. Lewis. London, 1853. 12°. 5702
Brazer, J. Sermons. Boston, 1849. 12°. 3337
Brazil, Cape Colony, &c., Travels in. J. Holman. London, 1840. 8°. 1986, 2

Brazil in 1828–29. R. Walsh. Boston, 1831. 2 v. 12°. 2106
Rambles in. A. R. M. Payne. New York, 1854. 12°. . . . 5809
Residence and Travels in. D. P. Kidder. Phil. 1845. 2 v. 12°. . 2280
Travels in the Interior of. J. Mawe. Philadelphia, 1816. 8°. . 1597
Breck, J. Flower Garden; or, Book of Flowers. Boston, 1851. 12°. . 3822
Bremer, Fredrika. Brothers and Sisters. New York, 1848. 8°. . . 3208
Home. New York, 1844. 8°. 2087
Homes of the New World. New York, 1853. 2 v. 12°. . . 5537
Neighbors. Boston, 1843. 2 v. 12°. 1716
Parsonage of Mora. New York, 1845. 8°. 2618
President's Daughters. Boston, 1843. 12°. 1725
Sketches of Every-day Life. New York, 1848. 8°. 2072
Brenton, E. P. Naval History of Great Britain. London, 1823. 8°. . 5904
Brewer, Complete Practical. M. L. Byrn. Philadelphia, 1852. 12°. . 5007
Brewer, J. Residence at Constantinople in 1827. N. Haven, 1830. 12°. 341
Brewer, T. M. (Editor). Wilson's Am. Ornithology. N. Y. 1852. 8°. . 5924
Brewer, W. A. Recreations of a Merchant. Boston, 1836. 12°. . . 280
Brewster, Sir D. Life of Sir I. Newton. New York, 1831. 12°. . . 1
Life of Sir Isaac Newton. (H. F. L.) N. York, 1846. 12°. 3683, 26
Martyrs of Science. New York, 1841. 12°. 1627
The same. (H. F. L.) New York, 1846. 12°. . . 3683, 130
Natural Magic. New York, 1845. 12°. 2433
The same. (H. F. L.) New York, 1848. 12°. . 3683, 50
Brian O'Linn. W. H. Maxwell. New York, 1848. 8°. 3204
Briancourt, M. Organization of Labor & Association. N. Y. 1847. 12°. 2439
Bricks and Tiles, Treatise on. E. Dobson. London, 1850. 12°. . . 6051
Bridal of Triermain, &c. Sir W. Scott. Edinburgh, 1848. 12°. . 4102, 11
The same. Philadelphia, 1839. 12°. 860, 4
Bride of Lammermoor. Sir W. Scott. Boston, 1848. 2 v. 12°. . 999, 13, 14
The same. Edinburgh, 1849. 2 v. 12°. . . 4100, 13, 14
The same. Edinburgh, 1850. Roy. 8°. . . . 4531, 4
Bride of Omberg. Emilie F. Carlen. New York, 1853. 12°. . . 5373
Bridge, H. Journal of an African Cruiser. New York, 1853. 12°. . 2398
*Bridges, Brit. & Conway Tubular. E. Clark. Lond. 1850. 2 v. 8°. 1 v. fol. 1673
Tubular and Iron. G. D. Dempsey. London, 1850. 12°. . . 6065
Bridgman, T. Epitaphs from Copp's Hill. Boston, 1851. 12°. . . 4466
Epitaphs in Grave Yards of Northampton. Northamp. 1850. 12°. 4215
Epitaphs in King's Chapel Burial Ground. Boston, 1853. 12°. . 5596
Brigands of the Revolution. New York, 1852. 8°. 629
Briggs, Caroline A. Utterance; a Collection of Poems. Bost. 1852. 12°. 4620
Brigham, A. Influence of Religion upon Health. Boston, 1835. 12°. . 1773
Brisbane, A. Association, & Re-organization of Industry. Phil. 1840. 12°. 2136
Bristed, C. A. Five Years in an English University. N. Y. 1852. 2 v. 12°. 4763
Upper Ten Thousand. New York, 1852. 12°. 4852
Britain Redeemed and Canada Preserved. F. A. Wilson. Lond. 1850. 8°. 5414
*Britannia & Conway Tub. Bridges. E. Clark. Lond. 1850. 2 v. 8°. 1 v. fol. 1673
British America, History of. H. Murray, &c. N.Y. 1846. 2 v. 12°. 3683, 101–2
British Angler's Manual. T. C. Hofland. London, 1848. Post 8°. . 4972

British Armies, Victories of. W. H. Maxwell. London, 1847. 12°. . 3133

British Cabinet in 1853. Philadelphia, 1853. 12°. 5368

British Cicero; a Selection of Speeches. T. Browne. Phil. 1810. 3 v. 8°. 2175

British Colonies, History of. R. M. Martin. London, 1843. Roy. 8°. . 2843

British Drama. — See *Drama.*

British Dramatists, Lives of. T. Campbell & others. Phil. 1846. 2 v. 12°. 2992

British Eloquence, Select. C. A. Goodrich. New York, 1852. Roy. 8°. 5083

British Empire, History of, 1792–93. F. Plowden. Dublin, 1794. 8°. . 742

British Encyclopædia. — See *Encyclopædia.*

British Female Missionaries, Memoirs of. T. Timpson. Lond. 1841. 12°. 2446

British Female Poets. G. W. Bethune. Philadelphia, 1848. 8°. . . 3191

British Gazetteer. B. Clarke. London, 1852. 3 v. roy. 8°. . . . 5169

British History, &c., Illustrations of. E. Lodge. London, 1838. 3 v. 8°. 4676

The same. London, 1838. 3 v. 8°. 5087

British India, Historical and Descriptive Account of. N. Y. 1842. 3 v. 12°. 1857

History of. J. Mill. London, 1830. 6 v. 8°. 2230

See also *India.*

British Manly Exercises. D. Walker. Philadelphia, 1850. 12°. . . 2200

British Museum, Antiquities and Marbles in. London, 1848. 18°. . 4776

British Poets, with Prefaces. J. Aiken and J. Frost. Phil. 1843. 3 v. 8°. 1962

Vol. 1. Chronological Series, Ben Jonson to Beattie.
2. " " Falconer to Scott.
3. " " Southey to Croly.

British Plutarch; or, Lives of Eminent Statesmen. Lond. 1791. 8 v. 12°. 158

British Senate. R. Grant. Philadelphia, 1838. 2 v. 12°. . . . 971

British Spy. Letters of W. Wirt. New York, 1836. 12°. . . . 2133

British Statesmen, Lives of. J. Forster and others. Lond. 1831. 7 v. 12°. 1831

For Contents, see *Lives.*

British Trade over Caspian Sea. J. Hanway. London, 1753. 3 v. 4°. . 2002

Britons, Ancient; a Tale of Primeval Life. London, 1851. 12°. . . 4610

Brittany, Popular Legends of. Boston, 1854. 12°. 5617

Broad Pennant; or, Cruise of U. S. Flag Ship. F.W.Taylor. N.Y. 1848. 12°. 3082

*Brockedon, W. Illust. of Passes of the Alps. Lond. 1838. 2 v. 4°. . 4829

Brocklesby, J. Views of the Microscopic World. New York, 1851. 12°. 4427

Broderip, W. J. Leaves from Note Book of a Naturalist. Bost. 1852. 8°. 4808

Zoölogical Recreations. Philadelphia, 1849. 12°. 4411

Broken Bracelet, & other Poems. Mrs. C. H. W. Esling. Phil. 1850. 12°. 4048

Bronchitis, and Kindred Diseases. W. W. Hall. New York, 1852. 12°. 4786

Bronson, C. P. Elocution. Louisville, 1845. 8°. 4955

Bronte, Caroline. Jane Eyre; an Autobiography. New York, 1848. 8°. 2876

Shirley; a Tale. New York, 1850. 8°. 2865

Villette. New York, 1853. 8°. 5158

Bronte, Miss. (Sister to above.) Agnes Grey. Philadelphia, 1850. 8°. 3523

Tenant of Wildfell Hall. New York, 1848. 12°. 3155

Wuthering Heights. New York, 1848. 12°. 3106

Bronte, Misses. (Three Sisters.) Poems. Philadelphia, 1848. 12°. . 3156

Brooks, C. Elements of Ornithology. Boston, 1847. 12°. 3508

Brooks, C. T. Schiller's Homage of the Arts, &c. Boston, 1847. 12°. . 2944

Brookes, R. General Gazetteer. London, 1821. 8°. 769
Brothers; a Tale of the Fronde. H. W. Herbert. N. Y. 1835. 2 v. 12°. 1073
Brothers and Sisters. Fredrika Bremer. New York, 1848. 8°. . . 3208
Brougham, H. (Lord). Men of Letters and Science. Phil. 1845. 2 v. 12°. 2524

Vol. 1. Voltaire; Rousseau; Hume; Robertson; Black; Watt; Priestley; Cavendish; Davy; Simson.
2. Johnson; Adam Smith; Lavoisier; Gibbon; Banks; D'Alembert.

On Education. New York, 1839. 12°. 1891
Opinions of. Philadelphia, 1839. 2 v. 12°. 1066
Political Philosophy. London, 1849. 3 v. 8°. 1239
Speeches. Edinburgh, 1838. 4 v. 8°. 3588
Speeches. Philadelphia, 1841. 2 v. 8°. 1954
Statesmen of Time of George III. Philadelphia, 1854. 2 v. 12°. . 6186
The same. 2d and 3d series. N. York, 1839–44. 3 v. 12°. 983
Brown, C. B. Edgar Huntley. London, 1853. 12°. 5699
Life. W. H. Prescott. Boston, 1838. 12°. 1076, 1
Wieland; or, the Transformation. New York, 1846. 8°. . . 2715
Brown, G. Grammar of English Grammars. New York, 1851. 8°. . 4699
Brown, J. Discourses on First Epistle of Peter. New York, 1851. 8°. 4723
Brown, J. N. (Ed.) Encyclop. of Religious Knowl. Phil. 1850. Roy. 8°. 4729
Brown, J. R. Etchings of a Whaling Cruise. New York, 1850. 8°. . 2753
Yusef; or, the Journey of the Frangi. New York, 1853. 12°. . 5292
Brown, S. R. Western Gazetteer. Auburn, 1817. 8°. 757
Brown, T. W. Minnie Hermon. Auburn, 1854. 12°. 5793
Why am I a Temperance Man? Auburn, 1853. 12°. . . . 5331
Browne, J. Hist. of the Highlands & Highland Clans. Lond. 1851, 4 v. 8°. 5094
Browne, R. W. History of Greek Literature. Philadelphia, 1852. 12°. 4562
Browne, Sir T., Selections from Works of. Cambridge, 1831. 12°. . 383, 3
Works. Edited by S. Wilkin. London, 1852, 3 v. post 8°. . . 5014

Vol. 1. Johnson's Life of Author, and Memoir by Editor; Four books of Vulgar Errors.
2. Three last books of Vulgar Errors; Religio Medici; Garden of Cyrus.
3. Urn Burial; Christian Morals; Miscellanies; Correspondence, &c.

Browne, T. British Cicero; a Selection of Speeches. Phil. 1810. 3 v. 8°. 2175
Browne, W. Britannia's Pastorals. London, 1845. 24°. . . . 2411
Browning, C. A. Convict Ship. Philadelphia, 1850. 12°. . . . 3576
Browning, Elizabeth B. Poems. New York, 1850. 2 v. 12°. . . 4498
Prometheus Bound, and other Poems. New York, 1851. 12°. . 4870
Browning, R. Poems. Boston, 1850. 2 vols. 12°. 3457
Browning, W. S. History of the Huguenots. Philadelphia, 1845. 8°. . 3530
Brownson, O. A. Charles Elwood. Boston, 1840. 1809
New Views of Christianity. Boston, 1836. 12°. 1776
Spirit Rapper. Boston, 1854. 6246
Bruce, J. Classic and Historic Portraits. New York, 1854. 12°. . . 5776
Bruce, J. Life and Travels. Sir F. B. Head. (H. F. L.) N.Y. 1846. 12°. 3683, 128
Travels into Abyssinia. Boston, 1798. 12°. 319
Brummell, G. Life. Capt. Jesse. Philadelphia, 1844. 8°. . . . 2757
Brunton, Mary. Discipline. London, 1850. 12°. 5651
Self-Control. Boston, 1848. 12°. 3128

Brunton, Mary. Self-Control. London, 1850. 12°. 5650
Bryan, D. Appeal for Suffering Genius; a Poem. Wash. 1826. 8°. . 3223
Lay of Gratitude. Philadelphia, 1826. 8°. 1406
Bryant, E. What I Saw in California, 1846–47. New York, 1849. 12°. 3144
Bryant, W. C. Fountain, and other Poems. New York, 1842. 12°. . 1722
Letters of a Traveller. New York, 1850. 12°. 3836
Poems. Philadelphia, 1848. 12°. 3327
The same. Philadelphia, 1848. 12°. 1538
(Editor.) Selec. from Am. Poets. (H. F. L.) N.Y. 1846, 12°. 3683, 111
Brydone, P. Tour through Sicily and Malta. London, 1775. 2 v. 8°. . 681
The same. London, 1773. 2 v. 8°. 5907
Bryne, O. Metal Worker's Assistant. Philadelphia, 1851. 8°. . . 4542
Bubbles from the Brunnen of Nassau. Sir F. B. Head. N.Y. 1845. 12°. 2487
Bubbleton Parish, Records of. Boston, 1854. 12°. 6151
Buccaneer. Mrs. S. C. Hall. London, 1853. 12°. 5723
Buccaneers, History of. (H. F. L.) New York, 1848. 12°. . . 3683, 30
of America, History of. Boston, 1853. 8°. 5171
Buchanan, C., Memoir of. H. Pearson. New York, n. d. 12°. . . 100
Buchanan, W. Memoirs of Painting. London, 1824. 2 v. 8°. . . 4824
Bucke, C. Beauties, Harmonies, &c., of Nature. Phil. 1833. 8°. . 1357, 3
The same. (H. F. L.) New York, 1848. 12°. . . 3683, 145
Ruins of Ancient Cities. (H. F. L.) N.Y. 1846. 2 v. 12°. 3683, 134–5
Buckeye Abroad in Europe. S. S. Cox. New York, 1852. 12°. . . 3754
Buckingham, H. A. Harry Burnham, the Young Continental. N.Y. 1851. 8°. 4520
Buckingham, J. S. Claims on the East India Company. Lond. 1834. 8°. 1238
Buckingham, J. T. Memoirs of Editorial Life. Boston, 1852. 2 v. 12°. 4909
Annals of Mass. Char. Mechanic Association. Boston, 1853. 8°. 5493
(Editor.) New England Magazine. Boston, 1831–35. 9 v. 8°. . 1760
Specimens of Newspaper Literature. Boston, 1850. 2 v. 12°. . 3916
Buckminster, J. & J. S. Memoirs. Mrs. E. B. Lee. Boston, 1849. 12°. 3376
Budget of the Bubble Family. E. L. Bulwer, N.Y. 1840. 2 v. 12°. . 928
of Letters; or, Things I saw Abroad. Boston, 1847. 12°. . . 3044
of Wit and Humor. Dr. W. Valentine. New York, 1849. 12°. 3282
Buenos Ayres, Travels in. J. A. B. Beaumont. London, 1828. 8°. . 5010
Buffum, E. G. Six Months in the Gold Mines. Phil. 1850. 12°. . . 3859
Builder's Pocket Companion. A. C. Smeaton. Philadelphia, 1852. 12°. 5003
Building, Art of. E. Dobson. London, 1854. 12°. 6050
Rudiments of the Art of. E. Dobson. New York, 1853. 12°. . 5530
Bulfinch, T. Hebrew Lyrical History. Boston, 1853. 12°. . . . 5072
Bullard, Mrs. A. T. J. Sights and Scenes in Europe. St. Louis, 1852. 12°. 5189
Bulgárin, T. Ivan Vejeeghen; or, Life in Russia. Phil. 1832. 2 v. 12°. 1163
Bullock, J. American Cottage Builder. New York, 1854. 12°. . . 6168
(Editor.) History and Rudiments of Architecture. N.Y. 1853. 12°. 5507
(Editor.) Rudiments of the Art of Building. N.Y. 1853. 12°. . 5530
Bulwer, Sir E. L. Alice; Sequel to Ernest Maltravers. N.Y. n. d. 8°. . 932
Asmodeus at Large. Philadelphia, 1833, 12°. 1208
Athens; its Rise and Fall. New York, 1852. 2 v. 12°. . . 153
Budget of the Bubble Family. New York, 1840. 2 v. 12°. . . 928

Bulwer, Sir E. L. Caxtons. New York, 1850. 8°. 3459
Conversations with an Ambitious Student. New York, 1832. 12°. 1046
Critical and Miscellaneous Writings. Philadelphia, 1841. 2 v. 12°. 1667
Devereux. New York, 1829. 2 v. 12°. 1494
Disowned. New York, 1829. 2 v. 12°. 1661
England and the English. New York, 1833. 2 v. 12°. . . 1150
Ernest Maltravers. New York, 1837. 2 v. 12°. 909
Eugene Aram. New York, n. d. 8°. 1488
The same. London, 1853. 12°. 5701
Falkland. Philadelphia, 1843. 8°. 1757
Godolphin. New York, 1840. 2 v. 12°. 274
Harold. New York, 1848. 8°. 3199
Last Days of Pompeii. New York, 1847. 8°. 1257
The same. London, 1853. 12°. 5721
Last of the Barons. New York. 1843. 8°. 1712
Leila; or, the Siege of Grenada. New York, 1838. 12°. . . 929
The same. London, 1850. 8°. 5914
Lucretia; or, the Children of Night. New York, 1846. 8°. . 2763
My Novel; or, Varieties in English Life. New York, 1852. 8°. . 5152
New Timon. Philadelphia, 1849. 12°. 5854
Night and Morning. New York, 1850. 8°. 1593
Paul Clifford. New York, 1830. 2 v. 12°. 1191
The same. London, 1853. 12°. 5706
Pelham. Boston, 1850. 8°. 838
Pilgrims of the Rhine. Boston, 1837. 24°. 1562
Rebel, and other Tales. New York, 1835. 12°. 1147
Rienzi. New York, 1836. 2 v. 12°. 1119
The same. Philadelphia, 1836. 8°. 2228, 1
Siamese Twins. New York, 1831. 12°. 549
Zanoni. New York, 1842. 2 v. 12°. 1681
Bulwer, Lady Lytton. Behind the Scenes. New York, 1854. 12°. . 5849
Cheveley; or, Man of Honor. New York, 1839. 2 v. 12°. . . 492
Miriam Sedley. London, 1851. 3 v. 12°. 4241
Peer's Daughters. New York, 1850. 8°. 4314
Bunbury, C. J. F. Residence at Cape of Good Hope. London, 1848. 12°. 4573
Bungay, G. W. Crayon Sketches. Boston, 1852. 12°. 813
Off-Hand Takings. Boston, 1854. 12°. 6245
Bungener, L. Julian; or, the End of the Era. Boston, 1855. 2 v. 12°. 6219
Preacher and the King. Boston, 1853. 12°. 5247
Priest and the Huguenot. Boston, 1853. 2 v. 12°. . . . 5574
Voltaire and his Times. Boston, 1855. 12°. 6220
Bunker Hill Battle. R. Frothingham, jun. Boston, 1851. 8°. . . 3518
S. Swett. Boston, 1818. 12°. 190
Bunn, A. Old England and New England. Philadelphia, 1853. 12°. . 5594
The Stage; Before and Behind the Curtain. Phil. 1840. 2 v. 12°. 419
Bunner, E. History of Louisiana. (H. F. L.) N.Y. 1848. 2 v. 12°. 3683, 176
Bunyan, J. Pilgrim's Progress. Philadelphia, 1844. 12°. . . . 148
Works. Philadelphia, 1836. 2 v. 8°. 1797

Burbury, Mrs. Florence Sackville. New York, 1852. 8°. 3983
Burdett, C. Elliott Family; or, Trials of N.Y. Seamstresses. N.Y.1850. 12°. 3675
Burges, T. Battle of Lake Erie. Boston, 1839. 12°. 417
Burgess, G. Last Enemy; Conquering and Conquered. Phil. 1850. 12°. 4752
Burgoyne, Sir J. Blasting and Quarrying Stone. London, 1852. 12°. . 6058
Burke, E. Memoir. J. Prior. Boston, 1854. 2 v. 12°. 5542
Selection of Speeches. London, 1853. Roy. 8°. 5482
On the Sublime and Beautiful. New York, 1846. 12°. . . 299
Works. Boston, 1839. 9 v. 8°. 1588
Works, with a Memoir. New York, 1835. 3 v. 8°. 446
Burke, P. Celebrated Trials of the Aristocracy. London, 1849. 8°. . 4522
Burleigh, J. B. Legislative Guide. Philadelphia, 1852. 8°. . . . 4815
Burman Slave Girl. Mrs. D. B. L. Wade. Boston, n. d. 18°. . . 1508
Burnap, G. W. Lectures on Christianity. Boston, 1848. 12°. . . 4920
Life of Leonard Calvert. Boston, 1848. 12°. . . . 1076, 19
Miscellaneous Writings. Baltimore, 1845. 12°. 2517
Burnet, G. (Bishop). History of his Own Time. London, 1850. Roy. 8°. 5459
History of Reformation of the Church of Eng. N. Y. 1843. 3 v. 8°. 2057
The same. London, 1841. 4 v. roy. 8°. 3993
Burnett, C. M. Philosophy of Spirits. London, 1850. 8°. 5410
Burnett, J. Notes on Early Settlement of N. W. Territory. Cin.1847. 8°. 2795
Burney, C., Memoirs of. Mde. D'Arblay. Philadelphia, 1833. 18°. . 1241
Burney, Frances. Camilla; or, a Picture of Youth. Bost.1797. 3 v. 12°. 2361
Evelina. New York, 1852. 2 v. 12°. 4890
Burn, J. I. Treatise on Marine Insurance. London, 1801. 12°. . . 172
Burnell, G. R. Treatise on Hydraulic Engineering. London, 1852. 12°. 6045
Treatise on Limes, Cements, &c. London, 1850. 12°. . . 6067
Burns, J. Mothers of the Wise and Good. Boston, 1850. 12°. . . 3851
Burns, R., as a Poet, and as a Man. S. Tyler. New York, 1848. 12°. . 3177
Genius and Character of. J. Wilson. Philadelphia, 1854. 12°. . 2484
*Life and Correspondence. (Illustrated.) London, 1840. 4°. . 4855
Life and Land of. A. Cunningham. New York, 1841. 12°. . 1754
Life and Works. Edited by R. Chambers. N. Y. 1852. 4 v. 12°. 4765
Life and Works. Ed. by A. Cunningham. Boston, 1834. 4 v. 12°. 888
Burr, A. Memoirs. M. L. Davis. New York, 1836. 2 v. 8°. . . 713
Burritt, E. Miscellaneous Writings. Part I. Worcester, 1850. 12°. . 3319
Thoughts and Things at Home and Abroad. Boston, 1854. 12°. . 6143
Burton; or, the Sieges. J. H. Ingraham. New York, 1847. 2 v. 12°. . 958
Burton, J. H. Life and Corres. of David Hume. Edin. 1846. 2 v. 8°. . 5149
Burton, R. Anatomy of Melancholy. Philadelphia, 1836. 2 v. 8°. . 1960
Burton, R. F. Goa and the Blue Mountains. London, 1851. 12°. . . 4577
Burton, W. Cheering Views of Man and Providence. Boston, 1832. 12°. 1528
District School as it Was. Boston, 1850. 12°. 3775
The same, and other Writings. Boston, 1852. 12°. . . 1516
White Slavery. Worcester, 1839. 12°. 1489
Bury, Lady B. de. Germania; its Courts, Camps, &c. Lon.1850. 2 v. 8°. 4302
Bury, Lady Charlotte. The Divorced. Philadelphia, n. d. 8°. . . 961
Diary of the Times of George IV. London, 1839. 4 v. 8°. . . 5144

Bury, Lady Charlotte. Two Sisters. New York, 1849. 8°. . . . 3463
Bury, T. T. Styles of Architecture. London, 1853. 12°. . . . 6047
Bush, Mrs. F. Memoirs of the Queens of France. Phil. 1851. 2 v. 12°. 2985
Bush, G. Anastasis; or, the Resurrection of the Body. N. Y. 1845. 12°. 2522
Life of Mahomet. (H. F. L.) New York, 1843. 12°. . 3683, 10
The Soul; or, Scriptural Psychology. New York, 1845. 12°. . 3610
Bushnell, H. Argument on Christian Nurture. Hartford, 1847. 8°. . 3197
Christ in Theology. Hartford, 1851. 12°. 4166
Fathers of New England. An Oration. New York, 1850. 12°. . 3926
God in Christ. Three Discourses. Hartford, 1849. 12°. . . 3283
Views of Christian Nurture. Hartford, 1848. 12°. . . . 3159
Bushnan, J. S. Fishes, their Structure and Uses. Edin. 1843. 12°. 4901, 35
Business, Practical Treatise on. E. T. Freedley. Philadelphia, 1852. 12°. 4898
Busy Moments of an Idle Woman. Mrs. King. New York, 1854. 12°. 5575
Butler, A. Lives of the Saints. New York, 1845. 8°. 5996
Butler, C. Historical Outline. Boston, 1823. 12°. 368, 2
Life of Erasmus, and Literature in the Middle Ages. Lon. 1825. 8°. 2609
Life of Fénélon. Philadelphia, 1811. 12°. 1834
Butler, Mrs. C. H. Life in Varied Phases. Boston, 1851. 12°. . . 4452
Butler, F. Compend of General History. Hartford, 1818. 16°. . . 38
Universal History. Hartford, 1822. 12°. 439
Butler, Frances Anna, Journal of. Philadelphia, 1835. 2 v. 12°. . . 225
Poems. Philadelphia, 1844. 12°. 2325
Year of Consolation. New York, 1847. 2 v. 12°. . . . 3002
Butler, J. Analogy of Religion. New York, 1843. 12° 1779
Criticism on. D. Wilson. Boston, 1834. 12°. . . . 1479
Butler, S. Hudibras; with Notes and Memoir of Author. N.Y. 1847. 12°. 2946
Butt, Martha H. Antifanaticism; a Tale of the South. Phil. 1853. 12°. 5338
Butterflies, British. J. Duncan. Edinburgh, 1843. 12°. . . 4901, 29
Foreign. J. Duncan. Edinburgh, 1843. 12°. . . . 4901, 31
Buxton, Sir T. F. African Slave Trade. Philadelphia, 1839. 12°. . 1527
Memoirs. C. Buxton. Philadelphia, 1849. 8°. 3253
Sketch of. T. Binney. Boston, 1851. 12°. 3776
Byrn, M. L. Complete Practical Brewer. Philadelphia, 1852. 12°. . 5007
Byron, Lord, and his Contemporaries. L. Hunt. London, 1828. 2 v. 8°. 2291
Conversations at Pisa, 1821–22. T. Medwin. N. Y. 1824. 12°. . 548
Conversations with Lady Blessington. Philadelphia, 1836. 8°. 2228, 2
Don Juan. Philadelphia, 1852. 12°. 1624
Letters and Journals. T. Moore. New York, 1830. 2 v. 8°. . 743
Life. J. Galt. New York, 1830. 18° 125
The same. (H. F. L.) New York, 1843. 12°. . . 3683, 9
Works, in Verse and Prose. New York, 1840. Roy. 8°. . . 1434
Works. Philadelphia, 1839. 8 v. 12°. 2114

Vol. 1. Hours of Idleness; English Bards and Scotch Reviewers, &c.
2. Prophecy of Dante; Age of Bronze, &c.
3. Giaour; Bride of Abydos.
4. Manfred; Marino Faliero; Heaven and Earth; Sardanapalus.
5. Two Foscari; Deformed Transformed; Cain; Werner.
6. Childe Harold's Pilgrimage.
7, 8. Don Juan.

C.

Cabin and Parlor; or, Slaves & Masters. J. T. Randolph. Phil. 1852. 12°. 5000
Cabin Book. C. Sealsfield. London, 1852. 12°. 2088
Cabinet of Curiosities. London, n. d. 8°. 5096
Cabinet of Freedom. Cond. by W. Jay and others. N. Y. 1836. 3 v. 12°. 1548
Cabot, J. E. Narrative of Lake Superior Tour. Boston, 1850. 8°. . 3604
Cabot, S. Life. C. Hayward, jun. Boston, 1844. 12°. . . 1076, 9
Cæsar, C. Julius. Commentaries. Literally trans. Lond. 1851. Post 8°. 4181
Commentaries. Trans. by W. Duncan. N. Y. 1842. 2 v. 12°. 1854, 6, 7
History of. J. Abbott. New York, 1850. 12°. 3381
Cæsars, The. T. De Quincey. Boston, 1851. 12°. 3817
Cairo, Jerusalem, &c., Excursion to. G. Jones. New York, 1836. 12°. 967
Cakes and Ale. D. Jerrold. London, 1851. 12°. 6234, 4
Calabrella, Baroness de. Double Oath. London, 1850. 3 v. 12°. . . 4249
Calavar; or, Knight of the Conquest. R. M. Bird. N. York, 1854. 12°. 6136
Calculus, Differential. W. S. B. Woolhouse. London, 1854. 12°. . 6108
Examples in. J. Haddon. London, 1851. 12°. . . 6111
and Integral. Cambridge, 1824. 8°. 1366
Calculus, Integral. H. Cox. London, 1852. 12°. 6109
Examples in. J. Hann. London, 1850. 12°. . . . 6110
Calcutta, Three Years in. G. W. Johnson. London, 1843. 2 v. 12°. . 4966
Calderon de la Barca, Mde. Life in Mexico. London, 1843. 8°. . . 1713
Caldicott, T. F. Hannah Corcoran. Boston, 1853. 16°. . . . 5370
Caldwell, C. Discourse on H. Holley. Boston, 1828. 8°. . . . 1387
Caleb Field; a Tale of the Puritans. Mrs. Oliphant. N. Y. 1851. 12°. 4220
Caleb Williams. W. Godwin. New York, 1831. 2 v. 12°. 402
The same. London, 1853. 12°. 5695
Calhoun, J. C. Speeches. New York, 1843. 8°. 1950
Works. Edited by R. K. Cralle. New York, 1853–54. 4 v. 8°. . 5987

Vol. 1. Disquisition on Government; Discourse on the Constitution and Government of the United States.
2–4. Speeches in Congress.

Calico Printing and Dyeing. New York, 1841. 8°. 2786
California, Adventures in. B. Taylor. New York, 1850. 2 v. 12°. . 3835
and its Gold Regions. F. Robinson. New York, 1849. 12°. . 3335
and Oregon in 1848. J. Q. Thornton. N. York, 1849. 2 v. 12°. . 3279
and Oregon, History of. R. Greenhow. Boston, 1845. 8°. . . 2270
and Oregon, with Maps. C. Wilkes. Philadelphia, 1849. 8°. . 3296
and Oregon Trail. F. Parkman, jun. New York, 1849. 12°. . 3351
Debates in Constitutional Convention of. Washington, 1850. 8°. 2752
Excursion to. W. Kelly. London, 1851. 2 v. 12°. . . . 4618
History of. E. S. Capron. Boston, 1854. 12°. 5833
Life and Adventures in. T. J. Farnham. New York, 1849. 8°. . 2756
Life in. A. Robinson. New York, 1846. 12°. 2549
Sights in the Gold Region. T. T. Johnson. N. York, 1849. 12°. 3434

California, Personal Adventures in. W. R. Ryan. Lond. 1850. 2 v. 12°. 4232
Six Months in the Mines. E. G. Buffum. Phil. 1850. 12°. . 3859
Sixteen Months in Gold Diggings. D. B. Woods. N. Y. 1851. 12°. 4597
Three Years in. W. Colton. New York, 1850. 12°. . . . 3903
Tour of Duty in. J. W. Revere. New York, 1849. 12°. . . 3345
What I Saw in, 1846–47. E. Bryant. New York, 1849. 12°. . 3144
Callcott, J. W. Musical Grammar. Boston, 1838. 12°. . . . 1473
Callery and Yvan. Insurrection in China. New York, 1853. 12°. . 5565
Callicot, T. C. Handbook of Universal Geography. N. York, 1853. 12°. 5232
Calmet, A. Dictionary of the Bible. Boston, 1843. Roy. 8°. . . 1439
Phantom World, Philosophy of Spirit, &c. Phil. 1850. 12°. . 3883
Calvert, G. H. Scenes and Thoughts in Europe. New York, 1846. 12°. 2591
Calvert, L. Life. G. W. Burnap. Boston, 1848. 12°. . . 1076, 19
Calvin, J. Institutes of the Christian Religion. Phil. 1850. 2 v. 8°. . 4707
Life. T. Beza. Philadelphia, 1836. 12°. 1935
Life. T. H. Dyer. New York, 1850. 8°. 3648
Life and Times of. Paul Henry. New York, 1851. 2 v. 8°. . 4123
Calvinistic and Socinian Systems. A. Fuller. Boston, 1815. 12°. . 197
Cambridge (Eng.) Prize Poems. London, 1847. 12°. 3134
Cambridge, W. G. Henri; or, the Web and Woof of Life. Bost. 1853. 12°. 5362
Camel Hunt. J. W. Fabens. New York, 1853. 12°. 4621
Camilla; or, a Picture of Youth. Miss F. Burney. Bost. 1797. 3 v. 12°. 2361
Camoens, L. de. Poems. Trans. by Lord Strangford. Balt. 1808. 12°. 2391
Camp, C. S. Democracy. (H. F. L.) New York, 1847. 12°. . 3683, 138
Camp and March, Treatise on. H. D. Grafton. Boston, 1854. 12°. . 5615
Camp-Fires of the Revolution. H. C. Watson. Philadelphia, 1850. 8°. 3828
Campan, Mde. Court of Marie Antoinette. London, 1850. 2 v. 12°. . 3834
Campbell, G. Philosophy of Rhetoric. N. York, 1844. 12°. . . 2304
Four Gospels, with Dissertations and Notes. And. 1837. 2 v. 8°. 4703
Campbell, J. Travels in South Africa. Andover, 1816. 8°. . . 756
Campbell, J. (Lord). Lives of Chief Justices of Eng. Lond. 1849. 2 v. 8°. 3519
Lives of Lord Chancellors of England. London, 1848. 7 v. 8°. . 3590
Campbell, Jane C. Money Maker. New York, 1854. 12°. . . . 6142
Campbell, Maria. Life of Gen. Wm. Hull. New York, 1848. 8°. . 2863
Campbell, T. Gertrude of Wyoming. New York, 1841. 12°. . . 2966
(Editor.) Frederick the Great and his Times. Lond. 1845. 2 v. 12°. 3187
Letters from the South. Philadelphia, 1836. 12°. . . . 252
Life and Letters. Edited by W. Beattie. N. York, 1850. 2 v. 12°. 3895
Life of Petrarch. Philadelphia, 1841. 8°. 2250
Life of Mrs. Siddons. New York, 1834. 12°. 1165
Poetical Works. Philadelphia, 1836. 8°. 580
The same. New York, 1847. 12°. 3477
The same. Edited by Epes Sargent. Boston, 1854. 12°. . 5743
Specimens of British Poets. Philadelphia, 1853. Roy. 8°. . . 5443
Campbell, W. Old Forest Ranger. New York, 1853. 12°. . . . 5319
Campbell, W. W. Border Warfare of New York. N.Y. 1849. 12°. . 3292
Life and Writings of De Witt Clinton. New York, 1849. 8°. . 3355
Robin Hood and Captain Kidd. New York, 1853. 12°. . . 5284

Campaign with Zumalacarregui. C. T. Henningsen. Phil. 1836. 8°. 2228, 2
in Northern Mexico in 1846–47. M. E. Curwen. N. Y. 1853. 12°. 5803
in Russia. R. K. Porter. Baltimore, 1806. 8°. 690
Sketches of the Mexican War. W. S. Henry. N. Y. 1847. 12°. 3091
Canada and United States, Travels in. F. Hall. Boston, 1818. 12°. . 1190
Conquest of. Captain Warburton. New York, 1850. 2 v. 12°. . 3839
Debates in House of Commons on, 1774. London, 1839. 8°. . 3549
in 1837–38. E. A. Theller. Philadelphia, 1841. 2 v. 12°. . . 3130
Preserved, and Britain Redeemed. F. A. Wilson. Lond. 1850. 8°. 5414
Upper, Geographical View of. M. Smith. Phil. 1813. 12°. . 484
Canadas, Travels through. G. Heriot. Philadelphia, 1813. . . . 485
Canning, G. Life. R. Bell. New York, 1846. 12°. 2904
Select Speeches. Philadelphia, 1835. 12°. 2248
Canot, T. Twenty Years of an African Slaver. New York, 1854. 12°. 6199
Canterbury Tales. Misses S. and H. Lee. London, 1850. 2 v. 12°. . 5649
Cap Sheaf; a Fresh Bundle. G. C. Hill. New York, 1853. 12°. . . 5054
Cape of Good Hope, Residence at. C. J. F. Bunbury. Lond. 1848. 12°. 4573
Capital Punishment. C. Spear. Boston, 1844. 12°. 1938
its Authority and Expediency. G. B. Cheever. N.Y. 1849. 12°. 2576
Capitalist; or, Fortune's Frolics. T. E. Hook. New York, 1844. 8°. 2167, 2
Capper, S. Acknowledged Doctrines of Church of Rome. Lond. 1850. 8°. 5412
Capron, E. S. History of California. Boston, 1854. 12°. . . . 5833
Captain Blake. W. H. Maxwell. London, 1851. 12°. 5668
Captain Kyd. J. H. Ingraham. New York, 1847. 2 v. 12°. . . 525
Captains of the Old World. H. W. Herbert. New York, 1851. 12°. . 4496
Captains of the Roman Republic. H. W. Herbert. N.Y. 1854. 12°. . 6215
Captive in Patagonia. B. F. Bourne. Boston, 1853. 12°. . . . 5215
Cardinal's Daughter. R. M. Daniel. New York, 1850. 8°. . . . 3461
Carey, Alice. Clovernook. New York, 1852. 12°. 4757
Clovernook Children. Boston, 1854. 12°. 6233
Hagar; a Story of To-day. New York, 1852. 12°. . . . 4910
Lyra, and other Poems. New York, 1852. 12°. 4783
and Phœbe. Poems. Philadelphia, 1850. 12°. 1089
Carey, H. C. Past, Present, and Future. Philadelphia, 1848. 8°. . 2882
Principles of Political Economy. Philadelphia, 1837. 3 v. 8°. . 1787
Carey's Library of Choice Literature. — See *Library*.
Carl Krinken. Anna Warner. New York, 1854. 12°. 5626
Carlén, Emilie F. Birthright. London, 1851. 3 v. 12°. . . . 4616
Bride of Omberg. New York, 1853. 12°. 5373
Gustavus Lindorm. New York, 1853. 12°. 5557
Home in the Valley. New York, 1854. 12°. 6214
Ivar; the Skjuts-Boy. New York, 1852. 8°. 4809
John; a Novel. New York, 1854. 8°. 5496
Marie Louise; or, Opposite Neighbors. London, 1853. 12°. . 5382
One Year; a Tale of Wedlock. New York, 1853. 12°. . . . 5311
Rose of Tistelon. New York, 1844. 8°. 2743
Whimsical Woman. New York, 1854. 12°. 5814
Carleton, W. Miser; or, Convicts of Lisnamona. Phil. 1840. 2 v. 12°. 1660

Carleton, W. Squanders of Castle Squander. London, 1852. 2 v. 12°. 5030
Valentine M'Clutchy, the Irish Agent. New York, 1846. 12°. . 2927
Carlington Castle; a Tale of the Jesuits. New York, 1854. 12°. . . 5779
Carlton, R. New Purchase. New York, 1843. 2 v. 12°. 1729
Carlyle, T. Chartism. Boston, 1840. 12°. 6242
Critical and Miscellaneous Essays. Boston, 1838. 4 v. 12°. . 1080

Vol. 1. Jean Paul Friedrich Richter; German Literature; Life and Writings of Werner; Goethe's Helena; Goethe; Burns; Life of Heyne; German Playwright.
2. Voltaire; Novalis; Signs of the Times; Jean Paul Friedrich Richter; History; Luther's Psalm; Schiller; Nibelungen Lied; German Literature of the Fourteenth and Fifteenth Centuries.
3. German Poetry; Characteristics; Goethe's Poetry; Biography; Boswell's Johnson; Death of Goethe; Goethe's Works; Corn Law Rhymes; Diderot; History.
4. Count Cagliostro; Edward Irving; Diamond Necklace; Mirabeau; French Revolution; Sir Walter Scott; Von Ense's Memoirs; Copyright Bill.

The same. Philadelphia, 1848. 8°. 3418, 5
Heroes and Hero-Worship. New York, 1849. 12°. . . . 1595
French Revolution of 1789. Boston, 1838. 2 v. 12°. . . . 944
Letters and Speeches of Oliver Cromwell. N.Y. 1845. 2 v. 12°. 2538
Life of F. Schiller. New York, 1846. 12°. 2498
Life of John Sterling. Boston, 1851. 12°. 4486
Past and Present. New York, 1844. 12°. 1743
Sartor Resartus. Boston, 1837. 12°. 346
Specimens of German Romance. Boston, 1841. 2 v. 12°. . . 2108
Carmichael, A. Life and Philosophy of J. G. Spurzheim. Bost. 1833. 12°. 564
Carmichael, Mrs. Domestic Manners at West Indies. Phil. 1833. 8°. 1357, 2
Carnes, J. A. Voyage to the West Coast of Africa. Boston, 1852. 12°. 4798
Caroline; a Franconia Story. J. Abbott. New York, 1855. 12°. . 5297
Carpenter, W. B. Use and Abuse of Alcoholic Liquors. Bost. 1851. 12°. 4099
Carpenter, W. H. History of Massachusetts. Philadelphia, 1853. 12°. 5320
Ruth Emsley, the Betrothed Maiden. Philadelphia, 1850. 12°. . 3891
Carpenter, W. W. Travels and Adventures in Mexico. N.Y. 1851. 12°. 4432
Carpenter of Rouen. J. S. Jones. Boston, 1849. 12°. 3124
Carr, J. Northern Summer round the Baltic. Hartford, 1806. 12°. . 833
Stranger in France. Brattleboro', 1806. 12°. 177
Carriers, Law of. J. K. Angell. Boston, 1848. 8°. 4022
Carthaginians, Hist. Researches on. A. H. L. Heeren. Ox. 1838. 2 v. 8°. 2657
Carver, J. Sketches of New England. New York, 1842. 12°. . . 1679
Case, W. Poems; Revolutionary Memorials. New York, 1852. 12°. . 943
Cass, L. France; its King, Court, and Government. N.Y. 1848. 8°. 3148
Caspar Hauser, Account of. P. J. A. Feuerbach. Boston, 1832. 16°. . 821
Caspian, Sketches of the Shores of. W. R. Holmes. London, 1845. 8°. 4642
Castilian, The. New York, 1829. 12°. 1209
Castle Dangerous. Sir W. Scott. Boston, 1848. 2 v. 12°. . . 999, 47, 48
The same. Edinburgh, 1849. 2 v. 12°. . . 4100, 47, 48
The same. Edinburgh, 1850. Roy. 8°. . . . 4531, 12
Castle of Ehrenstein. G. P. R. James. N.Y. 1847. 8°. 2784
Castle of Otranto. H. Walpole. London, 1853. 12°. 5702
Castles in the Air; a Novel. Mrs. Gore. New York, 1848. 8°. . . 3237

Castlereagh, Viscount. Journey to Damascus. London, 1847. 2 v. 12°. 4580
Correspondence and Despatches. London, 1851. 4 v. 8°. . . . 5408
Catacombs of Rome. W. I. Kip. New York, 1854. 12°. 5819
Catalogue of Am. Publications, 1820–52. O. A. Roorback. N. Y. 1852. 8°. 5993
of Books on the Masonic Institution. Boston, 1852. 8°. . . . 330
of the Boston Athenæum. Boston, 1827. 8°. 2907
of the Boston Library Society. Boston, 1844. 8°. 2276
of Cambridge High School Lib. E. Abbot, jun. Camb. 1853. 8°. 5986
of the Library of the Brothers in Unity. New Haven, 1851. 8°. . 5983
of the Cincinnati Mercantile Library. Cincinnati, 1846. 8°. . 5969
of the Hartford Young Men's Institute. Hartford, 1844. 8°. . 2275
of Harvard College Library. Cambridge, 1830–34. 5 v. 8°. . . 5998
of the Library of Young Men's Assoc. of Albany. Alb. 1848. 8°. 3140
of the Mercantile Library of Baltimore. Baltimore, 1851. 8°. . 4946
of the New York Mercantile Library. New York, 1837. 8°. . 1200
The same. New York, 1844. 8°. 1200
The same. New York, 1850. 8°. 1200
of the Mercantile Library Co. Philadelphia, 1850. 8°. . . 4333
of the Providence Athenæum. Providence, 1853. 8°. . . . 5954
of the Public Library of Boston. Boston, 1854. 8°. . . . 5979
of the Richest Men of Massachusetts. Boston, 1851. 8°. . . 4533
of the St. Louis Mercantile Library. St. Louis, 1850. 8°. . . 4308
of the Society Library, New York. New York, 1852. 8°. . . 5997
Catherine de Medicis. L. S. Costellow. London, 1853. 12°. . . 5739
Catholic Church, Acknowledged Doctrines of. S. Capper. Lond. 1850. 8°. 5412
and Modern Society. E. Quinet. Tr. by C. E. Lester. N.Y. 1845. 12°. 2512
Faith and Morality of. J. Curr. Boston, 1850. 24°. . . . 3756
Catholic Doctrine, Grounds of. Boston, 1847. 24°. 3758
Catholic History of the Bible. J. Reeve. Boston, 1849. 12°. . . 3681
Catholic Inquisition, History of. Philadelphia, 1835. 12°. . . . 910
Catholicism, Trials of a Mind in Progress to. L. S. Ives. Bost. 1854. 12°. 5839
Catlin, G. North American Indians. New York, 1844. 2 v. 8°. . . 1780
Catteau, M. General View of Sweden. London, 1790. 8°. . . . 653
Cattermole R. Book of Raphael's Cartoons. London, 1845. 8°. . . 5095
Catullus and Tibullus. Poems, translated. London, 1854. Post 8°. . 5876
Caucasus, Tour of the. G. L. Ditson. New York, 1850. 8°. . . 3522
Caudle Lectures. D. Jerrold. London, 1851. 12°. . . . 6234, 3
Caulfield, J. Remarkable Characters. London, 1819. 8°. . . . 5897
Caunter, R. Confessions and Crimes. Philadelphia, 1836. 8°. . 2228, 2
Cavaliers of England. H. W. Herbert. New York, 1852. 12°. . . 1020
Cavendish; or, the Patrician at Sea. Philadelphia, 1835. 2 v. 12°. . 293
Caxton, W. Life. London, 1833. 8°. 602
Caxtons; a Family Picture. E. L. Bulwer. New York, 1850. 8°. . 3459
Ceba, A. Citizen of a Republic. New York, 1845. 12°. . . . 2489
Cecil, J. Life and Works of John Newton. Philadelphia, 1839. 2 v. 8°. 4706
Cecil; or, the Adventures of a Coxcomb. Mrs. Gore. N. Y. 1845. 8°. 2240
Cecil, R. (Earl of Salisbury). Life. P. Courtenay. Lond. 1831. 12°. 1831, 5
Cecil, W. (Lord Burleigh). Life. London, 1831. 12°. . . . 1831, 1

Cecil Hyde; a Novel. Philadelphia, 1834. 2 v. 12°. 1186
Cecilia Howard. T. S. Arthur. Philadelphia, 1851. 8°. 4537
Celebrated Trials of the Aristocracy. P. Burke. London, 1849. 8°. . 4522
Celestial Scenery. T. Dick. Philadelphia, 1845. 12°. . . . 2357, 7
The same. (H. F. L.) New York, 1846. 12°. . . 3683, 83
Cellini, B., Memoirs of, by Himself. Tr. by T. Roscoe. N. Y. 1845. 2 v. 12°. 2497
*Cemeteries, Designs for Monuments in. J. J. Smith. N. Y. 1846. 4°. 4857
Census of the United States, 1840, Compendium of. Wash. 1842. Folio. 2033
1850. Washington, 1853. 4°. 5890
Central America, Travels in. J. L. Stephens. New York, 1848. 2 v. 8°. 1635
Central Society of Education. London, 1838. 2 v. 12°. 5040
Cervantes, M. de. Don Quixote. Boston, 1848. 2 v. 8°. 3094
The same. Philadelphia, 1846. 4 v. 24°. 30
Ceylon, Eleven Years in. Major Forbes. London, 1840. 2 v. 8°. . . 4681
Recollections of. J. Selkirk. London, 1844. 8°. 4650
Chadwick, E. Report on Interment in Towns. London, 1843. 8°. . 3390
Chainbearer; or, Littlepage MSS. J. F. Cooper. N. York, 1845. 2 v. 8°. 2509
Chairolas, Prince of Paida, and other Tales. Philadelphia, 1836. 12°. . 972
Challenge of Barletta. M. D'Azeglio. New York, 1845. 12°. . . 2483
Chalmers, A. Hist. and Biograph. Preface to Tatler. N. Y. 1809. 12°. 894, 1
Chalmers, G. Revolt of the American Colonies. Boston, 1845. 2 v. 8°. 2264
Chalmers, T. Application of Christianity to Affairs of Life. N.Y. 1821. 8°. 1305
Institutes of Theology. New York, 1849. 2 v. 12°. . . . 3415
Memoirs of Life and Writings. New York, 1850. 3 v. 12°. . 3656
Political Economy. New York, 1832. 12°. 533
Posthumous Works. Edited by W. Hanna. N. Y. 1848. 5 v. 12°. 3147
Select Works. New York, 1850. 4 v. 8°. 3539

Vol. 1. Miscellanies.
2. Lectures on Romans.
3. Miscellaneous Sermons.
4. Sermons on Depravity of Human Nature; Application of Christianity to Commerce, &c.; Sermons at St. John's Church, Glasgow; Christian Revelation and Modern Astronomy; Evidences of Christianity.

Chambers, R. Cyclopædia of English Literature. Bost. 1851. 2 v. roy. 8°. 2636
Select Writings. Edinburgh, 1847. 7 v. 12°. 4056
(Editor). Life and Works of Robert Burns. N. Y. 1852. 4 v. 12°. 4765
Chambers's Edinburgh Journal. Edinburgh, 1844–53. 20 v. roy. 8°. . 709
Information for the People. Philadelphia, 1849. 2 v. roy. 8°. . 2787
Library of Biography. Boston, 1849. 2 v. 12°. 3314
Miscellany. Edited by R. Chambers. Boston, 1847. 10 v. 12°. . 2457
Papers for the People. Edinburgh, 1850–51. 12 v. 12°. . . 4076

Vol. 1. Bonaparte Family; Sepulchres of Etruria; Valerie Dulcos; Education of the Citizen; The Myth; Sunken Rock, a Tale of the Mediterranean; Popular Cultivation of Music; Ebenezer Elliott.
2. Sanitary Movement; Washington and his Contemporaries; Edmund Atherton, a Tale; Memorabilia of the Seventeenth Century; Ruined Cities of Central America; Ivory Mine, a Tale; Secret Societies of Modern Europe; Francis Jeffrey.
3. Arctic Explorations; Social Utopias; Speculator, a Tale of Mammon-worship; Carthage and the Carthagenians; Recent Discoveries in Astronomy; White Swallow, an Indian Tale; Mechanics' Institutions; Thomas Campbell.
4. Bourbon Family; California; Black Pocket-book, a Tale; Fénélon; Every-day Life of the Greeks; Lady Marjory St. Just; Science of the Sunbeam; Sir Robert Peel.

Chambers's Papers for the People. — *Continued.*

Vol. 5. Secret Societies of the Middle Ages; Rajah Brooke and Borneo; Last of the Ruthvens; Education Movement; Antarctic Explorations; Queen of Spades; Jewish Life in Central Europe; Wm. Wordsworth.
6. Microscope and its Marvels; Pre-Columbian Discovery of America; Hermann, a Tale; Public Libraries; Australia and Van Dieman's Land; Lone Star, a Tale; Religion of the Greeks; Heyne.
7. Water Supply of Towns; Ancient Scandinavia; Lost Letter, the Somnambule; Life in an Indiaman; Law of Storms; Santillian's Choice, a Tale; Isthmus of Panama; Daniel De Foe.
8. Ocean Routes; Cromwell and Contemporaries; Life at Græfenburg; Black Gondola, a Tale; Ancient Philosophic Sects; Wonders of Human Folly; Mary Wortley Montagu.
9. Recent Decorative Art; Alchemy and the Alchemists; Lost Laird, a Tale of '45; German Poets and Poetry; Deserts of Africa; Sigismund Temple, a Tale; Electric Communications; Fichte, a Biography.
10. Ancient Rites and Mysteries; Siberia, and the Penal Settlements; Harriette, a Tale; Childhood of Experimental Philosophy; Confucius; The Temptation; Siam and the Siamese; Thomas Moore.
11. Isthmus of Suez; Animal Instincts and Intelligence; Realized Wishes, a Tale; Troubadours and Trouveres; New Zealand; Tower of Fontenay; Industrial Investments and Associations; Lord Brougham.
12. Railway Communications; Incas of Peru; Marfreda, or the Icelanders; What is Philosophy? European Intercourse with Japan; Half-caste, a Tale; Progress of America; Duke of Wellington.

Pocket Miscellany. Boston, 1852. 9 v. 12°. 864
Repository of Instruc. and Amusing Papers. Bost. 1854. 4 v. 12°. 5209
Chamier, F. Arethusa. Philadelphia, 1837. 2 v. 12°. 276
Ben Brace. London, 1852. 12°. 5671
Cruise of the Midge. New York, 1851. 8°. 1075
Green Hand; a Short Yarn. New York, 1851. 8°. . . . 4501
Life of a Sailor. London, 1852. 12°. 5689
Review of the French Revolution. London, 1849. 2 v. 8°. . . 4541
Tom Cringle's Log. New York, 1845. 8°. 1091
Unfortunate Man. New York, 1835. 2 v. 12°. 406
Young Muscovite. New York, 1834. 4 v. 12°. 1106
Chancellors of England. Lives. Lord Campbell. Lond. 1848. 7 v. 8°. 3590
Chandler, Eliz. M. Poetical Works, with Life. B. Lundy. Phil. 1836. 12°. 1533
Chandler, Ellen L. This, That, and the Other. Boston, 1854. 12°. . 5841
Chandler, Mary G. Elements of Character. Boston, 1854. 12°. . . 6144
Chandler, P. W. American Criminal Trials. Boston, 1841–44. 2 v. 12°. 1921
Channing, E. T. Life of William Ellery. Boston, 1840. 12°. . 1076, 6
Channing, W. E. Conversations in Rome. Boston, 1847. 12°. . . 2437
Discourses, Reviews, and Miscellanies. Boston, 1837. 8°. . . 794
Memoirs. Boston, 1848. 3 v. 12°. 3113
Slavery. Boston, 1835. 12°. 1118
Works. Boston, 1847. 6 v. 12°. 1798

Vol. 1. Milton; Napoleon; Fénélon; Calvinism; National Literature; Association; The Union; Education.
2. Slavery; Abolitionists; Annexation of Texas; Catholicism; Creeds; Temperance; Self-culture.
3. Discourses; Duties of Children; Honor due all Men; Evidences of Christianity.
4. Character of Christ; Christianity a Rational Religion; Spiritual Freedom; Self-denial; Imitableness of Christ's Character; Evil of Sin; Immortality; Love to Christ; Future Life; War; Ministry for the Poor; Christian Worship; Sunday-school; N. Worcester.
5. Slavery Question; War; Elevation of the Laboring Community; C. Follen; Charges at Ordinations; Miscellanies; Appendix.
6. Emancipation; J. Tuckerman; Present Age; The Church; Duty of the Free States; Address at Lenox.

Channing, W.H. (Ed.) Life & Writings of J.H.Perkins. Bos.1851. 2 v. 12°. 4094
Chanticleer; a Thanksgiving Story. Boston, 1850. 12°. . . . 4071
Chapel of the Hermits, and other Poems. J. G. Whittier. Bos.1853. 12°. 5207
Chapin, E. H. Characters in the Gospels. New York, 1852. 12°. . 36
Duties of Young Men. Boston, 1840. 12°. 1463
Duties of Young Women. Boston, 1850. 12°. 2451
Chapman, J. Cotton and Commerce of India. London, 1850. 8°. . 4328
Chapone, Hester. Works. Boston, 1809. 4 v. 16°. 65
Letters on Improvement of the Mind. Boston, 1822. 16°. . . 83
Chaptal, J. A. Chemistry applied to Agriculture. Boston, 1835. 12°. . 665
Elements of Chemistry. Boston, 1806. 8°. 774
Characteristics, after Rochefoucault's Maxims. W. Hazlitt. Lond.1837. 12°. 2368
of Women. Mrs. A. Jameson. Boston, 1846. 12°. . . . 266
Characters in the Gospels. E. H. Chapin. New York, 1852. 12°. . 36
Charcoal Sketches. J. C. Neal. New York, 1849. 2 v. 12°. . . . 2145
Charicles; or, Private Life of Greeks. W. A. Becker. Lond, 1854. 12°. 5831
Charities of London. S. Low. London, 1850. 12°. 937
Charity and the Clergy; Review of Colwell's 'New Themes.' Phil.1853. 12°. 5208
and its Fruits. J. Edwards. New York, 1852. 12°. . . . 4753
Charity Sister, and other Tales. Mrs. E. Norton. N. Y. 1840. 12°. . 1566
Charlemagne, History of. G. P. R. James. (H. F. L.) N.Y.1848. 12°. 3683, 60
or, Church Delivered; a Poem. L. Bonaparte. Phil. 1815. 2 v. 16°. 75
Charles I., History of. J. Abbott. New York, 1848. 12°. . . . 2463
Reign of; Fairfax Corres. Ed. by G. W. Johnson. Lon.1848. 4 v. 8°. 4690
Charles II., Beauties of the Court of. Mrs. A. Jameson. Bost. 1834. 8°. 2083
Diary of the Times of. H. Sidney. London, 1843. 2 v. 8°. . 4673
History of. J. Abbott. New York, 1849. 12°. 3767
Memoirs of Court of. Count Grammont. London, 1846. Post 8°. 2952
Charles V., Cloister Life of. W. Stirling. Boston, 1853. 12°. . . 5359
History of the Reign of. W. Robertson. Phil. 1812. 3 v. 8°. . 1294
The same. New York, 1829. 8°. 1392
Charles VIII., History of. P. de Segur. Philadelphia, 1842. 2 v. 12°. . 3081
Charles XII., History of. F. M. A. de Voltaire. New York, 1851. 16°. 5183
Charles Chesterfield. Mrs. F. Trollope. New York, 1851. 8°. . . 4524
Charles Elwood; or, Infidel Converted. O. A. Brownson. Bost. 1840. 12°. 1809
Charles John, of Sweden and Norway. W. G. Meredith. Lond. 1829. 8°. 1116
Memoirs and Campaigns. J. Philippart. London, 1814. 8°. . 589
Charles Observator, Life and Reflections of. E. R. Sabin. Bost.1816. 12°. 214
Charles O'Malley, the Irish Dragoon. C. Lever. Philadelphia, 1841. 8°. 1608
Charles Tyrrell. G. P. R. James. New York, 1839. 2 v. 12°. . . 976
Charles Vincent; or, the Two Clerks. New York, 1839. 2 v. 12°. . . 178
Charleston Book, a Miscellany. Charleston, 1845. 12°. 2319
Charlotte Elizabeth. — See *Tonna, Mrs. C. E.*
Charlotte Temple. Mrs. Rowson. New York, 1814. 12°. . . . 1864
Charms and Counter Charms. Maria J. McIntosh. N. Y. 1850. 12°. . 3150
Charnock, J. Memoirs of Lord Nelson. Boston, 1806. 8°. . . . 664
Chase, L. B. History of the Polk Administration. N. Y. 1850. 8°. . 3645
Chasles, P. Anglo-American Literature and Manners. N.Y. 1852. 12°. 4905

Chasles, P. Notabilities in France and England. New York, 1853. 12°. 5340
Chastellux, Marquis de. Travels in North America. N. Y. 1828. 8°. . 1339
Children of Love. E. Sue. New York, 1850. 8°. 3966
Chili, Geograph. Nat., & Civil Hist. of. J. I. Molina. Middlet. 1808. 2 v. 8°. 744
Chateaubriand, F. A. de. Jerusalem & Holy Land. Lond. 1835. 2 v. 12°. 4568
Recollections of Italy, England, and America. Phil. 1816. 8°. . 740
Travels in Greece, Palestine, &c., 1806–7. Phil. 1813. 8°. . . 1320
Mémoires d'Outre-Tombe. New York, 1848. 2 v. 8°. . . 5399
Chatterton, T. Works, with Life. G. Gregory. London, 1803. 3 v. 8°. 2222
Chaucer, G. Poems, Modernized. London, 1841. 12°. 2384
Poetical Works, with an Essay. T. Tyrwhitt. London, 1843. 8°. 2611
Chauncy, C. Scriptural Account of the Fall. London, 1785. 8°. . . 1225
Cheever, G. B. American Common-Place Book of Poetry. Phil. 1843. 12°. 1775
(Editor.) Journal of the Pilgrims, 1620. New York, 1848. 12°. . 3325
Hill Difficulty, and other Miscellanies. New York, 1849. 12°. . 3357
Pilgrim in the Shadow of the Jungfrau Alp. N. Y. 1846. 12°. . 2533
Punishment by Death. New York, 1849. 12°. 2576
Right of the Bible in our Public Schools. New York, 1854. 12°. 5749
River of the Water of Life. New York, 1849. 12°. . . . 3432
Wanderings in the Shadow of Mont Blanc. N. Y. 1845. 12°. . 2495
Cheever, N. Biography. H. T. Cheever. New York, 1851. 12°. . 4494
Cheever, H. T. Island World of the Pacific. New York, 1851. 12°. . 4095
Life and Trials of N. Cheever. 1851. 12°. 4494
Life in the Sandwich Islands. New York, 1851. 12°. . . 4453
Memoir of W. Colton. New York, 1851. 12°. 4439
Memorials of Captain O'Congar. New York, 1851. 12°. . . 4156
(Editor.) Reel in a Bottle. New York, 1852. 12°. . . . 3753
(Editor.) Voices of Nature to the Soul of Man. N. Y. 1852. 12°. 4918
Whale and his Captors. New York, 1850. 12°. 3317
Chelmsford, History of. W. Allen. Haverhill, 1820. 8°. . . . 667
Cherokee Nation, Case of, *vs.* Georgia. R. Peters. Phil. 1831. 8°. . 1260
Chemical Arts, Improvements in. J. C. Boothe & C. Morfit. Wash. 1852. 8°. 5163
Chemical Technology. F. Knapp. London, 1848. 2 v. 8°. . . . 4137
Chemistry, Animal. J. Liebig. Cambridge, 1843. 12°. . . . 1752
Applied to Agriculture. J. A. Chaptal. Boston, 1835. 12°. . 665
Applied to Arts and Manufactures. F. Knapp. Lond. 1848. 2 v. 8°. 4137
Applied to Dyeing. J. Napier. Philadelphia, 1853. 12°. . . 5566
Conversations on. New Haven, 1813. 12°. 288
Elements of. J. A. Chaptal. Boston, 1806. 8°. 774
Elements of. J. L. Comstock. New York, 1841. 12°. . . 1740
Elements of. T. Graham. Philadelphia, 1852. 8°. . . . 5967
Elements of. E. Turner. Philadelphia, 1835. 12°. . . . 3507
Familiar Lectures on. J. Liebig. London, 1851. 12°. . . 4276
First Principles of. B. Silliman, jun. Philadelphia, 1849. 12°. . 3015
Handbook of. F. A. Abel & C. L. Bloxam. Phil. 1854. 8°. . 5934
Principles of. J. A. Stockhardt. Cambridge, 1850. 12°. . . 3927
Treatise on. G. Fownes. London, 1853. 12°. 6036
Chemist's Assistant, Analytical. F. Woehler. Philadelphia, 1852. 12°. 5024

Cheney, Mrs. H. V. Peep at the Pilgrims in 1636. Bost. 1826. 2 v. 12°. 2115
The same. Boston, 1850. 12°. 4051
Chesebro', Caroline. Children of Light. New York, 1853. 12°. . . 5064
Dream-Land by Day-Light. New York, 1851. 12°. . . . 4769
Isa; a Pilgrimage. New York, 1852. 12°. 950
Chesney, F. R. Russo-Turkish Campaigns. New York, 1854. 12°. . 5830
Chesnut Wood; a Tale. New York, 1854. 12°. 6179
Chess-Player's Companion. H. Staunton. London, 1849. Post 8°. . 3567
Chess-Player's Handbook. H. Staunton. London, 1847. Post 8°. . 3566
Chest, Diseases of. J. A. Swett. New York, 1852. 8°. 4804
Chesterfield, Earl of. Life and Letters. New York, 1845. . . . 1690
Selections from Letters to his Son. Boston, 1801. 12°. . . 338
Chevalier, M. Society and Manners in United States. Boston, 1839. 8°. 691
Chevalier D'Harmental. A. Dumas. New York, 1846. 8°. . . . 2697
Chevaliers of France. H. W. Herbert. New York, 1853. 12°. . . 5056
Cheveley; or, Man of Honor. Lady Bulwer. N.Y. 1839. 2 v. 12°. . 492
Cheverus, Cardinal de. Life. J. H. Doubourg. Phil. 1839. 12°. . 1135
Chickering, Jesse. Immigration into the United States. Bost. 1848. 8°. 4035
Population of Massachusetts, 1765–1840. Boston, 1846. 8°. . 2816
Chickering, Jonas, Tribute to. R. G. Parker. Boston, 1854. 12°. . 5802
Chief Justices of England, Lives of. Lord Campbell. Lond. 1849. 2 v. 8°. 3519
Child, L. Maria. Appeal in Favor of Africans. New York, 1836. 12°. 322
Biographies of Lady Russell and Mde. Guyon. Boston, 1832. 12°. 2376
Biographies of Mde. de Staël and Mde. Roland. Bost. 1832. 12°. 2153
Fact and Fiction; a Collection of Stories. New York, 1846. 12°. 2937
Good Wives. Boston, 1833. 12°. 1839
History of the Condition of Women. Boston, 1838. 2 v. 12°. . 1880
Hobomok. Boston, 1824. 12°. 870
Isaac T. Hopper; a True Life. New York, 1853. 12°. . . 5381
Letters from New York. New York, 1843–45. 2 v. 12°. . . 1732
Philothea; a Grecian Romance. New York, 1848. 12°. . . 2373
Rebels; or, Boston before the Revolution. 1850. 12°. . . 3869
Child of the Islands; a Poem. Mrs. C. E. S. Norton. N.Y. 1846. 12°. 2567
Child's First History of Rome. E. M. Sewell. New York, 1849. 12°. 3310
Child's History of England. C. Dickens. New York, 1854. 2 v. 12°. 5829
Children of the Abbey. R. M. Roche. Phil. n. d. 24°. . . . 25
Children of Light. Caroline Chesebro'. New York, 1853. 12°. . . 5064
Chillingworth, W. Works. Philadelphia, 1844. Roy. 8°. . . . 2168
Chimes; a Goblin Story. C. Dickens. Philadelphia, 1845. 16°. . . 808
The same. New York, 1848. 12°. 2204
China, and the Chinese. H. C. Sirr. London, 1849. 2 v. 8°. . . 4822
and the Chinese, Points and Pickings about. London, 1844. 12°. 5642
and the English. New York, 1843. 16°. 4602
Consular Cities of. G. Smith. London, 1847. 8°. . . . 4960
Embassy to. H. Ellis. Philadelphia, 1818. 8°. 2612
Embassy to. G. Staunton. Philadelphia, 1799. 2 v. 8°. . . 1270
Embassy to the Emperor of. G. Staunton. London, 1799. 8°. . 716
Insurrection in. Callery and Yvan. New York, 1853. 12°. . 5565

China, New Zealand, &c., Travels in. J. Holman. London, 1840. 8°. 1986, 4
Pictorial, Descriptive, and Historical. London, 1853. Post 8°. . 5503
Political, Commercial, and Social. R. M. Martin. Lond. 1847. 2 v. 8°. 4341
Travels in. J. Barrow. Philadelphia, 1805. 8°. . . . 763
Two Voyages to the Coast of. C. Gutzlaff. New York, 1833. 12°. 2152
Visit to Consular Cities of. G. Smith. New York, 1847. 12°. . 3083
Chinese History, Sketch of. C. Gutzlaff. New York, 1834. 2 v. 12°. . 1916
Chinese Empire, and its Inhabitants. S. W. Williams. N.Y. 1848. 2 v. 12°. 3102
Chinese Repository. Vols. 5, 7, 10–12. Canton, 1836–43. 5 v. 8°. . 1606
Chinese, The. J. F. Davis. New York, 1845. 2 v. 12°. . . . 2443
The same. (H. F. L.) New York, 1846. 2 v. 12°. 3683, 80, 81
Chitty, J. Law of Bills of Exchange, Checks, &c. Portland, 1807. 8°. 1159
Chivalry, History of. G. P. R. James. (H. F. L.) N.Y. 1847. 12°. 3683, 20
History of. C. Mills. Philadelphia, 1826. 2 v. 8°. . . . 1400
Romance, and the Drama. Sir W. Scott. Edin. 1834. 12°. 4101, 6
The same. Boston, 1829. 12°. 399, 6
Cholera, Boston Report on. Boston, 1849. 8°. 3953
Chorley, H. F. Memorials of Mrs. F. Hemans. Philadelphia, 1836. 12°. 973
Sketches of a Seaport-Town. Philadelphia, 1836. 2 v. 12°. . 436
Choules, J. O. Cruise of the North Star. Boston, 1854. 12°. . . 5770
Origin and History of Missions. Boston, 1838. 2 v. 4°. . . 1999
(Editor.) Young Americans Abroad. Boston, 1852. 12°. . . 4638
Christ before the Flood. J. Cumming. Boston, 1854. 12°. . . . 5822
Character of. E. Smith. Boston, 1814. 12°. 310
Glory of. G. Spring. New York, 1852. 2 v. 8°. . . . 1002
His Person and his Kingdom. R. Whately. London, 1845. 8°. 2653
History and Evidence of the Resurrec. of. G. West. Bost. 1834. 12°. 1478
in History. R. Turnbull. Boston, 1854. 12°. 5603
in Theology. H. Bushnell. Hartford, 1851. 12°. . . . 4166
Life. A. Neander. New York, 1848. 8°. 4716
Our Example. Caroline Fry. New York, 1852. 12°. . . 930
Pathways & Abiding Places of. J. M. Wainwright. N.Y. 1851. 8°. 4008
Preciousness of. J. Thornton. Boston, 1834. 12°. . . . 1480
Testimony of his Second Appearing. Union Village (O.), 1823. 12°. 3052
Christian Biography, Studies in. S. Osgood. New York, 1850. 12°. . 3670
Christian Courtesy, Principles of. G. W. Hervey. New York, 1852. 12°. 4781
Christian Examiner. Vols. 1–55 [continued]. Boston, 1824–53. 8°. . 1289
Christian Duty, Pastoral Addresses on. J. A. James. N.Y. 1852. 16°. 4754
Christian Faith, Essays on the Dangers to. R. Whately. Lond. 1839. 8°. 2652
Christian Father's Present. J. A. James. New York, 1854. 12°. . 5588
Christian Life and Spirit, Discourses on. C. A. Bartol. Bost. 1850. 12°. 3844
Christian Morals. Hannah More. New York, 1818. 18°. . . . 126
Christian Nurture, Views of. H. Bushnell. Hartford, 1848. 12°. . . 3159
Christian Philosopher. T. Dick. Brookfield, 1828. 12°. . . . 519
The same. Philadelphia, 1845. 12°. 2357, 2
Christian Purity, Nature and Blessedness of. R. S. Foster. N.Y. 1851. 12°. 4158
Christian Religion. E. Swedenborg. Boston, 1833. 8°. . . . 797
Evidence of the Truth of. A. Keith. Philadelphia, 1850. 12°. . 4746

Christian Religion, Institutes of. J. Calvin. Philadelphia, 1850. 2 v. 8°. 4707
Evidences, Doctrines, and Duties of. O. Gregory. N.Y. 1826. 2 v. 12°. 1550
Christian Retrospect and Register. R. Baird. New York, 1851. 12°. . 4206
Christian Review. Vols. 1-18 [continued]. New York, 1836-53. 8°. 3737
Christian Theology, Lectures on. G. C. Knapp. New York, 1850. 8°. 4709
Christian World Unmasked. J. Berridge. Boston, 1854. 12°. . . . 5606
Christians, History of the Early. S. Eliot. Bost. 1853. 2 v. 12°. Part II. 5238
Christianity, Application of, to Affairs of Life. T. Chalmers. N.Y. 1821. 8°. 1305
The same. New York, 1850. 8°. 3539, 4
Contrasted with Infidelity. E. Neale. Philadelphia, 1850. 12°. 4169
Defence of. E. Everett. Boston, 1814. 12°. 2110
Early Conflicts of. W. I. Kip. New York, 1850. 12°. . . 3506
Evidences of. A. Alexander. Philadelphia, 1850. 12°. . . 4744
Evidences of. W. J. Bolton. Boston, 1854. 12°. . . . 5863
Evidences of. T. Chalmers. New York, 1850. 8°. . . 3539, 4
Evidences of. M. Hopkins. Boston, 1847. 8°. 2856
Evidences of. W. Paley. Boston, 1803. 12°. 392
Evidences of. J. G. Palfrey. Boston, 1843. 2 v. 8°. . . . 2251
Evidences of. D. Wilson. Boston, 1845. 2 v. 12°. . . . 4745
Evidences of. Lectures at University of Virginia. N.Y. 1852. 8°. 4802
History of. A. Neander. Boston, 1849-54. 5 v. 8°. . . . 3527
History of. H. H. Milman. New York, 1842. 8°. . . . 1952
History of, for 325 Years, A.D. J. L. Mosheim. N.Y. 1852. 2 v. 8°. 4841
Lectures on. G. W. Burnap. Boston, 1848. 12°. . . . 4920
Present State of. F. Shoberl. New York, 1828. 12°. . . 552
Revived in the East. H. G. O. Dwight. New York, 1850. 12°. 3936
Tracts concerning. A. Norton. Cambridge, 1852. 8°. . . 4847
True Theory of. W. S. Grayson. New York, 1853. 12°. . . 5601
Truth of, Demonstrated. H. Newcomb. Boston, 1842. 12°. . 977
Views of. C. Bonnet. London, 1787. 12°. 187
Christine Van Amberg, &c. Countess d'Arbouville. N.Y. 1853. 12°. 5290
Christmas, Book of; Customs, &c. T. K. Hervey. New York, 1845. 12°. 2590
Christmas, H. Echoes of the Universe. Philadelphia, 1850. 12°. . . 3917
Cradle of Twin-Giants, Science and History. Lon. 1849. 2 v. 12°. 4579
Shores and Islands of the Mediterranean. London, 1851. 3 v. 12°. 4289
Christmas, Miss. (Editor.) Hist. of Papal Persecutions. Lond. 1851. 12°. 4613
Christmas Stories. C. Dickens. New York, 1848. 12°. . . . 2204
Christmas Carol; The Chimes; Cricket on the Hearth; Battle of Life.

Christopher North. — See *Wilson, Prof. John.*
Christopher under Canvass. J. Wilson. Philadelphia, 1850, 12°. . . 3879
Christopher Tadpole, Adventures of. Albert Smith. N. York, 1848. 8°. 2897
Chronicle, Anglo-Saxon. London, 1847. Post 8°. 4365
of Battel Abbey. Trans. by M. A. Lover. London, 1851. 8°. . 4321
of the Cid. Translated by R. Southey. Lowell, 1846. 8°. . . 2672
Chronicles of Canongate. 1st s. Sir W. Scott. Bost. 1848. 2 v. 12°. 999, 39, 40
The same. Edinburgh, 1849. 12°. 4100, 41
The same. Edinburgh, 1850. Roy. 8°. 4531, 10
2d series. Sir W. Scott. Bost. 1848. 2 v. 12°. 999, 41, 42

Chronicles of Canongate. 2d s. Sir W. Scott. Edin. 1849. 2 v. 12°. 4100, 42–3
The same. Edinburgh, 1850. Roy. 8°. 4531, 11
The same. New York, 1827. 2 v. 12°. 365
of Clovernook. D. Jerrold. London, 1853. 12°. . . 6234, 6
of Crime; or, Newgate Calendar. London, 1842. 2 v. 8°. . . 2769
of the Crusades. London, 1848. Post 8°. 3564
of Europe. Sir J. Froissart. Trans. by T. Johnes. N. Y. 1845. 4°. 2027
of Monstrelet. Trans. by T. Johnes. Lond. 1849. 2 v. roy. 8°. . 1219
Six Old English. Edited by J. A. Giles. London, 1848. Post 8°. 4367

Ethelwerd's Chronicle; Asser's Life of Alfred; Geoffrey of Monmouth's British History; Gildas; Nennius; Richard of Cirencester.

Chronology and History, Handbook of. G. P. Putnam. N. Y. 1852. 8°. 2041
of History, Art, Literature, &c. London, 1854. 12°. . . . 6124
Chrysostom, J. Life. F. M. Perthes. Boston, 1854. 12°. . . . 6240
Chubbuck, Emily. Alderbrook. Boston, 1848. 2 v. 12°. . . . 2941
Trippings in Author Land. New York, 1846. 12°. . . . 2506
See also *Judson, Emily.*
Church, E. New System of Teaching French. Boston, 1845. 8°. . . 1136
Church and State. S. T. Coleridge. New York, 1853. 12°. . . 5561, 6
and State, Union of. B. W. Noel. New York, 1849. 12°. . . 3275
before the Flood. J. Cumming. Boston, 1854. 12°. . . . 5822
Book of the. R. Southey. Boston, 1825. 2 v. 8°. . . . 3612
Dictionary. W. F. Hook. Philadelphia, 1854. 8°. . . . 5430
Establishments, National. R. Wardlaw. London, 1839. 8°. . 1419
History of the Apostolic. P. Schaff. New York, 1853. 8°. . 5448
History of New England, 1602–1804. J. Backus. Bost. 1804. 12°. 5560
Members, Advice to. W. Innes. Boston, 1833. 12°. . . . 1475
of England. History of. T. V. Short. Philadelphia, 1843. 8°. . 3606
of England, Reformation of. G. Burnet. London, 1841. 4 v. 8°. 3993
The same. New York, 1843. 3 v. 8°. 2057
Churchill, C. H. Mt. Lebanon; a Ten Years' Residence. Lond. 1853. 3 v. 8°. 5426
Cicero, M. T. Life. C. Middleton. Boston, 1818. 3 v. 8°. . . . 1345
Life and Letters. London, 1848. Roy. 8°. 5481
Lettres de. Paris, 1738. 6 v. 12°. 389
Offices. Trans. by T. Cockman. New York, 1854. 12°. . 1854, 10
Offices; Three Books. Tr. by C. R. Edmonds. Lond. 1850. Post 8°. 4386
Orations. Trans. by W. Duncan. New York, 1844. 2 v. 12°. 1854, 8, 9
Oratory and Orators. London, 1808. 2 v. 8°. 5011
Cicilia Howard. T. S. Arthur. New York, 1844. 12°. . . . 2138
*Cincinnati Directory, 1853. Cincinnati, 1853. 8°. 5888
Cinq-Mars; a Conspiracy under Louis XIII. A. de Vigny. N. Y. 1847. 8°. 2773
Circassia; a Tour of the Caucasus. G. L. Ditson. New York, 1850. 8°. 3522
Circumnavigation of the Globe. (H. F. L.) New York, 1846. 12°. 3683, 82
Cities of the Western Continent. C. A. Goodrich. Hartford, 1848. 8°. 3622
Ruins of Ancient. C. Bucke. (H.F.L.) N.Y. 1846. 2 v. 12°. 3681, 134–5
Citizen of Prague. Mary Howitt. New York, 1846. 8°. . . . 2661
Citizen of a Republic. A. Ceba. New York, 1845. 12°. . . . 2489
City and Country Life. Mary I. Torrey. Boston, 1853. 12°. . . 5329

City Architecture. N. Field. New York, 1853. 8°. 5438
City Merchant; or, Mysterious Failure. J. B. Jones. Phil. 1851. 12°. . 3800
City of the Magyar. Miss Pardoe. 1840. 3 v. 12°. 3122
of the Sultan. Miss Pardoe. Philadelphia, 1837. 2 v. 12°. . 941
Civil Engineering, Encyclopædia of. E. Cresy. London, 1847. 8°. . 4529
Treatise on. H. Law. London, 1852. 12°. 6044
Civil Liberty and Self Government. F. Lieber. Philadelphia, 1853. 12°. 5552
Civil War in the Vendée. Paris, 1802. 8°. 574
Civilization in Europe, History of. M. Guizot. New York, 1838. 12°. . 1035
Clap, R. Memoirs, 1630. Reprinted, Boston, 1844. 12°. 4925
Clapp, W. W., jun. Record of the Boston Stage. Boston, 1853. 12°. . 5523
Clapperton, H. Second Expedition into Africa. Philadelphia, 1829. 8°. 1335
Clarence; a Tale of our own Times. C. M. Sedgwick. N. Y. 1849. 12°. 3423
Clarendon, E. H. (Earl of). History of the Rebellion. Oxford, 1826. 8 v. 8°. 2256
Claret and Olives. A. B. Reach. New York, 1852. 12°. 830
Claridge, R. T. Cold Water, Tepid Water, & Friction Cure. N.Y. 1849. 12°. 3404
Clarissa Harlowe. S. Richardson. London, 1764. 8 v. 12°. . . . 1832
Clark, D. A. Complete Works, with Life. G. Shepard. N.Y. 1848. 2 v. 8°. 4721
*Clark, E. Brit. & Conway Tub. Bridges. Lon. 1850. 2 v. 8°. plates 1 v. fol. 1673
Clark, J. A. Glimpses of the Old World. Philadelphia, 1840. 2 v. 12°. 1319
Clark, L. G. Knick-Knacks from an Editor's Table. N. Y. 1852. 12°. 5028
Knickerbocker Sketch-Book. New York, 1845. 12°. . . . 2374
Clark, R. W. Lectures to Young Men. Boston, 1853. 12°. . . . 5543
Memoir of John Edwards Emerson. Boston, 1852. 12°. . . 4921
Clark, W. G. Literary Remains. Ed. by L. G. Clark, N.Y. 1844. 8°. 2077
Clarke, B. British Gazetteer. London, 1852. 3 v. roy. 8°. . . . 5169
Clarke, E. D. Life and Remains. W. Otter. London, 1825. 8°. . . 5485
Travels. London, 1816. 11 v. 8°. 5486

Vols. 1, 2. Russia, Tartary, and Turkey.
3-8. Greece, Egypt, and the Holy Land.
9-11. Scandinavia.

Clarke, H. English Grammar. London, 1852. 12°. 6115
Clarke, F. L., & W. Dunlap. Life of Duke of Wellington. N.Y. 1814. 8°. 615
Clarke, J. F. Eleven Weeks in Europe. Boston, 1852. 12°. . . . 4773
Clarke, Mary C. *Concordance to Shakspeare. Boston, 1854. Roy. 8°. 5973
Girlhood of Shakspeare's Heroines. New York, 1852. 2 v. 12°. . 4450
Iron Cousin; or, Mutual Influence. New York, 1853. 12°. . 6141
Clarke, Sara J. Greenwood Leaves. Boston, 1850-52. 2 v. 12°. . . 3456
Haps and Mishaps in Europe. Boston, 1854. 2 v. 12°. . . 5624
History of my Pets. Boston, 1851. 12°. 4091
Poems. Boston, 1851. 12°. 4067
See also *Lippincott, Mrs. Sara J.*
Clarkson, T. History of Abolition of the Slave Trade. N.Y. 1836. 3 v. 12°. 1548
Public and Private Life of Wm. Penn. Dover, 1827. 8°. . . 1410
Classic and Historic Portraits. J. Bruce. New York, 1854. 12°. . . 5776
*Classical Dictionary. C. Anthon. New York, 1850. 8°. 2840
The same. New York, 1847. Roy. 8°. 1243
W. Smith. Edited by C. Anthon. New York, 1851. Roy. 8°. . 4347

Classical Gazetteer. W. Hazlitt. London, 1851. 12°. 4222
Classical Library, Harper's. (Translations.) N. Y. 1833–44. 36 v. 12°. 1854

Vols. 1, 2. Xenophon.
3, 4. Demosthenes.
5. Sallust.
6, 7. Cæsar.
8–10. Cicero.
11, 12. Virgil.
13. Æschylus.
15–17. Euripides.
14. Sophocles.
Vols. 18, 19. Horace and Phædrus.
20, 21. Ovid.
22, 23. Thucydides.
24–28. Livy.
29–31. Herodotus.
32–34. Homer.
35. Juvenal and Persius.
36. Pindar and Anacreon.

Classical Literature, History of. R. W. Browne. Phil. 1852. 8°. . . 4562
Clausing, L., Life of. S. F. B. Morse. New York, 1836. 16°. . . 42
Clay, C. M. Writings. New York, 1848. 8°. 3209
Clay, H. Biography. G. D. Prentice. Hartford, 1831. 12°. . . 393
Life and Speeches. Ed. by D. Mallory. New York, 1844. 2 v. 8°. 1789
Life and Times of. C. Cotton. New York, 1846. 2 v. 8°. . . 2675
Clay Lands and Loamy Soils. Prof. Donaldson. London, 1852. 12°. . 6079
Cleaveland P. Mineralogy and Geology. Boston, 1816. 8°. . . . 1380
Clement, J. (Editor.) Noble Deeds of Am. Women. Buffalo, 1851. 12°. 4217
Cleopatra, History of. J. Abbott. New York, 1851. 12°. . . . 4212
Clerk's Guide; or, Commercial Correspon. B. F. Foster. Bos. 1837. 12°. 1544
Cleveland, H. R. Life of Henry Hudson. Boston, 1844. 12°. . 1076, 10
Cleveland, R. J. Voyages and Commer. Enterprises. Camb. 1842. 2 v. 12°. 897
Clifford Family; a Tale of the Old Dominion. New York, 1852. 12°. . 4896
Climate in America. H. Williamson. New York, 1811. 8°. . . . 662
Clinch, J. H. Captivity in Babylon, and other Poems. Bost. 1840. 12°. 167
Clinton; a Book for Boys. W. Simonds. Boston, 1854. 12°. . . 5620
Clinton, De Witt. Discourse at New York, May 4, 1814. N. Y. 1815. 8°. 1824
Life. J. Renwick. New York, 1840. 12°. 1470
The same. (H. F. L.) New York, 1846. 12°. . . 3683, 125
Life and Writings. W. W. Campbell. New York, 1849. 8°. . 3355
Tribute to the Memory of. Albany, 1828. 12°. 210
Clinton Bradshaw. F. W. Thomas. Philadelphia, 1835. 2 v. 12°. . 1101
Clio; or, Discourse on Taste. Dublin, 1778. 12°. 145
Clock and Watch Making. E. B. Denison. London, 1850. 12°. . . 6080
T. Reid. Philadelphia, 1832. Roy. 8°. 1646
Clockmaker. T. C. Haliburton. Philadelphia, 1837. 12°. . . . 924
The same. Philadelphia, 1846. 12°. 3348
Cloister Life of Charles V. W. Stirling. Boston, 1853. 12°. . . 5359
Closing Scene; or, Christianity and Infidelity. E. Neale. Phil. 1850. 12°. 4169
Cloudesley. W. Godwin. New York, 1830. 2 v. 12°. 1927
Clouds and Sunshine. New York, 1853. 12°. 5326
Clovernook. Alice Carey. New York, 1852. 12°. 4757
Clovernook Children. Alice Carey. Boston, 1855. 12°. 6233
Club-Book; Tales by various Authors. New York, 1831. 2 v. 12°. . 3162
Coal, and Coal Pits, and the People in them. London, 1854. 12°. . . 5847
Statistics of. R. C. Taylor. Philadelphia, 1848. 8°. 3240
Coale, W. E. Hints on Health. Boston, 1852. 12°. 4764
Coast Survey Reports, 1851–52. Washington, 1852–53. 8°. . . . 2716
Cobb, J. B. Mississippi Scenes. Philadelphia, 1851. 12°. . . . 3782

Cobbett, W. Advice to Young Men. New York, 1844. 12°. . . . 26
Political Works. Ed. by J. M. & J. P. Cobbett. Lond. 1835. 6 v. 8°. 5136
Reformation in England and Ireland. Philadelphia, n. d. 12°. . 1777
Cobbold, H. Freston Tower. London, 1850. 3 v. 12°. 4275
Cobden, J. C. White Slaves of England. Auburn, 1853. 8°. . . . 5385
Cobden, R. Russia and the Eastern Question. Boston, 1854. 12°. . 5794
Cochin-China, Siam, & Muscat, Embassy to. E. Roberts. N. Y. 1837. 8°. 945
Cockburn, Lord. Life of F. Jeffrey. Philadelphia, 1852. 2 v. 8°. . 996
Cockburn, Sir G. Napoleon's Voyage to St. Helena. Boston, 1833. 12°. 1057
Cockton, H. George St. George Julian. Philadelphia, 1842. 8°. . . 2771
Lady Felicia. New York, 1852. 8°. 650
Love Match. New York, 1845. 8°. 2620
Sisters; or, the Fatal Marriages. New York, 1851. 8°. . . 4151
Stanley Thorn. New York, 1852. 8°. 1638
Steward; a Romance of Real Life. New York, 1852. 8°. . . 4549
Sylvester Sound, the Somnambulist. New York, 1849. 8°. . . 2216
Valentine Vox, the Ventriloquist. Philadelphia, 1848. 8°. . . 1650
Codman, J. Memoir. W. Allen. Boston, 1853. 8°. 5449
Cœlebs in Search of a Wife. Hannah More. London, 1852. 12°. . 374
Coffin, J. Hist. of Newbury, Newburyport, & W. Newbury. Bost. 1845. 8°. 2662
Coggeshall, G. Voyages from 1777 to 1844. New York, 1851. 8°. . 4303
Coincidences in Old and New Testaments. J. J. Blunt. N. Y. 1851. 8°. 4704
Coins, Money, & Exchange. Treatise on. J. Hewitt. Lond. 1755. 8°. 1223
New Gold & Silver. J. R. Eckfeldt & W. E. Dubois. N. Y. 1851. 8°. 4144
Coke, Sir E. Life. London, 1833. 8°. 602
Coke, E. T. Subaltern's Furlough. New York, 1833. 2 v. 12°. . . 1195
Cold Water, Tepid Water, & Friction Cure. R. T. Claridge. N.Y. 1849. 12°. 3404
Cole, T. Course of Empire, &c. L. L. Noble. New York, 1853. 12°. . 5334
Coleridge, S. T. Aids to Reflection. Burlington, 1840. 8°. . . . 1992
and R. Southey, Reminiscences of. J. Cottle. N.Y. 1847. 12°. 3016
Biographia Literaria. New York, 1852. 12°. 1032
Complete Works. New York, 1853. 7 v. 12°. 5561

Vol. 1. Aids to Reflection; Statesman's Manual.	Vol. 4. Shakspeare and the Dramatists.
2. The Friend; Miscellaneous.	5. Literary Remains.
3. Biographia Literaria.	6. Church and State.
	7. Poetical and Dramatic.

The Friend; a Series of Essays. Burlington, 1831. 8°. . . 1948
Poetical Works. Philadelphia, 1844. 8°. 581
Table-Talk. New York, 1835. 2 v. 12°. 1249
Works, in Prose and Verse. Philadelphia, 1849. 8°. . . . 2339
Coles, L. B. Beauties and Deformities of Tobacco-Using. Bost. 1851. 12°. 4477
Philosophy of Health. Boston, 1854. 12°. 5881
Colin Clink. C. Hooton. Philadelphia, 1840. 2 v. 12°. . . . 1551
*Collection de Mammifers. Paris, 1808. 4°. 5980
Collections of the Mass. Historical Society. Boston, 1806. 10 v. 8°. . 2631
The same. Second series. Boston, 1838. 10 v. 8°. . . 2631
The same. Third series. Boston, 1846. 10 v. 8°. . . 2631
College Words and Customs, Collection of. Cambridge, 1851. 12°. . 4410
Collier, J. P. Notes and Emendations on Shakspeare. N.Y. 1853. 12°. 5286

Collier, J. P. (Collector.) Shakspeare's Library. London, 1843. 2 v. 8°. 4656
(Editor.) Works of Shakspeare. New York, 1853. Roy. 8°. . 5432
Collins, A. Maria. Mrs. Ben Darby. Cincinnati, 1854. 12°. . . 5604
Collins, L. Historical Sketches of Kentucky. Maysville, 1847. 8°. . 3246
Collins, S. Miscellanies. Philadelphia, 1842. 12°. 1698
Collins, W. Poetical Works. New York, 1844. 12°. 12
Collins, W. W. Antonina; or, the Fall of Rome. New York, 1850. 8°. 3988
Basil; a Story of Modern Life. New York, 1853. 12°. . . 5058
*Collot, A. G. French and English Dictionary. Philadelphia, 1852. 8°. 1668
Colman Family, Memoirs of. R. B. Peake. London, 1841. 2 v. 8°. . 2605
Colman, H. European Agriculture & Rural Economy. Bos. 1849. 2 v. 8°. 3268
European Life and Manners. Boston, 1849. 2 v. 12°. . . . 3272
Third Mass. Report on Wheat and Silk. Boston, 1840. 8°. . 1607
Historical Geography of the Bible. Philadelphia, 1849. 12°. . 3428
Colonial Magazine. Ed. by P. L. Simonds. Vols. 1–5. Lond. 1845–46. 8°. 3218
Colonial Policy of Great Britain. Philadelphia, 1816. 12°. . . . 477
Colonies, History of the American. J. Marshall. Philadelphia, 1824. 8°. 1987
of the British Empire, Hist. of. R. M. Martin. Lon. 1843. Roy. 8°. 2843
Colonization and Anti-Slavery Societies. W. Jay. New York, 1838. 12°. 1526
Colors, Philosophy of Permanent. E. Bancroft. Phil. 1814. 2 v. 8°. . 654
Colquhoun, Lady Janet. Memoir. J. Hamilton. New York, 1850. 12°. 3491
Colquhoun, P. Police of London. London, 1800. 8°. . . . 729
Colt, J. C. Bookkeeping, Double Entry. Cincinnati, 1838. Roy. 8°. . 1995
Colton, C. Public Economy in the United States. New York, 1848. 8°. 3211
Four Years in Great Britain. New York, 1835. 2 v. 12°. . . 1258
Life and Times of Henry Clay. New York, 1846. 2 v. 8°. . 2675
Colton, C. C. Lacon; or, Many Things in Few Words. N.Y. 1836. 16°. 1856
Colton, W. Deck and Port. New York, 1850. 12°. 3659
Land and Lee in the Bosphorus and Ægean. N. Y. 1851. 12°. 4219
Memoir. H. T. Cheever. New York, 1851. 12°. 4439
Sea and the Sailor; Notes on France and Italy, &c. N.Y. 1851. 12°. 4439
Ship and Shore. New York, 1851. 12°. 1084
Three Years in California. New York, 1850. 12°. . . . 3903
Columbia River, Adventures on. R. Cox. New York, 1832. 8°. . 3215
Columbus, C., Life and Voyages. New York, 1828. 3 v. 8°. . . . 1347
The same (abridged). New York, 1829. 12°. . . . 2141
and Companions, Life and Voyages. W. Irving. N.Y. 1848. 3 v. 12°. 3360
The same. New York, 1849. 3 v. 12°. 800
First Voyage to America. Boston, 1827. 8°. 1332
Colville Family. F. Smedley. New York, 1853. 12°. 5517
Colwell, S. New Themes for Protestant Clergy. Philadelphia, 1852. 12°. 5025
Combe, A. Guide to Health. Buffalo, 1848. 12°. 3393
Life and Correspondence. G. Combe. Philadelphia, 1850. 12°. . 3862
Physiology applied to Health, &c. (H. F. L.) N.Y. 1846. 12°. 3683, 71
The same. New York, 1851. 12°. 2211
Combe, G. Constitution of Man. Boston, 1839. 12°. 555
Lectures on Phrenology. London, 1839. 12°. 434
Life and Correspondence of Andrew Combe. Phil. 1850. 12°. . 3862

Combe, G. Moral Philosophy. New York, 1843. 12°. 1460
The same. New York, 1848. 12°. 3771
Notes on the United States, 1838–40. Phil. 1841. 2 v. 12°. . 1603
System of Phrenology. New York, 1843. 12°. 1758
and R. Cox. Moral and Intellectual Science. New York, 1848. 8°. 3264
Combustion. R. A. Coffin. Boston, 1836. 12°. 898
Comedies, Italian. Trans. from Goldoni & others. New York, 1849. 12°. 3378
Comer, G. N. Bookkeeping by Double Entry. Boston, 1850. 8°. . 2731
Comets. J. Winthrop and A. Oliver, jun. Boston, 1811. 12°. . . 875
Comic Writers, Lectures on the English. W. Hazlitt. Lond. 1841. 12°. 1874
Coming of the Mammoth, and other Poems. H. B. Hirst. Bost. 1845. 12°. 2470
Commander of Malta. E. Sue. New York, 1849. 8°. 3299
Commentaries on American Law. J. Kent. New York, 1844. 4 v. 8°. . 2056
Commerce. J. R. M'Culloch. London, 1843. 8°. 2541
*Annuaire du. Paris, 1851. 4°. 21
by Sea and Land, Book of. Philadelphia, 1836. 12°. . . . 2113
Code of, translated from the French. Edinburgh, 1826. 12°. . 2545
*Cyclopædia of. W. Waterston. London, 1846. 8°. . . . 3996
The same. London, 1846. 8°. 3544
Dictionnaire de. Copenhagen, 1759. 4 v. folio. 2019
Dictionnaire Universel de. Paris, 1805. 2 v. 4°. . . . 2029
European. C. W. Rördansz. Boston, 1819. 8°. . . . 639
European. J. J. Oddy. Philadelphia, 1807. 2 v. 8°. . . . 720
de la France, Tableau Général. Paris, 1844. 2 v. 4°. . . 2035
History of British. G. L. Craik. London, 1844. 3 v. 18°. . 2413
of Greece. F. Beaujour. London, 1800. 8°. 715
of the Mediterranean. J. Jackson. New York, 1806. 12°. . 1222
of the Prairies. J. Gregg. New York, 1844. 2 v. 12°. . . 2098
Origin and History of. A. Anderson. London, 1764. 2 v. folio. 2025
Politics, and Finance, Lectures on. T. Mortimer. Lond. 1801. 8°. 575
Commercial Dictionary. J. R. M'Culloch. Phil. 1845. 2 v. roy. 8°. . 1691
J. Montefiore. Philadelphia, 1804. 3 v. 8°. . . . 1367
Commercial Law, Leading Cases in. J. P. Holcombe. N.Y. 1847. 8°. . 4304
Principles and Administration of. L. Levi. Lond. 1851. 2 v. 4°. 4837
Commercial Regulations of Foreign Nations. Washington, 1824. 8°. . 789
Commercial Review of the South and West. Vols. 4, 5. N.O. 1847–48. 8°. 2911
Commercial Statistics of all Nations. J. Macgregor. Lond. 1850. 5 v. roy. 8°. 5469
For Contents, See *Macgregor, J.*
*Commercial Tables. J. Hartshorn. Boston, 1852. Folio. . . . 5394
Commissioner; or, De Lunatico Inquirando. G. P. R. James. N.Y. 1851. 8°. 4116
Common Place Book. R. Southey. New York, 1849. 8°. . . . 3389
Companion of the Tour of France. Mde. Dudevant. N.Y. 1847. 12°. 3036
Companions of my Solitude. A. Helps. Boston, 1852. 12°. . . . 6204
Comparative Physiognomy. J. W. Redfield. New York, 1852. 8°. . 4947
Comstock, J. L. Elements of Chemistry. New York, 1841. 12°. . 1740
History of Precious Metals. Hartford, 1849. 12°. . . . 3007
Comte, A. Philosophy of Mathematics. New York, 1851. 8°. . . 4134
Philosophy of the Sciences. Ed. by G. H. Lewes. Lond. 1853. 8°. 5936

Comte, M. le. Mémoire sur les Etats-Généraux. Paris, 1789. 12°. . 1418
Con Cregan, Confessions of. C. Lever. New York, 1851. 8°. . . 4532
Conchologist's First Book. E. A. Poe. Philadelphia, 1839. 12°. . 840
Concord, Mass., History of. L. Shattuck. Boston, 1835. 8°. . . 2811
Concord & Merrimack Rivers, a Week on. H. D. Thoreau. Bost. 1849. 12°. 3374
*Concordance to Shakspeare. Mary C. Clarke. Boston, 1854. Roy. 8°. 5973
Condé, J. A. Arabs in Spain. Tr. by Mrs. J. Foster. Lond. 1854–55. 3 v. 8°. 5939
Condé, L. (Prince of). Life. Lord Mahon. New York, 1845. 2 v. 12°. 2513
Confessions of an Attorney. S. Warren. New York, 1852. 12°. . . 4772
of Con Cregan. C. Lever. New York, 1851. 8°. . . . 4532
of Cuthburt, and other Poems. S. Melmoth. Boston, 1827. 16°. 834
of an Elderly Lady and Gent. Lady Blessington. Phil. 1838. 2v. 12°. 456
of Fitz-Boodle, &c. W. M. Thackeray. New York, 1852. 12°. 5060
of a Housekeeper. T. S. Arthur. Philadelphia, 1851. 12°. . 4460
of an Opium-Eater. T. de Quincey. Boston, 1850. 12°. . . 3911
Confidential Disclosures. A. Lamartine. New York, 1849. 12°. . . 3349
Confessor; an Historical Novel. New York, 1851. 8°. 4509
Conflict of Ages. E. Beecher. Boston, 1853. 12°. 5528
Congar, O., Autobiography & Memorials of. H. T. Cheever. N.Y. 1851. 12°. 4156
Congregational Year Book, 1854. New York, 1854. 8°. . . . 5491
Congregationalism, History of. G. Punchard. Salem, 1841. 12°. . 2118
Congress, Acts of the First Session of, 1791. Philadelphia, n. d. 8°. . 760
Debates and Proceedings in, 1789–1837. Wash. 1834–37. 29 v. 8°. 4903
History of. H. G. Wheeler. New York, 1848. 2 v. 8°. . . 3200
Journals of, from Jan. 1, 1776, to Jan. 1, 1777. Yorktown, 1778. 8°. 618
Reminiscences of. C. W. March. New York, 1850. 12°. . . 3919
Congressional Globe [incomplete]. Wash. 1844–53. 12 v. 4°. . . 3225
Congreve, W. Dramatic Works. Ed. by L. Hunt. Lond. 1851. Roy. 8°. 4527
Coningsby. B. Disraeli. New York, 1845. 8°. 2282
Conjugial Love. E. Swedenborg. Boston, 1833. 8°. 798
Conkling, Margaret C. Mother and Wife of Washington. Aub. 1850. 12°. 3849
Connecticut, Educational Documents of. Hartford, 1853. 8°. . . 5971
Historical Collections of. J. W. Barber. N. Haven, 1836. 8°. . 652
History of. Theo. Dwight, jun. (H. F. L.) N.Y. 1846. 12°. 3683, 133
Conquest and Self-Conquest. Maria J. McIntosh. N.Y. 1846. 18°. . 2420
Conquest of Grenada. W. Irving. Philadelphia, 1829. 2 v. 12°. . 1182
The same. W. Irving. New York, 1850. 12°. . . 3369
of Mexico, History of. W. H. Prescott. N.Y. 1850. 3 v. 8°. . 1759
of Peru, History of. W. H. Prescott. New York, 1847. 2 v. 8°. 2793
Consolations of Travel. Sir H. Davy. London, 1831. 12°. . . . 2546
Consolation, Sermons of. F. W. P. Greenwood. Boston, 1842. 12°. . 1707
Conspiracy of Pontiac, History of. F. Parkman, jun. Boston, 1851. 8°. 4519
of the Spaniards against Venice, 1618. Boston, 1838. 18°. . . 1484
Conspirator, The. A. E. Dupuy. New York, 1850. 12°. . . . 4047
Constant, A. Last Incarnation. Trans. by F. G. Shaw. Bost. 1848. 12°. 3131
Constant, B. Philosophical Miscellaneous. Boston, 1838. 12°. . . 962, 2
Constantia de Valmont. H. Lee. Philadelphia, 1799. 12°. . . . 152
Constantinople in 1836. Miss Pardoe. Philadelphia, 1837. 2 v. 12°. . 941

Constantinople in 1836. Miss Pardoe. (Select Cir. Lib.) Phil. 1837. 4°. 2034, 1837
Month at. A. Smith. Boston, 1852. 12°. 391
Residence at, in 1827. J. Brewer. New Haven, 1830. 12°. . 341
Constitution of Man. G. Combe. Boston, 1839. 12°. 555
Constitution of the United States. Edited by W. Hickey. Phil. 1847. 12°. 3075
The same. Philadelphia, 1848. 12°. 4098
and the several States. Charlestown, 1812. 12°. 316
*The same. New York, 1852. 8°. 5902
Commentaries on. J. Story. Boston, 1833. 3 v. 8°. . . . 1796
The same. Boston, 1851. 2 v. roy. 8°. 4312
Writings on. J. Marshall. Boston, 1839. 8°. 2054
Constitutions, Generative Prin. of Political. J. de Maistre. Bost. 1847. 12°. 3024
Constitutional Convention, 1787, Secret Debates in. Rich. 1839. 12°. . 587
of Massachusetts. — See *Massachusetts.*
Constitutional Jurisprudence of U. S. W. A. Duer. N.Y. 1848. 12°. 3683, 160
Constitutional Text Book. L. Blake. New York, 1854. 12°. . . 5780
Consulate and Empire, History of. A. Thiers. New York, 1852. 2 v. 8°. 2754
Consuelo. Mde. Dudevant. Trans. by F. G. Shaw. Bost. 1850. 3 v. 12°. 2603
Sequel to (Countess of Rudolstadt.) Boston, 1847. 2 v. 12°. . 2956
Consumption, and Diseases of the Chest. J. A. Swett. N. Y. 1852. 8°. 4804
Forestalled and Prevented. W. M. Cornell. Bost. 1846. 12°. . 2418
Contarini Fleming. B. Disraeli. New York, 1832. 2 v. 12°. . . 409
The same. Philadelphia, 1845. 8°. 2689
Contemporary Portraits. London, 1825. 12°. 2288
Contentment better than Wealth. Alice B. Neal. New York, 1853. 12°. 5009
Continental Adventures; a Novel. Boston, 1826. 3 v. 12°. . . . 1152
Contracts, Law of. D. Gibbons. London, 1850. 12°. 6070
not under Seal, Law of. W. W. Story. Boston, 1844. 8°. . . 2219
Contributions of Q. Q. Jane Taylor. Boston, 1831. 2 v. 12°. . . 862
The same. New York, 1850. 2 v. 12°. 3664
Convention at Philadelphia, 1787, Secret Debates in. Rich. 1839. 12°. . 587
Convent; a Narrative. R. McCrindell. New York, 1850. 16°. . . 4401
Conversations in Rome. W. E. Channing. Boston, 1847. 12°. . . 2437
on the Old Poets. J. R. Lowell. Cambridge, 1845. 12°. . . 2306
with an Ambitious Student. E. L. Bulwer. N. York, 1832. 12°. 1046
Convict; or, Hypocrite Unmasked. G. P. R. James. N. York, 1847. 8°. 2869
Convict Ship. C. A. Browning. Philadelphia, 1850. 12°. . . . 3576
Conybeare, W. J., & Howson. Life & Epistles of Paul. N. Y. 1854. 2 v. 8°. 5992
Cook, J. Voyage, 1776–80. London, 1783. 2 v. 8°. 1348
Voyages Round the World. Philadelphia, n. d. 2 v. 24°. . . 3
The same. London, 1853. 2 v. roy. 8°. 5457
Cook, Eliza. Melaia, and other Poems. New York, 1844. 12°. . . 2348
*Cooke, W. B. Rome, and the Surrounding Scenery. Lond. 1840. 4°. 5455
Cooley, A. J. Cyclopædia of 6000 Receipts. New York, 1846. 8°. . 3537
Cooley, J. E. American in Egypt, &c., 1839–40. New York, 1842. 8°. 1692
Cooper, ——. Hist. of Greece, Rome, N. & S. America. Plym. 1818. 12°. 317
Cooper, J. F. Afloat & Ashore; or, Miles Wallingford. Phil. 1844. 4 v. 12°. 1898
American Democrat. Cooperstown, 1838. 12°. 1009

Cooper, J. F. Bravo. Philadelphia, 1848. 2 v. 12°. 332
Chainbearer; or, Littlepage MSS. New York, 1845. 2 v. 12°. . 2509
Crater; or, Vulcan's Peak. New York, 1847. 2 v. 12°. . . 3050
Deerslayer; or, First War-Path. New York, 1852. 12°. . . 1632
(Editor.) Elinor Wyllys. Phil. 1846. 2 v. 12°. 2534
Gleanings in Europe: England. Philadelphia, 1837. 2 v. 12°. . 905
Gleanings in Europe: France. Philadelphia, 1837. 12°. . . 273
Headsman. Philadelphia, 1848. 2 v. 12°. 1188
Heidenmauer. Philadelphia, 1841. 2 v. 12°. 1162
The same. London, 1853. 12°. 5710
Home as Found. Philadelphia, 1838. 2 v. 12°. 1143
Homeward Bound. New York, 1845. 2 v. 12°. 851
Jack Tier; or, the Florida Reef. New York, 1852. 2 v. 12°. . 3104
Last of the Mohicans. New York, 1850. 12°. 1038
Leather Stocking Tales. — The order of the series is as follows:

1. Deerslayer. — 2. Pathfinder. — 3. Last of the Mohicans.
4. Pioneers. — 5. Prairie.

Lionel Lincoln; or, the Leaguer of Boston. Phil. 1841. 2 v. 12°. 2314
Lives of American Naval Officers. Auburn, 1846. 2 v. 12°. . 2560

Vol. 1. Bainbridge; Somers; Shaw; Shubrick; Preble.
2. Jones; Woolsey; Perry; Dale.

Memorial of. New York, 1852. 12°. 1197
Mercedes of Castile. New York, 1845. 2 v. 12°. 2961
Monikins. Philadelphia, 1835. 2 v. 12°. 2307
Naval History of the United States. Philadelphia, 1839. 2 v. 8°. 1298
The same, abridged. Philadelphia, 1845. 12°. 1280
The same, continued to 1853. New York, 1853. 8° . 1298, 3
Ned Myers; or, a Life before the Mast. Philadelphia, 1843. 12°. 1751
Notions of the Americans. Philadelphia, 1832. 2 v. 12°. . . 3778
Oak Openings; or, the Bee Hunter. New York, 1848. 12°. . 3164
Pathfinder. New York, 1852. 12°. 1581
Pilot. New York, 1851. 12°. 348
Pioneers. Philadelphia, 1843. 2 v. 12°. 440
Prairie. New York, 1852. 12°. 1004
Precaution. New York, 1852. 2 v. 12°. 2960
Red Rover. New York, 1845. 2 v. 12°. 412
Redskins; the Conclusion of the Littlepage MSS. N.Y. 1846. 2 v. 12°. 2604
Satanstoe; or, the Littlepage MSS. New York, 1845. 2 v. 12°. . 2472
Sea Lions; or, the Lost Sealers. New York, 1849. 12°. . . 3350
Sketches of Switzerland. Philadelphia, 1836. 4 v. 12°. . . 229
Spy. New York, 1852. 12°. 421
Two Admirals. New York, 1851. 12°. 1683
Water Witch. Philadelphia, 1838. 2 v. 12°. 1168
Ways of the Hour. New York, 1850. 12°. 3674
Wept of Wish-Ton-Wish. Philadelphia, 1833. 2 v. 12°. . . 850
Wing-and-Wing. Philadelphia, 1842. 2 v. 12°. . . . 1703
Wyandotte; or, the Hutted Knoll. New York, 1843. 2 v. 12°. . 1734
Cooper, Susan F. Rural Hours. New York, 1850. 12°. . . . 3896

Coote, C. History of Modern Europe. Philadelphia, 1822. 2 v. 8°. 1998, 5, 6
The same. Philadelphia, 1811. 8°. 1377
Copway, G. Hist. and Sketches of the Ojibway Nation. Bost. 1851. 12°. 4176
Life, Letters, and Speeches. New York, 1850. 12°. . . . 3902
Running Sketches in England, France, &c. New York, 1851. 12°. 4435
Coquerel, A. Protestantism in France. Boston, 1854. 12°. 6145
Corcoran, H., Conversion & Abduction of. T. F. Caldicott. Bost. 1853. 16°. 5370
Corinthians, First Epistle to, Notes on. A. Barnes. N. Y. 1851. 12°. . 4733
Second Epistle to, Notes on. A. Barnes. New York, 1851. 12°. 4734
Corinne; or, Italy. Mde. de Staël. New York, 1847. 12°. . . . 895
The same. London, 1853. 12°. 5700
The same. (In French.) New York, 1851. 12°. . . 2099
Corkran, J. F. Hist. of National Constituent Assem., 1848. N.Y. 1849. 12°. 2935
Cormenin, L. de. Orators of France. New York, 1847. 12°. . . 3008
Corneille, P., and his Times. M. Guizot. New York, 1852. 12°. . 5195
Corneille, T. Poëmes Dramatiqes. Paris, 1738. 5 v. 12°. . . . 398
Cornell, W. M. Consumption Forestalled and Prevented. Bost. 1846. 12°. 2418
Corrected Proofs. H. H. Weld. Boston, 1836. 12°. 2151
Corner, Julia. English Envoy at Court of Nicholas I. N. Y. 1854. 12°. 6178
Corner Stone. J. Abbott. New York, 1852. 12°. 6205
Cornwall, Barry. — See *Proctor, B. W.*
Corse de Leon; or, the Brigand. G. P. R. James. N.Y. 1841. 2 v. 12°. 1600
Correspon. of the Am. Revolution. Ed. by J. Sparks. Bost. 1853. 4 v. 8°. 5389
Corson, J. W. Loiterings in Europe. New York, 1848. 12°. . . 3142
Cortez, H. Life. New York, 1850. 16°. 3316
Cosmos. A. von Humboldt. New York, 1849–52. 4 v. 12°. . . 3565
Cossacks, Characteristic Portraits and Costumes of. Lond. 1820. 4°. . 2761
Costellow, Louisa S. Catherine de Medicis. London, 1853. 12°. . 5739
Falls, Lakes, and Mountains of North Wales. London, 1845. 12°. 2388
Memoirs of Eminent Englishwomen. London, 1844. 4 v. 8°. . 4342
Cottage Builder, American. J. Bullock. New York, 1854. 12°. . . 6168
Cottage Building. C. B. Allen. London, 1854. 12°. 6064
Cottage Residences. A. J. Downing. New York, 1847. 8°. . . 2804
Cottages & Villas, 200 Designs for. T. U. Walter & J. J. Smith. Phil. 1847. 4°. 2980
Cottin, Mde. Saracen. New York, 1810. 2 v. 12°. 855
Cottle, J. Reminiscences of S. T. Coleridge & R. Southey. N.Y. 1847. 12°. 3016
Cotton and Commerce of India. J. Chapman. London, 1850. 8°. . 4328
in India, Culture and Commerce in. J. F. Royle. Lond. 1851. 8°. 4327
History of the Manufacture. G. S. White. Philadelphia, 1836. 8°. 1237
Cotton Spinner, American. R. H. Baird. Philadelphia, 1851. 12°. . 4263
Practical. R. Scott and O. Byrne. Philadelphia, 1851. 8°. . 4539
Count Julian; or, Last Days of the Goth. W. G. Simms. Balt. 8°. . 2738
Count Monte Leone. H. de S. Georges. New York, 1852. 8°. . . 413
Count of Monte Christo. A. Dumas. New York, 1850. 2 v. 8°. . . 2735
Count Robert of Paris. Sir W. Scott. Boston, 1848. 2 v. 12°. . 999, 45, 46
The same. Edinburgh, 1849. 12°. 4100, 46
The same. Edinburgh, 1850. Roy. 8°. . . . 4531, 12
Countess, and other Tales. Philadelphia, 1836. 2 v. 12°. . . . 1128

Countess Ida; a Tale of Berlin. T. S. Fay. New York, 1840. 2 v. 12°. 1584
Countess of Rodolstadt (Seq. to Consuelo). Mde. Dudevant. Bost. '47. 2 v. 12°. 2956
Countess of Salisbury. A. Dumas. New York, 1851. 8°. . . . 4334
Counting-House Assistant. J. C. Gilleland. Pittsburgh, 1818. 12°. . 358
Counting-House Companion. London, 1763. 8°. 696
Countries I have Seen. Sara J. Lippincott. Boston, 1852. 12°. . . 6232
of Europe Described. Philadelphia, 1849. 12°. 3313
Country Curate. G. R. Gleig. London, 1853. 12°. 5703
Country Hospitalities. Cath. Sinclair. Philadelphia, 1851. 12°. . . 4016
Country Merchant, Life and Adventures of. J. B. Jones. Phil. 1854. 12°. 5844
Country Stories. M. R. Mitford. Philadelphia, 1846. 8°. . . . 1637
Country Year Book. W. Howitt. New York, 1850. 12°. . . . 4054
Course of English Reading. J. Kent. New York, 1853. 12°. . . 5203
J. Pycroft. New York, 1845. 12°. 2297
Course of Time; a Poem. R. Pollok. Boston, 1842. 16°. . . . 1021
Cousin, V. Hist. of Modern Philos. Tr. by O. W. Wight. N.Y. 1852. 2v. 8°. 998
History of Philosophy. Tr. by H. G. Linberg. Boston, 1832. 8°. 1435
Philosophical Miscellanies. Boston, 1838. 2 v. 12°. . . 962, 1, 2
The True, the Beautiful, and the Good. New York, 1854. 12°. . 6153
Cousin Franck's Household. Mrs. C. H. Pearson. Boston, 1853. 12°. 5197
Court and Cabinet of St. Cloud, Secret History of. Philadelphia, 1806. 8°. 349
of England under the Stuarts. J. H. Jesse. Phil. 1840. 2 v. 12°. 2148
The same, continued, under Cromwell. Phil. 1840. 2 v. 12°. 2149
of London, Residence at. R. Rush. Philadelphia, 1845. 8°. . 2646
of Queen Elizabeth. Lucy Aikin. Philadelphia, 1823. 8°. . 671
Courtesy, Principles of. G. W. Hervey. New York, 1852. 12°. . . 4781
Courtenay, T. P. Historical Plays of Shakspeare. Lond. 1840. 2 v. 12°. 1112
Courtier of the Days of Charles II. G. P. R. James. N.Y. 1839. 2 v. 12°. 1072
Covenanters, Traditions of. R. Simpson. Edinburgh, 1850. 12°. . . 4265
Covetousness, Essay on. T. Dick. New York, 1836. 12°. . . . 261
The same. Philadelphia, 1845. 12°. 2357, 6
Cowell, J. Thirty Years among the Players. New York, 1845. 8°. . 1821
Cowper, W. Life. R. Southey. Boston, 1839. 2 v. 12°. . . . 1204
Life. T. Taylor. Philadelphia, 1834. 12°. 423
Life and Letters. London, 1835. 8°. 2169
Poems. Boston, 1826. 3 v. 18°. 39
The Task. Baltimore, 1804. 12°. 144
Works. Edited by T. S. Grimshawe. New York, 1849. Roy. 8°. 4348
Cox, F. A. Life of Philip Melancthon. Boston, 1835. 12°. . . . 1065
Cox, H. Integral Calculus. London, 1853. 12°. 6109
Cox, R. Adventures on the Columbia River. New York, 1832. 8°. . 3215
Cox, S. H. Interviews; Memorable and Useful. New York, 1853. 12°. 5262
Cox, S. S. Buckeye abroad in Europe. New York, 1852. 12°. . . 3754
Coxe, W. History of the House of Austria. London, 1847. 3 v. post 8°. 3553
Memoirs of Duke of Marlborough. London, 1847. 3 v. post 8°. . 3557
Crabb, G. Dictionary of General Knowledge. New York, 1835. 12°. . 3513
English Synonymes. Boston, 1819. 8°. 1292
Crabbe, G. Tales of the Hall. (Poems.) London, 1819. 2 v. 8°. . . 683

Cradle of the Twin Giants, Science & Hist. H. Christmas. Lond. 1849. 2 v. 4579
Craik, G. L. History of British Commerce. London, 1844. 3 v. 18°. . 2413
Pursuit of Knowledge. (H. F. L.) N. Y. 1846. 2 v. 12°. 3683, 94, 95
Cranch, C. P. Poems. Philadelphia, 1844. 12°. 2371
Cranes & Machinery, Construction of. J. Glynn. London, 1849. 12°. . 6060
Cranford; a Tale. Mrs. Gaskell. New York, 1853. 12°. 5374
Cranmer, T. Life. London, 1831. 12°. 1831, 1
Life and Times of. Mrs. H. F. Lee. Boston, 1841. 12°. . . 1653
Crater; or, Vulcan's Peak. J. F. Cooper. New York, 1847. 2 v. 12°. . 3050
Cravat, Art of Tying the. H. le Blanc. New York, 1829. 16°. . . 64
Crawfurd, J. Embassy to Court of Ava. London, 1834. 2 v. 8°. . . 4817
Embassy to Siam and Cochin China. London, 1830. 2 v. 8°. . 4816
History of the Indian Archipelago. London, 1820. 3 v. 8°. . 4818
Crayon Miscellany. W. Irving. Philadelphia, 1835. 3 v. 12°. . . 1070
The same. New York, 1849. 12°. 3362
Crayon Sketches & Off-Hand Takings. G. W. Bungay. Bost. 1852. 12°. 813
Cream of Scientific Knowl. Enlarged by G. N. Wright. Lond. 1841. 16°. 2400
Creamer, Hannah G. Eleanor; or, Life without Love. Bost. 1850. 12°. 3841
Creasy, E. S. Fifteen Decisive Battles of the World. Lond. 1851. 2 v. 12°. 4442
Creation, Course of. J. Anderson. Cincinnati, 1851. 12°. . . . 4196
Epoch of. E. Lord. New York, 1851. 12°. 4431
Picturesque Sketches of. D. T. Ansted. Philadelphia, 1847. 12°. 3054
Vestiges of the Natural History of. New York, 1845. 12°. . . 2316
Creator, Indications of the. W. Whewell. Philadelphia, 1845. 12°. . 2359
G. Taylor. New York, 1851. 12°. 4456
Crescent & the Cross; or, East. Trav. E. Warburton. N.Y. 1845. 2 v. 12°. 2377
Crests from the Ocean World. A. Tripp. Boston, 1853. 12°. . . 5239
Cresy, E. Encyclopædia of Civil Engineering. London, 1847. 8°. . 4529
Crichton; a Novel. W. H. Ainsworth. New York, 1846. 2 v. in 1. . 122
Crichton, A. History of Arabia. (H. F. L.) N.Y. 1848. 2 v. 12°. 3683, 68, 69
History of Scandinavia. New York, 1844. 2 v. 12°. . . . 1859
Cricket Field; or, History and Science of Cricket. London, 1851. 12°. . 4266
Cricket on the Hearth. C. Dickens. New York, 1846. 12°. . . . 2547
Crime, Chronicles of; or, Newgate Calendar. London, 1841. 2 v. 8°. . 2769
Rationale of, and its Treatment. M. B. Sampson. N. Y. 1846. 12°. 2933
Crimes of the Borgias. A. Dumas. New York, 1847. 8°. 2801
Criminal Cases Tried before Judge Thacher, 1823–43. Boston, 1845. 8°. 2774
Criminal Trials, American. P. W. Chandler. Boston, 1841–44. 2 v. 12°. 1921
Remarkable. P. J. A. von Feuerbach. New York, 1846. 12°. . 2584
Crimora; or, Love's Cross. G. L. Ditson. Boston, 1852. 12°. . . 3263
Critic of Pure Reason. I. Kant. London, 1838. 8°. 2260
Criticism, Elements of. Lord Kames. New York, 1823. 2 v. 8°. . . 706
The same. New York, 1836. 8°. 1450
Criticisms on Art. W. Hazlitt. London, 1843. 12°. 1870
Critics, Specimens of the British. J. Wilson. Philadelphia, 1846. 12°. . 2559
Crock of Gold, and other Tales. M. F. Tupper. New York, 1849. 12°. 2480
Crofton D. Genesis and Geology. Boston, 1853. 12°. 5264
Crockett, D. Sketches and Eccentricities. New York, 1847. 12°. . 3129

Crockett, D. Tour to the North and Down East. Phil. 1835. 12°. . 1145
Croker, J. W. (Editor.) Boswell's Life of Johnson. Lond. 1848. Roy. 8°. 1139
The same. New York, 1841. 2 v. roy. 8°. . . . 1253
Croly, G. Life and Times of George IV. New York, 1842. 12°. . . 1868
Life of George IV. (H. F. L.) New York, 1843. 12°. . 3683, 15
Salathiel. Cincinnati, 1847. 2 v. 12°. 3149
Cromwell, O., History of. M. Guizot. Philadelphia, 1854. 2 v. 12°. . 5917
Letters and Speeches. T. Carlyle. New York, 1845. 2 v. 12°. . 2538
Life. J. Forster. London, 1838. 12°. 1831, 6, 7
Life. J. T. Headley. New York, 1848. 12°. 3139
Life. M. Russell. (H. F. L.) New York, 1848. 2 v. 12°. 3683, 62, 63
Life. New York, 1850. 16°. 3316
A Vindication. J. H. M. D'Aubigné. New York, 1847. 12°. . 3019
Croppy; a Tale. J. Banim. Philadelphia, 1839. 12°. 1153
Crosby, E. Memoirs of. H. L. Barnum. New York, 1828. 8°. . . 1363
Crosby, H. Lands of the Moslem. New York, 1851. 8°. . . . 4120
Crosland, Mrs. N. Lydia; a Woman's Book. Boston, 1852. 12°. . 4912
Memorable Women. Boston, 1854. 12°. 6229
Croswell, H. Memoir of Wm. Croswell. New York, 1853. 8°. . . 5434
Crowe, Catherine. Linny Lockwood. New York, 1854. 8°. . . 5497
Light and Darkness; or, Mysteries of Life. New York, 1851. 8°. 4003
Night Side of Nature. New York, 1852. 12°. 3907
Crowell, B. Spirit of '76 in Rhode Island. Boston, 1850. 8°. . . 3646
Cruikshank, G., at Home. London, 1845. 4 v. 12°. 5039
(Illust.) Three Courses and a Dessert. London, 1850. Post 8°. 4392
Cruise in the Pacific, 1812–14. D. Porter. Philadelphia, 1815. 2 v. 12°. 636
in a Whale Boat. J. A. Rhodes. New York, 1848. 8°. . . 3206
of the Midge. Captain Chamier. New York, 1851. 8°. . . 1075
of the North Star. J. O. Choules. Boston, 1854. 12°. . . 5770
of the Potomac, 1831–34. F. Wassiner. New York, 1835. 12°. 1256
J. N. Reynolds. New York, 1835. 8°. 1980
Cruising in the last War. C. J. Peterson. Philadelphia, 1850. 2 v. 8°. 3990
Crumpe, S. Providing Employment for the People. London, 1795. 8°. 608
Crusades, Chronicles of. London, 1848. Post 8°. 3564
History of. C. Mills. Philadelphia, 1826. 8°. 779
History of. J. F. Michaud. New York, 1853. 2 v. 12°. . . 5278
Crystal Palace (Lond.), Architecture, &c. of. Berlyn & Fowler. Lon. 1851. 8°. 4310
See also *Exhibition of* 1851.
Crystal Palace (N.Y.), Art & Industry at. Ed. by H. Greeley. N.Y. 1854. 12°. 5643
a Day at. W. C. Richards. N.Y. 1853. 12°. 5618
*World of Science, Art, and Industry at. New York, 1854. 4°. . 5946
Crystaline. F. W. Shelton. New York, 1854. 12°. 5813
Crystallography, System of. J. J. Griffin. Glasgow, 1841. 8°. . . 1185
Cuba and the Cubans. New York, 1850. 12°. 3657
Gan Eden; or, Pictures of. W. H. Hurlbut. Boston, 1854. 12°. 6160
History of. M. M. Ballou. Boston, 1854. 12°. 6165
Letters from the Interior of. A. Abbot. Boston, 1829. 8°. . 1309
Porto Rico, and the Slave Trade. D. Turnbull. Lond. 1840. 8°. 4680

Culprit Fay, and other Poems. J. R. Drake. New York, 1835. 8°. . 2267
Cumberland, R. John de Lancaster. New York, 1809. 2 v. 12°. . 184
Memoirs of his own Life. New York, 1806. 8°. . . . 1346
Cumming, J. Apocalyptic Sketches. Philadelphia, 1854. 2 v. 12°. . 5821
Benedictions; or, the Blessed Life. Boston, 1854. 12°. . . 5753
Church before the Flood. Boston, 1854. 12°. 5822
Lectures on the Miracles. Philadelphia, 1854. 12°. . . . 5852
Lectures on the Parables. Philadelphia, 1854. 12°. . . . 5874
Lectures on Romanism. Boston, 1854. 12°. 6155
Minor Works. Philadelphia, 1854. 12°. 6200
Finger of God; Christ our Passover; The Comforter.
Sabbath Morning Readings: Genesis. Boston, 1854. 12°. . . 5872
Exodus. Boston, 1854. 12°. 6239
Tent and the Altar. Boston, 1854. 12°. 5873
Voices of the Dead. Boston, 1854. 12°. 5823
Cumming, R. G. Hunter's Life in South Africa. N.Y. 1850. 2 v. 12°. 3933
Cummings, A. Memoir of E. Payson. New York, 1830. 12°. . . 503
Cummings, Maria. Lamplighter. Boston, 1854. 12°. 5775
Cummings, J. A. Introduction to Geography. Boston, 1813. 12°. . 301
Cunningham, A. Life and Land of Robert Burns. N. Y. 1841. 12°. . 1754
Life of Robert Burns. Boston, 1834. 12°. 888, 1
Lives of British Painters and Sculptors. N.Y. 1840. 5 v. 12°. . 2430
The same. (H. F. L.) N.Y. 1843. 5 v. 12°. 3683, 17–19, 66, 67
Cunynghame, A. Glimpses of the United States. London, 1850. 8°. . 5411
Recollections of Opium War in China. Phil. 1845. 16°. . . 2409
Curiosities of Human Nature. S. G. Goodrich. Boston, 1849. 12°. 4900, 3
of Literature. I. Disraeli. Boston, 1834. 3 v. 12°. . . . 1234
of Nature and Art. New York, 1831. 8°. 579
Curling, J. B. Corps of Gentlemen-at-Arms. London, 1850. 8°. . 5409
Curr, J. Faith and Morality of the Catholic Church. Bost. 1849. 24°. . 3756
Curran, J. P., and his Contemporaries. C. Phillips. N.Y. 1851. 12°. . 4174
The same. New York, 1818. 8°. 1322
Currencies, Regulation of. J. Fullarton. London, 1844. 8°. . . 4640
Currency, Massachusetts, Historical Account of. J. B. Felt. Bost. 1839. 8°. 1252
Currer Bell. — See *Bronte, Caroline.*
Curse of Clifton; a Tale. Mrs. E. D. E. N. Southworth. Phil. 1853. 12°. 5229
Curtis, G. T. Inventor's Manual of Legal Principles. Bost. 1851. 12°. 4298
Curtis, G. W. Howadji in Syria. New York, 1852. 12°. . . . 4799
Lorgnette; or, Studies of the Town. New York, 1851. 2 v. 12°. 3908
Lotus Eating; a Summer Book. New York, 1852. 12°. . . 4888
Nile Notes of a Howadji. New York, 1851. 12°. . . . 3823
Potiphar Papers. New York, 1853. 12°. 5612
Curtis, Miss. Jessie's Flirtations. New York, 1846. 8°. . . . 2685
Curwen, S. Journal and Letters. New York, 1842. 8°. . . . 2849
Curzon, R. Armenia; a Year at Erzeroom. New York, 1854. 12°. . 6138
Curzon, R., jun. Monasteries of the Levant. New York, 1849. 12°. . 3273
Cushing, L. S. Reports on Contested Elections of Mass. Bost. 1853. 8°. 5178
Rules in Deliberative Assemblies. Boston, 1850. 12°. . . . 13

Cushing, C. Reminiscences of Spain. Boston, 1833. 2 v. 12°. . . . 2134
Custine, Marquis de. Russia. New York, 1854. 12°. 6146
Cutter, W. Life of Israel Putnam. New York, 1846. 12°. . . . 2984
Cuvier, Baron. Animal Kingdom. New York, 1831. 4 v. 8°. . . 1990
Cycle of Celestial Objects. W. H. Smyth. London, 1844. 2 v. 8°. . 5466
Cyclopædia of Anecdotes. K. Arvine. Boston, 1851. Roy. 8°. . . 3379
of Biography. P. Godwin. New York, 1852. 12°. . . . 4489
of Biblical Literature. J. Kitto. New York, 1850. 2 v. roy. 8°. 3526
The same, condensed. Boston, 1851. Roy. 8°. . . . 4332
*of Commerce, &c. W. Waterston. London, 1846. 8°. . . 3996
The same. London, 1846. 8°. 3544
of English Literature. R. Chambers. Boston, 1851. 2 v. roy. 8°. 2636
of the Industry of all Nations. C. Knight. New York, 1851. 8°. 4506
of Lit. and the Fine Arts. G. Ripley & B. Taylor. N.Y. 1852. 12°. 4488
of Moral and Religious Anecdotes. K. Arvine. N.Y. 1850. 8°. . 4551
of 6000 Receipts. A. J. Cooley. New York, 1846. 8°. . . 3537
of Useful Arts. T. Antisell. New York, 1852. 12°. . . . 4603
Standard Library. London, 1848. 4 v. post 8°. 4390
Cyril Thornton. T. Hamilton. New York, 1832. 2 v. 12°. . . . 2143
Cyrilla; a Tale. New York, 1854. 8°. 5951
Czar, his Court and People. J. S. Maxwell. New York, 1848. 12°. . 3115
and the Sultan. A. Gilson. New York, 1853. 12°. . . . 5571

D.

Dacre, Lady. Recollections of a Chaperon. London, 1852. 12°. . . 5685
Tales of the Peerage and Peasantry. New York, 1835. 2 v. 12°. . 239
The same. London, 1852. 12°. 5687
Dadd, G. H. Modern Horse Doctor. Boston, 1854. 12°. . . . 5838
Daguerreotype, The; a Magazine. Vols. 1–3. Boston, 1847–49. Roy. 8°. 2874
Daguerreotype Process, Treatise on. G. C. H. Halleur. Lond. 1852. 12°. 6087
Dahcotah; Life, &c., of the Sioux. Mary H. Eastman. N. Y. 1849. 12°. 3359
Dahlmann, F. E. Hist. of the English Revolution of 1688. Lond. 1844. 8°. 4678
Dakota Language, Gram. and Dict. of. S. K. Riggs. Wash. 1852. 4°. 1756, 4
Daily Bible Illustrations. J. Kitto. New York, 1850–53. 7 v. 12°. . 4296
For Contents, see *Kitto, J.*
Daisy Burns; a Tale. Julia Kavanagh. New York, 1853. 12°. . . 5233
D'Alembert, J. le R. Miscellanies in Literature, &c. Lond. 1764. 12°. 191
Dall, Caroline W. H. Essays and Sketches. Boston, 1849. 12°. . . 3340
Dalrymple, Sir J. Memoirs of Gt. Britain and Ireland. Lond. 1771. 2 v. 4°. 3630
Daltons; or, Three Roads in Life. C. Lever. New York, 1852. 8°. . 4812
Damascus and Palmyra. C. G. Addison. Philadelphia, 1838. 2 v. 12°. 835
Journey to. Viscount Castlereagh. London, 1847. 2 v. 12°. . 4580
Damberger, C. F. Travels in Interior of Africa. Charlestown, 1801. 8°. 215
Damer, Mrs. G. L. D. Tour in Greece, Turkey, &c. Lond. 1842. 2 v. 12°. 3660
Damsel of Darien. W. G. Simms. Philadelphia, 1839. 2 v. 12°. . . 1181
Dana, R. H. Poems and Prose Writings. New York, 1850. 2 v. 12°. . 2185

Dana, R. H. jun. Seaman's Friend, Dict. of Sea Terms, &c. Bost. 1851. 12°. 4254
Two Years before the Mast. New York, 1840. 12°. 1491
The same. (H. F. L.) New York, 1846. 12°. . . 3683, 106
Dancing Feather. J. H. Ingraham. New York, 1851. 8°. 4534
Dandolo, E. Italian Volunteers & Lombard Rifle Brigade. Lon. 1851. 12°. 4445
Dando, J. Bookkeeping by Double Entry. Philadelphia, 1842. 4°. . 3550
Danforth, J. N. Gleanings of a Pastor's Portfolio. N. Y. 1852. 12°. . 4747
Dangeau, Marquis de. Court of France, 1684–1720. Lond. 1825. 2 v. 8°. 5127
Daniel, Notes on. A. Barnes. New York, 1853. 12°. 5538
Daniel, R. M. Cardinal's Daughter. New York, 1850. 8°. 3461
Daniell, J. F. Elements of Meteorology. London, 1845. 2 v. 8°. . . 5473
Dante. Trans. by I. C. Wright; illust. by J. Flaxman. Lon. 1854. Post 8°. 5938
The Vision. Translated by H. F. Cary. New York, 1845. 12°. . 2246
Danvers, Mass. Centennial Celebration, June 16, 1852. Bost. 1852. 8°. 5161
History of. J. W. Hanson. Danvers, 1848. 12°. 3120
D'Anville, M. Compendium of Ancient Geography. N. Y. 1814. 2 v. 8°. 1344
D'Arblay, Mde. F. Diary and Letters. Philadelphia, 1842. 2 v. 8°. . 2254
Memoirs of Dr. C. Burney. Philadelphia, 1833. 8°. 1241
Darby, W. Tour from New York to Detroit, 1818. New York, 1819. 8°. 1374
Darien; or, The Merchant Prince. E. Warburton. New York, 1852. 8°. 3324
Darius, History of. J. Abbott. New York, 1850. 12°. 3765
Dark Scenes of History. G. P. R. James. New York, 1850. . . . 3495
Darlington, W. Memorials of J. Bartram and H. Marshall. Phil. 1849. 8°. 2864
Darnell, W. N. Memoir and Corres. of Isaac Basire. London, 1831. 8°. 1490
Darnley. G. P. R. James. New York, 1830. 2 v. 12°. 1808
The same. London, 1853. 12°. 5707
Dartmoor Prison, Journal at. Boston, 1816. 12°. 3320
The same. Milledgeville, 1816. 12°. 1069
Darwin, C. Researches in Nat. Hist. and Geology. N.Y. 1846. 2 v. 12°. 2594
Darwin, E. Memoirs. Anna Seward. Philadelphia, 1804. 8°. . . 712
Dashes of American Humor. H. Paul. New York, 1853. 12°. . . 5784
*Dates, Dictionary of. J. Haydn. London, 1847. 8°. 3959
Dictionary of. G. P. Putnam. New York, 1852. 8°. 2041
D'Aubigné, J. H. M. History of the Reformation. N.Y. 1843–53. 5 v. 12°. 1717
Oliver Cromwell; a Vindication. New York, 1847. 12°. . . 3019
Protestant Church in Hungary. Philadelphia, 1854. 12°. . . 5853
Daughter at School. J. Todd. Northampton, 1854. 12°. . . . 5535
Daughter of the Night. S. W. Fullom. London, 1851. 3 v. 12°. . . 4247
Daughters of England. Mrs. S. Ellis. New York, 1843. 8°. . . 1826
Davenport, R. A. Dictionary of Biography. Boston, 1832. 8°. . . 805
History of the Bastile and its Captives. Philadelphia, 1846. 12°. 2595
Perilous Adventures. (H. F. L.) New York, 1848. 12°. . 3683, 159
David Copperfield. C. Dickens. Philadelphia, 1851. 8°. 4002
Davidson, D. Connection of Sacred and Profane History. N. Y. 1849. 8°. 3517
Davidson, Lucretia M. Life. C. M. Sedgwick. Boston, 1844. 12°. 1076, 7
Poetical Remains, and Memoir. C. M. Sedgwick. Phil. 1843. 12°. 2572
The same. New York, 1851. 12°. 1613
Davidson, Marg. M. Biog. & Poetical Remains. W. Irving. N.Y. 1851. 12°. 1613

Davidson, Mrs. M. M. Selections from her Writings. Phil. 1843. 12°. . 2163
Davidson, S. Introduction to New Testament. London, 1848. 3 v. 8°. 5112
Treatise on Biblical Criticism. Boston, 1853. 2 v. 8°. . . . 5119
Davie, W. R. Life. F. M. Hubbard. Boston, 1848. 12°. . . 1076, 25
Davies, B. System of Modern Geography. Philadelphia, 1805. 2 v. 12°. 300
Davies, C. Logic and Utility of Mathematics. New York, 1850. 8°. . 3900
Davies, C. M. History of Holland. London, 1851. 3 v. 8° . . . 5135
Davis, A. J. Principles of Nature; her Divine Revelations. N.Y. 1850. 8°. 3943
Davis, E. History of the Half Century. Boston, 1851. 12°. . . 3784
Davis, J. F. The Chinese. (H. F. L.) New York, 1846. 2 v. 12°. 3683, 80, 81
The same. New York, 1845. 2 v. 12°. 2443
Davis, M. L. Memoirs of Aaron Burr. New York, 1836. 2 v. 8°. . 713
Davis, Z. A. Freemason's Monitor. Philadelphia, 1847. 12°. . . 385
Davy, Sir H. Consolations in Travel. London, 1839. 12°. . . . 2546
Davy, J. Ionian Islands and Malta. London, 1842. 2 v. 8°. . . 5472
Dawes, R. Geraldine, and other Poems. New York, 1839. 12°. . . 1133
Day, Julia. Old Engagement. Boston, 1852. 12°. 4797
Day, S. Historical Collections of Pennsylvania. Phil. 1843. 8°. . 2727
Days of Bruce. Grace Aguilar. New York, 1852. 2 v. 12°. . . 4790
D'Azeglio, M. Challenge of Barletta. New York, 1845. 12°. . . 2483
Dead Sea Expedition. W. F. Lynch. Philadelphia, 1849. 8°. . . 2850
Edited by E. P. Montague. Philadelphia, 1849. 12°. . 3288
Deaf and Dumb, and their Education. E. J. Mann. Boston, 1836. 12°. 281
Deafness and Blindness; The Lost Senses. J. Kitto. N. Y. 1852. 12°. 4863
Dean's Daughter; or, the Days we Live in. Mrs. Gore. N. Y. 1853. 12°. 5224
Deane, S. History of Scituate, Mass. Boston, 1831. 8°. . . . 1446
Dearborn, N. Boston Notions, 1630–1847. Boston, 1848. 16°. . . 2453
Reminiscences of Boston, and Guide. Boston, 1851. 18°. . . 4209
Death; the Last Enemy. G. Burgess. Philadelphia, 1850. 12° . . 4752
Death's Doings; in Verse and Prose. Boston, 1828. 2 v. 8°. . . . 1291
Debates & Proceedings in Congress, 1789–1837. Wash. 1834–37. 29 v. 8°. 4903
of Mass. Constitutional Convention, 1853. Bost. 1853. 3 v. roy. 8°. 5916
Debater, The. F. Rowton. London, 1846. 12°. 4055
De Bode, C. A. Travels in Luristan and Arabistan. Lond. 1845. 2 v. 8°. 4689
De Bow, J. D. B. Commercial Review. Vols. 4, 5. N. O. 1847–48. 8°. 2911
Debtor and Creditor, Law of. J. P. Holcombe. New York, 1849. 8°. . 4306
Decatur, S. Life. A. S. Mackenzie. Boston, 1848. 12°. . . 1076, 21
Deck and Port. W. Colton. New York, 1850. 12°. 3659
Deck of the Crescent City. W. G. Dix. New York, 1853. 12°. . . 5271
Declarations, American Precedents of. J. Anthon. Brookfield, 1821. 8°. 1402
Deer, Antelopes, &c. Sir W. Jardine. Edinburgh, 1843. 12°. . 4901, 21
Deerbrook. H. Martineau. New York, 1839. 2 v. 12°. . . . 981
Deerslayer; or, First War-Path. J. F. Cooper. New York, 1852. 12°. . 1632
De Foe, D. Novels and Miscellaneous Works. London, 1854. Post 8°. 6195

Vol. 1. Life of Captain Singleton; Life of Colonel Jack.
2. Memoirs of a Cavalier; Memoirs of Captain Carleton; Dickory Cronke.
[Remaining volumes of this edition not yet published.]

Robinson Crusoe. New York, 1847. 8°. 2848

De Foe, D. Robinson Crusoe. New York, n. d. 12°. 48
Works. [Vol. 1 missing.] London, 1841. 3 v. roy. 8°. . . . 2654
Degerando, J. M. (Baron). Self-Education. Boston, 1832. 12°. . . 2255
Deists, Short Method with the. C. Leslie. New York, n. d. 12°. . . 504
Déjean, M. Traité Raisonné de la Distillation. Paris, 1777. 12°. . 377
De Kroyft, S. H. Place in thy Memory. New York, 1850. 12°. . . 3931
Delano, A. Voyages and Travels. Boston, 1817. 8°. 640
Dellon, M. Inquisition at Goa. Boston, 1815. 16°. 27
De Lolme, J. L. Treatise on the Eng. Constitution. Lond. 1838. 2 v. 8°. 5474
Deloraine. W. Godwin. Philadelphia, 1833. 2 v. 12°. . . . 1926
De l'Orme. G. P. R. James. New York, 1830. 2 v. 12°. . . . 2901
The same. London, 1853. 12°. 5709
Delusions, Extraordinary Popular. C. Mackay. Phil. 1850. 2 v. 12°. . 3668
Demetrius; an Epic Poem. A. Eustaphieve. Boston, 1818. 12°. . 479
Demonology and Witchcraft, Letters on. Sir W. Scott. N.Y. 1830. 16°. 817
The same. (H. F. L.) New York, 1843. 12°. . . 3683, 11
Ghosts, and Apparitions. J. Thacher. Boston, 1831. 12°. . . 839
Democracy. C. S. Camp. (H. F. L.) New York, 1847. 12°. . 3683, 138
in America. A. de Tocqueville. New York, 1839. 2 v. 8°. . 948
Progress of, in France. A. Dumas. New York. 1841. 12°. . 1910
Democratic Review. Vols. 20–31. New York, 1847–52. 8°. . . 2819
Demosthenes. Orations. Trans. by T. Leland. N.Y. 1831. 2 v. 12°. 1854, 3, 4
Dempsey, G. D. Drainage of Districts and Lands. London, 1854. 12°. 6125
Treatise on Drainage of Towns and Streets. London, 1849. 12°. 6054
Tubular and Iron Bridges. London, 1850. 12°. 6065
Dendy, W. C. Philosophy of Mystery. New York, 1845. 12°. . . 2504
Denison, E. B. Clock and Watch-Making. London, 1850. 12°. . . 6080
Denison, Mary A. Home Pictures. New York, 1853. 12°. . . . 5354
Denmark, Norway, and Sweden. (H. F. L.) N.Y. 1847. 2 v. 12°. 3683, 136–7
Dennings and their Beaux, &c. Miss Leslie. Philadelphia, 1851. 8°. . 4149
Denon, V. Travels in Egypt. New York, 1803. 2 v. 8°. . . . 1199
Denounced, The. J. Banim. New York, 1830. 2 v. 12°. . . . 543
Dental Medicine, Practical Treatise on. T. E. Bond. Phil. 1852. 8°. . 5106
Dental Surgery, Principles & Practice of. C. A. Harris. Phil. 1853. 8°. 5105
De Puy, H. W. Kossuth and his Generals. Buffalo, 1852. 12°. . . 978
De Quincey, T. Autobiographic Sketches. Boston, 1853. 12°. . . 5514
Biographical Essays. Boston, 1850. 12°. 3939

Shakspeare; Pope; Lamb; Goethe; Schiller.

Cæsars. Boston, 1851. 12°. 3817
Confessions of an English Opium Eater. Boston, 1850. 12°. . 3911
Essays on the Poets. Boston, 1853. 12°. 5220

Wordsworth; Shelley; Keats; Goldsmith; Pope; Godwin; Foster; Hazlitt; Landor.

Historical and Critical Essays. Boston, 1853. 2 v. 12°. . . 5268

Vol. 1. Philosophy of Roman History; The Essenes; Philosophy of Herodotus; Plato's Republic; Homer and the Homeridæ.
2. Cicero; Style; Rhetoric; Secret Societies.

Letters to a Young Man; and other Papers. Boston, 1854. 12°. . 5771

De Quincey, T. Life and Manners. Boston, 1851. 12°. 4404

Early Days; London; Ireland; The Irish Rebellion; Premature Manhood; Travelling; My Brother; Oxford; German Literature.

Literary Reminiscences. Boston, 1852. 2 v. 12°. 4458

Vol. 1. Literary Novitiate; Sir Humphrey Davy; William Godwin; Mrs. Grant; Recollections of Charles Lamb; Walladmor; Coleridge; Wordsworth.
2. Wordsworth and Southey; Recollections of Grasmere; The Saracen's Head; Society of the Lakes; Charles Lloyd; Walking Stewart; Edward Irving; Talfourd; The London Magazine; Junius; Clare; Cunningham; Attack by a London Journal; Duelling.

Miscellaneous Essays. Boston, 1851. 12°. 4024

Knocking at the Gate, in Macbeth; Murder as one of the Fine Arts; Joan of Arc; English Mail Coach; Vision of Sudden Death; Dinner, Real and Reputed.

Philosophical Writers. Boston, 1854. 2 v. 12°. 5744

Vol. 1. Hamilton; Mackintosh; Kant; Herder; Richter; Lessing.
2. Bentley; Parr.

Narrative and Miscellaneous Papers. Boston, 1853. 2 v. 12°. . 5065

Vol. 1. Household Wreck; Spanish Nun; Flight of a Tartar Tribe.
2. Heavens as revealed by Rosse's Telescopes; Modern Superstition; Coleridge and Opium Eating; Temperance Movement; On War; Last Days of Immanuel Kant.

Theological Essays. Boston, 1854. 2 v. 12°. 5828

Vol. 1. Christianity as an Organ of Political Movement; Protestantism; Scriptural Expression for Eternity; Judas Iscariot; Hume's Argument against Miracles; Casuistry; Greece under the Romans.
2. Secession from Church of Scotland; Toilette of the Hebrew Lady; Milton; Charlemagne; Modern Greece; Lord Carlisle on Pope.

De Retz, Cardinal, and others. Lives. G. P. R. James. Phil. 1337. 2 v. 12°. 2315
De Rohan; or, the Court Conspirator. E. Sue. New York, 1845. 8°. 2838
Desert Home. M. Reid. Boston, 1852. 12°. 926
Deserted Wife. Mrs. E. D. E. N. Southworth. New York, 1850. 8°. . 3970
Designs for Cottages & Villas. T. U. Walter & J. J. Smith. Phil. 1847. 4°. 2980
for Gate Cottages, Lodges, &c. P. T. Robinson. Lond. 1837. 4°. 2890
*for Monuments and Mural Tablets. J. J. Smith. N.Y. 1846. 4°. 4857
*for Shop Fronts and Door Cases. London, n. d. 4°. . . . 1580
De Smet, P. J. Oregon Missions, 1845–46. New York, 1847. 12°. . 3061
De Soto, H. Conquest of Florida. T. Irving. New York, 1851. 12°. . 4105
Despotism in America. R. Hildreth. Boston, 1840. 12°. . . . 1132
The same. Boston, 1854. 12°. 5926
Destiny; or, Chief's Daughter. Susan Ferrier. London, 1852. 12°. . 5676
Desultoria; or, Recovered MSS. of an Eccentric. New York, 1850. 12°. 3503
Desultory Man. G. P. R. James. New York, 1830. 2 v. 12°. . . 268
De Vere; or, the Man of Independence. R. P. Ward. N.Y. 1831. 2 v. 12°. 350
De Vere, A. Picturesque Sketches of Greece and Turkey. Phil. 1850. 12°. 3909
De Vere, M. S. Outlines of Comparative Philology. N.Y. 1853. 12°. . 5568
Devereux; a Tale. E. L. Bulwer. New York, 1829. 2 v. 12°. . . 1494
Devotional Guides. R. Philip. New York, 1848. 2 v. 12°. . . . 4751
Devotions at Home. W. Wilberforce. Boston, 1838. 12°. . . . 1485
Dew, T. Digest of Laws, Customs, &c., of all Nations. N.Y. 1853. 8°. 5121
D'Ewes, Sir S., Autobiography and Correspond. London, 1845. 2 v. 8°. 5477

De Wette, W. M. L. Human Life; or, Prac. Ethics. Bos. 1842. 2 v. 12°. 962, 12, 13
Theodore; or, the Skeptic's Conversion. Bost. 1841. 2 v. 12°. 962, 10, 11
Dewey, C. Report on Herbaceous Plants of Mass. Cambridge, 1840. 8°. 1969
Dewey, O. Discourses. Boston, 1840. 3 v. 12°. 1558

Vol. 1. Explanation and Discussions of Unitarianism.
2. Moral Views of Commerce, Society, and Politics.
3. Discourses on Various Subjects.

Dexter, Lord Timothy. Life. S. L. Knapp. Newburyport, 1848. 12°. 881
D'Haussez, Baron. Great Britain in 1833. Philadelphia, 1833. 2 v. 12°. 1203
D'Homergue, J. Silk Culturist's Manual. Philadelphia, 1839. 12°. . 1625
Dial of Love. Mary Howitt. Philadelphia, 1854. 12°. 5583
Dialogues, Familiar. W. B. Fowle. Boston, 1846. 12°. 3347
Diana of Meridor. A. Dumas. New York, 1846. 8°. 2867
Diary of a Blasé. F. Marryat. Philadelphia, 1836. 12°. 272
of an Ennuyée. Mrs. A. Jameson. Philadelphia, 1826. 12°. . 2363
of a Désennuyée. Philadelphia, 1836. 12°. 1141
of a late Physician. S. Warren. New York, 1838. 3 v. 12°. . 2191
of the Times of George IV. Lady C. Bury. London, 1838. 4 v. 8°. 4652
The same. London, 1839. 4 v. 8°. 5144
Diaz del Castillo, B. Autobiog. and Conquest of Mexico. Lon. 1844. 2 v. 8°. 4547
Dibdin, T. F. Introd. to Greek and Latin Classics. Lond. 1827. 2 v. 8°. 5089
Dick Lawson; or, the Mocking Bird. New York, 1844. 8°. . . 2171
Dick, T. Celestial Scenery. (H. F. L.) New York, 1846. 12°. . 3683, 83
Christian Philosopher. Brookfield, 1828. 12°. 519
Diffusion of Knowledge. (H. F. L.) New York, 1848. 12°. 3683, 59
Essay on Covetousness. New York, 1836. 12°. 261
Practical Astronomer. New York, 1846. 12°. 2532
Sidereal Heavens. (H. F. L.) New York, 1846. 12°. . 3683, 99
Works. Philadelphia, 1845. 8 v. 12°. 2357

Vol. 1. Philosophy of a Future State.
2. Christian Philosopher.
3. Philosophy of Religion.
4. Diffusion of Knowledge.
Vol. 5. Mental Illumination.
6. Essay on Covetousness.
7. Celestial Scenery.
8. Sidereal Heavens.

Dickens, C. American Notes. New York, 1842. 8°. 1689
Battle of Life; a Love Story. New York, 1847. 12°. . . 2958
Barnaby Rudge. Philadelphia, 1849. 8°. 1674
Bleak House. Philadelphia, 1853. 8°. 5428
Child's History of England. New York, 1854. 2 v. 12°. . . 5829
Chimes; a Goblin Story. Philadelphia, 1845. 16°. . . . 808
Christmas Stories. New York, 1848. 12°. 2204

Christmas Carol; The Chimes; Cricket on the Hearth; Battle of Life.

Cricket on the Hearth. New York, 1846. 12°. 2547
David Copperfield. Philadelphia, 1851. 8°. 4002
Dombey and Son. New York, 1847. 2 v. 12°. 2884
Hard Times. New York, 1854. 8°. 5974
(Editor.) Household Words. Vols. 1–9 (con.). N.Y. 1850–54. 8°. 4129
Martin Chuzzlewit. Philadelphia, 1849. 8°. 2069
Master Humphrey's Clock, Old Curiosity Shop, &c. Phil. 1849. 8°. 1605
Memoirs of Grimaldi. Philadelphia, 1838. 2 v. 12°. 820

Dickens, C. Nicholas Nickleby. Philadelphia, 1850. 8°. 526
Oliver Twist. Philadelphia, 1853. 8°. 1338
Pickwick Papers. Philadelphia, 1854. 8°. 804
Pictures from Italy. New York, 1846. 12°. 2578
Sketches of Every-Day Life. Philadelphia, 1849. 8°. 843
Tuggs's at Ramsgate, and other Tales. Philadelphia, 1837. 12°. . 911
Dickinson, R. Elements of Geography. Boston, 1813. 8°. 630
Dictionnaire de Commerce. Copenhagen, 1759. 4 v. folio. . . . 2019
Universel de Commerce. Paris, 1805. 2 v. 4°. 2029
Dictionary, Classical. C. Anthon. New York, 1847. Roy. 8°. . . 1243
*The same. New York, 1850. Roy. 8°. 2840
W. Smith. Edited by C. Anthon. N. Y. 1851. Roy. 8°. 4347
English Pronouncing. J. Walker. New York, 1823. 8°. . . 660
Geographical, Statistical, &c. J. R. M'Culloch. N.Y. 1845. 2 v. roy. 8°. 2221
of Arts, Manufactures, and Mines. A. Ure. New York, 1849. 8°. 1687
*The same. New York, 1853. 2 v. 8°. 1687
of Commerce. J. R. M'Culloch. Philadelphia, 1845. 2 v. roy. 8°. 1691
*of Dates. J. Haydn. London, 1847. 8°. 3959
of the English Language. J. Barclay. London, n. d. 4°. . . 2024
S. Maunder. London, 1848. 12°. 4106
*C. Richardson. Philadelphia, 1851. 2 v. 4°. . . . 4902
J. Walker. Philadelphia, 1811. 8°. 1287
N. Webster. Springfield, 1845. 2 v. roy. 8°. . . . 2231
*The same. Springfield, 1849. 4°. 2040
J. E. Worcester. Boston, 1848. Roy. 8°. 2888
of General Knowledge. G. Crabb. New York, 1830. . . 460
The same. New York, 1835. 12°. 3513
of Geography. A. K. Johnson. London, 1850. 8°. . . . 4353
*of Greek & Roman Biog. & Mythology. W. Smith. Lon. 1849. 3 v. 8°. 3957
*of Machines, Mechanics, &c., Appleton's. N.Y. 1851. 2 v. roy. 8°. 4124
of Merchandise in all Languages. London, 1803. 8°. . . 765
*of Painters and Engravers. M. Bryan. London, 1849. Roy. 8°. 3960
of Quotations from Latin, French, Spanish, &c. Phil. 1851. 12°. 4425
of Science, Literature, & Art. W. T. Brande. N.Y. 1848. Roy. 8°. 2641
of the Scottish Language. J. Jamieson. Edinburgh, 1846. 8°. . 5137
of Shakspearian Quotations. Philadelphia, 1851. 12°. . . 4454
of Synonymes. J. Rawson. Philadelphia, 1850. 12°. . . 3577
of Terms of Art, &c. J. Weale. London, 1850. 12°. . . 6061
of the Wonders of Art and Nature. J. Hardie. N.Y. 1819. 12°. 347
Rhyming. J. Walker. Phil. 1852. 8°. 500
Didimus, H. New Orleans as I Found it. New York, 1845. 8°. . 2241
Dies Boreales; or, Christopher under Canvass. J. Wilson. Phil. 1850. 12°. 3879
Digest of Laws, Customs, &c., of all Nations. T. Dew. N.Y. 1853. 8°. 5121
Digestion and Dyspepsia. W. Sweetser. Boston, 1837. 12°. . . 1090
Dignities, Privilege, and Precedence, Manual of. C. R. Dodd. Lon. 1843. 12°. 3602
The same. London, 1344. 12°. 2444
Dill, E. M. Ireland's Miseries; their Cause and Cure. N.Y. 1852. 12°. 4793
Dillaway, C. K. Roman Antiquities and Mythology. Boston, 1831. 12°. 155

Diosma; a Perennial. H. F. Gould. Boston, 1851. 12°. 4087
Diplomatic Correspondence of the U. S., 1783–89. Wash. 1833. 6 v. 8°. 3615
of the Am. Revolution. Ed. by J. Sparks. Boston, 1829. 12 v. 8°. 3613
Discarded Daughter. Mrs. E. D. E. N. Southworth. Phil. 1852. 2 v. 12°. 4851
Discipline. Mary Brunton. London, 1850. 12°. 5651
Discipline of Life. Ellinor Ponsonby. New York, 1848. 8°. . . . 3238
Discovery and Adventure in the Polar Seas. New York, 1831. 16°. . 818
The same. (H. F. L.) New York, 1848. 16°. . . 3683, 14
Diseases of the Chest, Treatise on. J. A. Swett. New York, 1852. 8°. . 4804
of the Mind. B. Rush. Philadelphia, 1830. 8°. 2164
Disgrace to the Family. W. B. Jerrold. Philadelphia, 1848. 8°. . . 3203
*Disney, J. Museum Disneianum. London, 1849. 4°. 5107
Disowned, The. E. L. Bulwer. New York, 1829. 2 v. 12°. . . . 1661
Disraeli, B. Coningsby. New York, 1845. 8°. 2282
Contarini Fleming. New York, 1832. 2 v. 12°. 409
Sybil; or, the Two Nations. New York, 1845. 8°. . . . 2283
Tancred; or the New Crusade. New York, 1848. 8°. 2778
Venetia. Philadelphia, 1837. 2 v. 12°. 565
Vivian Gray. Baltimore, 1833. 2 v. 12°. 1149
Wondrous Tale of Alroy. Philadelphia, 1833. 2 v. 12°. . . . 1179
Works of Fiction. Philadelphia, 1845. Roy. 8°. 2689

Vivian Grey; Young Duke; Contarini Fleming; Wondrous Tale of Alroy; Rise of Iskander; Henrietta Temple; Venetia.

Disraeli, I. Amenities of Literature. New York, 1841. 2 v. 12°. . . 1878
Miscellanies of Literature. London, 1840. 8°. 2768

Literary Miscellanies; Quarrels of Authors; Calamities of Authors; Character of James I.; The Literary Character.

Curiosities of Literature. Boston, 1834. 3 v. 12°. 1234
Quarrels of Authors. New York, 1814. 2 v. 12°. 453
Distinguished Men of Modern Times. H. Malden. N.Y. 1846. 2 v. 12°. 3683, 123–4
District School as it Was. W. Burton. Boston, 1850. 12°. 3775
The same, and other Writings. Boston, 1852. 12°. . . 1516
Disturnell, J. Railroad, Steamboat, and Telegraph Book. N.Y. 1849. 12°. 55
Ditson, G. L. Circassia; a Tour to the Caucasus. New York, 1850. 8°. 3522
Crimora; or, Love's Cross. Boston, 1852. 12°. 3263
Divine Government, Method of. J. M'Cosh. New York, 1852. 8°. . 4725
Divorced, The. Charlotte Bury. Philadelphia, n. d. 8°. . . . 961
Dix, J. A. Winter in Madeira, and Summer in Spain, &c. N.Y. 1850. 12°. 4085
Dix, J. R. History of a Wasted Life. Boston, 1853. 12°. 5508
Pen and Ink Sketches. Boston, 1845. 12°. 2476
Pen Pictures of Popular English Preachers. London, 1852. 12°. 6243
Pulpit Portraits. Boston, 1853. 12°. 5584
Dix, W. G. Deck of the Crescent City. New York, 1853. 12°. . . . 5271
Wreck of the Glide. Boston, 1846. 12°. 2917
Dixon, E. S. Dovecote and Aviary. London, 1854. 12°. 5858
Dixon, G. Voyage autour du Monde, 1785–88. Paris, 1789. 2 v. 8°. . 1245
Dixon, H. Life of John Howard. New York, 1850. 12°. 3472
Dobson, E. Art of Building. New York, 1853. 12°. 5530

Dobson, E. Art of Building. London, 1854. 12°. 6050
Treatise on Bricks and Tiles. London, 1850. 12°. . . . 6051
Treatise on Foundations and Concrete Works. London, 1850. 12°. 6066
Treatise on Masonry and Stone-cutting. London, 1849. 12°. . 6052
Doctor, The. R. Southey. New York, 1836. 2 v. 12°. 1082
Doctrines, History of. K. R. Hagenbach. Edinburgh, 1850. 8°. . . 5151
Dodd, C. R. Manual of Dignities, Privilege, &c. London, 1843. 12°. . 3602
The same. London, 1844. 12°. 2444
Dodd, W. Beauties of Shakspeare. London, n. d. 18°. 2207
Life and Beauties of Shakspeare. Boston, 1850. 12°. . . . 880
Thoughts in Prison. Boston, n. d. 12°. 463
Dodd Family Abroad. C. Lever. New York, 1854. 8°. . . . 5949
Doddridge, P. Lectures on Ethics, Divinity, &c. London, 1799. 2 v. 8°. 1271
Life and Labors. J. Stoughton. Boston, 1853. 12°. . . . 5075
Dog, The. With Illustrations. London, n. d. Roy. 8°. . . . 3635, 2
W. Youatt. Philadelphia, 1847. 8°. 2764
Dogs, "Dinks" on. Edited by H. W. Herbert. New York, 1850. 12°. 4070
Natural History of. C. H. Smith. Edinburgh, 1843. 2 v. 12°. 4901, 18, 19
Dollars and Cents. Amy Lothrop. New York, 1852. 2 v. 12°. . . 4789
Dombey and Son. C. Dickens. New York, 1847. 2 v. 12°. . . . 2884
Domestic Manners of the Americans. Mrs. F. Trollope. N.Y. 1832. 8°. . 2078
Domestic Medicine. J. C. Gunn. New York, 1851. 8°. . . . 4701
Surgery, &c. F. G. Smith. 1851. 12°. 474
Domesticated Animals of British Islands. D. Low. London, 1853. 8°. 5453
Don Juan. Lord Byron. Philadelphia, 1852. 12°. 1624
Don Quixote. M. de Cervantes. Boston, 1848. 8°. 3094
The same. Philadelphia, 1846. 4 v. 24°. 30
Donaldson, Prof. Clay Lands and Loamy Soils. London, 1822. 12°. . 6079
Dongola and Sennaar, Expedition to. G. B. English. Boston, 1823. 8°. 1378
Donn, J. Catalogue of Plants in Cambridge Botanic Garden. Lon. 1845. 8°. 3545
Donnavan, C. Adventures in Mexico. Boston, 1848. 8°. . . . 3270
Donne, Wotton, and others, Lives of. I. Walton. Cambridge, 1831. 12°. 383, 5, 6
Doom of Devorgoil; a Melodrama. Sir W. Scott. New York, 1838. 12°. 537
The same. Philadelphia, 1839. 12°. 860, 6
Doomed, The. Philadelphia, 1834. 2 v. 12°. 541
D'Orsay, A. Treatise on Etiquette. Philadelphia, 1854. 8°. . . 5915
Dorsey, Mrs. A. H. Woodreve Manor. Philadelphia, 1852. 12°. . . 4879
Dost Mohammed Kahn. Life. Mohan Lal. London, 1846. 2 v. 8°. . 4677
Double Oath. Lady De Calabrella. London, 1850. 3 v. 12°. . . 4249
Doubourg, J. H. Life of Cardinal de Cheverus. Phil. 1839. 12°. . 1135
Douglas, R. Adventures of a Medical Student. N. York, 1848. 2 v. 12°. 3153
Dove and the Eagle; a Poem. Boston, 1851. 12°. 3801
Dovecote; or, Heart of the Homestead. G. C. Hill. Boston, 1854. 12°. 5619
Dovecote and Aviary. E. S. Dixon. London, 1854. 12°. . . . 5858
Dover, Lord. Life of Frederick II. New York, 1835. 2 v. 12°. . . 131
The same. (H. F. L.) New York, 1846. 2 v. 12°. 3680, 41, 42
Dow, L. Life, Experience, and Travels. New York, 1850. Roy. 8°. . 4357
Dowling, J. History of Romanism. New York, 1845. Roy. 8°. . . 2619

Downing, A. J. Architecture of Country Houses. New York, 1850. 8°. 3968
Cottage Residences. New York, 1847. 8°. 2804
Fruits and Fruit Trees of America. New York, 1847. 12°. . . 3029
Landscape Gardening. New York, 1844. 8°. 2227
Rural Essays; with Memoir of Author. New York, 1853. 8°. . 5175
Drainage of Towns and Buildings. G. D. Dempsey. London, 1849. 12°. 6054
of Districts and Lands. G. D. Dempsey. London, 1854. 12°. . 6125
Drake, Sir F., Cavendish, & Dampier. Lives & Voyages. Lond. 1849. 16°. 4584
The same. (H. F. L.) New York, 1848. 12°. . 3683, 30
Drake, J. R. Culprit Fay, and other Poems. New York, 1835. 8°. . 2267
Drake, N. Shakspeare and his Times. Paris, 1838. 8°. . . . 4513
Drake, S. G. History and Antiq. of Boston. Boston, 1854. Roy. 8°. . 5929
History of Philip's War. Exeter, 1836. 12°. 179
Drama, Ancient British. London, 1810. 3 v. roy. 8°. 3940
Defence of. R. Mansel and Caffaro. New York, 1826. 12°. . 133
in Pokerville, &c. J. M. Field. Philadelphia, 1847. 12°. . . 4074
Minor; a Collection of Popular Comedies. N.Y. 1847–54. 6 v. 12°. 3032

Vol. 1. Irish Attorney; Boots at the Swan; How to pay the Rent; Loan of a Lover; Dead Shot; Last Legs; Invisible Prince; Golden Farmer.—With Portrait and Memoir of John Sefton.
2. Pride of the Market; Used up; Irish Tutor; Barrack Room; Luke the Laborer; Beauty and the Beast; St. Patrick's Eve; Captain of the Watch.—With Portrait and Memoir of Miss C. Wemyss.
3. Secret; White Horse of the Peppers; Jacobite; Bottle; Box and Cox; Bamboozling; Widow's Victim; Robert Macaire.—With Portrait and Memoir of Francis S. Chanfrau.
4. Secret Service; Omnibus; Irish Lion; Maid of Croissey; Old Guard; Raising the Wind; Slasher and Crasher; Naval Engagement.—With Portrait and Memoir of Miss Rose Telbin.
5. Cocknies in California; Bombastes Furioso; Irish Ambassador; Weathercock; Who Speaks First?; Macbeth Travestie; Delicate Ground; All that Glitters is not Gold; Portrait and Memoir of William A. Goodall.
6. Grimshaw, Bagshaw, and Bradshaw; Bloomer Costume; Born to Good Luck; 'Twould Puzzle a Conjurer; Rough Diamond; Two Bonnycastles; Kiss in the Dark; Kill or Cure.—With Portrait and Memoir of Frederick M. Kent.

Modern British. London, 1811. 5 v. roy. 8°. 3941
Modern Standard. New York, 1846–54. 12 v. 12°. 2531

Vol. 1. Ion; Fazio, or the Italian Wife; Lady of Lyons; Richelieu, or the Conspiracy; The Wife, a Tale of Mantua; Honeymoon; School for Scandal; Money.—With Portrait and Memoir of Anna C. Mowatt.
2. Stranger; Grandfather Whitehead; Richard III.; Love's Sacrifice; Gamester; Cure for the Heartache; Hunchback; Don Cæsar de Bazan.—With Portrait and Memoir of Charles Kean.
3. The Poor Gentleman; Hamlet; Charles II., or the Merry Monarch; Venice Preserved; Pizarro; Love-Chase; Othello; Lend Me Five Shillings.—With Portrait and Memoir of Wm. E. Burton.
4. Virginius; King of the Commons; London Assurance; Rent-Day; Two Gentlemen of Verona; Jealous Wife; Rivals; Perfection.—With Portrait and Memoir of J. H. Hackett.
5. A New Way to Pay Old Debts; Look Before You Leap; King John; Nervous Man; Damon and Pythias; Clandestine Marriage; William Tell; The Day after the Wedding.—With Portrait and Memoir of George Colman the Elder.
6. Speed the Plough; Romeo and Juliet; Feudal Times; Charles the Twelfth; Bridal; Follies of a Night; Iron Chest; Faint Heart Never Won Fair Lady.—With Portrait and Memoir of Sir E. Bulwer Lytton.
7. Road to Ruin; Macbeth; Temper; Evadine; Bertram; Duenna; Much Ado About Nothing; Critic.—With Portrait and Memoir of Richard B. Sheridan.
8. Apostate; Twelfth Night; Brutus; Simpson & Co.; Merchant of Venice; Old Heads and Young Hearts; Mountaineers; Three Weeks After Marriage.—With Portrait and Memoir of George H. Barrett.

Drama, Modern Standard, *continued.*

9. Love; As You Like It; Elder Brother; Werner; Gisippus; Town and Country; King Lear; Blue Devils. — With Portrait and Memoir of Mrs. Shaw.
10. Henry the Eighth; Married and Single; Henry the Fourth (Part 1.); Paul Pry; Guy Mannering; Sweethearts and Wives; The Serious Family; She Stoops to Conquer. — With Portrait and Memoir of Charlotte Cushman.
11. Julius Cæsar; Vicar of Wakefield, Leap Year; The Catspaw; Passing Cloud; Drunkard; Rob Roy; George Barnwell. — With Portrait and Memoir of Mrs. John Sefton.
12. Ingomar; Sketches in India; Two Friends; Jane Shore; Corsican Brothers; Mind your Own Business; Writing on the Wall; Heir at Law. — With Portrait and Memoir of Thomas S. Hamblin.

Drama of Exile, and other Poems. E. B. Barrett. N. Y. 1845. 2 v. 12°. 2179
Dramas, Historical. F. Schiller. London, 1847. Post 8°. . . . 3555
Dramatic and Oratorical Expression. J. A. Fowler. Phil. 1833. 12°. . 5226
Dramatic Art and Literature, Lectures on. A. W. Schlegel. Phil. 1833. 8°. 1958
Dramatic Literature, Lectures on. W. Hazlitt. London, 1840. 12°. . 1871
Dramatic Poets, Specimens of English. C. Lamb. N. Y. 1845. 2 v. 12°. 2402
Dramatists, Lives of the British. T. Campbell, &c. Phil. 1846. 2 v. 12°. 2992
Drawing, Theory of Effect in. Philadelphia, 1851. 12°. . . . 3816
Drayton, J. View of South Carolina. Charleston, 1802. 8°. . . 1379
Dream; and other Poems. Mrs. C. E. S. Norton. New York, 1845. 16°. 2527
Dream-Land by Daylight. Caroline Chesebro'. New York, 1851. 12°. 4769
Dream Life. D. G. Mitchell. New York, 1851. 12°. 4636
Dream of a Day, and other Poems. J. G. Percival. N. Haven, 1843. 12°. 2327
Dreamer and the Worker. R. H. Horne. London, 1851. 2 v. 12°. . 4231
Druggist's General Receipt Book. H. Beasley. Philadelphia, 1853. 12°. 5063
The same. Philadelphia, 1850. 12°. 3672
Drugs, Medicine, &c., Examinations of. C. H. Peirce. Camb. 1852. 12°. 3875
Druitt, R. Modern Surgery. Philadelphia, 1851. 8°. 5991
Drury, Anna H. Eastbury; a Tale. New York, 1851. 12°. . . 4255
Light and Shade; or, Young Artist. New York, 1853. 12°. . 5205
Dryden, J., Criticism on. J. Wilson. Philadelphia, 1846. 12°. . . 2559
Life. Sir W. Scott. Boston, 1829. 12°. 399, 1
The same. Edinburgh, 1834. 12°. 4101, 1
Works, in Prose & Verse; with Life by J. Mitford. N.Y. 1837. 2v. 8°. 2730
Dublin University, History of. W. B. S. Taylor. London, 1845. 8°. . 4663
Dubois, J. A. Character of the People of India. Phil. 1818. 2 v. 8°. . 725
Du Bourg; or, the Mercuriale. M. A. S. Barber. London, 1851. 12°. . 4608
Duchess; or, Woman's Love and Woman's Hate. Phil. 1851. 8°. . 4011
Dudevant, Mde. Consuelo. Trans. by F. G. Shaw. Bost. 1850. 3 v. 12°. 2603
Countess of Rudolstadt (Sequel to Consuelo). Bost. 1847. 2 v. 12°. 2956
Jacques. New York, 1847. 2 v. 12°. 2957
Journeyman Joiner. New York, 1847. 12°. 3036
Duer, W. A. Constitutional Jurisp. of U. States. N. Y. 1848. 12°. 3683, 160
Life of W. Alexander (Earl of Sterling). New York, 1847. 8°. . 2800
Duffield, J. T. Princeton Pulpit. New York, 1852. 8°. . . . 4842
Duke of Monmouth. G. Griffin. Philadelphia, 1837. 2 v. 12°. . . 923
Dukes of Normandy. J. Duncan. London, 1839. 12°. 4563
Dumas, A. Amaury. New York, 1845. 8°. 2634

Dumas, A. Ascanio; or, the Sculptor's Apprentices. New York, 1846. 8°. 2643
(3) Bragelonne, the Son of Athos. New York, 1850. 8°. 3806
Chevalier D'Harmental. New York, 1846. 8°. 2697
Count of Monte-Cristo. New York, 1850. 2 v. 8°. 2735
Sequel to. — See *Edmond Dantes.*
Countess of Salisbury. New York, 1851. 8°. 4334
Crimes of the Borgias. New York, 1847. 8°. 2801
Diana of Meridor. New York, 1846. 8°. 2867
Foresters. New York, 1854. 12°. 5789
Emmanuel-Philibert. New York, 1854. 8°. 5988
Forty-Five Guardsmen. New York, 1848. 8°. 2895
Genevieve; or, Chevalier of Maison Rouge. New York, 1846. 8°. 2758
(4) Iron Mask. Philadelphia, 1850. 8°. 3979
(5) Louise la Valliere. Philadelphia, 1851. 2 v. 8°. 3807
Marguerite de Valois. New York, 1850. 8°. 2705
(*a*) Memoirs of a Physician. Philadelphia, 1851. 8°. 4338
Progress of Democracy in France. New York, 1841. 12°. . . 1910
(*b*) Queen's Necklace. Philadelphia, 1851. 2 v. 8°. 4037
Regent's Daughter. New York, 1845. 8°. 2229
Secret Belt of the Invisibles. New York, 1848. 8°. 3534
(*c*) Six Years Later. Philadelphia, 1853. 8°. 5407
Sketches in France. Philadelphia, 1852. 8°. 4693
(1) Three Guardsmen. New York, 1846. 8°. 2686
(2) Twenty Years After. New York, 1846. 8°. 2687
Dumourier, General. Autobiography. Philadelphia, 1794. 8°. . . 1304
Duncan, James. Bees. Edinburgh, 1843. 12°. 4901, 34
Beetles. Edinburgh, 1843. 12°. 4901, 33
British Butterflies. Edinburgh, 1843. 12°. . . . 4901, 29
British Moths, Sphinxes, &c. Edinburgh, 1843. 12°. . . 4901, 30
Exotic Moths. Edinburgh, 1843. 12°. 4901, 32
Foreign Butterflies. Edinburgh, 1843. 12°. 4901, 31
Introduction to Entomology. Edinburgh, 1843. 12°. . . 4901, 28
Duncan, John. Travels in Western Africa. London, 1847. 2 v. 12°. . 4965
Duncombe, C. Free Banking. Cleveland, 1841. 12°. 992
Dunglinson, R. Human Physiology. Philadelphia, 1844. 2 v. 8°. . 1795
Dunlap, W. History of the American Theatre. New York, 1832. 8°. . 1993
Dunlavy, J. Manifesto of the Church of Christ. New York, 1847. 8°. 2829
Dunlop, J. History of Fiction. Philadelphia, 1842. 2 v. 12°. . . 1912
Memoirs of Spain, from 1621 to 1700. Edinburgh, 1834. 2 v. 8°. 4545
Dupuy, A. E. Conspirator. New York, 1850. 12°. 4047
Durbin, J. P. Observations in Europe. New York, 1844. 2 v. 12°. . 2137
Observations in the East. New York, 1845. 2 v. 12°. . . 2499
Durham Village; a Temperance Tale. Boston, 1854. 12°. . . . 5842
Durivage, F. A. Life Scenes. Boston, 1853. 12°. 5549
Dutchman's Fireside. J. K. Paulding. New York, 1831. 2 v. 12°. . 415
Duxbury, Mass., History of. J. Winsor. Boston, 1849. 8°. . . . 2579
Dwight, H. G. O. Christianity Revived in the East. N.Y. 1850. 12°. . 3936
Dwight, Theo. Character of Thomas Jefferson. Boston, 1839. 12°. . 1012

Dwight, Theo. Roman Republic of 1849. New York, 1851. 12°. . 4262
History of the Hartford Convention. New York, 1833. 8°. . . 746
Summer Tours; or, Notes of a Traveller. New York, 1847. 12°. 3037
Dwight, Theo., jun. Hist. of Conn. (H. F. L.) N.Y. 1846. 12°. 3683, 133
Dwight, Timothy. Life. W. B. Sprague. Boston, 1844. 12°. . 1076, 14
Theology Explained and Defended. New York, 1854. 4 v. 8°. . 5999
Dyce, A. Remarks on Collier's & Knight's Shakspeare. London, 1844. 8°. 1115
Dyeing, Calico Printing, &c. E. Bancroft. Philadelphia, 1814. 2 v. 8°. 654
Practical Treatise on. New York, 1846. 8°. 2786
Chemistry applied to. J. Napier. Philadelphia, 1853. 12°. . 5566
Dyer, T. H. Life of John Calvin. New York, 1850. 8°. . . . 3648
Dymond, J. Essays on the Principles of Morality. New York, 1844. 8°. 2265
War, and the Principles of Christianity. Philadelphia, 1834. 12°. 2129
Dynamics of Magnetism, Heat, &c. C. von Reichenbach. Lond. 1851. 8°. 4159
Dyspepsia and Digestion. W. Sweetser. Boston, 1837. 12°. . . 1090

E.

Eagle Pass; or, Life on the Border. C. Montgomery. N.Y. 1852. 12°. 4989
Earl, G. W. Voyages in Eastern Seas, 1832–34. London, 1837. 8°. . 4688
Native Races of Indian Archipelago. London, 1853. 12°. . . 5741
Earl's Daughter. E. M. Sewell. New York, 1850. 12°. . . . 3886
Earlswood. Charlotte Anley. New York, 1853. 12°. 4999
Early Called. Mrs. C. Southey. New York, 1842. 12°. . . . 1045
Early Engagements. Sarah M. Hayden. Cincinnati, 1854. 12°. . . 5800
Early Rising, Advantages of. W. A. Alcott. Boston, 1836. 12°. . 898
Earnestness; or, Life of an English Bishop. C. B. Tayler. N.Y. 1850. 12°. 3913
Earth, The. R. Mudie. Philadelphia, 1836. 12°. 321
and Man. A. Guyot. Boston, 1852. 12°. 5213
its Condition & Phenom. W. M. Higgins. (H.F.L.) N.Y. 1846. 12°. 3683, 78
Pre-Adamite. J. Harris. Boston, 1849. 12°. 3304
Theory of. S. Fish. Boston, 1836. 12°. 898
Earths in our Solar System. E. Swedenborg. Boston, 1828. 12°. . 14
Earthquake; a Tale. J. Galt. New York, 1821. 2 v. 12°. . . . 1903
East and West; a Novel. F. W. Thomas. Philadelphia, 1836. 2 v. 12°. 271
East, The, Observations in. J. P. Durbin. New York, 1845. 2 v. 12°. 2499
1001 Days in. F. Bodenstedt. London, 1851. 2 v. 12°. . . 4444
Sketches of Travels in. J. A. Spencer. New York, 1850. 8°. . 3546
Thirty Years Changes in. W. Goodell. New York, 1853. 12°. . 5332
East Indian Recreations. W. Tennant. London, 1804. 2 v. 8°. . . 969
Eastbury; a Tale. Anna H. Drury. New York, 1851. 12°. . . 4255
Eastern Europe and Emperor Nicholas. London, 1846. 3 v. 12°. . . 4422
Eastern Life, Present and Past. Harriet Martineau. Phil. 1848. 12°. . 3118
Eastern Seas, Voyages in, 1832–34. G. W. Earl. Lond. 1837. 8°. . 4688
Eastern States, Letters on. New York, 1820. 12°. 462
Eastman, Mary H. Aunt Phillis's Cabin. Philadelphia, 1852. 12°. . 4853
Dahcotah; or, Life and Legends of the Sioux. N. Y. 1849. 12°. 3359

Easy Nat; or, the Three Apprentices. A. L. Stimson. N. Y. 1854. 12°. 6173
Eaton, A. Manual of Botany. Albany, 1824. 12°. 458
Eaton, C. Annals of Warren (Maine). Hallowell, 1851. 12°. . . . 959
Eaton, J. H. Life of Andrew Jackson. Philadelphia, 1824. 8°. . . 1061
Eaton, W. Life. Brookfield, 1813. 8°. 1337
Life. C. C. Felton. Boston, 1844. 12°. 1076, 9
Eben Erskine; or, the Traveller. J. Galt. Philadelphia, 1833. 2 v. 12°. 1924
Ecarté; or, the Salons of Paris. Major Richardson. N. Y. 1851. 8°. . 4556
Eccentric Biography. Boston, 1825. 18°. 128
Ecclesiastes, Lectures on. J. Hamilton. New York, 1851. 12°. . . 4297
Ecclesiastical History. Socrates (the Advocate). Lond. 1853. Post 8°. . 5747
of England. Bede. London, 1847. Post 8°. 4365
Ecclesiastical Polity, Laws of. R. Hooker. Oxford, 1843. 2 v. 8°. . 1961
Echoes of a Belle; or, a Voice from the Past. New York, 1853. 12°. . 5325
Echoes of the Universe. H. Christmas. Philadelphia, 1850. 12°. . 3917
Eckermann, J. P. Conversations with Goethe. Boston, 1839. 12°. . 3585
The same. Boston, 1839. 12°. 962, 4
Eckfeldt, J. R., & W. Dubois. New Gold and Silver Coins. N.Y. 1851. 8°. 4144
Eclectic Magazine. Vol. 17-32 [continued]. N. York, 1849-54. 8°. . 3616
Eclipse of Faith. H. Rogers. Boston, 1852. 12°. 4915
Defence of. H. Rogers. Boston, 1854. 12°. 5840
Eddy, D. C. Heroines of Missionary Enterprise. Boston, 1850. 12°. . 3678
Edgar, J. G. Footprints of Famous Men. New York, 1854. 12°. . 6154
Edgar, S. Variations of Popery. New York, 1852. 8°. 416
Edgar Clifton; or, Right and Wrong. C. Adams. N. York, 1853. 12°. 6344
Edgar Huntley. C. B. Brown. London, 1853. 12°. 5699
Edgeworth, Maria. Frank. Cambridge, 1822. 2 v. 12°. 487
Helen. New York, 1850. 12°. 935
The same. London, 1852. 12°. 5669
Tales and Novels. New York, 1845. 10 v. 12°. 1811

Vol. 1. Castle Rackrent; Essay on Irish Bulls.
2. Moral Tales.
3. Moral Tales.
4. Manœuvring; Almeria; Vivian.
5. Absentee; Madame de Fleury; Emilie de Coulanges; Modern Griselda.
6. Belinda.
7. Leonora; Letters on Female Education; Patronage.
8. Patronage; Comic Dramas.
9. Harrington; Thoughts on Bores; Ormond.
10. Helen.

Works. (Vols. 1, 5-8 wanting.) Boston, 1824-25. 13 v. 8°. . 1273

Vol. 2. Letters to Literary Ladies; Castle Rackrent; Leonora; Essay on Irish Bulls.
3. Belinda.
4. Vivian; Emilie de Coulanges; Absentee.
9. Modern Griselda; Moral Tales.
10. Parent's Assistant; Comic Dramas.
11. Early Lessons; Harry and Lucy; Rosamond.
12. Early Lessons; Frank and Sequel.
13. Harry and Lucy, concluded; Comic Dramas.

Edgeworth, R. L., Memoirs, by Himself and Daughter. Boston, 1821. 8°. 1412
Edinburgh, New Picture of. Edinburgh, n. d. 16°. 61
Edinburgh Journal, Chambers's. Edinburgh, 1844-53. 20 v. roy. 8°. . 709
Edinburgh to Dublin, Excursion. A. Bigelow, 1817. Boston, 1821. 12°. 444

*Edinburgh Review. Vols. 1–97 [continued]. Edinburgh, 1802–53. 8°. 1301
*Index to vols. 1–20. Edinburgh, 1813. 8°.
*Index to vols. 21–50. Edinburgh, 1832. 8°.
*Index to vols. 51–80. Edinburgh, 1850. 8°.
The same. Vols. 75–97. New York, 1842–53. 8°. . . 1301
Contributions to. F. Jeffrey. London, 1844. 4 v. 8°. . . 2608
The same. Philadelphia, 1848. 8°. 3418, 6
Selections from. Edited by M. Cross. Paris, 1835. 6 v. 8°. . 1913
Edleston, J. (Ed.) Corres. of Sir I. Newton and R. Cotes. Lond. 1850. 8°. 4330
Edmond Dantes; a Sequel to Monte-Cristo. G. W. Noble. Phil. 1853. 8°. 5492
Edmonds, J. W., and G. T. Dexter. Spiritualism. New York, 1853. 8°. 5447
Education. Lord Brougham. New York, 1839. 12°. 1891
American Journal of, 1830. Boston, 8°. 666
Central Society of. London, 1838. 2 v. 12°. 5040
Connecticut Documents. Hartford, 1853. 8°. 5971
Elementary Principles of. G. Spurzheim. Boston, 1836. 12°. . 146
Essays on Practical. London, 1836. 2 v. 12°. 5041

Vol. 1. Ascham, R. Schoolmaster.
Milton, J. Education.
Locke, J. Thoughts on Education.
Butler, Bishop. Charity-Schools.
Wayland, F. Introductory Discourse.
Sainteville, J. de. Moral Education.
Barwell, Mrs. Early Education.
Warren, J. C. Physical Education.
Long, G. Discipline of Schools.
Parkhurst, J. L. Motives to Study.
Oliver, H. K. Monitorial System.
Wittich, W. Prussian Schools.
2. Baker, C. Teaching Reading.
Thayer, G. F. Spelling of Words.
Long, G. Teaching by Pictures.
Study of Geography.
Study of Latin and Greek.
De Morgan, A. Teaching Arithmetic.
Teaching Fractional Arithmetic.
Teaching Geometry.
Mathematical Instruction.
Study of Natural Philosophy.
Vieusseux, A. Study of Italian.
Geography and Statistics.
Teaching the Italian.
Durgin, C. Study of Natural History.
Barwell, Mrs. Learning Singing.
Baker, C. Yorkshire Deaf and Dumb Inst.

History of. H. I. Schmidt. (H. F. L.) N. Y. 1848. 12°. 3683, 156
Home. I. Taylor. New York, 1838. 12°. 2356
Lectures on. H. Mann. Boston, 1848. 12°. 2323
Massachusetts Report, 1850. Boston, 1850. 8°. 3770
Massachusetts Reports, Twelve. H. Mann. Bost. 1838–48. 2 v. 8°. 4121
National, in Europe. H. Barnard. New York, 1854. 8°. . . 5960
Popular. I. Mayhew. New York, 1850. 12°. 4069
Self. Baron Degerando. Boston, 1832. 12°. 2255
Some Thoughts on. J. Locke. London, 1693. 12°. . . . 195
System of Popular. E. C. Wines. Philadelphia, 1838. 12°. . 1452
Educator, The; Prize Essays on Education. London, 1839. 12°. . . 5042
By J. Lalor; J. A. Heraud; E. Higginson; J. Simpson; Mrs. G. R. Porter.
Edward, D. B. History of Texas. Cincinnati, 1836. 12°. . . . 304
Edwards, B. B. Biography of Self-taught Men. Boston, 1832. 12°. . 1803
Writings; with Memoir. E. A. Park. Boston, 1853. 2 v. 12°. . 5289
(Editor.) Year Book; or, Manual of Reference. Phil. 1838. 12°. 2125
Edwards, B. British Colonies in West Indies. London, 1794. 2 v. 4°. . 2004
Edwards, Jona. Charity and its Fruits. New York, 1852. 16°. . . 4753
Life of Brainerd, abridged. Boston, 1821. 12°. 205
Religious Affections. New York, n. d. 16°. 311
History of Redemption. New York, n. d. 12°. 430

Edwards, Jona. Life. S. Miller. Boston, 1844. 12°. 1076, 8
Works; with Life. New York, 1830. 10 v. 8°. 1793

Vol. 1. Life; Farewell Sermon; Notes on Natural Science.
2. Inquiry into the Freedom of the Will; Doctrine of Original Sin Defended.
3. End for which God created the World; Nature of True Virtue; History of the Work of Redemption; Prayer; Marks of a Work of the Spirit of God.
4. Narrative of Surprising Conversions; Revival of 1740; Qualifications for Communion; Reply to Williams.
5. Religious Affections; Justification by Faith Alone; Pressing into the Kingdom of God; Ruth's Resolution; Justice of God in the Damnation of Sinners; Excellency of Jesus Christ.
6. Sermons.
7, 8. Sermons; Miscellaneous Theological Discussions.
9. Types of the Messiah; Notes on the Bible.
10. Memoirs of David Brainerd.

Edwards, Jona., 2d. Works and Life. T. Edwards. Bost. 1850. 2 v. 8°. 547
Edwards, W. H. Voyage up the Amazon. New York, 1847. 12°. . 3003
Edwin the Fair, & Isaac Comnenus. (Dramas.) H. Taylor. Lon. 1845. 24°. 2412
Effect in Drawing, Colors, &c., Theory of. Philadelphia, 1851. 12°. . 3816
Egeria; or Voices of Thoughts & Counsel. W. G. Simms. Phil. 1853. 12°. 5527
Egypt, American in, 1839–40. J. E. Cooley. New York, 1842. 8°. . 1692
Ancient, under the Pharaohs. J. Kendrick. N.Y. 1852. 2 v. 12°. 4930
and Candia, Rambles in. C. R. Scott. London, 1837. 2 v. 8°. . 3195
and the Holy Land, Travels in. H. Crosby. New York, 1851. 8°. 4120
G. Fisk. New York, 1848. 12°. 3573
J. A. Spencer. New York, 1850. 8°. . . . 3546
J. Thomas. Philadelphia, 1853. 12°. . . . 5304
and Nubia, Discoveries in. G. Belzoni. London, 1822. 2 v. 8°. 2655
Arabia Petræa, and the Holy Land. D. Millard. N.Y. 1849. 12°. 3290
S. Olin. New York, 1843. 2 v. 12°. . . . 1919
J. L. Stephens. New York, 1837. 2 v. 12°. . . 1054
Asia Minor, Syria, &c. C. J. Monk. London, 1851. 2 v. 12°. . 4233
Ethiopia, and Sinai, Letters from. R. Lespius. Lond. 1853. 12°. 5579
Handbook for Travellers in. G. Wilkinson. London, 1847. 12°. 60
History of. M. Russell. (H. F. L.) New York, 1846. 12°. 3683, 23
Memoirs relative to. London, 1800. 8°. 1282
Modern History and Condition of. W. H. Yates. Lond. 1843. 2 v. 8°. 3994
Monuments of. F. L. Hawks. New York, 1850. 8°. . . . 3446
Nile Boat. W. H. Bartlett. New York, 1851. Roy. 8°. . . . 4516
Nubia, & Palestine, Pilgrimage to. Mrs. Romer. Lon. 1846. 2 v. 8°. 4647
Palestine, Syria, &c., Travels in. J. P. Durbin. N.Y. 1845. 2 v. 12°. 2499
Photographic Views of. J. P. Thompson. New York, 1854. 12°. 5869
Pilgrimage to. J. V. C. Smith. Boston, 1852. 12°. 254
Travels in. V. Denon. New York, 1803. 2 v. 8°. 1199
under the Ptolomies, History of. S. Sharpe. London, 1838. 4°. . 3611
Village Life in. B. St. John. Boston, 1853. 2 v. 12°. . . . 4998
Egyptian Antiquities and Hieroglyphics. Marquis Spineto. Lond. 1845. 8°. 4667
Egyptians, Ancient. Sir J. G. Wilkinson. London, 1837. 3 v. 8°. . 2656
The same, revised and abridged. New York, 1854. 2 v. 12°. 5752
Hist. Researches concerning. A. H. L. Heeren. Ox. 1838. 2 v. 8°. 2657
1851; or, the Sandboys at the Great Exhibit. H. Mayhew. N.Y. 1852. 8°. 4807

Eighteenth Century, History of. F. C. Schlosser. London, 1843. 8 v. 8°. 5148
Elder, W. Periscopics; or, Current Subjects. New York, 1854. 12°. . 6188
Eldon, J. (Lord). Public and Private Life. H. Twiss. Phil. 1844. 2 v. 8°. 2089
Eldorado; or, Adven. in California. B. Taylor. N.Y. 1850. 2 v. 12°. 3835
Eleanor; or, Life without Love. Hannah G. Creamer. Bost. 1850. 12°. 3841
Electric Telegraph, Anecdotes of. London, n. d. 24°. 5047
Historical Sketch of. A. Jones. New York, 1852. 8°. . . 4845
Treatise on. E. Highton. London, 1852. 12°. 6059
Electricity, Treatise on. Sir W. S. Harris. London, 1853. 12°. . . 6041
Electro-Metallurgy, Elements of. A. Smee. New York, 1852. 12°. . 985
Manual of. J. Napier. Philadelphia, 1853. 12°. . . . 5567
Electrotype Manipulation. C. V. Walker. Philadelphia, 1852. 12°. . 5005
Elegant Extracts. Compiled by V. Knox. Vols. 2–4. Boston, 1826. 8°. 1407
from Eminent Poets. Boston, 1826. 6 v. 16°. 77
from Eminent Prose Writers. Boston, 1826. 6 v. 16°. . . 62
in Poetry. London, 1791. 8°. 593
Elements of Character. Mary G. Chandler. Boston, 1854. 12°. . . 6144
Elephant, Natural History of. (H. F. L.) New York, 1846. 12°. 3683, 164
Elenor Wyllys; a Tale. Ed. by J. F. Cooper. Phil. 1846. 2 v. 12°. . 2534
Eliot, John. Biog. Dic. of First Settlers of New Eng. Salem, 1809. 8°. 1313
Eliot, John (the Apostle). Life. C. Francis. Boston, 1840. 12°. . 1076, 5
Eliot, Sir John. Life. London, 1831. 12°. 1831, 2
Eliot, S. History of Liberty. Boston, 1353. 4 v. 12°. 5238
Part I. Ancient Romans, 2 v.—Part II. Early Christians, 2 v.
Liberty of Rome. New York, 1849. 2 v. 8°. 3419
Passages from the History of Liberty. Boston, 1847. 12°. . . 2965
Eliot, S. A. Sketch of Harvard College. Boston, 1848. 12°. . . 5330
Eliot, W. G., jun. Lectures to Young Men. Boston, 1854. 12°. . . 5639
Lectures to Young Women. Boston, 1853. 12°. 5553
Elizabeth, Queen, History of. J. Abbott. New York, 1849. 12°. . . 3766
History of. Agnes Strickland. Philadelphia, 1853. 2 v. 12°. 3524, 6, 7
The same. Philadelphia, 1843. 2 v. 12°. . . . 1911, 6, 7
Memoirs of the Court of. Lucy Aiken. Philadelphia, 1823. 8°. . 671
Elkswatawa; or, the Prophet of the West. New York, 1836. 2 v. 12°. . 232
Ella Stratford; or, the Orphan Child. Lady Blessington. Phil. 1850. 8°. 3460
Ellen Linn; a Franconia Story. J. Abbott. New York, 1850. 12°. . 5296
Ellen Middleton; a Tale. Lady G. Fullerton. New York, 1849. 12°. . 3175
Ellen Wareham; or, Love and Duty. Ellen Pickering. Phil. 1849. 8°. 3294
Ellery, W. Life. E. T. Channing. Boston, 1840. 12°. . . 1076, 6
Ellet, C., jun. Mississippi and Ohio Rivers. Phil. 1853. Roy. 8°. . 5391
Ellet, Mrs. E. F. Characters of Schiller. Boston, 1839. 12°. . . 988
Domestic History of the American Revolution. N.Y. 1850. 12°. 3923
Evenings at Woodlawn. New York, 1849. 12°. . . . 3414
Family Pictures from the Bible. New York, 1849. 12°. . . 3442
Pioneer Women of the West. New York, 1852. 12°. . . . 4919
Women of the American Revolution. New York, 1848. 2 v. 12°. 3170
Elliott, C. W. Mysteries; or, the Supernatural. New York, 1852. 12°. 4895
Elliott, E. Poetical Works. London, 1844. 3 v. 12°. 2312

Elliott Family; or, the N. Y. Seamstresses. C. Burdett. N. Y. 1850. 12°. 3675
Ellis, G. Specimens of the Early English Poets. London, 1845. 3 v. 12°. 5043
Specimens of Early Eng. Metrical Romances. Lond. 1848. Post 8°. 4370
Ellis, G. E. Life of Anne Hutchinson. Boston, 1845. 12°. . . . 1076, 16
Life of John Mason. Boston, 1844. 12°. 1076, 13
Life of William Penn. Boston, 1848. 12°. 1076, 22
Ellis, H. Journal of an Embassy to China. London, 1840. 8°. . . 2612
Ellis, Sir H. Letters Illustrative of Eng. History. 3d s. Lon. 1846. 4 v. 12°. 4581
Ellis, J., Letters to, 1686–88. Edited by Lord Dover. Lond. 1831. 2 v. 8°. 1492
Ellis, Mrs. Sarah. Fireside Stories. New York, 1850. 16°. . . . 3315
Hearts and Homes; or Social Distinction. New York, 1850. 2 v. 8°. 3397
Home; or, the Iron Rule. New York, 1843. 12°. 250
Look to the End; or, the Bennets Abroad. New York, 1845. 8°. 2242
Pretension. Philadelphia, 1837. 2 v. 12°. 942
Prevention better than Cure. New York, 1847. 12°. 2995
Select Works. New York, 1844. 8°. 1826
Women of England; Wives of England; Daughters of England; Poetry of Life.
Self-Deception; or, the History of a Human Heart. N.Y. 1851. 3 v. 8°. 4014
Summer and Winter, in the Pyrenees. London, 1841. 12°. . . 4571
Elocution. C. P. Bronson. Louisville, 1845. 8°. 4955
Art of. G. Vandenhoff. London, 1846. 12°. 2352
Exercises in. W. Russell. Boston, 1841. 12°. 2128
Lectures on. T. Sheridan. London, 1798. 8°. 5012
Vocal Culture in. J. E. Murdoch and W. Russell. Bost. 1845. 12°. 2351
Lessons in. Wm. Scott. Boston, 1814. 12°. 957
Elocutionist, American. W. Russell. Boston, 1844. 12°. . . . 2142
a First-class Rhetorical Reader. J. S. Knowles. N.Y. 1844. 12°. 2159
Eloquence of the British Senate. W. Hazlitt. Brooklyn, 1810. 2 v. 8°. 621
Principles of. Abbé Maury. (H. F. L.) N.Y. 1848. 12°. 3683, 184
Select British. C. A. Goodrich. New York, 1852. Roy. 8°. . 5083
Elves; and other Tales. L. Tieck. Trans. by T. Carlyle. N.Y. 1846. 8°. 2679
Elvira, the Nabob's Wife. Mrs. Monkland. Philadelphia, 1839. 2 v. 12°. 995
Elwes, A. Grammar of the Italian Language. London, 1852. 12°. . 6119
Grammar of the Spanish Language. London, 1852. 12°. . . 6120
Emancipation in the W. Indies. J. A. Thome & J. H. Kimball. N.Y. 1838. 8°. 699
Embanking Lands from the Sea. J. Wiggins. London, 1852. 12°. . 6089
Embassy to China. H. Ellis. London, 1840. 8°. 2612
G. Staunton. London, 1797. 8°. 716
to Cochin-China, Siam, and Muscat. E. Roberts. N.Y. 1837. 8°. 945
to Court of Ava. J. Crawfurd. London, 1834. 2 v. 8°. . . 4817
Embury, Mrs. E. C. Glimpses of Home Life. New York, 1848. 12°. . 3180
Emerson, B. D. Academical Speaker. Philadelphia, 1835. 12°. . . 1807
Emerson, G. B. Report on Trees and Shrubs of Mass. Boston, 1846. 8°. 2803
Emerson, J. E. Memoir. R. W. Clark. Boston, 1852. 12°. . . 4921
Emerson, R. W. Essays. 1st and 2d series. Boston, 1841–45. 2 v. 12°. 1601
Nature: Addresses and Lectures. Boston, 1849. 12°. . . . 3478
Poems. Boston, 1847. 12°. 2947
Representative Men. Boston, 1850. 12°. 3484

Emigrant, The. Sir F. B. Head. New York, 1847. 12°. 2951
Emma; a Novel. Jane Austen. Philadelphia, 1838. 8°. . . 1585, 2
The same. London, 1853. 12°. 5692
Emmanuel-Philibert. A. Dumas. New York, 1854. 8°. . . . 5988
Emmet, T. A., Memoir of. C. G. Haines. New York, 1829. 12°. . 220
Emmons, E. Report on Quadrupeds of Mass. Cambridge, 1840. 8°. 1969
Emmons, N. Works; with Life. Ed. by J. Ide. Boston, 1842. 6 v. 8°. 1686

Vol. 1. Autobiography; Additional Memoir; Recollections of a Visitor, by Prof. E. A. Park; Sermons on the Christian Ministry.
2. Sermons on Social and Civil Duties.
3. Instructions to the Afflicted.
4. Systematic Theology, viz.: God; Divine Revelation; Trinity; Standard of Moral Obligation; Revealed Character of God; Decrees of God; Divine and Human Agency; Angels; Original State of Man; Apostacy of Man; Present State of Man; Character of Christ.
5. Work of Christ; Justification; Work of the Spirit; Christian Character; Holiness; Prayer; Perseverance of the Saints; The Sabbath; The Church; Baptism; Lord's Supper; Future State.
6. Miscellaneous.

Emory, W. H. Military Reconnoissance to California. Wash. 1848. 8°. 3267
Employment for the People, Providing. S. Crumpe. London, 1795. 8°. 608
Encyclopædia Americana. Edited by F. Lieber. Phil. 1830–47. 14 v. 8°. 1384

Vol. 1. A to Bat.
2. Bat to Cat.
3. Cat to Cra.
4. Cra to Eve.
5. Eve to Gre.
6. Gre to Ind.
7. Ind to Lin.
Vol. 8. Lin to Mon.
9. Mon to Pen.
10. Pen to Rev.
11. Rev to Ste.
12. Ste to Vis.
13. Vis to Zwi, and Appendix.
14. Supplement.

*Britannica. Seventh edition. Edinburgh, 1842. 21 v. 4°. . . 2030

Vol. 1. Dissertations.
2. A to Ana.
3. Ana to Ast.
4. Ast to Bor.
5. Bor to Cal.
6. Cal to Clo.
7. Clo to Dia.
8. Dia to Eng.
9. Eng to Fox.
10. Fra to Gro.
11. Gro to Hyd.
Vol. 12. Hyd to Kyr.
13. Lab to Mag.
14. Mag to Mex.
15. Mey to Nav.
16. Nav to Pan.
17. Pan to Pla.
18. Pla to Quo.
19. Rab to Scu.
20. Scu to Swr.
21. Swr to Z.

British. W. Nicholson. Philadelphia, 1819–21. 12 v. 8°. . . 687

Vol. 1. Aba to Are.
2. Are to Buб.
3. Buc to Con.
4. Con to Ell.
5. Ell to Gil.
6. Gil to Iron.
Vol. 7. Iron to Med.
8. Med to Nic.
9. Nic to Pho.
10. Pho to Ryn.
11. Ryn to Sur.
12. Sur to Zyg.

Family. J. S. Blake. New York, 1837. 8°. 1884
Farmer's. C. W. Johnson. Philadelphia, 1850. Roy. 8°. . . 4358
National. — See *National Cyclopædia.*
of Architecture. J. Gwilt. London, 1851. 8°. 4528
of Civil Engineering. E. Cresy. London, 1847. 8°. . . . 4529
of Geography. H. Murray. Philadelphia, 1837. 3 v. roy. 8°. . 2010
of Music. J. W. Moore. Boston, 1854. Roy. 8°. 5961
of Religious Knowl. Ed. by J. N. Brown. Bratt. 1850. Roy. 8°. 4729
of Trees and Shrubs. J. C. Loudon. London, 1842. 8°. . . 5893

Encyclopædia, Penny. London, 1833–43. 28 v. in 14. Roy. 8°. . . 5100
Supplement. London, 1846. 2 v. roy. 8°. . . . 5100

Vols. 1, 2. A to Ath.
3, 4. Ath to Blo.
5, 6. Blo to Cha.
7, 8. Cha to Dio.
9, 10. Dio to Fru.
11, 12. Fue to Int.
13, 14. Int to Mas.
15, 16. Mas to Org.
Vols. 17, 18. Org to Pri.
19, 20. Pri to Sca.
21, 22. Sca to Ste.
23, 24. Ste to Tit.
25, 26. Tit to Wal.
27, 28. Wal to Zyg.
Sup. 1. Aba to Gyr.
2. Hab to Zum.

Endless Amusement; a Collection of 400 Experiments. Phil. 1847. 12°. 2440
Endymion; a Tale of Greece. H. B. Hirst. Boston, 1848. 12°. . . 3127
Enemies of the Constitution Discovered, &c. New York, 1835. 12°. . 1535
Enfield, W. History of Philosophy. London, 1839. 8°. 1426
England, American in. A. S. Mackenzie. New York, 1835. 2 v. 12°. . 1108
and the Continent. Travels in. J. H. Sherburne. Phil. 1847. 12°. 2978
and the English. E. L. Bulwer. New York, 1833. 2 v. 12°. . 1150
and France, under the House of Lancaster. London, 1852. 8°. . 5140
and its People, First Impression of. H. Miller. Bost. 1851. 12°. 4193
and Wales. J. G. Kohl. Philadelphia, 1844. 8°. . . . 2684
by an American. J. F. Cooper. Philadelphia, 1837. 2 v. 12°. . 905
Child's History of. C. Dickens. New York, 1854. 2 v. 12°. . 5829
Chronicle of Kings of. William of Malmesbury. Lon. 1847. Post 8°. 3563
Comment. on the Laws of. Sir W. Blackstone. N.Y. 1849. 2 v. 8°. 3592
The same. New York, 1844. 2 v. 8°. 2218
Condition and Fate of. C. E. Lester. New York, 1843. 2 v. 12°. 1708
Constitution of. J. L. de Lolme. Ed. by Stephens. Lond. 1810. 8°. 695
Constitutional History of. H. Hallam. Paris, 1841. 3 v. 8°. . 1823
Court of, under the Stuarts. J. H. Jesse. Phil. 1840. 2 v. 12°. . 2148
Court of, under Cromwell. J. H. Jesse. Phil. 1840. 2 v. 12°. . 2149
Ecclesiastical History of. Bede. London, 1847. Post 8°. . . 4365
Fame and Glory of, Vindicated. New York, 1842. 12°. . . 1682
France, &c., Running Sketches in. G. Copway. N. Y. 1851. 12°. 4435
Glory and Shame of. C. E. Lester. New York, 1841. 2 v. 12°. . 1654
History of. J. Bigland. Boston, 1815. 2 v. 8°. 698
History of. O. Goldsmith. Philadelphia, 1850. 12°. . . 285
The same, continued by C. Coote. London, 1812. 4 v. 8°. 4981
History of. D. Hume. Boston, 1851. 6 v. 12°. 3499
The same. Boston, 1854. 6 v. 8°. 5499
The same. New York, 1846. 2 v. 8°. 705
Continued. T. Smollett. Phil. 1846. 8°. . . 705, 3
The same. Philadelphia, 1832. 8°. . . . 730
Continued. J. R. Miller. Philadelphia, 1844. 8°. . 705, 4
The same. Philadelphia, 1832. 8°. . . . 755
History of. T. Keightley. Boston, 1840. 2 v. 8°. 1786
The same. (H. F. L.) N. York, 1846. 5 v. 12°. 3683, 114–18
History of. J. Lingard. Paris, 1840. 8 v. 8°. 3542
History of. J. Mackintosh. Philadelphia, 1830. 3 v. 12°. . . 76
History of. Lord Mahon. New York, 1849. 2 v. 8°. 3262
History of, 1816–1846. H. Martineau. Lond. 1849. 2 v. roy. 8°. 3793

England, History of. T. B. Macaulay. New York, 1849. 2 v. 8°. . 3257
History of Rebellion. Earl Clarendon. Oxford, 1826. 8 v. 8°. . 2256
History of the Reign of George III. R. Bisset. Alb. 1816. 2 v. 8°. 1264
History of, to 1235. R. de Wendover. Lond. 1849. 2 v. post 8°. 4366
in 16th, 17th, & 18th Centuries. F. von Raumer. Lond. 1837. 2v. 8°. 2842
Ireland, and France, Tour in. Pückler Muskau. Phil. 1833. 8°. 2723
Lec. on Const. and Laws of. F. S. Sullivan. Portl. 1805. 2 v. 12°. 3584
Letters from. M. A. Espriella. Boston, 1808. 12°. . . . 425
Letters on. J. E. White. Philadelphia, 1816. 2 v. 8°. . . 1375
Month in. H. T. Tuckerman. New York, 1854. 12°. . . 5748
Outline History of. W. D. Hamilton. London, 1852. 12°. . 6113
Pictorial History of. New York, 1847. 4 v. roy. 8°. . . . 2899
Queens of. Agnes Strickland. Philadelphia, 1843. 11 v. 12°. . 1911
The same. Philadelphia, 1849. 12 v. 12°. 3524
Recollections of. F. A. de Chateaubriand. Phil. 1816. 8°. . 740
Retrospect of Public Affairs for 1831. Boston, 1831. 2 v. 12°. . 1013
Royal Prerogative Power in. J. Allen. London, 1849. 8°. . 5415
Rural Life in. W. Howitt. Philadelphia, 1841. 8°. . . . 2061
under the House of Hanover. T. Wright. London, 1848. 2 v. . 5159
under Seven Administrations. A. Fonblanque. Lon. 1837. 3 v. 12°. 2379
Views of. M. Pillet. Boston, 1818. 12°. 181
White Slaves of. J. C. Cobden. Auburn, 1853. 8°. . . . 5385
English, G. B. Expedition to Dongola and Sennaar. Boston, 1823. 8°. 1378
English Chronicles, Six Old. Ed. by J. A. Giles. Lond. 1848. Post 8°. 4367

Ethelwerd's Chronicle; Asser's Life of Alfred; Geoffrey of Monmouth's British History; Gildas; Nennius; Richard of Cirencester.

English Comic Writers, Lectures on. W. Hazlitt. London, 1841. 12°. . 1874
English Composition, Aids to. R. G. Parker. Boston, 1844. 12°. . 1922
Exercises in. R. G. Parker. Boston, 1835. 12°. . . . 1810
English Constitution and Laws. F. S. Sullivan. Portl. 1805. 2 v. 12°. 3584
Book of. T. Stephen. Glasgow, n. d. 8°. 2859
Rise and Progress of. J. L. De Lolme. Ed. by A. J. Stephens. Lond. 5474
English Envoy at Court of Nicholas I. Julia Corner. N. Y. 1854. 12°. 6178
English Dramatic Poets, Specimens of. C. Lamb. N. Y. 1845. 2 v. 12°. 2402
English Grammar. H. Clarke. London, 1852. 12°. 6115
J. P. Wilson. Philadelphia, 1817. 12°. 586
English Grammars, Grammar of. G. Brown. New York, 1851. 8°. . 4699
English History, Tales from. Agnes Strickland. New York, 1854. 12°. 5630
English Humorists of the 18th Century. W. M. Thackeray. N.Y. 1853. 12°. 5342
English in America, Rule and Misrule of. T. C. Haliburton. N.Y. 1851. 12°. 4467
English Items. M. F. Ward. New York, 1853. 12°. 5211
English Language, Gram. Structure of. J. Mulligan. N.Y. 1852. 8°. 5122
English Literature, Cyclopædia of. R. Chambers. Bost. 1851. 2 v. roy. 8°. 2636
History of. W. Spalding. New York, 1853. 12°. . . . 5265
Outlines of. T. B. Shaw. Philadelphia, 1849. 12°. . . . 3277
English Metrical Romances, Specimens of Early. G. Ellis. Lond. 1848. 8°. 4370
English Poetry, History of. T. Warton. London, 1840. 3 v. 8°. . . 5476
English Poets, Lectures on. W. Hazlitt. London, 1841. 12°. . . 1875

English Poets. Lives of. S. Johnson. London, 1810. 2 v. 8°. . . . 686
English Preachers, Sketches of Popular. J. R. Dix. Lond. 1852. 12°. 6243
English Reading, Course of. J. Kent. New York, 1853. 12°. . . . 5203
J. Pycroft. New York, 1845. 12°. 2297
English Reformation, Original Letters on. Camb. (Eng.), 1846. 2 v. 8°. 5912
See also *Reformation.*
English Revolution of 1640, History of. F. Guizot. N.Y. 1846. 2 v. 12°. 2565
of 1688, History of. F. E. Dahlmann. London, 1844. 8°. 4678
of 1688, History of. Sir J. Mackintosh. Lond. 1846. 8°. 2703, 2
English Soldier in the U. S. Army, Autobiography of. N.Y. 1853. 12°. 5274
English Stage, History of. T. Betterton. Boston, 1814. 8°. 2074
View of. W. Hazlitt. London, 1818. 8°. 2289
English Synonymes. G. Crabb. Boston, 1819. 8°. 1292
G. F. Graham. New York, 1847. 12°. 3004
English Versification, System of. Erastus Everett. New York, 1848. 12°. 3108
English University, Five Years in an. C. A. Bristed. N.Y. 1852. 2 v. 12°. 4763
English Words, Thesaurus of. P. M. Roget. Boston, 1854. 12°. . . 5781
Englishwoman in Egypt. Mrs. S. Poole. Philadelphia, 1845. 16°. . 2405
Englishwomen, Memoirs of Eminent. L. S. Costellow. Lond. 1844. 4 v. 8°. 4342
Enterprise, Industry, & Art of Man. S. G. Goodrich. Bost. 1849. 12°. 4900, 18
Entertaining Knowledge, Youth's Handbook of. Lond. 1844. 2 v. 12°. . 4261
Entertaining Naturalist. Mrs. Loudon. London, 1850. 12°. . . 4565
Euthanasy; or, Happy Talk, &c. W. Mountford. Boston, 1848. 12°. . 3174
Enthusiasm, Natural History of. I. Taylor. Boston, 1830. 12°. . . 1923
The same. New York, 1849. 12°. 3609
Entomology. — See *Naturalist's Library.*
Entz, J. F. Exchange & Cotton Trade between Eng. & U. S. N.Y. 1840. 8°. 1651
Enunciation, Lessons in. W. Russell. Boston, 1843. 12°. . . . 1889
Envy. E. Sue. New York, 1848. 8°. 3214
Eoline; or, Magnolia Vale. Caroline L. Hentz. Philadelphia, 1852. 12°. 5221
Eöthen; or, Travels in the East. R. Kinglake. New York, 1845. 12°. 2330
Eötvös, Baron. Village Notary; a Hungarian Romance. N.Y. 1850. 8°. 3643
Ephesians, Philip., and Colos., Notes on. A. Barnes. N. Y. 1851. 12°. 4735
Epicurian, The. T. Moore. Boston, 1831. 16°. 46
Episcopal Church, Dictionary of. W. Staunton. New York, 1839. 12°. 2447
Episodes of Insect Life. New York, 1851. 3 v. 8°. 4128
Epitaphs from Copp's Hill. T. Bridgman. Boston, 1851. 12°. . . 4466
in Graveyards of Northampton. T. Bridgman. North. 1850. 12°. 4215
in King's Chapel Burial Ground. T. Bridgman. Bost. 1853. 12°. 5596
Epistolary Correspondence, Gems of. R. A. Willmott. Lon. 1846. 2 v. 12°. 4569
Equestrian Manual, Lady's. Philadelphia, 1854. 12°. 5836
Erasmus. Life. C. Butler. London, 1825. 8°. 2609
Erman, A. Travels in Siberia. Philadelphia, 1850. 2 v. 12°. . . . 3853
Ernest Maltravers. E. L. Bulwer. New York, 1837. 2 v. 12°. . . 909
Sequel to (Alice). E. L. Bulwer. New York, n.d. 8°. . . . 932
Erskine, T. (Lord). Selection of Speeches. London, 1853. Roy. 8°. . 5482
Speeches; with Memoir, by Lord Brougham. Lond. 1847. 2 v. 8°. 5484
Speeches on Liberty of the Press, &c. New York, 1813. 2 v. 8°. 2668

Esling, Mrs. C. H. W. Broken Bracelet, and other Poems. Phil. 1850. 12°. 4048
Espriella, M. A. Letters from England. Boston, 1808. 12°. . . 425
Espy, J. P. Philosophy of Storms. Boston, 1841. 8°. 1981
Essays & Tracts on Theology. Ed. by J. Sparks. Boston, 1823. 2 v. 12°. 368
For Contents, see *Sparks, J.*
for Summer Hours. C. Lanman. New York, 1853. 12°. . . 5365
from the London Times. New York, 1852. 2 v. 12°. . . . 262
of Elia. C. Lamb. New York, 1852. 12°. 3453
on the Formation of Opinions. S. Bailey. Philadelphia, 1831. 12°. 2160
The same. Boston, 1854. 12°. 5855
on the Pursuit of Truth. S. Bailey. Philadelphia, 1831. 12°. . 2156
The same. Boston, 1854. 12°. 5855
Written in the Intervals of Business. London, 1842. 16°. . . 2184
Estray; a Collection of Poems. Boston, 1847. 12°. 2948
Essayists, Modern British. Philadelphia, 1848. 8 v. 8°. . . . 3418

Vol. 1. T. B. Macaulay.
2. Sir A. Alison.
3. Sydney Smith.
4. John Wilson (Chris. North).
Vol. 5. Thomas Carlyle.
6. Francis Jeffrey.
7. T. N. Talfourd; J. Stephen.
8. Sir James Mackintosh.

Ethel Churchill; or, the Two Brides. L. E. Landon. Phil. 1847. 8°. 1343, 2
Ether Controversy, Statements on. W. T. G. Morton. Wash. 1853. 8°. 5160
Ethical Philosophy, Progress of. Sir J. Mackintosh. Phil. 1845. 8°. . 3608
Ethics, Introduction to. T. Jouffroy. Boston, 1841. 2 v. 12°. . 962, 5, 6
Manual of Political. F. Lieber. Boston, 1838. 2 v. 8°. . . 1783
of Aristotle. Trans. by R. W. Browne. London, 1850. Post 8°. 4388
Ethiopia, Highlands of. W. C. Harris. New York, 1845. 8°. . . 2271
Ethiopians, Hist. Researches concerning. A. H. L. Heeren. Ox. 1838. 2 v. 8°. 2657
Ethnology, Progress of. J. R. Bartlett. New York, 1847. 8°. . . 2792
Ethnological Society, Transactions of the American. N.Y. 1845. 2 v. 8°. 3384
Etiquette, Treatise on. A. D'Orsay. Philadelphia, 1854. 8°. . . 5915
Etruria, History of. Mrs. H. Gray. London, 1843. 2 v. 12°. . . 3788
Euclid, Elements of. Edited by H. Law. London, 1853. 12°. . . 6098
Edited by J. Playfair. New York, 1828. 8°. . . . 617
Edited by R. Simson. Philadelphia, 1825. 8°. . . . 694
(in French.) Paris, 1746. 12°. 1541
Eugene Aram. E. L. Bulwer. New York, 1832. 2 v. 12°. . . . 1488
The same. London, 1853. 12°. 5701
Eugénie, the Young Laundress. M. de La Voye. Lond. 1851. 3 v. 12°. 4251
Euler, L. Letters on Nat. Philosophy. (H.F.L.) N.Y. 1848. 2v. 12°. 3683, 55, 56
Euripides, Tragedies. Trans. by T. A. Buckley. Lond. 1850. 2 v. post 8°. 4387
Trans. by R. Potter. New York, 1842. 3 v. 12°. 1854, 15–17
The same. New York, 1848. 3 v. 12°. . . . 3761
Europe, after Congress of Aix-la-Chapelle. M. de Pradt. Phil. 1820. 8°. 1388
and the East, Travels in. V. Mott. New York, 1842. 8°. . . 1710
Budget of Letters from. Boston, 1847. 12°. 3044
Countries of, Described. Philadelphia, 1849. 12°. . . . 3313
during the Middle Ages. H. Hallam. New York, 1837. 8°. . 1395
Eleven Weeks in. J. F. Clarke. Boston, 1852. 12°. . . . 4773
a General Survey. A. H. Everett. Boston, 1822. 8°. . . 1359

Europe, Glances at. H. Greeley. New York, 1851. 12°. 4497
Gleanings in: England. J. F. Cooper. Phil. 1837. 2 v. 12°. . 905
Gleanings in: France. J. F. Cooper. Philadelphia, 1837. 2 v. 12°. 273
Handbook for American Travellers in. R. Park. N.Y. 1853. 12°. 5312
History of, 1789–1815. A. Alison. New York, 1842. 4 v. 8°. . 1735
History of, from 1815 to 1852. Sir A. Alison. N. York, 1853. 8°. 5156
History of Ancient. W. Russell. Philadelphia, 1801. 2 v. 8°. . 1966
History of Modern, to 1763. W. Russell. Phil. 1822. 4 v. 8°. . 1998
The same, abridged. Hanover, 1810. 12°. 1023
The same, con. to 1815. C. Coote. Phil. 1822. 2 v. 8°. 1998, 5, 6
The same. Philadelphia, 1811. 8°. 1377
Holidays Abroad in. Mrs. C. M. Kirkland. N. Y. 1819. 2 v. 12°. 3375
in a Hurry. G. Wilkes. New York, 1852. 12°. 5021
Letters from. Cath. M. Sedgwick. New York, 1841. 2 v. 12°. . 1626
Letters from, 1849. New York, 1851. 12°. 4031
Loiterings in. J. W. Corson. New York, 1848. 12°. . . 3142
Men and Things in. N. Murray. New York, 1853. 12°. . . 5569
Observations in. J. P. Durbin. New York, 1844. 2 v. 12°. . 2137
Observations in, 1843–44. J. Mitchell. New York, 1845. 2 v. 12°. 2491
Past and Present. F. H. Ungewitter. New York, 1850. 12°. . 3897
Rambles in. M. Trafton. Boston, 1852. 12°. 4591
Reminiscences of an Old Traveller in. Edinburgh, 1833. 12°. . 1574
Scenes and Thoughts in. G. H. Calvert. New York, 1846. 12°. 2591
Sights and Scenes in. Mrs. A. T. J. Bullard. St. Louis, 1852. 12°. 5189
Tour in; Old Sights with New Eyes. New York, 1854. 12°. . 5599
Travels in. W. Fisk. New York, 1841. 8°. 2051
Travels in. W. Furniss. New York, 1850. 12°. . . . 3441
Travels in. A. McFarland. Boston, 1851. 12°. . . . 5291
Travels in, 1837–38. J. A. Clark. Philadelphia, 1840. 2 v. 12°. . 1319
Travels in. Mrs. S. J. Lippincott. Boston, 1854. 2 v. 12°. . 5624
Travels in, 1805–6. B. Silliman. New Haven, 1820. 3 v. 12°. . 378
Travels in. Mrs. H. B. Stowe. Boston, 1854. 2 v. 12°. . . 6156
Vanderbilt's Steam Excursion to. J. O. Choules. Bost. 1854. 12°. 5770
Views A-Foot. B. Taylor. New York, 1852. 12°. 2940
Visit to. H. P. Tappan. New York, 1852. 2 v. 12°. . . 4872
Visit to. A. Tripp. Boston, 1853. 12°. 5239
Visit to, in 1851. B. Silliman. New York, 1853. 2 v. 12°. . 5519
Visit to Northern. R. Baird. New York, 1841. 2 v. 12°. . . 2119
Young Americans in. Ed. by J. O. Choules. Boston, 1852. 12°. 4638
European Agriculture & Rural Economy. H. Colman. Bost. 1849. 2 v. 8°. 3268
European Capitals, Sketches of. W. Ware. Boston, 1851. 12°. . . 4426
European Commerce. C. W. Rördansz. Boston, 1819. 8°. . . . 639
European Hist., Lights and Shadows of. S. G. Goodrich. Bost. 1849. 12°. 4900, 8
European Life and Manners. H. Colman. Boston, 1849. 2 v. 12°. . 3272
Eustaphieve, A. Demetrius; an Epic Poem. Boston, 1818. 12°. . . 479
Evangeline; a Tale of Acadie. H. W. Longfellow. Boston, 1847. 12°. 3055
Evans, E. Pedestrious Tour of 4000 Miles. Concord, 1819. 12°. . 443
Evans, R. M. Story of Joan of Arc. New York, 1847. 12°. . . 3089

Evans, R. W. Rectory of Valehead. Philadelphia, 1832. 12°. . . . 1501
Evarts, J. Life. E. C. Tracy. Boston, 1845. 8°. 4714
Eve of the Deluge. H. W. V. Stuart. London, 1851. 12°. . . . 4256
Evelina. Miss F. Burney. New York, 1852. 2 v. 12°. . . . 4890
Evelyn, C. (Ed.) Table Talk of Books, Men, & Manners. N. Y. 1853. 12°. 5032
Evelyn, J. Diary and Correspondence. London, 1850. 4 v. 8°. . . 5756
Life of Mrs. Godolphin. New York, 1847. 12°. . . . 2436
Evening Book. Mrs. C. M. Kirkland. New York, 1853. 12°. . . 5328
Evenings at Donaldson Manor. Maria J. McIntosh. N. York, 1851. 8°. 4309
The same. New York, 1853. 12°. 4926
at Home. J. Aikin and Mrs. Barbauld. New York, 1850. 12°. . 3445
at Sea; from Blackwood. London, 1853. 12°. 5631
at Woodlawn. Mrs. E. F. Ellet. New York, 1849. 12°. . . 3414
Eventide; Tales and Poems. Miss Harper. Boston, 1854. 12°. . . 6237
Everest, C. W. Poets of Connecticut. New York, 1844. 8°. . . 2268
Everett, A. H. America; a General Survey. Philadelphia, 1827. 8°. . 1354
Critical and Miscellaneous Essays. Boston, 1845. 12°. . . 2526

Vol. 1. Mde. de Sévigné; Who Wrote Gil Blas? Life of B. de St. Pierre; Life and Writings of Schiller; French Dramatic Literature; Private Life of Voltaire; Art of Being Happy; Life and Works of Canova; Sir James Mackintosh; Cicero on Government; Dialogue on Government between Franklin and Montesquieu; Chinese Manners; The Sabbath; Poems.

2. Harro Harring; Mde. de Staël; Musæus's Popular Tales; Irving's Columbus; De Gerando's History of Philosophy; Greenough's Statue of Washington; Stewart's Philosophy; Jean J. Rousseau; Havana; History of Intellectual Philosophy; Lord Vapourcourt.

Europe; a General Survey. Boston, 1822. 8°. 1359
Life of Patrick Henry. Boston, 1844. 12°. 1076, 11
Life of Joseph Warren. Boston, 1844. 12° 1076, 10
Everett, Edward, Beauties of; with Sketch of Life. Boston, 1839. 24°. 1497
Biography of Daniel Webster. Boston, 1851. 8°. . . . 1648, 1
Defence of Christianity. Boston, 1814. 14°. 2110
Eulogy on J. Q. Adams. Boston, 1848. 8°. 3533
Life and Character of John Lowell, jun. Boston, 1843. 8°. . 2251, 1
Life of John Stark. Boston, 1838. 12°. 1076, 1
Orations and Speeches. Boston, 1836. 8°. 795
The same. Boston, 1850. 2 v. 8°. 3973
Everett, Erastus. System of English Versification. New York, 1848. 12°. 3108
Every-Day Book. New York, 1842. 12°. 1887
Evidences of Christianity. — See *Christianity*.
Evil, Origin, Uses, and Remedies of. W. Burton. Boston, 1832. 12°. . 1528
Ewbank, T. Hydraulics and Mechanics. New York, 1846. 8°. . . 2790
Examiner, The. August, 1849, to May, 1850. London, 4°. . . . 3732
Examples of Life and Death. Mrs. L. H. Sigourney. N.Y. 1852. 12°. . 4748
Exchange between England and U. S. J. F. Entz. N. Y. 1840. 8°. . 1651
Interest, Money, &c., Essays on. J. R. McCulloch. Bost. 1850. 8°. 3984

Interest, and the Effect of the Usury Laws; Foreign and Domestic Exchange; Money, Coins, Bullion, Currency, Seignorage, Degradation of Standard, &c.; Tables.

Excursion, The; a Poem. W. Wordsworth. New York, 1849. 12°. . 3436

Exhibition of 1851. C. Babbage. London, 1851. 8°. 4345
Lectures on the Results of. London, 1852. 8°. 4849

Whewell, W. Inaugural Lecture.	Solly, E. Vegetable Substances.
De la Beche, Sir H. Mining, &c.	Willis, R. Machines.
Owen, R. Animal Products.	Glaisher, J. Philosophical Instruments.
Bell, J. Chemical Processes.	Hensman, R. Civil Engineering.
Playfair, L. Industrial Education.	Royle, J. F. Manufactures of India.
Lindley, J. Substances used as Food.	Washington, Capt. Life-Boats.

Official Catalogue. London, 1851. 8°. 4339
Exile into Siberia. A. von Kotzebue. New York, 1802. 12°. . . 871
Exiles, The. Mrs. Robinson (Talvi). New York, 1853. 12°. . . 5513
Expectant, The; a Novel. E. Pickering. Philadelphia, 1842. 2 v. 12°. 1697
Expedition of the British Fleet to Sicily, 1718–20. London, 1739. 12°. . 493
to the Dead Sea. — See *Dead Sea.*
to River Jordan and Dead Sea. W. F. Lynch. Phil. 1849. 8°. . 2850
to the Rocky Mountains. J. C. Fremont. Buffalo, 1851. 12°. . 2639
to the Sources of the Mississippi. Z. M. Pike. Phil. 1810. 8°. . 1341
Experience of Life. E. M. Sewell. New York, 1853. 12°. . . . 5196
Experiences of a Barrister. S. Warren. New York, 1852. 12°. . . 4771
of a Gaol Chaplain. London, 1850. 12°. 5686
Explanatory Bible Atlas. W. Jenks. Boston, 1847. 4°. . . . 3232
Exploring Expedition, U.S., 1838–42. C. Wilkes. Phil. 1845. 5 v. roy. 8°. 2244
Exploring Expeditions, U. States. J. S. Jenkins. Auburn, 1850. 8°. . 3620
Exposition of the Weakness of the Govt. of the U. States. 1845. 12°. . 2906
Extemporaneous Preaching, Hints on. H. Ware, jun. Boston, 1831. 12°. 1882
Extracts from the Best Authors. New York, 1827. 5 v. 12°. . . 408
Extraordinary Men. W. Russell. London, 1853. 12°. 5343

F.

Fabens, J. W. Camel Hunt. New York, 1853. 12°. 4621
Life on the Isthmus. New York, 1853. 12°. 5073
Faber, G. S. Difficulties of Infidelity. New York, 1853. 12°. . . 5346
Fable for Critics. J. R. Lowell. New York, 1848. 12°. . . . 3182
Fables, Æsop's; Illustrated. Edited by T. James. London, 1848. 8°. . 4536
Fables. J. La Fontaine. Trans. by E. Wright. Boston, 1842. 2 v. 12°. 1746
*The same. Boston, 1841. 8°. 2334
Illustrated by Facts. W. O. Bourne. New York, 1853. 12°. . 5022
Select. T. and J. Bewick. Newcastle, 1820. 8°. . . . 5899
Fact and Fiction; a Collection of Stories. L. M. Child. N.Y. 1846. 12°. 2937
Fadette; a Domestic Story. Trans. by Matilda M. Hays. N.Y. 1851. 12°. 4039
Faerie Queene. E. Spenser. Boston, 1839. 12°. 1920, 1
and Spenser. J. S. Hart. Philadelphia, 1854. 12°. . . . 6223
Faesch, G. R. L'Art de la Guerre. Leipzig, 1771. 2 v. 8°. . . . 710
Faggot of French Sticks. Sir F. B. Head. New York, 1852. 12°. . 4755
Fair Maid of Perth. Sir W. Scott. Boston, 1848. 2 v. 12°. . . 999, 41, 42
The same. Edinburgh, 1849. 2 v. 12°. . . 4100, 42, 43
The same. Edinburgh, 1851. Roy. 8°. . . . 4531, 11

Fairbairn, P. Typology of Scripture. Philadelphia, 1852. 2 v. 8°. . 4710
Fairfax Correspondence. Edited by G. W. Johnson. Lond. 1848. 4 v. 8°. 4690
Fairy Land, Adventures in. R. H. Stoddard. Boston, 1853. 12°. . 5234
Fairy Mythology. T. Keightley. London, 1849. Post 8°. . . . 4368
Fairy Tales and Romances. Count A. Hamilton. London, 1849. Post 8°. 3447
Faith, Develop.; Discipline and Fruits of. G. B. Cheever. N.Y. 1849. 12°. 3432
Falcon Family; or, Young Ireland. M. W. Savage. Boston, 1848. 8°. 2898
Falkland; a Novel. E. L. Bulwer. Philadelphia, 1843. 8°. . . . 1757
Fall of the Indian, and other Poems. I. McLellan, jun. Boston, 1830. 12°. 502
Fall of Man, Scriptural Account of. C. Chauncy. London, 1785. 8°. . 1225
Falls, Lakes, and Mounts. of N. Wales. L. S. Costellow. Lond. 1845. 12°. 2388
False Heir. G. P. R. James. New York, 1843. 8°. 1726
Fame and Glory of England Vindicated. New York, 1842. 12°. . . 1682
Family Book; or, Instructions on the Relations of Life. N.Y. 1835. 12°. 2112
Family Pictures from the Bible. Mrs. E. F. Ellet. New York, 1849. 12°. 3442
Family Tourist. C. A. Goodrich. Hartford, 1848. 8°. 3622
Famine in Ireland, 1847–49. Mrs. A. Nicholson. New York, 1851. 12°. 4161
Famous Men and Places. N. P. Willis. New York, 1854. 12°. . . 6184
of Ancient Times. S. G. Goodrich. Boston, 1849. 12°. . 4900, 2
of Modern Times. S. G. Goodrich. Boston, 1849. 12°. . 4900, 1
Fanaticism. I. Taylor. New York, 1834. 12°. 1848
Fanny; with other Poems. F. G. Halleck. New York, 1839. 12°. . 1530
Fanny Forester. — See *Chubbuck, Emily;* and *Judson, Mrs. Emily.*
Farley, Harriet. Happy Nights at Hazel Nook. Boston, 1854. 12°. . 5525
Farm Implements. J. J. Thomas. New York, 1854. 12°. . . . 5884
Farmer, J. Genealog. Reg. of New England Settlers. Lancas. 1829. 8°. 2070
Farmer's Boy; a Rural Poem. R. Bloomfield. New York, 1803. 12°. . 2354
Farmer's Encyclopædia. C. W. Johnson. Philadelphia, 1850. Roy. 8°. 4358
Farmer's Library: Animal Economy. London, n. d. 2 v. roy. 8°. . 3635

Vol. 1. The Ox; The Horse.
2. Sheep; The Dog; The Hog; Poultry; Bees.

Farmingdale. Caroline Thomas. New York, 1854. 12°. . . . 5868
Farnham, Eliza W. Life in Prairie Land. New York, 1846. 12°. . 3011
Farnham, T. J. Life and Adventures in California. N.Y. 1849. 8°. . 2756
Farquhar, G. Dramatic Works. Ed. by L. Hunt. Lond. 1851. Roy. 8°. 4527
Farrington, Mrs. Sarah P. Fern Leaves. Auburn, 1853. 12°. . . 5336
Fern Leaves. Second series. Auburn, 1854. 12°. . . . 5865
Little Ferns. Auburn, 1854. 12°. 5607
Fashion and Famine. Ann S. Stephens. New York, 1854. 12°. . . 6157
Fast of St. Magdalen. Anna M. Porter. New York, 1819. 2 v. 12°. . 395
Fate; a Tale of Stirring Times. G. P. R. James. New York, 1851. 8°. 4503
Father Clement. Grace Kennedy. Philadelphia, 1853. 12°. . . . 811
Father's Instructions. T. Percival. Richmond, 1800. 12°. . . . 136
Fathers and Sons. T. E. Hook. Philadelphia, 1842. 2 v. 12°. . . 900
Fathers of the Desert. H. Ruffner. New York, 1850. 2 v. 12°. . . 4062
Faust. J. W. von Goethe. Trans. by A. Hayward. Lowell, 1845. 12°. 2320
Fawn of the Pale Faces. J. P. Brace. New York, 1853. 12°. . . 5380
Fay, T. S. Countess Ida; a Tale of Berlin. New York, 1840. 2 v. 12°. 1584

Fay, T. S. Norman Leslie. New York, 1836. 2 v. 12°. . . . 1092
Hoboken; a Romance of New York. New York, 1843. 2 v. 12°. 1731
Fear of the World. Bros. Mayhew. New York, 1850. 8°. 3641
Federal Government, Hist. of, 1789-1839. A. Bradford. Bost. 1840. 8°. 1587
Federalist, The. A. Hamilton, J. Jay, and J. Madison. Phil. 1818. 8°. 697
Feejee, Life in. Mrs. M. D. Wallis. Boston, 1851. 12°. . . . 4160
Feet, Book of the. J. S. Hall. New York, 1847. 12°. 4420
Felltham, O. Resolves. Cambridge, 1832. 12°. 383, 4
Felt, J. B. Annals of Salem. Salem, 1845-49. 2 v. 12°. . . . 2521
Historical Account of Massachusetts Currency. Boston, 1839. 8°. 1252
Felton, C. C. Life of William Eaton. Boston, 1844. 12°. . . 1076, 9
(Editor.) Memorial of John S. Popkin. Cambridge, 1852. 12°. . 4883
Female Biography. S. L. Knapp. Philadelphia, 1836. 12°. 1840
Female Characters of Scotland. J. Anderson. New York, 1851. 12°. . 4471
Female Jesuit, and Sequel. Mrs. S. Luke. New York, 1851-53. 2 v. 12°. 4165
Female Poets, British. G. W. Bethune. Philadelphia, 1848. 8°. . . 3191
of America. R. W. Griswold. Philadelphia, 1849. 8°. . . 3252
of America. Caroline May. Philadelphia, 1848. 8°. . . . 3535
Female Sovereigns, Memoirs of. Mrs. A. Jameson. N.Y. 1844. 2 v. 12°. 2404
The same. (H. F. L.) New York, 1846. 2 v. 12°. 3683, 33, 34
Fénélon, F. de S. de L. Life. C. Butler. Philadelphia, 1811. 12°. . 1834
Life. J. Cormack. New York, 1843. 12°. 2423
Lives of the Ancient Philosophers. New York, 1843. 12°. . . 2423
The same. (H. F. L.) New York, 1847. 12°. . 3683, 140
Télémaque. Trans. by G. Bagnall. Dublin, 1792. 2 v. 12°. . 170
The same. Trans. by J. Hawkesworth. N.Y. 1847. 2 v. 12°. 2238
Fenn, J. (Editor.) Paston Letters. London, 1849. 8°. . . . 4371
Fennell, J., Apology for the Life of. Philadelphia, 1814. 8°. . . 588
Ferdinand and Isabella, History of. W. H. Prescott. N.Y. 1851. 3 v. 8°. 947
Ferdinand Count Fathom. T. Smollett. Philadelphia, 1851. 8°. . 801, 1
Fergus, H. Class Book of Natural Theology. Boston, 1837. 12°. . 1454
Ferguson, A. Hist. of Rome, abridged. (H. F. L.) N.Y. 1848. 12°. 3683, 187
Ferguson, J. Introduction to Astronomy. Philadelphia, 1805. 12°. . 337
Ferguson, R. Works; with Life. London, 1851. 12°. 5036
Fern Leaves. Mrs. Sarah P. Farrington. Auburn, 1854. 12°. . . 5336
The same. Second series. Auburn, 1854. 12°. . . 5865
Fernley Manor; or, Edith, the Inconstant. Mrs. M. Daniel. N.Y. 1851. 8°. 4540
Ferrier, Susan. Destiny; or, the Chief's Daughter. London, 1852. 12°. 5676
Inheritance. London, 1853. 12°. 5725
Marriage. New York, 1848. 8°. 303
The same. London, 1853. 12°. 5724
Ferris, B. G. Utah and the Mormons. New York, 1854. 12°. . . 6150
Fessenden, T. G. Register of Arts. Philadelphia, 1808. 8°. . . . 738
Terrible Tractoration, and other Poems. Boston, 1836. 12°. . 736
Festivals, Games, &c. Horatio Smith. (H. F. L.) N.Y. 1846. 12°. 3683, 25
Festus; a Poem. P. J. Bailey. Boston, 1849. 12°. 2396
Feuerbach, P. J. A. von. Account of Caspar Hauser. Boston, 1832. 16°. 821
Remarkable Criminal Trials. New York, 1846. 12°. . . . 2584

Fichte, J. G., Memoir. W. Smith. Boston, 1846. 12°. . . . 2905
Fiction, History of. J. Dunlop. Philadelphia, 1842. 2 v. 12°. . . 1912
Field, G. Painter's Art and Coloring. London, 1850. 12°. . . . 6053
Field, H. M. Irish Confederates and Rebellion of 1798. N.Y. 1851. 12°. 4115
Field, J. M. Drama of Pokerville, &c. Philadelphia, 1847. 12°. . . 4074
Field, M. City Architecture. New York, 1853. 8°. 5438
Field Sports of United States. H. W. Herbert. N. York, 1849. 2 v. 8°. 3266
Fielding, H. Select Works. Philadelphia, 1843. 2 v. roy. 8°. . . 1232

Vol. 1. Tom Jones.
2. Joseph Andrews; Amelia; Jonathan Wild.

Fielding; or, Society. R. P. Ward. Philadelphia, 1837. 3 v. 12°. . 907
The same. London, 1843. 2 v. 12°. 4564, 2, 3
Fields, J. T. Poem before Boston M. L. Association. Boston, 1838. 8°. 1739
Poems. Boston, 1849. 12°. 3346
Poems. Boston, 1854. 18°. 6254
Fifteen Hundred and Seventy-Two. P. Merimée. New York, 1830. 12°. 1220
Fifty Years in Both Hemispheres. V. Nolte. New York, 1854. 12°. . 6176
Firmilian; a Spasmodic Tragedy. W. E. Aytoun. N. York, 1854. 12°. 6212
Fine Arts, General View of. D. Huntington. New York, 1851. 12°. . 4060
History of. B. J. Lossing. (H. F. L.) N. York, 1846. 12°. 3683, 103
in Great Britain. W. B. S. Taylor. London, 1841. 2 v. 12°. . 4628
Outline History of. B. J. Lossing. New York, 1840. 12°. . 2429
Fireside Lectures for Sabbath Evenings. F. Horton. Boston, 1850. 12°. 3880
Fireside Stories. Mrs. S. Ellis. New York, 1850. 16°. . . . 3315
First and Second Love. H. C. Crawford. New York, 1844. 8°. . 2167, 1
First Class Standard Reader. Epes Sargent. Boston, 1854. 12°. . . 5816
First Things; a Series of Lectures. G. Spring. N. York, 1851. 2 v. 8°. 4117
Fish and Fishing in the United States. H. W. Herbert. N. Y. 1850. 8°. 3417
Fishes, British. R. Hamilton. Edinburgh, 1843. 2 v. 12°. . 4901, 36, 37
their Uses and Structure. J. S. Bushnan. Edin. 1843. 12°. 4901, 35
of Guiana. R. H. Schomburgk. Edin. 1843. 2 v. 12°. 4901, 39, 40
of Massachusetts. D. H. Storer. Boston, 1839. 8°. . . . 722
of the Perch Family. Sir W. Jardine. Edinburgh, 1843. 12°. 4901, 38
Fisher, A. Petrel; or, Love on the Ocean. Philadelphia, 1851. 8°. . 4511
Ralph Rutherford; a Nautical Romance. New York, 1851. 8°. . 4502
Fisk, G. Sevenfold Aspect of Popery. London, 1851. 12°. . . . 4213
Travels in Egypt and the Holy Land. New York, 1848. 12°. . 3573
Fisk, W. Travels in Europe. New York, 1841. 8°. 2051
Fitch, J. Life. C. Whittlesey. 1076, 16
Fitzgeorge; a Novel. Philadelphia, 1833. 2 v. 12°. 1160
Fitzgerald, E., Life and Death of. T. Moore. New York, 1831. 2 v. 12°. 464
Fitzosborne's Letters. W. Melmoth. Boston, 1815. 12°. . . . 1025
Five Years in an English University. C. A. Bristed. N. York, 1852. 12°. 4763
Flag Ship; or, Voy. round the World. F. W. Taylor. N.Y. 1840. 2 v. 12°. 2116
Flagg, E. Venice; the City of the Sea. New York, 1853. 2 v. 12°. . 5518
Fleetwood. W. Godwin. Alexandria, 1805. 2 v. 12°. . . . 1607
The same. London, 1851. 12°. 5654
Fleming and Tibbins's French & English Dictionary. Phil. 1846. Roy. 8°. 2782

Fleming, J. Molluscous Animals. Edinburgh, 1837. 12°. 4968
Fletcher, J. History of Poland. New York, 1831. 12°. 139
The same. (H. F. L.) New York, 1846. 12°. . 3683, 24
Fletcher, J. P. Notes from Nineveh. Philadelphia, 1850. 12°. . . 3852
Flies in Amber. Miss Pardoe. London, 1850. 3 v. 12°. . . . 4277
Flint, G. L. Agriculture of Massachusetts. Boston, 1854. 8°. . . 5955
Flint, T. History and Geog. of Mississippi Valley. Cincin. 1832. 2 v. 8°. 1955
Indian Wars of the West. Cincinnati, 1833. 12°. . . . 1456
(Ed.) Personal Narrative of Jas. O. Pattie. Cincinnati, 1833. 8°. 2601
Recollections in the Valley of the Mississippi. Boston, 1826. 8°. . 1411
Flora Lyndsay. Mrs. S. Moodie. New York, 1854. 12°. . . . 6137
Florence; the Parish Orphan. Eliza B. Lee. Boston, 1852. 12°. . . 4491
Florence Egerton; or, Sunshine and Shadow. New York, 1854. 12°. . 6180
Florence Sackville; or, Self-Independence. Mrs. Burbury. N.Y. 1852. 8°. 3983
Florentine Histories. N. Machiavelli. New York, 1845. 2 v. 12°. . 2482
Florian, M. Moors in Spain. (H. F. L.) New York, 1848. 12°. 3683, 177
Florida, Conquest of. T. Irving. New York, 1851. 12°. . . . 4105
Florida War, History of. J. T. Sprague. New York, 1848. 8°. . . 2873
Flower, Fruit, and Thorn Pieces. J. P. F. Richter. Boston, 1845. 2 v. 12°. 2321
Flower Garden; or, Book of Flowers. J. Breck. Boston, 1851. 12°. . 3822
Flower of the Family. New York, 1854. 12°. 5597
Flowers of History. Roger de Wendover. London, 1849. 2 v. post 8°. 4366
of Modern Travels. Rev. J. Adams. Boston, 1816. 2 v. 12°. . 1652
of Wit. H. Kett. Hartford, 1825. 18°. 130
Flush Times in Alabama. J. G. Baldwin. New York, 1853. 12°. . 5602
Fluxions, Doctrine of. Cambridge, 1824. 8°. 1366
Flying Dutchman; a Legend of the High Seas. Phil. 1840. 2 v. 12°. . 1596
Follen, C. Works, with Memoir. Boston, 1842. 5 v. 12°. . . . 1937
Follen, Eliza L. Sketches of Married Life. Boston, 1841. 12°. . . 1866
Folsom, B. Biog. of Officers of the Am. Navy. Newburyport, 1814. 8°. 758
Fonblanque, A. Eng. under Seven Administrations. Lond. 1837. 3 v. 12°. 2379
Fontaine, J. Memoirs of a Huguenot Family. New York, 1853. 12°. . 5067
Food, History of. A. Soyer. Boston, 1853. 8°. 5460
Vegetable Substances as. (H.F. L.) New York, 1846. 12°. 3683, 169
Foote, A. H. Africa and the American Flag. New York, 1854. 12°. . 5826
Footpath and Highway. B. Moran. Philadelphia, 1853. 12°. . . 5204
Foot-Prints of the Creator. H. Miller. Boston, 1850. 12°. . . . 4043
of Famous Men. New York, 1854. 12°. 6154
Footsteps of our Forefathers. J. G. Miall. Boston, 1852. 12°. . . 4995
Forbes, J. Eleven Years in Ceylon. London, 1840. 2 v. 8°. . . 4681
*Oriental Memoirs. Lond. 1834. 2 v. 8°. 1 v. plates, 4°. . . 3796
Forbes, J. D. Travels in the Alps of Savoy. Edinburgh, 1845. Roy. 8°. 5470
Forbes, R. B. Shipwreck by Lightning. Boston, 1853. 8°. . . . 5404
Voyage of the Jamestown. Boston, 1847. 8°. 2799
*Forbin, Comte de, Portefeuille du. Paris, 1843. 4°. 3740
Ford, J., and P. Massinger. Dramatic Works. London, 1848. Roy. 8°. 1788
Ford, R. Spaniards and their Country. New York, 1847. 2 v. 12°. . 2993
Ford, T. History of Illinois from 1818–47. Chicago, 1854. 12°. . 6198

Foreign Quarterly Review. Vols. 14–37. New York, 1834–46. Roy. 8°. 2827
Foreign Reminiscences. Lord Holland. New York, 1851. 12°. . . . 3797
Foreign Standard Literature, Specimens of. — See *Specimens.*
Foreign Travel, Sketches of. C. Rockwell. Boston, 1842. 2 v. 8°. . 1684
Forest, The. J. V. Huntington. New York, 1852. 12°. 5217
Forest Days. G. P. R. James. New York, 1843. 8°. 1718
Forest Life. C. M. Kirkland. New York, 1844. 12°. 1705
and Forest Trees. J. S. Springer. New York, 1851. 12°. . . 4459
Forester, Frank. — See *Herbert, H. W.*
Forester, T. (Editor.) Norway and its Scenery. London, 1853. Post 8°. 5360
Foresters, The. A. Dumas. New York, 1854. 12°. 5789
Foresters, The. John Wilson. Boston, 1845. 12°. 1469
Forgery; a Tale. G. P. R. James. New York, 1848. 8°. . . . 3250
Forster, J., and others. Eminent British Statesmen. Lond. 1831. 7 v. 12°. 1831
For Contents, see *Lives.*
Life and Adventures of Oliver Goldsmith. London, 1848. 8°. . 5172
Forsyth, W. Napoleon at St. Helena. New York, 1853. 2 v. 12°. . 5611
Fortescue; a Novel. J. S. Knowles. New York, 1846. 8°. . . . 2772
Fortification and Artillery, Treatise on. H. Straith. Lond. 1850. 2 v. 8°. 4823
Fortune Hunter. Anna Cora Mowatt. Philadelphia, 1854. 8°. . . 5922
Fortunes of Nigel. Sir W. Scott. Boston, 1848. 2 v. 12°. . 999, 25, 26
The same. Edinburgh, 1849. 2 v. 12°. . . 4100, 26, 27
The same. Edinburgh, 1850. Roy. 8°. . . . 4531, 7
Forty-five Guardsmen. A. Dumas. New York, 1848. 8°. . . . 2895
Fosdick, D., jun. Sermons at Hollis-street Church. Boston, 1847. 8°. 3197
Fosgate, B. Sleep Psychologically Considered. New York, 1850. 12°. 3894
*Fossil Remains, Pictorial Atlas of. G. A. Mantell. London, 1850. 4°. 4351
Foster, B. F. Clerk's Guide; or, Commercial Correspondence. Bos. 1837. 12°. 1544
Commercial Bookkeeping. Boston, 1839. 8°. 1350
Foster, B. W. Bookkeeping, Double and Single Entry. Bost. 1844. 8°. 1709
Foster, Mrs. M. E. Handbook of Mod. European Literature. Phil. 1850. 12°. 3498
Foster, J. Essays in a Series of Letters. Boston, 1839. 12°. . . . 1487

On a Man's Writing Memoirs of Himself; Decision of Character; Application of the Epithet Romantic; Aversion of Men of Taste to Evangelical Religion.

The same. Boston, 1811. 12°. 211
Essays on the Evils of Popular Ignorance. New York, 1850. 12°. 3662
Life & Correspondence. Ed. by J. E. Ryland. N.Y. 1846. 2 v. 12°. 2918
Foster, R. S. Nature & Blessedness of Christian Purity. N.Y. 1851. 12°. 4158
Foster Brother; a Tale. Edited by L. Hunt. New York, 1846. 8°. . 2648
Fouché, J., Memoirs of. Boston, 1825. 8°. 1355
Fouqué, F. de la M. Thiodolf the Icelander. New York, 1845. 12°. . 2581
Undine. New York, 1839. 12°. 1560
The same. New York, 1845. 12°. 2332
Foundations and Concrete Works. E. Dobson. London, 1850. 12°. . 6066
Fountain, and other Poems. W. C. Bryant. New York, 1842. 12°. . 1722
Four Pillars; or, Truth of Christianity. H. Newcomb. Bost. 1842. 12°. 977
Fourier, C. Life. C. Pellarin. New York, 1848. 12°. . . . 3179
Fowle, W. B. Familiar Dialogues. Boston, 1846. 12°. . . . 3347

Fowler, J. A. Dramatic and Oratorical Expression. Phil. 1853. 12°. . 5226
Fowler, O. S. Phrenology applied to Matrimony. New York, 1842. 8°. 1844
Fownes, G. Treatise on Chemistry. London, 1853. 12°. 6036
Fox, C. J., Recollections of Life of. B. C. Walpole. N.Y. 1807. 12°. . 468
Speeches. London, 1853. 8°. 5468
Fox, G., Popular Life of. J. Marsh. Philadelphia, 1848. 12°. . . 3332
France. Lady S. Morgan. Philadelphia, 1817. 8°. 1261
and England, Notabilities in. P. Chasles. New York, 1853. 12°. 5340
and the French. London, 1851. 12°. 4292
and Italy, Journey through. W. Hazlitt. London, 1826. 8°. . 2286
and Italy, Travels through. T. Smollett. London, 1778. 2 v. 12°. 866
and its Revolutions. G. Long. London, 1850. Roy. 8°. . . 5901
and Switzerland, Pedestrian in. G. Barrell, jun. N.Y. 1853. 12°. 5376
Civil War in the Vendée. Paris, 1802. 8°. 574
Civil Wars and Monarchy in. L. Ranke. New York, 1853. 12°. 5345
Consulate and Empire. A. Thiers. New York, 1852. 2 v. 8°. . 2754
Court of, 1684–1720. Marquis de Dangeau. Lond. 1825. 2 v. 8°. 5127
Democracy in. M. Guizot. New York, 1849. 12°. 3342
History of. J. Michelet. Tr. by G. H. Smith. N. Y. 1847. 2. v. 8°. 2627
History of the Girondists. A. Lamartine. N. Y. 1849. 3 v. 12°. 3030
Hist. of the National Assem., 1848. J. F. Corkran. N.Y. 1849. 12°. 2935
History of Ten Years, 1830–40. Louis Blanc. Phil. 1848. 2 v. 8°. 2883
in 1829–30. Lady S. Morgan. New York, 1830. 2 v. 12°. . 527
its King, Court, and Government. L. Cass. New York, 1848. 8°. 3148
Lectures on the History of. Sir J. Stephen. New York, 1852. 8°. 4697
Memoirs of the Queens of. Mrs. F. Bush. Phil. 1847. 2 v. 12°. 2985
Orators of. L. de Cormenin. New York, 1847. 12°. . . . 3008
Protestantism in. A. Coquerel. Boston, 1854. 12°. 6145
Restoration of Monarchy. A. Lamartine. N. Y. 1851. 3 v. 12°. 5198
Revolution of 1789. Philadelphia, 1794. 12°. 553
Savoy, Switzerland, &c., Letters from. T. Raffles. N. Y. 1818. 12°. 974
Stranger in. J. Carr. Brattleboro', 1806. 12°. 177
Prussia, Switzerland, &c., Travels in. S. Laing. Phil. 1846. 8°. 2690
Protestant Reformation in. Mrs. Marsh. London, 1847. 2 v. 8°. 4643
Sketches in. A. Dumas. Philadelphia, 1852. 8°. 4693
Sketches of Living Characters in. R. M. Walsh. Phil. 1841. 12°. 2296
Travels in, 1787–89. A. Young. London, 1792. 4°. . . . 2007
The same. Dublin, 1793. 2 v. 8°. 605
Woman in, in the 18th Century. Julia Kavanagh. Phil. 1850. 12°. 3855
Fox, G. T. Memoir of Henry W. Fox. New York, 1851. 12°. . . 4171
Fox, J. History of Christian Martyrdom. London, 1837. 8°. . . 1941
Fragments of Voyages and Travels. Capt. B. Hall. London, 1842. 8°. . 2610
Framingham, Mass., History of. W. Barry. Boston, 1847. 8°. . . 2834
Francesca Carrara. Letitia E. Landon. Philadelphia, 1847. 8°. . 1343, 1
Franchere, G. Voyage to N. W. Coast of America. N. York, 1854. 12°. 5818
Francia, Dr., Reign of Terror. J.P. & W.P. Robertson. Phil. 1839. 2 v. 12°. 979
Francis, C. Life of John Eliot. Boston, 1840. 12°. 1076, 5
Life of Sebastian Rale. Boston, 1848. 12°. 1076, 17

Francis-Eugene, Prince of Savoy, History of. London, 1754. 12°. . 182
Francis, G. H. Orators of the Age. New York, 1847. 12°. . . 3001
Francis, J. Chronicles and Characters of Stock Exchange. Bost. 1850. 8°. 3949
Francis Berrian; or, the Mexican Patriot. Boston, 1826. 2 v. 12°. . 551
Frank. Maria Edgeworth. Cambridge, 1822. 2 v. 12°. . . . 487
Frank Fairlegh. F. Smedley. New York, 1850. 8°. 3997
Frank Forester. — See *Herbert, H. W.*
Frank Freeman's Barber Shop. B. R. Hall. New York, 1852. 12°. . 5034
Frank Heartwell; or, Fifty Years Ago. New York, 1844. 8°. . 2167, 1
Frank Mildmay. F. Marryat. New York, 1848. 8°. . . . 1766, 2
Frankenstein. Mrs. M. W. Shelley. London, 1853. 12°. . . . 5698
The same. Philadelphia, 1833. 2 v. 12°. 2333
Franklin, B. Autobiography and Life. H. H. Weld. N. Y. 1848. 8°. 3265
Autobiography and Select Writings. N. Y. 1846. 2 v. 12°. 3683, 92, 93
Life. M. L. Weems. Philadelphia, 1829. 12°. 1019
Select Works. Edited by E. Sargent. Boston, 1853. 12°. . . 5637
Works; with Notes and Life. J. Sparks. Boston, 1840. 10 v. 8°. 1792

Vol. 1. Autobiography; Life continued, by Sparks.
2. Essays on Religious and Moral Subjects, and the Economy of Life; Essays on Politics, Commerce, and Political Economy.
3. Essays and Tracts, Historical and Political, before the American Revolution; Constitution and Government of Pennsylvania.
4. Essays and Tracts continued.
5. Political Papers during and after the American Revolution; Letters and Papers on Electricity.
6. Letters and Papers on Philosophical Subjects.
7. Correspondence: Part 1. Private Letters to the Time of the Author's First Mission to England, 1725-57. Part 2. Letters, Private and Official, from the Time of the Author's First Mission to England to the Beginning of the American Revolution, 1757-75.
8. Correspondence: Part 2 continued, 1757-75. Part 3. Letters, Private and Official, from the Beginning of the Revolution to End of the Author's Mission to France, 1775-85; Appendix; Fragment of Polybius on the Athenian Government; Memoir of Sir John Dalrymple.
9. Correspondence: Part 3 continued; Journal of the Negotiation of the Treaty of Peace.
10. Correspondence: Part 3 continued; Part 4. Private Letters, from the Termination of the Author's Mission to France to the End of his Life, 1785-90; Supplement; Indexes; Chronological List of the Author's Writings.

Franklin, Sir J., and the Arctic Regions. P. L. Simmonds. Buff. 1852. 12°. 968
Frascati's; or, Scenes in Paris. Philadelphia, 1836. 2 v. 12°. . . 259
Fraser, J. B. History of Persia. (H. F. L.) New York, 1848. 12°. 3683, 70
Mesopotamia and Assyria. (H. F. L.) New York, 1848. 12°. 3683, 157
Fraser's Magazine. Vol. 47. London, 1853. 8°. 5419
Freaks of Fortune; or, Ned Lorn. J. B. Jones. Philadelphia, 1854. 12°. 6258
Frederick the Great; his Court & Times. T. Campbell. Lon. 1845. 2 v. 12°. 3187
Life. Lord Dover. New York, 1835. 2 v. 12°. . . . 131
The same. (H. F. L.) New York, 1846. 2 v. 12°. 3683, 41, 42
Free Trade Advocate. Ed. by C. Raguet. Philadelphia, 1829. 2 v. 8°. . 1216
Freedley, E. T. Practical Treatise on Business. Philadelphia, 1852. 12°. 4898
Freeman, S. American Clerk's Magazine. Boston, 1814. 12°. . . 327
*Freeman, S. Art of Horsemanship. London, 1806. 4°. . . . 4828
Freeman's Guide; con. Const. of U. S. & the States. Charlestown, 1812. 12°. 316
Freemasonry, Genius of; a Defence. S. L. Knapp. Prov. 1828. 12°. . 2120
its Pretensions Exposed. New York, 1828. 8°. 1382

Freemason's Manual. K. J. Stewart. Philadelphia, 1851. 12°. . . 4191
Freemason's Monitor. Z. A. Davis. Philadelphia, 1847. 12°. . . 385
Frémont, J. C. Expedition to the Rocky Mountains. Buffalo, 1851. 12°. 2639
Map of the above Expedition. 2879
French and Eng. Dictionary. Fleming and Tibbins. Phil. 1846. Roy. 8°. 2782
*A. G. Collot. Philadelphia, 1852. 8°. 1668
*A. Spiers. New York, 1852. Roy. 8°. 4935
G. Surenne. New York, 1851. 12°. 4873
French Grammar. J. Rowbotham. Boston, 1841. 12°. 283
G. L. Strauss. London, 1853. 12°. 6116
French History, Stories from. Sir W. Scott. Bost. 1848. 2 v. 12°. 999, 53, 54
The same. Edinburgh, 1849. 2 v. 12°. . . 4101, 27, 28
French in Algiers. C. Lamping and M. de France. N. York, 1845. 12°. 2365
French, Letters on the Manners of. Dublin, 1791. 12°. 151
French Literature, Modern. L. R. de Vericour. Boston, 1848. 12°. . 3158
French National Constituent Assembly. J. F. Corkran. N. Y. 1849. 12°. 2935
French Language, New System of Teaching. E. Church. Bost.1845. 8°. 1136
Ollendorff's Method of Learning. New York, 1851. 12°. . . 5191
French Phrases, Manual of. N. M. Hentz. Boston, 1822. 12°. . . 865
French Protestants, History of. C. Weiss. New York, 1854. 2 v. 12°. . 5799
French Republic, Constitution of (in French and Eng.). N.Y. 1850. 12°. 5351
Past, Present, and Future of. A. Lamartine. N. Y. 1850. 12°. . 3865
The same (in French). Paris, 1850. 8°. 5398
French Revolution of 1789. C. MacFarlane. London, 1844. 4 v. 12°. . 3093
History of. T. Carlyle. Boston, 1838. 2 v. 12°. . . 944
History of. L. Blanc. Philadelphia, 1848. 2 v. 12°. . 3623
History of. A. Thiers. Philadelphia, 1842. 4 v. 8°. . 1724
Letters on. H. M. Williams. New York, 1794. 4 v. 12°. 1043
of 1830, Annals of. M. Moses. New York, 1830. 12°. . . 517
of 1848. F. Chamier. London, 1849. 2 v. 8°. 4541
P. B. St. John. New York, 1848. 12°. 2454
History of. A. Lamartine. Boston, 1849. 2 v. 12°. . 3424
French Sergeant, Adventures of. R. Guillemard. Phil. 1826. 12°. . 1068
French Writers, Lives of Eminent. Mrs. Shelley. Phil. 1840. 2 v. 12°. 1140
Fresh Gleanings of Europe. D. G. Mitchell. New York, 1851. 12°. . 3026
Freston Tower. R. Cobbold. London, 1850. 3 v. 12°. 4275
Friend, The; a Series of Essays. S. T. Coleridge. Burlington, 1831. 8°. 1948
The same. New York, 1853. 12°. 5561, 2
Friends in Council. A. Helps. Boston, 1849. 12°. 3373
Friends of Christ in the New Testament. N. Adams. Boston, 1853. 8°. 5118
Fright, The. E. Pickering. Philadelphia, 1847. 8°. 2186
Frisbie, L., Life and Writings of. A. Norton. Boston, 1823. 8°. . 1427
Fritz Harold; or, the Temptation. Sarah A. Myers. N.Y. 1854. 12°. . 6192
Froissart, Sir J. Chronicles of Europe. Tr. by T. Johnes. N.Y. 1845. 4°. 2027
Fromberg, E. O. Treatise on Painting on Glass. London, 1851. 12°. . 6063
Frontenac; a Metrical Romance. A. B. Street. New York, 1849. 12°. 3413
Frost, J. American Speaker. Philadelphia, 1844. 12°. . . . 1806
Book upon the American Colonies. New York, 1846. 12°. . 2515

Frost, J. H. Book of Anecdotes. New York, 1847. 12°. 2939
Book of the Army. New York, 1845. 12°. 2180
Book of the Indians. New York, 1845. 12°. 2210
Book of the Navy. New York, 1845. 12°. 2208
Continuation of Aikin's British Poets. Phil. 1843. 2 v. 8°. 1962, 2, 3

Vol. 2. Chronological Series, Falconer to Scott.
3. ,, ,, Southey to Croly.

Heroic Women of the West. Philadelphia, 1854. 12°. . . . 5765
Pictorial History of the United States. Phil. 1846. 4 v. roy. 8°. . 2777
Self-Made Men of America. New York, 1848. 12°. 3176
(Compiler.) Wild Scenes in a Hunter's Life. Auburn, 1851. 12°. 4216
Frothingham, N. L. Sermons of a Twelvemonth. Boston, 1852. 12°. . 4787
Frothingham, R., jun. History of the Siege of Boston. Bost. 1851. 8°. 3518
Fruit Culturist, American. J. J. Thomas. Auburn, 1852. 12°. . . 5078
Fruit Garden. P. Barry. New York, 1851. 12°. 4164
Fruits and Fruit Trees of America. A. J. Downing. N.Y. 1847. 12°. 3029
Fry, Caroline. Autobiography and Letters. Philadelphia, 1849. 12°. . 3285
Christ our Example. New York, 1852. 12°. 930
The Listener. Philadelphia, 1837. 2 v. 12°. 2206
Fryxell, A. History of Sweden. London, 1844. 2 v. 12°. 4578
Fudge Doings. D. G. Mitchell. New York, 1854. 2 v. 12°. . . 6217
Fuel, Economy of. T. S. Prideaux. London, 1853. 12°. . . . 6085
Fuller, A. Calvinistic and Socinian Systems. Boston, 1815. 12°. . 197
Memoir of Samuel Pearce. New York, n. d. 16°. 475
Works; with Memoir by A. G. Fuller. Philadelphia, 1845. 3 v. 8°. 4720

Vol. 1. Memoir; Sermons and Sketches; Illustrations of Scripture; Passages Apparently Contradictory; Letters on Systematic Divinity; Thoughts on Preaching.
2. The Gospel its own Witness; Calvinistic and Socinian Systems as to their Moral Tendency; Socinianism Indefensible; Universal Salvation; The Gospel worthy of all Acceptation; Defence of the same; Reality and Efficacy of Divine Grace; Strictures on Sandemanianism; Dialogues and Letters between Crispus and Gaius; Conversations between Peter, James, and John; Controversy with Rev. A. Booth; Antinomianism; Apology for the Missions in India.
3. Expository Discourses on Genesis and the Apocalypse; Circular Letters; Memoirs of Rev. Samuel Pearce; Essays, Letters, &c., on Ecclesiastical Polity; Miscellaneous Tracts, Essays, Letters, &c.; Reviews; Answers to Queries; Fugitive Pieces; Sermons; Index.

Fuller, M. V. Senator's Son; or, the Maine Law. Cleveland, 1853. 12°. 5324
Fuller, S. Margaret. Memoirs. J. F. Clarke & others. Bost. 1852. 2 v. 12°. 4766
Papers on Literature and Art. New York, 1846. 2 v. 12°. . . 2921
Summer on the Lakes. Boston, 1844. 12°. 2104
Woman in the Nineteenth Century. New York, 1845. 12°. . 2313
Fuller, T. Holy and Profane States. Cambridge, 1831. 12°. . 383, 1
Fullarton, J. Regulation of Currencies. London, 1844. 8°. . . 4640
Fullerton, Lady Georgiana. Ellen Middleton. New York, 1849. 12°. . 3175
Grantley Manor. New York, 1848. 12°. 3151
Lady Bird. New York, 1853. 12°. 5202
Fullom, S. W. Daughter of the Night. London, 1851. 3 v. 12°. . . 4247
Fulton, R. Life. C. D. Colden. New York, 1817. 8°. 732
Life. J. Renwick. Boston, 1844. 12°. 1076, 10
Fun, Phantasmagoria of. London, 1843. 2 v. 12°. 5632

Fun-Jottings; or, Laughs I have taken a Pen to. N. P. Willis. N.Y. 1853. 12°. 5534
Fur Trade, History of. A. Mackenzie. Philadelphia, 1802. 8°. . . 766
Furlong, L. American Coast Pilot. Newburyport, 1798. 8°. . . 1221
Furniss, W. Land of the Cæsar and Doge. New York, 1853. 12°. . 5216
Old World; or, Scenes & Cities in Foreign Lands. N.Y. 1850. 12°. 3441
Waraga; or, the Charms of the Nile. New York, 1850. 12°. . 3485
Future State, Philosophy of a. T. Dick. Philadelphia, 1845. 12°. 2357, 1

G.

Gabriel; a Story of Wichnor Wood. Mary Howitt. N. York, 1850. 18°. 3667
Gaieties and Gravities. Horace Smith. New York, 1852. 12°. . . 1011
Galatians, Epistle to, Notes on. A. Barnes. New York, 1851. 12°. . 4734
Gale Middleton. Horace Smith. Philadelphia, 1834. 2 v. 12°. . . 606
Gales and Seaton's Reg. of Debates, 1789–1837. Wash. 1834–37. 29 v. 8°. 4903
Galileo. Life. London, 1833. 8°. 602
Tycho Brahe, and Kepler. Lives. D. Brewster. N.Y. 1841. 12°. 1627
Gall, J. Literature of the Blind, and their Education. Edin. 1834. 8°. 1156
Gallaghar, J. Pilgrimage of Adam and David. Boston, 1849. 12°. . 3400
*Gallery of Illustrious Americans. Ed. by C. E. Lester. N.Y. 1850. Folio. 1715
of Literary Portraits. G. Gilfillan. New York, 1846. 2 v. 12°. . 2530
*of 100 British Engravings. London, n. d. 4°. 5896
*of Nature, Pictorial and Descriptive. T. Milner. London, 1846. 8°. 2044
The same. London, 1849. Roy. 8°. 4526
Gallus; or, Roman Scenes. W. A. Becker. London, 1849. 12°. . . 5646
Galt, J. Autobiography. Philadelphia, 1834. 2 v. 12°. . . . 323
The same. Philadelphia, 1833. 8°. 1357, 3
Adam Blair. Boston, 1822. 12°. 352
Ayrshire Legatees. New York, 1823. 12°. 1906
Earthquake. New York, 1821. 2 v. 12°. 1903
Eben Erskine; or, the Traveller. Philadelphia, 1833. 2 v. 12°. . 1924
History and Adventures of Pen Owen. New York, 1851. 8°. . 3808
Last of the Lairds. New York, 1827. 12°. 491
Lawrie Todd. New York, 1830. 2 v. 12°. 1931
The same. London, 1850. 12°. 5653
Life of Lord Byron. New York, 1830. 18°. 125
The same. (H. F. L.) New York, 1843. 12°. . 3683, 9
Life and Studies of Benjamin West. Philadelphia, 1816. 8°. . 1327
Lives of the Players. Boston, 1831. 2 v. 12°. 345
Omen; a Tale of Real Life. New York, 1844. 8°. . . 2167, 3
Provost. New York, 1822. 12°. 1940
Ringan Gilhaize. New York, 1823. 2 v. 12°. 1902
Rothelan; a Romance of English Histories. N.Y. 1825. 2 v. 12°. 1929
Southennan. New York, 1830. 2 v. 12°. 1930
Spaewife; a Tale of Scottish Chronicles. Phil. 1824. 2 v. 12°. . 1932
Stanley Buxton; or the Schoolfellows. Phil. 1833. 2 v. 12°. . 1925
Steamboat. New York, 1823. 12°. 1907

Galvanism and Electro-Metallurgy. A. Smee. New York, 1852. 12°. . 985
Gambier, J. E. Guide to the Study of Moral Evidence. Bost. 1834. 12°. 1482
Game, American, in its Season. H. W. Herbert. New York, 1853. 12°. 5327
of Life. L. Ritchie. New York, 1844. 8°. 2176, 3
The same. Philadelphia, 1833. 8°. 1357, 1
Games. E. Hoyle. Philadelphia, 1838. 24°. 2417
Handbook of. Edited by H. G. Bohn. London, 1850. Post 8°. . 4362
History and Science of Cricket. London, 1851. 12°. . . . 4266
Gammell, W. History of American Baptist Missions. Boston, 1849. 12°. 3504
Life of Roger Williams. Boston, 1844. 12°. 1076, 14
Life of Samuel Ward. Boston, 1848. 12°. 1076, 19
Gan Eden; or, Pictures of Cuba. W. H. Hurlbut. Boston, 1854. 12°. 6160
Gaol Chaplain, Experiences of a. London, 1852. 12°. 5686
Garbett, E. L. Principles of Design in Architecture. London, 1850. 12°. 6048
Garden Walks with the Poets. Mrs. C. M. Kirkland. N. Y. 1852. 12°. 5027
Gardening Landscape. A. J. Downing. New York, 1844. 8°. . . 2227
*Gardens and Chateaux of France. Paris, 1808. Folio. . . . 2048
Gardiner, W. (Editor.) Lives of Haydn and Mozart. Boston, 1839. 12°. 471
Music of Nature. Boston, 1841. 8°. 1447
Gardner, A. K. Spare Hours of a Student in Paris. N. York, 1848. 12°. 3086
Gardner, C. K. Dictionary of the Army of U. S. New York, 1853. 12°. 5242
Garland, H. A. Life of John Randolph. New York, 1850. 2 v. 8°. . 3999
Gas Works, Treatise on. S. Hughes. London, 1853. 12°. 6092
Gaskell, Mrs. Cranford. New York, 1853. 12°. 5374
Mary Barton. New York, 1849. 8°. 3245
Ruth. Boston, 1853. 12°. 5223
Gass, P. Journal of Voyages and Travels. Philadelphia, 1811. 12°. . 160
Gautier, T. Wanderings in Spain. London, 1853. 12°. 5638
Gavazzi, A. Lectures; with Life. G. B. Nicolini. N. York, 1854. 12°. 5357
Gayarré, C. Louisiana; its Colonial History & Romance. N. Y. 1851. 8°. 3827
Romance of the History of Louisiana. New York, 1848. 12°. . 3107
Gazetteer, American. J. Morse. Charlestown, 1804. 8°. 628
British. B. Clarke. London, 1852. 3 v. roy. 8°. . . . 5169
General. R. Brookes. London, 1821. 8°. 769
of the Eastern Continent. J. Morse. Charlestown, 1802. 8°. . 1268
of Indiana. Indianapolis, 1849. 12°. 3496
of Massachusetts, J. Hayward. Boston, 1849. 12°. . . . 3027
of New Hampshire. J. Hayward. Boston, 1849. 12°. . . 5555
*of United States. J. Hayward. Hartford, 1853. 8°. . . 5402
*of United States. T. Baldwin and J. Thomas. Phil. 1854. 8°. . 5494
of Vermont. J. Hayward. Boston, 1849. 12°. 5556
of the World. T. C. Callicot. New York, 1853. 12°. . . 5232
of the World. A. K. Johnston. London, 1850. 8°. . . . 4353
Universal. S. Maunder. London, 1848. 12°. 4106
Universal Pronouncing. T. Baldwin. Philadelphia, 1847. 12°. . 2973
Western. S. R. Brown. Auburn, 1817. 8°. 757
Gebir, Count Julian, and other Poems. W. S. Landor. Lond. 1831. 12°. 2544
Gebel Teir. Boston, 1829. 12°. 560

Gems by the Wayside. Mrs. L. G. Abell. New York, 1850. 12°. . 4088
 from Fable Land. W. O. Bourne. New York, 1853. 12°. . 5022
 from New Hampshire Authors. F. A. Moore. Manches. 1850. 12°. 3887
 of Epistolary Correspondence. R. A. Willmott. Lond. 1846. 12°. 4569
 of Mod. Poets; with Biog. Notices. S. C. Hall. Phil. 1842. 12°. 1666
Genealogical Register, New England. Boston, 1847–53. 7 v. 8°. . . 2845
 of the First Settlers of New England. J. Farmer. Lancas. 1829. 8°. 2070
Genealogy of the Abbot Family. Boston, 1847. 8°. 2846
 of the Prentice or Prentiss Family. C. J. F. Binney. Bos. 1852. 8°. 4813
 of the Stetson Family. J. S. Barry. Boston, 1847. 8°. . . 3046
Genesis and Geology. D. Crofton. Boston, 1853. 12°. . . . 5264
Genevieve. A. Lamartine. London, 1850. 12°. 4419
Genevieve; or, Chevalier of Maison Rouge. A. Dumas. N.Y. 1846. 8°. 2758
Genevra; or, History of a Portrait. Philadelphia, 1851. 8°. . . . 4152
Genius, Illustrations of. H. Giles. Boston, 1854. 12°. 6228
 Infirmities of. R. R. Madden. Philadelphia, 1833. 2 v. 12°. . 2551
 of Italy. R. Turnbull. New York, 1849. 12°. 3301
 of Scotland. R. Turnbull. New York, 1847. 12°. . . . 3017
Genlis, Mde. de. Memoirs of her own Life. New York, 1825. 8°. . 1385
Gentleman of the Old School. G. P. R. James. N.Y. 1839. 2 v. 12°. . 465
Gentleman's Daughter. Mrs. A. Opie. New York, 1844. 8°. . 2167, 2
Gentleman's Magazine, Selections from. London, 1811. 4 v. 8°. . . 610
Gentleman's Miscellany. G. Wright. Exeter, 1797. 12°. . . . 828
Gentlemen-at-Arms, Corps of. J. B. Curling. London, 1850. 8°. . 5409
Geographical Dictionary. J. R. M'Culloch. New York, 1845. 2 v. roy. 8°. 2221
 of the United States. J. Scott. Philadelphia, 1805. 8°. . . 1269
Geographical, Hist. and Commer. Grammar. W. Guthrie. Lond. 1792. 8°. 737
  The same. T. Salmon. London, 1799. 8°. 1342
Geographical Science, Manual of. London, 1852. 8°. 5498

O'Brien, M. Mathematical Geography.
Ansted, D. T. Physical Geography.
Jackson, J. R. Chartography.
Nicolay, C. G. Description and Geographical Terminology.

Geography, Ancient. M. D'Anville. New York, 1814. 2 v. 8°. . . 1344
 Ancient and Mediæval. C. Anthon. New York, 1850. Roy. 8°. 3514
 Atlas to Walker's. London, 1806. 8°. 689
 Dictionary of. A. K. Johnston. London, 1850. 8°. 4353
 Dictionary of Ancient. W. Hazlitt. London, 1851. 12°. . . 4222
 Elements of. R. Dickinson. Boston, 1813. 8°. 630
 Elements of Ancient & Modern. J. E. Worcester. Bost. 1844. 12°. 3867
 Encyclopædia of. H. Murray. Phil. 1837. 3 v. roy. 8°. . . . 2010
 Handbook of Universal. T. C. Callicot. New York, 1853. 12°. 5232
 Introduc. to Ancient and Mod. J. A. Cummings. Bost. 1813. 12°. 301
 of the State of New York. J. H. Mather. Hartford, 1847. 12°. 3866
 Physical. Mary Somerville. Philadelphia, 1848. 12°. . . 3168
 System of Modern. B. Davies. Philadelphia, 1805. 2 v. 12°. . 300
 Universal. J. Morse. Charlestown, 1819. 2 v. 8°. 620
 Universal, on System of Malte-Brun and Balbi. Lond. 1851. 8°. 5900
Geological Account of the United States. J. Mease. Phil. 1807. 16°. . 85

Geological Map of the United States. J. Marcou. Boston, 1853. 8°. . 5417
Geological Soc. of Penn., Trans. of. Vol. 1, parts 1, 2. Phil. 1835. 8°. 2868
*Geological Survey of Wisconsin, Iowa, &c. R. D. Owen. Phil. 1852. 4°. 5167
Geology and Genesis. D. Crofton. Boston, 1853. 12°. . . . 5264
  and Mineralogy. P. Cleaveland. Boston, 1816. 8°. . . . 1380
  and Natural History, Researches in. C. Darwin. N.Y. 1846. 2 v. 12°. 2594
  and Revelation; Two Records. H. Miller. Boston, 1854. 12°. . 5796
  Elements of. C. A. Lee. (H. F. L.) New York, 1848. 12°. 3683, 178
  Elements of. J. R. Loomis. Boston, 1852. 12°. 4791
  Elements of. Sir C. Lyell. Boston, 1841. 2 v. 12°. . . . 2519
  Elements of. S. St. John. New York, 1851. 12°. . . . 4438
  Manual of Elementary. Sir C. Lyell. London, 1851. 8°. . . 4356
  of Bass Rock. H. Miller. New York, 1851. 12°. . . . 4269
  of the Globe, Outline of. E. Hitchcock. Boston, 1853. 8°. . 5439
  of Isle of Wight. G. A. Mantell. London, 1854. Post 8°. . . 5937
  of Maine, Second Report. C. T. Jackson. Augusta, 1838. 8°. . 3248
  of Mass., Final Report. E. Hitchcock. Amherst, 1841. 2 v. 4°. 2026
  Principles of. Sir C. Lyell. Boston, 1842. 3 v. 12°. . . . 2520
    The same. Philadelphia, 1837. 2 v. 8°. 784
    The same. Eighth edition, revised. London, 1854. 8°. . 3986
    The same. Ninth edition, revised. Boston, 1853. 8°. . 2520
  Religion of. E. Hitchcock. Boston, 1851. 12°. 4207
  Scripture Doctrine and. E. Lord. New York, 1851. 12°. . 4431
  Treatise on. J. E. Portlock. London, 1853. 12°. . . . 6038
  Wonders of. S. G. Goodrich. Boston, 1849. 12°. . . 4900, 14
Geometry, Analytical. J. Hann. London, 1853. 12°. 6099
  Descriptive. J. F. Heather. London, 1851. 12°. . . . 6084
  Elements of Euclid. Edited by H. Law. London, 1853. 12°. . 6098
    The same. Edited by J. Playfair. New York, 1828. 8°. . 617
    The same. Edited by R. Simson. Philadelphia, 1825. 8°. 694
  Leçons de. M. Mauduit. Paris, 1790. 8°. 1445
  Plane. F. J. Grund. Boston, 1830. 12°. 496
George, Anita. Queens of Spain. New York, 1850. 12°. . . . 3505
George II., Memoirs of the Reign of. J. Hervey. Phil. 1848. 2 v. 12°. 3157
George III., his Court and Family. London, 1824. 2 v. 8°. . . . 5145
  History of the Reign of. J. Adolphus. London, 1802. 3 v. 8°. . 5908
    R. Bisset. Albany, 1816. 2 v. 8°. 1264
  Life. E. Holt. London, 1820. 2 v. 8°. 1285
  Memoirs of the Reign of. H. Walpole. Phil. 1845. 2 v. 8°. . 2617
George IV., Diary of the Times of. Lady C. Bury. Lond. 1838. 4 v. 8°. 4652
    The same. London, 1839. 4 v. 8°. 5144
    Continuation of same. Ed. by J. Galt. Phil. 1838. 2 v. 12°. 963
  Life and Times of. G. Croly. New York, 1832. 12°. . . 1868
    The same. (H. F. L.) New York, 1843. 12°. . 3683, 15
George Barnwell. T. S. Surr. Boston, 1826. 12°. 18
George St. George Julian. H. Cockton. Philadelphia, 1842. 8°. . 2771
Georges, H. de St. Count Monte Leone. New York, 1852. 8°. . . 413
Georgia, History of. T. S. Arthur and W. H. Carpenter. Phil. 1852. 12°. 4866

Georgia, History of. W. B. Stevens. Vol. 1. New York, 1847. 8°. . 2858
Georgian Era; Memoirs of Eminent Persons. London, 1833. 4 v. 12°. . 3000
Geraldine, and other Poems. R. Dawes. New York, 1839. 12°. . . 1133
Geraldine; or, Modes of Faith and Practice. Boston, 1824. 2 v. 12°. . 452
Geraldine; a Sequel to Coleridge's Christabel. M.F.Tupper. Bost. 1846. 12°. 2510
Gerard, A. Journey in Himalaya Mountains. London, 1846. 8°. . 4021
German and English Dictionary. G. F. Adler. New York, 1849. 8°. . 3525
German Emigrants, Fortunes of some. F. Gerstæcker. N. Y. 1848. 12°. 3114
German Grammar. G. L. Strauss. London, 1852. 12°. 6117
German in America. F. W. Bogen. Boston, 1851. 18°. . . . 4403
German Language, Ollendorff's Method of Learning. N. Y. 1852. 12°. 5192
German Life, Lights and Shadows of. Philadelphia, 1833. 2 v. 12°. . 2102
German Literature. W. Menzel. Boston, 1840. 3 v. 12°. . . 962, 7–9
German Lyric Poets. Trans. by C. T. Brooks. Boston, 1842. 12°. 962, 14
German Poetry, Historic Survey of. W. Taylor. London, 1830. 3 v. 8°. 5467
German Poets, Translations from. C. T. Brooks. Boston, 1847. 12°. . 2944
German Popular Tales. Bros. Grimm. New York, 1853. 2 v. 12°. . 5608
German Prose Writers. Fragments, trans. by S. Austin. N. Y. 1841. 12°. 2101
German Reader. G. L. Strauss. London, 1852. 12°. 6118
German Romance, Specimens of. T. Carlyle. Boston, 1841. 2 v. 12°. 2108
German Tales. Translated by N. Greene. Boston, 1837. 2 v. 12°. . 917
Germania; its Courts, Camps, &c. Lady B. de Bury. Lond. 1850. 2 v. 8°. 4302
Germany. Mde. de Staël. London, 1814. 3 v. 12°. 2607
History, Literature, &c. of. B. Hawkins. London, 1838. 8°. . 3193
History of. F. Kohlrausch. New York, 1845. Roy. 8°. . . 2642
History of. W. Menzel. London, 1848. 3 v. post 8°. . . 3554
History of the Thirty Years' War. F. Schiller. N. Y. 1846. 12°. 2954
Home Life in. C. L. Brace. New York, 1853. 12°. . . 5308
Pictorial History of. F. Kugler. London, 1845. Roy. 8°. . . 3599
Poetry of. Translated by A. Baskerville. New York, 1854. 12°. 6257
Prose Writers of. F. H. Hedge. Philadelphia, 1848. 8°. . . 2872
Ramble in. London, 1827. 8°. 1943
The same. Boston, 1827. 12°. 841
Rural and Domestic Life of. W. Howitt. New York, 1842. 8°. 1719
Student-Life of. W. Howitt. Philadelphia, 1842. 8°. . . 2075
Tour in, 1820–22. J. Russell. Boston, 1825. 8°. 631
Gerry, E. Life. J. T. Austin. Boston, 1828. 2 v. 8°. . . . 1311
Gerstæcker, F. Fortunes of some German Emigrants. N. Y. 1848. 12°. 3114
Voyage Round the World. New York, 1853. 12°. . . . 5372
Gertrude; a Novel. E. M. Sewell. New York, 1845. 12°. . . 2481
Gertrude Leslie; or, the Queen's Vengeance. New York, 1850. 8°. . 674
Gesner, A. New Brunswick; with Notes for Emigrants. Lond. 1847. 8°. 3954
Gessert, M. A. Treatise on Glass Staining. London, 1851. 12°. . . 6062
Gesta Romanorum, Select Tales from. New York, 1845. 12°. . . 2375
Gesture, Rudiments of. W. Russell. Boston, 1838. 12°. . . . 1899
Ghost-Seer. F. Schiller. London, 1849. Post 8°. 3560
The same. London, 1853. 2 v. 12°. 5698, 5699
Giafar al Barmeki; a Tale. G. Spring, jun. New York, 1836. 2 v. 12°. 294

Gibbon, E. Autobiography. Ed. by Lord Sheffield. N. York, 1846. 2 v. 2577
Decline and Fall of the Roman Empire. Boston, 1850. 6 v. 12°. 3872
The same. New York, 1826. 6 v. 8°. 775
Memoirs of Alexander I. Baltimore, 1818. 12°. 478
Gibbons, D. Law of Contracts. London, 1850. 12°. 6070
Gibbs, G. Administrations of Washington & Adams. N. Y. 1846. 2 v. 8°. 2728
Gibraltar, History of the Siege of. Philadelphia, 1789. 12°. . . . 98
Giddings, J. R. Speeches in Congress. Boston, 1853. 12°. . . . 5293
Gideon Giles, the Roper. T. Miller. London, 1841. 8°. 2892
*Gift Book of the Republic. Edited by C. E. Lester. N.Y. 1850. Folio. 1715
Gil Blas. A. R. Le Sage. Trans. by T. Smollett. Hartford, 1847. 3 v. 12°. 1037
Gilbart, J. W. Practical Treatise on Banking. London, 1849. 2 v. 8°. 3802
Gilbert, L. (Ed.) Beauties & Wonders of Nature & Science. Lon. n. d. 8°. 2839
Gilbert Gurney. T. E. Hook. Philadelphia, 1845. 8°. 1124
The same. London, 1852. 12°. 5677
Sequel (Gurney Married). Philadelphia, 1839. 2 v. 12°. . . 2516
Giles, H. Lectures and Essays. Boston, 1850. 2 v. 12°. . . . 3568

Vol. 1. Falstaff; Crabbe; Moral Philosophy of Byron's Life; Moral Spirit of Byron's Genius; Ebenezer Elliott; Oliver Goldsmith; Spirit of Irish History.

2. Ireland and the Irish; Worth of Liberty; True Manhood; The Pulpit; Patriotism; Economics; Music; Young Musician; Day in Springfield; Chatterton; Carlyle; Savage and Dermody.

Illustrations of Genius. Boston, 1854. 12°. 6228

Cervantes; Don Quixote; Scarlet Letter; Fiction; Public Opinion; Philanthropic Sentiment; Music; Cost of a Cultivated Man; Conversation; Wordsworth; Robert Burns; Thomas De Quincey.

Gilfillan, G. Gallery of Literary Portraits. New York, 1846. 2 v. 12°. 2530
Modern Literature and Literary Men. New York, 1850. 12°. . 3511
Gilleland, J. C. Counting-House Assistant. Pittsburg, 1818. 12°. . 358
Gillespie, W. M. Principles and Practice of Road-Making. N.Y.1847. 8°. 3076
Rome as seen by a New Yorker. New York, 1845. 12°. . . 2311
Gilliam, A. M. Travels in Mexico, 1843–44. Philadelphia, 1846. 8°. . 2673
Gillies, J. Life of Geo. Whitefield. Boston, 1813. 12°. . . . 208
Gillies, R. P. Memoirs of a Literary Veteran. London, 1851. 3 v. 12°. 4248
Gilliss, J. M. Magnetical and Meteorological Observations. Wash.1845. 8°. 2813
Gilman, Caroline. Oracles from the Poets. New York, 1849. 12°. . 2338
New England Bride and Southern Matron. New York, 1852. 12°. 4993
Recollections of a Housekeeper. New York, 1842. 12°. . . 1861
Gilson, A. Czar and the Sultan. New York, 1853. 12°. . . . 5571
Gipsy; a Tale. G. P. R. James. New York, 1835. 2 v. 12°. . . 1071
Girlhood of Shakspeare's Heroines. Mary C. Clarke. N.Y. 1852. 2 v. 12°. 4450
Girls, Physical Education of. Elizabeth Blackwell. N.Y. 1852. 12°. . 4885
Girondists, History of. A. Lamartine. New York, 1849. 3 v. 12°. . 3030
Gironière, P. de la. Twenty Years in the Philippines. London, 1853. 12°. 5848
Glass Painting, Ancient. Oxford, 1847. 2 v. 8°. 4821
Glass, Painting on. E. O. Fromberg. London, 1851. 12°. . . . 6063
Glass Staining, Treatise on. M. A. Gessert. London, 1851. 12°. . . 6062
*Gleason's Pictorial. Vols. 1–6. Boston, 1851–54. 4°. 4859
Glenns; a Family History. J. L. M'Connel. New York, 1851. 12°. . 4189

Gleig, G. R. Country Curate. London, 1853. 12°. 5703
History of the Bible. (H. F. L.) New York, 1843. 2 v. 12°. 3683, 12, 13
Memoirs of Warren Hastings. London, 1841. 3 v. 8°. . . 1453
Story of the Battle of Waterloo. New York, 1847. 12°. . . 3023
Glide, Wreck of the. W. G. Dix. Boston, 1846. 12°. 2917
Glimpses of Home Life. Mrs. E. C. Embury. New York, 1848. 12°. . 3180
Globes, Treatise on the Use of. T. Keith. New York, 1815. 12°. . . 538
Use of. J. Lathrop, jun. Boston, 1812. 12°. 1006
Glory of Christ. G. Spring. New York, 1852. 2 v. 8°. . . . 1002
Glynn, J. Constructing Cranes and Machinery. London, 1849. 12°. . 6060
Power of Water. London, 1853. 12°. 6090
Goa and the Blue Mountains. R. F. Burton. London, 1851. 12°. . 4577
Goats, Sheep, Oxen, &c. Sir W. Jardine. Edinburgh, 1843. 12°. 4901, 22
God in Christ; Three Discourses. H. Bushnell. Hartford, 1849. 12°. . 3283
Wisdom of, in Works of Creation. J. Ray. London, 1732. 12°. 5559
Worship and Love of. E. Swedenborg. Boston, 1832. 12°. . 904
Goddard, T. H. Hist. of the Prominent Banks in Europe. N.Y. 1831. 8°. 749
Godey's Lady's Book. Vols. 39–47 [continued]. Phil. 1849–53. 8°. . 1428
Godfrey Malvern. T. Miller. New York, 1850. 8°. 4331
Godman, J. D. Rambles of a Naturalist. Philadelphia, 1833. 12°. . 67
Godolphin; a Novel. E. L. Bulwer. New York, 1840. 2 v. 12°. . 274
Godolphin, Mrs. Life. J. Evelyn. New York, 1847. 12°. . . . 2436
Godwin, P. Handbook of Universal Biography. New York, 1852. 12°. 4489
Vala; a Mythological Tale. New York, 1851. 8°. . . . 4803
Godwin, W. Caleb Williams. New York, 1831. 2 v. 12°. . . . 402
The same. London, 1853. 12°. 5695
Cloudesley. New York, 1830. 2 v. 12°. 1927
Deloraine. Philadelphia, 1833. 2 v. 12°. 1926
Fleetwood. Alexandria, 1805. 2 v. 12°. 1867
The same. London, 1851. 12°. 5654
Lives of the Necromancers. New York, 1847. 12°. . . . 3025
Mandeville; a Tale. Philadelphia, 1818. 2 v. 12°. . . . 1908
St. Leon. London, 1850. 12°. 5647
Goethe, J. W. von. Autobiography. New York, 1824. 8°. . . . 2649
The same. London, 1849. Post 8°. 4376
The same. Ed. by P. Godwin. New York, 1846. 4 v. 12°. 3021
Characteristics of. Trans. by S. Austin. Phil. 1841. 2 v. 12°. . 1620
Conversations with. J. P. Eckermann. Boston, 1839. 12°. . 3585
The same. Boston, 1839. 12°. 962, 4
Correspondence with a Child. Lowell, 1841. 2 v. 12°. . . 2583
Essays on Art. Trans. by S. G. Ward. Boston, 1845. 12°. . 2367
Faust. Trans. by A. Hayward. Lowell, 1845. 12°. . . . 2320
Iphigenia in Tauris; a Drama. New York, 1850. 12°. . . 4084
Letters from Switzerland and Italy. London, 1849. Post 8°. . 4376
Novels and Tales. London, 1854. Post 8°. 5942
Wilhelm Meister's Apprenticeship. Boston, 1851. 2 v. 12°. . 1802
and Schiller, Correspondence of. New York, 1845. 2 v. 12°. . 2341
and Schiller. Select Minor Poems. Boston, 1839. 12°. . . 962, 3

Gold Diggings, Sixteen Months in. D. B. Woods. N. York, 1851. 12°. 4597
Gold Region, Sights in the. T. T. Johnson. New York, 1849. 12°. . 3434
Gold Worshippers; a Novel. New York, 1851. 8°. 4150
Golden Dreams and Leaden Realities. New York, 1853. 12°. . . 5581
Golden Horn; Sketches of Asia Minor, &c. C. J. Monk. Lon. 1851. 2 v. 12°. 4233
Golden Legend. H. W. Longfellow. Boston, 1852. 12°. . . . 4606
Golden Sands of Mexico; a Tale. Philadelphia, 1850. 12°. . . . 3863
Golden Steps for Youth. J. M. Austin. Auburn, 1850. 12°. . . 3860
Goldenlink; or, Tales and Poems. W. O. Bourne. N. York, 1854. 12°. 5572
Goldsmith, J. Manners, Customs, &c., of Nations. Phil. 1818. 2 v. 12°. 1016
Goldsmith, O. History of England. London, 1812. 4 v. 8°. . . 4981
The same; improved by Pinnock. Philadelphia, 1850. 12°. 285
History of Greece. London, 1812. 2 v. 8°. 4982
The same. Philadelphia, 1818. 2 v. 12°. 203
History of Rome. London, 1812. 2 v. 8°. 4983
The same. Philadelphia, 1818. 12°. 290
Life. W. Irving. New York, 1840. 2 v. 12°. 2425
The same. (H. F. L.) N. York, 1846. 2 v. 12°. 3683, 121–2
The same. New York, 1849. 12°. 3367
Life. J. Prior. Philadelphia, 1837. 8°. 726
Life and Adventures. J. Forster. London, 1848. 8°. . . . 5172
Miscellaneous Works. Ed. by J. Prior. N. York, 1850. 4 v. 12°. 3454

Vol. 1. The Bee; Essays; State of Polite Learning in Europe; Prefaces and Introductions.
2. Letters from a Citizen of the World; Study of Natural History.
3. Vicar of Wakefield; Biographies; Miscellaneous Criticism.
4. Poems; Miscellaneous Pieces; Dramas; Criticisms.

Miscellaneous Works. Edinburgh, 1833. 4 v. 12°. . . . 1835

Vol. 1. Life; Commendatory Verses.
2. Poems; Plays; Letters.
3. Vicar of Wakefield.
4. State of Polite Learning in Europe; The Bee; History of Cyrillo Padovano; Life of Dr. Parnell; Life of Lord Bolingbroke; Prefaces and Introductions; Appendix.

Vicar of Wakefield. New York, 1845. 12°. 2
Goldsmith of Paris. C. F. W. Hoffman. New York, 1844. 8°. . 2167, 1
Good, J. M. Book of Nature. Boston, 1826. 2 v. 8°. 1263
Goodell, W. Changes of Thirty Years in the East. N. York, 1853. 12°. 5332
Goodman, G. Court of James I. London, 1839. 2 v. 8°. . . . 4651
Good Wives. Mrs. L. M. Child. Boston, 1833. 12°. 1839
Goodrich, Chas. A. History of United States. Hartford, 1826. 12°. . 68
Lives of the Signers of the Dec. of Ind. Hartford, 1842. 12°. . 3069
Visit to the Cities of Western Continent. Hartford, 1848. 8°. . 3622
Goodrich, Chauncey A. Select British Eloquence. N. Y. 1852. Roy. 8°. 5083
Goodrich, S. G. History of all Nations. Boston, 1851. 2 v. roy. 8°. . 4318
Parley's Cabinet Library. Boston, 1849. 20 v. 12°. 4900

Vol. 1. Famous Men of Modern Times.
2. Famous Men of Ancient Times.
3. Curiosities of Human Nature.
4. Lives of Benefactors.
5. Lives of Celebrated Indians.
6. Lives of Celebrated Women.
7. Lights and Shadows of American History.
8. Lights and Shadows of European History.

Goodrich, S. G. Parley's Cabinet Library, *continued*,

Vol. 9. Lights and Shadows of Asiatic History.
10. Lights and Shadows of African History.
11. History of the American Indians.
12. Manners and Customs of the Indians.
13. Glance at the Physical Sciences.
14. Wonders of Geology.
15. Anecdotes of the Animal Kingdom.
16. Glance at Philosophy.
17. Ancient and Modern Literature.
18. Enterprise, Industry, and Art of Man.
19. Manners and Customs of Nations.
20. World and its Inhabitants.

Parley's Present for all Seasons. New York, 1854. 12°. . . . 5570
Pictorial History of America. Philadelphia, 1854. 12°. . . . 1362
Sketches from a Student's Window. Boston, 1841. 12°. . . . 2302
Gordon, A. Lives of Pope Alexander VI. & Cæsar Borgia. Phil. 1844. 8°. 2894
Gordon, T. History of the Greek Revolution. Edinburgh, 1844. 2 v. 8°. 4826
Gordon, Wm., Closing Scenes in the Life of. N. Hall. Phil. 1852. 12°. 4780
Gordon, Wm. Hist. of the Independence of the U. S. Lond. 1788. 4 v. 8°. 578
Gore, Mrs. C. Castles in the Air. New York, 1848. 8°. 3237
Cecil; or the Adventures of a Coxcomb. New York, 1845. 8°. . 2240
Dean's Daughter; or, the Days we Live in. N. York, 1853. 12°. 5224
Hamiltons. London, 1852. 12°. 5688
Heir of Selwood. Philadelphia, 1838. 2 v. 12°. 1455
Mothers and Daughters. London, 1851. 12°. 5660
Peers and Parvenus. New York, 1846. 8°. 2710
Percy Ranthorpe. New York, 1848. 8°. 2875
Preferment. New York, 1840. 2 v. 12°. 1556
Progress and Prejudice. New York, 1854. 12°. 6260
(Editor.) Queen of Denmark. New York, 1846. 8°. . . . 2681
Soldier of Lyons. London, 1852. 12°. 5675
Story of a Royal Favorite. New York, 1846. 8°. 2664
Görgei, A. My Life and Acts in Hungary. New York, 1852. 12°. . 5244
Gorton, J. Biographical Dictionary. London, 1847. 3 v. 8°. . . 3597
Gorton, S. Life. J. M. Mackie. Boston, 1845. 12°. 1076, 15
Gospels, The Four, Notes on. A. Barnes. New York, 1851. 2 v. 12°. . 4730
Notes on. A. A. Livermore. Boston, 1854. 2 v. 12°. . . 6261
with Dissertations and Notes. G. Campbell. And. 1837. 2 v. 8°. 4703
Gosse, P. H. Sacred Streams; or, Rivers of the Bible. N. Y. 1852. 12°. 4482
Goth and the Hun. A. A. Paton. London, 1851. 8°. 4325
Gothic Architecture, Specimens of. A. Pugin. London, 1821. 2 v. 4°. 5101
Terms in, with 1700 Woodcuts. Oxford, 1852. 2 v. 8°. . . 2052
Government, Discourses on. Algernon Sidney. N. Y. 1805. 3 v. 8°. . 793
Gowrie; or, the King's Plot. G. P. R. James. New York, 1848. 8°. . 3212
Gould, A. A. Naturalist's Library. Boston, 1853. 8°. 2071
Report on Invertebrata of Mass. Cambridge, 1841. 8°. . . 1970
*U. S. Ex. Exped. Report on Mollusca and Shells. Bost. 1852. 4°. 5978
Gould, E. S. The Very Age; a Comedy. New York, 1850. 12°. . 3764
Gould, Hannah F. Diosma; a Perennial. Boston, 1851. 12°. . . . 4087
New Poems. Boston, 1850. 12°. 3492
Poems. Boston, 1839. 3 v. 12°. 1846

Gould, N. D. Church Music in America. Boston, 1853. 12°. . . 5061
Goulding, F. R. Young Marooners on the Florida Coast. Phil. 1852. 16°. 5185
Gouraud, F. F. Art of Memory. New York, 1845. Roy. 8°. . . 2269
Grace Greenwood. — See *Clarke, Sara J.*; and *Lippincott, Mrs. S. J.*
Grace Seymour. New York, 1830. 2 v. 12°. 520
Grafton, H. D. Treatise on the Camp and March. Boston, 1854. 12°. . 5615
Graham, G. F. English Synonymes. New York, 1847. 12°. . . 3004
Graham, T. Elements of Chemistry. Philadelphia, 1852. 8°. . . 5967
Graham's Magazine. Vols. 35–44 [continued]. Phil. 1849–54. Roy. 8°. 2783
Grahame, J. History of the United States. London, 1833. 2 v. 8°. . 1617
Grahame; or, Youth and Manhood. New York, 1850. 12°. . . . 4199
Grammar, Essay on. J. P. Wilson. Philadelphia, 1817. 12°. . . 586
of English Grammars. G. Brown. New York, 1851. 8°. . . 4699
Grammatical Structure of the Eng. Language. J. Mulligan. N.Y. 1852. 8°. 5122
Grammont, Count. Memoirs. A. Hamilton. Philadelphia, 1836. 8°. . 1317
Memoirs of the Court of Charles II. London, 1846. Post 8°. . 2952
Grandmother's Recollections. Ella Rodman. New York, 1852. 12°. . 4188
Granite Rock. S. Fish. Boston, 1836. 12°. 898
Grant, A., and the Nestorians. T. Laurie. Boston, 1853. 12°. . . 5305
Grant, J. British Senate. Philadelphia, 1838. 2 v. 12°. . . . 971
Every-Day Life in London. Philadelphia, 1839. 12°. . . 1582
Great Metropolis. New York, 1837. 2 v. 12°. 1901
Impressions of Ireland and the Irish. Philadelphia, 1845. 16°. . 2408
Random Recollections of House of Commons. Phil. 1836. 12°. . 226
The same. Philadelphia, 1836. 8°. 2228, 1
Random Recollections of House of Lords. Phil. 1836. 12°. . 1933
The same. Philadelphia, 1836. 8°. 2228, 2
Sketches of London. Philadelphia, 1839. 2 v. 12°. . . . 518
Walks in the World of Literature. Phil. 1840. 2 v. 12°. . . 867
Grant, J. Jane Seton; or, the King's Advocate. New York, 1853. 12°. 5529
Grant, Mrs. (of Laggan). Memoir & Corres. J. P. Grant. Lon. 1844. 3 v. 12°. 2397
Memoirs of an American Lady. New York, 1846. 12°. . . 2500
Grantley Manor; a Tale. Lady G. Fullerton. New York, 1848. 12°. . 3151
Grattan, H., Life and Times of. H. Grattan. London, 1839. 5 v. 8°. . 4977
The same. London, 1849. 5 v. 8°. 3624
Speeches. New York, 1813, 2 v. 8°. 731
Grattan, T. C. Heiress of Bruges. New York, 1831. 2 v. 12°. . . 357
The same. London, 1851. 12°. 5661
High-Ways and By-Ways. Boston, 1824. 2 v. 12°. . . . 143
The same. Boston, 1840. 3 v. 12°. 2131
History of the Netherlands. Philadelphia, 1831. 12°. . . 428
Jacqueline of Holland. London, 1853. 12°. 5726
Legends of the Rhine. London, 1853. 12°. 5738
Traits of Travel. Boston, 1829. 12°. 292
Graves, Mrs. A. J. Woman in America. (H.F.L.) N.Y. 1848. 12°. 3683, 166
Gray, F. C. Prison Discipline in America. Boston, 1847. 8°. . . 2860
Gray, Mrs. H. Emperors of Rome. London, 1850. 12°. . . . 4282
History of Etruria. London, 1843. 2 v. 12°. 3788

Gray, T. Letters and Poems. New York, 1827. 16°. 12
Poetical Works. New York, 1844. 16°. 12
Gray, T., jun. The Vestal. Boston, 1830. 12°. 483
Graydon, A. Memoirs of his own Time. Philadelphia, 1846. 8°. . 2722
Grayson, E. Overing; or, Heir of Wycherly. New York, 1852. 12°. 4871
Standish, the Puritan. New York, 1850. 12°. 3848
Grayson, W. S. True Theory of Christianity. New York, 1853. 12°. . 5601
Great Britain, Four Years in. C. Colton. New York, 1835. 2 v. 12°. . 1258
and Ireland, Memoirs of. Sir. J. Dalrymple. Lond. 1771. 2 v. 4°. 3630
History of. R. Henry. London. 1788. 12 v. 8°. 3631
in 1833. Baron D'Haussez. Philadelphia, 1833. 2 v. 12°. . . 1203
Popular Antiquities of. J. Brand. London, 1848. 3 v. post 8°. . 4369
Tour in, 1810–11. L. Simond. Edinburgh. 1817. 2 v. 8°. . 677
Great Commanders, Memoirs of. G. P. R. James. Phil. 1835. 2 v. 12°. 1087
Great Events, described by Historians. F. Lieber. Boston, 1840. 12°. . 2139
Great Hoggarty Diamond. W. M. Thackeray. New York, 1848. 8°. . 3244
Great Metropolis. R. Grant. New York, 1837. 2 v. 12°. . . . 1901
Great Salt Lake, Valley of. H. Stansbury. Washington, 1853. 8°. . 4939
Great Truths by Great Authors. Philadelphia, 1853. 12°. . . . 5387
Greece, and the Golden Horn. S. Olin. New York, 1854. 12°. . . 5862
and Rome, History of. — Cooper. Plymouth. 1818. 12°. . 317
and Turkey, Picturesque Sketches of. A. De Vere. Phil. 1850. 12°. 3909
Commerce of. F. Beaujour. London, 1800. 8°. 715
First History of. E. M. Sewell. New York, 1853. 18°. . . 5201
History of. O. Goldsmith. London, 1812. 2 v. 8°. . . . 4982
The same. Philadelphia, 1818. 2 v. 12°. 203
History of. G. Grote. London, 1849–50. 8 v. 8°. . . . 3962
The same, continued. Vols. 9–11. N. Y. 1853. 3 v. 12°. 3962
History of. W. Mitford. Boston, 1823. 8 v. 8°. 772
History of. W. Robertson. Edinburgh, 1793. 8°. . . . 724
History of. Wm. Smith. Boston, 1854. 12°. 5763
History of. C. Thirlwall. London, 1843. 7 v. 12°. . . . 1879
Memoirs of the Affairs of. J. Millingen. London, 1831. 8°. . 3194
Modern, History of. Sir J. E. Tennent. London, 1845. 2 v. 8°. . 5138
Outline History of. W. D. Hamilton. London, 1853. 12°. . 6114
Palest., Egypt, &c., Travels in. F.A.D.Chateaubriand. Phil.1813. 8°. 1320
Politics of Ancient. A. H. L. Heeren. Boston, 1824. 8°. . . 1299
Turkey,Egypt,&c.,Tour in. Mrs.G.L.D.Damer. Lon.1842. 2 v. 12°. 3660
Turkey, Russia, &c., Travels in. J. L. Stephens. N.Y. 1843. 2 v. 12°. 879
Gregg, J. Commerce of the Prairies. New York, 1844. 2 v. 12°. . 2098
Gregg, W. P., and B. Pond. Railroad Laws of U. S. Bost. 1851. 2 v. 8°. 4317
Gregory, G. Elements of a Polite Education. Boston, 1801. 12°. . 338
Letters on Literature, Taste, and Composition. Phil. 1809. 12°. . 371
Gregory, O. Evidences, Doctrines, &c., of Christianity. N.Y. 1826. 2v.12°. 1550
*Greek and Roman Antiquities, Dict. of. W. Smith. London, 1849. 8°. 3958
*Greek and Roman Biog. and Mythology. W. Smith. Lond.1849. 3 v. 8°. 3957
Greek and Latin Classics, Introduction to. T. F. Dibdin. Lon.1827. 2 v. 8°. 5089
Greek Grammar. H. C. Hamilton. London, 1854. 12°. . . . 6121

Greek Lexicon. H. R. Hamilton. London, 1852. 12°. 6122
H. G. Liddell and R. Scott. New York, 1849. Roy. 8°. . 3543
of the New Testament. E. Robinson. New York, 1850. Roy. 8°. 4349
Greek Literature, History of. R. W. Browne. Philadelphia, 1852. 12°. 4562
Greek Reader. F. Jacobs. Boston, 1835. 12°. 1459
Greek Revolution, History of. T. Gordon. Edinburgh, 1844. 2 v. 8°. . 4826
Historical Sketch of. S. G. Howe. New York, 1828. 12°. . 3580
Greek Testament; with Notes. S. T. Bloomfield. Phil. 1848. 2 v. 8°. . 4705
Greeks, Theatre of. Cambridge (Eng.), 1827. 8°. 5910
and Turks, Wayfaring Sketches among. London, 1849. 12°. . 4967
Greeley, H. Glances at Europe. New York, 1851. 12°. . . . 4497
(Editor.) Art and Industry at Crystal Palace. N.Y. 1854. 12°. 5643
Hints towards Reforms. New York, 1850. 12°. 3856
Green, T. J. Texan Expedition against Mier. New York, 1845. 8°. . 2623
Green Book. J. C. O'Callaghan. Boston, 1849. 12°. . . . . 3682.
Green Hand; a Short Yarn. F. Chamier. New York, 1851. 8°. . . 4501
Green Hand's First Cruise. Boston, 1841. 12°. 1706
Green Mountain Boys. D. P. Thompson. Boston, 1854. 12°. . . 3117
Green Mountain Spring. Vol. 1. Brattleboro', 1846. 8°. . . . 3224
Greene, G. W. Historical Studies. New York, 1850. 12°. . . . 3572

Petrarch; Machiavelli; Reformation in Italy; Italian Literature; Manzoni; Hopes of Italy; Historical Romance in Italy; Libraries; Verrazzano; Charles Edward; Contributions to the Pope.

Life of Nathaniel Greene. Boston, 1848. 12°. 1076, 20
Greene, N., Life. G. W. Greene. Boston, 1848. 12°. . . . 1076, 20
Life. W. G. Simms. New York, 1849. 12°. 3665
Greenbank, T. K. Periodical Library. Philadelphia, 1833. 3 v. 8°. . 1357
Greenhow, R. History of California and Oregon. Boston, 1845. 8°. . 2270
Greenough, H., Memorial of. H. T. Tuckerman. New York, 1853. 12°. 5377
Greenwood, J. Treatise on Navigation. London, 1850. 12°. . . 6073
Greenwood, F. W. P. History of King's Chapel. Boston, 1833. 12°. . 1053
Miscellaneous Writings. Boston, 1846. 12°. 2915
Sermons of Consolation. Boston, 1842. 12°. 1707
Greenwood Leaves. Sara J. Clarke. Boston, 1850–52. 2 v. 12°. . . 3456
Greer, Mrs. J. R. Society of Friends; Domestic Narrat. N.Y. 1853. 12°. 5248
Grenada, Conquest of. W. Irving. Philadelphia, 1829. 2 v. 12°. . . 1182
The same. New York, 1850. 12°. 3369
Grey, Maria G. Thoughts on Self-Culture. Boston, 1851. 12°. . . 4195
Grey, Mrs. Alice Seymour. Philadelphia, 1854. 8°. 6001
Duke and the Cousin. Philadelphia, 1848. 8°. 6003
Old Country House. New York, 1850. 8°. 3982
Rectory Guest. New York, 1849. 8°. 6005
Sybil Lennard. Philadelphia, 1848. 8°. 6002
Greyslaer; a Romance of the Mohawk. C. F. Hoffman. Phil. 1841. 2 v. 12°. 845
Griffin, F. Junius Discovered. Boston, 1854. 12°. 5786
Griffin, G. Duke of Monmouth. Philadelphia, 1837. 2 v. 12°. . . 923
Tales of my Neighborhood. Philadelphia, 1836. 2 v. 12°. . . 2183
Griffin, J. J. System of Crystallography. Glasgow, 1841. 8°. . . 1185

Grillparzer, F. Sappho; a Tragedy. Boston, 1846. 12°. . • . 2916
Grimaldi, J., Memoirs of. C. Dickens. Philadelphia, 1838. 2 v. 12°. . 820
Grimké, Angelina E. Letters on Slavery. Boston, 1838. 12°. . . 1531
Grimm, Bros. German Popular Tales. New York, 1853. 2 v. 12°. . 5608
Grimshawe, T. S. (Editor.) Works of Wm. Cowper. N.Y. 1849. Roy. 8°. 4348
Grimshaw, W. History of the United States. Philadelphia, 1821. 12°. 331
Grinnell Exploring Expedition. E. K. Kane. New York, 1854. 8°. . 5892
Griscom, J. H. Animal Mechanism and Physiology. N. Y. 1846. 12°. 3683, 85
Griswold, R. W. Female Poets of America. Philadelphia, 1849. 8°. . 3252
Poets and Poetry of America. Philadelphia, 1847. 8°. . . 1685
Poets and Poetry of England. Philadelphia, 1845. 12°. . . 2213
Prose Writers of America. Philadelphia, 1847. 8°. . . . 2775
Sacred Poets of England and America. New York, 1850. 8°. . 4700
Grote, G. History of Greece. London, 1849–50. 8 v. 8°. . . . 3962
The same, continued. Vols. 9–11. N. York, 1853. 3 v. 12°. 3962
Grumbler; a Novel. Ellen Pickering. New York, 1844. 8°. . . 1968
Grummett's Log. Philadelphia, 1835. 12°. 554
Grund, F. J. The Americans. Boston, 1837. 12°. 445
Elements of Natural Philosophy. Boston, 1832. 12°. . . 1457
Merchant's Assistant. Boston, 1834. 8°. 1767
Plane Geometry. Boston, 1830. 12°. 496
Guardian, The. Addison, Steele, and others. Glasgow, 1746. 2 v. 12°. 869
The same. Philadelphia, 1803. 2 v. 12°. 149
and Tatler. Addison, Steele, and others. New York, 1842. 8°. . 792, 3
The same. New York, 1852. Roy. 8°. . . . . • 4840
The same. New York, 1853. 12°. 5562, 3
Guerre, L'Art de la. G. R. Faesch. Leipzig, 1771. 2 v. 8°. . . 710
Guide for Young Disciples. J. G. Pike. New York, n. d. 18°. . . 343
Guide through Northern States and Canada. O. L. Holley. N.Y. 1844. 12°. 2599
Guide-Book of the New York and Erie Railroad. New York, 1851. 12°. 4208
Guido and Julius. F. A. G. Tholuck. Boston, 1854. 12°. . . . 6221
Guillemard, R. Adventures of a French Sergeant. Phil. 1826. 12°. . 1068
Guizot, M. Corneille and his Times. New York, 1852. 12°. . . 5195
Democracy in France. New York, 1849. 12°. 3342
Essay on Washington. Boston, 1840. 12°. 66
History of Civilization in Europe. New York, 1838. 12°. . . 1035
History of the English Revolution of 1640. N. Y. 1846. 2 v. 12°. 2565
History of Oliver Cromwell. Philadelphia, 1854. 2 v. 12°. . 5917
Shakspeare and his Times. New York, 1852. 12°. . . . 5194
Gulliver Joi; his Three Voyages. Ed. by E. Perce. N. Y. 1851. 16°. . 4472
Gulliver's Travels. J. Swift. New York, 1847. 12°. 2982
Gunn, J. C. Domestic Medicine. New York, 1851. 8°. . . . 4701
Gunnison, J. W. History of the Mormons. Philadelphia, 1852. 12°. . 4892
Guns and Shooting. P. Hawker. Philadelphia, 1853. 8°. . . . 5933
Gurney, J. J. Winter in the West Indies. New York, 1840. 8°. . . 1286
Gurney Married; Seq. to Gilbert Gurney. T. E. Hook. Phil. 1839. 2 v. 12°. 2516
Gurouski, Count de. Russia as it Is. New York, 1854. 12°. . . 5919
Gustavus Lindorm. Emilie F. Carlen. New York, 1853. 12°. . . 5557

Gutch, J. W. (Ed.) Robin Hood Garlands & Ballads. Lon. 1850. 2 v. 8°. 5471
Guthrie, W. Geograph. Hist. & Commercial Grammar. Lond. 1792. 8°. 737
Gutzlaff, C. Sketch of Chinese History. New York, 1834. 2 v. 12°. . 1916
Two Voyages to the Coast of China. New York, 1833. 12°. . 2152
Guy Fawkes. W. H. Ainsworth. Philadelphia, 1843. 8°. 2064
Guy Mannering. Sir W. Scott. Boston, 1848. 2 v. 12°. . . . 999, 3, 4
The same. Edinburgh, 1849. 2 v. 12°. . . . 4100, 3, 4
The same. Edinburgh, 1850. Roy. 8°. 4531, 1
Guyon, Mde., and Lady Russell. Lives. L. M. Child. Bost. 1832. 12°. 2376
Guyot, A. Earth and Man. Boston, 1852. 12°. 5213
Gwilt, J. Encyclopædia of Architecture. London, 1851. 8°. . . 4528
Gwynne, T. Nannette and her Lovers. New York, 1854. 12°. . . 5882
School for Fathers. New York, 1852. 12°. 4923
Gymnastic Exercises. M. Roth. Boston, 1853. 12°. 6139
Gypsies in Spain. G. Borrow. Philadelphia, 1844. 8°. . . . 2124
Gypsy Chief. G. W. M. Reynolds. New York, 1851. 8°. . . . 4500

H.

Hackett, H. B. Commentary on the Acts of the Apostles. Boston, 1852. 8°. 4724
Hackle, P. Hints on Angling. London, 1846. 8°. 5098
Hactenus. M. F. Tupper. Boston, 1848. 12°. 2448
Haddock, C. B. Addresses and Miscellaneous Writings. Cam. 1846. 8°. 2699
Haddock, J. W. Somnolism and Psycheism. Lond. 1851. 12°. . . 4286
Haddon, J. Examples in Differential Calculus. London, 1851. 12°. . 6111
Treatise on Algebra. London, 1850. 12°. 6097
Treatise on Bookkeeping. London, 1851. 12°. 6091
Hagar; a Story of To-Day. Alice Carey. New York, 1852. 12°. . . 4910
Hagenbach, K. R. History of Doctrines. Edinburgh, 1850. 2 v. 8°. . 5151
Hague, W. Discourse on J. Q. Adams. Boston, 1848. 8°. . . . 3533
Historical Discourse at Providence, 1839. Boston, 1839. 12°. . 1568
Hahn-Hahn, Ida (Countess). Travels in Sweden. London, 1845. 24°. 2419
Haines, C. G. Memoir of T. A. Emmet. New York, 1829. 12°. . . 220
Hair and the Skin, Treatise on. E. Wilson. Philadelphia, 1854. 12°. . 6177
Hajji Baba in England. J. Morier. London, 1853. 12°. . . . 5705
Hajji Baba of Ispahan. J. Morier. London, 1853. 12°. . . . 5704
Halcyon Luminary and Theological Repository. Vol. 1. N.Y. 1812. 8°. 783
Hale, C. (Editor.) To-Day; a Literary Journal. Boston, 1852. 2 v. 8°. 5418
Hale, D. Memoir. J. P. Thompson. New York, 1850. 12°. . . 3452
Hale, E. E. Kanzas and Nebraska. Boston, 1854. 12°. . . . 6255
Hale, S. Hist. of the U. States. (H. F. L.) N.Y. 1846. 2 v. 12°. 3683, 119, 120
Hale, Sarah J. *Dictionary of Poetical Quotations. Phil. 1851. 8°. . 2683
Liberia; or, Mr. Peyton's Experiments. New York, 1853. 12°. . 5614
Northwood; or, Life North and South. New York, 1852. 12°. . 4991
The same. Boston, 1827. 2 v. 12°. 1201
Sketches of American Character. Boston, 1829. 18°. . . . 176
Woman's Record. New York, 1853. Roy. 8°. 5104

Half-Century, History of. E. Davis. Boston, 1851. 12°. . . . 3784
Half-Hours with the Best Authors. C. Knight. N.Y. 1847. 3 v. 12°. . 3034
Haliburton, T. C. Clockmaker. Philadelphia, 1837. 12°. 924
Rule and Misrule of the English in America. New York, 1851. 12°. 4467
Yankee Stories. Philadelphia, 1849. 12°. 3348
Yankee Yarns and Letters. Philadelphia, 1852. 12°. . . . 1573
Hall, B. (Capt.). Fragments of Voyages and Travels. London, 1842. 8°. 2610
Patchwork. Philadelphia, 1841. 2 v. 12°. 2107
Skimmings; or, a Winter at Schloss Hainfield. Phil. 1836. 12°. 340
Hall, B. R. Frank Freeman's Barber Shop. New York, 1852. 12°. . 5034
Hall, E. Puritans, and their Principles. New York, 1847. 8°. . . 3529
Hall, E. B. Memoir of Mary L. Ware. Boston, 1853. 12°. . . . 5076
Hall, J. Legends of the West. New York, 1853. 12°. 5287
Wilderness and the War Path. New York, 1846. 12°. . . 2580
Life of Thomas Posey. Boston, 1848. 12°. 1076, 19
Hall, J. S. History of Boots and Shoes. New York, 1847. 12°. . . 4420
Hall, N. Closing Scenes in the Life of Wm. Gordon. Phil. 1852. 12°. 4780
Hall, R. Modern Infidelity. New York, 1853. 12°. 5346
Works; with Life. Ed. by O. Gregory. N. York, 1844. 4 v. 8°. 2076

Vol. 1. Sermons and Charges.
2. Political and Miscellaneous Tracts; Articles from the Eclectic Review; Miscellaneous Pieces.
3. Life, by O. Gregory; His Character as a Preacher, by John Foster; Notes of Sermons; Letters; Sermons.
4. (Edited by J. Belcher.) Reminiscences of Rev. Robert Hall, by John Greene; Notes of Sermons; Expository Discourses on the Epistle to the Philippians; Letters; Gleanings.

Hall, S. C. Gems of Modern Poets. Philadelphia, 1842. 12°. . . 1666
Hall, Mrs. S. C. Buccaneer. London, 1853. 12°. 5723
Lights and Shadows of Irish Life. Philadelphia, 1838. 2 v. 12°. 249
Marian; or, the Young Maid's Fortunes. New York, 1840. 2 v. 12°. 1523
Outlaw. London, 1852. 12°. 5682
Sketches of Irish Character. New York, 1829. 12°. . . . 2105
Whiteboy; a Story of Ireland. New York, 1845. 8°. . . 2640
and Mrs. J. Foster. Stories from History. New York, 1852. 12°. 4996
Hall, W. W. Bronchitis and Kindred Diseases. New York, 1852. 12°. . 4786
Hall and the Hamlet. W. Howitt. Philadelphia, 1847. 12°. . . 3053
Hallam, H. Constitutional History of England. Paris, 1841. 3 v. 8°. . 1823
Europe during the Middle Ages. New York, 1837. 8°. . . 1395
Liter. of Europe in 15th, 16th, & 17th Centuries. Par. 1837. 4 v. 8°. 584
Halleck, F. G. Alnwick Castle, and other Poems. New York, 1845. 12°. 2324
Fanny, with other Poems. New York, 1839. 12°. . . . 1530
Poetical Works. New York, 1852. 12°. 4867
(Ed.) Selec. from Br. Poets. (H. F. L.) N.Y. 1846. 2 v. 12°. 3683, 112, 113
Halleur, G. C. H. Treatise on Photography. London, 1854. 12°. . 6087
Halliwell, J. O. Autobiog. & Corres. of Sir S. D'Ewes. Lon. 1845. 2 v. 8°. 5477
Hallucinations, Apparitions, &c. A. B. de Boismont. Phil. 1853. 8°. . 5423
Halsted, Caroline A. Richard III. Philadelphia, 1844. 8°. . . . 2266
Hamilton, Alexander. Life. J. C. Hamilton. New York, 1840. 3 v. 8°. 1791
Life. H. B. Renwick. New York, 1841. 12°. 183

Hamilton, A. Life. H. B. Renwick. (H. F. L.) N. Y. 1845. 12°. 3683, 129
Works. Edited by J. C. Hamilton. New York, 1851. 7 v. 8°. . 4805

Vol. 1. Correspondence.
2. Political Miscellanies.
3. Papers as Secretary of the Treasury.
4. Cabinet Papers.
5. Cabinet Papers; Military Papers; Correspondence.
6. Correspondence and Political Papers.
7. Political and Law Papers; Index.

J. Jay, and J. Madison. The Federalist. Philadelphia, 1818. 8°. 697
Hamilton, Count A. Fairy Tales and Romances. London, 1849. Post 8°. 3447
Memoirs of Count Grammont. Philadelphia, 1836. 8°. . . . 1317
Hamilton, Elizabeth. Letters to the Daughter of a Nobleman. Salem, 1821. 12°. 1007
Hamilton, H. C. Greek Grammar. London, 1854. 12°. 6121
Hamilton, H. R. Greek Lexicon. London, 1852. 12°. 6122
Hamilton, J. Memoir of Lady Janet Colquhoun. New York, 1850. 12°. 3491
Royal Preacher. New York, 1851. 12°. 4297
Hamilton, R. British Fishes. Edinburgh, 1843. 2 v. 12°. . 4901, 36, 37
Amphibious Carnivora. Edinburgh, 1843. 12°. 4901, 25
Whales. Edinburgh, 1843. 12°. 4901, 26
Hamilton, T. Annals of the Peninsular Campaigns. Phil. 1831. 3 v. 12°. 1189
Cyril Thornton. New York, 1832. 2 v. 12°. 2143
Men and Manners in America. Philadelphia, 1833. 2 v. 12°. . 1166
Hamilton, Sir W. Discussions on Philosophy and Literature. N.Y. 1853. 8°. 5427
Philosophy. Edited by O. W. Wight. New York, 1853. 12°. . 5371
Hamilton, W. D. Outline History of England. London, 1852. 12°. . 6113
Outline History of Greece. London, 1853. 12°. 6114
Hamilton King; or, the Smuggler and the Dwarf. Phil. 1839. 2 v. 12°. 1040
Hamiltons, The. Mrs. C. Gore. London, 1852. 12°. 5688
Hamlin, E. Lady Lee's Widowhood. New York, 1853. 8°. . . . 5442
Hamlin, Mrs. H. A. L. Memoir. Mrs. M. W. Lawrence. Bost. 1854. 12°. 5545
Hammond, J. D. Polit. Parties of N.Y. State. Cooperstown, 1846. 2 v. 8°. 2847
Hammond, S. H. Hills, Lakes, and Forest Streams. N.Y. 1854. 12°. . 5878
Hampden, J. Life. J. Forster. London, 1837. 12°. 1831, 3
Handbook for American Travellers in Europe. R. Park. N.Y. 1853. 12°. 5312
for Central Italy. O. Blewitt. London, 1850. 12°. 74
for the Continent. London, 1851. 12°. 117
for Northern Europe. London, 1849. 2 v. 12°. 119
for Northern Italy. London, 1847. 12°. 71
for Readers and Students. A. Potter. New York, 1843. . . 2197
The same. (H. F. L.) New York, 1848. 12°. . 3683, 165
for Travellers in Egypt. G. Wilkinson. London, 1847. 12°. . 60
to the Galleries of London. Mrs. Jameson. London, 1845. 12°. 51
Handy Andy; a Tale of Irish Life. S. Lover. New York, 1850. 8°. . 1711
Hann, J. Analytical Geometry. London, 1850. 12°. 6099
Examples in Integral Calculus. London, 1850. 12°. . . . 6110
Plane Trigonometry. London, 1854. 12°. 6101
Spherical Trigonometry. London, 1849. 12°. 6100
Hanna, W. Memoirs of Thomas Chalmers. New York, 1850. 3 v. 12°. 3656
Hannah, J. (Ed.) Poems by Wotton, Raleigh, and others. Lond. 1845. 12°. 2505

Hannay, J. Singleton Fontenoy. New York, 1851. 8°. 4006
Hannibal, History of. J. Abbott. New York, 1849. 12°. 2467
Hanson, J. H. Lost Prince (Rev. E. Williams). New York, 1854. 12°. 5623
Hanson, J. W. History of Danvers, Mass. Danvers, 1848. 12°. . . 3120
Hanway, J. British Trade of Caspian Sea. London, 1753. 3 v. 4°. . 2002
Happiness, Conditions of Human. H. Spencer. London, 1851. 8°. . 4153
Essay on the Pursuit of. B. L. Oliver. Cambridge, 1818. 8°. . 1333
Haps and Mishaps in Europe. Mrs. S. J. Lippincott. Bost. 1854. 2 v. 12°. 5624
Happy Nights at Hazel Nook. Harriet Farley. Boston, 1854. 12°. . 5525
Harbaugh, H. Heaven; the Abode of the Sainted Dead. Phil. 1851. 12°. 4053
Hard Times. C. Dickens. New York, 1854. 8°. 5974
Hardie, J. Dictionary of the Wonders of Art & Nature. N.Y. 1819. 12°. 347
Hardwicke, Lord. Life. G. Harris. London, 1847. 3 v. 8°. . . . 5906
Hare, F. Study of the Scriptures. Boston, 1823. 12°. . . 368, 2
Harmon, D. W. Voyages and Travels in N. America. Andover, 1820. 8°. 1349
Harold; the Last of the Saxon Kings. E. L. Bulwer. N. York, 1848. 8°. 3199
Harold the Dauntless. Sir W. Scott. Philadelphia, 1839. 12°. . . 860, 6
Harpe, Mde. de la. Œuvres. Paris, 1778. 4 v. 8°. 641
Harper, Miss. Eventide; Tales and Poems. Boston, 1854. 12°. . . 6237
Harper, R. G. Select Works. Vol. 1. Baltimore, 1814. 8°. . . . 1328
Harper's Family Library. New York, 1843–48. 187 v. 12°. . . . 3683

Vols. 1–3. Milman, H. H. History of the Jews.
4, 5. Lockhart, J. G. Life of Napoleon Bonaparte.
6. Southey, R. Life of Horatio Lord Nelson.
7. Williams, J. Life of Alexander the Great.
8, 74. Natural History of Insects.
9. Galt, J. Life of Byron.
10. Bush, G. Life of Mohammed.
11. Scott, Sir W. Letters on Demonology and Witchcraft.
12, 13. Gleig, G. R. History of the Bible.
14. Leslie, Sir J., and others. Discovery in the Polar Seas.
15. Croly, G. Life of George IV.
16. Murray, H., and others. Discovery and Adventure in Africa.
17–19, 66, 67. Cunningham, Allan. British Painters, Sculptors, and Architects.
20. James, G. P. R. History of Chivalry and the Crusades.
21, 22. Bell, H. G. Life of Mary, Queen of Scots.
23. Russell, M. History of Egypt.
24. Fletcher, Jas. History of Poland.
25. Smith, H. Festivals, Games, and Amusements.
26. Brewster, Sir D. Life of Sir Isaac Newton.
27. Russell, M. History of Palestine.
28. Memes, J. S. Memoirs of the Empress Josephine.
29. Court and Camp of Bonaparte.
30. Lives and Voyages of Drake, Cavendish, and Dampier.
31. Barrow, J. Pitcairn's Island; and Mutiny of the Bounty.
32, 72, 84. Turner, S. Sacred History of the World.
33, 34. Jameson, Anna. Memoirs of Celebrated Female Sovereigns.
35, 36. Lander, R. & J. Travels in Africa.
37. Abercrombie, J. Inquiries concerning the Intellectual Powers.
38–40. St. John, J. A. Lives of Celebrated Travellers.
41, 42. Dover, Lord. Life of Frederick the Great.
43, 44. Smedley, E. Sketches from Venetian History.
45, 46. Thatcher, B. B. Indian Biography.
47–49. Murray, H., and others. Account of British India.
50. Brewster, Sir D. Letters on Natural Magic.
51, 52. Taylor, W. C. History of Ireland.
53. Tytler, P. F. Discovery on the more Northern Coasts of America.
54. MacGillivray, W. Life and Travels of Humboldt.
55, 56. Euler, L. Letters to a Princess on Natural Philosophy.
57. Mudie, R. Popular Guide to the Observation of Nature.
58. Abercrombie, J. Philosophy of the Moral Feelings.
59. Dick, T. Improvement of Society by Diffusion of Knowledge.
60. James, G. P. R. History of Charlemagne.
61. Russell, M. History of Nubia and Abyssinia.
62, 63. Russell, M. Life of Oliver Cromwell.

Harper's Family Library, *continued.*

Vol. 64. Montgomery, J. Letters on Poetry, Literature, &c.
65. Barrow, J. Life of Peter the Great.
68, 69. Crichton, A. History of Arabia.
70. Fraser, J. B. History of Persia.
71. Combe, A. Physiology applied to Health and Education.
73. Russell, M. History of the Barbary States.
75, 76. Paulding, J. K. Life of George Washington.
77. Ticknor, C. Philosophy of Living.
78. Higgins, W. M. The Earth; its Condition and Phenomena.
79. Sforzozi, L. History of Italy.
80, 81. Davis, J. F. The Chinese.
82. Historical Account of the Circumnavigation of the Globe.
83. Dick, T. Celestial Scenery.
85. Griscom, J. H. Animal Mechanism and Physiology.
86–91. Tytler, A. F., and Nares, E. Universal History.
92, 93. Franklin, B. Life of Himself, and Select Writings.
94, 95. Craik, G. L. Pursuit of Knowledge under Difficulties.
96, 97. Paley, Wm. Natural Theology; with Notes.
98. Rennie, J. Natural History of Birds.
99. Dick, T. Sidereal Heavens.
100. Upham, T. C. Imperfect or Disordered Mental Action.
101, 102. Murray, H., and others. History of British America.
103. Lossing, B. J. History of the Fine Arts.
104, 164. Ogilby, Martin, and Knight, C. Quadrupeds.
105. Park, Mungo. Writings, Life, and Travels of.
106. Dana, R. H., jun. Two Years Before the Mast.
107, 108. Parry, Sir W. E. Three Voyages for Discovery of Northwest Passage.
109, 110. Johnson, S. Life of; with Selections from his Works.
111. Bryant, W. C. (Editor.) Selections from American Poets.
112, 113. Halleck, F. G. (Editor.) Selections from the British Poets.
114–118. Keightley, T. History of England.
119, 120. Hale, S. History of the United States.
121, 122. Irving, W. Life of Goldsmith; with Select Writings.
123, 124. Malden, H. Distinguished Men of Modern Times.
125. Renwick, J. Life of De Witt Clinton.
126, 127. Mackenzie, A. S. Life of Oliver Hazard Perry.
128. Head, Sir F. B. Life and Travels of Bruce.
129. Renwick, H. B. Lives of John Jay and Alexander Hamilton.
130. Brewster, Sir D. Martyrs of Science.
131. Iceland, Greenland, and the Faroe Islands.
132. Manners and Customs of the Japanese.
133. Dwight, T., jun. History of Connecticut.
134, 135. Bucke, Chas. Ruins of Ancient Cities.
136, 137. Crichton, A., and Wheaton, H. Denmark, Norway, and Sweden.
138. Camp, G. S. Democracy.
139. Lanman, J. H. History of Michigan.
140. Fénélon, F. de S. de L. Lives of the Ancient Philosophers.
141, 142. Segur, Count P. de. Napoleon's Expedition to Russia.
143, 144. Henry, C. S. (Trans.) History of Philosophy.
145. Bucke, Chas. Beauties of Nature.
146. Lieber, F. Essays on Property and Labor.
147. White, G. Natural History of Selborne.
148. Wrangell, F. Expedition to the Polar Seas.
149, 150. Hazen, E. Popular Technology.
151–153. Spalding, W. Italy and the Italian Islands.
154, 155. Lewis, M., and Clarke, W. Travels West of the Mississippi.
156. Schmidt, H. I. History of Education.
157. Fraser, J. B. Mesopotamia and Assyria.
158. Russell, M. History of Polynesia.
159. Davenport, R. A. Perilous Adventures.
160. Duer, W. A. Constitutional Jurisprudence of the United States.
161–163. Belknap, J. American Biography.
164. Natural History of the Elephant.
165. Potter, A. Hand-Book for Readers and Students.
166. Graves, Mrs. A. J. Woman in America.
167, 168. Stone, W. L. Border Wars of the Revolution.
169. Vegetable Substances used for Food.
170. Michelet, J. Elements of Modern History.
171. Bacon, F. Essays; and, J. Locke, On the Understanding.
172. Voyages Round the World; from the Death of Captain Cook.
173. Murray, H. Travels of Marco Polo.
174, 175. American Adventure.
176. Bunner, E. History of Louisiana.
177. Florian, M. Moors of Spain.
178. Lee, A. Chas. Elements of Geology.
179. Potter, A. Objects and Uses of Science and Literature.

Harper's Family Library, *continued.*

Vol. 180. Moseley, H. Illustrations of Mechanics.
181, 182. Spectator in Miniature.
183. Potter, A. Political Economy.
184. Maury, Abbé. Principles of Eloquence.
185. Robertson, W. History of America; abridged.
186. Robertson, W. History of the Reign of Charles V.; abridged.
187. Ferguson, Adam. History of Rome; abridged.

Harper's New Monthly Magazine. Vols. 1–9 [con.] N. Y. 1850–54. 8°. 3735
Harring, H. Poland under the Dominion of Russia. Boston, 1834. 12°. 711
Harris, C. A. Principles and Practice of Dental Surgery. Phil. 1853. 8°. 5105
Harris, G. Life of Lord Hardwicke. London, 1847. 3 v. 8°. . . . 5906
Harris, J. Man Primeval. Boston, 1849. 12°. 3358
Pre-Adamite Earth. Boston, 1849. 12°. 3304
Harris M. System of Practical Bookkeeping. Hartford, 1838. 8°. . 1991
Harris, Sir W. S. Treatise on Electricity. London, 1853. 12°. . . 6041
Treatise on Magnetism. London, 1853. 12°. 6042
Harris, T. Life and Services of Com. W. Bainbridge. Phil. 1837. 8°. . 627
Harris, T. M. Tour through the North West Territory. Bost. 1805. 8°. 1310
Harris, T. W. Insects Injurious to Vegetation. Cambridge, 1842. 8°. . 1738
The same. Boston, 1852. 8°. 5116
Harris, W. C. Adventures in Africa. Philadelphia, 1850. 8°. . . 3946
Highlands of Ethiopia. New York, 1845. 8°. 2271
*Wild Sports of Southern Africa. London, 1852. 8°. 5093
Harrison, W. H. Tales of a Physician. Philadelphia, 1853. 2 v. 12°. . 856
Harrison, Wm. Henry, Life of. Boston, 1839. 16°. 80
Harry Ashton. J. F. Smith. New York, 1853. 8°. 5465
Harry Burnham, the Continental. H. A. Buckingham. N. Y. 1851. 8°. 4520
Harry Coverdale's Courtship. F. Smedley. New York, 1853. 12°. . 5363
Harry Lorrequer, Confessions of. C. Lever. New York, 1842. 8°. . 1589
Harry Muir; a Story of Scottish Life. Mrs. Oliphant. N. Y. 1853. 12°. 5263
Hart, A. M. History of Mississippi Valley. Cincinnati, 1853. 12°. . 5310
Hart, J. C. Romance of Yachting. New York, 1848. 12°. . . . 3185
Hart, J. S. Spenser and the Fairy Queen. Philadelphia, 1854. 12°. . 6223
Hartford Convention, History of. Theo. Dwight. New York, 1833. 8°. 746
*Hartshorn, J. Commercial Tables. Boston, 1852. Folio. . . . 5394
Harvard College. History of. J. Quincy. Cambridge, 1840. 2 v. 8°. . 2237
Sketch of. S. A. Eliot. Boston, 1848. 12°. 5330
Harverty, M. Wanderings in Spain, in 1843. London, 1844. 2 v. 12°. 4630
Hastings, W. Memoirs of. G. R. Gleig. London, 1841. 3 v. 8°. . 1453
Hatchie, the Guardian Slave. W. T. Ashton. Boston, 1853. 12°. . 5228
Haverhill; or, Memoirs of an Officer. J. A. Jones. N. Y. 1831. 2 v. 12°. 1187
Hawes, J. Lectures to Young Men. Hartford, 1830. 16°. . . . 90
Hawes, Virginia. Alone. Richmond, 1854. 12°. 5832
Hawk Chief. J. T. Irving, jun. Philadelphia, 1837. 12°. . . . 915
Hawker, P. Guns and Shooting. Philadelphia, 1853. 8°. . . . 5933
Hawkins, J. Voyage to the Coast of Africa. Philadelphia, 1797. 12°. . 831
Hawks, F. L. Monuments of Egypt; with Voy. up the Nile. N.Y. 1850. 8°. 3446
(Translator.) Peruvian Antiquities. New York, 1853. 8°. . 5440
Hawkesworth, J. Voyage of Discovery. Perth, 1789. 4 v. 12°. . . 169

Hawkins, B. History, Literature, &c., of Germany. London, 1838. 8°. 3193
Hawks of Hawk-Hollow. R. M. Bird. Philadelphia, 1835. 2 v. 12°. . 1096
Hawthorne, N. Blithedale Romance. Boston, 1852. 12°. . . . 4881
House of the Seven Gables. Boston, 1851. 12°. 4113
(Ed.) Journal of an African Cruiser. H. Bridge. N.Y. 1853. 12°. 2398
Life of Franklin Pierce. Boston, 1852. 12°. 4917
Mosses from an Old Manse. Boston, 1854. 2 v. 12°. . . . 3105
Scarlet Letter. Boston, 1850. 12°. 3653
Tanglewood Tales. Boston, 1853. 12°. 5506
Snow-Image, and other Tales. Boston, 1852. 12°. . . . 4598
True Stories from History and Biography. Boston, 1851. 12°. . 3774
Twice-Told Tales. Boston, 1851. 12°. 418
Wonder-Book for Girls and Boys. Boston, 1852. 12° . . . 4601
Hayden, Sarah M. Early Engagements. Cincinnati, 1854. 12°. . . 5800
Haydn and Mozart, Lives of. L. A. C. Bombet. Boston, 1839. 12°. . 471
*Haydn, J. Dictionary of Dates. London, 1847. 8°. 3959
Haydon, B. R. Autobiography. Ed. by T. Taylor. N. Y. 1853. 2 v. 12°. 5591
Lectures on Painting and Design. London, 1844. 2 v. 8°. . . 4674
Hays, Matilda M. (Trans.) Fadette; a Domestic Story. N. Y. 1851. 12°. 4039
Hayward, C., jun. Life of Sebastian Cabot. Boston, 1844. 12°. . 1076, 9
Hayward, J. Book of Religions. Boston, 1842. 12°. 2095
Gazetteer of Massachusetts. Boston, 1849. 12°. 3027
Gazetteer of New Hampshire. Boston, 1849. 12°. . . . 5555
*Gazetteer of United States. Hartford, 1853. 8°. 5402
Gazetteer of Vermont. Boston, 1849. 12°. 5556
Haywarde, R. Prismatics. New York, 1853. 12°. 5282
Hazen, E. Popular Technology. (H. F. L.) N. Y. 1848. 2 v. 12°. 3683, 149–50
Hazlitt, W. Characters of Shakspeare's Plays. Boston, 1818. 12°. . 2154
Characteristics, after Rochefoucault's Maxims. London, 1837. 12°. 2368
Classical Gazetteer. London, 1851. 12°. 4222
Conversations of James Northcote. London, 1830. 12°. . . 2317
Criticisms on Art. London, 1844. 12°. 1870
Eloquence of the British Senate. Brooklyn, 1810. 2 v. 8°. . . 621
Essays on the Principles of Human Action. London, 1841. 12°. 1876
Journey through France and Italy. London, 1826. 8°. . . 2286
The same. Philadelphia, 1833. 8°. 1357, 1
Lectures on Dramatic Literature. London, 1840. 12°. . . 1871
Lectures on the English Comic Writers. London, 1841. 12°. . 1874
Lectures on the English Poets. London, 1841. 12°. . . . 1875
Life of Napoleon. London, 1830. 4 v. 8°. 2262
Literary Remains. New York, 1836. 8°. 2082
Plain Speaker. Vol. 2. London, 1826. 8°. 2258
Political Essays. London, 1819. 8°. 2259
Round Table; a Collection of Essays. London, 1841. 12°. . 1872
Select Poets of Great Britain. London, 1825. 8°. . . . 2245
Sketches and Essays. London, 1839. 12°. 1873
Table-Talk. London, 1824. 2 v. 8°. 2290
The same. New York, 1845. 2 v. 12°. 2372

Hazlitt, W. View of the English Stage. London, 1818. 8°. . . . 2289
Head, Sir F. B. Bubbles from the Brunnen of Nassau. N.Y. 1845. 12°. 2487
The Emigrant. New York, 1847. 12°. 2951
Faggot of French Sticks. New York, 1852. 12°. 4755
Fortnight in Ireland. New York, 1853. 12°. 5199
Journey to the Pampas and Andes. Boston, 1827. 12°. . . . 508
Life and Travels of Bruce. (H. F. L.) New York, 1846. 12°. 3683, 128
Narrative, from Upper Canada. London, 1839. 8°. 1177
Head, Sir G. Tour in Manufacturing Districts of Eng. N.Y. 1847. 12°. 3038
Head of the Family. Miss Muloch. New York, 1852. 8°. 194
Headley, J. T. Alps and the Rhine. New York, 1847. 12°. . . . 2529
Imperial Guard of Napoleon. New York, 1851. 12°. 4625
Letters from Italy. New York, 1851. 12°. 2399
Life of Oliver Cromwell. New York, 1848. 12°. 3139
Lives of Gens. W. Scott and A. Jackson. New York, 1852. 12°. 4985
Miscellaneous Works. New York, 1849. 2 v. 12°. 3488

Vol. 1. Biographical Sketch of Author; Rome; Pope Pius IX. and Italy; Rambles through Paris; Rambles about London; Rambles in England and Wales; St. Regis Indians; Adaptation of One's Intellectual Efforts, &c.; Washington; Battle of Monmouth.
2. Waldenses; Paul Jones; Oliver Cromwell; Theirs's French Revolution; Alison's History of Europe; Waterloo; The One Progressive Principle.

Napoleon and his Marshals. New York, 1850. 2 v. 12°. . . . 2596
Power of Beauty. New York, 1850. 12°. 4041
Sacred Mountains. New York, 1847. 12°. 2989
Sacred Scenes and Characters. New York, 1850. 12°. . . . 3833
Second War with England. New York, 1853. 2 v. 12°. . . . 5533
Sketches and Rambles. New York, 1850. 12°. 3655
Washington and his Generals. New York, 1847. 2 v. 12°. . 2975
Headley, P. C. Life of Josephine. Auburn, 1850. 12°. 3910
Life of Louis Kossuth. Auburn, 1852. 12°. 4760
Life of Lafayette. Auburn, 1851. 12°. 4114
Women of the Bible. Auburn, 1850. 12°. 3846
Headlong Hall, and other Tales. G. Peacock. London, 1851. 12°. . 5665
The same. New York, 1845. 12°. 2358
Heads of the People; or, Portraits of the English. Phil. 1841. 8°. . 1604
Headsman; a Tale. J. F. Cooper. Philadelphia, 1848. 2 v. 12°. . 1188
Health, and Longevity, Code of. Sir J. Sinclair. London, 1844. 8°. . 4944
Guide to. A. Combe. Buffalo, 1849. 12°. 3393
Hints on. W. E. Coale. Boston, 1852. 12°. 4764
Influence of Religion upon. A. Brigham. Boston, 1835. 12°. . 1773
Lectures on. W. A. Alcott. Boston, 1853. 12°. 5256
Library of. Edited by W. A. Alcott. Boston, 1837. 2 v. 12°. . 955
Philosophy of. L. B. Coles. Boston, 1854. 12°. 5881
Physiology applied to. A. Combe. New York, 1851. 12°. . 2211
The same. (H. F. L.) New York, 1846. 12°. . 3683, 71
Preservation of. B. N. Comings. New York, 1854. 12°. . . 6189
Preservation of. J. C. Warren. Boston, 1854. 12°. . . . 5797
Report on, in Massachusetts. Boston, 1850. 8°. 3791

Health Report of the American Medical Association. Phil. 1849. 8°. . 3987
Health-Trip to the Tropics. N. P. Willis. New York, 1853. 12°. . 5577
Heart-Histories and Life-Pictures. T. S. Arthur. New York, 1853. 12°. 5180
Heart of Mid-Lothian. Sir W. Scott. Boston, 1848. 2 v. 12°. 999, 11, 12
The same. Edinburgh, 1849. 3 v. 12°. . . 4100, 11-13
The same. Edinburgh, 1850. Roy 8°. 4531, 3
Hearts and Faces; or, Home Life. J. T. Trowbridge. Boston, 1853. 12°. 5532
Hearts and Homes; or, Social Distinction. Mrs. Ellis. N.Y. 1850. 2 v. 8°. 3397
Hearts Unveiled. S. E. Saymore. New York, 1852. 12°. . . . 816
Heather, J. F. Descriptive Geometry. London, 1851. 12°. . . . 6084
Mathematical Instruments. London, 1851. 12°. . . . 6056
Heaven; the Abode of the Sainted Dead. H. Harbaugh. Phil. 1851. 12°. 4053
Heavenly Arcana. E. Swedenborg. Boston, 1837. 4 v. 8°. . . . 668
Heavens, The. R. Mudie. Philadelphia, 1836. 12°. 914
Architecture of. J. P. Nichol. New York, 1842. 12°. . . 2309
Heber, R. (Bishop.) Journey in India. Philadelphia, 1829. 2 v. 12°. . 1212
Life of. Boston, 1829. 18°. 129
Hebrew and English Lexicon. J. Parkhurst. London, 1799. Roy. 8°. . 1449
Hebrew Lyrical History. T. Bulfinch. Boston, 1853. 12°. . . . 5072
Hebrew Tales. H. Hurwitz. New York, 1847. 12°. 3084
Hebrews, Epistle to, Notes on. A. Barnes. New York, 1851. 12°. . 4737
Hebrews, Laws of the Ancient. E. C. Wines. New York, 1853. 8°. . 5390
Hector O'Halloran. W. H. Maxwell. New York, 1843. 8°. . . 1762
The same. London, 1852. 12°. 5683
Hedge, F. H. Prose Writers of Germany. Philadelphia, 1848. 8°. . 2872
Heeren, A. H. L. Politics of Ancient Greece. Boston, 1824. 8°. . . 1299
Carthaginians, Ethiopians, and Egyptians. Oxford, 1838. 2 v. 8°. 2657
Heidelberg; a Romance. G. P. R. James. New York, 1846. 8°. . . 2740
Heidenmauer; or, the Benedictions. J. F. Cooper. Phil. 1841. 2 v. 12°. 1162
The same. London, 1853. 12°. 5710
Heighway, O. W. T. Leila Ada. New York, 1854. 12°. . . . 6149
Heir of Redclyffe. New York, 1853. 2 v. 12°. 5246
Heir of Selwood. Mrs. C. Gore. Philadelphia, 1838. 2 v. 12°. . . 1455
Heir of Wast-Wayland. Mary Howitt. New York, 1851. 12°. . . 4210
Heiress. Ellen Pickering. Philadelphia, 1847. 8°. 470
Heiress of Bruges. T. C. Grattan. New York, 1831. 2 v. 12°. . . 357
The same. London, 1851. 12°. 5661
Heirs of Derwentwater. E. L. Blanchard. New York, 1851. 8°. . . 4127
Helen. Maria Edgeworth. New York, 1850. 12°. 935
The same. London, 1851. 12°. 5669
Helen and Arthur. Mrs. C. L. Hentz. Philadelphia, 1854. 12°. . . 5769
Helen Mulgrave; or, Jesuit Executorship. New York, 1853. 12°. . . 5585
Heloise; or, the Unrevealed Secret. Mrs. Robinson. N.Y. 1850. 12°. . 3870
Helps, A. Companions of my Solitude. Boston, 1852. 12°. . . . 6204
Friends in Council. Boston, 1849. 12°. 3373
Helvetic Union, Destruction of. J. Mallet. Boston, 1799. 12°. . . 180
Hemans, Mrs. Felicia, Memorials of. H. F. Chorley. Phil. 1836. 12°. . 973
Poetical Works. Philadelphia, 1836. 8°. 934

Hemans, Mrs. Felicia. Works; with Memoir. Phil. 1842. 7 v. 12°. . 2566
Henningsen, C. F. Campaign with Zumalacarregui. Phil. 1836. 8°. 2228, 2
The same. Philadelphia, 1836. 12°. 224
Henri; or, the Web and Woof of Life. W. G. Cambridge. Bost. 1853. 12°. 5362
Henri Quatre; or, Days of the League. G. P. R. James. N.Y. 1834. 2 v. 12°. 1074
Henrietta Temple. B. Disraeli. Philadelphia, 1845. 8°. . . . 2689
Henry II., History of. G. (Lord) Lyttleton. London, 1769. 6 v. 8°. . 5911
Henry IV., Life. G. P. R. James. New York, 1847. 2 v. 12°. . . 3065
Henry VIII. and his Contemporaries. B. Bensley. London, 1844. 12°. 2395
Henry, C. S. (Trans.) Hist. of Philosophy. N.Y. 1847. 2 v. 12°. 3683, 143, 144
Henry, Patrick. Life. A. H. Everett. Boston, 1844. 12°. . . 1076, 11
Life and Character of. W. Wirt. Hartford, 1852. 8°. . . 594
Henry, Paul. Life and Times of John Calvin. New York, 1851. 2 v. 8°. 4123
Henry, R. History of Great Britain. London, 1788. 12 v. 8°. . . 3631
Henry, W. S. Campaign Sketches of Mexican War. N. Y. 1847. 12°. 3091
Henry Esmond, History of. W. M. Thackeray. New York, 1852. 8°. . 5111
Henry Masterton. G. P. R. James. New York, 1832. 2 v. 12°. . . 171
The same. London, 1853. 12°. 5713
Henry of Guise. G. P. R. James. New York, 1839. 2 v. in 1. 12°. . 96
Henry Smeaton. G. P. R. James. New York, 1851. 8°. . . . 4010
Hentz, Caroline L. Eoline; or, Magnolia Vale. Philadelphia, 1852. 12°. 5221
Helen and Arthur. Philadelphia, 1854. 12°. 5769
Linda; or, the Young Pilot. Philadelphia, 1852. 12°. . . 3840
Marcus Warland. Philadelphia, 1852. 12°. 3574
Mob Cap, and other Tales. Philadelphia, 1852. 8°. . . . 4811
Planter's Northern Bride. Philadelphia, 1854. 2 v. 12°. . . 5787
Rena; or, the Snowbird. Philadelphia, 1851. 12°. . . . 4428
Ugly Effie, and other Tales. Philadelphia, 1853. 8°. . . . 5157
Victim of Excitement. Philadelphia, 1854. 12°. 5767
Wild Jack; or, the Stolen Child. Philadelphia, 1854. 12°. . . 5768
Hentz, N. M. Manual of French Phrases. Boston, 1822. 12°. . . 865
Heraldry, Curiosities of. M. A. Lower. London, 1845. 8°. . . . 3598
*Book of Family Crests. London, 1853. 2 v. 12°. . . . 6275
*General Armory. J. and J. B. Burke. London, 1853. 8°. . . 6006
Herbaceous Plants of Mass., Report on. C. Dewey. Camb. 1848. 8°. . 1969
Herbert, C. Relic of the Revolution. Boston, 1847. 12°. . . . 3049
Herbert, H. W. American Game in its Seasons. New York, 1853. 12°. 5327
Brothers. New York, 1835. 2 v. 12°. 1073
Captains of the Old World. New York, 1851. 12°. . . . 4496
Captains of the Roman Republic. New York, 1854. 12°. . . 6215
Cavaliers of England. New York, 1852. 12°. 1020
Chevaliers of France. New York, 1853. 12°. 5056
(Editor.) "Dinks" on Dogs. New York, 1850. 12°. . . 4070
Field Sports of United States. New York, 1849. 2 v. 8°. . . 3266
Fish and Fishing in the United States. New York, 1850. 8°. . 3417
Knights of England, France, and Scotland. New York, 1852. 12°. 4794
Marmaduke Wyvil. New York, 1853. 12°. 5317
Persons and Pictures from History. New York, 1854. 12°. . 5870

Herbert, H. W. Roman Traitor. New York, 1853. 12°. 5516
Warwick Woodlands. New York, 1851. 12°. 3842
Herbert Tracy; or, Trials of Mercantile Life. New York, 1851. 12°. . 5008
Herbert Wendall; a Tale of the Revolution. New York, 1835. 2 v. 12°. 1134
Heretic, The. M. Lajĕtchnikoff. New York, 1844. 8°. 2749
Heriot, G. Travels through the Canadas. Philadelphia, 1813. . . . 485
Hermit's Dell. New York, 1854. 12°. 6202
Herndon, Mary E. Louise Elton. Philadelphia, 1853. 12°. 5348
Herndon, W. L. Valley of the Amazon. Washington, 1854. 8°. . 5462
Herodotus. Translated by W. Beloe. New York, 1844. 3 v. 12°. 1854, 29–31
The same. New York, 1828. 3 v. 16°. 1500
Translated by H. Cary. London, 1850. Post 8°. 4378
Heroic Women of the West. J. Frost. Philadelphia, 1854. 12°. . . 5765
Heroines of History. Mrs. O. F. Owen. London, 1854. 12°. . . 5846
of the Missionary Enterprise. D. C. Eddy. Boston, 1850. 12°. . 3678
of Sacred History. Mrs. Steele. New York, 1850. 12°. . . 4045
Heroes and Hero-Worship. T. Carlyle. New York, 1849. 12°. . . 1595
Herschel, J. F. W. Outlines of Astronomy. Philadelphia, 1849. 8°. . 3471
Hervey, A. Ten Years in India. London, 1850. 3 v. 12°. . . 4239
Hervey, G. W. Principles of Courtesy. New York, 1852. 12°. . . 4781
Hervey, J. Letters; with Life and Character. Boston, n. d. 12°. . . 1026
Meditations and Contemplations. Philadelphia, 1808. 12°. . . 164
Hervey, J. (Lord.) Memoirs of Reign of George II. Phil. 1848. 2 v. 12°. 3157
Hervey, N. Memory of Washington. Boston, 1852. 16°. . . . 4595
Hervey, T. K. Book of Christmas; Descrip. of Customs, &c. N.Y. 1845. 12°. 2590
Heustis, D. D. (Capt.), Adventures and Sufferings of. Boston, 1847. 12°. 3067
Hewes, G. R. T. Memoir. New York, 1835. 12°. 1471
Hewitt, J. Treatise on Coins, Money, and Exchange. London, 1755. 8°. 1223
Hicks, Rebecca. Lady Killer. Philadelphia, 1851. 12°. 4635
Hieroglyphics and Egyptian Antiqui. Marquis Spineto. Lond. 1845. 8°. 4667
Higgins, W. M. Earth; its Condition & Phen. (H.F.L.) N.Y.1846. 12°. 3683, 78
High Life in New York. New York, 1854. 12°. 6211
Highland Widow, &c. Sir W. Scott. Boston, 1848. 12°. . . . 999, 39
The same. Edinburgh, 1849. 12°. 4100, 41
The same. Edinburgh, 1850. Roy. 8°. 4531, 10
Highlands and Highland Clans, Hist. of. J. Browne. Lond. 1851. 4 v. 8°. 5094
with Anecdotes of Rob Roy. Philadelphia, 1818. 16°. . . . 70
Highlands of Ethiopia. W. C. Harris. New York, 1845. 8°. . . 2271
Highton, E. Treatise on the Electric Telegraph. London, 1852. 12°. . 6059
High-Ways and By-Ways. T. C. Grattan. Boston, 1840. 3 v. 12°. . 2131
The same. Boston, 1824. 2 v. 12°. 143
Hildreth, R. Despotism in America. Boston, 1840. 12°. 1132
The same. Boston, 1854. 12°. 5926
History of the United States. New York, 1849–51. 6 v. 8°. . 2851
Memoirs of Archy Moore. Boston, 1839. 2 v. 12°. 1194
Theory of Morals. Boston, 1844. 12°. 1000
White Slave; or, Memoirs of a Fugitive. Boston, 1852. 12°. . 4882
Hildreth, S. P. Pioneer History; Ohio Valley, &c. Cincinnati, 1848. 8°. 3231

Hill, A. Familiar Letters. London, 1767. 8°. 573
Hill, G. Ruins of Athens, and other Poems. Boston, 1839. 8°. . . 1255
Hill, G. C. Cap Sheaf; a Fresh Bundle. New York, 1853. 12°. . . 5054
Dovecote; or, Heart of the Homestead. Boston, 1854. 12°. . 5619
Hill Difficulty, and other Miscellanies. G. B. Cheever. N. Y. 1849. 12°. 3357
Hillard, G. S. Life of Capt. John Smith. Boston, 1838. 12°. . 1076, 2
Oration on Daniel Webster. Boston, 1853. 8°. 5114
Six Months in Italy. Boston, 1853. 2 v. 12°. 5505
(Editor.) Works of Spenser. Boston, 1839. 5 v. 12°. . . . 1920
Hillhouse, J. A. Dramas, Discourses, &c. Boston, 1839. 2 v. 12°. . 1622
Hilliard, F. Elements of Law. Boston, 1835. 8°. 807
Hills, Lakes, and Forest Streams. S. P. Hammond. N. Y. 1854. 12°. . 5878
Hill-Side and Border Sketches. W. H. Maxwell. New York, 1847. 8°. 2780
Himalaya Mountains, Journey in. Sir W. Lloyd. London, 1846. 8°. . 4021
Hind, J. R. Solar System. New York, 1852. 12°. 4880
Hindoo Rajah, Letters of a. Trans. by E. Hamilton. Bost. 1819. 2 v. 12°. 127
Hindostan, Scenes & Characteristics in. E. Roberts. Phil. 1836. 2 v. 12°. 1123
The same. Philadelphia, 1836. 8°. 2228, 1
Hinton, J. H. History and Topography of U. States. Bost. 1834. 2 v. 4°. 2028
Hints and Helps for the Home Circle. New York, 1844. 12°. . . 2138
Hipsley, W. Equational Arithmetic. London, 1852. 12°. . . . 6096
Hirscher, J. B. von. Sympathies of the Continent. Oxford, 1852. 12°. 5237
Hirst, H. B. Coming of the Mammoth, and other Poems. Bost. 1845. 12°. 2470
Endymion; a Tale of Greece. Boston, 1848. 12°. . . . 3127
Historic Doubts relative to Napoleon. R. Whately. N. Y. 1853. 12°. . 6203
Hist. Causes and Effects, from 476 to 1517. W. Sullivan. Bost. 1838. 12°. 922
Historical Collections. — See *Collections*.
Historical Proof, Process of. I. Taylor. London, 1828. 8°. . . . 2287
History, Ancient. C. Rollin. New York, 1845. 2 v. roy. 8°. . . 704
and General Policy, Lectures on. J. Priestley. Phil. 1803. 2 v. 8°. 598
Catechetical Compend of General. F. Butler. Hartford, 1818. 16°. 38
Christ in. R. Turnbull. Boston, 1854. 12°. 5603
Compend of. S. Whelpley. New York, 1844. 12°. . . . 333
Connexion of Sacred and Profane. D. Davidson. N.Y. 1849. 8°. 3517
Elements of General. A. F. Tytler. New York, 1818. 8°. . 566
Epitomized. B. Tucker. Richmond, 1806. 12°. . . . 324
of New York. W. Irving. New York, 1849. 12°. 1051
Manual of Ancient and Modern. W. C. Taylor. N.Y. 1845. 8°. 2253
Modern, Elements of. J. Michelet. (H.F.L.) N.Y. 1848. 12°. 3683, 170
Modern, Lectures on. T. Arnold. London, 1845. 8°. . . 2615
Modern, Lectures on. F. Schlegel. London, 1849. Post 8°. . 4375
Modern, Lectures on. W. Smyth. Cambridge, 1841. 2 v. 8°. . 1677
of all Nations. S. G. Goodrich. Boston, 1851. 2 v. roy. 8°. . 4318
of the World. Sir W. Raleigh. London, 1677. Folio. . . 3749
Outlines of. Philadelphia, 1831. 12°. 441
Outlines of Universal. Edited by F. Bowen. Boston, 1853. 8°. 5165
Philosophically Illustrated. G. Miller. London, 1849. 4 v. post. 8°. 4393
Philosophy of. F. Schlegel. London, 1846. Post 8°. . . 2343

History, Study and Use of. Lord Bolingbroke. Paris, 1808. 8°. . . 790
Study and Use of Ancient and Modern. J. Bigland. Phil. 1806. 8°. 648
Treasury of. S. Maunder. London, 1850. 12°. 4107
Universal. F. Butler. Hartford, 1822. 12°. 439
Universal. A. F. Tytler. Boston, 1850. 2 v. 8°. . . . 692
Universal. A.F.Tytler & E. Nares. (H.F.L.) N.Y.1846. 6 v.12°. 3683,86–91
Hitchcock, D. Poetical Works. Boston, 1806. 12°. 1458
Hitchcock, D. K. Preservation of the Teeth. Boston, 1840. 24°. . . 1499
Hitchcock, E. Final Report on Geology of Mass. Amherst, 1841. 2 v. 4°. 2026
(Editor.) Life of Mary Lyon. Northampton, 1852. 12°. . . 4624
Outline of the Geology of the Globe. Boston, 1853. 8°. . . 5439
Religion of Geology. Boston, 1851. 12°. 4207
Hits and Dashes by "Cymon." Boston, 1852. 12°. 4590
Hive of the Bee-Hunter. T. B. Thrope. New York, 1854. 12°. . . 5867
Hoadly, B., Selections from Works of. Boston, 1823. 12°. . . . 368, 1
Hobbes, T. Analysis of Aristotle's Rhetoric. London, 1850. Post 8°. . 4381
Tripos, in Three Discourses. London, 1840. 8°. 2284
Hoboken; a Romance of New York. T. S. Fay. N.Y. 1843. 2 v. 12°. 1731
Hobomok; a Tale of Early Times. Mrs. L. M. Child. Bost. 1824. 12°. 870
Hochelaga; or, Eng. in the New World. E. Warburton. N.Y. 1846. 2 v. 12°. 2914
Hodgson, R. Life of Beilby Porteus. New York, 1811. 12°. . . 192
Hofland, T. C. British Angler's Manual. London, 1848. Post 8°. . 4972
Hoffman, C. F. Greyslaer. Philadelphia, 1841. 2 v. 12°. 845
Life of Jacob Leisler. Boston, 1844. 12°. 1076, 13
Vigil of Faith, and other Poems. New York, 1845. 18°. . . 2415
Wild Scenes of the Forest and Prairie. New York, 1843. 2 v. 12°. 1727
Hoffman, C. F. W. Goldsmith of Paris. New York, 1844. 8°. . 2167, 1
Rolandsitten. New York, 1844. 8°. 2167, 1
Hofland, Mrs. Young Pilgrim. New York, 1828. 12°. . . . 353
Hog, The, with Illustrations. London, n. d. Roy. 8°. . . . 3635, 2
Hogarth, G. Musical Drama. London, 1850. 8°. 5141
Musical History, Biography, and Criticism. New York, 1848. 8°. 3261
*Hogarth, W. Works, with Descriptions by Trusler. Lond. n. d. 2 v. 4°. 4819
Hogg, J. Songs. New York, 1832. 12°. 857
Winter Evening Tales. Hartford, 1847. 2 v. 12°. 1461
Holcombe, J. P. Law of Debtor and Creditor. New York, 1849. 8°. . 4306
Leading Cases in Mercantile Law. New York, 1847. 8°. . . 4304
Holidays Abroad. Mrs. C. M. Kirkland. New York, 1849. 2 v. 12°. . 3375
Holland, History of. C. M. Davies. London, 1851. 3 v. 8°. . . . 5135
Holland, E. G. Essays; and Drama in Five Acts. Boston, 1852. 12°. . 5081
Holland, H. R. (Lord). Foreign Reminiscences. New York, 1851. 12°. 3797
Holland, W. M. Life and Polit. Opin. of M. Van Buren. Hart. 1836. 12°. 1847
Holley, H., Discourse on. C. Caldwell. Boston, 1828. 8°. . . . 1387
Holley, O. L. Guide through East. States and Canada. N.Y. 1844. 12°. 2599
Hollis-street Church Controversy, 1838–39. Boston, 1839. 8°. . . 1615
Holman, J. Travels in Madeira, Brazil, &c. London, 1840. 4 v. 8°. . 1986
Holmes, A. American Annals. Cambridge, 1805. 2 v. 8°. . . . 1618
Annals of America. Cambridge, 1829. 2 v. 8°. 1403

Holmes, A. Life of Ezra Stiles. Boston, 1798. 8°. 714
Holmes, J. Art of Rhetoric; or, Elements of Oratory. Phil. 1849. 12°. 3305
Holmes, Mary J. Tempest & Sunshine; or, Life in Kentucky. N.Y. 1854. 12°. 5804
Holmes, O. W. Astræa; a Poem. Boston, 1850. 12°. 4040
Poems. Boston, 1849. 12°. 258
Holmes, W. R. Sketches of the Shores of the Caspian. Lond. 1845. 8°. 4642
Holstein, H. L. V. D. Memoirs of Simon Bolivar. Boston, 1829. 8°. . 1390
Holt, E. Life of George III. London, 1820. 2 v. 8°. 1285
Holy and Profane States. T. Fuller. Cambridge, 1831. 12°. . 383, 1
Holy Land. — See *Palestine*.
Holy Living and Dying. Jeremy Taylor. Philadelphia, 1843. 12°. . 2406
Homans, J. S. Sketches of Boston, Past and Present. 1851. 16°. . 2725
Home. Catherine M. Sedgwick. Boston, 1841. 18°. 2196
Home; or, Family Cares and Joys. F. Bremer. New York, 1844. 8°. 2087
Home; or, the Iron Rule. Mrs. Ellis. New York, 1843. 12°. . . 250
Home and Social Philosophy: from "Household Words." N.Y. 1852. 12°. 4758
Home as Found. J. F. Cooper. Philadelphia, 1838. 2 v. 12°. . . 1143
Home Education. I. Taylor. New York, 1838. 12°. 2356
Home Influence. Grace Aguilar. New York, 1848. 12°. . . . 3167
Home in the Valley. Emilie Carlen. New York, 1854. 12°. . . . 6214
Home is Home; a Domestic Tale. New York, 1851. 12°. . . . 4416
Home Life; or, Causes and Consequences. Mrs. E. C. Embury. N.Y. 1848. 12°. 3180
Home Life in Germany. C. L. Brace. New York, 1853. 12°. . . 5308
Home Narratives: from "Household Words." New York, 1852. 12°. . 858
Home Pictures. Mary A. Denison. New York, 1853. 12°. 5354
Home Scenes and Heart Studies. Grace Aguilar. New York, 1853. 12°. 5066
Home Scenes and Home Sounds. Mrs. H. M. Stephens. Bost. 1854. 12°. 5627
Homes and Haunts of British Poets. W. Howitt. N. Y. 1847. 2 v. 12°. 3009
of American Authors. New York, 1853. 8°. 5452
of the New World. Fredrika Bremer. New York, 1853. 2 v. 12°. 5537
Homer, Iliad. Translated by T. A. Buckley. London, 1851. Post 8°. . 4179
Iliad. Translated by G. Chapman. London, 1843. 2 v. 12°. . 2696
Iliad. Translated by W. Cowper. New York, 1850. 12°. . . 3468
Odyssey. Trans. by T. A. Buckley. London, 1851. Post 8°. . 4180
Works. Translated by A. Pope. Philadelphia, 1841. 8°. . . 2674
The same. New York, 1844. 3 v. 12°. . . 1854, 32–34
Homeward Bound. J. F. Cooper. New York, 1845. 2 v. 12°. . . 851
Homiletics; or, Theory of Preaching. A. Vinet. New York, 1854. 12°. 5742
Homœopathic Domestic Physician. J. H. Pulte. New York, 1852. 12°. 4801
Homœopathy, Theory and Practice of. I. G. Rosenstein. Louisv. 1840. 12°. 1892
Honan, M. B. Our own Correspondent in Italy. New York, 1852. 12°. 4922
Hone, W. Ancient Mysteries and Miracle-Plays. London, 1823. 8°. . 2694
Every-Day Book. London, 1841. 3 v. 8°. 2277
Honeymoon, and other Comicalities, from Punch. New York, 1854. 12°. 6164
Hood, G. History of Music in New England. Boston, 1846. 13°. . 2553
Hood, T. Hood's Own. With Comic Illustrations. New York, 1852. 12°. 2854
Poems. New York, 1846. 12°. 2900
Prose and Verse. New York, 1852. 12°. 2485

Hood, T. Tylney Hall. Philadelphia, 1844. 8°. 2798
The same. London, 1852. 12°. 5673
Up the Rhine. New York, 1852. 12°. 4875
Whims and Oddities, in Prose and Verse. New York, 1852. 12°. 4990
Whimsicalities. New York, 1852. 12°. 4759
Hook, T. E. All in the Wrong. London, 1852. 12°. 5679
Births, Deaths, and Marriages. Philadelphia, 1839. 2 v. 12°. . 989
Capitalist; or, Fortune's Frolics. New York, 1844. 8°. . 2167, 2
Fathers and Sons. Philadelphia, 1842. 2 v. 12°. 900
Gilbert Gurney. Philadelphia, 1845. 8°. 1124
The same. London, 1852. 12°. 5677
Gurney Married: Sequel to Gilbert Gurney. Phil. 1839. 2 v. 12°. 2516
Jack Brag. Philadelphia, 1837. 2 v. 12°. 844
The same. London, 1852. 12°. 5670
Maxwell. London, 1851. 12°. 5659
Parson's Daughter. London, 1851. 12°. 5663
Snowdon; a Novel. New York, 1845. 8°. 2665
Widow and the Marquis. London, 1852. 12°. 5678
Hook, W. F. Church Dictionary. Philadelphia, 1854. 8°. . . . 5430
Hooker, R. Works; with Life, by I. Walton. Oxford, 1843. 2 v. 8°. . 1961
Hooker, W. Lessons from the Hist. of Medical Delusions. N.Y. 1850. 12°. 4049
Physician and Patient. New York, 1849. 12°. 3430
Hooper, J. H. Widow Rugby's Husband. Philadelphia, 1851. 12°. . 4173
Hooper, Jane W. Arbell; a Tale. New York, 1853. 12°. . . . 5313
Hooton, C. Colin Clink. Philadelphia, 1840. 2 v. 12°. . . . 1551
Hope, T. Anastasius. Paris, 1831. 2 v. 8°. 432
Hope Leslie. Cath. M. Sedgwick. New York, 1842. 2 v. 12°. . . 188
Hopes and Helps for the Young. G. S. Weaver. New York, 1853. 12°. 5269
Hopkins, M. Essays and Discourses. Boston, 1847. 8°. . . . 2855

Mystery; Argument from Nature of the Divine Existence; Human Happiness; Originality; Connection between Taste and Morals; Addresses and Sermons.

Lectures on the Evidences of Christianity. Boston, 1847. 8°. . 2856
Hopkins, S. Works; with Memoir. Ed. by E. A. Park. Bos. 1852. 3 v. 8°. 4940
Hopkinson, F. Miscellaneous Essays. Philadelphia, 1792. 3 v. 8°. . 1308
Hopper, I. T.; a True Life. Mrs. L. M. Child. New York, 1853. 12°. 5381
Hoppin, J. M. Notes of a Theological Student. New York, 1854. 12°. 6183
Horace in London. H. and J. Smith. Boston, 1813. 18°. . . . 162
Horace, Q. F. Origin. Views of Passages in. J. Murray. Dublin, 1851. 8°. 5416
Works. Translated by C. Smart. London, 1850. Post 8°. . . 4384
Works. Translated by P. Francis. New York, 1825. 2 v. 12°. . 23
The same. New York, 1840. 2 v. 12°. . . 1854, 18, 19
Horace Templeton; an Autobiography. C. Lever. Phil. 1850. 8°. .. 3981
Horace Vernon; or, Fashionable Life. Philadelphia, 1839. 2 v. 12°. . 2144
Horæ Paulinæ. W. Paley. New York, 1851. 8°. 4704
Hordynski, J. History of the Polish Revolution. Boston, 1833. 8°. . 622
Horne, R. H. Dreamer and the Worker. London, 1851. 2 v. 12°. . 4231
New Spirit of the Age. New York, 1844. 12°. 2123

Horne, R. H. Orion; an Epic Poem. London, 1843. 12°. . . . 2473
Horner, F. Memoir and Corres. Ed. by L. Horner. Bost. 1853. 2 v. 8°. 5446
Horse, The; with Illustrations. London, n. d. Roy. 8°. . . 3635, 1
and his Rider. R. Springfield. London, 1847. 12°. 5835
Structure and Diseases of. W. Youatt. New York, 1852. 12°. . 5077
Horse-Doctor, Modern. G. H. Dadd. Boston, 1854. 12°. 5838
Horse-Shoe Robinson. J. P. Kennedy. Philadelphia, 1845. 2 v. 12°. . 1107
Horses, Asses, &c., Natural History of. C. H. Smith. Edin. 1843. 12°. 4901, 20
Horsemanship, for Ladies. J. Allen. London, 1825. 8°. 5956
*Art of. S. Freeman. London, 1806. 4°. 4828
Lady's Equestrian Manual. Philadelphia, 1854. 12°. . . . 5836
Method of. F. Baucher. Philadelphia, 1852. 12°. 5834
Horton, F. Fireside Lectures for Sabbath Evenings. Boston, 1850. 12°. 3880
Hosmer, W. H. C. The Months. Boston, 1847. 12°. 3039
Hotchkin, J. H. History of Western New York. New York, 1848. 8°. 3216
Hot-Houses, Practical Treatise on. R. B. Leuchars. Boston, 1851. 12°. 4081
House I Live in. W. A. Alcott. Boston, 1842. 12°. 1027
House of Commons, Lives of the Speakers of. J. A. Manning. Lon. 1851. 8°. 5147
Random Recollections of. J. Grant. Philadelphia, 1836. 12°. . 226
The same. Philadelphia, 1836. 8°. 2228, 1
House of Lords, Random Recollections of. J. Grant. Phil. 1836. 12°. . 1933
The same. Philadelphia, 1836. 8°. 2228, 2
House of the Seven Gables. N. Hawthorne. Boston, 1851. 12°. . . 4113
Household Surgery. J. F. South. London, 1851. 18°. 4774
Household Words. Con. by C. Dickens. Vols. 1–9 [con.]. N.Y. 1850–54. 8°. 4129
Housekeeper, Trials of an American. Philadelphia, 1854. 12°. . . 5812
Houssaye, A. Men and Women of the 18th Century. N.Y. 1852. 2 v. 12°. 3736
Philosophers and Actresses. New York, 1852. 2 v. 12°. . . 4927
Houstoun, Mrs. Texas and Gulf of Mexico. Philadelphia, 1845. 16°. . 2189
How to Observe. H. Martineau. New York, 1838. 12°. . . . 246
Howadji in Syria. G. W. Curtis. New York, 1852. 12°. . . . 4799
on the Nile. G. W. Curtis. New York, 1851. 12°. . . . 3823
Howard, E. Jack Ashore. Philadelphia, 1840. 2 v. 12°. . . . 964
Old Commodore. Philadelphia, 1837. 2 v. 12°. 931
Outward Bound. Philadelphia, 1838. 2 v. 12°. 823
Ratlin the Reefer. London, 1851. 12°. 5667
Howard, F. Illustrations of Shakspeare. London, 1833. 5 v. 8°. . . 5480
Howard, H. R. History and Adventure of V. A. Stewart. N.Y. 1836. 12°. 233
Howard, J. Life. H. Dixon. New York, 1850. 12°. 3472
Memoirs. Boston, 1830. 12°. 112
Howe, F. Oriental and Sacred Scenes. New York, 1854. 12°. . . 5751
Howe, H. Historical Collections of Ohio. Cincinnati, 1847. 8°. . . 2814
Historical Collections of Virginia. Charleston, 1845. 8°. . . 2719
Memoirs of Eminent American Mechanics. New York, 1847. 12°. 2990
Howe, S. G. Hist. Sketch of the Greek Revolution. N.Y. 1828. 12°. . 3580
Howe, Mrs. S. G. Passion Flowers. Boston, 1854. 12°. . . . 5773
Howie, J. Scots Worthies. Glasgow, 1839. 2 v. 8°. 2059
The same. New York, 1853. 8°. 4938

Howitt, Anna M. Art Student at Munich. Boston, 1854. 12°. . . 5805
Howitt, Mary. Artist Wife, and other Tales. New York, 1853. 12°. . 5504
Ballads, and other Poems. New York, 1847. 12°. . . . 2959
Citizen of Prague. New York, 1846. 8°. 2661
Dial of Love. Philadelphia, 1854. 12°. 5583
Gabriel; a Story of Wichnor Wood. New York, 1850. 18°. . 3667
Heir of Wast-Wayland. New York, 1851. 12°. 4210
Midsummer Flowers. Philadelphia, 1854. 12°. 6252
Pictorial Calendar of the Seasons. London, 1854. Post 8°. . . 5920
Strive and Thrive. Boston, 1841. 18°. 2161
Wood Leighton. Philadelphia, 1837. 3 v. 12°. 965
Howitt, R. Impressions of Australia Felix. London, 1845. 12°. . . 2392
Howitt, W. Book of the Seasons; or, Calendar of Nature. Phil. 1831. 12°. 1048
Country Year Book. New York, 1850. 12°. 4054
Hall and the Hamlet. Philadelphia, 1847. 12°. 3053
History of Priestcraft. New York, 1833. 12°. 2111
Homes and Haunts of British Poets. New York, 1847. 2 v. 12°. 3009
Madam Dorrington of the Dene. London, 1851. 3 v. 12°. . . 4619
Rural and Domestic Life of Germany. New York, 1842. 8°. . 1719
Rural Life of England. Philadelphia, 1841. 8°. 2061
Story of Peter Schlemihl. New York, 1844. 8°. . . . 2167, 2
Student-Life of Germany. Philadelphia, 1842. 8°. . . . 2075
Visits to Remarkable Places. Philadelphia, 1842. 8°. . . . 1764
and Mary. Stories of English & Foreign Life. Lon. 1853. Post 8°. 5944
Howitt's Journal. Ed. by W. & M. Howitt. Vols. 1, 2. Lond. 1847. 8°. 2880
Hoyle, E. Games. Philadelphia, 1838. 24°. 2417
Hubback, Mrs. Wife's Sister; or, Forbidden Marriage. N. Y. 1851. 8°. 4131
Hubbard, F. M. Life of W. R. Davie. Boston, 1848. 12°. . . 1076, 25
Hubbard, W. General History of New England. Boston, 1815. 8°. . 2632
Hubbell, Mrs. M. S. Shady Side; or, Life in a Parsonage. Bost. 1853. 12°. 5252
Huc, M. Journey to Tartary, Thibet, &c., 1844–46. N. Y. 1852. 2 v. 12°. 946
Hudibras. S. Butler. With Notes and Memoir. New York, 1847. 12°. 2946
Hudson, H. Life. H. R. Cleveland. Boston, 1844. 12°. . . 1076, 10
Hudson, H. N. Lectures on Shakspeare. New York, 1848. 2 v. 12°. . 3112
Hudson River and Vicinity, Letters about. F. Hunt. N. Y. 1837. 18°. 161
Hudson's Bay. R. M. Ballantyne. Edinburgh, 1848. 12°. . . . 5550
Hudson's Bay Co.'s Discoveries, 1836–39. T. Simpson. Lond. 1843. 8°. 4344
Hufeland, C. W. Art of Prolonging Life. Boston, 1854. 12°. . . 5589
Hughes, S. Treatise on Gas Works. London, 1853. 12°. . . . 6092
Hughs, T. New American Speaker. Philadelphia, 1835. 12°. . . 2158
Hugo, V. Hunchback of Notre Dame. New York, 1848. 8°. . . 3249
The same. London, 1851. 12°. 5658
The Rhine. New York, 1845. 12°. 2508
Huguenot; a Tale. G. P. R. James. New York, 1839. 2 v. 12°. . . 1114
Huguenot Family, Memoirs of. J. Fontaine. New York, 1853. 12°. . 5067
Huguenots, in France and America. H. F. Lee. Boston, 1852. 2 v. 12°. 5057
History of. W. S. Browning. Philadelphia, 1845. 8°. . . 3530
History of. Mrs. Marsh. London, 1847. 2 v. 8°. . . . 4643

Hull, W. Revolu. Services and Civil Life. M. Campbell. N.Y. 1848. 8°. 2863
Hulse, Georgie A. Sunbeams and Shadows. New York, 1851. 12°. . 4429
Human Action, Principles of. W. Hazlitt. London, 1841. 12°. . . 1876
Human Body, as Connec. with Man, J. J. G. Wilkinson. Phil. 1851. 12°. 4487
Human Life; or, Pract. Ethics. W. M. L. DeWette. Bost. 1842. 2 v. 12°. 962, 12, 13
 Science of. S. Graham. Boston, 1836. 12°. 898
 View of. F. Petrarch. London, 1797. 8°. 591
Human Magnetism. W. Newnham. New York, 1845. 12°. . . 2342
Human Physiology. R. Dunglison. Philadelphia, 1844. 2 v. 8°. . . 1795
Human Progression, Theory of. Boston, 1851. 12°. 4433
Human Species, Natural History of. C. H. Smith. Boston, 1851. 12°. . 4476
Human Rights, Essays on. E. P. Hurlbut. New York, 1850. 12°. . 3125
Humane Society of Massachusetts, History of. Boston, 1845. 8°. . . 2629
Humboldt, A. von. Biography. Prof. Klencke. New York, 1853. 12°. 5243
 Aspects of Nature in Different Lands. Philadelphia, 1849. 12°. . 3469
 Cosmos. New York, 1849–1852. 4 v. 12°. 3565
 Life and Travels. (H. F. L.) New York, 1848. 12°. . 3683, 54
 Personal Narrative of Travels. London, 1853. 3 v. post 8°. . 5384
 Political Essay on New Spain. New York, 1811. 2 v. 8°. . . 604
 Travels and Researches, condensed. New York, 1843. 16°. . . 1852
 Views of Nature. London, 1850. Post 8°. 4364
Humboldt, W. von. Life. Schlesier. New York, 1853. 12°. . . 5243
 Religious Thoughts and Opinions. Boston, 1851. . . . 5757
Humbugs of New York. D. M. Reese. New York, 1838. 12°. . . 960
Hume, D. Essays and Treatises. Vol. 1. London, 1788. 8°. . . 2079
 History of England. New York, 1846. 2 v. 8°. 705
  The same. Boston, 1854. 6 v. 8°. 5499
  The same. Boston, 1851. 6 v. 12°. 3499
 Life and Correspondence. J. H. Burton. Edin. 1846. 2 v. 8°. . 5149
 Philosophical Works. Boston, 1854. 4 v. 8°. 5957
 Private Correspondence. London, 1820. 4°. 2031
Humphrey Clinker. T. Smollett. New York, 1835. 12°. . . . 396
  The same. Philadelphia, 1851. 8°. 801, 2
Humphreys, D. Life of Israel Putnam. Boston, 1818. 12°. . . 190
 Miscellaneous Works. New York, 1790. 8°. 642
Humorous Speaker. New York, 1853. 12°. 5500
Hunchback of Notre Dame. V. Hugo. New York, 1848. 8°. . . 3249
  The same. London, 1851. 12°. 5658
Hungarian Brothers. Anna M. Porter. Philadelphia, 1809. 2 v. 12°. . 355
  The same. London, 1850. 12°. 5648
Hungarian War and Kossuth. Philadelphia, 1851. 12°. . . . 4633
Hungary and her Institutions. Miss Pardoe. 1840. 3 v. 12°. . . 3122
 and Kossuth. B. F. Tefft. Philadelphia, 1852. 12°. . . . 4626
 in 1851. C. L. Brace. New York, 1852. 12°. 980
 My Life and Acts in. A. Görgei. New York, 1852. 12°. . . 5244
 Protestant Church in. J. H. M. D'Aubigné. Phil. 1854. 12°. . 5853
 Revelations of. Baron Prochazka. London, 1851. 12°. . . 4228
 Tales and Traditions of. Theresa Pulszky. London, 1851. 12°. . 4240

Hungary, War of Independence in. Gen. Klapka. Lond. 1850. 2 v. 12°. 4634
Hunt, F. Letters about the Hudson River. New York, 1837. 18°. . 161
(Editor.) Merchant's Magazine. Vols. 1–30. N. Y. 1839–54. 8°. 1586
Hunt, L. Autobiography. New York, 1850. 2 v. 12°. . . . 3905
Book for a Corner. New York, 1852. 2 v. 12°. 1088
Essays : The Indicator and the Seer. London, 1841. Roy. 8°. . 2614
Essays and Miscellanies : Indicator and Companion. Phil. 1854. 12. 5764
(Editor.) Foster Brother ; a Tale. New York, 1846. 8°. . . 2648
Imagination and Fancy. New York, 1845. 12°. 2331
The Indicator. London, 1842. 8°. 2234
Lord Byron and his Contemporaries. London, 1828. 2 v. 8°. . 2291
Men, Women, and Books. New York, 1847. 2 v. 12°. . . 3013
Rimini, and other Poems. Boston, 1844. 12°. 2410
Sir Ralph Esher. London, 1850. 12°. 5737
Stories from the Italian Poets. New York, 1846. 12°. . . . 2564
Table Talk. London, 1851. 12°. 6274
Wit and Humor. New York, 1846. 12°. 2587
Hunt R. Elementary Physics. London. 1851. 12°. 5051
Panthea, or Spirit of Nature. London, 1850. 12°. . . . 5097
Poetry of Science. Boston, 1850. 12°. 4082
Hunter, H. Sacred Biography. Philadelphia, 1832. 8°. . . . 1288
'Hunter Naturalist. C. W. Webber. Philadelphia, 1851. Roy. 8°. . 1340
Hunter's Life in South Africa. R. G. Cumming. N. Y. 1850. 2 v. 12°. 3933
Hunting the Romantic. J. Sandeau. New York, 1852. 12°. . . 4878
Huntingdon, Selina, Countess of, and her Friends. N. Y. 1853. 12°. . 5634
Life and Times of. London, 1844. 2 v. 8°. 5134
Huntington, D. General View of the Fine Arts. New York, 1851. 12°. 4060
Huntington, J. V. Alban. New York, 1851. 12°. 4448
Forest. New York, 1852. 12°. 5217
Lady Alice ; or, the New Una. New York, 1849. 2 v. 12°. . 3382
Hurlbut, E. P. Essays on Human Rights. New York, 1850. 12°. . 3125
Hurlbut, W. H. Gan Eden ; or, Pictures of Cuba. Boston, 1854. 12°. 6160
Hurry-Graphs. N. P. Willis. New York, 1851. 12°. 4162
Hursthouse, C., jun. Settlement of New Zealand. London, 1849. 12°. 4291
Hurton, W. Voyage from Leith to Lapland, 1850. Lond. 1851. 2 v. 12°. 4257
Hurwitz, H. Hebrew Tales. New York, 1847. 12°. 3084
Huskisson, W. Speeches. London, 1831. 3 v. 8°. 4657
and W. Windham. Select Speeches. Philadelphia, 1837. 8°. . 1817
Hutchinson, Anne. Life. G. E. Ellis. Boston. 1076, 16
Hutchinson, Lucy. Life of Col. Hutchinson. London, 1846. Post 8°. . 3558
Hutchinson, T. Hist. of Massachusetts, 1628–1750. Bost. 1795. 2 v. 8°. 1284
Hutted Knoll. J. F. Cooper. New York, 1843. 2 v. 12°. . . . 1734
Hydraulic Engineering, Treatise on. G. R. Burnell. Lond. 1852. 12°. 6045
Hydraulics and Mechanics. T. Ewbank. New York, 1846. 8°. . . 2790
Hydropathy. R. T. Claridge. New York, 1849. 12°. 3404
Hylton House, and its Inmates. New York, 1850. 8°. 3944
Hypatia ; or, New Foes, &c. C. Kingsley, jun. Boston, 1854. 2 v. 12°. 5576
Hyperion ; a Romance. H. W. Longfellow. Boston, 1850. 12°. . . 1078

I.

Iceland, Greenland, and Faroe Islands. (H. F. L.) N. Y. 1846. 12°. 3683, 131
Journey to. Ida Pfeiffer. New York, 1852. 12°. 1005
Letters on. U. von Troil. Dublin, 1780. 8°. 596
Rambles in. P. Miles. New York, 1854. 12°. 5963
Idle Man. Vol. 1. New York, 1821–22. 8°. 1302
Idler, The. S. Johnson. New York, 1816. 12°. 522
The same. New York, 1843. Roy. 8°. 1984, 1
Ignorance, Popular Essay on the Evils of. J. Foster. N. Y. 1850. 12°. 3662
Ike Marvel. — See *Mitchell, D. G.*
Iliad. — See *Homer*.
Illinois, History of. W. H. Carpenter and T. S. Arthur. Phil. 1854. 12°. 6283
History of, from 1818–47. T. Ford. Chicago, 1854. 12°. . . 6198
*Illustrated American Biography. A. D. Jones. Vol. 2. N.Y. 1854. Roy. 8°. 5889
Illustrated London Almanack, 1845–50. London, 4°. 5102
*Illustrated London News. London, 1844, '45, '48, '49. 4 v. 4°. . . 4834
Illustrated Magazine of Art. Vols. 1–3 [con.] N. Y. 1853–54. Roy. 8°. 5887
*Illustrated News (Barnum & Beech's). New York, 1853. 2 v. 4°. . 5984
Illustrated Parlor Miscellany. London, 1849. 8°. 3416
Illustrations of Genius. H. Giles. Boston, 1854. 12°. 6228
Image of his Father. Bros. Mayhew. New York, 1848. 12°. . . 3173
Imaginary Conversations. W. S. Landor. London, 1826. 5 v. 8°. . 2261
Imagination and Fancy. L. Hunt. New York, 1845. 12°. . . . 2331
Imitations of Celebrated Authors. London, 1844. 12°. 2570
Immigration into the United States. Jesse Chickering. Boston, 1848. 8°. 4035
Imperial Guard of Napoleon. J. T. Headley. New York, 1851. 12°. . 4625
Improvisatore. H. C. Andersen. New York, 1845. 8°. . . . 2243
The same. London, 1853. 12°. 5736
Improvisatrice, and other Poems. Letitia E. Landon. Phil. 1847. 8°. 1343, 2
In Memoriam. A. Tennyson. Boston, 1850. 12°. 3888
Incarnation; or, Pictures of the Virgin & her Son. C. Beecher. N.Y. 1849. 12°. 3306
Inchbald, Mrs. Eliza, Memoirs of. J. Boaden. London, 1833. 2 v. 8°. . 2293
Simple Story. London, 1852. 12°. 5655
Incidents in a Pastor's Life. W. Wisner. New York, 1851. 12°. . 4436
Index of Books Prohibited by Gregory XVI. J. Mendham. Lon. 1840. 12°. 3066
to Periodical Literature. W. F. Poole. New York, 1853. Roy. 8°. 5444
to Subjects in Periodicals. W. F. Poole. New York, 1848. 8°. . 3210
India and the Hindoos. F. De W. Ward. New York, 1850. 12°. . 3935
British. H. Murray and others. (H. F. L.) N.Y. 1848. 3 v. 12°. 3683, 47–49
British; Historical and Descriptive Account of. N.Y. 1842. 3 v. 12°. 1857
Character, Manners, &c., in. J. A. Dubois. Phil. 1818. 2 v. 8°. 725
Condition and Char. of the Natives. R. Rickards. Lon. 1829. 2 v. 8°. 3955
Continental. J. W. Massie. London, 1840. 2 v. 8°. 4543
Cotton and Commerce of. J. Chapman. London, 1850. 8°. . 4328
Goa, and the Blue Mountains. R. F. Burton. London, 1851. 12°. 4577

India, History of British. J. Mill. London, 1830. 6 v. 8°. . . . 2230
Historical Disquisition on. W. Robertson. London, 1804. 8°. . 535
The same. Philadelphia, 1812. 8°. 1295
Journey to. (No titlepage.) 12°. 204
Overland Journey to. Major Skinner. Philadelphia, 1837. 12°. . 913
Rise and Progress of Brit. Power in. P. Auber. Lon. 1837. 2 v. 8°. 4660
*Seventeen Years in. J. Forbes. Lond. 1834. 2 v. 8°. 1 v. plates, 4°. 3796
Six Years in. Mrs. C. Mackenzie. New York, 1853. 12°. . . 5548
Stranger in. G. W. Johnson. London, 1843. 2 v. 12°. . . 4966
Ten Years in. A. Hervey. London, 1850. 3 v. 12°. . . . 4239
Travels in. R. Heber. Philadelphia, 1829. 2 v. 12°. . . . 1212
Indian Archipelago, History of. J. Crawfurd. Edin. 1820. 3 v. 8°. . 4818
Native Races of. G. W. Earl. London, 1853. 12°. . . . 5741
Voyages in, 1832–34. G. W. Earl. Lond. 1837. 8°. . . . 4688
Indian Biography. B. B. Thacher. New York, 1843. 2 v. 12°. . . 2427
The same. (H. F. L.) New York, 1846. 2 v. 12°. 3683, 45, 46
Indian Sketches. J. T. Irving, jun. Philadelphia, 1835. 2 v. 12°. . 1895
Indian Tales and Legends. H. R. Schoolcraft. New York, 1839. 2 v. 12°. 240
*Indian Tribes of N. Amer. H. R. Schoolcraft. Wash. 1851–54. 4 v. 4°. 1723
Thirty Years' Residence with. H. R. Schoolcraft. Phil. 1851. 8°. 4544
Indian Wars. H. Trumbull. Boston, 1833. 8°. 1334
The same. Boston, 1841. 8°. 759
of the West. T. Flint. Cincinnati, 1833. 12°. 1456
Indians, Book of. J. Frost. New York, 1845. 12°. 2210
History of. S. G. Goodrich. Boston, 1849. 12°. . . 4900, 11
League of the Ho-dé-no-sau-nee. L. H. Morgan. Roch. 1851. 8°. 3825
Lives of Celebrated. S. G. Goodrich. Boston, 1849. 12°. 4900, 5
Manners and Customs of. S. G. Goodrich. Boston, 1849. 12°. 4900, 12
North American. G. Catlin. New York, 1844. 2 v. 8°. . . 1780
Notes on the Iroquois. H. R. Schoolcraft. Albany, 1847. 8°. . 2841
Ojibway Nation. G. Copway. Boston, 1851. 12°. 4176
Origin of the North American. J. McIntosh. New York, 1853. 8°. 1841
Travels among. T. L. M'Kenney. New York, 1846. 8°. . . 2765
Indiana Gazetteer. Indianopolis, 1849. 12°. 3496
Indications of the Creator. G. Taylor. New York, 1851. 12°. . . 4456
Indicator, The. L. Hunt. London, 1841. Roy. 8°. 2614
The same. London, 1842. 8°. 2234
Inductive Sciences, History of. W. Whewell. London, 1837. 3 v. 8°. . 2273
Philosophy of. W. Whewell. London, 1840. 2 v. 8°. . . 2692
Industry of all Nations, Cyclopædia of. C. Knight. New York, 1851. 8°. 4506
Infidelity, Aspects, Causes, and Agencies of. T. Pearson. N.Y. 1854. 8°. 5435
Common Maxims of. H. A. Rowland. New York, 1850. 12°. . 3493
Counsels to Young Men on Modern. J. Morison. Bost. 1834. 12°. 1477
Difficulties of. G. S. Faber. New York, 1853. 12°. . . . 5346
Modern. R. Hall. New York, 1853. 12°. 5346
Treatises against. New York, n. d. 12°. 504
Infirmities of Genius. R. R. Madden. Philadelphia, 1833. 2 v. 12°. . 2551
Influence; or, the Evil Genius. Miss M. Planche. London, 1853. 12°. 6292

Ingersoll, C. J. History of the War of 1812. 2d series. Phil. 1852. 2 v. 8°. 5177
Ingoldsby Legends. 1st series. R. H. Barham. New York, 1852. 12°. 4775
Ingraham, J. H. Burton; or, the Sieges. New York, 1847. 2 v. 12°. . 958
Captain Kyd. New York, 1847. 2 v. 12°. 525
Dancing Feather. New York, 1851. 8°. 4534
Lafitte. New York, 1836. 2 v. 12°. 263
Quadroon; or St. Michael's Day. New York, 1847. 2 v. 12°. . 1599
South-West. New York, 1835. 12°. 1100
Inheritance. Susan Ferrier. London, 1853. 12°. 5725
Initials; a Story of Modern Life. Philadelphia, 1850. 8°. 3971
The same. Philadelphia, 1852. 12°. 4876
Inklings of Adventure. N. P. Willis. New York, 1836. 2 v. 12°. . 223
Innes, W. Advice to Church Members. Boston, 1833. 12°. . . . 1475
Inquisition, Dealings with the. G. Achilli. New York, 1851. 12°. . 4175
at Goa. M. Dellon. Boston, 1815. 16°. 27
History of. Compiled by C. Mason. Philadelphia, 1835. 12°. . 910
History of. Edited by Miss Christmas. London, 1851. 12°. . 4613
Imprisonment of J. Van Halen, at Madrid. New York, 1828. 8°. 741
Insanity, Medical Jurisprudence of. I. Ray. Boston, 1853. 8°. . . 5386
Inscriptions in Graveyards. — See *Epitaphs*.
Insect Architecture. Boston, 1830. 12°. 110
Insect Life, Episodes of. New York, 1851. 3 v. 8°. 4128
Insects Injurious to Vegetation. T. W. Harris. Camb. 1842. 8°. . 1738
The same. Boston, 1852. 8°. 5116
Natural History of. (H.F. L.) New York, 1843. 12°. . 3683, 8, 74
Insurance, Law of. S. Marshall. Boston, 1805. 8°. 1389
Marine. Adjustments of Losses. Stevens & Benecke. Bos. 1833. 8°. 2060
Marine, Laws of. J. A. Park. Boston, 1799. 8°. . . . 782
Insurgents; an Historical Novel. Philadelphia, 1835. 2 v. 12°. . . 939
Intellectual Powers. J. Abercrombie. Boston, 1839. 12°. . . . 1572
The same. (H. F. L.) New York, 1846. 12°. . 3683, 37
Essays on. T. Reid. Cambridge, 1850. 12°. 3571
Interment in Towns, Report on. E. Chadwick. London, 1843. 8°. . 3390
Interviews, Memorable and Useful. S. H. Cox. New York, 1853. 12°. 5262
International Magazine. Vols. 1–5. New York, 1850–52. 8°. . . 3734
International Law, Elements of. H. Wheaton. Philadelphia, 1846. 8°. 3538
Invalide; or, Pictures of the French Rev. C. Spindler. N. Y. 1844. 8°. 2726
Inventions, Discoveries, &c., Hist. of. J. Beckmann. Lon. 1846. 2v. post 8°. 3090
History of Wonderful. New York, 1849. 12°. 3372
Inventor's Manual of Legal Principles. G. T. Curtis. Boston, 1851. 12°. 4298
Invertebrata, Anatomy of. C. T. v. Siebold. Boston, 1854. 8°. . . 5891
of Mass., Report on. A. A. Gould. Cambridge, 1841. 8°. . . 1970
Io; a Tale of the Olden Fane. K. Barton. New York, 1851. 12°. . 4437
Ion; a Tragedy. T. N. Talfourd. New York, 1846. 12°. . . . 2403
The same. New York, 1850. 12°. 2531, 1
Ionian Islands and Malta, Notes on. J. Davy. London, 1842. 2 v. 8°. . 5472
Iphigenia in Tauris; a Drama. J. W. von Goethe. N. York, 1850. 12°. 4084
Ireland and the Irish, Impressions of. J. Grant. Phil. 1845. 16°. . . 2408

Ireland, as I Saw it. W. S. Balch. New York, 1850. 12°. 3489
Catechism of the History of. W. J. O. Daunt. Bost. 1850. 24°. 3759
Excursion through, 1844–45. A. Nicholson. N. York, 1847. 12°. 3031
Famine in, 1847–49. Mrs. A. Nicholson. New York, 1851. 12°. 4161
Fortnight in. Sir F. B. Head. New York, 1853. 12°. . . . 5199
Gazetteer of. J. M. Wilson and J. P. Lawson. Dub. n. d. 2 v. 12°. 5038
Gleanings in the West of. S. G. Osborne. London, 1850. 12°. . 4290
History of. Abbé MacGeoghegan. Dublin, 1844. Roy. 8°. . 3964
History of. T. Mooney. Boston, 1845. 2 v. roy. 8°. . . . 2670
History of. T. Moore. Philadelphia, 1843. 8°. . . . 1982
History of. W. C. Taylor. (H. F. L.) N. Y. 1848. 2 v. 12°. 3683, 51, 52
Legends, Tales, and Stories of. Philadelphia, 1837. 2 v. 12°. . 908
Memoir on Native & Saxon. D. O'Connell. Vol. 1. N.Y. 1843. 12°. 1851
Miseries of; their Cause and Cure. E. M. Dill. N. Y. 1852. 12°. 4793
National Education, Reports on. Dublin, 1844. 8°. . . . 2628
Patriotic Sketches of. Miss Owenson. Baltimore, 1809. 12°. . 199
Saxon in. London, 1851. 12°. 4230
Irish Agent. W. Carleton. New York, 1846. 12°. 2927
*Irish Almanac and Directory for 1851. A. Thorn. Dublin, 1851. 8°. . 11
Irish Bar, Sketches of. R. L. Sheil. New York, 1854. 2 v. 12°. . . 5755
Irish Confederates and Rebellion of 1798. H. M. Field. N. Y. 1851. 12°. 4115
Irish Gentleman. Trav. in Search of a Religion. T. Moore. Balt. 1847. 12°. 3680
Irish Guardian. Dublin, 1776. 2 v. 12°. 121
Irish Sketch Book. W. M. Thackeray. Philadelphia, 1843. 8°. . . 1750
The same. New York, 1846. 8°. 2171
Irishmen, Lives of Illustrious. J. Wills. Dublin, 1839. 6 v. 8°. . 3591
Iron Cousin and Mutual Influence. Mary C. Clarke. N. Y. 1853. 12°. 6141
Iron, Manufacture of. F. Overman. Philadelphia, 1850. 8°. . . 3520
Iron Mask. A. Dumas. Philadelphia, 1850. 8°. 3979
Iron Roads, English. F. S. Williams. London, 1852. 8°. . . . 5084
Iroquois, League of Ho-dé-no-sau-nee. L. H. Morgan. Roch. 1851. 8°. 3825
Notes on the. H. R. Schoolcraft. Albany, 1847. 8°. . . 2841
Irving, D. Lives of the Scottish Writers. Edin. 1850. 2 v. 12°. . . 6269
Irving, E. Oracles of God; Four Orations. New York, 1825. 8°. . 1368
Irving, J. J. Quod Correspondence. Boston, 1842. 2 v. 12°. . . 1699
Irving, J. T., jun. Hawk Chief. Philadelphia, 1837. 12°. . . . 915
Indian Sketches. Philadelphia, 1835. 2 v. 12°. 1895
Irving, T. Conquest of Florida. New York, 1851. 12°. . . . 4105
Irving, W. Alhambra. New York, 1851. 12°. 532
Astoria; or, Adventures beyond Rocky Mount. N. Y. 1851. 12°. 595
The same. New York, 1849. 12°. 3361
(Ed.) Bonneville's Journal to Rocky Mount. Phil. 1837. 2 v. 12°. 510
The same. New York, 1849. 12°. 3366
Bracebridge Hall. New York, 1851. 12°. 369
The same. New York, 1851. 12°. 3365
Conquest of Grenada. Philadelphia, 1829. 2 v. 12°. . . . 1182
The same. New York, 1850. 12°. 3369
Crayon Miscellany. Philadelphia, 1835. 3 v. 12°. . . . 1070

Irving, W. Crayon Miscellany. New York, 1849. 12°. 3362
History of New York. New York, 1849. 12°. 1051
The same. New York, 1849. 12°. 3363
Life and Voyages of Columbus. New York, 1828. 3 v. 8°. . . 1347
The same, abridged. New York, 1829. 12°. 2141
Life and Voyages of Columbus and Companions. N.Y. 1848. 3 v. 12°. 3360
The same. New York, 1849. 3 v. 12°. 800
Life of Oliver Goldsmith. New York, 1840. 2 v. 12°. . . . 2425
The same. New York, 1849. 12°. 3367
The same. (H. F. L.) New York, 1846. 2 v. 12°. 3683, 121–22
Mahomet and his Successors. New York, 1850. 2 v. 12° . . 3368
Memoir and Remains of Margaret M. Davidson. N. Y. 1851. 12°. 1613
Sketch Book. New York, 1850. 12°. 1206
The same. New York, 1850. 12°. 3370
Tales of a Traveller. New York, 1851. 12°. 3364
and J. K. Paulding. Salmagundi. New York, 1835. 2 v. 12°. . 1813
Isa; a Pilgrimage. Caroline Chesebro'. New York, 1852. 12°. . . 950
Isabel Carrolton; a Personal Retrospect. Boston, 1854. 12°. . . . 6236
Isaiah, Notes on. A. Barnes. New York, 1851. 2 v. 12°. . . . 4739
Translated and Explained. J. A. Alexander. N. Y. 1851. 2 v. 12°. 4742
Island Home; or, the Young Castaways. Ed. by C. Romaunt. Bos. 1852. 12°. 4639
Island of Life; an Allegory. Boston, 1851. 16°. 4201
Island World of the Pacific. H. T. Cheever. New York, 1851. 12°. . 4095
Israel, Lectures on the Children of. R. Alliott. London, 1849. 12°. . 3395
of the Alps. A. Muston. London, 1852. 12°. 5260
Israelitish Nation, History of. A. Alexander. Philadelphia, 1853. 8°. 5155
Isthmus, Life on the. J. W. Fabens. New York, 1853. 12°. . . 5073
of Tehuantepec. J. J. Williams. New York, 1852. 2 v. 8°. . 4843
Italian Comedies. Translated from Goldoni & others. N.Y. 1849. 12°. 3378
Italian Grammar. A. Elwes. London, 1852. 12°. 6119
Italian Language, Ollendorff's Method of Learning. N.Y. 1851. 12°. . 5190
Italian Life, Scenes from. L. Mariotti. London, 1850. 12°. . . . 4227
Italian Poets, Stories from. L. Hunt. New York, 1846. 12°. . . 2564
Italian Republics, History of. J. C. L. de Sismondi. Lond. 1832. 12°. 2382
Italian Sketch Book. H. T. Tuckerman. New York, 1848. 12°. . . 3121
Italian Volunteers & Lombard Rifle Brigade. E. Dandolo. Lond. 1851. 12°. 4445
Italy. Lady S. Morgan. London, 1824. 3 v. 8°. 4682
The same. New York, 1821. 2 v. 8°. 1972
and the Italian Islands. W. Spalding. Edinburgh, 1841. 3 v. 16°. 4589
The same. (H. F. L.) New York, 1848. 3 v. 12°. 3683, 151, 3
Compendious History of. Trans. by N. Greene. N.Y. 1836. 12°. 120
England and America. F. A. de Chateaubriand. Phil. 1816. 8°. 740
Genius of. R. Turnbull. New York, 1849. 12°. . . . 3301
Handbook for Central. O. Blewitt. London, 1850. 12°. . . 74
Handbook for Northern. London, 1847. 12°. 71
History of. L. Sporzozi. (H. F. L.) New York, 1846. 12°. 3683, 79
Idler in. Lady Blessington. Philadelphia, 1839. 2 v. 12°. . 486
Letters from. J. W. von Goethe. London, 1849. Post 8°. . . 4376

Italy, Letters from. J. T. Headley. New York, 1851. 12°. . . . 2399
Literary & Scientific Men of. Mrs. Shelley, &c. Phil. 1841. 2 v. 12°. 2135

Dante; Petrarch; Boccacio; Lorenzo de Medici; Bojardo; Berni; Ariosto; Machiavelli.

Notes on. R. Peale. Philadelphia, 1831. 8°. 1329
Observations on. J. Bell. Boston, 1826. 12°. 495
Our Own Correspondent in. M. B. Honan. New York, 1852. 12°. 4922
Past and Present. L. Mariotti. London, 1848–49. 2 v. 12°. . 3356
Pictures from. C. Dickens. New York, 1846. 12°. . . . 2578
Romance of History. C. Macfarlane. New York, 1832. 2 v. 12°. 1549
Scenes & Events in, 1847–49. Gen. Pepe. Lond. 1850. 2 v. 12°. 4235
Six Months in. G. S. Hillard. Boston, 1853. 2 v. 12°. . . 5505
Six Years in the Monasteries of. S. I. Mahoney. Phil. 1836. 12°. 227
Spain, and Portugal. W. Beckford. New York, 1845. 2 v. 12°. 2913
Switzerland, France, &c., Travels in. T. A. Trollope. Lond. 1850. 12°. 4224
Ivanhoe. Sir W. Scott. Boston, 1848. 2 v. 12°. . . . 999, 15, 16
The same. Edinburgh, 1849. 2 v. 12°. . . 4100, 16, 17
The same. Edinburgh, 1850. Roy. 8°. . . . 4531, 4
Ivar; or, the Skjuts-Boy. Emilie F. Carlen. New York, 1852. 8°. . 4809
Ivan Vejeeghen; or, Life in Russia. T. Bulgárin. Phil. 1832. 2 v. 12°. 1163
Ives, L. S. Trials in Progress to Catholicism. Boston, 1854. 12°. . 5839
Izard, R. Correspondence, with Memoir. New York, 1844. 12°. . 3035

J.

Jack Ashore. E. Howard. Philadelphia, 1840. 2 v. 12°. 964
Jack Brag. T. E. Hook. Philadelphia, 1837. 2 v. 12°. 844
The same. London, 1852. 12°. 5670
Jack Downing's Life and Writings. Boston, 1833. 12°. 2157
Jack Hinton, the Guardsman. C. Lever. Philadelphia, 1847. 8°. . 1688
Jack Tier; or, the Florida Reef. J. F. Cooper. N.Y. 1852. 2 v. 12°. . 3104
Jackson, A. Life. J. H. Eaton. Philadelphia, 1824. 8°. . . . 1061
Life and Public Services. J. S. Jenkins. Buffalo, 1850. 12°. . 4061
Memoirs. Boston, 1828. 16°. 819
and Winfield Scott. Lives. J. T. Headley. N.Y. 1852. 12°. . 4985
Jackson, C. T. Second Report on the Geology of Maine. Augus. 1838. 8°. 3248
Jackson, J. Commerce of the Mediterranean. New York, 1806. 12°. . 1222
Jackson, J., jun. Memoir. J. Jackson. Boston, 1836. 12°. . . 99
Jacksonism, Review of; or, the Political Mirror. New York, 1835. 12°. 1517
Jacob Faithful. F. Marryat. Philadelphia, 1847. 8°. 401
The same. Philadelphia, 1847. 8°. 1766, 1
The same. London, 1853. 12°. 5715
Jacobites, History of. Mrs. Thompson. London, 1845. 3 v. 8°. . . 4672
Jacobs, F. Greek Reader. Boston, 1835. 12°. 1459
Jacobs, Sarah S. Nonantum and Natick. Boston, 1854. 12°. . . 5600
Jacobs, T. J. Voyage of the Margaret Oakley. New York, 1844. 12°. . 2170
Jacqueline of Holland. T. C. Grattan. London, 1853. 12°. . . 5726

Jacqueline Pascal; or, Convent Life at Port-Royal. N. York, 1854. 12°. 5587
Jacquerie, The. G. P. R. James. New York, 1842. 2 v. 12°. . . . 1675
Jacques. Mde. Dudevant. New York, 1847. 2 v. 12°. 2957
Jahn, J. Biblical Archæology. Trans. by T. C. Upham. N. Y. 1849. 8°. 3528
Jamaica in 1850. J. Bigelow. New York, 1851. 12°. 4072
James, G. P. R. Agincourt. New York, 1844. 8°. 2217
Agnes Sorel. New York, 1853. 8°. 5173
Aims and Obstacles. New York, 1851. 8°. 4550
Ancient Régime. New York, 1841. 2 v. 12°. 1602
Arabella Stuart. New York, 1847. 8°. 1761
Arrah Neil; or, Times of Old. New York, 1848. 8°. . . . 2172
Attila; a Romance. New York, 1837. 2 v. 12°. 202
Beauchamp; or, the Error. New York, 1847. 8°. 2766
Castle of Ehrenstein. New York, 1847. 8°. 2784
Charles Tyrrell. New York, 1839. 2 v. 12°. 976
Chivalry and the Crusades. (H. F. L.) New York, 1847. 12°. 3683, 20
Commissioner. New York, 1851. 8°. 4116
Convict; or, Hypocrite Unmasked. New York, 1847. 8°. . . 2869
Corse de Leon; or, the Brigand. New York, 1841. 2 v. 12°. . 1600
Courtier of the Days of Charles II., &c. N. York, 1839. 2 v. 12°. 1072
Dark Scenes of History. New York, 1850. 3495
Darnley. New York, 1830. 2 v. 12°. 1808
The same. London, 1853. 12°. 5707
De l'Orme. New York, 1830. 2 v. 12°. 2901
The same. London, 1853. 12°. 5709
Desultory Man. New York, 1836. 2 v. 12°. 268
False Heir. New York, 1843. 8°. 1726
Fate; a Tale of Stirring Times. New York, 1851. 8°. . . 4503
Forest Days. New York, 1843. 8°. 1718
Forgery. New York, 1848. 8°. 3250
Gentleman of the Old School. New York, 1839. 2 v. 12°. . . 465
Gipsy. New York, 1835. 2 v. 12°. 1071
Heidelberg. New York, 1846. 8°. 2740
Henri Quatre; or, Days of the League. New York, 1834. 2 v. 12°. 1074
Henry Masterton. New York, 1832. 2 v. 12°. 171
The same. London, 1853. 12°. 5713
Henry of Guise. New York, 1839. 2 v. 12°. 96
Henry Smeaton. New York, 1851. 8°. 4010
History of Charlemagne. (H. F. L.) New York, 1848. 12°. 3683, 60
Huguenot; a Tale of the French Protestants. N. Y. 1839. 2 v. 12°. 1114
Jacquerie. New York, 1842. 2 v. 12°. 1675
John Marston Hall. New York, 1834. 2 v. 12°. 1008
King's Highway. New York, 1840. 2 v. 12°. 1522
Life of De Retz, Colbert, De Witt, &c. Philadelphia, 1837. 2 v. 12°. 2315
Life of Henry IV. New York, 1847. 2 v. 12°. 3065
Life of Richard Cœur-de-Lion. New York, 1842. 2 v. 12°. . 1877
Lives of Richelieu and others. Philadelphia, 1836. 12°. . . 247
Man-at-Arms. New York, 1840. 2 v. 12°. 420

James, G. P. R. Man-at-Arms. London, 1853. 12°. 5727
Margaret Graham. New York, 1847. 8°. 2808
Mary of Burgundy. New York, 1833. 2 v. 12°. 1036
Memoirs of Great Commanders. Philadelphia, 1835. 2 v. 12°. . 1087
Morley Ernstein. New York, 1842. 2 v. 12°. 1693
Old Oak Chest. New York, 1850. 8°. 3945
One in a Thousand. New York, 1836. 2 v. 12°. . . . 986
The same. Philadelphia, 1836. 8°. 2228, 1
Pequinillo. New York, 1852. 8°. 6204
Philip Augustus. New York, 1836. 2 v. 12°. 1563
The same. London, 1853. 12°. 5711
Richelieu. New York, 1847. 2 v. 12°. 2305
Robber. New York, 1835. 2 v. 12°. 1111
Rose d'Albret. New York, 1844. 8°. 2068
Russell; a Tale of the Reign of Charles II. New York, 1847. 8°. 2797
Sir Theodore Broughton. New York, 1848. 8°. 2887
Smuggler. New York, 1847. 8°. 2616
Step-Mother. New York, 1846. 2 v. 8°. 2678
Story without a Name. New York, 1852. 8°. 375
Thirty Years Since; or, the Ruined Family. New York, 1848. 8°. 3239
Ticonderoga; or, the Black Eagle. New York, 1854. 8°. . . 5975
Whim, and its Consequences. New York, 1848. 8°. . . . 3220
Woodman. New York, 1847. 8°. 2802
and M. B. Field. Adrian; or, Clouds of the Mind. N. Y. 1852. 12°. 4599
James I., Court of. G. Goodman. London, 1839. 2 v. 8°. . . . 4651
Memoirs of the Court of. Lucy Aiken. Boston, 1822. 2 v. 8°. . 1217
James, H. Lectures and Miscellanies. New York, 1852. 12°. . . 982
James, J. A. Christian Father's Present. New York, 1854. 12°. . . 5588
Pastoral Addresses on Christian Duty. New York, 1852. 16°. . 4754
James, W. Naval History of Great Britain. London, 1837. 6 v. 8°. . 2606
James Mountjoy; or, I've Been Thinking. A. S. Roe. N.Y. 1850. 12°. 3501
Jameson, Mrs. Anna. Beauties of the Court of Charles II. Bost. 1834. 8°. 2083
Characteristics of Women. Boston, 1846. 8°. 266
Diary of an Ennuyée. Philadelphia, 1826. 12°. 2363
Handbook to the Galleries of London. London, 1845. 12°. . 51
Memoirs and Essays. New York, 1846. 12°. 2902
Memoirs of Celebrated Female Sovereigns. N.Y. 1844. 2 v. 12°. 2404
The same. (H. F. L.) N.Y. 1846. 2 v. 12°. 3683, 33, 34
Memoirs of the Loves of the Poets. Philadelphia, 1844. 12°. . 2364
Visits and Sketches at Home and Abroad. N.Y. 1834. 2 v. 12°. 2369
Winter Studies and Summer Rambles. New York, 1839. 2 v. 12°. 1060
Jamestown, Settlement of. New York, 1806. 12°. 442
Jamestown, Voyage of the. R. B. Forbes. Boston, 1847. 2 v. 12°. . 2799
Jamie Gordon; or, the Orphan. New York, 1852. 12°. 384
Jamieson, J. Dictionary of the Scottish Language. Edinburgh, 1846. 8°. 5337
Jane Bouverie. Catherine Sinclair. New York, 1851. 12°. . . . 3798
Jane Eyre; an Autobiography. Caroline Bronte. New York, 1848. 8°. 2876
Jane Seton; or, the King's Advocate. J. Grant. New York, 1853. 12°. 5529

January and June. B. F. Taylor. New York, 1853. 12°. 5633
Japan, Geograph. and Hist. Account of. C. MacFarlane. N.Y. 1852. 12°. 4907
Japanese, Manners and Customs of. (H. F. L.) New York, 1846. 12°. 3683, 132
Japhet in Search of a Father. F. Marryat. Philadelphia, 1837. 2 v. 12°. 1120
The same. Philadelphia, 1847. 8°. 1766, 2
The same. London, 1853. 12°. 5716
Jardine, Sir W. British Birds. Edinburgh, 1843. 4 v. 12°. 4901, 1–4
Deer, Antelopes, &c. Edinburgh, 1843. 12°. 4901, 21
Fishes of Perch Family. Edinburgh, 1843. 12°. 4901, 38
Gallinaceous Birds. Edinburgh, 1843. 12°. 4901, 14
Game Birds. Edinburgh, 1843. 12°. 4901, 8
Goats, Sheep, Oxen, &c. Edinburgh, 1843. 12°. 4901, 22
Humming Birds. Edinburgh, 1843. 2 v. 12°. 4901, 6, 7
Lions, Tigers, &c. Edinburgh, 1843. 12°. 4901, 16
Monkeys. Edinburgh, 1843. 12°. 4901, 27
Sun Birds. Edinburgh, 1843. 12°. 4901, 5
Thick-Skinned Animals. Edinburgh, 1843. 12°. 4901, 23
(Editor). — See *Naturalist's Library*.
Jarves, J. J. History of Sandwich Islands. Boston, 1844. 8°. 1748
The same. Boston, 1843. 12°. 2298
Jay, J. Life. W. Jay. New York, 1833. 2 v. 8°. 1790
Life. H. B. Renwick. New York, 1841. 12°. 183
The same. (H. F. L.) New York, 1846. 12°. 3683, 129
Jay, W. Federal Government in behalf of Slavery. N.Y. 1839. 12°. 1547
Inquiry into Colonization & Anti-Slavery Societies. N. Y. 1838. 12°. 1526
Memoirs of Cornelius Winter. New York, 1811. 12°. 1018
Miscellaneous Writings on Slavery. Boston, 1853. 12°. 5333
Review of the Mexican War. Boston, 1849. 12°. 3303
Jay, Rev. W. Works. New York, 1849. 3 v. 8°. 4708
Jeames's Diary, and other Papers. W. M. Thackeray. N. Y. 1853. 12°. 5277
Jeans, G. Practical Astronomy. London, n. d. 12°. 5050
Jeans, H. W. Navigation and Nautical Astronomy. London, 1853. 12°. 6107
Jebb, Col. Management of Convict Prisons. London, 1851. 8°. 5109
Jefferson, T., Character of. Theo. Dwight. Boston, 1829. 12°. 1012
Life. G. Tucker. Philadelphia, 1837. 2 v. 8°. 1432
Manual of Parliamentary Practice. Philadelphia, 1843. 12°. 1890
Memoir, Corres. &c. Ed. by T. J. Randolph. Bost. 1830. 4 v. 8°. 1405
Memoirs. New York, 1809. 2 v. 8°. 752
Notes on the State of Virginia. Boston, 1801. 8°. 568
Jeffrey, F. Contributions to the Edin. Review. London, 1844. 4 v. 8°. 2608

Vol. 1. General Literature and Biography, viz.: Alison's Essay on Taste; Mde. de Staël; Benjamin Franklin; Jona. Swift; Mde. du Deffand and Mlle. de Lespinasse; Goethe's Wilhelm Meister; Correspondence of Samuel Richardson; Baron de Grimm; Victor Alfieri; Wm. Cowper; Colonel Hutchinson; Samuel Pepy's Diary.

2. History and Historical Memoirs, viz.: Fox's Reign of James II.; J. S. Bailly's Memoirs; Mde. de Staël's French Revolution; Mde. de Larochejaquelein; Margravine of Bareith; Irving's Life of Columbus; Memoirs of Muhammed Baber. — Poetry, viz.: Campbell's British Poets; Ford's Dramatic Works; Hazlitt's Characters of Shakspeare; Byron's Tragedies; Byron's Manfred; Reliques of Robert Burns; Campbell's Gertrude of Wyoming; Campbell's Theodric; Scott's Lay of the Last Minstrel; Scott's Lady of the Lake.

Jeffrey, F. Contributions to the Edinburgh Review, *continued.*

3. Poetry, continued; Crabbe's Poems, Borough, Tales, Tales of the Hall; Keats's Endymion, &c.; Rogers's Human Life; Southey's Roderick; Byron's Childe Harold; Moore's Lalla Rookh; Wordsworth's Excursion, and White Doe of Rylstone; Hemans's Poems. — Philosophy of the Mind, Metaphysics, and Jurisprudence, viz.: Bentham's Legislation; Stewart's Life of Reid; Priestley's Memoirs; Drummond's Academical Questions; Forbes's Life of Dr. Beattie; Stewart's Philosophical Essays. — Novels, Tales, and Prose Fictions, viz.: Edgeworth's Tales of Fashionable Life; Scott's Waverley, Tales of My Landlord, Rob Roy, Ivanhoe, Fortunes of Nigel; Galt's Novels; Lockhart's Novels.

4. General Politics and Miscellaneous, viz.: Leckie on British Government; Restoration of the Bourbons; State of Parties, 1810; O'Driscol's Ireland; Moore's Life of Sheridan; Walsh's Appeal; Irving's Bracebridge Hall; Clarkson on Quakerism; Clarkson's Life of Penn; Correspondence of Lord Collingwood; Bishop Heber's India; Sketches of India, Egypt, and Italy; Warburton's Letters; Life of Earl of Charlemont; Buxton on Prison Discipline; Memoirs of R. Cumberland; Lady Mary W. Montagu; Life of J. P. Curran; Simond's Switzerland; Rejected Addresses; Mde. de Staël; Sir James Mackintosh; Notices of Henry Erskine, Prof. Playfair, and James Watt.

The same. Philadelphia, 1848. 8°. 3418, 6

Life. Lord Cockburn. Philadelphia, 1852. 2 v. 8°. 996

Jeffreys, Judge. Life. H. W. Woolrych. Philadelphia, 1852. 12°. . 4862

Jenkins, J. S. Life of Silas Wright. Auburn, 1847. 12°. . . . 3178

United States Exploring Expeditions. Auburn, 1850. 8°. . . 3620

Jenks, W. Explanatory Bible Atlas. Boston, 1847. 4°. . . . 3232

Jenner, E. Life and Doctrines. J. Baron. London, 1838. 2 v. 8°. . 4552

Jenyns, S. Internal Evidence of Christianity. New York, n. d. 12°. . 504

Jeremiah Parkes. Ellen Pickering. New York, 1849. 8°. . . . 3462

Jerrmann, E. Pictures of St. Petersburg. New York, 1852. 12°. . . 5062

Jerrold, D. Man made of Money. New York, 1849. 8°. . . . 3297

Writings. London, 1851–54. 8 v. 12°. 6234

Vol. 1. St. Giles and St. James.
2. Men of Character.
3. Caudle Lectures; Story of a Feather; Sick Giant and the Doctor Dwarf.
4. Cakes and Ale.
5. Punch's Letters to his Son; Punch's Complete Letter Writer; Sketches of the English.
6. Man made of Money; Chronicles of Clovernook.
7. Comedies, viz.: Bubbles of the Day; Time Works Wonders; Catspaw; Prisoner of War; Retired from Business; St. Cupid.
8. Comedies and Dramas, viz.: Rent Day; Nell Gwynne; Housekeeper; Wedding Gown; Schoolfellows; Doves in a Cage; Painter of Ghent; Black-ey'd Susan.

Jerrold, W. B. Disgrace to the Family. Philadelphia, 1848. 8°. . 3203

Jerusalem, and Holy Land. F. A. de Chateaubriand. Lon. 1835. 2 v. 12°. 4568

History and Topography of. G. Williams. London, 1849. 2 v. 8°. 4655

Jerusalem Delivered. T. Tasso. Tr. by J. H. Wiffen. N.Y. 1850. 12°. 16

The same. Translated by E. Fairfax. Lon. 1844. 2 v. 12°. 16

The same. Tr. by J. Hoole. Newburyport, 1810. 2 v. 8°. 748

Jesse, E. Gleanings from Natural History. Philadelphia, 1833. 12°. . 2193

Jesse, J. H. Court of England under the Stuarts. Phil. 1840. 2 v. 12°. 2148

Court of England under Cromwell. Philadelphia, 1840. 2 v. 12°. 2149

London and its Celebrities. London, 1850. 2 v. 8°. . . . 4959

Memoirs of the Pretenders. Philadelphia, 1846. 2 v. 16°. . . 2573

Memorials of London. London, 1847. 2 v. 8°. 4679

Jessie's Flirtations. Miss Curtis. New York, 1846. 8°. . . . 2685

Jesuit in the Family. A. Steinmetz. London, 1847. 12°. . . . 1110

Jesuit Missions in North America, Early. W. I. Kip. N.Y. 1846. 12°. 2928
Jesuitism, Americans Warned of. J. C. Pitrat. New York, 1851. 12°. 4186
Jesuits at Rome, Mornings among. M. H. Seymour. N.Y. 1849. 12°. . 3401
History of. G. B. Nicolini. London, 1854. Post 8°. . . . 6197
History of. A. Steinmetz. Philadelphia, 1848. 2 v. 8°. . . 3165
Year among the English. A. Steinmetz. New York, 1846. 12°. 2945
Jesus Christ. — See *Christ.*
Jew, The. C. Spindler. New York, 1844. 8°. 2751
Jewish Scriptures and Antiquities. J. G. Palfrey. Bost. 1840–52. 4 v. 8°. 1642
Jews, Antiquities of. F. Josephus. Philadelphia, 1841. 2 v. 8°. . . 1610
History of. Hannah Adams. Boston, 1812. 2 v. 12°. . . 883
History of. A. Alexander. Philadelphia, 1853. 8°. 5155
History of. H. H. Milman. (H. F. L.) N.Y. 1843. 3 v. 12°. 3683, 1–3
in Great Britain. M. Margoliouth. London, 1851. 3 v. 12°. . 4287
Lectures on. R. Alliott. London, 1849. 12°. 3395
Stories from the History of. New York, 1853. 12°. . . . 5628
Jewsbury, G. E. History of an Adopted Child. New York, 1853. 12°. 5225
Jewsbury, Maria J. Three Histories. Boston, 1831. 12°. . . . 542
The same. Philadelphia, 1833. 8°. 1357, 3
Jilt, The; a Novel. New York, 1844. 8°. 2745
Joan of Arc. Life. D. W. Bartlett. Auburn, 1854. 12°. . . . 6277
Story of. R. M. Evans. New York, 1847. 12°. 3089
Job, Notes on. A. Barnes. New York, 1850. 2 v. 12°. . . . 4740
John; a Novel. Emilie F. Carlen. New York, 1854. 8°. . . . 5496
John Decastro, and his Brother Bat. Boston, 1815. 3 v. 12°. . . 874
John de Lancaster. R. Cumberland. New York, 1809. 2 v. 12°. . . 184
John Marston Hall. G. P. R. James. New York, 1834. 2 v. 12°. . 1008
Johnson, C. W. Farmers' Encyclopædia. Philadelphia, 1850. Roy. 8°. 4358
Johnson, E. Life, Health, and Disease. New York, 1850. 12°. . . 3433
Johnson, G. W. Stranger in India. London, 1843. 2 v. 12°. . . 4966
(Editor.) Fairfax Correspondence. London, 1848. 4 v. 8°. . . 4690
Johnson, L. D. Spirit of Roger Williams. Boston, 1839. 12°. . . 49
Johnson, S. Idler. New York, 1816. 12°. 522
Life. R. Anderson. London, 1795. 12°. 513
Life. J. Boswell. London, 1821. 5 v. 12°. 1154
The same. Edited by J. W. Croker. Lond. 1848. Roy. 8°. 1139
The same. Edited by J. W. Croker. N.Y. 1841. 2 v. roy. 8°. 1253
Life and Maxims of. Boston, 1834. 12°. 901
Life and Selections from. (H. F. L.) N.Y. 1846. 2 v. 12°. 3683, 109, 110
Lives of the English Poets. London, 1810. 2 v. 8°. . . . 686
Religious Life, and his Death. New York, 1850. 12°. . . 3884
Rambler. Philadelphia, 1812. 4 v. 16°. 22
Rasselas. Boston, 1811. 12°. 291
Works; with Essay on, by A. Murphy. N. Y. 1843. 2 v. roy. 8°. 1984

Vol. 1. Essay on the Life and Genius of Dr. Johnson; The Rambler; The Adventurer; The Idler; Rasselas; Tales of Imagination; Letters; Irene, a Tragedy; Miscellaneous Poems.

2. Lives of the Poets; Lives of Eminent Persons; Political Tracts; Philological Tracts; Miscellaneous Tracts; Opinions on Questions of Law; Reviews and Criticisms; Journey to the Western Islands of Scotland; Prayers and Meditations.

Johnson, T. T. Sights in the Gold Region. New York, 1849. 12°. . 3434
Johnsoniana; Anecdotes & Sayings of Dr. Johnson. London, 1845. 12°. 4974
Johnston, A. K. Dictionary of Geography. London, 1850. 8°. . . 4353
Johnston, C. Travels in Southern Abyssinia. London, 1844. 2 v. 8°. . 4691
Johnston, J. F. W. Notes on North America. Boston, 1851. 2 v. 12°. 4172
Johnston, R. Travels in Russia and Poland. New York, 1816. 8°. . 1397
Johnstone, J. (Editor.) Works of Samuel Parr. London, 1828. 8 v. 8°. 5903
Jomini, Baron de. Art of War. New York, 1854. 12°. 5774
Jonathan Wild. H. Fielding. Philadelphia, 1843. 8°. . . 1232, 2
Jones, A. Historical Sketch of the Electric Telegraph. N.Y. 1852. 8°. 4845
*Jones, A. D. Illustrated American Biography. N.Y. 1854. 2 v. roy. 8°. 5889
Jones, G. Excursions to Cairo, Jerusalem, &c. New York, 1836. 12°. 967
Jones, J. A. Haverhill. New York, 1831. 2 v. 12°. 1187
Jones, J. B. City Merchant; or, Mysterious Failure. Phil. 1851. 12°. . 3800
Freaks of Fortune; or, Ned Lorn. Philadelphia, 1854. 12°. . 6258
Life and Adventures of a Country Merchant. Phil. 1854. 12°. . 5844
Spanglers and Tinglers; or, Rival Belles. Boston, 1850. 8°. . 372
Jones, J. Paul. Biography. S. P. Waldo. Hartford, 1823. 8°. . . 651
Life. A. S. Mackenzie. Boston, 1841. 12°. 1905
Life and Character. J. H. Sherburne. Wash. 1825. 8°. . . 679
The same. New York, 1851. 8°. 4316
Life and Correspondence. Philadelphia, 1846. 12°. . . . 2593
Jones, J. S. Carpenter of Rouen. Boston, 1849. 12°. 3124
Jones, Sir J. T. Sieges of Wellington in Spain. London, 1846. 3 v. 8°. 5132
Jones, S. Practical Phrenology. Boston, 1836. 12°. 237
Jones, S. S. Beatrice; or, the Influence of Words. London, 1850. 12°. 4229
Jones, Sir W. Life. Lord Teignmouth. London, 1804. 8°. . . 762
The same. London, 1807. 8°. 1974
Jonson, Ben. Works; with Memoir by B. W. Proctor. London, 1838. 8°. 1437
The same, with Memoir by W. Gifford. London, 1843. 8°. 1437
Joseph, Story of; or, the Patriarchal Age. Philadelphia, 1851. 12°. . 4182
Joseph Andrews. H. Fielding. Philadelphia, 1843. 8°. . . 1232, 2
Josephine, History of. J. S. C. Abbott. New York, 1851. 12°. . . 4402
Life. P. C. Headley. Auburn, 1850. 12°. 3910
Memoirs. J. S. Memes. New York, n. d. 16°. 2194
The same. (H. F. L.) New York, 1846. 12°. . . 3683, 28
Memoirs. M. A. Le Normand. Philadelphia, 1850. 2 v. 12°. . 3103
Josephine; or, the Edict. Grace Aguilar. Philadelphia, 1850. 12°. . 4025
Josephus, F. Works. Trans. by W. Whiston. Phil. 1841. 2 v. 8°. . 1610
Jouffroy, T. Introduction to Ethics. Boston, 1841. 2 v. 12°. . 962, 5, 6
Philosophical Miscellanies. Boston, 1838. 12°. . . . 962, 1, 2
Journal at Dartmoor Prison. Milledgeville, 1816. 12°. 1069
of an African Cruiser. H. Bridge. New York, 1853. 12°. . 2398
of Agriculture. Edited by W. S. King. Vol. 1. Bost. 1851. 8°. 257
of Design and Manufactures. Vol. 1. London, 1849. 8°. . . 4326
of the Franklin Institute. Vols. 1, 2. New series. Phil. 1828. 8°. 1356
of Law. Vol. 1. Philadelphia, 1830. 8°. 2702
of a Naturalist. Philadelphia, 1831. 12°. 219

Journal of a Summer Tour. E. M. Sewell. New York, 1852. 12°. . 4914
on Board an American Privateer. Boston, 1816. 12°. 3320
Journey from Aleppo to Jerusalem. H. Maundrell. Boston, 1836. 16°. 86
from Cornhill to Grand Cairo. W. M. Thackeray. N.Y. 1846. 12°. 2561
to Rome and Naples, in 1817. New York, 1818. 12°. 320
Journeyman Joiner. Mde. Dudevant. New York, 1847. 12°. . . 3036
Joyce, J. Scientific Dialogues. London, 1846. Post 8°. 4363
Juan, G., & A. de Ulloa. Voyage to South America. Lond. 1758. 2 v. 8°. 5909
Judd, S. Life and Character. Boston, 1854. 12°. 6298
Philo; an Evangeliad. Boston, 1850. 12°. 3481
Margaret; a Tale of the Real and Ideal. Boston, 1851. 2 v. 12°. . 2523
Richard Edney and the Governor's Family. Boston, 1850. 12°. . 4073
Judicial History of Massachusetts. E. Washburn. Boston, 1840. 8°. . 2090
Judson, A. Memoir. F. Wayland. Boston, 1853. 2 v. 12°. . . 5536
Judson, Mrs. Anna H. Memoir. J. D. Knowles. Boston, 1853. 12°. . 5745
Judson, Mrs. Emily. Kathayan Slave, and other Papers. Bost. 1853. 12°. 5227
Olio of Domestic Verses. New York, 1852. 12°. 4906
Jukes, J. B. Excursions in Newfoundland, 1839–40. Lond. 1842. 2 v. 12°. 3138
Julia Howard; a Romance. Mrs. M. Bell. London, 1850. 3 v. 12°. . 4273
Julia of Baiæ; or, the Days of Nero. New York, 1843. 12°. . . 1700
Julian; or, the End of the Era. L. Bungener. Boston, 1855. 2 v. 12°. 6219
Julian; or, Scenes in Judea. W. Ware. New York, 1841. 2 v. 12°. . 1631
Julienne, the Daughter of the Hamlet. H. de Normand. Aub. 1854. 12°. 6163
Junius Discovered. F. Griffin. Boston, 1854. 12°. 5786
Identity of, with Sir P. Francis. J. Taylor. New York, 1818. 8°. 1326
Letters. Boston, 1853. 12°. 1976
Letters, and Authorship of. J. Wade. London, 1850. 2 v. post 8°. 4374
Junot, Mde. Memoirs of Celebrated Women. Phil. 1835. 2 v. 12°. . 1030
Justin, Nepos, & Eutropius. Trans. by J. S. Watson. Lond. 1853. Post 8°. 5941
Juvenal and Perseus. Trans. by C. Badham. New York, 1841. 12°. 1854, 35
Satires. Translated by W. Gifford. Philadelphia, 1803. 2 v. 8°. 1323
Juvenile Emigrants; a Novel. London, 1799. 2 v. 12°. 313

K.

Kaleidoscope of Anecdotes & Aphorisms. Cath. Sinclair. Lond. 1851. 12°. 4400
Kaloolah; or, Journeyings of the Djébel Kumri. W. S. Mayo. N.Y. 1849. 12°. 2909
Kamenski, B. Age of Peter the Great. London, 1851. 12°. . . 4615
Kane, E. K. Grinnell Exploring Expedition. New York, 1854. 8°. . 5892
Kant, I. Critick of Pure Reason. London, 1838. 8°. 2260
Kanzas and Nebraska. E. E. Hale. Boston, 1854. 12°. 6255
Kate Bouverie, and other Tales. Mrs. Norton. Philadelphia, 1835. 2 v. 12°. 557
Kate Walsingham; a Novel. Ellen Pickering. Philadelphia, 1848. 8°. 3233
Kater, H., and D. Lardner. Treatise on Mechanics. Boston, 1831. 12°. 473
Katharine Ashton. E. M. Sewell. New York, 1854. 2 v. 12°. . . 6167
Katherine Walton. W. G. Simms. New York, 1854. 12°. 5877
The same. Philadelphia, 1851. 8°. 4514

Kathay; Cruise in the China Seas. W. H. Macaulay. N.Y. 1852. 12°. 5080
Kathayan Slave, and other Papers. Emily Judson. Boston, 1853. 12°. 5227
Katmandu, Journey of. L. Oliphant. New York, 1852. 12°. . . . 4850
Kavanagh; a Tale. H. W. Longfellow. Boston, 1849. 12°. 3302
Kavanagh, Julia. Daisy Burns. New York, 1853. 12°. . . . . 52[illegible]3
 Madeleine. New York, 1852. 12°. 949
 Nathalie; a Tale. New York, 1851. 12°. 4111
 Woman in France in the 18th Century. Philadelphia, 1850. 12°. 3855
 Women of Christianity. New York, 1852. 12°. 4762
Kavanagh, M. Discovery of the Science of Languages. Lon. 1844. 2 v. 8°. 4962
Kames, Lord. Elements of Criticism. New York, 1823. 2 v. 8°. . . 706
 The same. New York, 1836. 8°. 1450
Kean, E. Life. New York, 1835. 12°. 2903
Keate, G. Account of the Pelew Islands. Boston, 1796. 12°. . . . 163
Keats, J. Poetical Works. Philadelphia, 1844. 8°. 581
Keeping up Appearances. T. S. Arthur. New York, 1847. 16°. . . 2435
Keightley, T. Fairy Mythology. London, 1850. Post 8°. 4368
 History of England. Boston, 1840. 2 v. 8°. 1786
 The same. (H. F. L.) New York, 1846. 5 v. 12°. 3683, 114–18
 History of Rome. New York, 1851. 12°. 1768
Keith, A. Evidence of the Truth of the Christian Religion. Phil. 1850. 12°. 4746
Keith, T. Treatise on the Use of Globes. New York, 1815. 12°. . . 538
Kelly, W. Excursion to California. London, 1851. 2 v. 12°. . . . 4618
Kelly, W. K. History of Russia. London, 1854. 2 v. post 8°. . . . 6196
 Life of the Duke of Wellington, for Boys. London, 1853. 12°. . 6272
 Syria and the Holy Land. London, 1844. 8°. 3190
Kemble, Frances A. Poems. Philadelphia, 1844. 12°. 2325
 See also *Butler, Mrs. Frances A.*
Kendall, E. A. Travels in United States, 1807–8. N. Y. 1809. 3 v. 8°. 571
Kendall, G. W. Texan Santa Fé Expedition. New York, 1850. 2 v. 12°. 1765
 *Mexican War Illustrated. New York, 1851. Folio. 1665
Kendrick, J. Ancient Egypt under the Pharaohs. N. Y. 1852. 2 v. 12°. 4930
Kenilworth. Sir W. Scott. Boston, 1848. 2 v. 12°. 999, 21, 22
 The same. Edinburgh, 1849. 2 v. 12°. . . . 4100, 22, 23
 The same. Edinburgh, 1850. Roy. 8°. 4531, 6
Kennard, J., jun. Selections from Writings. Boston, 1849. 12°. . . 3338
Kennedy, Grace. Father Clement. Philadelphia, 1853. 12°. . . . 811
Kennedy, J. P. Horse-Shoe Robinson. Philadelphia, 1845. 2 v. 12°. . 1107
 Memoirs of Wm. Wirt. Philadelphia, 1850. 2 v. 12°. 3443
 Rob of the Bowl. New York, 1854. 12°. 1104
 Swallow Barn. Philadelphia, 1832. 2 v. 12°. 1207
Kenneth; a Romance of the Highlands. G.W.M. Reynolds. N.Y. 1852. 8°. 4696
Kent, J. Commentaries on American Law. New York, 1844. 3 v. 8°. . 2056
 Course of English Reading. N. Y. 1853. 12°. 5203
Kentucky, Hist. of. T. S. Arthur and W. H. Carpenter. Phil. 1852. 12°. 4864
 Historical Sketches of. L. Collins. Maysville, 1847. 8°. . . . 3246
Kepler, J. Life. London, 1833. 8°. 602
Kerr, R. Hist. and Collec. of Voyages and Travels. Edin. 1854. 18 v. 8°. 5489

Kett, H. Flowers of Wit. Hartford, 1825. 18°. 130
Kettell, S. Specimens of American Poetry. Boston, 1839. 3 v. 12°. . 1184
Key to Uncle Tom's Cabin. Mrs. H. B. Stowe. Boston, 1853. 8°. . 5174
Kickleburys on the Rhine. W. M. Thackeray. New York, 1851. 12°. 3812
Kidd, Capt., and Robin Hood. W. W. Campbell. New York, 1853. 12°. 5284
Kidder, D. P. Residence and Travels in Brazil. Phil. 1845. 2 v. 12°. . 2280
Kimball, R. B. Romance of Student Life Abroad. N. York, 1853. 12°. 5055
St. Leger; or, Threads of Life. New York, 1850. 12°. . . 3474
Kincaid, J. Adventures of the Rifle Brigade. Philadelphia, 1836. 8°. 2228, 1
King, J. A. Twenty-four Years in the Argentine Republic. N.Y. 1846. 12°. 2597
King, Mrs. Busy Moments of an Idle Woman. New York, 1854. 12°. 5575
King, W. R., Obituary Addresses on. Washington, 1854. 8°. . . 5923
King of the Hurons. P. H. Myers. New York, 1850. 12°. . . 3473
Kinglake, R. Eöthen; or, Traces of Eastern Travels. N. Y. 1845. 12°. 2330
Klapka, Gen. War of Independence in Hungary. Lond. 1850. 2 v. 12°. 4634
Klencke, Prof. Biography of Alex. von Humboldt. N. Y. 1853. 12°. . 5243
Kings and Queens. J. S. C. Abbott. New York, 1848. 12°. . . 3146
King's Chapel, Boston, History of. F. W. P. Greenwood. Bost. 1833. 12°. 1053
Epitaphs in Burial Ground. T. Bridgman. Boston, 1853. 12°. . 5596
King's Highway. G. P. R. James. New York, 1840. 2 v. 12°. . . 1522
King's Own. F. Marryat. Philadelphia, 1834. 2 v. 12°. . . . 1196
The same. Philadelphia, 1847. 8°. 1766, 1
The same. London, 1853. 12°. 5717
Kingsley, C., jun. Alton Locke, Tailor and Poet. New York, 1850. 12°. 4065
Hypatia; or New Foes, &c. Boston, 1854. 2 v. 12°. . . . 5576
Twenty-five Village Sermons. Philadelphia, 1854. 12°. . . 5592
Yeast; a Problem. New York, 1851. 12°. 4218
Kingsley, J. L. Life of Ezra Stiles. Boston, 1847. 12°. . . 1076, 16
Kingston, W. H. G. Peter the Whaler. New York, 1852. 12°. . . 4480
Kinsman; or, Black Riders of Congaree. W. G. Simms. Phil. 1841. 2 v. 12°. 1598
Kip, W. I. Catacombs of Rome. New York, 1854. 12°. . . . 5819
Early Conflicts of Christianity. New York, 1850. 12°. . . 3506
Early Jesuit Missions in North America. New York, 1846. 12°. . 2928
Kipping, R. Masting, Mastmaking, & Rigging of Ships. Lon. 1854. 12°. 6072
Kirby, W. History, Habits, and Instinct of Animals. Phil. 1836. 8°. . 1422
Kirby's Wonderful Museum. London, 1820. 5 v. 8°. 4669
Kirkland, Mrs. C. M. Evening Book. New York, 1853. 12°. . . 5328
Forrest Life. New York, 1844. 12°. 1705
Garden Walks with the Poets. New York, 1852. 12°. . . 5027
Holidays Abroad; or, Europe from the West. N.Y. 1849. 2 v. 12°. 3375
New Home: Who 'll Follow? New York, 1839. 12°. . . 429
Western Clearings. New York, 1845. 12°. 2525
Kirkland, J. T., Discourse on. A. Young. Boston, 1840. 8°. . . 2225
Kirkland, S. Life. S. K. Lothrop. Boston, 1848. 12°. . . 1076, 25
Kirkman, T. P. Mnemonical Lessons in Geom., Algeb., &Trig. Lon. 1852. 12°. 6112
"Kirwan" [N. Murray]. Letters on Romanism. New York, 1852. 12°. 1095
Letters to Bishop Hughes. New York, 1849. 12°. . . . 3666
Men and Things in Europe. New York, 1853. 12°. . . . 5569

Kitto, J. Cyclopædia of Biblical Literature. New York, 1850. 2 v. roy. 8°. 3526
The same, condensed. Boston, 1851. Roy. 8°. 4332
Daily Bible Illustrations. New York, 1850-53. 7 v. 12°. . . 4296
History of Palestine. Boston, 1852. 12°. 35
Lost Senses: Deafness and Blindness. New York, 1852. 12°. . 4863
Scripture Lands; with 24 Maps. London, 1850. Post 8°. . . 4391
Knapen, D. M. Mechanic's Assistant. New York, 1849. 12°. . . 3403
Knapp, F. Chemical Technology. London, 1848. 2 v. 8°. . . . 4137
Knapp, G. C. Lectures on Christian Theology. New York, 1850. 8°. . 4709
Knapp, S. L. Female Biography. Philadelphia, 1836. 12°. . . . 1840
Advice in the Pursuits of Literature. New York, 1832. 12°. . 326
Genius of Masonry. Providence, 1828. 12°. 2120
Life of Lord Timothy Dexter. Newburyport, 1848. 12°. . . 881
Lives of Lawyers, Statesmen, &c. Boston, 1821. 8°. . . . 659
Knickerbocker, The. Vols. 1-43 [continued]. New York, 1833-54. 8°. 933
Knickerbocker Sketch-Book. L. G. Clark. New York, 1845. 12°. . 2374
Knickerbocker's History of New York. W. Irving. N.Y. 1809. 2 v. 12°. 1051
The same. New York, 1849. 12°. 3363
Knick-Knacks from an Editor's Table. L. G. Clark. N. York, 1852. 12°. 5028
Knight, C. Half Hours with the Best Authors. N.York, 1847. 3 v. 12°. 3034
Cyclopædia of the Industry of All Nations. New York, 1851. 8°. 4506
London. London, 1851. 6 v. roy. 8°. 4827
Studies of Shakspeare. London, 1851. 8°. 5464
Wm. Shakspeare; a Biography. London, 1851. 8°. . . . 5463
Knight and Gwynne. C. Lever. Philadelphia, 1847. 8°. . . . 2796
Knights of England, France, and Scotland. H.W. Herbert. N.Y. 1852. 12°. 4794
of Malta, Achievements of. A. Sutherland. Phil. 1846. 2 v. 12°. 2996
Knorr, J. Two Roads. Philadelphia, 1854. 12°. 5811
Knorring, Baroness. Peasant and Landlord. New York, 1848. 12°. . 3126
Knout and the Russians. G. de Lagny. New York, 1854. 12°. . . 5857
Knowledge, Diffusion of. T. Dick. Philadelphia, 1845. 12°. . 2357, 4
The same. (H. F. L.) New York, 1848. 12°. . . 3683, 59
Pursuit of, under Difficulties. G. L. Craik. N.Y. 1844. 2 v. 16°. 824
The same. (H. F. L.) New York, 1846. 2 v. 12°. 3683, 94, 95
Knowles, J. D. Memoir of Mrs. Ann H. Judson. Boston, 1853. 12°. . 5745
Memoir of Roger Williams. Boston, 1834. 12°. 563
Knowles, J. S. Elocutionist; a Rhetorical Reader. N. York, 1844. 12°. 2159
Fortescue. New York, 1846. 8°. 2772
Select Tales and Dramas. New York, 1837. 2 v. 16°. . . . 2575
Knox, J. Life. T. M'Crie. Edinburgh, 1840. 12°. 1800
Kohl, J. G. Works. Philadelphia, 1844. 8°. 2684

Austria, Vienna, and Prague; England and Wales; Russia and the Russians in 1842; Scotland.

Kohlrausch, F. History of Germany. New York, 1845. Roy. 8°. . 2642
Koran; with Notes and Discourse, by G. Sale. London, 1844. 8°. . 2003
Körner, C. G. Life, Poems, and Prose Tales. Philadelphia, 1833. 8°. 1357, 1
Songs and Ballads. Boston, 1842. 12°. 962, 14
and Schiller, Correspondence of. London, 1849. 3 v. 12°. . . 4585

Kossuth, L., and his Generals. H. W. de Puy. Buffalo, 1852. 12°. . 978
and Hungary. B. F. Tefft. Philadelphia, 1852. 12°. 4626
and the Hungarian War. Philadelphia, 1851. 12°. 4633
Life. P. C. Headley. Auburn, 1852. 12°. 4760
Life and Speeches. New York, 1851. 8°. 4555
Life and Speeches in England. London, 1851. 8°. 4145
in New England. Boston, 1852. 8°. 4894
Kotzebue, A. von. Exile into Siberia. New York, 1802. 12°. . . 871
Krummacher, F. A. Parables. Philadelphia, 1854. 8°. . . . 6000
Krusenstern, A. J. von. Voyage round the World. Lond. 1813. 2 v. 4°. 2016
Kugler, F. Pictorial History of Germany. London, 1845. Roy. 8°. . 3599
Kurten, P. Art of Manufacturing Soaps. Philadelphia, 1854. 12°. . 5761
Kyd, S. Law of Bills of Exchange and Promis. Notes. Alb. 1800. 12°. 884

L.

Labor and Love; a Tale of English Life. Boston, 1853. 12°. . . . 5250
Organization of, and Association. M. Briancourt. N.Y. 1847. 12°. 2439
Laboring Classes of England. W. Dodd. Boston, 1847. 12°. . . 3063
Labree, L. Rebels and Tories. New York, 1851. 8°. 4337
Lacon; or, Many Things in Few Words. C. C. Colton. N.Y. 1836. 16°. 1856
Laconia; or, Legends of White Mount. I. W. Scrivener. Bost. 1854. 12°. 6238
Laconics; or, Best Words of the Best Authors. London, 1840. 3 v. 16°. 5049
World's; or, Best Thoughts, &c. E. Berkeley. N. Y. 1853. 12°. 5029
Lacroix, F. Mysteries of Russia. Boston, 1848. 8°. 3236
Ladies of the Covenant, Memoirs of. J. Anderson. New York, 1851. 12°. 4471
Ladies' Repository. Vols. 12, 13 [continued]. Cincinnati, 1852–53. 8°. 5125
Lady Alice; or, the New Una. J. V. Huntington. N.Y. 1849. 2 v. 12°. 3382
Lady and the Priest. Mrs. Maberly. New York, 1851. 8°. . . . 4525
Lady at Home. Philadelphia, 1844. 12°. 2138
Lady-Bird; a Tale. Lady G. Fullerton. New York, 1853. 12°. . . 5202
Lady Felicia. H. Cockton. New York, 1852. 8°. 650
Lady Jane Grey; an Historical Romance. T. Miller. Phil. 1840. 2 v. 12°. 1521
Lady Killer. Rebecca Hicks. Philadelphia, 1851. 12°. 4635
Lady Lee's Widowhood. E. Hamlin. New York, 1853. 8°. . . . 5442
Lady of the Lake. Sir W. Scott. Philadelphia, 1839. 12°. . . 860, 3
The same. Edinburgh, 1848. 12°. 4102, 8
Lady of Milan. Edited by Mrs. Thompson. New York, 1846. 8°. . 2644
Lady's Book. L. A. Godey. Vols. 39–48 [continued]. Phil. 1849–54. 8°. 1428
Lady's Equestrian Manual. Philadelphia, 1854. 12°. 5836
Lady's Gift. Jane K. Stanford. Philadelphia, 1836. 12°. . . . 896
Lafayette, Marquis de, Complete History of. Hartford, 1847. 12°. . . 3073
in America, in 1824–25. A. Levasseur. Phil. 1829. 2 v. 12°. . 351
Life. P. C. Headley. Auburn, 1851. 12°. 4114
Memoirs, Correspondence, and MSS. of. New York, 1837. 8°. . 1425
La Fontaine, J., Fables of. Trans. by E. Wright. Boston, 1842. 2 v. 12°. 1746
*The same. Boston, 1841. 8°. 2334

Lafitte, the Pirate of the Gulf. J. H. Ingraham. N.Y. 1836. 2 v. 12°. . 263
Lagny, G. de. Knout and the Russians. New York, 1854. 12°. . . 5857
Laing, S. Travels in France, Prussia, Switzerland, &c. Phil. 1846. 8°. 2690
Laird of Logan; or, Wit and Humor of Scotland. Glasgow, 1841. 12°. 3466
Lajétchnikoff, M. The Heretic. Trans. by T. B. Shaw. N.Y. 1844. 8°. 2749
Lake Superior, Description of. L. Agassiz & J. E. Cabot. Bost. 1850. 8°. 3604
Lakes, Life on the. New York, 1836. 2 v. 12°. 361
Summer on the. S. Margaret Fuller. Boston, 1844. 12°. . . 2104
Lalla Rookh; an Oriental Romance. T. Moore. New York, 1847. 12°. 72
Lamar, J. B. Polly Peablossom's Wedding, & other Tales. Phil. 1851. 12°. 3811
Lamartine, A. de. Atheism among the People. Boston, 1850. 12°. . 3877
Confidential Disclosures. New York, 1849. 12°. . . . 3349
Genevieve. London, 1850. 12°. 4419
History of the French Revolution of 1848. Boston, 1849. 2 v. 12°. 3424
History of the Girondists. New York, 1849. 3 v. 12°. . . 3030
Les Confidences. New York, 1849. 8°. 5397
Le Passé, le Présent, l'Avenir de la République. Paris, 1850. 8°. 5398
Past, Present, and Future of the Republic. New York, 1850. 12°. 3865
Raphael; or, Life at Twenty. New York, 1849. 12°. . . . 3344
Restoration of Monarchy in France. New York, 1851. 3 v. 12°. 5198
Travels in the East. Edinburgh, 1850. 2 v. 12°. 1126
Lamb, C. Essays of Elia. New York, 1852. 12°. 3453
Last Essays of Elia. Philadelphia, 1833. 8°. . . . 1357, 1
Literary Sketches and Letters. T. N. Talfourd. N.Y. 1848. 12°. 3213
Poetical Works. Philadelphia, 1836. 8°. 580
Specimens of English Dramatic Poets. New York, 1845. 2 v. 12°. 2402
Works; with Life by T. N. Talfourd. New York, 1845. 2 v. 12°. 356
Lambert, T. S. Popular Anatomy and Physiology. N. Y. 1850. 12°. . 3625
Lamp to the Path. W. K. Tweedie. Boston, 1854. 12°. . . . 5824
Lamplighter. Maria Cummings. Boston, 1854. 12°. 5775
Lamson, D. R. Two Years among the Shakers. West Boylston, 1848. 12°. 2456
Lancashire Dialect. Illustrated by G. Cruikshank. London, 1828. 12°. 1293
Lancashire Witches. W. H. Ainsworth. New York. 1849. 8°. . . 3293
Lancaster, House of, England and France under. London, 1852. 8°. . 5140
Lancaster, Mass. Address at 200th Anniver. J. Willard. Bost. 1853. 8°. 5456
Land of the Cæsar and Doge. W. Furniss. New York, 1853. 12°. . 5216
Lander, R. and J. Exploration of the Niger. New York, 1842. 2 v. 12°. 1883
The same. (H. F. L.) New York, 1846. 2 v. 12°. 3683, 35, 36
Landis, R. W. Liberty's Triumph; a Poem. New York, 1849. 12°. . 3398
Landon, Letitia E. Romance and Reality. London, 1852. 12°. . . 5684
Life, and Literary Remains. L. Blanchard. Phil. 1841. 2 v. 12°. 1623
Works. Philadelphia, 1847. 2 v. roy. 8°. 1343

Vol. 1. Romance and Reality; Francesca Carrara; Traits and Trials of Early Life.
2. Ethel Churchill; Book of Beauty; Poetical Works.

Landor, W. S. Gebir, Count Julian, and other Poems. Lond. 1839. 12°. 2544
Imaginary Conversations. London, 1836. 5 v. 8°. 2261
Pentameron and Pentalogia. London, 1837. 12°. 2318

Landor, W. S. Pericles and Aspasia. Philadelphia, 1839. 2 v. 12°. . 1236
Lands of the Moslem; Oriental Travel. H. Crosby. N. York, 1851. 8°. 4120
Landscape Gardening. A. J. Downing. New York, 1844. 8°. . . 2227
Laneton Parsonage. E. M. Sewell. New York, 1846. 2 v. 12°. . . 2912
Languages, Discovery of Science of. M. Kavanagh. Lond. 1844. 2 v. 8°. 4962
Lanman, C. Essays for Summer Hours. New York, 1853. 12°. . . 5365
Letters from the Alleghany Mountains. New York, 1849. 12°. . 3405
Private Life of Daniel Webster. New York, 1852. 12°. . . 5052
Lanman, J. H. History of Michigan. New York, 1841. 12°. . . 1858
The same. (H. F. L.) New York, 1847. 12°. . 3683, 139
Lanzi, L. History of Painting in Italy. London, 1847. 3 v. post 8°. . 3551
Laplace, P. S. Exposition du Système du Monde. Paris, 1813. 4°. . 3322
Traité de Mécanique Céleste. Paris, 1800–5. 4 v. 4°. . . . 3321
Lapland, Voyage from Leith to. W. Hurton. London, 1851. 2 v. 12°. 4257
Lardner, D. Lectures on Science and Art. New York, 1846. 2 v. 8°. . 2677
Lectures on the Steam Engine. New York, 1828. 12°. . . 1176
Railway Economy. New York, 1850. 12°. 3874
Treatise on the Steam Engine. London, 1853. 12°. . . . 6057
Lardner, N. Works; with Life by A. Kippis. London, 1838. 10 v. 8°. 4806

Vols. 1–4. Credibility of Gospel History.
5. The same, concluded; History of the Apostles and Evangelists.
6. The same, concluded; Jewish and Heathen Testimonies as to the Truth of the Christian Religion.
7. The same, continued.
8. The same, concluded; State of Gentilism under Christian Emperors; History of Heretics.
9. Sermons; Posthumous Sermons; Two Schemes of the Trinity, and the Divine Unity.
10. Vindication of the Miracles; Dissertations on two new Epistles ascribed to Clement of Rome; Remarks on Dr. Ward's Dissertations.

Lares & Penates; or, Cilicia & its Governors. W. B. Barker. Lon. 1853. 8°. 5461
Larochejaquelein, Marchioness de. Memoirs. Philadelphia, 1816. 8°. . 1242
Las Cases, M. J. E. Napoleon at St. Helena. Boston, 1823. 4 v. 8°. . 718
Last Days of Pompeii. E. L. Bulwer. New York, 1847. 8°. . . 1257
The same. London, 1853. 12°. 5721
Last Incarnation. A. Constant. Boston, 1848. 12°. 3131
Last Judgment. E. Swedenborg. Boston, 1828. 12°. 8
Last Leaf from Sunny Side. Mrs. E. S. Phelps. Boston, 1853. 12°. . 5307
Last of the Barons. E. L. Bulwer. New York, 1843. 8°. 1712
Last of the Lairds. J. Galt. New York, 1827. 12°. 491
Last of the Mohicans. J. F. Cooper. New York, 1850. 12°. . . . 1038
Latham, R. G. Elementary English Grammar. Cambridge, 1853. 12°. 6295
Handbook of the English Language. New York, 1853. 12°. . 6296
Man and his Migrations. New York, 1852. 12°. 4594
Lathrop, J., jun. Treatise on the Use of Globes. Boston, 1812. 12°. . 1006
Latimer, H. Sermons. Cambridge, 1832. 12°. 383, 7
Latin Dictionary, Ainsworth's, abridged. London, 1763. 2 v. 8°. . . 1353
Companion of. A. Rich. London, 1849. 12°. 5645
Latin Lexicon. Edited by F. P. Leverett. Boston, 1849. Roy. 8°. . 3603
Founded on Freund. E. A. Andrews. New York, 1851. Roy. 8°. 4350
Latitude and Longitude, the Compass, &c. T. Truxtun. Phil. 1794. 4°. 2009
Latreaumont; or, the Court Conspirator. E. Sue. Phil. 1849. 8°. . 3300

Latrobe, C. J. Rambler in Mexico. New York, 1836. 12°. . . . 265
Lauder, Sir T. D. Royal Progress in Scotland. Edinburgh, 1843. 4°. . 4954
Launcelot Graves. T. Smollett. Philadelphia, 1851. 8°. . . . 801, 2
Laurent (de l'Ardèche). History of Napoleon. New York, 1851. 8°. . 4346
La Vendée; an Historical Romance. A. Trollope. Lond. 1850. 3 v. 12°. 4281
Lavengro; the Scholar, Gipsy, and Priest. G. Borrow. N. Y. 1851. 12°. 3785
La Voye, M. de. Eugénie, the Young Laundress. Lond. 1851. 3 v. 12°. 4251
Law, and the Testimony. Anna Warner. New York, 1853. Roy. 8°. . 5424
Compendium of Mercantile. J. W. Smith. New York, 1850. 8°. 4305
Commentaries on American. J. Kent. New York, 1844. 3 v. 8°. 2056
Dictionary of the United States. J. Bouvier. Phil. 1848. 2 v. 8°. 3596
Elements of. F. Hilliard. Boston, 1835. 8°. 807
Elements of International. H. Wheaton. Philadelphia, 1846. 8°. 3538
Leading Cases in Commercial. J. P. Holcombe. N.Y. 1847. 8°. 4304
of Bills of Exchange. J. Story. Boston, 1847. 8°. . . . 3594
of Carriers. J. K. Angell. Boston, 1849. 8°. 4022
of Contracts. D. Gibbons. London, 1850. 12°. 6070
of Contracts not under Seal. W. W. Story. Boston, 1847. 8°. . 2219
of Debtor and Creditor. J. P. Holcombe. New York, 1849. 8°. 4306
of Merchant Ships and Seamen. C. Abbott. Phil. 1802. 8°. . 1365
of Nations. E. de Vattel. Dublin, 1792. 8°. 601
of Partnership. J. Story. Boston, 1846. 8°. 3595
of Promissory Notes. J. Story. Boston, 1847. 8°. . . . 3593
of Sales of Personal Property. W. W. Story. Boston, 1847. 8°. 3792
of Sales of Personal Property. G. Long. Boston, 1839. 8°. . 2062
Law, H. Elements of Euclid. London, 1853. 12°. 6098
Treatise on Civil Engineering. London, 1852. 12°. . . . 6044
Treatise on Common Roads. London, 1850. 12°. . . . 6068
Treatise on Logarithms. London, 1853. 12°. 6103
Law, W. Serious Call to a Holy and Devout Life. Boston, 1818. 12°. . 329
Law-Student; or, Guide to the Study of Law. J. Anthon. N.Y. 1850. 8°. 4307
Lawrence, Mrs. M. W. Light on the Dark River. Boston, 1853. 12°. . 5545
Lawrence, W. Lectures on Comparative Anatomy, &c. Lon. 1848. Post 8°. 4395
Laurie, T. Dr. A. Grant and the Nestorians. Boston, 1853. 12°. . . 5305
Lawrie Todd. J. Galt. New York, 1830. 2 v. 12°. 1931
The same. London, 1850. 12°. 5653
Laws of England, Comment. on. Sir W. Blackstone. N.Y. 1844. 2 v. 8°. 2218
The same. New York, 1849. 2 v. 8°. 3592
of the United States. Philadelphia, 1796, 1801. 5 v. 8°. . . 1214
Spirit of the. C. Montesquieu. Worcester, 1802. 2 v. 8°. . . 1799
The same. Worcester, 1808. 8°. 796
Lawson, J. P. Gazetteer of Scotland. Edinburgh, n. d. 12°. . . 5037
Lawson, W. J. History of Banking. London, 1850. 8°. 4646
Lawyers, Lives of Eminent British. H. Roscoe. Phil. 1841. 2 v. 12°. . 2162
Moral and Professional Duties of. S. Warren. N.Y. 1849. 12°. . 2464
Statesmen, &c., Lives of. S. L. Knapp. Boston, 1821. 8°. . . 659
Lawyer's Story; or, the Orphan's Wrongs. New York, 1853. 12°. . 5509
Lay, W., and C. M. Hussey. Mutiny of the "Globe." New Lond. 1828. 12°. 852

Lay of the Last Minstrel. Sir W. Scott. Boston, 1845. 12°. . . 69
The same. Philadelphia, 1839. 12°. 860, 1
The same. Edinburgh, 1848. 12°. 4102, 6
Layard, A. H. Nineveh and its Remains. New York, 1850. 2 v. 8°. . 3269
Discoveries in Nineveh and Babylon. New York, 1853. 8°. . 5162
Lays of the Kirk and Covenant. Mrs. A. S. Menteath. N.Y. 1851. 12°. 4170
Lays of the Scottish Cavaliers. W. E. Aytoun. New York, 1853. 12°. 6227
Lead Mines of Missouri. H. R. Schoolcraft. New York, 1819. 8°. . 1369
Leake, W. M. Travels in the Morea. London, 1830. 3 v. 8°. . . 5128
Leather Stocking and Silk; a Tale of Virginia. New York, 1854. 12°. . 6152
Leather Stocking Tales. J. F. Cooper. Viz.: —
Deerslayer. New York, 1852. 12°. 1632
Pathfinder. New York, 1852. 12°. 1581
Last of the Mohicans. New York, 1850. 12°. . . . 1038
Pioneers. Philadelphia, 1843. 2 v. 12°. 440
Prairie. New York, 1852. 12°. 1004
Leather Work, Ornamental. Boston, 1854. 12°. 5837
Leaves from Margaret Smith's Journal, 1678-9. Boston, 1849. 12°. . 3339
Lebanon, Mt.: a Ten Years' Residence. C.H.Churchill. Lon. 1853. 3 v. 8°. 5426
Lectures before the Ch. of Eng. Young Men's Society. London, 1851. 12°. 4267

Hoare, E. Civil and Religious Liberty.
Pym, W. W. The Lost Tribes.
Seymour, M. H. Church of Rome in Eng.
Dallas, A. R. C. Protestantism in Ireland.
Cadman, W. Eng. in Reign of James II.
Cumming, J. The Bible.
Dallas, A. R. C. Christ of Romanism.

on Evidences of Christianity, at University of Va. N. Y. 1852. 8°. 4802
to Young Men. W. G. Eliot, jun. Boston, 1854. 12°. . . 5639
to Young Men. J. Hawes. Hartford, 1830. 16°. . . . 90
to Young Men. H. W. Beecher. Indianapolis, 1844. 12°. . . 2181
to Young Women. W. G. Eliot, jun. Boston, 1854. 12°. . . 5553
before Young Men's Christian Association. Lond. 1850. 2 v. 12°. 4204

Vol. 1. Stowell, H. The Bible Self-Evidential.
Alexander, W. L. Influence of Romanism.
Hamilton, J. Literary Attractions of the Bible.
Mahan, A. Christianity and Freedom of Thought.
Arthur, W. Church in the Catacombs.
Seymour, M. H. Nature of Romanism.
M'Neile, H. The Bible.
Brock, W. The Apostle Paul.
Martin, S. Money.
Cumming, J. Music in its Relation to Religion.
Sherman, J. William Allen.
Burgess, R. French Protestantism.
2. Bickersteth, R. National Obligation to the Bible.
Stowell, H. The Age we Live in.
Duff, A. India, and its Evangelization.
Noel, B. W. A Revival of Religion.
Cumming, J. God in Science.
Villiers, H. M. Life in London.
Arthur W. Heroes.
Brock, W. Daniel, a Model for Young Men.
Hamilton, J. Solomon the Prince, and Solomon the Preacher.
Martin, S. Instincts of Industry.
Melson, J. B. Cherubic Symbol.
Candlish, R. S. Authority and Inspiration of the Holy Scriptures.

Ledyard, J. Life. J. Sparks. Boston, 1848. 12°. 1076, 24
Lee, A. Life. R. H. Lee. Boston, 1829. 2 v. 8°. 1408
Lee, C. Life. J. Sparks. Boston, 1848. 12°. 1076, 18

Lee, C. A. Elements of Geology. (H. F. L.) New York, 1848. 12°. 3683, 178
Lee, D. K. Master Builder; or, Life at a Trade. New York, 1852. 12°. 4889
Merrimack; or, Life at the Loom. New York, 1854. 12°. . . 5918
Summerfield; or, Life on a Farm. Auburn, 1852. 12°. . . 4796
Lee, Eliza B. Florence, the Parish Orphan. Boston, 1852. 12°. . . 4491
Memoirs of J. and J. S. Buckminster. Boston, 1849. 12°. . . 3376
Naomi; or, Boston 200 Years Ago. Boston, 1848. 12°. . . 3095
Lee, H. Memoirs of the War in the Southern Department. Wash. 1827. 8°. 899
Lee, Harriet. Constantia de Valmont. Philadelphia, 1799. 12°. . . 152
Lee, Mrs. H. F. Huguenots of France & America. Bost. 1852. 2 v. 12°. 5057
Life and Times of Thomas Cranmer. Boston, 1841. 12°. . . 1653
Life and Times of Martin Luther. Boston, 1839. 12°. . . 1629
Sketches and Stories from Life. Boston, 1850. 12°. . . . 3490
Sketches of Sculpture and Sculptors. Boston, 1854. 2 v. 12°. . 5590
Sketches of the Old Painters. Boston, 1838. 12°. . . . 379
Tales. Boston, 1842. 12°. 1658
Lee, Misses S. and H. Canterbury Tales. London, 1850. 2 v. 12°. . 5649
Lee, Mrs. R. African Crusoes. Philadelphia, 1854. 12°. . . . 6262
Anecdotes of Birds, Reptiles, and Fishes. Philadelphia, 1853. 12°. 5510
Anecdotes of Habits and Instincts of Animals. Phil. 1853. 12°. . 5511
Australian Wanderings. Philadelphia, 1854. 12°. . . . 6263
Lee, R. H. Life of Arthur Lee. Boston, 1829. 2 v. 8°. . . . 1408
Leech, S. Voice from the Main Deck. Boston, 1843. 16°. . . . 1744
Leeds, W. H. Orders of Architecture. London, 1854. 12°. . . . 6046
Legaré, H. S. Writings; with Memoir. Charleston, 1841. 2 v. 8°. . 2698
Legend of Montrose. Sir W. Scott. Boston, 1848. 2 v. 12°. . 999, 14
The same. Edinburgh, 1849. 12°. 4100, 15
The same. Edinburgh, 1850. Roy. 8°. . . . 4531, 4
Legend of the Waldenses, & other Tales. Mary J. Windle. Phil. 1852. 12°. 4605
Legends and Stories of Ireland. S. Lover. Philadelphia, 1835. 12°. . 124
of the Library at Lilies. Philadelphia, 1833. 2 v. 12°. . . . 1180
of the Rhine. T. C. Grattan. London, 1853. 12°. . . . 5738
of the West. J. Hall. New York, 1853. 12°. 5287
of the White Mountains. I. W. Scrivener. Boston, 1854. 12°. . 6238
Leggett, W. Polit. Writings. Ed. by T. Sedgwick, jun. N.Y. 1840. 12°. 1769
Legislation, Principles of. J. Bentham. Boston, 1830. 8°. . . . 786
Legislative Guide. J. B. Burleigh. Philadelphia, 1852. 8°. . . . 4815
Leibnitz, G. W. von. Life. J. M. Mackie. Boston, 1845. 12°. . . 2326
Leigh, Lord. Poems. London, 1839. 12°. 2390
Leigh, S. New Picture of London. London, 1830. 24°. . . . 5071
Leighton, R. Works; with Life by J. N. Pearson. New York, 1844. 8°. 2252
Leila; or, the Island. Ann F. Tytler. New York, 1853. 12°. . . 5318
Leila; or, Siege of Grenada. E. L. Bulwer. London, 1850. 8°. . . 5914
The same. Philadelphia, 1838. 12°. 929
Leila Ada. O. W. T. Heighway. New York, 1854. 12°. . . . 6149
Leisler, Jacob. Life. C. F. Hoffman. Boston, 1844. 12°. . . 1076, 13
Leisure Hours; Readings in Prose. E. A. Andrews. Boston, 1844. 12°. 2303
The same. Boston, 1835. 12°. 1747

Le Normand, M. A. Memoirs of Josephine. Philadelphia, 1850. 2 v. 12°. 3103
Leo X., Life and Pontificate of. W. Roscoe. London, 1846. 2 v. post 8°. 2930
Leonilla Lynmore, and other Tales. Miss Leslie. Philadelphia, 1847. 8°. 3202
Lepsius, R. Letters from Egypt, Ethiopia, and Sinai. Lond. 1853. 12°. 5579
Le Sage, A. R. Asmodeus; or, Devil on Two Sticks. Lond. 1845. 12°. 2426
Bachelor of Salamanca. Philadelphia, 1854. 12°. 6209
Gil Blas. Trans. by T. Smollett. Hartford, 1844. 3 v. 12°. . 1037
Leslie, C. Short Method with the Deists. New York, n. d. 12°. . . 504
Leslie, Miss. Behavior Book. Philadelphia, 1854. 12°. 5880
Dennings, and their Beaux, &c. Philadelphia, 1851. 8°. . . 4149
Leonilla Lynmore, and other Tales. Philadelphia, 1847. 8°. . 3202
Maid of Canal-street and the Bloxhams. Philadelphia, 1851. 8°. 3810
Mrs. Washington Potts and Mr. Smith. Philadelphia, 1843. 8°. 2167, 1
Pencil Sketches. Philadelphia, 1852. 2 v. 12°. 4877
Leslie, Sir J., and others. Discovery in Polar Seas. (H.F.L.) N.Y.1843. 12°. 3683,14
L'Esprit des Beaux Arts. Paris, 1753. 2 v. 12°. 297
Lester, C. E. Artist, Merchant, and Statesman. N.Y. 1845. 2 v. 12°. . 2501
Condition and Fate of England. New York, 1843. 2 v. 12°. . 1708
*(Editor.) Gallery of Illustrious Americans. N.Y. 1850. Folio. . 1715
Glory and Shame of England. New York, 1841. 2 v. 12°. . . 1654
Life and Voyages of Americus Vespucius. New York, 1846. 8°. 2712
Letter Writing, History of. W. Roberts. London, 1843. 8°. . . 4530
Letters from the Levant. Lady M. W. Montagu. London, 1838. 12°. . 2445
from New York. L. M. Child. New York, 1843–45. 2 v. 12°. . 1732
from Paris during the Reign of Napoleon. London, 1816. 2 v. 8°. 754
from Switzerland and Italy, 1801–2. Philadelphia, 1805. 2 v. 8°. . 684
from the Mountains. Boston, 1809. 2 v. 12°. 459
from the Shores of the Baltic. London, 1844. 12°. 2392
from the South. New York, 1835. 2 v. 12°. 1093
from the South [of Europe]. T. Campbell. Philadelphia, 1836. 12°. 252
from Three Continents. New York, 1851. 12°. 4031
Illustrative of Eng. History. 3d s. Sir H. Ellis. Lon. 1846. 4 v. 12°. 4581
of a Traveller. London, 1798. 8°. 613
of a Traveller. W. C. Bryant. New York, 1850. 12°. . . 3836
of the British Spy. W. Wirt. New York, 1836. 12°. . . 2133
on the Eastern States. New York, 1820. 12°. 462
on Literature, Taste, & Composition. G. Gregory. Phil. 1809. 12°. 371
on the Manners of the French. Dublin, 1791. 12°. . . . 151
to the Daughter of a Nobleman. Eliz. Hamilton. Salem, 1821. 12°. 1007
to a Young Man, &c. T. De Quincey. Boston, 1854. 12°. . 5771
to a Young Man. Mrs. West. Charlestown, 1803. 2 v. 12°. . 286
to My Pupils. Mrs. L. H. Sigourney. New York, 1851. 12°. . 4424
to a Young Lady. J. Bennett. Philadelphia, 1793. 2 v. 12°. . 185
Lettice Arnold; a Novel. Mrs. Marsh. New York, 1850. 8°. . . 3947
Leuchars, R. B. Practical Treatise on Hot-Houses. Boston, 1851. 12°. 4081
Levasseur, A. Lafayette in America, in 1824–25. Phil. 1829. 2 v. 12°. 351
Lever, C. Arthur O'Leary. Philadelphia, 1846. 8°. 2215
Confessions of Con Cregan. New York, 1851. 8°. 4532

Lever, C. Confessions of Harry Lorrequer. New York, 1842. 8°. . 1589
Daltons; or, Three Roads in Life. New York, 1852. 8°. . . 4812
Dodd Family Abroad. New York, 1854. 8°. 5949
Horace Templeton; an Autobiography. Philadelphia, 1850. 8°. . 3981
Jack Hinton, the Guardsman. Philadelphia, 1847. 8°. . . 1688
Knight of Gwynne. Philadelphia, 1847. 8°. 2796
Maurice Tierney. New York, 1852. 8°. 3991
Nevilles of Garretstown. New York, 1844. 8°. 2621
O'Donoghue; a Tale of Ireland. Philadelphia, 1846. 8°. . . 2645
Roland Cashel. New York, 1850. 8°. 3521
Sir Jasper Carew, Knt. New York, 1854. 8°. 5965
Tom Burke of "Ours." Philadelphia, 1846. 8°. . . . 2177
Leverett, F. P. (Ed.) Lexicon of the Latin Language. Bost. 1849. Roy. 8°. 3603
Levi, L. Principles and Administ. of Commercial Law. Lon. 1851. 2 v. 4°. 4837
Leviticus, Commentary on. A. A. Bonar. New York, 1851. 8°. . . 4715
Lewes, G. H. Life of M. I. Robespierre. Philadelphia, 1849. 12°. . 3077
Three Sisters and Three Fortunes. New York, 1848. 8°. . . 3230
Lewie; or, the Bended Twig. Auburn, 1853. 12°. 5740
Lewis, A. Poems. Boston, 1831. 12°. 516
Lewis, E. J. Hints to Sportsmen. Philadelphia, 1851. 12°. . . . 4167
Lewis, M., and W. Clarke. Exped. to Rocky Mount. N.Y. 1843. 2 v. 12°. 1745
The same. (H. F. L.) New York, 1848. 2 v. 12°. 3683, 154–5
Lewis, M. G. Bravo of Venice. London, 1853. 12°. 5702
Life and Correspondence. London, 1839. 8°. 4645
Lewis, R. B. Light and Truth. Portland, 1836. 16°. 1503
Lewis Arundel; or, Railroad of Life. F. Smedley. N. York, 1851. 8°. 4518
Lexington, Lord. Papers. Ed. by H. M. Sutton. London, 1851. 8°. . 4300
Liberia; or, Mr. Peyton's Experiments. Sarah J. Hale. N. Y. 1853. 12°. 5614
Liberties of America. H. W. Warner. New York, 1853. 12°. . . 5356
Liberty. History of. S. Eliot. Boston, 1853. 4 v. 12°. . . . 5238
Part I. Ancient Romans, 2 v. — Part II. Early Christians, 2 v.
Passages from the History of. S. Eliot. Boston, 1847. 12°. . 2965
of Rome; a History. S. Eliot. New York, 1849. 2 v. 8°. . . 3419
The same. Boston, 1853. 2 v. 12°. 5238
Liberty's Triumph; a Poem. R. W. Landis. New York, 1849. 12°. . 3398
Library, Classical. — See *Classical.*
Harper's Family. — See *Harper's Family Library.*
Library Manual, Appleton's. New York, 1847. 8°. 2830
Library of Choice Literature, Carey's. Philadelphia, 1836. 2 v. roy. 8°. . 2228
Vol. 1. Mackintosh, R. J. Life of Sir J. Mackintosh.
Kincaid, J. Adventures in the Rifle Brigade.
Roberts, Emma. Scenes in Hindostan.
James, G. P. R. One in a Thousand.
Bulwer, E. L. Rienzi.
Grant, J. Random Recollections of House of Commons.
2. Baillie, Joanna. Dramas.
Caunter, R. Confessions and Crimes.
Ritchie, L. Russia and the Russians.
Grant, J. Random Recollections of House of Lords.
Henningsen, C. F. Campaign in Navarre.
Rankin, F. H. Visit to Sierra Leone, 1834.
Byron, Lord. Conversations with Lady Blessington.
Tin Trumpet.
Village Sayings and Doings.

Library of Health. Edited by W. A. Alcott. Boston, 1837. 2 v. 12°. . 955
of Old English Prose Writers. Cambridge. 1831. 9 v. 12°. . 383

Vol. 1. Fuller, T. Holy and Profane States.
2. Sidney, Sir P. Defence of Poesy.
Selden, J. Table Talk.
3. Browne, Sir T., Selections from Works of.
4. Felltham, O. Resolves.
5, 6. Walton, I. Lives of Donne, Wotton, and others.
7. Latimer, H. Sermons.
8. Taylor, Jeremy, Selections from Works of.
9. More, Sir T. Utopia, and History of Richard III.

Libyan Desert, Adventures in. B. St. John. New York, 1849. 12°. . 3287
Liddell, H. G., and R. Scott. Greek Lexicon. New York, 1849. Roy. 8°. 3543
Lieber, F. Civil Liberty and Self-Government. Philadelphia, 1853. 12°. 5552
Essays on Property and Labor. (H. F. L.) N.Y. 1848. 12°. 3683, 146
Great Events described by Historians. Boston, 1840. 12°. . . 2139
Manual of Political Ethics. Boston, 1838. 2 v. 8°. 1783
Lieber, O. M. Assayer's Guide. Philadelphia, 1852. 12°. . . . 5006
(Translator.) Analytical Chemist's Assistant. Phil. 1852. 12°. . 5024
Liebig, J. Animal Chemistry. Cambridge, 1843. 12°. 1752
Familiar Lectures on Chemistry. London, 1851. 12°. . . . 4276
Life and Health, Lectures on. W. A. Alcott. Boston, 1853. 12°. . . 5256
and its Aims. Philadelphia, 1854. 12°. 5871
and Manners. T. De Quincey. Boston, 1851. 12°. . . . 4404
at the Water Cure; or, Month at Malvern. R.J.Lane. Lon. 1846. 12°. 4964
Art of Prolonging. C. W. Hufeland. Boston, 1854. 12°. . . 5589
Health, and Disease. E. Johnson. New York, 1850. 12°. . . 3433
Here and There. N. P. Willis. New York, 1850. 12°. . . 3924
in Earnest. C. B. Smith. Hartford, 1848. 12°. 3172
in the Far West. G. F. Ruxton. New York, 1849. 12°. . . 3438
in London. New York, 1848. 8°. 2755
in the New World; by Seatsfield. New York, 1844. 8°. . . 2081
in the Sick-Room. H. Martineau. Boston, 1844. 12°. . . 1843
in Prairie Land. Eliza W. Farnham. New York, 1846. 12°. . 3011
in Varied Phases. Mrs. C. H. Butler. Boston, 1851. 12°. . . 4452
Laws of, and Education of Girls. Eliz. Blackwell. N.Y. 1852. 12°. 4885
of a Sailor. F. Chamier. London, 1852. 12°. 5689
on the Isthmus. J. W. Fabens. New York, 1853. 12°. . . 5073
on the Lakes; a Trip to Lake Superior. New York, 1836. 2 v. 12°. 361
on the Ocean; or, 20 Years at Sea. G. Little. Boston, 1846. 12°. 2209
Life Scenes. F. A. Durivage. Boston, 1853. 12°. 5549
Life's Discipline; a Tale of Hungary. Mrs. Robinson. N.Y. 1851. 12°. 4030
Life's Lesson; a Tale. New York, 1854. 12°. 6251
Lift for the Lazy. New York, 1849. 8°. 3391
Light and Darkness; or, Mysteries of Life. Cath. Crowe. N.Y. 1851. 8°. 4003
and Shade; or, Young Artist. Anna H. Drury. N.Y. 1853. 12°. 5205
of Nature Pursued. A. Tucker. Cambridge, 1831. 4 v. 8°. . 2226
on the Dark River. Mrs. M. W. Lawrence. Boston, 1853. 12°. . 5545
Lighthouses, Report on. Washington, 1852. 8°. 2744
Treatise on. A. Stevenson. London, 1850. 12°. 6069
Lights and Shadows of German Life. Philadelphia, 1833. 2 v. 12°. . 2102

Lights and Shadows of Irish Life. S. C. Hall. Phil. 1838. 2 v. 12°. . 249
 and Shadows of Scottish Life. J. Wilson. New York, 1849. 12°. 394
Lillian, and other Poems. W. M. Praed. New York, 1852. 12°. . . 4784
Lily and the Bee. S. Warren. New York, 1851. 16°. 4468
Lily and the Totem. W. G. Simms. New York, 1850. 12°. . . . 3921
Lily Gordon; or, the Young Housekeeper. New York, 1854. 12°. . 6266
Limes, Cements, &c. G. R. Burnell. London, 1850. 12°. . . . 6067
Lincoln, R. W. Lives of the Presidents of the U.S. N. York, 1842. 8°. 1825
Lincoln, W. History of Worcester, Mass. Worcester, 1837. 8°. . . 3201
Lincoln, W. S. Alton Trials for Riot. New York, 1838. 12°. . . 1545
Lind, Jenny, in America. C. G. Rosenberg. New York, 1851. 12°. . 4409
 Memoranda of the Life of. N. P. Willis. Philadelphia, 1851. 12°. 4097
Linda; or, the Young Pilot. Caroline L. Hentz. Phil. 1852. 12°. . 3840
Lingard, J. Antiquities of the Anglo-Saxon Church. Phil. n. d. 8°. . 2084
 History of England. Paris, 1840. 8 v. 8°. 3542
Linny Lockwood; a Novel. Catherine Crowe. New York, 1854. 8°. . 5497
Linwoods; or, Sixty Years Since. C. M. Sedgwick. N.Y. 1835. 2 v. 12°. 1086
Lionel Lincoln; or, the Leaguer of Boston. J.F.Cooper. Phil. 1841. 2 v. 12°. 2314
Lion's Skin and Lover Hunt. C. de Bernard. New York, 1853. 12°. . 5241
Lippard, G. Washington and his Generals. Philadelphia, 1847. 8°. . 2831
Lippincott, Sara J. Countries I have Seen. Boston, 1855. 12°. . . 6232
Listener, The. Caroline Fry. Philadelphia, 1837. 2 v. 12°. . . . 2206
Literary and Educational Register. C. B. Norton. New York, 1854. 12°. 5783
Literary Recreations and Miscellanies. J. G. Whittier. Bost. 1854. 12°. 6222
Literary Reminiscences. T. De Quincey. Boston, 1851. 2 v. 12°. . 4458
Literary World. Vols. 3–5, 11. New York, 1848–52. 4°. . . . 3729
Literati, The. E. A. Poe. New York, 1850. 12°. 3929
Literature, Advice in the Pursuits of. S. L. Knapp. N. York, 1832. 12°. 326
 Amenities of. I. Disraeli. New York, 1841. 2 v. 12°. . . 1878
 Ancient and Modern. S. G. Goodrich. Boston, 1849. 12°. 4900, 17
 and Fine Arts, Handbook of. G. Ripley & B. Taylor. N.Y.1852. 12°. 4488
 and Literary Men, Modern. G. Gilfillan. New York, 1850. 12°. 3511
 and Literary Men of Great Britain. A. Mills. N.Y. 1851. 2 v. 8°. 4515
 Characteristics of. H. T. Tuckerman. Philadelphia, 1849. 12°. . 3377
 Curiosities of. I. Disraeli. Boston, 1834. 3 v. 12°. . . . 1234
 Cyclopædia of English. R. Chambers. Boston, 1851. 2 v. roy. 8°. 2636
 History of English. W. Spalding. New York, 1853. 12°. . . 5265
 Lectures on the History of. F. Schlegel. New York, 1844. 12°. 2344
 Modern European. Mrs. M. E. Foster. Philadelphia, 1850. 12°. 3498
 of Europe in 15th to 17th Centuries. H. Hallam. Paris, 1837. 4°. 584
 of South of Europe. J. C. L. S. de Sismondi. Lond. 1823. 4 v. 8°. 2233
 Outlines of English. T. B. Shaw. Philadelphia, 1849. 12°. . 3277
 Specimens of Foreign Standard. — See *Specimens*.
 Taste, and Composition, Letters on. G. Gregory. Phil. 1809. 12°. 371
 Walks in the World of. R. Grant. Philadelphia, 1840. 2 v. 12°. 867
Littell's Living Age. Vols. 1–42 [continued]. Boston, 1844–51. 8°. . 2214
Little, G. American Cruiser's Own Book. New York, 1851. 12°. . 2949
 Life on the Ocean; or, Twenty Years at Sea. Boston, 1846. 12°. 2209

Little Drummer. G. Nieritz. New York, 1853. 12°. 5540
Little Ferns. Mrs. S. P. Farrington. Auburn, 1854. 12°. . . . 5607
Little Pedlington. J. Poole. New York, 1852. 2 v. 12°. . . . 4861
Little Savage. F. Marryat. New York, 1849. 12°. 3410
Live and Let Live. C. M. Sedgwick. New York, 1837. 12°. . . 918
Livermore, A. A. The Acts; with a Commentary. Boston, 1853. 12°. 6264
Discourses. Boston, 1854. 12°. 6256
Gospels; with a Commentary. Boston, 1854. 2 v. 12°. . . 6261
Review of the Mexican War. Boston, 1850. 12°. . . . 3509
Romans; with a Commentary. Boston, 1853. 12°. . . . 6265
Lives and Anecdotes of Illustrious Men. New York, 1850. 16°. . . 3316
of American Merchants. New York, 1846. 16°. 2198
of Benefactors. S. G. Goodrich. Boston, 1849. 12°. . 4900, 4
of Distinguished Shoemakers. Portland, 1849. 12°. . . . 3280
of Eminent Brit. Statesmen. J. Forster & others. Lon. 1831. 7 v. 12°. 1831

Vol. 1. Sir Thomas More; Cardinal Wolsey; Archbishop Cranmer; Wm. Cecil, Lord Burleigh.
2. Sir John Eliot; Thomas Wentworth, Earl of Strafford.
3. John Pym; John Hampden.
4. Sir Henry Vane, the Younger; Henry Marten.
5. Robert Cecil, Earl of Salisbury; Thos. Osborne, Earl of Danby.
6, 7. Oliver Cromwell.

of Eminent Persons. London, 1833. 8°. 602

Galileo; Kepler; Newton; Mahomet; Wolsey; Sir E. Coke; Lord Somers; Caxton; Blake; Adam Smith; Niebuhr; C. Wren; M. Angelo.

of the Felons; or, American Criminal Calendar. N.Y. 1846. 8°. 2734
of the Heroes of the American Revolution. Boston, 1847. 12°. . 3010
of Literary and Scientific Men. J. Wynne. New York, 1850. 12°. 3920

Benj. Franklin; Jonathan Edwards; Robert Fulton; John Marshall; David Rittenhouse; Eli Whitney.

of Men of Letters & Science. Lord Brougham. Phil. 1845. 2 v. 12°. 2524
For contents, see *Brougham.*
of Scottish Writers. D. Irving. Edinburgh, 1850. 12°. . . 6269
Living Age. Ed. by E. Littell. Vols. 1–42 [con.] Boston, 1844–54. 8°. 2214
Living, Philosophy of. H. Mayo. Philadelphia, 1852. 12°. . . . 4860
Philosophy of. C. Ticknor. (H. F. L.) New York, 1846. 12°. 3683, 77
Livy, T. History of Rome. Trans. by G. Baker. Phil. 1836. 8°. . 803
The same. New York, 1842. 5 v. 12°. . . 1854, 24–28
The same. Tr. by Spillan and Edmonds. Lon. 1849. 4 v. 8°. 4379
Lloyd, Sir W. Journey in Himalaya Mountains. Lond. 1846. 8°. . 4021
Loaded Dice. J. Banim. New York, 1844. 8°. 2167, 3
Local Loiterings in the Vicinity of Boston. Boston, 1845. 12°. . . 2539
Locke Amsden; or, the Schoolmaster. D. P. Thompson. Bost. 1850. 12°. 3041
Locke, J. Conduct of the Understanding. (H. F. L.) N.Y. 1848. 12°. 3683, 171
on Education. London, 1693. 12°. 195
Essay on the Human Understanding. Boston, 1803. 3 v. 12°. . 872
Paraphrase and Notes on the Epistles of Paul. Boston, 1832. 8°. 1818
Works. Vol. 1 (the only vol. yet pub.). London, 1854. Post 8°. 5875
Lockhart, J. G. Ancient Spanish Ballads. New York, 1842. 8°. . . 2349
Life of Napoleon. New York, 1843. 2 v. 12°. 2452

Lockhart, J. G. Life of Napoleon. (H. F. L.) N.Y. 1843. 2 v. 12°. 3683, 4, 5
Life of Sir W. Scott. Edinburgh, 1848. 10 v. 12°. 4103
The same. Philadelphia, 1837. 2 v. 8°. 1259
Peter's Letters to his Kinsfolk. New York, 1820. 8°. . . . 657
Reginald Dalton. New York, 1823. 2 v. 12°. 339
Locks, Treatise on. C. Tomlinson. London, 1853. 12°. . . . 6093
Locomotive Engineers, Handbook of. S. Norris. Phil. 1852. 12°. . 5315
Lodge, E. Illustrations of British History, &c. London, 1838. 3 v. 8°. 4676
The same. London, 1838. 3 v. 8°. 5087
Portraits of Illustrious Men of Great Britain. Lond. n. d. 8 v. 12°. 3476
Lofty and the Lowly. Maria J. McIntosh. New York, 1853. 2 v. 12°. 5200
Logarithms, Treatise on. H. Law. London, 1853. 12°. . . . 6103
Logic, Elements of. R. Whately. New York, 1839. 12°. . . . 1805
System of; Ratiocinative and Inductive. J. S. Mill. N.Y. 1850. 8°. 2232
for the Million. London, 1851. 12°. 4259
and Utility of Mathematics. C. Davies. New York, 1850. 8°. . 3900
Lolme, J. L. de. Constitution of England. London, 1810. 8°. . . 695
London. C. Knight. London, 1851. 6 v. roy. 8°. 4827
and its Celebrities. J. H. Jesse. London, 1850. 2 v. 8°. . . 4959
and its Vicinity in 1851. J. Weale. London, 1851. 12°. . . 4406
Anecdotes; Electric Telegraph. London, n. d. 24°. . . . 5047
Pictures and Painters. London, n. d. 24°. . . . 5048
Antiquarian Ramble in. J. T. Smith. London, 1846. 2 v. 8°. . 4343
Charities of. S. Low, jun. London, 1850. 937
Every-Day Life in. J. Grant. Philadelphia, 1839. 2 v. 12°. . 1582
Great Metropolis. J. Grant. New York, 1837. 2 v. 12°. . . 1901
Labor and London Poor. Vol. 1. H. Mayhew. N.Y. 1851. 8°. 5176
Leigh's New Picture of. London, 1830. 24°. 5071
Letters from, 1802-3. W. Austin. Boston, 1804. 8°. . . 733
Life, Oddities of. J. Poole. Philadelphia, 1838. 2 v. 12°. . . 245
Magazine. Vols. 1-36 (8, 9, 16, 21, 24-32 wanting). Lon. 1732-69. 8°. 3777
Memorials of. J. H. Jesse. London, 1847. 2 v. 8°. . . . 4679
Memories of. F. Saunders. New York, 1852. 12°. . . . 4756
Metropolitan Improvements. J. Elmes. London, 1837. 8°. . 2836
Missionary Society, Fathers of. J. Morrison. London, 1844. 8°. 4355
Police of. P. Colquhoun. London, 1800. 8°. 729
Sketches of. J. Grant. Philadelphia, 1839. 2 v. 12°. . . . 518
Times, Essays from. New York, 1852. 2 v. 12°. . . . 262
What I Saw in. D. W. Bartlett. Auburn, 1852. 12°. . . 4782
World of. J. F. Murray. London, 1845. 2 v. 12°. . . . 4566
*Vestiges of Old. J. W. Archer. London, 1851. 4°. . . . 5429
Londonderry, N.H., History of. E. L. Parker. Boston, 1851. 12°. . 5017
Lone Dove; a Legend of Revolutionary Times. Phil. 1850. 12°. . . 3864
Long, G. France and its Revolutions. London, 1850. Roy. 8°. . . 5901
Law of Sales of Personal Property. Boston, 1839. 8°. . . 2062
Longfellow, H. W. Ballads, and other Poems. Cambridge, 1844. 12°. . 1676
Belfry of Bruges, and other Poems. Cambridge, 1846. 12°. . 2535
Evangeline; a Tale of Acadie. Boston, 1847. 12°. . . . 3055

Longfellow, H. W. Golden Legend. Boston, 1852. 12°. 4606
Hyperion. Boston, 1850. 12°. 1078
Kavanagh; a Tale. Boston, 1849. 12°. 3302
Outre-Mer. Boston, 1835. 2 v. 12°. 1079
Poems. Boston, 1851. 2 v. 12°. 4405
Poets and Poetry of Europe. Philadelphia, 1845. Roy. 8°. . . 2281
Seaside and Fireside. Boston, 1850. 12°. 3482
Spanish Student. Cambridge, 1843. 12°. 2126
Voices of the Night. Cambridge, 1839. 12°. 94
Longfellow, S., & T. W. Higginson. (Editors.) Thalatta. Bost. 1853. 12°. 5306
Look to the End; or, the Bennets Abroad. Mrs. Ellis. N.Y. 1845. 8°. 2242
Looker on; a Periodical Paper. Philadelphia, 1796. 4 v. in 2. 12°. . 887
Loomis, E. Progress of Astronomy in United States. N.Y. 1851. 12°. . 4027
Loomis, J. R. Elements of Geology. Boston, 1852. 12°. 4791
Lord, E. Epoch of Creation. New York, 1851. 12°. 4431
Lord, W. W. Poems. New York, 1845. 12°. 2366
Lord and Lady Harcourt. Catherine Sinclair. Philadelphia, 1851. 12°. 4016
Lord of the Isles. Sir W. Scott. Philadelphia, 1839. 12°. . . 860, 5
The same. Edinburgh, 1848. 12°. 4102, 10
Lord's Prayer, Lectures on. W. R. Williams. Boston, 1851. 12°. . 4407
Lord's Supper, Bickersteth's Treatise on. Philadelphia, 1831. 16°. . 822
Lorenzo Benoni; or, Life of an Italian. G. Ruffini. N.Y. 1853. 12°. . 5512
Lorgnette; or, Studies of the Town. D. G. Mitchell. N.Y. 1851. 2 v. 12°. 3908
Loring, J. S. Hundred Boston Orators. Boston, 1852. 8°. 4832
Los Gringos; or, View of Mexico, California, &c. Lieut. Wise. N.Y. 1849. 12°. 3429
Lossing, B. J. History of the Fine Arts. (H. F. L.) N.Y. 1846. 12°. 3683, 103
Outline History of the Fine Arts. New York, 1840. 12°. . . 2429
Pictorial Field-Book of the Revolution. N.Y. 1851–52. 2 v. roy. 8°. 4130
1776; or, War of Independence. New York, 1847. 8°. . . 2818
Signers of Declaration of Independence. New York, 1848. 12°. 1778
Lost Heiress. Mrs. E. D. E. N. Southworth. New York, 1854. 8°. . 5985
Lost Prince [Rev. Eleazar Williams]. J. H. Hanson. N.Y. 1854. 12°. 5623
Lost Senses; Deafness and Blindness. J. Kitto. New York, 1852. 12°. 4863
Lost Ship; or, the Atlantic Steamer. W. J. Neale. New York, 1844. 8°. 2729
Lothrop, Amy. Dollars and Cents. New York, 1852. 2 v. 12°. . . 4789
Lothrop, S. K. Life of Samuel Kirkland. Boston, 1848. 12°. . 1076, 25
Lotus-Eating; a Summer Book. G. W. Curtis. New York, 1852. 12°. 4888
Loudon, J. C. Encyclopædia of Trees and Shrubs. London, 1842. 8°. 5893
Trees and Shrubs of Britain. London, 1844. 8 v. 8°. . . . 1514

Vol. 1. History, Geography, and Science, with Descriptions; from Ranunculaceæ to Staphyleaceæ.
2. Celastraceæ to Apocynaceæ.
3. Asclepiadaceæ to Corylaceæ.
4. Garryaceæ to the End.
5. (Plates.) Magnoliaceæ to Leguminosæ.
6. (Plates.) Rosaceæ to Oleaceæ.
7. (Plates.) Bignoniaceæ to Corylaceæ.
8. (Plates.) Corylaceæ to Cupressinæ.

Loudon, Mrs. Entertaining Naturalist. London, 1850. 12°. . . . 4565
Louis Napoleon. — See *Napoleon, Louis.*
Louis XIV., and Court, in 17th Cent. Miss Pardoe. N.Y. 1847. 2 v. 12°. 3040

Luther, M., Life and Times of. Mrs. H. F. Lee. Boston, 1839. 12°. . 1629
Luttrells; or, the Two Marriages. F. Williams. New York, 1851. 8°. 4005
Lycia, Travels in. T. A. B. Spratt and E. Forbes. Lond. 1847. 2 v. 8°. 4662
Lydia; a Woman's Book. Mrs. N. Crosland. Boston, 1852. 12°. . 4912
Lyell, Sir C. Elements of Geology. Boston, 1841. 2 v. 12°. . . 2519
Manual of Elementary Geology. London, 1851. 8°. . . . 4356
Principles of Geology. Philadelphia, 1837. 2 v. 8°. . . . 784
The same. Boston, 1842. 3 v. 12°. 2520
The same. Eighth edition, revised. London, 1850. 8°. . 3986
The same. Ninth edition revised. Boston, 1853. 8°. . 2520
Second Visit to United States. New York, 1849. 2 v. 12°. . . 3396
Travels in North America, 1841–42. New York, 1845. 2 v. 12°. . 2479
Lying, Illustrations of. Amelia Opie. Boston, 1827. 12°. . . . 201
Lyman, S. P. Life and Memorials of Danl. Webster. N. Y. 1853. 2 v. 12°. 5069
Lynch, Anne C. Rhode Island Book. Providence, 1841. 12°. . . 1728
Lynch, W. F. Expedition to Jordan and Dead Sea. Phil. 1849. 8°. . 2850
Midshipman. New York, 1851. 12°. 4483
Lynde Weiss; an Autobiography. G. H. Throop. Phil. 1852. 12°. . 140
Lyon, Mary. Life and Labors. Ed. by E. Hitchcock. Northampt. 1852. 12°. 4624
Lyra, and other Poems. Alice Carey. New York, 1852. 12°. . . 4783
Lyttleton, G. (Lord). Conversion of St. Paul. New York, n. d. 12°. . 504
History of Henry II. London, 1769. 6 v. 8°. 5911

M.

Mabel, the Actress. Baron St. Leger. New York, 1844. 8°. . 2167, 2
Maberly, Mrs. Lady and the Priest. New York, 1851. 8°. . . . 4525
Macaulay, T. B. Critical and Miscellaneous Essays. Phil. 1848. 8°. 3418, 1
The same. Philadelphia, 1851. 5 v. 12°. 278

Vol. 1. Milton; Machiavelli; Dryden; History; Hallam; Southey's Colloquies on Society; Byron; Bunyan's Pilgrim's Progress.
2. Boswell's Johnson; Hampden; Burghley; Mirabeau; War of the Succession; Walpole's Letters; Chatham; Bacon.
3. Mackintosh's English Revolution of 1688; Clive; Temple; Church and State; History of the Popes; Cowley and Milton; Mitford's Greece; Athenian Orators.
4. Comic Dramatists of the Restoration; Lord Holland; Hastings; Frederic the Great; Lays of Ancient Rome.
5. Mde. D'Arblay; Addison; Barere; Robt. Montgomery's Poems; Civil Disabilities of the Jews; Mill's Essay on Government; Bentham's Defence of Mill; Utilitarian Theory of Government.

Extracts from the Writings of. Buffalo, 1849. 12°. 3394
History of England from Accession of James II. N.Y. 1849. 2 v. 8°. 3257
Speeches. New York, 1853. 2 v. 12°. 5193
Macaulay, W. H. Kathay; Cruise in the China Seas. N.Y. 1852. 12°. 5080
MacCabe, W. B. Bertha; a Romance of the Dark Ages. Lon. 1851. 3 v. 12°. 4246
M'Cartney, W. Origin and Progress of United States. Phil. 1847. 12°. 3043
M'Cheyne, R. M. Works. New York, 1852. 2 v. 8°. 4726
McConnel, J. L. The Glenns; a Family History. New York, 1851. 12°. 4189
Grahame; or, Youth and Manhood. New York, 1850. 12°. . 4199
Talbot and Vernon; a Novel. New York, 1850. 12°. . . . 3847

McConnel, J. L. Western Characters. New York, 1853. 12°. . . 5563
M'Cosh, J. Method of Divine Government. New York, 1852. 8°. . 4725
M'Crie, T. Life of John Knox. Edinburgh, 1840. 12°. . . . 1800
McCrindell, R. Convent; a Narrative. New York, 1850. 12°. . . 4401
M'Culloch, J. R. Commerce. London, 1843. 8°. 2541
Dictionary of Commerce. Philadelphia, 1845. 2 v. roy. 8°. . 1691
Essays on Exchange, Interest, Money, &c. Boston, 1850. 8°. . 3984
Geographical Dictionary. New York, 1845. 2 v. roy. 8°. . . 2221
Literature of Political Economy. London, 1845. 8°. . . . 2625
McCulloch's Texas Rangers. S. C. Reid. Philadelphia, 1847. 12°. . 3085
McFarland, A. The Escape; Travels in Europe. Boston, 1851. 12°. . 5291
MacFarlane, C. Armenians; a Tale of Constantinople. Phil. 1830. 2 v. 12°. 1227
French Revolution of 1789. London, 1844. 4 v. 12°. . . . 3093
Japan; Geographical and Historical Account. N. Y. 1852. 12°. . 4907
Life of the Duke of Marlborough. London, 1852. 12°. . . 6281
Romance of History; Italy. New York, 1832. 2 v. 12°. . . 1549
Turkey and its Destiny. Philadelphia, 1850. 2 v. 12°. . . 3868
MacFarlane, R. Steam Navigation and Propellers. N.Y. 1851. 12°. . 4058
MacGavock, R. W. Tennessean Abroad. New York, 1854. 12°. . . 6279
Mac-Geoghegan, Abbé. History of Ireland. Dublin, 1844. Roy. 8°. . 3964
Macgillivray, W. History of British Birds. London, 1839. 2 v. 8°. . 3547
British Quadrupeds. Edinburgh, 1843. 12°. . . . 4901, 17
Macgregor, J. Commercial Statistics of all Nations. Lond. 1850. 5 v. roy. 8°. 5469

Vol. 1. Austria; Belgium; Denmark; France, and Colonies; Holland, and Colonies; Germanic Union; Italian States; Gibraltar; Malta; Ionian Islands.
2. Ottoman Empire; Greece; African States; Russia; Sweden and Norway; Spain, and Colonies; Portugal, and Colonies.
3. United States; Mexico; Central America; Mosquito Territory; New Grenada; Venzuela; British, French, and Dutch Guyana; Peru; Bolivia; Equador; Chili; Paraguay; Buenos Ayres; Monte Video; Patagonia.
4. Hayti; Cuba; Porto Rico; French, Dutch, and Danish West Indies; Brazil; British East Indies; Ceylon; Singapore; Malacca; Prince of Wales's Island.
5. Chinese Empire; British Possessions in Africa, Asia, and Australia; British North American Colonies; British West Indies; Falkland Islands; Sandwich Islands; British and Colonial Customs; Tariffs and Regulations; Dues and Charges in Seaports of Great Britain; Summary of British Navigation for One Hundred and Fifty Years; Supplements.

*Progress of America. London, 1847. 2 v. 8°. 4023
*Machines, Mechanics, &c., Appleton's Dictionary of. N.Y.1851. 2 v. roy. 8°. 4124
Machiavelli, N. Art of War. Albany, 1815. 8°. 1330
Florentine Histories. New York, 1845. 2 v. 12°. 2482
McIntosh, J. Origin of the North American Indians. N.Y. 1853. 8°. . 1841
McIntosh, Maria J. Aunt Kitty's Tales. New York, 1849. 12°. . . 3932
Conquest and Self-Conquest. New York, 1846. 18°. . . . 2420
Evenings at Donaldson Manor. New York, 1851. 8°. . . . 4309
The same. New York, 1853. 12°. 4926
Charms and Counter-Charms. New York, 1850. 12°. . . 3150
Lofty and the Lowly. New York, 1853. 2 v. 12°. . . . 5200
Two Lives; or, To Seem and To Be. New York, 1852. 12°. . 4868
Woman in America. New York, 1850. 12°. 3629

Mackay, C. Extraordinary Popular Delusions. Phil. 1850. 2 v. 12°. . 3668
M'Kenney, T. L. Memoirs and Travels. New York, 1846. 8°. . . 2765
Mackenzie, A. Voyages to Frozen and Pacific Oceans. Phil. 1802. 8°. 766
Mackenzie, A. S. American in England. New York, 1835. 2 v. 12°. . 1108
Life of Stephen Decatur. Boston, 1848. 12°. 1076, 21
Life of J. Paul Jones. Boston, 1841. 12°. 1905
Life of Oliver H. Perry. New York, 1840. 2 v. 12°. . . . 221
The same. (H. F. L.) New York, 1846. 2 v. 12°. 3683, 126–7
Year in Spain. New York, 1836. 3 v. 12°. 1193
Mackenzie, Mrs. C. Six Years in India. New York, 1853. 12°. . . 5548
Mackenzie, H. Memoir and Works (no titlepage). 12°. 235
Mackie, J. M. Life of G. W. von Leibnitz. Boston, 1845. 12°. . . 2326
Life of S. Gorton. Boston, 1844. 12°. 1076, 15
McKinnen, D. Tour through Brit. West India Islands. Lond. 1804. 12°. 196
Mackinnon, Capt. Atlantic and Transatlantic. New York, 1852. 12°. . 5018
McKinnon, W. C. St. George; or, Canadian League. Halif. 1852. 2 v. 12°. 189
Mackintosh, Sir J. History of England. Philadelphia, 1830. 2 v. 12°. . 76
Miscellaneous Works. Philadelphia, 1848. 8°. 3418, 8
The same. London, 1846. 3 v. 8°. 2703

Vol. 1. Progress of Ethical Philosophy; Philosophical Genius of Bacon and Locke; Law of Nature and Nations; Life of Sir Thomas More; Authorship of Icôn Basilikè; Affairs of Holland.
2. English Revolution of 1688; Partition of Poland; Administration and Fall of Struensee; Case of Donna Maria, of Portugal; Charles, First Marquis Cornwallis; Character of George Canning; Preface to a Reprint of the Edinburgh Review of 1755; Writings of Machiavelli; Lives of Milton's Nephews; Review of Rogers's Poems; Mde. de Staël's Germany; Discourse at the Literary Society of Bombay.
3. Defence of the French Revolution; State of France in 1815; Right of Parliamentary Suffrage; Defence of Jean Peltier; Charge to Grand Jury of Bombay. — Speeches, viz.: On Annexation of Genoa; On the State of Criminal Law; On Case of Missionary Smith; On Spanish-American States; On Civil Government of Canada; On Affairs of Portugal, 1829; On the Reform Bill, 1831.

Life. R. J. Mackintosh. Boston, 1853. 2 v. 8°. 5421
The same. Philadelphia, 1836. 8°. 2228, 1
Progress of Ethical Philosophy. Philadelphia, 1845. 8°. . . 3608
Mackintosh, John. Pathology and Practice of Medicine. Phil. 1844. 8°. 4702
MacLeod, D. The Bloodstone. New York, 1853. 12°. 5616
Life of Sir Walter Scott. New York, 1852. 12°. 5053
Pynnshurst. New York, 1852. 12°. 1031
McLellan, I., jun. Fall of the Indian, and other Poems. Bost. 1830. 12°. 502
McMullen, T. Handbook of Wines. New York, 1852. 12°. . . 4777
Macnish, R. Tales and Essays; with Life. D. M. Moir. Lon. 1844. 2 v. 12°. 4975
Macpherson, J. (Translator.) Poems of Ossian. New York, 1846. 12°. 2999
Macy, O. History of Nantucket. Boston, 1835. 12°. 1183
Madam Dorrington of the Dene. W. Howitt. London, 1851. 3 v. 12°. 4619
Madden, R. R. Infirmities of Genius. Philadelphia, 1833. 2 v. 12°. . 2551
Residence in the West Indies. Philadelphia, 1835. 2 v. 12°. . 1077
United Irishmen. Philadelphia, 1842. 2 v. 12°. 1936
Madeleine; a Tale of Auvergne. Julia Kavanagh. N. York, 1852. 12°. 949
Madeira and West Indies, Traveller's Guide to. Haddington, n. d. 8°. . 663
Sierra Leone, &c., Travels in. J. Holman. London, 1840. 8°. 1986, 1

Madeira, Spain, and Florence. J. A. Dix. New York, 1850. 12°. . 4085
Madison, J. Life. J. Q. Adams. Boston, 1850. 12°. 3934
Papers, Correspondence, and Reports. New York, 1841. 3 v. 8°. 1781
Madoc; a Poem. R. Southey. Boston, 1821. 2 v. 8°. 745
Madras, Ceylon, &c., Travels in. J. Holman. London, 1840. 8°. . 1986, 3
Madrid in 1835. New York, 1836. 2 v. 8°. 1431
Madrilenia; or, Spanish Life. H. D. Wolff. London, 1851. 12°. . . 5413
Magdalen Hepburn. Mrs. Oliphant. New York, 1854. 12°. . . . 6174
Magendie, F. Use of Prussic Acid in Disease of the Breast. N.H. 1820. 12°. 975
Magic and Sorcery, Narratives of. T. Wright. New York, 1852. 12°. . 4768
Natural, Letters on. Sir D. Brewster. New York, 1845. 12°. . 2433
The same. (H. F. L.) New York, 1848. 12°. . . 3683, 50
Philosophy of. E. Salverte. Ed. by A.T.Thomson. Lon.1846. 2 v. 8°. 4683
Magic of Kindness. Bros. Mayhew. New York, 1849. 12°. . . 3309
Magician Priest of Avignon. T. H. Usborne. London, 1851. 2 v. 12°. 4607
Magin, E. Piozziana. London, 1833. 8°. 2543
Maginn, W. Odoherty Papers. New York, 1855. 2 v. 12°. . . . 6241
Magnalia Christi Americana. Cotton Mather. Hartford, 1853. 2 v. 8°. . 5445
Magnetical and Meteorological Observations. J. M. Gilliss. Wash. 1845. 8°. 2813
Magnetism, Heat, &c., Dynamics of. C. von Ruchenbach. Lon. 1851. 8°. 4159
Human. W. Newnham. New York, 1845. 12°. . . . 2342
Popular Treatise on. Sir D. Brewster. Edinburgh, 1851. 12°. . 6271
Treatise on. Sir W. S. Harris. London, 1843. 12°. . . . 6042
Magoon, E. L. Living Orators of America. New York, 1850. 12°. . 3281
Proverbs for the People. Boston, 1849. 12°. 3186
Republican Christianity. Boston, 1849. 12°. 3354
Magyars, Poetry of. J. Bowring. London, 1830. 12°. 3092
Mahmoud; a Novel. Philadelphia, 1835. 2 v. 12°. 1121
Mahomedans and Hindoos, Strictures on. W. Tennant. Lon. 1804. 2 v. 8°. 969
Mahomet and his Successors. W. Irving. New York, 1850. 2 v. 12°. . 3368
and his Successors. S. Ockley. London, 1847. Post 8°. . . 3556
The Koran; Translated, with Discourse, by G. Sale. Lon. 1844. 8°. 2003
Life. London, 1833. 8°. 602
The same. Philadelphia, 1833. 8°. 1357, 2
Life. G. Bush. (H. F. L.) New York, 1843. 12°. . . 3683, 10
Life and Religion of. Trans. by J. L. Merrick. Bost. 1850. 12°. 3628
Mahon, Lord. History of England. New York, 1849. 2 v. 8°. . . 3262
Life of Belisarius. Philadelphia, 1832. 12°. 216
Life of Louis, Prince of Condé. New York, 1845. 2 v. 12°. . 2513
Mahoney, S. I. Six Years in the Monasteries of Italy. Phil. 1836. 12°. 227
Maid of Canal-street and the Bloxhams. Miss Leslie. Phil. 1851. 8°. . 3810
Maid of Orleans; a Romantic Tragedy. F. Schiller. London, n. d. 12°. 2979
Maillard, A. Marie. Miles Tremenhere. New York, 1853. 12°. . . 5375
Main, R. Treatise on Astronomy. London, 1852. 12°. 6104
Maine, History of. W. D. Williamson. Hallowell, 1832. 2 v. 8°. . . 569
History of the District of. J. Sullivan. Boston, 1795. 8°. . . 577
Geology of; Second Report. C. T. Jackson. Augusta, 1838. 8°. 3248
Maistre, J. de. Generative Principle of Polit. Constitutions. Bost. 1847. 12°. 3024

Major Jones's Courtship. Philadelphia, 1850. 12°. 3889
Major Jones's Sketches of Travel. Philadelphia, 1850. 12°. . . . 3890
Malcolm, Sir J. Sketches of Persia. London, 1845. 12°. 2389
Malcom, H. Christian's Rule of Marriage. Boston, 1834. 12°. . . . 1481
Travels in South-Eastern Asia. Boston, 1839. 2 v. 12°. . . 1250
Malden, H. Distinguished Men of Modern Times. N.Y. 1846. 2 v. 12°. 3683, 124–5
Malham, J. Naval Gazetteer. Boston, 1797. 2 v. 8°. 678
Mallet, M. Northern Antiquities. London, 1846. Post 8°. . . . 3561
Malleville ; a Franconia Story. J. Abbott. New York, 1850. 12°. . 4033
Malibran, Madame. Memoirs. Countess de Merlin. Lon. 1844. 2 v. 12°. 2386
Malta and Sicily, Travels in, 1827. A. Bigelow. Boston, 1831. 8°. . 787
Malthus, T. R. Essay on Population. Georgetown, 1809. 2 v. 8°. . 1973
*Mammifers, Collection de. Paris, 1808. 4°. 5980
Man and his Migrations. R. G. Latham. New York, 1852. 12°. . . 4594
and his Motives. G. Moore. New York, 1848. 12°. 2460
Constitution of. G. Combe. Boston, 1839. 12°. 555
History of; or, the Wonders of Human Nature. Perth, 1796. 12°. 118
in his Physical Structure & Adaptations. R. Mudie. Bost. 1838. 12°. 334
Natural History of. W. Lawrence. London, 1848. Post 8°. . 4395
Physical History of. J. C. Prichard. London, 1813. 8°. . . 1914
Primeval. J. Harris. Boston, 1849. 12°. 3358
Theories on Nat. History of. W. F. Van Amringe. N. Y. 1848. 8°. 4354
Man-at-Arms. G. P. R. James. New York, 1840. 2 v. 12°. . . 420
The same. London, 1844. 12°. 5727
Man Made of Money. D. Jerrold. New York, 1849. 12°. . . . 3297
The same. London, 1853. 12°. 6234, 6
Man of Two Lives ; written by Himself. Boston, 1829. 12°. . . . 390
Management of the Tongue. Boston, 1813. 12°. 137
Mandeville; a Tale. W. Godwin. Philadelphia, 1818. 2 v. 12°. . . 1908
Manhattaner in New Orleans. A. O. Hall. New York, 1851. 12°. . 4089
*Mankind, Types of. S. G. Morton. Ed. by Nott & Gliddon. Phil. 1854. 8°. 5928
Manly Exercises, British. D. Walker. Philadelphia, 1850. 12°. . . 2200
Mann, E. J. Deaf and Dumb, and their Education. Boston, 1836. 12°. 281
Mann, H. Lectures on Education. Boston, 1848. 12°. 2323
Slavery ; Letters and Speeches. Boston, 1851. 12°. . . . 4623
Twelve Reports on Education in Mass. Boston, 1838–48. 2 v. 8°. 4121
Mann, J. Bird-Keeper's Manual. Boston, 1848. 12°. 3308
Manners and Customs of Nations. S. G. Goodrich. Bost. 1849. 12°. 4900, 19
Customs & Curiosities of Nations. J. Goldsmith. Phil. 1818. 2 v. 12°. 1016
Manning, J. A. Lives of Speakers of House of Commons. Lon. 1851. roy. 8°. 5147
Manning, R. Shortest Way to end Disputes about Religion. Bost. 1850. 12°. 3832
Mansfield, E. D., Legal Rights and Duties of Women. Salem, 1845. 12°. 2574
Life of Gen. Winfield Scott. New York, 1846. 12°. . . . 2598
Mansfield, —. Up Country Letters. New York, 1852. 12°. . . . 4893
Mansfield Park. Jane Austen. London, 1853. 12°. 5693
The same. Philadelphia, 1838. 8°. 1585, 1
Mansie Wauch. New York, 1828. 12°. 524
Mantell, G. A. Geology of Isle of Wight. London, 1854. Post 8°. . 5937

*Mantell, G. A. Pictorial Atlas of Fossil Remains. London, 1850. 4°. 4351
Manual of Dignities, Privilege, and Precedence. C. R. Dodd. Lond. 1844. 12°. 2444
The same. London, 1843. 12°. 3602
Manufacturing Districts of England. Sir G. Head. New York, 1847. 12°. 3038
Manzoni, A. The Betrothed. London, 1851. 12°. 5662
The same. New York, 1845. 2 v. 12°. 2496
Mapleton; or, the Maine Law. P. Church. Boston, 1853. 12°. . . 5309
Maps. — See *Atlas.*
Marble, D., Biographical Sketch of. New York, 1851. 12°. . . . 4462
March, C. W. Reminiscences of Congress. New York, 1850. 12°. . 3919
Marchioness of Brinvilliers. A. Smith. London, 1852. 12°. . . 5680
Marcou, J. Geological Map of United States. Boston, 1853. 8°. . . 5417
Marcus Warland. Caroline Lee Hentz. Philadelphia, 1852. 12°. . 3574
Mardi; and a Voyage thither. H. Melville. New York, 1849. 2 v. 12°. 3276
Margaret; a Tale of the Real and Ideal. S. Judd. Boston, 1851. 2 v. 12°. 2523
Margaret; or, Prejudice at Home. New York, 1854. 12°. . . . 5788
Margaret Cecil; or, "I Can, because I Ought." New York, 1852. 12°. 4767
Margaret Graham. G. P. R. James. New York, 1847. 8°. . . . 2808
Margaret Maitland. Mrs. Oliphant. New York, 1851. 12°. . . . 4423
Margaret Percival in America; a Tale. Boston, 1850. 12°. . . . 3915
Margaret Smith's Journal, 1678–9. Boston, 1849. 12°. 3339
Margoliouth, M. History of the Jews in Great Britain. Lond. 1851. 3 v. 12°. 4287
Pilgrimage to the Land of my Fathers. London, 1850. 2 v. 8°. . 4324
Marguerite de Valois. A. Dumas. New York, 1850. 8°. . . . 2705
Marian; or, the Young Maid's Fortunes. Mrs. S. G. Hall. N.Y. 1840. 2 v. 12°. 1523
Marie Antoinette, Court of. Mde. Campan. London, 1850. 2 v. 12°. . 3834
History of. J. S. C. Abbott. New York, 1850. 12°. . . . 3380
Marie Louise; or, Opposite Neighbors. Emilie F. Carlen. Lond. 1853. 12°. 5382
Marie de Berniere. W. G. Simms. Philadelphia, 1853. 12°. . . . 5301
Marine Engines and Steam Vessels. R. Murray. London, 1852. 12°. . 6088
Marine Insurances, Law of. J. A. Park. Boston, 1799. 8°. . . . 782
Practical Treatise on. J. I. Burn. London, 1801. 12°. . . 172
Mariner, W. Account of Natives of Tonga Islands. Boston, 1820. 8°. 751
Mariner's Library of Popular Voyages. Boston, 1833. 12°. . . . 1169
Mariner's Sketches. N. Ames. Providence, 1830. 12°. . . . 590
Mariner's Technical Terms, Dictionary of. Washington, 1805. 12°. . 109
Marion, F. (Gen.). Life. P. Horry and M. L. Weems. Phil. 1841. 12°. 1894
Life. W. G. Simms. New York 1844. 12°. 2182
Mariotti, L. Blackgown Papers. London, 1846. 2 v. 12°. . . . 4970
Italy Past and Present. London, 1848–49. 2 v. 12°. . . . 3356
Scenes from Italian Life. London, 1850. 12°. 4227
Maritime Contracts, Treatise on. R. J. Pothier. Boston, 1821. 8°. . 1401
Mark Hurdlestone. Mrs. S. Moodie. New York, 1853. 12°. . . 5378
Marlborough, Duke of, History of. London, 1754. 12°. . . . 854
Letters and Despatches. London, 1845. 3 v. 8°. 2274
Life. C. MacFarlane. London, 1852. 12°. 6201
Memoirs. W. Coxe. London, 1847. 3 v. post 8°. . . . 3557
Marmaduke Herbert. Countess of Blessington. New York, 1849. 8°. . 2820

Marmaduke Lorrimer. J. Middleton. London, 1850. 12°. 4279
Marmaduke Wyvil. H. W. Herbert. New York, 1853. 12°. . . 5317
Marmion. Sir W. Scott. Philadelphia, 1839. 12°. 860, 2
The same. Edinburgh, 1848. 12°. 4102, 7
Marquette, Father. Life. J. Sparks. Boston, 1844. 12°. . . 1076, 10
Marquis de Letorière. E. Sue. New York, 1844. 8°. 2167, 2
Marriage; a Novel. Susan Ferrier. New York, 1848. 8°. 303
The same. London, 1853. 12°. 5724
Marriage, Christian's Rule of. H. Malcom. Boston, 1834. 8°. . . 1481
Marriage Contract. Harriet Raikes. Boston, 1850. 8°. 3640
Marryat, F. Ardent Troughton. New York, 1846. 8°. 2812
Diary in America. New York, 1839. 12°. 193
Diary of a Blasé. Philadelphia, 1836. 12°. 272
Jacob Faithful. Philadelphia, 1847. 8°. 401
The same. London, 1853. 12°. 5715
Japhet in Search of a Father. Philadelphia, 1837. 2 v. 12°. . 1120
The same. London, 1853. 12°. 5716
King's Own. Philadelphia, 1834. 2 v. 12°. 1196
The same. London, 1853. 12°. 5717
Little Savage. New York, 1849. 12°. 3410
Midshipman Easy. Philadelphia, n. d. 8°. 244
The same. London, 1853. 12°. 5718
Newton Forster. London, 1853. 12°. 5719
Novels. Philadelphia, 1847. 2 v. 8°. 1766

Vol. 1. Peter Simple; Jacob Faithful; King's Own; Pacha of Many Tales.
2. Snarleyyow, or Dog-Fiend; Midshipman Easy; Japhet in Search of a Father; Newton Forster; Frank Mildmay.

Pacha of Many Tales. London, 1853. 12°. 5720
The same. Philadelphia, 1847. 8°. 2964
Percival Keene. Philadelphia, 1846. 8°. 2714
The same. London, 1853. 12°. 5735
Peter Simple. Philadelphia, 1847. 8°. 449
The same. London, 1853. 12°. 5714
Phantom Ship. Philadelphia, 1839. 2 v. 12°. 481
The same. London, 1853. 12°. 5732
Pirate, and the Three Cutters. Philadelphia, 1847. 8°. . . . 1122
Poacher. London, 1853. 12°. 5731
Poor Jack. Philadelphia, n. d. 8°. 920
Snarleyyow; or, Dog-Fiend. Philadelphia, 1837. 2 v. 12°. . . 902
The same. London, 1853. 12°. 5733
Marsh, Mrs. Adelaide Lindsay. New York, 1850. 8°. 3976
Angela. New York, 1848. 12°. 3145
Aubury. New York, 1854. 8°. 5966
Lettice Arnold. New York, 1850. 8°. 3947
Mordaunt Hall. New York, 1849. 8°. 3295
Norman's Bride; or, the Modern Midas. New York, 1847. 8°. . 2815
Protestant Reformation in France. London, 1847. 2 v. 8°. . . 4643
Ravenscliffe. New York, 1852. 8°. 414

Marsh, Mrs. Tales of the Fields and Woods. New York, 1836. 12°. . 238
Time, the Avenger. New York, 1851. 8°. 3809
Two Old Men's Tales. New York, 1848. 8°. 3154
The same. London, 1853. 12°. 5728
Marsh, C. C. Bookkeeping by Double Entry. Phil. 1843. 8°. . . 1645
The same. New York, 1851. 8°. 4078
Single-Entry Bookkeeping. New York, 1843. 8°. 1614
Marsh, J. Popular Life of Geo. Fox. Philadelphia, 1848. 12°. . . 3332
Marshall, E. C. Book of Oratory. New York, 1851. 12°. . . . 4198
Marshall, J. History of the Colonies of North America. Phil. 1824. 8°. 1987
Life of George Washington. Philadelphia, 1805-7. 5 v. 8°. . 1267
Writings on the Federal Constitution. Boston, 1839. 8°. . . 2054
Marshall, S. Law of Insurance. Boston, 1805. 8°. 1389
Martell, Martha. Second Love. New York, 1851. 12°. 4157
Marten, H. Life. J. Forster. London, 1831. 12°. . . . 1831, 4
Martin, R. M. China, Political, Commercial, & Social. Lon. 1847. 2 v. 8°. 4341
History of Australia. London, n. d. Roy. 8°. 4941
History of the British Colonies. London, 1843. Roy. 8°. . . 2843
*(Editor.) Tallis's Illustrated Atlas. London, 1851. 4°. . . 4948
Martin, S. Useful Arts; their Birth and Development. Lond. 1851. 12°. 4214
Martin Chuzzlewit. C. Dickens. Philadelphia, 1849. 8°. . . . 2069
Martin Faber, and other Tales. W. G. Simms. Philadelphia, 1846. 2 v. 12°. 207
Martineau, Harriet. Deerbrook. New York, 1839. 2 v. 12°. . . 981
Eastern Life, Past and Present. Philadelphia, 1848. 12°. . . 3118
History of England, 1816-46. London, 1849. 2 v. roy. 8°. . . 3793
Illustrations of Political Economy. Philadelphia, 1834. 2 v. 24°. 1464

Vol. 1. Life in the Wilds; Hill and the Valley; Brooke and Brooke Farm; Demerara; Ella of Garveloch.
2. Weal and Woe in Garveloch; Manchester Strike; Cousin Marshall; Ireland; Hours Abroad.

Life in the Sick-Room. Boston, 1844. 12°. 1843
Morals and Manners. New York, 1838. 12°. 246
Retrospect of Western Travel. New York, 1838. 2 v. 12°. . . 1117
Society in America. New York, 1837. 2 v. 12°. 367
Martineau, J. Miscellanies. Boston, 1852. 12°. 4627

Joseph Priestley; Thomas Arnold; Church and State; Theodore Parker's Discourse; Phases of Faith; Church of England; Battle of the Churches.

Martyn, H. Journal & Letters. Ed. by S. Wilberforce. N.Y. 1851. 12°. 4168
Memoir. J. Sargent. New York, n. d. 12°. 447
Sermons. Boston, 1822. 12°. 1000
Martyr Wife. Philadelphia, 1844. 12°. 2138
The same. New York, 1844. 8°. 2171
Martyrdom, History of Christian. J. Fox. London, 1837. 8°. . . 1941
Martyrs of Science, Lives of. Sir D. Brewster. New York, 1841. 12°. 1627
The same. (H. F. L.) New York, 1847. 12°. . 3683, 130
Mary Barton; a Tale of Manchester Life. Mrs. Gaskell. N.Y. 1849. 8°. 3245
Mary Bell; a Franconia Story. J. Abbott. New York, 1850. 12°. . 4154
Mary Erskine; a Franconia Story. J. Abbott. New York, 1850. 12°. . 3814
Mary of Burgundy. G. P. R. James. New York, 1833. 2 v. 12°. . 1036

Mary, Queen of Scots, History of. J. Abbott. New York, 1848. 12°. . 2461
Life. H. G. Bell. New York, 1844. 2 v. 12°. 2401
The same. (H. F. L.) New York, 1847. 2 v. 12°. 3683, 21, 22
Recueil des Lettres de. London, 1844. 7 v. 12°. . . . 4517
Mary Schweidler, the Amber Witch. W. Meinhold. N.Y. 1845. 12°. . 2329
Mason, C. Discourse at New York University. New York, 1847. 8°. . 3197
National and State Governments of United States. Bost. 1842. 12°. 2155
Mason, E. Pastor's Legacy; with Memoir of Author. N.Y. 1853. 8°. . 5120
Mason, G. C. Newport Illustrated. New York, 1854. 12°. . . . 5964
Mason, J. Life. G. E. Ellis. Boston, 1844. 12°. . . . 1076, 13
Mason, J. M. Complete Works. New York, 1850. 4 v. 12°. . . 4750
Mason, L. Musical Letters from Abroad. New York, 1854. 12°. . . 5636
Masonic Institution, Catalogue of Books on. Boston, 1852. 8°. . . 330
Letters on. J. Q. Adams. Boston, 1847. 8°. 2857
Masonry, Opinions on Speculative. J. C. Odiorne. Boston, 1830. 12°. 1097
See also *Freemasonry*.
Masonry and Stone-cutting. E. Dobson. London, 1849. 12°. . . 6052
Massachusetts, Agriculture of. G. L. Flint. Boston, 1853. 8°. . . 5955
Agricultural Societies of, 1850. Boston, 1851. 8°. . . . 4360
Agricultural Societies of, 1851. Boston, 1852. 8°. . . . 5126
Bay, Chronicles of the Colony of. A. Young. Boston, 1846. 8°. 2733
Bay, History of, from 1748. G. R. Minot. Boston, 1798. 8°. . 673
Bay, Lives of Governors of. J. B. Moore. New York, 1848. 8°. 3228
Board of Education Report, 1850. Boston. 8°. 3770
Twelve Reports, 1838–48. H. Mann. Boston. 8°. . . 4121
Char. Mech. Asso., Annals of. J. T. Buckingham. Bost. 1853. 8°. 5493
Constitution of, Discussions on. Boston, 1854. 8°. . . . 5495
Constitutional Convention, 1779, Journal of. Boston, 1832. 8°. . 1785
Constitutional Convention, 1820; Journal & Debates. Bos. 1853. 8°. 791
Constitutional Convention, 1853, Debates in. Bost. 1853. 3 v. roy. 8°. 5916
Constitutional Convention, 1853, Journal of. Boston, 1853. 8°. . 5970
Currency, Historical Account of. J. B. Felt. Boston, 1839. 8°. . 1252
Gazetteer of. J. Hayward. Boston, 1849. 12°. 3027
General Hospital, History of. N. I. Bowditch. Boston, 1851. 8°. 4535
Geology of; Final Report. E. Hitchcock. Amherst, 1841. 2 v. 4°. 2026
Historical Collections of. J. W. Barber. Worcester, 1841. 8°. . 1964
Historical Society, Collections of. — See *Collections*.
History of. W. H. Carpenter. Philadelphia, 1853. 12°. . . 5320
History of, 1620–1820. A. Bradford. Boston, 1835. 8°. . . 767
History of, 1764–1775. A. Bradford. Boston, 1822. 8°. . . 761
History of, 1628–1750. T. Hutchinson. Boston, 1795. 2 v. 8°. . 1284
History of Land-Titles in. J. Sullivan. Boston, 1801. 8°. . . 747
Insurrections in 1786. G. R. Minot. Boston, 1810. 8°. . . 1336
Judicial History of. E. Washburn. Boston, 1840. 8°. . . 2090
Legislature, Patriotic Proceedings in, 1809. Boston, 1809. 8°. . 768
Lunatic Hospital Reports. Boston, 1837. 8°. 1590
Perpetual Laws of. Boston, 1789. 4°. 3639
Population of, 1765–1840. Jesse Chickering. Boston, 1846. 8°. . 2816

Massachusetts Quarterly Review. Vols. 1-3. Boston, 1848-50. 8°. . 3617
Register, 1839. Boston. 12°. 1472
Register; 1852-54. G. Adams. Boston, 3 v. 8°. . . . 256
Reports on Fishes, Reptiles, and Birds of. Boston, 1839. 8°. . 722

Storer, D. H. Reports on Ichthyology and Herpetology.
Peabody, W. B. O. Report on Ornithology.

Report on Herbaceous Plants of. C. Dewey. Camb. 1848. 8°. . 1969
Report on Insects Injurious to Vege. T. W. Harris. Camb. 1842. 8°. 1738
The same. Boston, 1852. 8°. 5116
Report on Invertebrata of. A. A. Gould. Camb. 1841. 8°. . 1970
Report on Quadrupeds of. E. Emmons. Cambridge, 1840. 8°. . 1969
Report on Trees and Shrubs of. G. B. Emerson. Boston, 1846. 8°. 2803
Reports on Contested Elections. L. S. Cushing. Boston, 1853. 8°. 5178
Revised Statutes. Boston, 1836. Roy. 8°. 1351
Supplements to the same, 1849. Roy. 8°. . . . 1351, 2
Sanitary Report. Boston, 1850. 8°. 3791
*Scenery of. Northampton, 1842. 4°. 3795
School Returns, 1838-39. Boston, 1839. 8°. 1616
Speeches of Governors, from 1765-75. Boston, 1818. 8°. . . 576
State Record. Vols. 1-4. Boston, 1847-50. 12°. . . . 3099
Statistics of Industry in. J. G. Palfrey. Boston, 1846. 8°. . 4359
Massey, G. Poems and Ballads. New York, 1854. 12°. . . . 6294
Massie, J. W. Continental India. London, 1840. 2 v. 8°. . . . 4543
Massillon, J. B., Morceaux Choisis de. Paris, 1812. 16°. . . . 81
Sermons. Boston, 1845. 8°. 3621
Massinger, P. Plays, Expurgated. New York, 1831. 3 v. 12°. . . 4474
and J. Ford. Dramatic Works. London, 1848. Roy. 8°. . . 1788
Master Builder; or, Life at a Trade. D. K. Lee. New York, 1852. 12°. 4889
Master Humphrey's Clock. C. Dickens. Philadelphia, 1849. 8°. . . 1605
Master's House; a Tale of Southern Life. New York, 1854. 12°. . . 6148
Masters and Workmen; a Tale. London, 1851. 3 v. 12°. . . . 4252
Masting, Mastmaking, and Rigging of Ships. R. Kipping. Lon. 1854. 12°. 6072
*Mastodon, Description of a Skeleton. J. C. Warren. Boston, 1852. 4°. 4937
Materia Medica and Therapeutics. A. T. Thomson. London, 1843. 8°. 4692
Materials for Thinking. London, 1812. 12°. 6273
Mathematical Instruments. J. F. Heather. London, 1851. 12°. . . 6056
Mathematics, Logic and Utility of. C. Davies, New York, 1850. 8°. . 3900
Philosophy of. A. Comte. New York, 1851. 8°. . . . 4134
Mather, Cotton. Life. W. B. O. Peabody. Boston, 1840. 12°. . 1076, 6
Magnalia; or Ecc. History of New England. Hart. 1853. 2 v. 8°. 5445
Mather, J. H. Geography of the State of New York. Hartf. 1847. 12°. 3866
Mathews, C. Big Abel, and the Little Manhattan. N. York, 1845. 12°. 2488
Memoirs. Mrs. Mathews. London, 1839. 4 v. 8°. . . . 2779
Moneypenny; or, Heart of the World. New York, 1850. 8°. . 3642
Motley Book. New York, 1840. 8°. 777
Various Writings. New York, 1843. 2247
Matilda Montgomerie. Major Richardson. New York, 1851. 8°. . . 4521
Matrimony, Phrenology applied to. O. S. Fowler. New York, 1842. 8°. 1844

Matthew, Lectures on. B. Porteus. Northampton, 1805. 8°. . . . 619
Matthias, B. Rules of Order in Deliberative Bodies. Phil. 1851. 18°. . 4761
Mattison, H. Spirit Rapping Unveiled. New York, 1853. 12°. . . 5281
Maturin, E. Montezuma; the Last of the Aztecs. N.Y. 1845. 2 v. 12°. 2528
Mauduit, M. Leçons de Géométrie. Paris, 1790. 8°. 1445
Maunder, S. Biographical Treasury. London, 1851. 12°. . . . 4470
Scientific and Literary Treasury. London, 1848. 12°. . . . 4109
Treasury of History. London, 1850. 12°. 4107
Treasury of Knowledge and Library of Reference. Lond. 1848. 12°. 4106
Treasury of Natural History. London, 1849. 12°. . . . 4108
Maundrell, H. Journey from Aleppo to Jerusalem. Boston, 1836. 16°. 86
Maurice and Berghetta; a Tale. Boston, 1820. 12°. 1173
Maurice, F. D. Religions of the World. Boston, 1854. 12°. . . 5605
Theological Essays. New York, 1854. 12°. 5772
Maurice Tiernay; or, the Soldier of Fortune. C. Lever. N.Y. 1852. 8°. 3991
Maury, Abbé. Principles of Eloquence. (H. F. L.) N.Y. 1848. 12°. 3683, 184
Maury, Sarah M. Statesmen of America in 1846. Phil. 1847. 12°. . 4469
Mawe, J. Travels in Interior of Brazil. Philadelphia, 1816. 8°. . . 1597
Maxims and Moral Sentences. F. Rochefoucauld. N. York, 1851. 12°. 404
Religious. T. C. Upham. Philadelphia, 1854. 18°. 6253
Maxwell; a Novel. T. E. Hook. London, 1851. 12°. 5659
Maxwell, J. S. The Czar; his Court and People. New York, 1848. 12°. 3115
Maxwell, W. H. Bivouac. London, 1853. 12°. 5722
Brian O'Linn. New York, 1848. 8°. 3204
Captain Blake. London, 1850. 12°. 5668
Hector O'Halloran. New York, 1843. 8°. 1762
The same. London, 1852. 12°. 5683
Hill-Side and Border Sketches. New York, 1847. 8°. 2780
Life of Duke of Wellington. London, 1845. 3 v. 8°. . . . 5092
Stories of Waterloo. London, 1851. 12°. 5657
Victories of British Armies. London, 1847. 12°. 3133
Wild Sports of the West. Philadelphia, 1846. 8°. 2663
The same. Philadelphia, 1851. 8°. 4125
May, Caroline. American Female Poets. Philadelphia, 1848. 8°. . . 3535
May, E. J. Louis's School Days. New York, 1851. 12°. . . . 4481
Sunshine of Greystone. New York, 1854. 12°. 5785
May, G. Birth-Town of Shakspeare. Evesham, 1847. 12°. . . . 4026
May Martin, and other Tales. D. P. Thompson. Boston, 1852. 12°. . 1064
May-Flowers. D. H. Howard. Boston, 1836. 12°. 898
May You Like it. C. B. Tayler. Philadelphia, 1851. 12°. . . . 4190
Mayer, B. (Editor.) Capt. Canot; or, 20 Years a Slaver. N.Y. 1854. 12°. 6199
Mayhew, Bros. Fear of the World. New York, 1850. 8°. 3641
Image of his Father. New York, 1848. 12°. 3173
Magic of Kindness. New York, 1849. 12°. 3309
Mayhew, H. 1851; or, the Sandboys at the Exhibition. N.Y. 1852. 8°. 4807
London Labor and London Poor. Vol. 1. New York, 1851. 12°. 5176
Model Men. New York, n. d. 16°. 2462
Mayhew, I. Popular Education. New York, 1850. 12°. . . . 4069

Mayo, H. Philosophy of Living. Philadelphia, 1852. 12°. 4860
Truths in Popular Superstitions. Edinburgh, 1851. 12°. . . 4221
Mayo, R. Ancient Geography and Ancient History. Phil. 1813. 8°. . 739
Mayo, W. S. Berber; a Tale of Morocco. New York, 1850. 12°. . 3901
Kaloolah; or, Journeyings to the Djébel Kumri. N.Y. 1849. 12°. 2909
Romance Dust from the Historic Placer. New York, 1851. 12°. . 4163
Mayor of Wind-Gap. J. Banim. New York, 1835. 12°. . . . 1146
Meagher, T. F. Speeches on Independence of Ireland. N.Y. 1853. 12°. 5222
Mease, J. Geological Account of the United States. Phil. 1807. 16°. . 85
Picture of Philadelphia. Philadelphia, 1811. 12°. . . . 289
Mechanics. F. Overman. Philadelphia, 1851. 12°. 4260
and Hydraulics. T. Ewbank. New York, 1846. 8°. . . . 2790
*Appleton's Dictionary of. New York, 1851. 2 v. roy. 8°. . . 4124
Illustrations of. H. Moseley. (H. F. L.) N. Y. 1844. 12°. 3683, 180
Memoirs of Eminent American. H. Howe. N. York, 1847. 12°. 2990
of Nature, Philosophy of. Z. Allen. New York, 1852. 8°. . 4538
Treatise on. C. Tomlinson. London, 1854. 12°. . . . 6040
Treatise on. H. Kater and D. Lardner. Boston, 1831. 12°. . 473
Mechanic's Assistant. D. M. Knapen. New York, 1849. 12°. . . 3403
Mechanic's Magazine, Appleton's. New York, 1851–52. 2 v. 8°. and 4°. 5395
Mechanic's Magazine. Vol. 1. Boston, 1830. 8°. 1396
Mécanique Céleste, Traité de. P. S. Laplace. Paris, 1800–5. 4 v. 4°. . 3321
Mechanism, Treatise on. T. Baker. London, 1852. 12°. . . . 6106
Medbery, Mrs. R. B. Memoir of Mrs. Sarah E. York. Bost. 1853. 12°. 5035
Medical Cases, What to Observe in. Philadelphia, 1853. 12°. . . 5754
Medical Delusions, Lessons from History of. W. Hooker. N.Y. 1850. 12°. 4049
Medici, L. de. Life. W. Roscoe. London, 1836. 12°. . . . 1742
Medical Formulary, American. J. J. Reese. Philadelphia, 1850. 12°. . 3671
Medical Jurisprudence of Insanity. I. Ray. Boston, 1853. 8°. . . 5386
Medical Student, Adventures of a. R. Douglas. N.Y. 1848. 2 v. 12°. . 3153
Medicine, Domestic. J. C. Gunn. New York, 1851. 8°. . . . 4701
Domestic. F. V. Raspail. London, 1853. 12°. 6123
Practice of, and Pathology. J. Mackintosh. Phil. 1844. 8°. . 4702
Surgery, and Materia Medica. F. G. Smith. 1851. 12°. . . 474
Meditations and Contemplations. J. Hervey. Philadelphia, 1808. 12°. . 164
Mediterranean, Shores and Islands of. H. Christmas. Lond. 1851. 3 v. 12°. 4289
Medwin, T. Conversations of Lord Byron. New York, 1824. 12°. . 548
Meikle, J. Solitude Sweetened. Pittsburg, 1818. 12°. 405
Meinhold, W. Amber Witch. New York, 1845. 12°. 2329
Melancholy, Anatomy of. R. Burton. Philadelphia, 1836. 2 v. 8°. . 1960
Melancthon, P. Life. F. A. Cox. Boston, 1835. 12°. . . . 1065
Melbourne and Chincha Islands. G. W. Peck. New York, 1854. 12°. . 5927
Melish, J. Travels in United States. Philadelphia, 1812. 2 v. 8°. . . 1321
Mellen, G. W. F. Unconstitutionality of Slavery. Boston, 1841. 12°. . 2094
Mellichampe; a Legend of the Santee. W. G. Simms. N.Y. 1854. 12°. 269
Melmoth, W. Fitzosborne's Letters. Boston, 1815. 12°. . . . 1025
Melmouth, S. Confessions of Cuthbert. Boston, 1827. 16°. . . . 834
Melville, H. Mardi, and a Voyage Thither. New York, 1849. 2 v. 12°. 3276

Melville, H. Moby-Dick; or, the Whale. New York, 1851. 12°. . 4600
Omoo: Adventures in the South Seas. New York, 1847. 12°. . 2977
Pierre; or, the Ambiguities. New York, 1852. 12°. 4897
Redburn; his First Voyage. New York, 1849. 12°. 3450
Typee; a Peep at Polynesian Life. New York, 1848. 12°. . . 2571
Memes, J. S. Memoirs of Josephine. (H. F. L.) N.Y. 1846. 12°. 3683, 28
History of Sculpture, Painting, & Architecture. Bost. 1834. 12°. 1003
Memoirs of an American Lady. Mrs. Grant. New York, 1846. 12°. . 2500
of a Literary Veteran. R. P. Gillies. London, 1851. 3 v. 12°. . 4248
of a Physician. A. Dumas. Philadelphia, 1851. 8°. . . . 4338
Relative to Egypt. London, 1800. 8°. 1282
Memorable Women. Mrs. N. Crosland. Boston, 1854. 12°. . . 6229
Memories of a Grandmother. Mrs. A. M. Richards. Boston, 1854. 12°. 6280
Memory, Art of. F. F. Gouraud. New York, 1845. Roy. 8°. . . 2269
Men and Manners in America. T. Hamilton. Phil. 1833. 2 v. 12°. . 1166
and Manners in Britain. G. Thornburn. New York, 1834. 12°. 2150
and Women of the 18th Century. A. Houssaye. N.Y. 1852. 2 v. 12°. 3736
of Character. D. Jerrold. London, 1851. 12°. 6234, 2
of Letters & Science, Lives of. Lord Brougham. Phil. 1845. 2 v. 12°. 2524
For contents, see *Brougham.*
of the Time. New York, 1852. 12°. 4887
Women, and Books. L. Hunt. New York, 1847. 2 v. 12°. . 3013
Men's Wives. W. M. Thackeray. New York, 1852. 12°. . . . 5001
Menageries, The. Quadrupeds. Boston, 1830. 16°. 826
Mendham, J. Index of Books Prohibited by Gregory XVI. Lon. 1840. 12°. 3066
Mensuration. T. Baker. London, 1850. 12°. 6102
Mental Action, Disordered. T. C. Upham. (H. F. L.) N.Y. 1848. 12°. 3683, 100
Mental Hygiene; or, Intellect and Passions. W. Sweetser. N.Y. 1850. 12°. 4050
Mental Illumination and Moral Improvement. T. Dick. Phil. 1845. 12°. 2357, 5
Mental Improvement. P. Wakefield. Philadelphia, 1819. 12°. . . 435
Menteath, Mrs. A. S. Lays of the Kirk and Covenant. N.Y. 1851. 12°. 4170
Menzel, W. German Literature. Boston, 1840. 3 v. 12°. . . 962, 7-9
History of Germany. London, 1848. 3 v. post 8°. . . . 3554
Mephistophiles in England. Philadelphia, 1835. 2 v. 12°. . . . 1226
Mercedes of Castile. J. F. Cooper. New York, 1845. 2 v. 12°. . . 2961
Mercantile Correspondence. W. Anderson. New York, 1851. 12°. . 4032
Mercantile Guide, European. C. W. Rördansz. Boston, 1819. 8°. . 639
Mercantile Law, Compendium of. J. W. Smith. New York, 1850. 8°. 4305
Digest of American. J. C. Gilleland. Pittsburg, 1818. 12°. . 358
*Mercantile Library Association of Boston; Reports, Addresses, &c. 1 v. 8°. 2823
Mercantile Morals. W. H. Van Doren. New York, 1852. 12°. . . 5020
Merchandise, Dictionary of, in all Languages. London, 1803. 8°. . . 765
Merchant, The Universal. W. J. Alldridge. Philadelphia, 1797. 8°. . 597
Merchant Ships and Seamen, Laws of. C. Abbott. Philadelphia, 1802. 8°. 1365
Merchant's Assistant. F. J. Grund. Boston, 1834. 8°. . . . 1767
Merchant's Clerk. S. Warren. New York, 1836. 12°. 457
Merchant's Directory. W. Beawes. London, 1783. Folio. . . . 2036
Merchants, Lives of American. New York, 1846. 16°. 2198

Merchant's Magazine, Hunt's. Vols. 1–30 [continued]. N.Y. 1839–53. 8°. 1586
Meredith, Mrs. C. My Home in Tasmania. New York, 1853. 12°. . 5275
Meredith, W. G. Memorials of Charles John of Sweden. Lond. 1829. 8°. 1116
Merimee, P. 1572; a Chronicle of Times of Charles IX. N.Y. 1830. 12°. 1220
Merivale, C. Hist. of the Romans under the Empire. Lon. 1852. 3 v. 8°. 5133
Merkland; or, Self-Sacrifice. Mrs. Oliphant. New York, 1853. 12°. . 5593
Merlin, Countess de. Memoirs of Madame Malibran. Lond. 1844. 2 v. 12°. 2386
Merrill, E. and P. Gazetteer of New Hampshire. Exeter, 1817. 8°. . 682
Merrimack; or, Life at the Loom. D. K. Lee. New York, 1854. 12°. 5918
Merovingian Era, Narratives of. A. Thierry. Philadelphia, 1845. 8°. . 2635
Merry-Mount; a Romance of Mass. J. L. Motley. Bost. 1849. 2 v. 12°. 3188
Mesmerism and Magnetism. J. W. Haddock. London, 1851. 12°. . 4286
Mesopotamia and Assyria. (H. F. L.) New York, 1845. 12°. . 3683, 157
Metal-Worker's Assistant. O. Byrne. Philadelphia, 1851. 8°. . . 4542
Metallic Wealth of the United States. J. D. Whitney. Phil. 1854. 8°. 5990
Metallurgy, Electro, Elements of. A. Smee. New York, 1852. 12°. . 985
  Manual of. J. Napier. Philadelphia, 1853. 12°. . . . 5567
  Treatise on. F. Overman. New York, 1852. 8°. . . . 4825
Meteorology and Physics, Principles of. J. Muller. London, 1847. 8°. . 4136
  The same. Philadelphia, 1848. 8°. 2893
  Elements of. J. F. Daniell. London, 1845. 2 v. 8°. . . . 5473
Methodism and Wesley. I. Taylor. New York, 1852. 12°. . . . 3906
  History of, and Life of J. Wesley. R. Southey. N.Y. 1847. 2 v. 12°. 3005
  Introduction into the Eastern States. A. Stevens. Bost. 1848. 12°. 3048
Methodist Quarterly Review. 4th s., vols. 2–5. New York, 1853–54. 8°. 5886
Metropolitan Improvements; or, London in 19th Century. Lond. 1837. 8°. 2836
Mexican War, and California. Emma Willard. New York, 1849. 12°. 3286
  Causes and Consequences of. W. Jay. Boston, 1849. 12°. . 3303
  History of. R. S. Ripley. New York, 1849. 2 v. 8°. . . 3516
  *Illustrated. G. W. Kendall. New York, 1851. Folio. . . 1665
  Mexican History of. Trans. by A. C. Ramsey. N.Y. 1850. 12°. 3487
  President's Messages and Documents on. Washington, 1848. 8°. 2742
  Review of. A. A. Livermore. Boston, 1850. 12°. . . . 3509
  Review of. C. T. Porter. Auburn, 1849. 12°. 3475
  Service Afloat and Ashore in. R. Semmes. Cincinnati, 1851. 12°. 4319
Mexico, Adventures in. C. Donnavan. Boston, 1848. 8°. . . . 3270
  and California, View of. Lieut. Wise. New York, 1849. 12°. . 3429
  and her Military Chieftains. F. Robinson. Phil. 1847. 12°. . 3033
  and Rocky Mount. Adventures in. G. F. Ruxton. N.Y. 1848. 12°. 3097
  and South America, View of. Montreal, 1827. 2 v. 12°. . . 200
  Campaign in Northern, 1846–47. New York, 1853. 12°. . . 5803
  Conquest of. B. Diaz del Castillo. London, 1844. 2 v. 8°. . 4547
  History of the Conquest of. W. H. Prescott. N. Y. 1850. 3 v. 8°. 1759
  Life in. Mde. Calderon de la Barca. London, 1843. 8°. . . 1713
  Political Essay on. A. von Humboldt. New York, 1811. 2 v. 8°. 604
  Rambler in. C. J. Latrobe. New York, 1836. 12°. . . . 265
  Recollections of. W. Thompson. New York, 1846. 8°. . . 2713
  Travels and Adventures in. W. W. Carpenter. N. Y. 1851. 12°. 4432

Mexico, Travels in, 1843-44. A. M. Gilliam. Philadelphia, 1846. 8°. . 2673
Trip to, and Ten Months' Ramble in, 1849-50. Lond. 1851. 12°. 4223
Miall, J. G. Footsteps of our Forefathers. Boston, 1852. 12°. . . . 4995
Memorials of Early Christianity. Boston, 1853. 12°. 5521
Michaelo and the Twins. Amalie Winter. Bath, n. d. 12°. 5640
Michaud, J. F. History of the Crusades. New York, 1853. 2 v. 12°. . 5278
Michelet, J. Elements of Modern History. (H. F. L.) N.Y. 1848. 12°. 3683, 170
History of the Roman Republic. New York, 1847. 12°. . . . 2969
Michigan, History of. J. H. Lanman. New York, 1841. 12°. . . . 1858
Microscope, Practical Treatise on. J. Quekett. London, 1848. 8°. . 4138
Microscopic World, Views of. J. Brocklesby. New York, 1851. 12°. . 4427
Middle Ages, Europe during the. H. Hallam. New York, 1837. 8°. . 1395
The World in the. A. L. Kœppen. New York, 1854. 2 v. 12°. . 6305
Middle Kingdom; or, China. S. W. Williams. New York, 1848. 2 v. 12°. 3102
Middleton, C. Life of Cicero. London, 1848. Roy. 8°. 5481
The same. Boston, 1818. 3 v. 8°. 1345
Middleton, J. Marmaduke Lorrimer. London, 1850. 3 v. 12°. . . . 4279
Midnight Harmonies. O. Winslow. New York, 1851. 12°. 4187
Midshipman. W. F. Lynch. New York, 1851. 12°. 4483
Midshipman Easy. F. Marryat. Philadelphia, n. d. 8°. 244
The same. Philadelphia, 1847. 8°. 1766, 2
The same. London, 1853. 12°. 5718
Midsummer Fays. Susan Pindar. New York, 1851. 12°. 3773
Midsummer Flowers. Mary Howitt. Philadelphia, 1854. 12°. . . . 6252
Miles, G. H. Mohammed; a Tragedy. Boston, 1850. 12°. 3861
Miles, P. Rambles in Iceland. New York, 1854. 12°. 5963
Miles Tremenhere. A. Marie Maillard. New York, 1853. 12°. . . . 5375
Military Adventure, Twelve Years of. London, 1840. 2 v. 8°. . . . 4649
Military Career of John Shipp. New York, 1829. 2 v. 12°. 528
Military Expedition to Navajo Country. J. H. Simpson. Phil. 1852. 8°. 3586
Military Journal during the Am. Revolution. J. Thacher. Bost. 1823. 8°. 637
during the American Revolution. J. G. Simcoe. N. Y. 1844. 8°. 1983
Military Maxims of Napoleon. New York, 1845. 12°. 3068
Military Reconnoissance to California. W. H. Emory. Wash. 1848. 8°. 3267
Military Tactics, Artillery & Infantry. C. P. Kingsbury. N.Y. 1849. 12°. 3412
Camp and March. H. D. Grafton. Boston, 1854. 12°. . . . 5615
Mill, James. History of British India. London, 1840. 6 v. 8°. . . . 2230
Mill, John. Fossil Spirit; a Dream of Geology. New York, 1854. 16°. 6303
Mill, J. S. Principles of Political Economy. Boston, 1848. 2 v. 8°. . 3229
System of Logic, Ratiocinative and Inductive. N. Y. 1850. 8°. . 2232
Millard, D. Travels in Egypt, Arabia Petræa, &c. N. Y. 1849. 12°. . 3290
Millengen, J. G. Passions; or, Mind and Matter. London, 1848. 8°. . 5090
Miller, G. History Philosophically Illustrated. Lond. 1849. 4 v. post 8°. 4393
Miller, H. First Impressions of England and its People. Bost. 1851. 12°. 4193
Footprints of the Creator. Boston, 1850. 12°. 4043
Geology of Bass Rock. New York, 1851. 12°. 4269
My Schools and Schoolmasters. Boston, 1854. 12°. 5795
Old Red Sandstone. Boston, 1851. 12°. 3783

Miller, H. Two Records, Mosaic and Geological. Boston, 1854. 12°. . 5796
Scenes and Legends of North of Scotland. Boston, 1851. 12°. . 4464
Miller, J. R. History of England, 1760–1821. Phil. 1844. 8°. . . 705, 4
The same. Philadelphia, 1832. 8°. 755
Miller, J. W. Poems and Sketches. Boston, 1830. 12°. . . . 467
Miller, S. Life of Jonathan Edwards. Boston, 1844. 12°. . . 1076, 8
Miller, T. Gideon Giles, the Roper. London, 1841. 8°. . . . 2892
Godfrey Malvern. New York, 1850. 8°. 4331
Lady Jane Grey; a Romance. Philadelphia, 1840. 2 v. 12°. . 1521
Pictures of Country Life. London, 1847. 12°. 5531
Royston Gower. Philadelphia, 1838. 2 v. 12°. 970
Millingen, J. Memoirs of the Affairs of Greece. London, 1831. 8°. . 3194
Million of Facts. Sir R. Phillips. New York, 1836. 12°. . . . 1010
Mills, A. Literature and Literary Men of G. Britain. N.Y. 1851. 2 v. 8°. 4515
Mills, C. History of the Crusades. Philadelphia, 1826. 8°. . . 779
History of Chivalry. Philadelphia, 1826. 2 v. 8°. . . . 1400
Mills, J. Our Country; a Tale. London, 1850. 3 v. 12°. . . . 4614
Milman, E. H. Arthur Conway; or, Scenes in the Tropics. N.Y. 1851. 8°. 4508
Milman, H. H. Belshazzar; a Poem. Boston, 1822. 12°. . . . 837
History of Christianity. New York, 1842. 8°. 1952
History of the Jews. (H. F. L.) New York, 1843. 3 v. 12°. 3683, 1–3
Milne, A. D. Uncle Sam's Farm Fence. New York, 1854. 12°. . . 5825
Milnes, R. M. Poems of Many Years. Boston, 1846. 12°. . . . 2518
*Milner, T. Descriptive Atlas of Astronomy. London, 1850. 4°. . 3965
Gallery of Nature, Pictorial and Descriptive. Lond. 1849. Roy. 8°. 4526
*The same. London, 1846. Roy. 8°. 2044
Milton, J. Paradise Lost. Boston, 1841. 12°. 173
The same. New York, 1850. 12°. 4063
Poetical Works. New York, 1841. 8°. 1672
Prose Works. Ed. by J. A. St. John. Lond. 1848–53. 5 v. post 8°. 4372

Vol. 1. Defence of the People of England; Second Defence; Eikonoklastes.
2. Tenure of Kings and Magistrates; Areopagitica; Tracts on the Commonwealth; Observations on Ormond's Peace; Letters of State, &c.; Notes on Dr. Griffith's Sermon; Reformation in England; Prelatical Episcopacy; The Reason of Church Government urged against Prelacy; True Religion, Heresy, Schism, and Toleration; Civil Power in Ecclesiastical Causes.
3. Likeliest Means to remove Hirelings out of the Church; Animadversions upon the Remonstrant's Defence against Smectymnuus; Apology for Smectymnuus; Doctrine and Discipline of Divorce; Judgment of Martin Bucer concerning Divorce; Tetrachordon; Colasterion; Tractate on Education; Declaration for the Election of John III. King of Poland; Familiar Letters.
4. First Book of a Treatise on Christian Doctrine.
5. Second Book of the same; History of Britain; History of Moscovia; Accedence commenced Grammar; Index to the 5 vols.

The same. Philadelphia, 1847. 2 v. 8°. 1828
Mind, Diseases of. B. Rush. Philadelphia, 1830. 8°. 2164
Improvement of. I. Watts. New York, 1819. 12°. . . . 1483
Inquiry into the Human. T. Reid. New York, 1824. 16°. . 88
Philosophy of the Human. D. Stewart. Boston, 1847. 2 v. 8°. . 1370
Mineral Region of Lake Superior, Map of. 2891
Mineralogy, Manual of. J. Nicol. Edinburgh, 1849. 12°. . . . 3878

Mineralogy and Geology. P. Cleaveland. Boston, 1816. 8°. . . . 1380
Treatise on. D. Varley. London, 1849. 12°. 6039
Ministering Children; a Tale. New York, 1854. 12°. 6182
Minstrelsy, Ancient and Modern. W. Motherwell. Bost. 1846. 2 v. 12°. 2592
of the Scottish Border. Sir W. Scott. Edinburgh, 1848. 4 v. 12°. 4102
Ministry of the Beautiful. H. J. Slack. Philadelphia, 1850. 12°. . . 4068
Minnesota, and its Resources. J. W. Bond. New York, 1853. 12°. . 5580
Sketches of. E. S. Seymour. New York, 1850. 12°. . . . 3512
Minnie Hermon. T. W. Brown. Auburn, 1854. 12°. 5793
Minor Drama. — See *Drama*.
Minorca, History of the Island of. J. Armstrong. London, 1756. 8°. . 2536
Minot, G. R. History of Mass. Bay from 1748. Boston, 1798. 8°. . 673
Insurrections in Massachusetts. Boston, 1810. 8°. 1336
Mirabeau; a Life History. J. S. Smith. Philadelphia, 1848. 12°. . . 3152
Miracles, Lectures on. J. Cumming. Philadelphia, 1854. 12°. . . 5852
of our Lord, Notes on. R. C. Trench. New York, 1852. 8°. . 4712
Starkie's Examination of Hume. New York, n. d. 12°. . . 504
Miriam Coffin; or, the Whale Fisherman. New York, 1834. 2 v. 12°. . 2178
Miriam Sedley; a Tale. Lady Bulwer. London, 1851. 3 v. 12°. . 4241
Miranda, F. de. Attempt to Revolutionize South America. Bost. 1808. 12°. 1063
Mirror, The; a Periodical Paper. Boston, 1792. 2 v. 16°. . . . 827
Mirror of Nature. G. H. Schubert. Philadelphia, 1849. 12°. . . 3343
Miscellanies, by Swift, Arbuthnot, Pope, and Gay. Lond. 1747. 4 v. 12°. 287
Miscellany, Chambers's. Boston, 1847. 10 v. 12°. 2457
Chambers's Pocket. Boston, 1852. 9 v. 12°. 864
Miser; or, Convicts of Lisnamona. W. Carleton. Phil. 1840. 2 v. 12°. 1660
Misers, Lives and Anecdotes of. London, 1851. 16°. 4294
Miser's Secret; or, Days of James I. London, 1850. 3 v. 12°. . . 4283
Miseries of Human Life; in Twelve Dialogues. Boston, 1807. 2 v. 12°. 1028
The same, in a New Dress. New York, 1853. 12°. . . 5210
Missionaries, Memoirs of British Female. T. Timpson. Lond. 1841. 12°. 2446
Missionary Enterprise, Heroines of. D. C. Eddy. Boston, 1850. 12°. . 3678
Missionary Herald. Vols. 47–49 [continued]. Boston, 1851–53. 3 v. 8°. 623
Missionary Magazine (Baptist). Vols. 32, 33. Boston, 1852–53. 2 v. 8°. 624
Missionary Memorial, American. H. W. Pierson. New York, 1853. 8°. 5113
Missions, History of American Baptist. W. Gammell. Bost. 1849. 12°. 3504
London Missionary Society's. J. Morison. London, 1844. 8°. . 4355
Origin and History of. J. O. Choules. Boston, 1838. 2 v. 4°. . 1999
Mississippi and Ohio Rivers. C. Ellet, jun. Philadelphia, 1853. Roy. 8°. 5391
Mississippi Scenes. J. B. Cobb. Philadelphia, 1851. 12°. . . . 3782
Mississippi Valley, Discovery and Explor. of. J. G. Shea. N.Y. 1852. 8°. 4953
Discovery and Settlement of. J. W. Monette. N. Y. 1846. 2 v. 8°. 2776
History and Geography of. T. Flint. Cincinnati, 1832. 2 v. 8°. 1955
History of. A. M. Hart. Cincinnati, 1853. 12°. 5310
*Monuments of. E. G. Squier and E. H. Davis. Wash. 1848. 4°. 1756, 1
Notes on the Upper. W. J. A. Bradford. New York, 1846. 12°. 2931
Recollections in. T. Flint. Boston, 1826. 8°. 1411
Mitchel, O. M. Orbs of Heaven. London, 1851. 12°. 4274

Mitchel, O. M. Planetary and Stellar Worlds. New York, 1848. 12°. . 3143
Mitchell, D. G. (Ike Marvel.) Battle Sumner. New York, 1850. 12°. 3486
Dream Life. New York, 1851. 12°. 4636
Fresh Gleanings in Europe. New York, 1851. 12°. . . . 3026
Fudge Doings. New York, 1854. 2 v. 12°. 6217
Lorgnette; or, Studies of the Town. New York, 1851. 2 v. . 3908
Reveries of a Bachelor. New York, 1850. 12°. 4086
Mitchell, J. Life of Wallenstein. London, 1840. 12°. 4567
Mitchell, Rev. J. Observations in Europe, 1843-44. N. Y. 1845. 2 v. 12°. 2491
Mitchell, J. K. Wisdom of God displayed in Water. Phil. 1833. 8°. 1357, 3
Mitford, Mary R. Atherton, and other Tales. Boston, 1854. 12°. . 5885
Recollections of a Literary Life. New York, 1852. 12°. . . 3752
Works; Prose and Verse. Philadelphia, 1846. 8°. 1637

Our Village; Belford Regis; Country Stories; Finden's Tableaux; Foscari; Julian; Rienzi; Charles I.

Mitford, W. History of Greece. Boston, 1823. 8 v. 8°. 772
Mnemonical Lessons in Geom., Algeb., &c. T.P.Kirkman. Lon. 1852. 12°. 6112
Mob Cap, and other Tales. Caroline L. Hentz. Philadelphia, 1852. 8°. 4811
Moby-Dick; or, the Whale. H. Melville. New York, 1851. 12°. . 4600
Model Men. H. Mayhew. New York, n. d. 18°. 2462, 4
Modern Accomplishments. Catherine Sinclair. New York, 1849. 12°. . 3426
Modern British Essayists. — See *Essayists.*
Modern Chivalry. H. H. Brackenridge. Pittsburg, 1819. 2 v. 12°. . 1067
Modern Flirtations. Catherine Sinclair. New York, 1853. 12°. . . 5335
Modern History, Lectures on. W. Smyth. Cambridge, 1841. 2 v. 8°. . 1677
Modern Lothario. Baroness M. la Fouqué. New York, 1844. 8°. 2167, 1
Modern Painters. J. Ruskin. New York, 1847. 3 v. 12°. 3018
Modern Philosopher; a Poem. T. G. Fessenden. Philadelphia, 1806. 8°. 736
Modern Society (Seq. to Mod. Accomp.). Cath. Sinclair. N.Y. 1849. 12°. 3425
Modern Standard Drama. — See *Drama.*
Mohammed. — See *Mahomet.*
Mohammed; a Tragedy. G. H. Miles. Boston, 1850. 12°. 3861
Mohan Lal. Life of Dost Mohammed Khan. London, 1846. 2 v. 8°. . 4677
Moir, D. M. Life, Tales, and Essays of Robt. Macnish. Lond. 1844. 2v.12°. 4975
Wounded Spirit. Philadelphia, 1833. 8°. 1357, 1
Molina, J. I. History of Chili. Middletown, 1808. 2 v. 8°. . . . 744
*Mollusca and Shells, U.S. Ex. Exped. Report on. A.A.Gould. Bost. 1852. 4°. 5978
Molluscous Animals. J. Fleming. Edinburgh, 1837. 12°. 4968
Monachism, Origin and Practice of. H. Ruffner. N.Y. 1850. 2 v. 12°. 4062
Monaldi; a Tale. W. Allston. Boston, 1841. 12°. 1655
Monasteries of Alcobaça and Batalha. W. Beckford. Phil. 1835. 12°. . 1081
of Italy, Six Years in. S. I. Mahoney. Philadelphia, 1836. 12°. 227
of the Levant. R. Curzon, jun. New York, 1849. 12°. . . 3273
Monastery. Sir W. Scott. Boston, 1848. 2 v. 12°. . . . 999, 17, 18
The same. Edinburgh, 1849. 2 v. 12°. . . 4100, 18, 19
The same. Edinburgh, 1850. Roy. 8°. 4531, 5
Monette, J.W. Discov. and Settle. of Mississippi Valley. N.Y.1846. 2 v. 8°. 2776
Money Maker. Jane C. Campbell. New York, 1854. 12°. 6142

Moneypenny; or, Heart of the World. C. Mathews. N.Y. 1850. 8°. . 3642

Monikins. J. F. Cooper. Philadelphia, 1835. 2 v. 12°. 2307

Monitor, The. Vol. 2. Boston, 1824. 12°. 1014

Monk, C. J. Golden Horn, Sketches of Asia Minor, &c. Lon. 1851. 2 v. 12°. 4233

Monk's Revenge; or, the Secret Enemy. S. Spring. N.Y. 1847. 8°. . 2791

Monkeys, Natural History of. Sir W. Jardine. Edinburgh, 1843. 12°. 4901, 27

Monkland, Mrs. Elvira, the Nabob's Wife. Phil. 1839. 2 v. 12°. . . 995

Monmerqué, L. J. N. Théatre Français au Moyen-Age. Paris, 1839. 8°. 3548

Monroe, J. Conduct of the Executive in Foreign Affairs. Phil. 1797. 8°. 1575

Life. J. Q. Adams. Boston, 1850. 12°. 3934

Tour in 1817. S. P. Waldo. Hartford, 1818. 12°. 315

Monstrelet, E. de, Chronicles of. Trans. by T. Johnes. Lon. 1849. 2 v. roy. 8°. 1219

Montagu, A. de. Etudes Sociales. Paris, 1851. 12°. 5524

Montagu, B. Selec. from the Works of Various Authors. N.Y. 1845. 12°. 2493

Montagu, Mrs. E. Letters. Boston, 1810. 16°. 95

Montagu, Lady M. W. Letters from the Levant. London, 1838. 12°. . 2445

Letters and Works. Ed. by Lord Wharncliffe. Paris, 1837. 2 v. 8°. 592

Montague, E. P. Dead Sea Expedition. Philadelphia, 1849. 12°. . 3288

Montaigne, M. de. Works; with Life by W. Hazlitt. Lond. 1845. 8°. 2285

The same. Philadelphia, 1850. Roy. 8°. 3420

Mont Blanc, Story of. Albert Smith. New York, 1853. 12°. . . 5515

Wanderings in the Shadow of. G. B. Cheever. N.Y. 1845. 12°. 2495

Monte-Cristo. A. Dumas. New York, 1850. 2 v. 8°. 2735

Monte Leone. H. de S. Georges. New York, 1852. 8°. 413

Montefiore, J. Commercial Dictionary. Philadelphia, 1804. 3 v. 8°. . 1367

Montesquieu, C. (Baron de.) Spirit of the Laws. Worces. 1802. 2 v. 8°. 1799

The same. Worcester, 1808. 8°. 796

Montezuma, the Last of the Aztecs. E. Maturin. N.Y. 1845. 2 v. 12°. 2528

Montgomery, C. Eagle Pass; or, Life on the Border. N.Y. 1852. 12°. 4989

Montémont, A. Voyages autour du Monde. Paris, 1853. Roy. 8°. . 5976

Montgomery, J. Lectures on Poetry, Lit., &c. (H.F.L.) N.Y. 1840. 12°. 3683, 64

Poetical Works. Boston, 1825. 4 v. 12°. 113

The same. Philadelphia, 1836. 8°. 580

Montgomery, Richard. Life. J. Armstrong. Boston, 1838. 12°. . 1076, 1

Montgomery, Robert. Universal Prayer, &c. Boston, 1829. 12°. . . 498

Monthly Anthology. Vol. 1. Boston, 1804. 8°. 1358

Monthly Review. Vols. 28–81 (34, 35, 40–45 wanting). Lon. 1763–89. 8°. 3738

The same, enlarged. Vols. 1–36. London, 1790–1801. 8°. 3739

Months, The. W. H. C. Hosmer. Boston, 1847. 12°. 3039

Monumental Brasses, Manual of. Oxford, 1848. 8°. 4980

*Monuments of the West. E. G. Squier & E. H. Davis. Wash. 1848. 4°. 1756, 1

Moodie, Mrs. S. Flora Lyndsay. New York, 1854. 12°. 6137

Mark Hurdlestone. New York, 1853. 12°. 5378

Roughing it in the Bush. New York, 1852. 12°. . . . 4874

Mooney, T. History of Ireland. Boston, 1845. 2 v. roy. 8°. . . . 2670

Moore, F. A. Gems from New Hampshire Authors. Manches. 1850. 12°. 3887

Moore, G. Body in Relation to Mind. New York, 1847. 12°. . . . 2943

Man and his Motives. New York, 1848. 12°. 2460

Moore, G. Power of the Soul over the Body. New York, 1847. 12°. . 3012
Moore, J. B. Lives of Governors of Plym. and Mass. Bay. N.Y. 1848. 8°. 3228
Moore, J. W. Encyclopædia of Music. Boston, 1854. Roy. 8°. . . 5961
Moore, T. The Epicurean. Boston, 1831. 16°. 46
History of Ireland. Philadelphia, 1843. 8°. 1982
Lalla Rookh. New York, 1847. 12°. 72
Letters and Journals of Lord Byron. New York, 1831. 2 v. 8°. . 743
Life and Death of Lord Edward Fitzgerald. N.Y. 1831. 2 v. 12°. 464
Memoirs of R. B. Sheridan. New York, 1853. 2 v. 12°. . . 1372
Poetical Works. Philadelphia, 1831. 8°. 1314
Songs, Ballads, and Sacred Songs. London, 1849. 12°. . . 3626
Travels in Search of a Religion. Baltimore, 1847. 12°. . . 3680
Moorland Cottage. Mrs. Gaskell. New York, 1851. 12°. . . . 3799
Moors in Spain. M. Florian. (H. F. L.) New York, 1848. 12°. 3683, 177
Moral and Intellectual Science. G. Combe and R. Cox. N.Y. 1848. 8°. 3264
Moral and Literary Dissertations. T. Percival. London, 1789. 12°. . 480
Moral and Political Philosophy. W. Paley. Philadelphia, 1814. 8°. . 735
Moral and Religious Anecdotes, Cyclopædia of. K. Arvine. N.Y. 1850. 8°. 4551
Moral and Religious Tracts. Boston, 1848. 12°. 2466
Moral and Spiritual Culture. R. C. Waterston. Boston, 1844. 12°. . 2130
Moral Class Book. W. Sullivan. Boston, 1831. 12°. 422
Moral Evidence, Guide to the Study of. J. E. Gambier. Bos. 1834. 12°. 1482
Moral Feelings, Philosophy of. J. Abercrombie. Boston, 1843. 12°. . 1570
Moral Philosophy. G. Combe. New York, 1843. 12°. 1460
The same. New York, 1848. 12°. 3771
Sketches of. Sydney Smith. New York, 1850. 12°. . . . 3899
Moral Science, Elements of. F. Wayland. Boston, 1839. 12°. . . 1448
Outlines of. A. Alexander. New York, 1852. 12°. . . . 4987
Moral Tales. S. G. Goodrich. Boston, 1840. 2 v. 16°. 44
Morality, Essays on the Principles of. J. Dymond. New York, 1844. 8°. 2265
and Polity, Elements of. W. Whewell. New York, 1845. 2 v. 12°. 2490
Morals, Theory of. R. Hildreth. Boston, 1844. 12°. 1900
and Manners. H. Martineau. New York, 1838. 12°. . . . 246
Moran B. Footpath and Highway. Philadelphia, 1853. 12°. . . . 5204
Mordaunt Hall. Mrs. Marsh. New York, 1849. 8°. 3295
More, Hannah. Christian Morals. New York, 1818. 18°. 126
Cœlebs in Search of a Wife. London, 1852. 12°. 374
Life. H. Thompson. Philadelphia, 1838. 2 v. 12°. . . . 1052
Poems. Boston, 1817. 16°. 7
Works. New York, 1847. 7 v. 12°. 3569

Vol. 1. Repository Tales.
2. Cœlebs in Search of a Wife; Essays; Moriana.
3. Christian Morals; Moral Sketches; Reflections on Prayer.
4. Practical Piety; Life and Writings of St. Paul.
5. The Manners of the Great; Estimate of Religion; Tragedies; Poems.
6. Strictures on Female Education; Sacred Dramas.
7. Hints for forming the Character of a Princess; Spirit of Prayer; Bible Rhymes.

The same. New York, 1843. 2 v. 8°. 1815
More, Sir T. Household of. New York, 1852. 12°. 936

More, Sir T. Life. London, 1831. 12°. 1831, 1
Utopia, and Richard III. Cambridge, 1834. 12°. . . . 383, 9
More Worlds than One. Sir D. Brewster. New York, 1854. 12°. . 6299
Morell, J. D. Speculative Philosophy of Europe. New York, 1851. 8°. 3422
Morfit, C. Tanning, Currying, and Leather-Dressing. Phil. 1852. 8°. . 4951
Morgan, L. H. League of Ho-dé-no-sau-nee, or Iroquois. Roch. 1851. 8°. 3825
Morgan, Lady S. Book of the Boudoir. New York, 1829. 2 v. 12°. . 530
France. Philadelphia, 1817. 8°. 1261
France in 1829-30. New York, 1830. 2 v. 12°. 527
Italy in 1819-20. London, 1824. 3 v. 8°. 4682
The same. New York, 1821. 2 v. 8°. 1972
O'Briens and the O'Flahertys. Philadelphia, 1828. 2 v. 12°. . 1178
Princess; or the Beguine. Philadelphia, 1835. 2 v. 12°. . . 1229
Morea, Travels in. W. M. Leake. London, 1830. 3 v. 8°. . . . 5128
Morier, J. Abel Allnutt. Philadelphia, 1837. 2 v. 12°. . . . 984
Hajji Baba in England. London, 1853. 12°. 5705
Hajji Baba of Ispahan. London, 1853. 12°. 5704
Zohrab. London, 1853. 12°. 5708
Morison, J. Counsels to Young Men on Mod. Infidelity. Bost. 1834. 12°. 1477
London Missionary Society's Founders. London, 1845. 8°. . . 4355
Morrison, J. H. Life of Jeremiah Smith. Boston, 1845. 12°. . . 2353
Morley, H. Life of Bernard Palissy. Boston, 1853. 2 v. 12°. . . 4997
Morley Ernstein. G. P. R. James. New York, 1842. 2 v. 12°. . . 1693
Mormons; or, Latter-Day Saints. London, 1852. 12°. 993
and Utah. B. G. Ferris. New York, 1854. 12°. . . . 6150
History of. J. W. Gunnison. Philadelphia, 1852. 12°. . . 4892
Morning-Land; or, 1001 Days in the East. F. Bodenstedt. Lon. 1851. 2v.12°. 4444
Morning Stars of the New World. H. F. Parker. New York, 1854. 12°. 5861
Morning Watch; a Poem. New York, 1850. 12°. 3930
Morocco, Account of the Empire of. Philadelphia, 1810. 12°. . . 284
Travels in, 1848. D. Urquhart. New York, 1850. 2 v. 12°. . 3854
Tripoli, &c., Travels in, 1803-7. Ali Bey. Phil. 1816. 2 v. 8°. 1265
Morpeth, Lord. Travels in America, and Poetry of Pope. N.Y. 1851. 12°. 4183
Morrell, Abby J. Narrative of a Voyage, 1829-31. N.Y. 1833. 12°. . 2805
Morrell, B. Voyage of the Margaret Oakley. New York, 1844. 12°. . 2170
Morris, G. Life. J. Sparks. Boston, 1832. 3 v. 8°. 1947
Morse, J. American Gazetteer. Charlestown, 1804. 8°. 628
Gazetteer of the Eastern Continent. Charlestown, 1802. 8°. . 1268
Universal Geography. Charlestown, 1819. 2 v. 8°. 620
and E. Parish. History of New England. Newburyport, 1809. 12°. 878
*Morse, S. E. North American Atlas. New York, 1842. 4°. . . . 2049
Morse, S. F. B. Proscribed German Student. New York, 1836. 16°. . 42
Mortimer, C. B. Morton Montagu. New York, 1850. 12°. 3651
Mortimer, G. W. Pyrotechnist's Companion. Philadelphia, 1852. 12°. 5004
Mortimer, T. Lectures on Commerce, Politics, & Finance. Lon. 1801. 8°. 575
Morton, N. New England's Memorial. Fifth edition. Boston, 1826. . 1619
*Morton, S. G. Types of Mankind. Nott & Gliddon, Ed's. Phil. 1854. Roy.8°. 5928
Morton, W. T. G. Statements on the Ether Controversy. Wash. 1853. 8°. 5160

Morton Montagu. C. B. Mortimer. New York, 1850. 12°. . . . 3651
Morton's Hope. J. L. Motley. New York, 1839. 2 v. 12°. . . . 1083
Mosaique, La; Nouveau Magasin Pittoresque. Paris, 1838. 8°. . . 5400
Moseley, H. Illustrations of Mechanics. (H. F. L.) N.Y. 1844. 12°. 3683, 180
Moses, M. Annals of the French Revolution of 1830. N.Y. 1830. 12°. 517
Mosheim, J. L. Hist. of Christianity for 325 Years. N.Y. 1852. 2 v. 8°. 4841
Mosses from an Old Manse. N. Hawthorne. Boston, 1854. 2 v. 12°. . 3105
Mother-in-Law. Mrs. E. D. E. N. Southworth. New York, 1851. 8°. 4122
Mothers and Daughters. Mrs. C. Gore. London, 1851. 12°. . . 5660
Mothers of the Wise and Good. J. Burns. Boston, 1850. 12°. . . 3851
Mother's Recompense. Grace Aguilar. New York, 1851. 12°. . . 4093
Motherwell, W. Minstrelsy, Ancient and Modern. Bost. 1846. 2 v. 12°. 2592
Poems, Narrative and Lyrical. Boston, 1841. 12°. . . . 1664
Posthumous Poems. Boston, 1851. 12°. 4457
Moths, British. J. Duncan. Edinburgh, 1843. 12°. . . . 4901, 30
Foreign. J. Duncan. Edinburgh, 1843. 12°. . . . 4901, 32
Motley Book; Tales of American Life. C. Mathews. N.Y. 1840. 8°. . 777
Motley, J. L. Merry-Mount; a Romance of Mass. Bost. 1849. 2 v. 12°. 3188
Morton's Hope. New York, 1839. 2 v. 12°. 1083
Mott, V. Travels in Europe and the East. New York, 1842. 8°. . . 1710
Moulder's and Founder's Pocket Guide. F. Overman. Phil. 1851. 12°. 4264
Mountford, W. Euthanasy; or, Happy Talk, &c. Boston, 1848. 12°. . 3174
Thorpe, a Quiet English Town. Boston, 1852. 12°. . . . 877
Mowatt, Anna Cora. Autobiography. Boston, 1854. 12°. . . . 5625
Fortune Hunter. Philadelphia, 1854. 8°. 5922
Moxon, E. Sonnets. London, 1837. 8°. 6013
Mozart, L. Life. E. Holmes. New York, 1845. 12°. 2550
and J. Haydn. Lives. L. A. C. Bombet. Boston, 1839. 12°. . 471
Mr. Brown's Letter to a Young Man. W. M. Thackeray. N.Y. 1853. 12°. 5235
Mr. Rutherford's Children. Anna Warner. New York, 1853. 12°. . 5547
Mrs. Ben Darby. A. Maria Collins. Cincinnati, 1853. 12°. . . . 5604
Mrs. Partington's Life and Sayings. B. P. Shillaber. N.Y. 1854. 12°. 5925
Mrs. Washington Potts and Mr. Smith. Miss Leslie. Phil. 1843. 8°. 2167, 1
Much Instruction from Little Reading. New York, 1827. 5 v. 12°. . 408
Mud Cabin. W. Isham. New York, 1853. 12°. 5526
Mudie, R. The Earth. Philadelphia, 1836. 12°. 321
Feathered Tribes of British Islands. London, 1854. 2 v. post 8°. . 5940
The Heavens. Philadelphia, 1836. 12°. 914
Man's Structure and Adaptations. Boston, 1838. 12°. . . . 334
Observations of Nature. (H. F. L.) New York, 1847. 12°. 3683, 57
Mügge, T. Afraja; a Norwegian and Lapland Tale. Phil. 1854. 12°. . 6301
Switzerland in 1847. London, 1848. 2 v. 12°. 4588
Muller, J. Physics and Meteorology. London, 1847. 8°. . . . 4136
The same. Philadelphia, 1848. 8°. 2893
Mulligan, J. Grammatical Structure of Eng. Language. N. Y. 1852. 12°. 5122
Muloch, Miss. Agatha's Husband. New York, 1853. 8°. . . . 5968
Head of a Family. New York, 1852. 8°. 194
Ogilvies; a Novel. New York, 1850. 8°. 3458

Muloch, Miss. Olive; a Novel. New York, 1851. 8°. 4004
Munn, L. C. American Orator. Boston, 1853. 12°. 5026
Murat, A. America and the Americans. New York, 1849. 12°. . . 2976
Murder Will Out. Mrs. A. Opie. New York, 1844. 8°. . . . 2167, 3
Murdoch, J. E., & W. Russell. Orthophony; or Elocution. Bost. 1845. 12°. 2351
Murphy, D. J. Wild Irish Boy. New York, 1808. 2 v. 12°. . . 306
Murray, A. (Com.). Biography. S. P. Waldo. Hartford, 1823. 8°. . 651
Murray, C. A. Prairie-Bird. New York, 1849. 8°. 2053
The same. London, 1853. 12°. 5730
Murray, H. Encyclopædia of Geography. Phil. 1837. 3 v. roy. 8°. . 2010
History of Br. America. (H. F. L.) N. Y. 1848. 2 v. 12°. 3683, 101–2
Pictorial History of the United States. Boston, 1851. 8°. . . 4007
Travels of Marco Polo. (H. F. L.) New York, 1845. 12°. 3683, 173
and others. British India. (H. F. L.) N. Y. 1848. 3 v. 12°. 3683, 47, 49
and others. Discovery in Africa. (H. F. L.) N. Y. 1846. 12°. 3683, 16
Murray, James. Sermons to Asses. London, 1819. 8°. . . . 1364
Murray, John. Handbooks. — See *Handbook.*
Original Views of Passages in Horace. Dublin, 1851. 8°. . . 5416
Murray, J. F. Picturesque Tour of the Thames. London, 1849. 8°. . 4659
World of London. London, 1845. 2 v. 12°. 4566
Murray, L. Power of Religion on the Mind. New York, 1818. 12°. . 198
Murray, R. Treatise on Marine Engines. London, 1852. 12°. . . 6088
Museum Disneianum. J. Disney. London, 1849. 4°. 5107
Museum, Kirby's Wonderful. London, 1820. 5 v. 8°. 4669
Musgrave, G. M. Excursion to Paris, Tours, and Rouen. Lon. 1849. 12°. 4414
Music, Church, in America. N. D. Gould. Boston, 1853. 12°. . . 5061
Book, People's. Part 2: Sacred. London, 1844. Roy. 8°. . . 6011
Easy Guide to Vocal. J. Turner. Boston, 1836. 12°. . . 1474
Encyclopædia of. J. W. Moore. Boston, 1854. Roy. 8°. . . 5961
for the Million. London, n. d. 12°. 6012
in New England, History of. G. Hood. Boston, 1846. 12°. . 2553
New England Village Choir. Boston, 1829. 12°. 1525
of Nature. W. Gardiner. Boston, 1841. 8°. 1447
Perfect Intonation in. H. W. Poole. New Haven, 1850. 8°. . 6016
Playing the Piano-Forte. C. C. Spencer. London, 1853. 12°. . 6082
Treatise on. C. C. Spencer. London, 1854. 12°. . . . 6081
Musical Biography. London, 1814. 2 v. 8°. 4979
Musical Cyclopædia. W. S. Porter. Boston, 1834. 16°. . . . 4417
Musical Drama, Memoirs of. G. Hogarth. London, 1838. 2 v. 8°. . 4685
Musical Grammar. Dr. J. W. Callcott. Boston, 1838. 12°. . . . 1473
Musical History, Biography, and Criticism. G. Hogarth. N. Y. 1848. 8°. 3261
Musical Letters from Abroad. L. Mason. New York, 1854. 12°. . . 5636
Mussulman, The. R. R. Madden. Philadelphia, 1830. 2 v. 12°. . . 451
Muston, A. History of the Persecutions of the Waldenses. Lon. 1852. 12°. 5260
Mutiny of the Bounty. J. Barrow. (H. F. L.) N. York, 1848. 12°. 3683, 31
Mutiny on board the Globe. W. Lay. New London, 1828. 12°. . . 852
Muzzey, A. B. Young Maiden. Boston, 1841. 12°. 1578
My Cousin Nicholas. R. H. D. Barnham. London, 1852. 12°. . . 5681

My Home in Tasmania. Mrs. C. Meredith. New York, 1853. 12°. . 5275
My Novel; or, Varieties in English Life. E. L. Bulwer. N.Y. 1852. 8°. 5152
My Peninsular Medal. New York, 1850. 8°. 3977
My Schools and Schoolmasters. H. Miller. Boston, 1854. 12°. . . 5795
Myers, P. H. King of the Hurons. New York, 1850. 12°. . . . 3473
Young Patroon. New York, 1849. 12°. 3326
Myers, Sarah A. Fitz Harold; or, the Temptation. N.Y. 1854. 12°. . 6192
Neighbor's Children, and Sequel. Philadelphia, 1854. 2 v. 12°. . 6259
Myrtis, and other Prose Writings. L. H. Sigourney. N. Y. 1846. 12°. 2932
Myrtle Wreath. "Minnie Myrtle." New York, 1854. 12°. . . 5845
Mysteries, Ancient, and Miracle Plays, described. W. Hone. Lon. 1823. 8°. 2694
of City Life. J. Rees. Philadelphia, 1849. 12°. . . . 3291
or, Glimpses of the Supernatural. C. W. Elliott. N.Y. 1852. 12°. 4895
of the Heaths. F. Soulié. New York, 1844. 8°. . . 2167, 1
of Paris. E. Sue. New York, 1843. 8°. 1749
of Russia. F. Lacroix. Boston, 1848. 8°. 3236
of Udolpho. Ann Radcliffe. Philadelphia, 1852. 24°. . . 1855
Mysterious Agents, Philosophy of. E. C. Rogers. Boston, 1853. 12°. . 5279
Mysterious Parchment. J. Wakeman. Boston, 1853. 12°. . . . 5522
Mystery, Philosophy of. W. C. Dendy. New York, 1845. 12°. . . 2504
Mythology, Ancient. C. K. Dillaway. Boston, 1831. 12°. . . . 155
*Dictionary of Greek and Roman. W. Smith. Lond. 1849. 3 v. 8°. 3957

N.

Nag's Head; or, Two Months among the Bankers. Phil. 1850. 12°. . 3914
Nan Darrell; or, the Gipsy Mother. Ellen Pickering. Phil. 1847. 8°. 2707
Nancrede, P. J. G. de. L'Abeille Françoise. Boston, 1792. 12°. . . 891
Nannette and her Lovers. T. Gwynne. New York, 1854. 12°. . . 5882
Nantucket, History of. O. Macy. Boston, 1835. 12°. 1183
Naomi; or, Boston 200 Years Ago. Eliza B. Lee. Boston, 1848. 12°. . 3095
Napier, Sir C. War in Syria. London, 1842. 2 v. 12°. . . . 3058
Napier, J. Chemistry applied to Dyeing. Philadelphia, 1853. 12°. . 5566
Manual of Electro-Metallurgy. Philadelphia, 1853. 12°. . . 5567
Napier, W. F. P. History of the War in the Peninsula. Phil. 1842. 4 v. 8°. 1951
Napoleon and his Marshals. J. T. Headley. New York, 1850. 2 v. 12°. 2596
and the Marshals of the Empire. Philadelphia, 1848. 2 v. 12°. . 3111
at St. Helena. B. E. O'Meara. Boston, 1823. 2 v. 12°. . . 366
The same. New York, 1853. 2 v. 12°. 5068
at St. Helena; Sir H. Low's Letters. W. Forsyth. N.Y. 1853. 2 v. 12°. 5611
Campaign in Russia. R. K. Porter. Baltimore, 1806. 8°. . . 690
Court and Camp of. (H. F. L.) New York, 1848. 12°. . 3683, 29
Expedition to Russia. P. de Segur. New York, 1845. 12°. . 325
The same. (H. F. L.) N. York, 1847. 2 v. 12°. 3683, 141, 142
Historic Doubts relative to. R. Whately. New York, 1853. 12°. 6203
History of. Laurent (de l'Ardeche). New York, 1851. 8°. . 4346
Imperial Guard of. J. T. Headley. New York, 1851. 12°. . 4625

Napoleon in Council. Baron Pelet. Trans. by B. Hall. Edin. 1837. 12°. 2717
Letters from Paris during Reign of. London, 1816. 2 v. 8°. . 754
Life. F. de Bourrienne. Philadelphia, 1832. 8°. 1373
Life. W. Hazlitt. London, 1830. 4 v. 8°. 2262
Life. J. G. Lockhart. New York, 1843. 2 v. 12°. . . . 2452
The same. (H. F. L.) New York, 1843. 2 v. 12°. . 3683, 4, 5
Life. Sir W. Scott. Philadelphia, 1827. 3 v. 8°. . . . 1612
The same. Edinburgh, 1834. 9 v. 12°. 4101, 8–16
Life. W. L. Van-Ess. Philadelphia, 1809. 4 v. 8°. 1628
Memoirs. Duchess d'Abrantes. New York, 1832. 8°. . . 5150
Memoirs. B. E. O'Meara. (No titlepage.) 8°. 1413
Military Maxims of. New York, 1845. 12°. 3068
on Board the Northumberland, &c. W. Warden. Bost. 1817. 16°. 815
Private Life at St. Helena. M. J. E. Las Cases. Bost. 1823. 4 v. 8°. 718
Recollections of, at St. Helena. Mrs. E. Abell. Lond. 1844. 12°. 3074
Voyage to St. Helena; Diary of Sir G. Cockburn. Bost. 1833. 12°. 1057
Napoleon, Louis. Political and Historical Works. Lond. 1852. 2 v. 8°. 4942
Sketches of, and Visit to. H. Wikoff. New York, 1849. 12°. . 3352
Napoleon Dynasty; or, History of the Bonaparte Family. N. Y. 1852. 8°. 4846
Narrien, J. Historical Account of Astronomy. London, 1850. 8°. . 1157
Nasology; or, Classification of Noses. E. Warwick. London, 1848. 12°. 4969
Nathalie; a Tale. Julia Kavanagh. New York, 1851. 12°. . . . 4111
National Cyclopædia of Useful Knowledge. London, 1847. 12 v. 8°. . 5099

Vol. 1. A to Arce.
2. Arch to Baut.
3. Bava to Cæs.
4. Cæs to Côtes.
5. Cotes to Evel.
6. Ever to Hano.
Vol. 7. Hans to Ligu.
8. Lila to North.
9. North to Quot.
10. R to Siege.
11. Sieg to Theb.
12. Theca to Zygo.

National Magazine. Vols. 1–4 [continued]. New York, 1852–54. 8°. . 5124
Nations, Progress of. E. C. Seaman. New York, 1852. 12°. . . 4984
Natural History, Edited by J. Wright. Boston, 1831. 5 v. 12°. . . 829
and Geology, Researches in. C. Darwin. N. York, 1846. 2 v. 12°. 2594
Boston Journal of. Vols. 1, 2. Boston, 1837–45. 8°. . . . 3619
Discourses on. London, 1757. 7 v. 12°. 1518
Elements of. W. S. W. Ruschenberger. Phil. 1850. 2 v. 12°. . 4299
Gleanings from. E. Jesse. Philadelphia, 1833. 12°. . . . 2193
Illustrated. A. B. Strong. New York, 1848. 2 v. 8°. . . 4512
Illustrated. J. G. Wood. New York, 1853. 12°. . . . 5609
Philosophy of. W. Smellie. Boston, 1829. 8°. 1414
Romance of. C. W. Webber. Philadelphia, 1852. 8°. . . 4814
Studies in. W. Rhind. Edinburgh, 1830. 12°. 2132
Treasury of. S. Maunder. London, 1849. 12°. 4108
of Insects. (H. F. L.) New York, 1843. 12°. . . . 3683, 8, 74
of Man. W. F. Van Amringe. New York, 1848. 8°. . . . 4354
of Quadrupeds. (H. F. L.) New York, 1846. 2 v. 12°. 3683, 104, 164
of Selborne. G. White. London, 1853. 12°. 2192
The same. London, 1851. Post 8°. 4178
The same. (H. F. L.) New York, 1847. 12°. . . 3683, 147

Natural History of Society. W. C. Taylor. New York, 1841. 2 v. 12°. 1849
of the Tower Menagerie. London, 1829. 12°. 6311
of Enthusiasm. I. Taylor. Boston, 1830. 12°. 1923
The same. New York, 1849. 12°. 3609
Natural Magic, Letters on. D. Brewster. New York, 1845. 12°. . . 2433
The same. (H. F. L.) New York, 1843. 12°. . . 3683, 50
Natural Philosophy. Elements of. N. Arnott. London, 1828. 8°. . 1989
Elements of. F. J. Grund. Boston, 1832. 12°. 1457
Introduction to. R. Hunt. London, 1851. 12°. 5051
Letters on. L. Euler. (H. F. L.) N. York, 1848. 2 v. 12°. 3683, 55, 56
Mathematical Elements of. London, 1731. 499
Treatise on. C. Tomlinson. London, 1853. 12°. . . . 6037
Natural Theology. W. Paley. New York, 1820. 12°. 861
The same. (H. F. L.) New York, 1846. 2 v. 12°. 3683, 96, 97
The same, illustrated by J. Paxton. Boston, 1851. 12°. . 1569
Class Book of. H. Fergus. Boston, 1837. 12°. 1454
Naturalist, Entertaining. Mrs. Loudon. London, 1850. 12°. . . 4565
Journal of a. Philadelphia, 1831. 12°. 219
Leaves from the Note-Book of a. W. J. Broderip. Bost. 1852. 8°. 4808
Naturalist's Library. A. A. Gould. Boston, 1853. 8°. 2071
Naturalist's Library. Ed. by Sir W. Jardine. Edinburgh, 1843. 40 v. 12°. 4901

Vols. 1-4. Jardine, Sir W. British Birds.
5. Jardine, Sir W. Sun Birds.
6, 7. Jardine, Sir W. Humming Birds.
8. Jardine, Sir W. Game Birds.
9. Selby, P. J. Pigeons.
10. Selby, P. J. Parrots.
11, 12. Swainson, W. Birds of Western Africa.
13. Swainson, W. Fly-Catchers.
14. Jardine, Sir W. Gallinaceous Birds.
15. Smith, C. H. Introduction to Mammalia.
16. Jardine, Sir W. Lions, Tigers, &c.
17. Macgillivray, W. British Quadrupeds.
18, 19. Smith, C. H. Dogs.
20. Smith, C. H. Horses, Asses, &c.
21. Jardine, Sir W. Deer, Antelopes, &c.
22. Jardine, Sir W. Goats, Sheep, Oxen, &c.
23. Jardine, Sir W. Thick-Skinned Quadrupeds.
24. Waterhouse, G. R. Marsupialia.
25. Hamilton, R. Amphibious Carnivora.
26. Hamilton, R. Whales, &c.
27. Jardine, Sir W. Monkeys.
28. Duncan, J. Introduction to Entomology.
29. Duncan, J. British Butterflies.
30. Duncan, J. British Moths, Sphinxes, &c.
31. Duncan, J. Foreign Butterflies.
32. Duncan, J. Exotic Moths.
33. Duncan, J. Beetles.
34. Dunbar, —. Bees.
35. Bushnan, J. S. Fishes; their Structure and Uses.
36, 37. Hamilton, R. British Fishes.
38. Jardine, Sir W. Fishes of the Perch Family.
39, 40. Schomburgk, R. H. Fishes of British Guiana.

Nature. Boston, 1836. 12°. 2205
and Science, Beauties and Wonders of. Ed. by L. Gilbert. Lon. n.d. 8°. 2839
Beauties, Harmonies, &c., of. C. Bucke. Phil. 1833. 8°. . 1357, 3
The same. (H. F. L.) New York, 1846. 12°. . 3683, 145
Book of. J. M. Good. Boston, 1826. 2 v. 8°. 1263
Book of; an Introduc. to the Sciences. T. Schoedler. Phil. 1853. 8°. 5441
Displayed; Discourses on Nat. History. London, 1757. 7 v. 12°. 1518

Nature, Gallery of. T. Milner. London, 1849. Roy. 8°. 4526
*The same. London, 1846. 8°. 2044
in Different Lands, Aspects of. A. von Humboldt. Phil. 1849. 12°. 3469
Observations of. R. Mudie. (H. F. L.) N.Y. 1847. 12°. . 3683, 57
Studies of. J. H. B. de St. Pierre. London, 1801. 4 v. 8°. . 708
Views of. A. von Humboldt. London, 1850. Post 8°. . . 4364
Nature's Divine Revelations. A. J. Davis. New York, 1850. 8°. . . 3943
Naval and Military Memoirs of G. Britain. R. Beatson. Lon. 1804. 6 v. 8°. 5905
Naval Architecture. J. Peake. London, 1850. 2 v. 12°. 6071
Naval Biography, American. I. Bailey. Providence, 1815. 12°. . . 209
Naval Gazetteer. J. Malham. Boston, 1797. 2 v. 8°. 678
Naval Heroes, Biographies of American. S. P. Waldo. Hartford, 1823. 8°. 651
Naval History of Great Britain. E. P. Brenton. London, 1823. 5 v. 8°. 5904
of Great Britain, 1793–1820. W. James. London, 1837. 6 v. 8°. 2606
of the United States. J. F. Cooper. Philadelphia, 1839. 2 v. 8°. 1298
The same, continued to 1853. New York, 1853. 8°. . 1298, 3
The same, abridged. Philadelphia, 1845. 12°. . . . 1280
Naval Officers, Biography of American. B. Folsom. Newbur. 1814. 8°. 758
Lives of American. J. F. Cooper. Auburn, 1846. 2 v. 12°. . 2560

Vol. 1. Bainbridge; Somers; Shaw; Shubrick; Preble.
2. Jones; Woolsey; Perry; Dale.

Naval Worthies of Queen Elizabeth's Reign. J. Barrow. Lond. 1845. 8°. 2666
Navigation and Nautical Astronomy. H. W. Jeans. London, 1853. 12°. 6107
Treatise on. J. Greenwood. London, 1850. 12°. . . . 6073
Navigator, Practical. N. Bowditch. New York, 1846. 8°. . . . 2249
Practical and Seaman's Assistant. (No titlepage.) 8°. . . . 1306
Navy, Battles of the British. J. Allen. London, 1852. 2 v. post 8°. . 5015
Book of the. J. Frost. New York, 1845. 12°. 2208
Royal, History of. Sir N. H. Nicolas. London, 1847. 2 v. 8°. . 4675
Neal, Alice B. All 's not Gold that Glitters. New York, 1853. 12°. . 5541
Contentment Better than Wealth. New York, 1853. 12°. . . 5009
No such Word as Fail. New York, 1852. 12°. 4631
Patient Waiting no Loss. New York, 1853. 12°. . . . 5070
Neal, D. History of the Puritans. New York, 1843. 2 v. 8°. . . 1820
Neal, J. Rachel Dyer. Portland, 1828. 12°. 521
Neal, J. C. Charcoal Sketches. New York, 1849. 2 v. 12°. . . . 2145
Peter Ploddy, and other Oddities. Philadelphia, 1844. 12°. . . 2300
Neale, E. Closing Scene; or, Christianity and Infidelity. Phil. 1850. 12°. 4169
Neale, F. A. Residence in Siam. London, 1852. 12°. 5261
Syria, Palestine, and Asia Minor, 1842–50. Lond. 1851. 2 v. 12°. 4446
Neale, W. J. Lost Ship; or, the Atlantic Steamer. N. York, 1844. 8°. 2729
Priors of Prague. Philadelphia, 1836. 2 v. 12°. 267
Neander, A. History of Christianity. Boston, 1849–54. 5 v. 8°. . . 3527
Life of Jesus Christ. New York, 1848. 8°. 4716
Necromancers, Lives of. W. Godwin. New York, 1835. 12°. . . 3025
Ned Myers; or, a Life before the Mast. J. F. Cooper. Phil. 1843. 12°. 1751
Neele, H. Literary Remains. New York, 1829. 8°. 669
Neighbors; a Story of Every-Day Life. F. Bremer. Bost. 1843. 2 v. 12°. 1716

Neighbor's Children, and Sequel. Sarah A. Myers. Phil. 1854. 12°. . 6259
Nelson, H. (Lord.) Dispatches and Letters. London, 1845. 2 v. 8°. . 2294
Life. R. Southey. New York, 1835. 12°. 154
The same. (H. F. L.) New York, 1843. 12°. . 3683, 6
Life and Naval Memoirs. J. M. Tucker. London, 1848. 8°. . 3467
Memoirs. J. Charnock. Boston, 1806. 8°. 664
Nepos, C. Lives of Illustrious Men. Oxford, 1684. 12°. . . . 386
Justin and Eutropius. Tr. by J. S. Watson. Lond. 1853. Post 8°. 5941
Nero, History of. J. Abbott. New York, 1853. 12°. 5267
Nestorians and Dr. A. Grant. T. Laurie. Boston, 1853. 12°. . . 5305
Netherlands, History of. T. C. Grattan. Philadelphia, 1831. 12°. . 428
History of the Revolt in. F. Schiller. New York, 1847. 12°. . 2953
Nevilles of Garretstown; a Tale of 1760. C. Lever. New York, 1844. 8°. 2621
New American Speaker. T. Hughs. Philadelphia, 1835. 12°. . . 2158
New American Speaker. J. C. Zachos. New York, 1852. 8°. . . 3587
New Brunswick; with Notes for Emigrants. A. Gesner. Lond. 1847. 8°. 3954
New England and her Institutions. Boston, 1835. 12°. . . . 1015, 1
and Middle States, Hist. & Antiq. of. J. W. Barber. Hart. 1846. 8°. 2721
Biograph. Dict. of First Settlers of. J. Eliot. Salem, 1809. 8°. . 1313
Bride and Southern Matron. Caroline Gilman. N.Y. 1852. 12°. 4993
Chronology, 1497–1820. A. Bradford. Boston, 1843. 12°. . 1838
Ecclesiastical History of, 1620–98. C. Mather. Hart. 1853. 2 v. 8°. 5445
Fathers, of. H. Bushnell. New York, 1850. 12°. . . . 3926
General History of. W. Hubbard. Boston, 1815. 8°. . . 2632
Hist. & Genealogical Register. Vols. 1–7 [con.]. Bos. 1847–53. 8°. 2845
History of. Hannah Adams. Dedham, 1799. 8°. . . . 585
History of. J. Morse and E. Parish. Newburyport, 1809. 12°. . 878
History of, from 1630–49. J. Winthrop. Boston, 1853. 2 v. 8°. 1784
Magazine. Ed. by J. T. Buckingham. Vols. 1–9. Bost. 1831–35. 8°. 1760
Mercantile Union Directory, 1849. New York, 1849. 8°. . . 1131
*Pilgrim Fathers of. W. H. Bartlett. London, 1853. Roy. 8°. . 6007
Quarterly Magazine. Vol. 2. Boston, 1802. 12°. . . . 559
Sketches of. J. Carver. New York, 1842. 12°. 1679
Tale, and Miscellanies. C. M. Sedgwick. New York, 1852. 12°. 4986
Village Choir, Memoirs of. Boston, 1829. 12°. 1525
New England's Memorial. N. Morton. Fifth edition. Boston, 1826. 8°. 1619
New Englander. Vols. 7–11 [continued]. New Haven, 1849–53. . . 3618
New Forest. Horace Smith. New York, 1829. 2 v. 12°. . . . 515
New Hampshire, Authors of. F. A. Moore. Manchester, 1850. 12°. . 3887
Book. Nashville, N.H., 1844. 12°. 2100
Festival, Nov. 7, 1849. Boston, 1850. 8°. 3532
Gazetteer of. E. and P. Merrill. Exeter, 1817. 8°. . . . 682
Gazetteer of. J. Hayward. Boston, 1849. 12°. 5555
History of. J. Belknap. Philadelphia, 1784. 3 v. 8°. . . . 583
The same. Dover, N.H., 1812. 3 v. 8°. 1303
History of. G. Barstow. Concord, 1842. 8°. 1975
New Holland and Caroline Islands. J. F. O'Connell. Bost. 1836. 12°. 1468
New Home; Who'll Follow? Mrs. C. M. Kirkland. N. Y. 1839. 12°. 429

New Ipswich, N.H., History of. Boston, 1852. 8°. 4952
New Jersey, Hist. Collections of. J. W. Barber & H. Howe. N.Y. 1845. 8°. 2720
History of. W. H. Carpenter and T. S. Arthur. Phil. 1854. 12°. 6284
New Mexico and Texas, Explorations in. J. R. Bartlett. N.Y. 1854. 2 v. 8°. 5950
Military Expedition through. J. H. Simpson. Phil. 1852. 8°. . 3586
New Mirror. Ed. by Morris & Willis. Vol. 3. N.Y. 1844. Roy. 8°. . 1822
New Monthly Magazine. Vols. 1-3. Boston, 1833-34. 8°. . . . 1307
New Netherland, History of. E. B. O'Callaghan. New York, 1846. 8°. 3540
New Purchase; or, Life in the Far West. R. Carlton. N.Y. 1843. 2 v. 12°. 1729
New Rome; or, the United States of the World. New York, 1853. 12°. 5314
New Spain, Political Essay on. A. von Humboldt. N.Y. 1811. 2 v. 8°. 604
New Spirit of the Age. Ed. by R. H. Horne. New York, 1844. 12°. . 2123
New Testament, and Book of Psalms. New York, 1848. 8°. . . . 4077
Commentary on. W. Trollope. London, 1842. 2 v. 8°. . . 4934
See also *Barnes, A.*, and *Livermore, A. A.*
Divine Authority of. D. Bogue. New York, n. d. 12°. . . 1022
Greek Lexicon of. E. Robinson. New York, 1850. Roy. 8°. . 4349
in Historical and Chron. Order. G. Townsend. Bost. 1840. Roy. 8°. 4728
Introduction to. S. Davidson. London, 1848. 3 v. 8°. . . 5112
New Timon; a Poem. E. L. Bulwer. Philadelphia, 1849. 12°. . . 5854
New York City. Alms House Report, 1852. New York, 1853. 8°. . 5405
Aristocracy; or, Gems of Japonica-dom. New York, 1851. 12°. . 342
*Directory, 1854-55. C. R. Rode. New York, 1854. 8°. . . 6015
History of. D. T. Valentine. New York, 1853. 8°. . . . 5479
in Slices. New York, 1849. 8°. 3298
Letters from. Mrs. L. M. Child. New York, 1843-45. 2 v. 12°. 1732
Mirror. Vols. 9, 11-14, 17. New York, 1831-37. 4°. . . 2021
New York State, Border Warfare of. W. W. Campbell. N,Y. 1849. 12°. 3292
Documentary History of. E. B. O'Callaghan. Alb. 1849. 2 v. 8°. 3383
Geography of. J. H. Mather. Hartford, 1847. 12°. . . . 3866
Historical Collections of. J. W. Barber. New York, 1851. 8°. . 2718
History of. W. H. Carpenter and T. S. Arthur. Phil. 1854. 12°. 6285
History of. W. Smith. Albany, 1814. 8°. 670
Knickerbocker's History of. W. Irving. New York, 1849. 12°. 1051
The same. New York, 1849. 12°. 3363
Political Parties of. J. D. Hammond. Cooperstown, 1846. 2 v. 8°. 2847
Purchase and History of Western. J. H. Hotchkin. N.Y. 1848. 8°. 3216
State Library, Catalogue of. Albany, 1846. 8°. 3386
The same. Albany, 1850. 8°. 3386
Reports of. Albany, 1847-53. 8°. 3385
under the Dutch. E. B. O'Callaghan. New York, 1846. 8°. . 3540
New York and Erie Railroad Guide-Book. New York, 1851. 12°. . 4208
New Orleans as I Found It. H. Didimus. New York, 1845. 8°. . . 2241
Book. Edited by R. G. Barnwell. New Orleans, 1851. 12°. . 3928
Manhattaner in. A. O. Hall. New York, 1851. 12°. . . . 4089
New Zealand, Settlement of. C. Hursthouse, jun. London, 1849. 12°. 4291
Southern Districts of. E. Shortland. London, 1851. 12°. . . 4463
New Zealanders. Boston, 1830. 12°. 882

Newbury, Newburyport, & W. Newbury, Hist. of. J. Coffin. Bost. 1845. 8°. 2662
Newcomb, H. Four Pillars; or, Truth of Christianity. Bost. 1842. 12°. 977
Newcombe, S. P. Pleasant Pages for Young People. Boston, 1853. 12°. 5214
Newfoundland, Excursions in, 1839–40. J. B. Jukes. Lond. 1842. 2 v. 12°. 3138
in 1842. Sir R. H. Bonnycastle. London, 1842. 2 v. 8°. . . 4963
Newnham, W. Human Magnetism. New York, 1846. 12°. . . 2342
Newport Illustrated. G. C. Mason. New York, 1854. 12°. . . . 5964
Newspaper Lit., Specimens of. J. T. Buckingham. Bost. 1850. 2 v. 12°. 3916
Newton, Sir I. Account of Two Corruptions of Scripture. Bost. 1823. 12°. 368, 2
Life. London, 1833. 8°. 602
Life. Sir D. Brewster. New York, 1831. 12°. 1
The same. (H. F. L.) New York, 1846. 12°. . . 3683, 26
and R. Cotes, Correspondence of. Ed. by J. Edleston. Lond. 1850. 8°. 4330
Newton, J. Pleasures of Personal Religion. Boston, 1839. 12°. . . 1486
Works; with Life. J. Cecil. Philadelphia, 1839. 2 v. 8°. . . 4706
Newton Forster. F. Marryat. Philadelphia, 1847. 8°. . . . 1766, 2
The same. London, 1853. 12°. 5719
Ney, M. (Marshal.) Memoirs. Philadelphia, 1834. 8°. 1399
Nicaragua; its People, Scenery, &c. E. G. Squier. N.Y. 1852. 2 v. 8°. 4560
Nichol, J. P. Architecture of the Heavens. New York, 1842. 12°. . 2309
Phenomena and Order of the Solar System. New York, 1843. 12°. 2308
Nicholas Nickleby. C. Dickens. Philadelphia, 1850. 8°. . . . 526
Nicholson, Mrs. A. Famine in Ireland, 1847–49. New York, 1851. 12°. 4161
Ireland's Welcome to the Stranger. New York, 1847. 12°. . . 3031
Nicholson, W. British Encyclopædia. — See *Encyclopædia.*
Nick of the Woods. R. M. Bird. New York, 1853. 12°. . . . 501
Nicol, J. Manual of Mineralogy. Edinburgh, 1849. 12°. . . . 3878
Nicolas, Sir N. H. History of the Royal Navy. Lond. 1847. 2 v. 8°. . 4675
Nicolini, G. B. History of the Jesuits. London, 1854. Post 8°. . . 6197
Niebuhr, B. G. History of Rome. Philadelphia, 1844. 5 v. . . . 2235
Lectures on the History of Rome. London, 1849. 3 v. 8°. . . 3600
Lectures on Ancient Ethnography and Geog. Boston, 1854. 2 v. 8°. 5454
Niebuhr, C. Life. London, 1833. 8°. 602
Nieritz, G. Little Drummer. New York, 1853. 12°. 5540
Niger Expedition, 1830. R. and J. Lander. New York, 1842. 2 v. 12°. 1883
The same. (H. F. L.) New York, 1846. 2 v. 12°. 3683, 35, 36
1841. W. Allen and T. R. H. Thomson. London, 1848. 2 v. 8°. 4641
Night and Morning. E. L. Bulwer. New York, 1850. 8°. . . . 1593
Night Thoughts. E. Young. New York, 1854. 12°. 4592
Night Side of Nature. Catherine Crowe. New York, 1852. 12°. . . 3907
Nights in a Block-House. H. C. Watson. Philadelphia, 1852. 12°. . 1198
Nights of the Round Table. Philadelphia, 1845. 16°. 2407
Nile Boat; or, Glimpses of Egypt. W. H. Bartlett. N.Y. 1851. Roy. 8°. 4516
Nile, Expedition to the White. F. Werne. London, 1849. 2 v. 12°. . 4019
Nile Notes of a Howadji. G. W. Curtis. New York, 1851. 12°. . . 3823
Niles, H. Principles and Acts of the Revolution. Balt. 1822. Roy. 8°. . 4000
Nina (Part II. of President's Daughters). F. Bremer. N.Y. 1845. 8°. . 1736
Nineteenth Century; a Quarterly Miscellany. Vols. 2–3. Phil. 1848. 8°. 3196

Nineteenth Century; or, the New Dispensation. New York, 1852. 12°. 4891
Nineveh and its Remains. A. H. Layard. New York, 1850. 2 v. 8°. . 3269
and Babylon, Discoveries in. A. H. Layard. N.Y. 1853. 8°. . 5162
Notes from. J. P. Fletcher. Philadelphia, 1850. 12°. . . 3852
Nix's Mate; a Romance of America. New York, 1839. 2 v. 12°. . . 1167
No Fiction. A. Reed. Hartford, 1821. 2 v. 16°. 37
No such Word as Fail. Alice B. Neal. New York, 1852. 16°. . . 4631
Noah and his Times. J. M. Olmstead. Boston, 1853. 12°. . . . 5582
Noble, L. L. T. Cole's Pictures, Letters, and Writings. N.Y. 1853. 12°. 5334
Noble Deeds of Amer. Women. Ed. by J. Clement. Buffalo, 1851. 12°. 4217
of Woman. Elizabeth Starling. Boston, 1850. 12°. . . . 3673
Noble Slaves. Mrs. Aubin. Boston, 1821. 16°. 45
Nobody's Son; or, Percival Mayberry. Philadelphia, 1851. 12°. . . 3780
Noctes Ambrosianæ. J. Wilson and others. Philadelphia, 1843. 4 v. 12°. 1801
The same. Ed. by S. Mackenzie. N.Y. 1854. 5 v. 12°. . 6235
Noel, B. W. Union of Church and State. New York, 1849. 12°. . 3275
Nolte, V. Fifty Years in both Hemispheres. New York, 1854. 12°. . 6176
Nonantum and Natick. Sarah S. Jacobs. Boston, 1853. 12°. . . 5600
Norman Leslie; a Tale. T. S. Fay. New York, 1850. 12°. . . . 1092
Norman Leslie; a Tale. "C. G. H." New York, 1850. 12°. . . 3850
Norman Maurice; a Drama. W. G. Simms. Philadelphia, 1853. 12°. . 5366
Norman's Bride; or, the Modern Midas. Mrs. Marsh. N. Y. 1847. 8°. 2815
Normand, H. de. Julienne, the Daughter of the Hamlet. Aub. 1847. 12°. 6163
Normandy, Dukes of. J. Duncan. London, 1839. 12°. . . . 4563
Norris, S. Handbook for Locomotive Engineers. Phil. 1852. 12°. . 5315
Northall, W. K. Before and Behind the Curtain. New York, 1851. 12°. 4110
North America, Notes on. J. F. W. Johnston. Boston, 1851. 2 v. 12°. 4172
Three Years in. J. Stuart. New York, 1833. 2 v. 12°. . . 1171
Tour in, 1831–2. H. Tudor. London, 1834. 2 v. 12°. . . 1231
Travels in. Marquis de Chastellux. New York, 1628. 8°. . . 1339
Travels in, 1841–42. Sir C. Lyell. New York, 1845. 2 v. 12°. . 2479
Travels in, 1825–26. Duke of Saxe-Weimar. Phil. 1828. 8°. . 1398
Travels in the Interior of. D. W. Harmon. Andover, 1820. 8°. 1349
*North American Atlas, Morse's. New York, 1842. 4°. . . . 2049
North American Miscellany. Vols. 1–3. Boston, 1851. 8°. . . . 4352
North American Review. Vols. 1–78 [continued]. Boston, 1815–54. 8°. 1290
Northanger Abbey. Jane Austen. Philadelphia, 1838. 8°. . . 1585, 2
The same. London, 1853. 12°. 5694
North British Review. Vols. 6–21 [continued]. N. Y. 1846–54. Roy. 8°. 2824
North Carolina, History of. H. Williamson. Philadelphia, 1812. 2 v. 8°. 680
North Star, Cruise of the. J. O. Choules. Boston, 1854. 12°. . . 5770
Northcote, J., Conversations of. W. Hazlitt. London, 1830. 12°. . . 2317
Life of Sir Joshua Reynolds. London, 1818. 2 v. 8°. . . . 2542
Life of Titian. London, 1830. 2 v. 8°. 2292
Northend, C. Teacher and the Parent. New York, 1853. 12°. . . 5358
Northern and Eastern Traveller's Guide. W. Williams. N.Y. 1853. 12°. 5353
Northern Antiquities. M. Mallet. London, 1847. Post 8°. . . . 3561
Northern Summer round the Baltic. J. Carr. Hartford, 1806. 12°. . 833

Northmen, History of the. H. Wheaton. Philadelphia, 1831. 8°. . . 2174
Northup, S. Twelve Years a Slave. Auburn, 1853. 12°. . . . 5501
Northwest, Travels through the. H. R. Schoolcraft. Albany, 1821. 8°. 771
North-West Territory, Early Settlement of. J. Burnett. Cinc. 1847. 8°. 2795
Early Settlement of. S. P. Hildreth. Cincinnati, 1848. 8°. . 3231
Notes on. W. J. A. Bradford. New York, 1846. 12°. . . 2931
Northwood; or, Life North and South. Mrs. S. J. Hale. N. Y. 1852. 12°. 4991
The same. Boston, 1827. 2 v. 12°. 1201
Norton, Mrs. C. E. S. Child of the Islands. New York, 1846. 12°. . 2567
Charity Sister, and other Tales. New York, 1840. 12°. . . 1566
Dream, and other Poems. New York, 1845. 16°. . . . 2527
Kate Bouverie, and other Tales. Philadelphia, 1835. 2 v. 12°. . 557
Stuart of Dunleath; a Tale. London, 1851. 3 v. 12°. . . . 4238
Undying One, and other Poems. New York, 1854. 12°. . . 5879
Norton, A. Life and Writings of L. Frisbie. Boston, 1823. 8°. . . 1427
Reasons for not believing in Trinitarianism. Cambridge, 1833. 12°. 1774
Tracts concerning Christianity. Cambridge, 1852. 8°. . . 4847
Norton, C. B. Literary Advertiser, 1852–53. New York. 4°. . . 5154
Literary and Educational Register. New York, 1853–54. 2 v. 12°. 5783
Norway and its Scenery. Edited by T. Forester. Lond. 1853. Post 8°. 5360
Denmark, & Sweden, Hist. of. (H.F.L.) N.Y. 1847. 2 v. 12°. 3683, 136, 137
Noses, Classification of. E. Warwick. London, 1848. 12°. . . . 4969
Notabilities in France and England. P. Chasles. New York, 1853. 12°. 5340
Notation, System of. W. Pelham. Boston, 1808. 12°. 461
Notes and Queries. Vols. 1–5. London, 1849–52. 8°. 4933
Notes of a Theological Student. J. M. Hoppin. New York, 1854. 12°. 6183
from Life, in Seven Essays. H. Taylor. Boston, 1853. 12°. . 5285

Money; Humility and Independence; Wisdom; Choice in Marriage; Children; The Life Poetic; The Ways of the Rich and Great.

Notions of the Americans. J. F. Cooper. New York, 1850. 2 v. 12°. . 3778
Nott, E., and Finances of Union College. J. C. Spencer. Alb. 1853. 8°. 5953
Nourse, J. D. The Past, and its Legacies to Am. Soc. Louisville, 1847. 12°. 3042
Novanglus and Massachusettensis. J. Adams & J. Sewall. Bost. 1819. 8°. 781
Novelists, Lives of the. Sir W. Scott. Boston, 1829. 2 v. 12°. . 399, 3, 4
The same. Boston, 1826. 2 v. 12°. 1151
The same. Edinburgh, 1834. 2 v. 12°. . . . 4101, 3, 4
Novelties of the New World. J. Banvard. Boston, 1852. 16°. . . 4632
Novitiate; or, Year among the Jesuits. A. Steinmetz. N. Y. 1846. 12°. 2945
Novum Organum. F. (Lord) Bacon. Philadelphia, 1844. Roy. 8°. 1996, 3
Now-a-Days. New York, 1854. 12°. 6250
Now and Then. S. Warren. New York, 1848. 12°. 3096
Nubia and Abyssinia, Hist. of. M. Russell. (H.F.L.) N. Y. 1848. 12°. 3683, 61
Nugent, T. Journey through Europe. London, 1756. 4 v. 12°. . . 836
Nursery Book for Young Mothers. Mrs. L. C. Tuthill. N. Y. 1849. 16°. 3307
Nye, G. jun. Tea and the Tea Trade. New York, 1850. 8°. . . 3942
Nystrom, J. W. Screw Propellers and their Steam Engines. Phil. 1852. 8°. 5085

O.

Oak Openings; or, the Bee Hunter. J. F. Cooper. New York, 1848. 12°. 3164
*Oakes, W. Scenery of the White Mountains. Boston, 1848. 4°. . 3747
O'Briens and the O'Flahertys. Lady S. Morgan. Phil. 1828. 2 v. 12°. 1178
O'Callaghan, E. B. Documentary Hist. of N. York. Alb. 1849. 2 v. 8°. 3383
History of New Netherland. New York, 1846. 8°. 3540
O'Callaghan, J. C. Green Book. Boston, 1849. 12°. 3682
Ocean Scenes; or, Perils and Beauties of the Deep. New York, 1848. 12°. 3088
Occult Sciences. E. Salverte. London, 1846. 2 v. 8°. 4683
Ockley, S. History of the Saracens. London, 1847. Post 8°. . . . 3556
O'Connell, D. Memoir on Native and Saxon Ireland. N.Y. 1843. 12°. 1851
O'Connell, J. F. Residence in N. Holland & Caroline Islands. Bos. 1836. 12°. 1468
Oddities of London Life. J. Poole. Philadelphia, 1838. 2 v. 12°. . 245
Oddy, J. J. European Commerce. Philadelphia, 1807. 2 v. 8°. . . 720
Odiorne, J. C. Opinions on Speculative Masonry. Boston, 1830. 12°. . 1097
Odoherty Papers. W. Maginn. New York, 1855. 2 v. 12°. . . . 6241
O'Donoghue; a Tale of Ireland. C. Lever. Philadelphia, 1841. 8°. . 2645
Odyssey of Homer. Trans. by T. A. Buckley. London, 1851. Post 8°. 4180
Translated by A. Pope. New York, 1844. 2 v. 12°. . 1854, 33, 34
The same. Philadelphia, 1841. 8°. 2674
Oehlenschlager, A. Corregio, a Tragedy; with Life. Boston, 1846. 12°. 2916
Off-Hand Takings. G. W. Bungay. New York, 1854. 12°. . . 6245
Ogden, G. W. Letters from the West. New Bedford, 1823. 12°. . 1175
Ogilvies; a Novel. Miss Muloch. New York, 1850. 8°. . . . 3458
Oglethorpe, J. Life. W. B. O. Peabody. Boston, 1844. 12°. . 1076, 12
Ohio, Geograph. and Hist. Account of. T. M. Harris. Boston, 1805. 8°. 1310
Historical Collections of. H. Howe. Cincinnati, 1847. 8°. . . 2814
History of. W. H. Carpenter and T. S. Arthur. Phil. 1854. 12°. 6286
Indiana Territory, and Louisiana, Description of. Bost. 1812. 12°. 282
Ohio Valley and North-West Territory. S. P. Hildreth. Cincin. 1848. 8°. 3231
Ojibway Nation, History and Sketches of. G. Copway. Bost. 1851. 12°. 4176
O'Keeffe, J. Autobiography. London, 1826. 2 v. 8°. 5129
Old Bell of Independence. H. C. Watson. Philadelphia, 1852. 12°. . 142
Old Brewery, and Mission House at Five Points. New York, 1854. 12°. 5759
Old Commodore. E. Howard. Philadelphia, 1837. 2 v. 12°. . . . 931
Old Continental; or, the Price of Liberty. J. K. Paulding. N.Y. 1846. 2 v. 12°. 2588
Old Country House; a Novel. Mrs. Gray. New York, 1850. 8°. . 3982
Old Curiosity Shop, and other Tales. C. Dickens. Phil. 1849. 8°. . 1605
Old Doctor; or Stray Leaves from my Journal. New York, 1853. 12°. 5578
Old Engagement. Julia Day. Boston, 1852. 12°. 4797
*Old England; a Pictorial Museum. London, n. d. 2 v. 4°. . . . 4831
and New England. A. Bunn. Philadelphia, 1853. 12°. . . 5594
Old English Chronicles. — See *Chronicles*.
Old Forest Ranger. W. Campbell. New York, 1853. 12°. . . . 5319
Old Hicks, the Guide. C. W. Webber. New York, 1848. 12°. . . 3160

Old House by the River. W. C. Prime. New York, 1853. 12°. . . 5347
Old Karl, the Cooper. E. Perce. New York, 1854. 16°. . . . 6218
Old Sights with New Eyes; Tour in Europe. New York, 1854. 12°. . 5599
Old Man's Bride. T. S. Arthur. New York, 1853. 12°. . . . 5276
Old Mortality. Sir W. Scott. Boston, 1848. 2 v. 12°. . . . 999, 9, 10
The same. Edinburgh, 1849. 3 v. 12°. . . . 4100, 9–11
The same. Edinburgh, 1850. Roy. 8°. . . . 4531, 2
Old Oak Chest. G. P. R. James. New York, 1850. 8°. . . . 3945
Old Portraits and Modern Sketches. J. G. Whittier. Boston, 1850. 12°. 3479
Old Red Sandstone. H. Miller. Boston, 1851. 12°. 3783
Old Testament in Hist. and Chron. Order. G. Townsend. Bos. 1839. 8°. 4727
Canon, History and Defence of. M. Stuart. Andover, 1845. 12°. 4749
and New Testament Connected. H. Prideaux. N.Y. 1850. 2 v. 8°. 4711
Old Wine in New Bottles. A. K. Gardner. New York, 1848. 12°. . 3086
Old World; or, Scenes & Cities in For. Lands. W. Furniss. N.Y. 1850. 12°. 3441
Olin, S. Greece and the Golden Horn. New York, 1854. 12°. . . 5862
Travels in Egypt, Arabia Petræa, &c. New York, 1843. 2 v. 12°. 1919
Works; Sermons, Sketches, and Lectures. N. Y. 1852. 2 v. 12°. 1044
Olio of Domestic Verses. Emily Judson. New York, 1852. 12°. . . 4906
Oliphant, L. Journey to Katmandu. New York, 1852. 12°. . . 4850
Russian Shores of the Black Sea. New York, 1854. 12°. . . 5791
Oliphant, Mrs. Caleb Field; Tale of the Puritans. N. York, 1851. 12°. 4220
Magdalen Hepburn. New York, 1854. 12°. 6174
Margaret Maitland. New York, 1851. 12°. 4423
Merkland; or Self-Sacrifice. New York, 1853. 12°. . . . 5593
Olive; a Novel. Miss Muloch. New York, 1851. 8°. 4004
Olive Leaves; Mrs. L. H. Sigourney. New York, 1852. 12°. . . 4479
Oliver, A., jun. Essay on Comets; with Author's Life. Bost. 1811. 12°. 875
Oliver, B. L., jun. Essay on the Pursuit of Happiness. Camb. 1818. 8°. 1333
Oliver Twist. C. Dickens. Philadelphia, 1853. 8°. 1338
Ollendorff's Method of Learning French. New York, 1851. 12°. . . 5191
Method of Learning German. New York, 1852. 12°. . . . 5192
Method of Learning Italian. New York, 1851. 12°. . . . 5190
Olmsted, D. Compendium of Astronomy. New York, 1841. 12°. . 1695
Letters on Astronomy. New York, 1847. 8°. 3226
Olmsted, F. L. Walks & Talks of an Amer. Farmer in Eng. N.Y. 1852. 12°. 147
Olmstead, J. M. Noah and his Times. Boston, 1853. 12°. . . . 5582
Olney, Captain S., Biography of. Mrs. C. R. Williams. Prov. 1839. 12°. 1571
O'Meara, B., Memoirs of Napoleon. (No titlepage.) 8°. . . . 1413
Napoleon at St. Helena. Boston, 1823. 2 v. 12°. 366
The same. New York, 1853. 2 v. 12°. 5068
Omen; a Tale of Real Life. J. Galt. New York, 1844. 8°. . . 2167, 3
Omnibus of Modern Romance (Six Inside). New York, 1844. 3 v. 8°. . 2167

Vol. 1. Frank Heartwell.
Crawford, H. C. First and Second Love.
Hoffman, C. F. W. Goldsmith of Paris.
Hoffman, C. F. W. Rolandsitten.
Leslie, Miss. Mr. Washington Potts and Mr. Smith.
Pichler, Caroline. Wife Hunter.
Fouqué, Baroness La M. Modern Lothario.
Soulié, F. Mysteries of the Heaths.

Omnibus of Modern Romance *continued.*

Vol. 2. St. Leger, Baron. Mabel the Actress.
St. Leger, Baron. Rescued Nun.
Hook, T. E. Capitalist.
Opie, Mrs. A. Gentleman's Daughter.
Howitt, W. Wonderful Story of Peter Schlemihl.
Sue, E. Marquis de Letoriere.
3. Ritchie, L. Game of Life.
Gore, Mrs. C. Marrying for Money.
Galt, J. The Omen; a Tale of Real Life.
Banim, J. The Loaded Dice.
Opie, Mrs. A. Murder Will Out.
James, G. P. R. Bertrand de la Croix.

Omoo; Adventures in the South Seas. H. Melville. N.Y. 1847. 12°. . 2977
Onderdonk, H., jun. Revolutionary Incid. of Queen's Co. N.Y. 1846. 12°. 3824
One in a Thousand. G. P. R. James. New York, 1836. 2 v. 12°. . 986
The same. Philadelphia, 1836. 8°. 2228, 1
Only a Fiddler, and O. T. H. C. Andersen. New York, 1846. 8°. . 2637
Opérations des Changes de l'Europe. (No titlepage.) 8°. . . . 1247
Opie, Amelia. Gentleman's Daughter. New York, 1844. 8°. . 2167, 2
Illustrations of Lying. Boston, 1827. 12°. 201
Works. Philadelphia, 1850. 3 v. 8°. 2885

Vol. 1. Madeline; Adeline Mowbray; Simple Tales; Father and Daughter; Happy Faces.
2. Tales of Real Life; New Tales.
3. Temper; Woman's Love and Wife's Duty; Two Sons; Opposite Neighbor; Love Mystery and Superstition; After the Ball; False or True; Confessions of an Odd Tempered Man; Illustrations of Lying, in all its Branches.

Opinions, Essays on Formation and Publica. of. S. Bailey. Phil. 1831. 12°. 2160
The same. Boston, 1854. 12°. 5855
Opium Eater, Confessions of an. T. De Quincey. Boston, 1850. 12°. . 3911
Opium War in China, Recollections of. A. Cunynghame. Phil. 1845. 16°. 2409
Optimist, The. H. T. Tuckerman. New York, 1850. 12°. 3658
Oracles from the Poets. Caroline Gilman. New York, 1849. 12°. . 2338
of God; Four Orations. E. Irving. New York, 1825. 8°. . 1368
Orations in Boston on the 5th March. Boston, 1785. 16°. 825
Orator, American. L. C. Munn. Boston, 1853. 12°. 5026
Orator's Own Book, American. Philadelphia, 1840. 24°. 1669
Oratorical and Dramatic Expression. J. A. Fowler. Phil. 1853. 12°. . 5226
Orators of America, Living. E. L. Magoon. New York, 1850. 12°. . 3281
of France. L. de Cormenin. New York, 1847. 12°. 3008
Sketches of English. G. H. Francis. New York, 1847. 12°. . 3001
Oratory, American. Philadelphia, 1849. 8°. 4139
and Orators. M. T. Cicero. London, 1808. 2 v. 8°. 5011
Book of. E. C. Marshall. New York, 1851. 12°. 4198
Elements of. J. Holmes. Philadelphia, 1849. 12°. 3305
Orbs of Heaven. O. M. Mitchel. London, 1851. 12°. 4274
Oregon and California, History of. R. Greenhow. Boston, 1845. 8°. . 2270
and California in 1848. J. Q. Thornton. N.Y. 1849. 2 v. 12°. . 3279
and North California, Expedition to. J. C. Fremont. N.Y. 1846. 8°. 2639
History and Discovery of. T. Twiss. New York, 1846. 12°. . 2997
Oregon Missions, and Rocky Mountains. P. J. De Smet. N.Y. 1847. 12°. 3061
Organic Christianity. L. A. Sawyer. Boston, 1854. 12°. 6249

Oriental and Sacred Scenes. F. Howe. New York, 1854. 12°. . . 5751
*Oriental Memoirs. J. Forbes. London, 1834. 2 v. 8°. 1 v. plates 4°. . 3796
Oriental Travel, Narrative of. H. Crosby. New York, 1851. 8°. . . 4120
Original Letters on English Reformation. Cambridge (Eng.), 1846. 2 v. 8°. 5912
Orion; an Epic Poem. R. H. Horne. London, 1842. 12°. . . . 2473
Orlando Furioso. L. Ariosto. Tr. by J. Hoole. Phil. 1816. 6 v. 18°. . 138
Orleans, House of, Memoirs of. W. C. Taylor. Phil. 1850. 2 v. 12°. . 3837
Ornamental Leather Work. Boston, 1854. 12°. 5837
Ornithology, American. A. Wilson. Ed. by T. M. Brewer. N.Y. 1852. 8°. 5924
Elements of. C. Brooks. Boston, 1847. 12°. 3508
Orphan Niece; a Novel. Ellen Pickering. Philadelphia, 1848. 8°. . 3221
Orthophony; or, Elocution. J. E. Murdoch and W. Russell. Bost. 1845. 12°. 2351
Osborn, S. Arctic Journal. New York, 1852. 12°. 4886
Osborne, S. G. Gleanings in the West of Ireland. London, 1850. 12°. 4290
Osborne, T. (Earl of Danby.) Life. T. P. Courtenay. Lond. 1831. 12°. 1831, 5
Osgood, Frances S. Poems. New York, 1846. 12°. 5230
Osgood, S. Studies in Christian Biography. New York, 1850. 12°. . 3670
Ossian. Poems. Translated by J. Macpherson. New York, 1846. 12°. 2999
Ossoli, Marg. Fuller. Memoirs. J.F. Clark and others. Bost. 1852. 2 v. 12°. 4766
Otis, Mrs. H. G. Barclays of Boston. Boston, 1854. 12°. . . . 5777
Otis, J. Life. F. Bowen. Boston, 1844. 12°. 1076, 12
Life. W. Tudor. Boston, 1823. 8°. 599
Otter, W. Life and Remains of E. D. Clarke. London, 1825. 2 v. 8°. . 5485
Otto, F. History of Russian Literature. Oxford, 1839. 8°. . . . 3789
Otway, T. Works. Vol. 1. London, 1712. 12°. 106
Our Campaign; or, Thoughts of Life. E. W. Reynolds. Bost. 1851. 12°. 4455
Our Country; a Tale. J. Mills. London, 1850. 3 v. 12°. . . . 4614
Our Folks at Home. E. Toliver. Philadelphia, 1855. 12°. . . . 6191
Our Island; comprising the Tales, Forgery and Lunatic. Phil. 1833. 2v. 12°. 1210
Our Parish; or, Annals of Pastor and People. Boston, 1854. 12°. . 5806
Our Village; Sketches of Rural Character. M. R. Mitford. Phil. 1846. 8°. 1637
Outlaw; a Novel. Mrs. S. C. Hall. London, 1852. 12°. . . . 5682
Outlines of History. Philadelphia, 1831. 12°. 441
Outre-Mer; a Pilgrimage. H. W. Longfellow. Boston, 1835. 2 v. 12°. 1079
Outward Bound. E. Howard. Philadelphia, 1838. 2 v. 12°. . . 823
Overing; or, the Heir of Wycherly. E. Grayson. New York, 1852. 12°. 4871
Overman, F. Manufacture of Iron. Philadelphia, 1850. 8°. . . 3520
Manufacture of Steel. Philadelphia, 1851. 12°. 4203
Mechanics. Philadelphia, 1851. 12°. 4260
Moulder's and Founder's Pocket Guide. Philadelphia, 1851. 12°. 4264
Treatise on Metallurgy. New York, 1852. 8°. 4825
Ovid, N. P. Works. Tr. by Dryden and others. N.Y. 1841. 2v. 12°. 1854, 20, 21
Owen, Mrs. O. F. Heroines of History. London, 1854. 12°. . . 5846
*Owen, R. D. Geological Survey of Wisconsin, Iowa, &c. Phil. 1852. 4°. 5167
Owenson, Miss. Patriotic Sketches of Ireland. Baltimore, 1809. 12°. . 199
Owl Creek Letters. W. C. Prime. New York, 1848. 12°. . . . 3411
Ox, The; with Illustrations. London, n. d. Roy. 8°. . . . 3635, 1
Ox Tribe, Delineations of. G. Vasey. London, 1851. 8°. . . . 4322

Oxford, Handbook for Visitors to. Oxford, 1847. 8°. 4654
Oxonians; a Novel. Philadelphia, 1852. 8°. 1202
Ozark Mountains, Adventures in. H. R. Schoolcraft. Phil. 1853. 8°. . 5393

P.

Pacha of Many Tales. F. Marryat. Philadelphia, 1847. 8°. . . 2964
The same. Philadelphia, 1847. 8°. 1766, 1
The same. London, 1853. 12°. 5720
Pacific, Island World of the. H. T. Cheever. New York, 1851. 12°. . 4095
Three Years in the. Philadelphia, 1834. 8°. 1415
Paddock, J. Shipwreck of the Oswego. New York, 1818. 8°. . . 1297
Pagés, M. de. Travels round the World. London, 1793. 3 v. 8°. . . 572
*Paine, R. Troup. Memoir, by his Parents. New York, 1852. 4°. . 4949
Paine, T. Life. J. Chatham. New York, 1809. 8°. 655
Political Writings. Charlestown, 1824. 2 v. 8°. 1814
Painter, Gilder, and Varnisher's Companion. Philadelphia, 1853. 12°. . 6278
Painters and Engravers, Anecdotes of. S. Spooner. N.Y. 1853. 3 v. 12°. 5750
*and Engravers, Dictionary of. M. Bryan. Lond. 1849. Roy. 8°. 3960
& Sculptors, Lives of British. A. Cunningham. N.Y. 1840. 5 v. 12°. 2430
The same. (H. F. L.) N.Y. 1843. 5. v. 12°. 3683, 17–19, 66, 67
Modern. J. Ruskin. New York, 1847. 3 v. 12°. . . . 3018
Sculptors, & Architects, Lives of. G. Vasari. Lond. 1850. 2 v. post 8°. 4185
Sketches of American. H. T. Tuckerman. New York, 1847. 12°. 3057
Sketches of the Old. H. F. Lee. Boston, 1838. 12°. 379
Painting, Ancient Glass. Oxford, 1847. 2 v. 8°. 4821
and Architecture, Lectures on. J. Ruskin. Phil. 1854. 12°. . 6170
and Design, Lectures on. B. R. Haydon. London, 1844. 2 v. 8°. 4674
Art of, and Coloring. G. Field. London, 1850. 12°. . . . 6053
History of, in Italy. L. Lanzi. London, 1847. 3 v. post 8°. . 3551
Lectures on. J. Barry, J. Opie, and H. Fuseli. Lond. 1848. Post 8°. 4361
Lectures on the History & Principles of. T. Phillips. Lond. 1833. 8°. 3963
Memoirs of. W. Buchanan. London, 1824. 2 v. 8°. 4824
on Glass, Treatise on. E. O. Fromberg. London, 1851. 12°. . 6063
Rise and Progress of the Art. Boston, 1846. 12°. 2998
Sculpture and Architecture, Hist. of. J. S. Memes. Bost. 1834. 12°. 1003
Treatise on Pigments. J. P. Ridner. New York, 1850. 12°. . 4059
Palestine and Syria, Travels in. G. Robinson. Paris, 1837. 12°. . . 2122
Biblical Researches in. E. Robinson. Boston, 1841. 3 v. 8°. . 1985
Descriptive Geography and Sketch of. J. Schwarz. Phil. 1850. 8°. 3985
Early Travels in. Ed. by T. Wright. London, 1848. Post 8°. . 3562
Egypt, and Italy, Visit to. Ida Pfeiffer. London, 1852. 12°. . 5259
History of. J. Kitto. Boston, 1852. 12°. 35
History of. M. Russell. (H. F. L.) New York, 1846. 12°. 3683, 27
Letters on. T. Wells. Boston, 1846. 12°. 2555
Pilgrimage to. J. V. C. Smith. Boston, 1853. 12°. . . . 5184
Scripture Lands; with 24 Maps. J. Kitto. Lond. 1850. Post 8°. 4391

Paley, W. Evidences of Christianity. Boston, 1803. 12°. 392
Horæ Paulinæ. New York, 1851. 8°. 4704
Moral and Political Philosophy. Philadelphia, 1814. 8°. . . . 735
Natural Theology. New York, 1820. 12°. 861
The same. (H. F. L.) New York, 1846. 2 v. 12°. 3683, 96, 97
The same. Illustrated by J. Paxton. Boston, 1851. 12°. 1569
Works; with Life. Philadelphia, 1831. 8°. 647
Palfrey, J. G. Evidences of Christianity. Boston, 1843. 2 v. 8°. . . 2251
Jewish Scriptures and Antiquities. Boston, 1838–52. 4 v. 8°. . 1642
Life of William Palfrey. Boston, 1848. 12°. 1076, 17
Sermons of the Duties of Private Life. Boston, 1834. 8°. . . 1641
Statistics of Industry in Massachusetts. Boston, 1846. 8°. . . 4359
Palfrey, W. Life. J. G. Palfrey. Boston, 1848. 12°. . . . 1076, 17
Palissy, B. Life. H. Morley. Boston, 1853. 2 v. 12°. . . . 4997
Palmer, J. Travels in United States. London, 1818. 8°. . . . 770
Pamela; or, Virtue Rewarded. S. Richardson. London, 1801. 4 v. 12°. 1833
Pampas and the Andes, Journey to. Sir F. B. Head. Boston, 1827. 12°. 508
Pamphlets. 31 vols. 625
relating to English Politics. 7 vols. 1244
Panama Mission, Documents relating to. Washington, 1826. 8°. . . 728
Panoplist. Vol. 4. New series. Boston, 1812. 8°. 773
Panthea; or, Spirit of Nature. R. Hunt. London, 1850. 12°. . . 5097
Pantheon of the Heathen Gods. A. Tooke. New York, 1816. 12°. . 159
Pantropheon; or, History of Food. A. Soyer. Boston, 1853. 8°. . 5460
Papal Persecutions, History of. Ed. by Miss Christmas. Lond. 1851. 12°. 4613
Papal Rome; her Priests and Jesuits. G. Achilli. New York, 1851. 12°. 4175
Paper Credit in Great Britain. H. Thornton. Philadelphia, 1807. 8°. . 656
Papers from the Quarterly Review. New York, 1852. 12°. . . . 4792
Para; or, Adventures on the Amazon. J. E. Warren. N.Y. 1851. 12°. 4258
Parables. F. A. Krummacher. Philadelphia, 1854. 8°. . . . 6000
Lectures on. J. Cumming. Philadelphia, 1854. 12°. . . . 5874
of our Lord, Notes on. R. C. Trench. New York, 1851. 8°. . 4713
Paradise Lost. J. Milton. New York, 1850. 12°. 4063
The same. New York, 1851. 8°. 173
Paraguay, Francia's Reign in. J. P. & W. P. Robertson. Phil. 1839. 2 v. 12°. 979
Pardee, R. G. Cultivation of the Strawberry. New York, 1854. 12°. . 6268
Pardoe, Miss. City of the Magyar. London, 1840. 3 v. 12°. . . 3122
City of the Sultan, in 1836. Philadelphia, 1837. 2 v. 12°. . . 941
The same. (Select Circ. Lib.) Philadelphia, 1837. 4°. 2034, 1837
Flies in Amber. London, 1850. 3 v. 12°. 4277
Louis XIV., and Court of France. New York, 1847. 2 v. 12°. . 3040
Reginald Lyle. New York, 1854. 12°. 6140
Rival Beauties; a Novel. New York, 1848. 8°. 3234
Romance of the Harem. Philadelphia, 1839. 2 v. 12°. . . 1049
Paris and the Parisians in 1835. Mrs. F. Trollope. New York, 1836. 8°. 607
*and its Environs. A. Pugin. London, 1833. 4°. 2014
Few Weeks in. Boston, 1814. 12°. 469
Frascati's; or, Scenes in. Philadelphia, 1836. 2 v. 12°. . . 259
in 1851. Sir F. B. Head. New York, 1852. 12°. 4755

Paris, Letters from, during the Reign of Napoleon. Lond. 1816. 2 v. 8°. 754
Purple Tints of. B. St. John. New York, 1854. 12°. . . 5808
Revisited in 1815. J. Scott. Boston, 1816. 12°. 174
Rollo in. J. Abbott. Boston, 1854. 12°. 5782
Sketch Book. W. M. Thackeray. New York, 1852. 2 v. 12°. . 2166
Sketches of, by an American. Philadelphia, 1838. 12°. . . 370
Spare Hours of a Student in. A. K. Gardner. N.Y. 1848. 12°. . 3086
Spectator. Philadelphia, 1816. 2 v. 18°. 54
Tours and Rouen, Excursion to. G. M. Musgrave. Lond. 1849. 12°. 4414
Parish Side. New York, 1854. 12°. 5851
Parisian Sights and French Principles. New York, 1852. 12°. . . 4988
Park, E. A. (Editor.) Works and Memoir of S. Hopkins. Bos. 1852. 3 v. 8°. 4940
Writings and Memoir of B. B. Edwards. Boston, 1853. 2 v. 12°. 5289
Park, H. G. Voice from the Parsonage. Boston, 1854. 12°. . . 5856
Park, J. A. Law of Marine Insurances. Boston, 1799. 8°. . . . 782
Park, M. Writings, Life, and Travels. (H. F. L.) N.Y. 1846. 12°. 3683, 105
Park, R. Handbook for Amer. Travellers in Europe. N.Y. 1853. 12°. 5312
Parker, E. L. History of Londonderry. Boston, 1851. 12°. . . 5017
Parker, H. F. Morning Stars of the New World. New York, 1854. 12°. 5861
Parker, R. G. Aids to English Composition. Boston, 1844. 12°. . . 1922
Exercises in English Composition. Boston, 1835. 12°. . . 1810
Tribute to Jonas Chickering. Boston, 1854. 12°. . . . 5802
Parker, S. Tour beyond the Rocky Mountains. Auburn, 1846. 12°. . 3028
Parker, Theo. Critical and Miscellaneous Writings. Boston, 1843. 12°. 1812
Discourse of Matters pertaining to Religion. Boston, 1842. 8°. . 1830
Miscellaneous Sermons and Discourses. Boston, 1845–48. 2 v. 8°. 3271
Sermons of Theism, Atheism, &c. Boston, 1853. 12°. . . . 6316
Speeches, Addresses, and Occasional Sermons. Bost. 1852. 2 v. 12°. 4561
Ten Sermons of Religion. Boston, 1853. 12°. 5186
Parkhurst, J. Hebrew and English Lexicon. London, 1799. Roy. 8°. . 1449
Parkman, F., jun. California and Oregon Trail. New York, 1849. 12°. 3351
History of the Conspiracy of Pontiac. Boston, 1851. 8°. . . 4519
Parkyns, M. Life in Abyssinia. New York, 1854. 2 v. 12°. . . 5859
Parley's Cabinet Library. — See *Goodrich, S. G.*
Parley's Present for all Seasons. S. G. Goodrich. New York, 1854. 12°. 5570
Parliamentary Practice, Manual of. J. B. Burleigh. Phil. 1852. 8°. . 4815
Manual of. T. Jefferson. Philadelphia, 1843. 12°. . . . 1890
Parlor Book. New York, 1842. 12°. 1886
Parlor-Book; or, Family Encyclopædia. J. L. Blake. N.Y. 1837. 8°. . 1884
Parnassian Shop. Boston, 1801. 12°. 488
Parnassus in Pillory; a Satire. New York, 1851. 12°. 3820
Parr, S. Works. Edited by J. Johnstone. London, 1828. 8 v. 8°. . 5903

Vol. 1. Memoirs.
2. Sermons.
3. Notice of Dr. Combe's Horace; Prefatio ad Bellendeni Libros; Remarks on Politics, Jurisprudence, Morals, &c.; Letter from Irenopolis; Warburtonian Tracts; Letter to Dr. Milner; Pamphlet on Dr. Combe's Horace; Notes on Rapin's Whigs and Tories.
4. Character of Charles James Fox; Note on Fox's History of Reign of James II.; Latin and English Inscriptions; Illustrations of the Inscriptions.
5, 6. Sermons.
7, 8. Correspondence with Dr. Parr.

Parricide, The; a Domestic Romance. Philadelphia, 1836. 2 v. 12°. . 222
Parrot, F. Journey to Ararat. Tr. by W. D. Cooley. N.Y. 1846. 12°. 2558
Parrots, Natural History of. P. J. Selby. Edinburgh, 1843. 12°. . 4901, 10
Parry, Sir W. E. Journal of Voyage of Discov., 1819-20. Phil. 1821. 8°. 1316
Second Voyage of Discovery, 1821-23. New York, 1824. 8°. . 1272
Three Voyages. Philadelphia, 1833. 8°. 1357, 3
The same. (H. F. L.) New York, 1846. 2 v. 12°. 3683, 107, 108
Parson, The, Pen and Pencil. G. M. Musgrave. London, 1849. 12°. . 4414
Parsonage of Mora. Fredrika Bremer. New York, 1845. 8°. . . 2618
Parsonage, Voice from the. Rev. H. G. Park. Boston, 1854. 12°. . 5856
Parson's Daughter. Theo. E. Hook. London, 1851. 12°. . . . 5663
Parsons, T. Essays [on Swedenborgianism]. Boston, 1845. 12°. . . 2346
Parsons, T. W. Poems. Boston, 1854. 12°. 6230
Partington, Mrs. Ruth. Life and Sayings. B. P. Shillaber. N.Y. 1854. 12°. 5925
Partisan; a Romance of the Revolution. W. G. Simms. N.Y. 1854. 12°. 1099
Partnership, Law of. J. Story. Boston, 1846. 8°. 3595
Party Leaders. J. G. Baldwin. New York, 1854. 12°. . . . 6247
Pascal, B. Provincial Letters. New York, 1850. 12°. 3444
Thoughts on Religion. London, 1836. 12°. 1860
Passages from the History of Liberty. S. Eliot. Boston, 1847. 12°. . 2965
from the History of a Wasted Life. J. A. Dix. Boston, 1853. 12°. 5508
in Life of Margaret Maitland. Mrs. Oliphant. N. Y. 1851. 12°. 4423
Passion, and other Tales. Mrs. J. Thayer. Boston, 1846. 12°. . . 2569
Passion Flowers. Mrs. S. G. Howe. Boston, 1854. 12°. . . . 5773
Passions; or, Mind and Matter. J. G. Millingen. London, 1848. 8°. . 5090
Past, The, and its Legacies to Am. Soc. J. D. Nourse. Louisville, 1847. 12°. 3042
and Present. T. Carlyle. New York, 1844. 12°. . . . 1743
Present, and Future. H. C. Carey. Philadelphia, 1848. 8°. . 2882
Paston Letters. Edited by J. Fenn. London, 1849. 8°. . . . 4371
Pastor's Fireside. Jane Porter. London, 1850. 2 v. 12°. . . . 5652
Pastor's Legacy. E. Mason. New York, 1853. 8°. 5120
Pastor's Sketches. I. S. Spencer. New York, 1853. 12°. . . . 5502
Patagonia, Captive in. B. F. Bourne. Boston, 1853. 12°. . . . 5215
Patchwork. Capt. B. Hall. Philadelphia, 1841. 2 v. 12°. . . . 2107
Patent Office, Guide to. G. T. Curtis. Boston, 1851. 12°. . . . 4298
Reports, 1844-53. Washington. 8°. 3222
Pathfinder; or, The Inland Sea. J. F. Cooper. New York, 1852. 12°. . 1581
Pathology and Practice of Medicine. J. Mackintosh. Phil. 1844. 8°. . 4702
Pathways and Abiding Places of our Lord. J.M.Wainwright. N.Y.1851. 8°. 4008
Pattie, J. O., Personal Narrative. Ed. by T. Flint. Cincinnati, 1833. 8°. 2601
Patient Waiting no Loss. Alice B. Neal. New York, 1853. 12°. . . 5070
Paton, A. A. Goth and the Hun. London, 1851. 8°. 4325
Patriarchal Age; or, the Story of Joseph. Philadelphia, 1851. 12°. . 4182
Patriotic Proceedings in Mass. Legislature, 1809. Boston, 1809. 8°. . 768
Paul, St., Difficulties in the Writings of. R. Whately. Lond. 1845. 8°. 2650
Horæ Paulinæ. W. Paley. New York, 1851. 8°. 4704
Life and Epistles. W. J. Conybeare and Howson. N.Y. 1854. 2v. 8°. 5992
Paraphrase and Notes on the Epistles. J. Locke. Boston, 1832. 8°. 1818

Paul and Virginia. B. de St. Pierre. Philadelphia, 1849. 18°. . . 4461
Paul, H. Dashes of American Humor. New York, 1853. 12°. . . 5784
Paul Clifford. E. L. Bulwer. New York, 1830. 2 v. 12°. . . . 1191
The same. London, 1853. 12°. 5706
Paul Periwinkle's Adventures. New York, 1851. 8°. 4335
Paul Pry's Journal of a Residence. J. Poole. Philadelphia, 1836. 12°. . 893
Paul Ulric; or, Adventures of an Enthusiast. New York, 1835. 2 v. 12°. 1105
Paul's Letters to his Kinsfolk. Sir W. Scott. Edinburgh, 1816. 8°. . 632
The same. Boston, 1829. 12°. 399, 5
The same. Edinburgh, 1843. 12°. 4101, 5
Paulding, J. K. Dutchman's Fireside. New York, 1831. 2 v. 12°. . 415
John Bull in America. New York, 1825. 12°. 255
Koningsmarke. New York, 1823. 2 v. 12°. 260
Letters from the South. New York, 1835. 2 v. 12°. . . . 1093
Life of Geo. Washington. (H. F. L.) N. Y. 1846. 2 v. 12°. 3683, 75, 76
Old Continental; or, Price of Liberty. N. York, 1846. 2 v. 12°. 2588
Puritan and his Daughter. New York, 1849. 12°. 3431
Slavery in the United States. New York, 1836. 16°. . . . 242
Tales of a Good Woman. New York, 1836. 2 v. 12°. . . . 264
Westward, Ho! New York, 1832. 2 v. 12° 431
and W. Irving. Salmagundi. New York, 1835. 2 v. 12°. . . 1813
Pauli, R. Life of Alfred the Great. London, 1853. Post 8°. . . 5364
Paxton, P. Stray Yankee in Texas. New York, 1853. 12°. . . 5258
Payne, A. R. M. Rambles in Brazil. New York, 1854. 12°. . . 5809
Payson, E. Memoir. A. Cummings. New York, 1830. 12°. . . 503
Payson, G. Totemwell. New York, 1854. 12°. 6312
Pazos, V. Letters on the United Provinces of S. America. N. Y. 1819. 8°. 1324
*Peabody, G. Dinner at London, 27th Oct. 1851. London, 1851. Roy. 8°. 4936
Peabody, W. B. O. Birds of Massachusetts. Boston, 1839. 8°. . . 722
Life of David Brainerd. Boston, 1844. 12°. 1076, 8
Life of Cotton Mather. Boston, 1840. 12°. 1076, 6
Life of James Oglethorpe. Boston, 1844. 12°. 1076, 12
Life of Alexander Wilson. Boston, 1838. 12°. 1076, 2
Life of John Sullivan. Boston, 1844. 12°. 1076, 13
Literary Remains. Ed. by Everett Peabody. Boston, 1850. 12°. . 3502
Sermons; with Memoir. Boston, 1849. 12°. 3329
Peace, Manual of. T. C. Upham. New York, 1836. 8°. 6014
Peace Societies, History of. W. Ladd. Boston, 1836. 12°. . . . 898
Peacock, G. Headlong Hall and Nightmare Abbey. N. York, 1845. 12°. 2358
The same. London, 1837. 12°. 5665
Peake, J. Naval Architecture. London, 1850. 2 v. 12°. . . . 6071
Peake, R. B. Memoirs of the Colman Family. London, 1841. 2 v. 8°. 2605
Peake, W. Austria during its Revolutionary Crisis. Lond. 1851. 2 v. 12°. 4617
Peale, R. Notes on Italy, 1829–30. Philadelphia, 1831. 8°. . . . 1329
Pearl-Fishing; Stories from Household Words. Auburn, 1854. 12°. . 5790
Pearce, R. R. Memoirs and Corres. of R. Wellesley. Lond. 1846. 3 v. 8°. 4661
Pearce, S. Memoir. A. Fuller. New York, n. d. 16°. . . . 475
Pears, S. A. Life and Times of Sir Philip Sidney. London, 1845. 8°. . 2667

Pearson, Mrs. C. H. Cousin Franck's Household. Boston, 1853. 12°. . 5197
Pearson, H. Memoir of C. Buchanan. New York, n. d. 12°. . . 100
Pearson, T. Infidelity; its Aspects, Causes, and Agencies. N.Y. 1854. 8°. 5435
Peasant and Landlord. Baroness Knorring. New York, 1848. 12°. . 3126
Peck, G. W. Melbourne and Chincha Islands. New York, 1854. 12°. 5927
Peck, J. M. Guide for Emigrants in Ill., Missou., &c. Bost. 1831. 12°. 1493
Life of Daniel Boone. Boston, 1847. 12°. 1076, 23
Pedestrious Tour of 4000 Miles. E. Evans. Concord, 1819. 12°. . . 443
Peel, Sir R., Life and Times of. W. C. Taylor. London, n. d. 2 v. 8°. 3632
and Duke of Wellington. Lives. New York, 1852. 12°. . . 4992
Peep at Number Five. Mrs. E. S. Phelps. Boston, 1852. 18°. . . 4778
Peep at the Pilgrims in 1636. Mrs. H. V. Cheney. Boston, 1826. 2 v. 12°. 2115
The same. Boston, 1850. 12°. 4051
Peep behind the Curtain. J. F. Leonard. Boston, 1850. 12°. . . 3892
Peer's Daughters. Lady Bulwer. New York, 1850. 8°. . . . 4314
Peers and Parvenus. Mrs. C. Gore. New York, 1846. 8°. . . . 2710
Peirce, C. H. Exam. of Drugs, Medicines, &c., as to Purity. Camb. 1852. 12°. 3875
Pelayo; a Story of the Goth. W. G. Simms. New York, 1838. 2 v. 12°. 1144
Pelet, Baron. Napoleon in Council. Tr. by B. Hall. Edinb. 1837. 12°. 2717
Pelew Islands, Account of. G. Keate. Boston, 1796. 12°. . . . 163
Pelham. E. L. Bulwer. Boston, 1850. 8°. 838
Pelham, W. System of Notation. Boston, 1808. 12°. 461
Pellarin, C. Life of Charles Fourier. New York, 1848. 12°. . . 3179
Pellew, G. Life and Corres. of Lord Sidmouth. London, 1847. 3 v. 8°. 4133
Pellico, S., Memoirs of; or, My Prisons. New York, 1844. 8°. . . 2171
The same. New York, 1833. 12°. 1218
Peloponnesus and Greek Islands. R. Anderson. Boston, 1830. 12°. . 544
Pen and Ink Sketches. J. R. Dix. Boston, 1845. 12°. 2476
Pen Owen, History and Adventures of. J. Galt. New York, 1851. 8°. 3808
Pen Pictures of Popular English Preachers. J. R. Dix. Lond. 1852. 12°. 6243
Pencil Sketches. Miss Leslie. Philadelphia, 1833–35. 2 v. 12°. . . 1094
The same. Philadelphia, 1852. 2 v. 12°. 4877
Pencillings by the Way. N. P. Willis. New York, 1852. 12°. . . 1130
Pendennis, History of. W. M. Thackeray. New York, 1850. 2 v. 8°. . 4034
Peninsular Campaigns, Annals of. T. Hamilton. Phil. 1831. 3 v. 12°. . 1189
Peninsular Medal, My. New York, 1850. 8°. 3977
Peninsular War, History of. W. F. P. Napier. Phil. 1842. 4 v. 8°. . 1951
Story of. C. W. Vane. New York, 1848. 12°. 3161
Penitentiary System in U. S. Beaumont & de Tocqueville. Phil. 1833. 8°. 1583
Penn, W. Life. George E. Ellis. Boston, 1848. 12°. . . . 1076, 22
Private and Public Life of. T. Clarkson. Dover, 1827. 8°. . 1410
Penny Encyclopædia. London, 1833–44. 30 v. roy. 8°. 5100
For contents, see *Encyclopædia, Penny.*
Penny Magazine, 1832–39, 1841–45. London, 12 v. roy. 8°. . . . 1438
Pennsylvania, Historical Collections of. S. Day. Philadelphia, 1843. 8°. 2727
History of. W. H. Carpenter and T. S. Arthur. Phil. 1854. 12°. 6287
Pennsylvania Hall, History of. Philadelphia, 1838. 8°. 1440
Pentameron and Pentalogia. W. S. Landor. London, 1837. 12°. . 2318

People I have Met. N. P. Willis. New York, 1850. 12°. 3483
*People's Journal. Vols. 1-4. Ed. by J. Saunders. Lond. 1846-49. 8°. 2760
People's Music Book. Part 2: Sacred. London, 1844. Roy. 8°. . . 6011
People's Own Book. F. de la Mennais. (Tr. by N. Greene.) Bost. 1839. 16°. 63
Pépé, G. Memoirs, by Himself. London, 1846. 3 v. 12°. 4570
Scenes and Events in Italy, 1847-49. London, 1850. 2 v. 12°. . 4235
Pepys, S. Life, Journals, and Correspondence. London, 1841. 2 v. 8°. 4668
Pequinillo; a Tale. G. P. R. James. New York, 1852. 8°. . . . 6004
Perce, E. (Editor.) Gulliver Joi; his Three Voyages. N.Y. 1851. 16°. . 4472
Last of his Name. New York, 1854. 12°. 6315
Old Karl, the Cooper. New York, 1854. 16°. 6218
Percival, J. G. Dream of a Day, and other Poems. N. Haven, 1843. 12°. 2327
Poems. New York, 1823. 8°. 2263
Percival, T. Father's Instructions. Richmond, 1800. 12°. . . . 136
Moral and Literary Dissertations. London, 1789. 12°. . . 480
Percival Keene. F. Marryat. Philadelphia, 1846. 8°. 2714
The same. London, 1853. 12°. 5735
Percival Mayberry. Philadelphia, 1851. 12°. 3780
Percy, S. & R. Anecdotes; with American Anecdotes. N.Y. 1847. 2 v. 8°. 1763
Percy, T. Reliques of Ancient English Poetry. London, 1847. 3 v. 12°. 1279
Percy Ranthorpe. Mrs. C. Gore. New York, 1848. 8°. . . . 2875
Peregrine Pickle. T. Smollett. Philadelphia, 1851. 8°. . . . 801, 1
Pericles and Aspasia. W. S. Landor. Philadelphia, 1839. 2 v. 12°. . 1236
Perilous Adventures. R. A. Davenport. New York, 1841. 12°. . . 2424
The same. (H. F. L.) New York, 1848. 12°. . . 3683, 159
Periodical Library. T. K. Greenbank. Philadelphia, 1833. 3 v. 8°. . 1357
Periodical Literature, Index to. W. F. Poole. N. Y. 1853. Roy. 8°. . 5444
Periodicals, Index to Subjects in. W. F. Poole. New York, 1848. 8° . 3210
Periscopics; or, Current Subjects. W. Elder. New York, 1854. 12°. . 6188
Perkins, E. T. Reef Rovings in South Seas. New York, 1854. 8°. . 5972
Perkins, J. H. Annals of the West. Cincinnati, 1846. 8°. . . . 3247
Memoir and Writings. Ed. by W. H. Channing. Bost. 1851. 12°. 4094
Perry, O. H. Life. A. S. Mackenzie. New York, 1840. 2 v. 12°. . 221
The same. (H. F. L.) New York, 1846. 2 v. 12°. . 3683, 126, 127
Persia, History of. J. B. Fraser. (H. F. L.) New York, 1848, 12°. 3683, 70
Sketches of. Sir J. Malcolm. London, 1845. 12°. . . . 2389
Person, W. Life and Letters. Cambridge, 1820. 12°. 123
Personal Property, Law of Sales of. G. Long. Boston, 1839. 8°. . . 2062
Law of Sales of. W. W. Story. Boston, 1847. 8°. . . . 3792
Persons and Pictures from History. H. W. Herbert. N. York, 1854. 12°. 5870
Perspective, Treatise on. G. Pyne. London, 1852. 12°. . . . 6049
Persuasion; a Novel. Jane Austen. Philadelphia, 1832. 2 v. 12°. . 531
The same. Philadelphia, 1838. 8°. 1585, 1
Perthes, F. M. Life of J. (St.) Chrysostom. Boston, 1854. 12°. . . 6240
Peru, History of the Conquest of. W. H. Prescott. N. Y. 1847. 2 v. 8°. 2793
Travels in. E. Temple. Philadelphia, 1833. 2 v. 12°. . . 1205
Travels in, 1838-42. J. J. von Tschudi. New York, 1847. 12°. . 2967
Peruvian Antiquities. M. E. Rivero and J. J. von Tschudi. N.Y. 1853. 8°. 5440

Pestalozzi, H. Life and Travels. E. Biber. Philadelphia, 1833. 8°. 1357, 1
Peter, First Epistle of, Discourses on. J. Brown. New York, 1851. 8°. 4723
Peter the Great, Age of. B. Kamenski. London, 1851. 12°. . . 4615
History of. London, n. d. 12°. 111
The same. Boston, 1814. 12°. 111
Life. P. de Segur. Philadelphia, 1833. 8°. . . . 1357, 1
Peter, W. Poets and Poetry of the Ancients. Philadelphia, 1847. 8°. . 2767
Peters, R. Case of the Cherokee Nation *vs.* Georgia. Phil. 1831. 8°. . 1260
(Editor.) Public Statutes at Large of U. S. Bost. 1845. Roy. 8°. 3243
Peter Pilgrim; or, Rambler's Recollections. R.M.Bird. Phil. 1838. 2 v. 12°. 105
Peter Ploddy, and other Oddities. J. C. Neal. Philadelphia, 1844. 12°. 2300
Peter Schlemihl in America. G. Wood. Philadelphia, 1848. 12°. . 4928
Peter Simple. F. Marryat. Philadelphia, 1847. 8°. 449
The same. Philadelphia, 1847. 8°. 1766, 1
The same. London, 1853. 12°. 5714
Peter the Whaler. W. H. G. Kingston. New York, 1852. 12°. . . 4480
Peter Wilkins, Adventures of. R. Pultock. London, 1844. 8°. . . 89
Peter's Letters to his Kinsfolk. J. G. Lockhart. New York, 1820. 8°. . 657
Peterson, C. J. Cruising in the Last War. Philadelphia, 1850. 2 v. 8°. 3990
Petrarch, F. Life. T. Campbell. Philadelphia, 1841. 8°. . . . 2250
View of Human Life. London, 1797. 8°. 591
Petrel; or, Love on the Ocean. A. Fisher. Philadelphia, 1851. 8°. . 4511
Pets, History of my. Sara J. Clarke. Boston, 1851. 12°. . . . 4091
Petticoat Government; a Novel. Mrs. Trollope. London, 1850. 3 v. 12°. 3980
Peuchet, J. Vocabulaire des Termes de Commerce. Paris, 1801. 8°. . 1248
Peveril of the Peak. Sir W. Scott. Boston, 1848. 2 v. 12°. . . 999, 27, 28
The same. Edinburgh, 1849. 3 v. 12°. . . 4100, 28–30
The same. Edinburgh, 1850. Roy. 8°. . . . 4531, 7
Peyrouse, M. de la. Voyage round the World. Boston, 1801. 16°. . 876
Pfeiffer, Ida. Journey to Iceland, &c. New York, 1852. 12°. . . 1005
Visit to the Holy Land, Egypt, and Italy. London, 1852. 12°. . 5259
Voyage round the World. New York, 1852. 12°. . . . 4596
Phantasmagoria of Fun. London, 1843. 2 v. 12°. 5632
Phantom Ship. F. Marryat. Philadelphia, 1839. 2 v. 12°. . . . 481
The same. London, 1853. 12°. 5732
Phantom World; Philosophy of Spirits, &c. A. Calmet. Phil. 1850. 12°. 3883
Phelps, Mrs. E. S. Last Leaf from Sunny Side. Boston, 1853. 12°. . 5307
Peep at Number Five. Boston, 1852. 18°. 4778
Sunny Side; or, Country Minister's Wife. Philadelphia, 1851. 18°. 4397
Tell-Tale; or, Home Secrets. Boston, 1853. 18°. 5188
Phelps, Mrs. L. Ida Norman; or, Trials and their Uses. N. Y. 1854. 12°. 6300
Philadelphia, as it Is in 1852. R. A. Smith. Philadelphia, 1852. 12°. . 4788
Picture of. J. Mease. Philadelphia, 1811. 12°. 289
Society of National Industry. Addresses of. Phil. 1819. 12°. . 512
Philip Augustus; or, Brothers in Arms. G.P.R.James. N.Y. 1831. 2 v. 12°. 1563
The same. London, 1853. 12°. 5711
Philip, R. Devotional Guides. New York, 1848. 2 v. 12°. . . . 4751
Philip II. of Spain, History of the Reign of. R. Watson. N.Y. 1818. 8°. 638

Philip Van Artevelde. H. Taylor. Cambridge, 1835. 12°. 2322
Philippart, J. Memoirs of Charles John. London, 1814. 8°. 589
Philippines, Twenty Years in. P. de la Gironière. London, 1853. 12°. 5848
Philip's War, History of. S. G. Drake. Exeter, 1836. 12°. 179
Phillips, C. Curran and his Contemporaries. New York, 1818. 8°. . 1322
The same. New York, 1851. 12°. 4174
Phillips, Sir R. Million of Facts. New York, 1836. 12°. 1010
Phillips, T. Lectures on History and Principles of Painting. Lon. 1833. 8°. 3963
Phillips, W. Average and Marine Insurance. Boston, 1833. 8°. . . 2060
Protection and Free Trade. Boston, 1850. 12°. 5270
Philo; an Evangeliad. S. Judd, jun. Boston, 1850. 12°. 3481
Philology, Outlines of Comparative. M. S. De Vere. N. Y. 1853. 12°. 5568
Philosophers, Lives of Ancient. F. de S. de L. Fénélon. N. Y. 1843. 12°. 2423
The same. (H. F. L.) New York, 1847. 12°. . 3683, 140
and Actresses. A. Houssaye. New York, 1852. 2 v. 12°. . . 4927
Philosophical Writers. T. De Quincey. Boston, 1854. 12°. . . . 5744
Philosophy, Easy Grammar of. D. Blair. Philadelphia, 1811. 16°. . 15
and Literature, Discussions in. Sir W. Hamilton. N. Y. 1853. 8°. 5427
Glance at. S. G. Goodrich. Boston, 1849. 12°. . . . 4900, 16
History of. W. Enfield. London, 1839. 8°. 1426
Hist. of. Tr. by C. S. Henry. (H.F.L.) N.Y. 1847. 2v. 12°. 3683, 143-4
Intellectual, Elements of. F. Wayland. New York, 1855. 12°. . 6319
Introduction to the History of. V. Cousin. Boston, 1832. 8°. . 1435
Modern, History of. V. Cousin. New York, 1852. 2 v. 8°. . 998
Moral. — See *Moral.*
of the Active and Moral Powers. D. Stewart. Camb. 1849. 12°. 3427
of History. F. von Schlegel. London, 1846. Post 8°. . . 2343
of Life and Language. F. von Schlegel. London, 1847. Post 8°. 3080
of Living. H. Mayo. Philadelphia, 1852. 12°. 4860
of Living. C. Ticknor. (H. F. L.) New York, 1846. 12°. 3683, 77
of Mystery. W. C. Dendy. New York, 1845. 12°. 2504
of the Sciences. A. Comte. Ed. by G. H. Lewes. Lon. 1853. Post 8°. 5936
Outline of. R. Park. Boston, 1836. 12°. 898
Progress of Ethical. Sir J. Mackintosh. Philadelphia, 1845. 8°. 3608
Speculative, of Europe in 19th Cent. J. D. Morell. N. Y. 1851. 8°. 3422
Philothea; a Grecian Romance. Mrs. L. M. Child. N. Y. 1848. 12°. . 2373
Phips, Sir W. Life. F. Bowen. Boston, 1840. 12°. 1076, 7
Photography, Treatise on. G. C. H. Halleur. London, 1854. 12°. . 6087
Phrenology. J. G. Spurzheim. Boston, 1832. 2 v. 8°. 1417
applied to Matrimony. O. S. Fowler. New York, 1842. 8°. . 1844
Examination of. T. Sewall. Washington, 1837. 8°. . . . 1647
Lectures on. G. Combe. London, 1839. 12°. 434
Practical. S. Jones. Boston, 1836. 12°. 237
System of. G. Combe. New York, 1843. 12°. 1758
with the Study of Physiognomy. J. G. Spurzheim. Bost. 1833. 8°. 2085
Phreno-Mnemotechny; or, Art of Memory. F.F.Gouraud. N.Y. 1845. 8°. 2269
Physical Education of Girls. Elizabeth Blackwell. New York, 1852. 12°. 4885
Physical Geography. Mary Somerville. Philadelphia, 1848. 12°. . . 3168

Physical History of Man. J. C. Prichard. London, 1813. 8°. . . . 1914
Physical Sciences, Connection of. Mary Somerville. London, 1842. 12°. 2540
Glance at. S. G. Goodrich. Boston, 1849. 12°. 4900, 13
Physician and Patient, Mutual Duties, &c., of. W.Hooker. N.Y.1849. 12°. 3430
Homœopathic Domestic. J. H. Pulte. New York, 1852. 12°. . 4801
Physics, Elementary. R. Hunt. London, 1851. 12°. 5051
Elements of. N. Arnott. London, 1828. 8°. 1989
and Meteorology, Principles of. J. Muller. Phil. 1848. 8°. . 2893
The same. London, 1847. 8°. 4136
Physiognomy, Comparative. J. W. Redfield. New York, 1852. 8°. . 4947
Physiological Effects of Alcoholic Drinks. Boston, 1848. 12°. . . 2450
Physiology. J. H. Griscom. (H. F. L.) New York, 1846. 12°. . 3683, 85
applied to Preservation of Health. A. Combe. N. Y. 1843. 12°. 2211
The same. (H. F. L.) New York, 1846. 12°. . . 3683, 71
Human. R. Dunglison. Philadelphia, 1844. 2 v. 8°. . . . 1795
of Taste. B. Savarin. Philadelphia, 1854. 12°. 5598
Physique et de Chymie, Nouvelles Découvertes de. Paris, 1786. 8°. . 1246
Physique Théorie de. P. du Phanjas. Paris, 1786. 4 v. 8°. . . . 1416
Piano-Forte, Treatise on Playing. C. C. Spencer. London, 1853. 12°. 6082
Picciola. X. B. Saintine. Philadelphia, 1849. 12°. 3838
Pickering, Ellen. Agnes Serle. Philadelphia, 1846. 8°. . . . 2709
Ellen Wareham. Philadelphia, 1849. 8°. 3294
Expectant. Philadelphia, 1842. 2 v. 12°. 1697
The Fright. Philadelphia, 1847. 8°. 2186
Grumbler. New York, 1844. 8°. 1968
Heiress. Philadelphia, 1849. 8°. 470
Jeremiah Parkes. New York, 1849. 8°. 3462
Kate Walsingham. Philadelphia, 1848. 8°. 3233
Nan Darrell; or, the Gipsy Mother. Philadelphia, 1847. 8°. . 2707
Orphan Niece. Philadelphia, 1848. 8°. 3221
Poor Cousin. Philadelphia, 1849. 8°. 3260
Prince and the Pedler. Philadelphia, 1848. 8°. 997
Secret Foe. Philadelphia, 1841. 2 v. 12°. 2708
Squire. New York, 1845. 8°. 2741
Who shall be Heir? Philadelphia, 1847. 8°. 2706
Pickings of a Reporter of the "New Orleans Picayune." Phil. 1847. 12°. 2563
Pickwick abroad in France. G. W. M. Reynolds. New York, 1851. 8°. 4313
Pickwick Papers. C. Dickens. Philadelphia, 1854. 8°. 804
Pic-Nic Papers, by various Hands. Philadelphia, 1841. 2 v. 12°. . . 1634
Pic-Nics; or, Legends and Stories of Ireland. Philadelphia, 1837. 2 v. 12°. 908
Pictorial Calendar of the Seasons. Mary Howitt. London, 1854. Post 8°. 5920
Pictorial Family Magazine; ed. by R. Sears. Vols. 3–5. N.Y. 1846–49. 8°. 4950
Pictorial Field-Book of the Revolution. B. J. Lossing. N.Y. 1851–52. 2 v. 8°. 4130
*Pictorial Gallery of the Useful and Fine Arts. London, 1847. 2 v. 4°. 4830
Pictorial Half-Hours. London, n. d. 8°. 4943
Pictorial History of England. New York, 1847. 4 v. roy. 8°. . . 2899
of Germany. F. Kugler. London, 1845. Roy. 8°. 3599
of the United States. J. Frost. Philadelphia, 1846. 4 v. roy. 8°. 2777

Pictorial History of the United States. H. Murray. Boston, 1851. 8°. . 4007
Pictorial Library; edited by R. Sears. New York, 1847. 8°. 4800
Picture of the Empire of Bonaparte, 1804–5. Middletown, 1807. 8°. . 734
Pictures and Painters, Anecdotes of. London, n. d. 24°. 5048
Pictures from Italy. C. Dickens. New York, 1846. 12°. 2578
of Country Life. T. Miller. London, 1847. 12°. 5531
Picturesque Tourist. O. L. Holley. New York, 1844. 12°. 2599
Piddington, H. Sailor's Horn Book. New York, 1848. 8°. 3241
Pierce, F. Life. N. Hawthorne. Boston, 1852. 12°. 4917
Pierce, J. Half-Century Sermon at Brookline. Boston, 1847. 8°. . 3197
Pierre; or, the Ambiguities. H. Melville. New York, 1852. 12°. . 4897
Pierre, J. H. G. Parisian Pastor's Glance at America. Boston, 1854. 12°. 6159
Pierpont, J. Airs of Palestine, and other Poems. Boston, 1840. 12°. . 1579
American First Class Book. Boston, 1834. 12°. 1564
Pierson, H. W. American Missionary Memorial. New York, 1853. 8°. 5113
Piety, Persuasives to Early. J. G. Pike. New York, 1830. 12°. . . 1502
Pigeons, Natural History of. P. J. Selby. Edinburgh, 1843. 12°. 4901, 9
Pike, J. G. Guide for Young Disciples. New York, 1823. 18°. . . 343
Persuasives to Early Piety. New York, 1830. 12°. 1502
Pike, Z. M. Expedition to the Sources of the Mississippi. Phil. 1810. 8°. 1341
Life. H. Whiting. 1076, 15
Pilgrim Celebration at Plymouth, Aug. 1, 1853. Boston, 1853. 8°. . 5425
Pilgrim Fathers, Chronicles of. A. Young. Boston, 1844. 8°. . . 1957
*of New England. W. H. Bartlett. London, 1853. 8°. . . 6007
Pilgrimage of Adam and David. J. Gallaher. Boston, 1849. 12°. . 3400
to the Land of my Fathers. M. Margoliouth. Lond. 1850. 2 v. 8°. 4324
Pilgrim's Progress. J. Bunyan. Philadelphia, 1844. 12°. . . . 148
Pilgrim's Journal of 1620. Edited by G. B. Cheever. N.Y. 1848. 12°. 3325
of the Rhine. E. L. Bulwer. Boston, 1837. 24°. 1562
of Walsingham. Agnes Strickland. New York, 1854. 12°. . 6147
Pillars of Hercules. D. Urquhart. New York, 1850. 2 v. 12°. . . 3854
The same. London, 1850. 2 v. 8°. 4653
Pillet, General. Views of England. Boston, 1818. 12°. 181
Pinkerton, J. Collection of Voyages and Travels. Phil. 1810. 6 v. 4°. 2000

Vol. 1. Willoughby's Russia and Siberia.
Dutch Voyages to North of Europe.
Regnard's Journey to Lapland.
Maupertuis's Journey to Polar Circle.
Outhier's Voyage to the North.
Ehrenmalm's Travels to West Nordland.
Leems's Account of Danish Lapland.
Allison's Voyage from Archangel.
New Account of Samoiedia.
Journals of Seamen at Spitsbergen.
Von Troil's Letters on Iceland.
Kerguelen's Voyage to the North.
Cumberland's Voyage to the Azores.
Raleigh's Engagement near the Azores.
De Chaste's Voyage to Tercera.
2. Gonzales's Voyage to Eng. and Scotland.
Shaw's Tour to West of England.
Bray's Tour into Derbyshire.
Ferber's Oryctography of Derbyshire.
Moritz's Travels in England.
Skrine's Tours in Wales.
Malkin's Tour in Wales.
Hassels's Tour to Isle of Wight.
Heath's Account of Islands of Scilly.
Robertson's Tour through Isle of Man.
3. Pennant's Tours in Scotland.
Garnet's Account of the Drosacks.
Martin's Western Islands.
Martin's Voyage to St. Kilda.
Brand's Orkneys and Shetland.
4. Young's Tour in Ireland.
Hamilton's Northern Coast of Ireland.
Lister's Journey to Paris, 1698.
Young's Travels in France.
Saussure's Ascent of Mont Blanc.
Ramond's Journey to Mont Perdu.
5. Spallanzani's Travels in Italy.
Dolomieu's Earthquakes in Calabria.
Bourgoanne's Travels in Spain.
Coxe's Travels in Switzerland.
6. Riesbeck's Travels through Germany.
Coxe's Travels in Denmark.
Coxe's Travels in Norway.
Fortia's Travels in Sweden.
Coxe's Travels in Russia.

Pilot, The. J. F. Cooper. New York, 1851. 12°. 348
Pindar. Odes. Translated by H. F. Cary. London, 1833. 12°. . . 2585
Odes. Translated by G. West. London, 1766. 3 v. 12°. . . 4976
and Anacreon. Odes. Tr. by C. A. Wheelwright. N.Y. 1837. 12°. 1854, 36
Pindar, Susan. Midsummer Fays. New York, 1851. 12°. . . . 3773
Pinkney, W. Life. W. Pinkney. New York, 1853. 8°. . . . 5433
Life. H. Wheaton. Boston, 1840. 12°. 1076, 6
Pioneer History; Account of Ohio Valley. S. P. Hildreth. Cin. 1848. 8°. 3231
Pioneer Women of the West. Mrs. E. F. Ellet. New York, 1852. 12°. 4919
Pioneer's Daughter. E. Bennett. New York, 1851. 8°. . . . 4336
Pioneers, The. J. F. Cooper. Philadelphia, 1843. 2 v. 12°. . . . 440
Piozziana; or, Recollections of Mrs. Piozzi. E. Magin. Lond. 1833. 8°. 2543
Pirate. Sir W. Scott. Boston, 1848. 2 v. 12°. . . . 999, 23, 24
The same. Edinburgh, 1849. 2 v. 12°. . . 4100, 24, 25
The same. Edinburgh, 1850. Roy. 8°. . . . 4531, 6
Pirate and the Three Cutters. F. Marryat. Philadelphia, 1847. 8°. . 1122
Pitcairn's Island; Mutiny of the Bounty. J. Barrow. N.Y. 1848. 12°. 3683, 31
Pitrat, J. C. Jesuits Unveiled. New York, 1851. 12°. 4186
Pitt, W. Correspondence. Vols. 3, 4. London, 1839. 2 v. 8°. . . 3192
Life. G. Tomline. Philadelphia, 1821. 2 v. 8°. 1978
Selection of Speeches. London, 1853. Roy. 8°. 5482
Speeches. London, 1817. 3 v. 8°. 2659
Plain Speaker. W. Hazlitt. Vol. 2. London, 1826. 8°. . . . 2258
Planché, Matilda. House on the Rock. Boston, 1852. 12°. . . . 6291
Influence on the Evil Genius. London, 1853. 12°. . . . 6292
Minor Tales. Boston, 1852–53. 2 v. 12°. 6293

Vol. 1. Trap to Catch a Sunbeam; Old Jolliffe; Sequel to Old Jolliffe; Cloud with a Silver Lining.
2. Dream Chintz; Only; Star in the Desert.

Planetary and Stellar Worlds. O. M. Mitchel. New York, 1848. 12°. . 3143
Planter; or, Thirteen Years at the South. Philadelphia, 1853. 12°. . 5272
Planter's Northern Bride. Mrs. C. L. Hentz. Philadelphia, 1854. 2 v. 12°. 5787
Plants and Quadrupeds of Mass., Reports on. Cambridge, 1840. 8°. . 1969
Catalogue of, in Camb. Botanic Gardens. J. Donn. Lon. 1845. 8°. 3545
of Boston and Vicinity. J. Bigelow. Boston, 1840. 12°. . . 1842
Plato. Divine Dialogues, and Apology of Socrates. London, 1847. 12°. 2378
Proclus on the Timæus. Trans. by T. Taylor. Lond. 1820. 2 v. 4°. 4858
Works. Tr. by Cary, Davis, and Burgess. Lon. 1848–54. 6 v. post 8°. 4385

Vol. 1. Apology of Socrates; Crito; Phædo; Gorgias; Protagoras; Phædrus; Theætetus; Euthyphron; Lysis.
2. Republic; Timæus; Critias.
3. Meno; Euthydemus; Sophist; Statesman; Cratylus; Parmenides; Banquet.
4. Philebus; Charmides; Laches; Menexenus; Hippias; Ion; Alcibiades; Theages; Rivals; Hipparchus; Minos; Clitopho; Epistles.
5. The Laws.
6. Epinomis; Axiochus; Eryxias; Virtue; Justice; Sisyphus; Demodocus; Definitions; Timæus Locrus.

Players, Lives of the. J. Galt. Boston, 1831. 2 v. 12°. . . . 845
Pleader's Guide; a Didactic Poem. J. Surrebutter. Phil. 1803. 8°. . 1296
Pleasant Memories of Pleasant Lands. L. H. Sigourney. Bost. 1844. 12°. 1837

Pleasant Pages for Young People. S. P. Newcombe. Boston, 1853. 12°. 5214
Pliny, the Consul, Letters of. Boston, 1809. 2 v. 12°. 328
Ploughboy, The. Vols. 1, 3, 4. Albany, 1819–21. 4°. 2013
Plough, Loom, and Anvil. Ed. by J. S. Skinner. Vol. 1. Phil. 1848. 8°. 3409
Plowden, F. History of the British Empire, 1792–93. Dublin, 1794. 8°. 742
Plurality of Worlds. W. Whewell. Boston, 1854. 12°. 5817
Reply to. Sir D. Brewster. New York, 1854. 12°. 6299
Plutarch. Lives of Illustrious Persons of Antiquity. New York, 1853. 8°. 2065
Select Lives. Philadelphia, 1810. 12°. 424
Le Vite di. Verona, 1772. 5 v. 4°. 3323
Plymouth and the Pilgrims. J. Banvard. Boston, 1851. 12°. . . . 4272
Guide to. W. S. Russell. Boston, 1846. 12°. 2974
Pneumatics, Treatise on. C. Tomlinson. London, 1852. 12°. . . . 6043
Poacher. F. Marryat. London, 1853. 12°. 5731
Pocket Miscellany, Chambers's. Boston, 1852. 9 v. 12°. 864
Poe, E. A. Conchologist's First Book. Philadelphia, 1839. 12°. . . 840
Literati. New York, 1850. 12°. 3929
Tales. New York, 1845. 12°. 2474
Tales of the Grotesque and Arabesque. Philadelphia, 1840. 2 v. 12°. 2310
Works. New York, 1850. 2 v. 12°. 3494

Vol. 1. Sketch of Edgar A. Poe, by J. R. Lowell; His Death, by N. P. Willis; Tales.
2. The Raven, and other Poems; Eureka; Rationale of Verse, and other Prose Articles.

Poems. T. W. Parsons. Boston, 1854. 12°. 6230
Poems, Cambridge (Eng.) Prize. London, 1847. 12°. 3134
of Established Reputation. Baltimore, 1804. 12°. 144
Poesche, T. & C. Goepp. New Rome; or, U.S. of the World. N.Y. 1853. 12°. 5314
Poesy, Defence of. P. Sidney. Cambridge, 1831. 12°. 383, 2
Poetical Magazine; or, Temple of the Muses. London, 1804. 12°. . 102
*Poetical Quotations, Dictionary of. Ed. by Mrs. S. J. Hale. Phil. 1851. 8°. 2683
Poetry, Common-Place Book of Am. G. B. Cheever. Phil. 1843. 12°. 1775
Elegant Extracts of. London, 1791. 8°. 593
English History of. T. Warton. London, 1840. 3 v. 8°. . . . 5476
German, Historic Account of. W. Taylor. Lond. 1830. 3 v. 8°. 5467
Reliques of Ancient English. T. Percy. London, 1847. 3 v. 12°. 1279
Specimens of American. S. Kettell. Boston, 1829. 3 v. 12°. . 1184
of the Anti-Jacobin. London, 1852. 12°. 5251
of Germany. Trans. by A. Baskerville. New York, 1854. 12°. . 6257
of Life. Sarah Stickney. Philadelphia, 1835. 2 v. 12°. . . . 1102
of Life. Mrs. Sarah Ellis. New York, 1843. 8°. 1826
of the Magyars. J. Bowring. London, 1830. 12°. 3092
of Science. R. Hunt. Boston, 1850. 12°. 4082
of the Vegetable World. M. J. Schleiden. Cincinnati, 1853. 12°. 5316
Poet's Pilgrimage to Waterloo; a Poem. R. Southey. Boston, 1816. 12°. 890
Poets and Poetry of America. R. W. Griswold. Phil. 1847. 8°. . . 1685
and Poetry of the Ancients. W. Peter. Phil. 1847. 8°. . . . 2767
and Poetry of England. R. W. Griswold. Phil. 1845. 12°. . 2213
and Poetry of Europe. H. W. Longfellow. Phil. 1845. Roy. 8°. 2281

Poets, American, Selections from. W. C. Bryant. N.Y. 1846. 12°. 3683, 111
British Female. G. W. Bethune. Philadelphia, 1848. 8° . . 3191
British, Selections from. F.G.Halleck. N.Y.1846. 2 v. 12°. 3683, 112, 113
British, with Prefaces. J. Aiken and J. Frost. Phil. 1843. 3 v. 8°. 1962

Vol. 1. Chronological Series, Ben Jonson to Beattie.
2. ,, ,, Falconer to Scott.
3. ,, ,, Southey to Croly.

Essays on the. T. De Quincey. Boston, 1853. 12°. . . . 5220
Female, of America. R. W. Griswold. Phil. 1849. 8°. . . 3252
Female, of America. Caroline May. Phil. 1848. 8°. . . . 3535
Garden Walks with the. Mrs. C. M. Kirkland. N. Y. 1852. 12°. 5027
Gems of Modern, with Biograph. Notices. S.C.Hall. Phil. 1842. 12°. 1666
Homes and Haunts of. W. Howitt. New York, 1847. 2 v. 12°. 3009
Lectures on the English. W. Hazlitt. London. 1841. 12°. . 1875
Lives of the English. S. Johnson. London, 1810. 2 v. 8°. . . 686
The same. New York, 1843. Roy. 8°. . . . 1984, 2
Lives of the Scottish. London, 1821. 3 v. 16°. 78
Memoirs of the Loves of the. Mrs. A. Jameson. Phil. 1844. 12°. 2364
of Connecticut. Ed. by C. W. Everest. New York, 1847. 8°. . 2268
of Great Britain; with Criticisms. W. Hazlitt. Lond. 1825. 8°. 2245
of Great Britain. S. Johnson. Dublin, 1795–1804. 7 v. 8°. . 780

Vol. 1. Lives of the Poets and Criticisms.
2. Cowley; Denham; Milton; Butler; Rochester; Roscommon; Otway; Waller; Pomfret; Dorset; Stepney; J. Phillips; Walsh.
3. Dryden; Smith; Duke; King; Sprat; Halifax.
4. (Missing.)
5. Granville; Yalden; Tickell; Swift; Hammond; Somerville; Parnell; Savage; Broome.
6. (Missing.)
7. Ed. Moore; Cawthorne; Collins; Dyer; Shenstone; Mallet; Akenside; Gray; Littleton; Gay.
8. Young; Churchill; Lloyd; Falconer; Thomson.

Sacred, of England and America. R. W. Griswold. N.Y. 1850. 8°. 4700
Specimens of British. T. Campbell. Philadelphia, 1853. Roy. 8°. 5443
Specimens of Dutch. J. Bowring & H. S. Van Dyk. Lon. 1824. 12°. 2416
Specimens of the Early English. G. Ellis. London, 1845. 3 v. 12°. 5043
Specimens of English Dramatic. C. Lamb. N.Y. 1845. 2 v. 12°. 2402
Thoughts on the. H. T. Tuckerman. New York, 1846. 12°. . 2589
Poisons, Culinary. F. Accum. Philadelphia, 1820. 18°. . . . 2428
Poivre, M. le. Travels of a Philosopher. Baltimore, 1818. 12°. . . 1029
Poland, Fall of. L. C. Saxton. New York, 1851. 2 v. 12°. . . . 4604
History of. J. Fletcher. New York, 1831. 12°. 139
The same. (H. F. L.) New York, 1846. 12°. . 3683, 24
History of the Revolution in. J. Hordynski. Boston, 1833. 8°. . 622
under the Dominion of Russia. H. Harring. Boston, 1834. 12°. 711
Polar Regions of the Western Continent. W. J. Snelling. Bost. 1831. 8°. 2671
Polar Seas, Expedition to. F. von Wrangell. London, 1844. 12°. . 5002
The same. (H. F. L.) N.Y. 1848. 12°. 3683, 148
Discovery in. Sir J. Leslie and others. (H. F. L.) N.Y. 1843. 12°. 3683, 14
The same. New York, 1831. 16°. 818
Police and Crimes of London. London, 1829. 8°. 6018

Police of London. P. Colquhoun. London, 1800. 8°. 729
Policeman, Recollections of a. T. Waters. New York, 1852. 12°. . 4770
Polish Chiefs; an Historical Romance. New York, 1832. 2 v. 12°. . 212
Polite Education, Elements of. G. Gregory. Boston, 1801. 12°. . . 338
Politiques de tous les Cabinets de l'Europe. Paris, 1793. 2 v. 12°. . 3579
Political Economy. T. Chalmers. New York, 1832. 12°. . . . 533
A. Potter. (H. F. L.) New York, 1848. 12°. . . 3683, 183
Theo. Sedgwick. New York, 1836. 2 v. 12°. . . . 1125
J. Wade. London, 1835. 12°. 2109
Conversations on. Philadelphia, 1817. 12°. 489
Elements of. F. Wayland. New York, 1837. 8°. . . . 799
Illustrations of. H. Martineau. Philadelphia, 1834. 2 v. 24°. . 1464
in the United States. C. Colton. New York, 1848. 8°. . . 3211
John Hopkins's Notions on. Boston, 1833. 12°. 1543
Literature of. J. R. M'Culloch. London, 1845. 8°. . . . 2625
Manual of. E. P. Smith. New York, 1853. 12°. . . . 5337
New Theory of. S. Simpson. Philadelphia, 1831. 8°. . . 4020
Past, Present, and Future. H. C. Carey. Philadelphia, 1848. 8°. 2882
Principles of. H. C. Carey. Philadelphia, 1837. 3 v. 8°. . . 1787
Principles of. J. S. Mill. Boston, 1848. 2 v. 8°. . . . 3229
Treatise on. J. B. Say. Philadelphia, 1836. 8°. . . . 1794
Wealth of Nations. Adam Smith. London, 1850. 8°. . . 676
Political Ethics, Manual of. F. Lieber. Boston, 1838. 2 v. 8°. . . 1783
Political Grammar of United States. E. D. Mansfield. N. Y. 1834. 12°. 2562
Political Magazine. Vol. 2. London, 1781. 8°. 1404
Political Mirror; or, Review of Jacksonism. New York, 1835. 12°. . 1517
Political Parties of N.Y., Hist. of. J. D. Hammond. Cooperst. 1846. 2 v. 8°. 2847
Political Philosophy. Lord Brougham. London, 1849. 3 v. 8°. . . 1239
Polk Administration, History of. L. B. Chase. New York, 1850. 8°. . 3645
Pollok, R. Course of Time; a Poem. Boston, 1842. 12°. . . . 1021
Polly Peablossom's Wedding, and other Tales. J. B. Lamar. Phil. 1851. 12°. 3811
Polo, Marco, Travels of. H. Murray. (H. F. L.) N.Y. 1848. 12°. 3683, 173
Polyanthos; a Monthly Magazine. Boston, 1807, 1812–14. 5 v. 18°. . 40
Polynesia, History of. M. Russell. (H.F. L.) N.Y. 1848. 12°. . 3683, 158
Ponsonby; a Tale of Troublous Times. London, 1850. 2 v. 12°. . . 4242
Ponsonby, Ellinor. Discipline of Life. New York, 1848. 8°. . . 3238
Pride and Irresolution. New York, 1850. 8°. 3992
Pontiac, History of the Conspiracy of. F. Parkman, jun. Bost. 1851. 8°. 4519
Poole, H. W. Perfect Intonation, and Euharmonic Organ. N.H. 1850. 8°. 6016
Poole, J. Little Pedlington. New York, 1852. 2 v. 12°. . . . 4861
Oddities of London Life. Philadelphia, 1838. 2 v. 12°. . . 245
Paul Pry's Journal of a Residence. Philadelphia, 1836. 12°. . 893
Sketches and Recollections. Philadelphia, 1835. 2 v. 12°. . . 1098
Poole, Mrs. S. Englishwoman in Egypt. Philadelphia, 1845. 12°. . 2405
Poole, T. E. Life in Sierra Leone and Gambia. London, 1850. 2 v. 12°. 4583
Poole, W. F. Index to Periodical Literature. New York, 1853. Roy. 8°. 5444
Index to Subjects in Periodicals. New York, 1848. 8°. . . 3210
Poor Cousin; a Novel. Ellen Pickering. Philadelphia, 1849. 8°. . 3260

Poor Jack. F. Marryat. Philadelphia, n. d. 8°. 920
Poor Rich Man and Rich Poor Man. C. M. Sedgwick. N.Y. 1836. 12°. 103
Poore, B. P. Rise and Fall of Louis Philippe. Boston, 1848. 12°. . 2422
Pope, A. Poetical Works. Philadelphia, 1841. 8°. 2674
Pope Alexander VI. and Cæsar Borgia. A. Gordon. Phil. 1844. 8°. . 2894
Pope Joan; or, the Female Pontiff. G. W. M. Reynolds. N.Y. 1851. 8°. 3805
Pope Leo X., Life and Pontificate of. W. Roscoe. Lond. 1846. 2 v. post 8°. 2930
Popery in Power. J. Turnley. London, 1850. 8°. 4301
its Character and its Crimes. W. E. Tayler. London, 1851. 12°. 4441
Sevenfold Aspect of. G. Fisk. London, 1851. 12°. . . . 4213
Variations of. S. Edgar. New York, 1852. 8°. . . . 416
Popes of Rome, History of. L. Ranke. Philadelphia, 1841. 2 v. roy. 8°. 1949
Popkin, J. S., Memoirial of. C. C. Felton. Cambridge, 1852. 12°. . 4883
Popular Antiquities of Great Britain. J. Brand. Lond. 1848. 3 v. post 8°. 4369
Popular Delusions, Memoirs of. C. Mackay. Phil. 1850. 2 v. 12°. . 3668
Popular Ignorance, Essays on the Evils of. J. Foster. N. Y. 1850. 12°. 3662
Popular Lectures on Science and Art. D. Lardner. N.Y. 1846. 2 v. 8°. 2677
Popular Legends of Brittany. Boston, 1854. 12°. 5617
Population, Essay on. T. R. Malthus. Georgetown, 1809. 2 v. 8°. . 1973
Porter, Anna M. Fast of St. Magdalen. New York, 1819. 2 v. 12°. . 395
Hungarian Brothers. Philadelphia, 1809. 2 v. 12°. . . . 355
The same. London, 1850. 12°. 5648
Roche-Blanche. Boston, 1822. 2 v. 12°. 382
Village of Mariendorpt. Boston, 1821. 4 v. 12°. . . . 302
Porter, Miss C. B. (Editor.) Silver Cup of Sparkling Drops. Buf. 1852. 12°. 4449
Porter, C. T. Review of the Mexican War. Auburn, 1849. 12°. . . 3475
Porter, D. Cruise in the Pacific, 1812–14. Philadelphia, 1815. 2 v. 12°. 636
Porter, Jane. Pastor's Fireside. London, 1850. 2 v. 12°. . . . 5652
Scottish Chiefs. Philadelphia, 1850. 3 v. in 1. 24°. . . . 29
The same. London, 1853. 2 v. 12°. 5697
Thaddeus of Warsaw. Hartford, 1848. 24°. 20
The same. London, 1853. 12°. 5696
Porter, R. K. Campaign in Russia. Baltimore, 1806. 8°. . . . 690
Porter, W. S. Musical Cyclopædia. New York, 1850. 12°. . . . 4417
Porter, W. T. (Editor.) Quarter Race in Kentucky. Phil. 1846. 12°. . 3893
Porteus, B. Lectures on St. Matthew. Northampton, 1805. 8°. . . 619
Life. R. Hodgson. New York, 1811. 12°. 192
Portfolio; a Monthly Miscellany. Philadelphia, 1809–12. 8 v. 8°. . . 717
Fourth series. Vols. 1–22. Philadelphia, 1816–27. 8°. . . 4899
Portfolio; View of Manners and Customs. London, 1812. 8°. . . 661
Portland, Hist. of; and Jour. of Smith & Deane. N. Willis. Port. 1849. 8°. 3605
Portlock, J. E. Treatise on Geology. London, 1853. 12°. . . . 6038
Portraits of Illustrious Men of Gt. Britain. E. Lodge. Lond. n.d. 8 v. 12°. 3476
*Ports & Harbors of Gt. Britain. W. H. Bartlett. Lond. 1842. 2 v. 4°. 3742
Portugal, Journal of Residence in. London, 1847. 2 v. 12°. . . . 4576
Posey, F. Life. J. Hall. Boston, 1846. 12°. 1076, 19
Post-Office Guide. E. Bowen. New York, 1851. 8°. 4507
Pothier, R. J. Treatise on Maritime Contracts. Boston, 1821. 8°. . . 1401

Potiphar Papers. G. W. Curtis. New York, 1853. 12°. 5612
Potomac, Voyage of the, 1831-34. J. N. Reynolds. New York, 1835. 8°. 1980
Voyage of the, 1831-34. F. Warriner. New York, 1835. 12°. . 1256
Potter, A. Handbook for Readers and Students. New York, 1843. . 2197
The same. (H. F. L.) New York, 1848. 12°. . 3683, 165
Objects and Uses of Science and Literature. N. Y. 1848. 12°. 3683, 179
Political Economy. (H. F. L.) New York, 1848. 12°. . 3683, 183
and G. B. Emerson. School and Schoolmaster. N.Y. 1844. 12°. 5074
Pottleton Legacy. Albert Smith. London, 1850. 12°. 5031
Poultry; with Illustrations. W. C. L. Martin. London, n. d. Roy. 8°. 3635, 2
Poultry Book. J. C. Bennett. Boston, 1850. 12°. 3663
Poussin, G. T. United States; its Power and Progress. Phil. 1851. 8°. 4320
Powell, T. Living Authors of England. New York, 1849. 12°. . . 3439
Power of Beauty. J. T. Headley. New York, 1850. 12°. 4041
Power of Instruction; or, the Guilty Tongue. Boston, 1833. 12°. . 1476
Powhatan; a Metrical Romance. Seba Smith. New York, 1841. 12°. . 157
Practical Helps towards Formation of Character. I. Taylor. Bost. 1838. 16°. 87
Practical Navigator. N. Bowditch. New York, 1846. 8°. 2249
and Seaman's Daily Assistant. (No titlepage.) 8°. 1306
Pradt, M. de. Europe after the Cong. of Aix-la-Chapelle. Phil. 1820. 8°. 1388
Praed, W. M. Lillian, and other Poems. New York, 1852. 12°. . . 4784
Prairie, The. J. F. Cooper. New York, 1852. 12°. 1004
Prairie-Bird. C. A. Murray. New York, 1849. 8°. 2053
The same. London, 1853. 12°. 5730
Prairie Land, Life in. Eliza W. Farnham. New York, 1846. 12°. . 3011
Prairiedom; Rambles in Texas. New York, 1845. 12°. 2502
Prairies, Commerce of the. J. Gregg. New York, 1844. 2 v. 12°. . 2098
Prandi, F. Memoirs of Father Ripa. New York, 1846. 12°. . . 2511
Pray, I. C., jun. Prose and Verse. Boston, 1836. 12°. 116
Prayer, Book of Common. Philadelphia, 1843. 12°. 2449
Preacher and the King. L. Bungener. Boston, 1853. 12°. 5247
Preaching, Theory of. A. Vinet. New York, 1854. 12°. 5742
Pre-Adamite Earth. J. Harris. Boston, 1849. 12°. 3304
Preble, E. (Com.). Biography. S. P. Waldo. Hartford, 1823. 8°. . 651
Life. L. Sabine. Boston, 1848. 12°. 1076, 22
Precaution; a Novel. J. F. Cooper. New York, 1852. 2 v. 12°. . . 2960
Precious Metals, History of. J. L. Comstock. Hartford, 1849. 12°. . 3007
Preferment; or, My Uncle the Earl. Mrs. C. Gore. N.Y. 1840. 2 v. 12°. 1556
Prelude; a Poem. W. Wordsworth. New York, 1850. 12°. . . 3904
Prentice, G. D. Biography of Henry Clay. Hartford, 1831. 12°. . . 393
Prentice or Prentiss Family, Genealogy of. C. J. F. Binney. Bost. 1852. 8°. 4813
Presbyterian Church in West. New York. J. H. Hotchkin. N.Y. 1848. 8°. 3216
Prescott, W. H. Biographical and Critical Miscellanies. Boston, 1845. 8°. 2676

Charles Brockden Brown; Asylum for the Blind; Irving's Conquest of Granada; Cervantes; Sir Walter Scott; Chateaubriand's English Literature; Bancroft's United States; Mde. Calderon's Life in Mexico; Molière; Italian Narrative Poetry; Poetry and Romance of the Italians; Scottish Song; Du Ponté's Observations.

History of the Conquest of Mexico. New York, 1850. 3 v. 8°. . 1759

Prescott, W. H. History of the Conquest of Peru. N. Y. 1847. 2 v. 8°. 2793
History of Ferdinand and Isabella. New York, 1851. 3 v. 8°. . 947
Life of Charles Brockden Brown. Boston, 1838. 12°. . . 1076, 1
Present for an Apprentice. London, 1742. 16°. 6
President's Daughters. Fredrika Bremer. Boston, 1843. 12°. . . 1725
Part 2. Nina. New York, 1845. 8°. 1736
Presidents of the United States, Lives of. R. W. Lincoln. N.Y. 1842. 8°. 1825
Addresses and Messages of. New York, 1842. 8°. . . . 1782
Addresses and Messages of. E. Williams. N. Y. 1846. 2 v. 8°. . 2781
Memoirs and Administrations of. E. Williams. N.Y. 1849. 8°. 2067
Preston, D. R. Wonders of Creation. Boston, 1807. 2 v. 12°. . . 206
Pretenders, Memoirs of the. J. H. Jesse. Philadelphia, 1846. 2 v. 16°. 2573
Pretension. Sarah Stickney [Mrs. Ellis]. Philadelphia, 1837. 2 v. 12°. 942
Prevention Better than Cure. Mrs. S. Ellis. New York, 1847. 12°. . 2995
Provost. J. Galt. New York, 1822. 12°. 1940
Price, T. Wisdom and Genius of Shakspeare. Philadelphia, 1839. 8°. 2458
Prichard, J. C. Physical History of Man. London, 1813. 8°. . . 1914
Pride and Irresolution. Ellinor Ponsonby. New York, 1850. 8°. . 3992
Pride and Prejudice. Jane Austen. Philadelphia, 1838. 8°. . 1585, 1
The same. London, 1853. 12°. 5691
Prideaux, H. Old and New Testament Connected. N.Y. 1850. 2 v. 8°. 4711
Prideaux, T. S. Economy of Fuel. London, 1853. 12°. . . . 6085
Priest and the Huguenot. L. Bungener. Boston, 1853. 2 v. 12°. . . 5574
Priestcraft, History of, in all Ages. W. Howitt. New York, 1833. 12°. 2111
Priest, J. American Antiquities. Albany, 1833. 8°. 2121
Anti-Universalist; or, Fallen Angels. Albany, 1839. 8°. . . 3786
Priestley, J. Lectures on History and General Policy. Phil. 1803. 2 v. 8°. 598
Prime, W. C. Old House by the River. New York, 1853. 12°. . . 5347
Owl Creek Letters. New York, 1848. 12°. 3411
Princess, The; a Medley. A. Tennyson. Boston, 1848. 12°. . . 3100
Princess; or, the Beguine. Lady Morgan. Phil. 1835. 2 v. 12°. . . 1229
Prince and the Pedler. Ellen Pickering. Philadelphia, 1848. 8°. . 997
Princeton Pulpit. Edited by J. T. Duffield. New York, 1852. 8°. . 4842
Pringle, T. Narrative of Residence in South Africa. London, 1840. 8°. 2613
Prinsep, H. T. Tibet, Tartary, and Mongolia. London, 1851. 12°. . 5369
Printing, Art of. T. C. Hansard. Edinburgh, 1851. 12°. . . . 6270
in America, History of. I. Thomas. Worcester, 1810. 2 v. 8°. . 1376
Dictionary of the Art of. W. Savage. London, 1841. 8°. . . 5088
Prior, J. Life of Oliver Goldsmith. Philadelphia, 1837. 8°. . . 726
Memoir of Edmund Burke. Boston, 1854. 2 v. 12°. . . . 5542
Priors of Prague. W. J. Neale. Philadelphia, 1836. 2 v. 12°. . . 267
Priscilla; or, Trials for the Truth. J. Banvard. Boston, 1854. 12°. . 5644
Prismatics. R. Haywarde. New York, 1853. 12°. 5282
Prison Discipline in America. F. C. Gray. Boston, 1847. 8°. . . 2860
Prison Discipline Society's Reports, 1826–34. Boston, 8°. . . . 3251
Prisoner's Friend. Edited by C. Spear. Vols. 1–4. Boston, 1848–52. 8°. 5945
Prisons, Management of Convict. Col. Jebb. London, 1851. 8°. . . 5109
Private Life, Sermons on the Duties of. J. G. Palfrey. Bost. 1834. 8°. 1641

Prize Essays on the Congress of Nations. Boston, 1840. 8°. . . . 6017
Prize Poems; Boston Theatre, Sept. 1823. Boston, 1824. 12°. . . 490
Probus; or, Rome in the Third Century. W. Ware. N.Y. 1838. 2 v. 12°. 1109
Proclus. Commentaries on the Timæus of Plato. London, 1820. 2 v. 4°. 4858
Prochazka, Baron. Revelations of Hungary. London, 1851. 12°. . 4228
Procrastination; or, the Vicar's Daughter. London, 1850. 12°. . . 4280
Proctor, B. W. English Songs, and other Poems. Boston, 1844. 12°. . 1737
Essays and Tales in Prose. Boston, 1853. 2 v. 12°. . . . 5059
Progress and Prejudice. Mrs. C. Gore. New York, 1854. 12°. . . 6260
Progress of Nations. E. C. Seaman. New York, 1852. 12°. . . 4984
Prometheus Bound, and other Poems. Eliz. B. Browning. N.Y. 1851. 12°. 4870
Promissory Notes, Commentaries on the Law of. J. Story. Bost. 1847. 8°. 3593
Propellers, Screw, and their Steam Engines. J.W.Nystrom. Phil. 1852. 8°. 5085
Property and Labor, Essays on. F. Lieber. (H.F.L.) N.Y. 1848. 12°. 3683, 146
Prophecy of the Santon, and other Poems. Worcester, 1847. 12°. . . 3056
Prose Writers of America. R. W. Griswold. Philadelphia, 1847. 8°. . 2775
of Germany. F. H. Hedge. Philadelphia, 1848. 8°. 2872
Pro-Slavery Arguments. Harper, Hammond, and others. Phil. 1853. 12°. 5361
Protection and Free Trade. W. Phillips. Boston, 1850. 12°. . . 5270
Protestant Annual. Edited by C. Sparry. New York, 1847. 8°. . . 2817
Protestant Clergy, New Themes for. S. Colwell. Phil. 1852. 12°. . 5025
Protestantism, Defence of. C. H. Wharton. New York, 1817. 8°. . 3636
in France. A. Coquerel. Boston, 1854. 12°. 6145
Protestant Lectures on Romanism. London, 1851. 12°. 4611
Protestant Reformation in France. Mrs. Marsh. London, 1847. 2 v. 8°. 4643
Protestants, History of the French. C. Weiss. New York, 1854. 2 v. 12°. 5799
Proverbial Philosophy. M. F. Tupper. Philadelphia, 1846. 12°. . . 2146
Proverbs for the People. E. L. Magoon. Boston, 1849. 12°. . . 3186
Lessons in. R. C. Trench. New York, 1853. 12°. . . . 5206
Prussic Acid, Use in Diseases of the Breast. F. Magendie. N. H. 1820. 12°. 975
Psalms, and the New Testament. New York, 1848. 8°. 4077
arranged in the Order of Events. T. Bulfinch. Boston, 1853. 12°. 5072
Translated and Explained. J. A. Alexander. N. Y. 1851. 3 v. 12°. 4412
Public Characters, Sketches of. I. L. Robertson. New York, 1830. 12°. 562
and Public Events, 1783–1815. W. Sullivan. Boston, 1834. 12°. 1228
Public Economy in the United States. C. Colton. New York, 1848. 8°. 3211
Public Men of the Revolution. W. Sullivan. Philadelphia, 1847. 8°. . 2809
Public Statutes at Large of U. S. Ed. by R. Peters. Bost. 1845. 8 v. roy. 8°. 3243
Pückler Muskau (Prince). Tutti Frutti. New York, 1834. 12°. . . 2602
Tour in England, Ireland, and France, 1826–29. Phil. 1833. 8°. 2723
Pugin, A. Specimens of Gothic Architecture. London, 1821. 2 v. 4°. . 5101
*Paris and its Environs. London, 1833. 4°. 2014
Pulpit, British. W. Suddards. New York, 1845. 2 v. 8°. . . . 6019
Pulpit Portraits. J. R. Dix. Boston, 1854. 12°. 5584
Pulpit Sketches of English Preachers. J. R. Dix. London, 1852. 12°. . 6243
Pulte, J. H. Homœopathic Domestic Physician. New York, 1852. 12°. 4801
Pultock, R. Adventures of Peter Wilkins. London, 1844. 8°. . . 89
Pulaski, Count. Life. J. Sparks. Boston, 1844. 12°. . . 1076, 14

Pulszky, F. and T. White, Red, Black. New York, 1853. 2 v. 12°. . 5245
Pulszky, Theresa. Tales and Traditions of Hungary. Lond. 1851. 12°. 4240
Punchard, G. History of Congregationalism. Salem, 1841. 12°. . . 2118
Punch's Complete Letter Writer. D. Jerrold. London, 1853. 12°. 6234, 5
Comic Blackstone. G. A. à Beckett. Philadelphia, 1844. 12°. . 6323
Letters to his Son. D. Jerrold. London, 1853. 12°. . . 6234, 5
Prize Novelists, &c. W. M. Thackeray. New York, 1853. 12°. . 5266
Punishment by Death. G. B. Cheever. New York, 1849. 12°. . . 2576
of Death. C. Spear. Boston, 1844. 12°. 1938
of Death. J. Sega. Boston, 1830. 12°. 3370
of Death, Report on. R. Rantoul, jun. Boston, 1836. 8°. . . 646
of Death, Selection of Papers on. London, 1836. 2 v. 12°. . 2455
Punctuation, Treatise on English. J. Wilson. Boston, 1855. 16°. . 3858
Puritan, The; a Series of Essays. L. Withington. Bost. 1836. 2 v. 12°. 400
and his Daughter. J. K. Paulding. New York, 1849. 12°. . 3431
Puritans, History of the. D. Neal. New York, 1843. 2 v. 8°. . . 1820
in England, and Pilgrim Fathers. New York, 1849. 12°. . . 3399
Sketches of the. J. Stoughton. New York, 1848. 12°. . . 3171
Pursuit of Knowledge under Difficul. G. L. Craik. N.Y. 1844. 2 v. 16°. 824
The same. (H. F. L.) New York, 1846. 2 v. 12°. 3683, 94, 95
Putnam, G. P. American Facts. London, 1845. 12°. 2695
*Book-Buyer's Manual. New York, 1848. 8°. 2045
World's Progress; a Dictionary of Dates. New York, 1852. 8°. . 2041
Putnam, I. (Gen.). Life. W. Cutter. New York, 1847. 12°. . . 2984
Life. D. Humphreys. Boston, 1818. 12°. 190
Life. O. W. B. Peabody. Boston, 1844. 12°. . . . 1076, 7
Putnam, S. Analytical Reader. Dover, 1830. 12°. 362
Sequel to Analytical Reader. Dover, 1832. 12°. 363
Putnam's Monthly Magazine. Vols. 1–3 [continued]. N. Y. 1853–54. 8°. 5392
Puzzledom; or, Charades, Conundrums, Puzzles, &c. Phil. 1853. 8°. . 6008
Pycroft, J. Course of English Reading. New York, 1845. 12°. . . 2297
Pyne, G. Treatise on Perspective. London, 1852. 12°. 6049
Pym, J. Life. J. Forster. London, 1831. 12°. 1831, 3
Pynnshurst; his Wanderings, &c. D. MacLeod. New York, 1852. 12°. 1031
*Pyramids of Gizeh. H. Wyse. London, 1840. 3 v. 4°. 3794
Pyrenees, Summer and Winter in. Mrs. S. Ellis. London, 1841. 12°. . 4571
Pyrrhus, History of. J. Abbott. New York, 1854. 12°. . . . 6171

Q.

Q. Q., Contributions of. Jane Taylor. New York, 1850. 2 v. 12°. . 3664
The same. Boston, 1831. 2 v. 12°. 862
Quadroon; or, St. Michael's Day. J. H. Ingraham. N. Y. 1847. 2 v. 12°. 1599
Quadrupeds. Boston, 1830. 16°. 826
British. W. Macgillivray. Edinburgh, 1843. 12°. . . 4901, 17
Natural History of. (H. F. L.) N. Y. 1846. 2 v. 12°. 3683, 104, 164
Quakerism, Apology for. R. Barclay. Philadelphia, 1805. 8°. . . 1918

Quakers, The. (No titlepage.) 12°. 218
History of. W. Sewel. New York, 1844. 2 v. 8°. 3217
Quarrels of Authors. I. Disraeli. New York, 1814. 2 v. 12°. . . . 453
Quarter Race in Kentucky. Ed. by W. T. Porter. Phil. 1846. 12°. . 3893
Quar. Jour. of Science. Vols. 1-5, 7, 16, 17, 19, 21. Lon. & N.Y. 1817-26. 8°. 3614
*Quarterly Review. Vols. 1-92. London, 1809-53. 8°. 2826
The Indexes are Vols. 20, 40, 60, 80.
The same. Vols. 52-93 [continued]. 1834-53. Roy. 8°. . 2826
Papers from. New York, 1852. 12°. 4792
Quatre Mois dans les Pays-bas. Paris, 1830. 3 v. 16°. 2438
Queechy. Anna Warner. New York, 1852. 2 v. 12°. 1050
Quekett, J. Practical Treatise on the Microscope. London, 1848. 8°. . 4138
Queen of Denmark. Edited by Mrs. Gore. New York, 1846. 8°. . 2681
Queen's Necklace. A. Dumas. Philadelphia, 1851. 2 v. 8°. 4037
Queens of England, Lives of. Agnes Strickland. Phil. 1843. 11 v. 12°. 1911
The same. Philadelphia, 1849. 12 v. 12°. 3524
For contents, see *Strickland.*
of France, Memoirs of. Mrs. F. Bush. Phil. 1847. 2 v. 12°. . 2985
of Scotland, Lives of. Agnes Strickland. N.Y. 1851-53. 4 v. 12°. 4028
of Spain, Annals of. Anita George. New York, 1850. 12°. . 3505
Quentin Durward. Sir W. Scott. Boston, 1848. 2 v. 12°. . . 999, 29, 30
The same. Edinburgh, 1849. 2 v. 12°. . . 4100, 31, 32
The same. Edinburgh, 1850. Roy. 8°. 4531, 8
Questions for Literary Societies. S. Bailey. London, 1823. 8°. . . 6009
Quiet Heart, from Blackwood. New York, 1854. 8°. 5952
Quiet Husband. Ellen Pickering. Philadelphia, 1840. 2 v. 12°. . . 2187
Quill, C. The Working-Man. Philadelphia, 1839. 12°. 1520
Quincy, E. Wensley; a Story without a Moral. Boston, 1854. 12°. . 5860
Quincy, J. History of the Boston Athenæum. Cambridge, 1851. 8°. . 3803
History of Harvard University. Cambridge, 1840. 2 v. 8°. . 2237
Life of Samuel Shaw. Boston, 1847. 8°. 2810
Memoir of Josiah Quincy, jun. Boston, 1825. 8°. 1383
Municipal History of Boston. Boston, 1852. 8°. 567
Quinet, E. Roman Church and Modern Society. New York, 1845. 12°. 2512
Quinten Matsys; or, Blacksmith of Antwerp. New York, 1852. 8°. . 217
Quod Correspondence. J. J. Irving. Boston, 1842. 2 v. 12°. . . 1699
Quotations from Latin, French, Spanish, &c., Dictionary of. Phil. 1851. 12°. 4425
*Poetical, Dictionary of. Ed. by Mrs. S. J. Hale. Phil. 1851. 8°. 2683

R.

Rabelais, F. Works. Trans. by Urquhart and Motteux. Lon. 1849. 2 v. 8°. 3552
Race for Riches. W. Arnot. Philadelphia, 1853. 12°. 5339
Races, Natural History of. C. H. Smith. Boston, 1851. 12°. . . 4476
of Indian Archipelago. G. W. Earl. London, 1853. 12°. . . 5741
Unity of the Human. C. Caldwell. New York, 1830. 12°. . 925
Unity of the Human. T. Smyth. New York, 1850. 12°. . . 3857

Rachel Dyer. J. Neal. Portland, 1828. 12°. 521
Rachel Kell. New York, 1853. 12°. 5303
Racine, J. Œuvres Complètes de. Paris, 1819. 3 v. 16°. . . . 2431
    Théâtre Complet. Paris, 1847. 12°. 5558
Radcliffe, Mrs. Ann. Mysteries of Udolpho. Philadelphia, 1852. 24°. . 1855
Raffles, T. Letters from France, Savoy, Switzerland, &c. N.Y. 1818. 12°. 974
Raffles, Sir T. S. Life and Services, by his Widow. Lond. 1835. 2 v. 8°. 4505
Raguet, C. Free Trade Advocate. Philadelphia, 1829. 2 v. 8°. . . 1216
Raikes, Harriet. Marriage Contract. Boston, 1850. 8°. . . . 3640
Railroad Accidents Prevented. L. Turnbull. Philadelphia, 1854. 12°. . 6224
Railroad Jubilee at Boston, Sept. 1851. Boston, 1852. 8°. . . . 778
Railroad Laws & Charters of U. S. Gregg & Pond. Bost. 1851. 2 v. roy. 8°. 4317
Railroad, Steamboat, and Telegraph Book. J. Disturnell. N.Y. 1849. 12°. 55
Railroads, Hist., Construct., & Influences of. F. S. Williams. Lon. 1852. 8°. 5084
    Practical Treatise on. N. Wood. London, 1838. 8°. . . . 4340
Railway Economy. D. Lardner. New York, 1850. 12°. . . . 3874
Railways, Treatise on. R. M. Stephenson. London, 1850. 12°. . . 6077
Rainbow in the North. S. Tucker. London, 1851. 12°. . . . 4270
Rale, S. Life. C. Francis. Boston, 1848. 12°. 1076, 17
Raleigh, Sir W. History of the World. London, 1677. Folio. . . 3749
    Life. P. F. Tytler. Philadelphia, 1833. 8°. 1357, 3
    Life of. Mrs. A. T. Thomson. Philadelphia, 1831. 12°. . . 410
    Poems. London, 1845. 12°. 2505
Ralph Rutherford; a Nautical Romance. A. Fisher. N.Y. 1851. 8°. . 4502
Ramble from Sydney to Southampton. London, 1851. 12°. . . . 4443
Rambler, The. S. Johnson. Philadelphia, 1812. 4 v. 16°. . . . 22
    The same. New York, 1843. Roy. 8°. 1984, 1
Rambles and Reveries. H. T. Tuckerman. New York, 1841. 12°. . 1633
    in Sweden and Gottland. London, 1847. 8°. 4146
    of a Naturalist. J. D. Godman. Philadelphia, 1833. 12°. . . 67
Ramsay, A. Works; with Life. G. Chalmers. London, 1851. 3 v. 12°. 5044
Ramsay, D. History of the American Revolution. Phil. 1789. 2 v. 8°. 675
Randolph, J. Biography. L. Sawyer. New York, 1844. 8°. . . 2724
    Letters to a Young Relative. Philadelphia, 1834. 8°. . . . 1251
    Life. H. A. Garland. New York, 1850. 2 v. 8°. . . . 3999
Randolph, J. T. Cabin and Parlor. Philadelphia, 1852. 12°. . . 5000
Randolph, T. J. Mem. and Corres. of T. Jefferson. Bost. 1830. 4 v. 8°. 1405
Random Shots and Southern Breezes. L. F. Tasistro. N.Y. 1842. 2 v. 12°. 1656
Rangers; or, the Tory's Daughter. D. P. Thompson. Bost. 1851. 2 v. 12°. 4104
Ranke, L. Civil Wars and Monarchy in France. New York, 1853. 12°. 5345
    History of the Popes of Rome. Philadelphia, 1841. 2 v. roy. 8°. 1949
    History of Servia. London, 1853. Post 8°. 5921
Rankin, F. H. Visit to Sierra Leone, 1834. Philadelphia, 1836. 8°. 2228, 2
Rankin, J. Letters on American Slavery. Boston, 1838. 12°. . . 1546
Rantoul, R., jun. Memoirs, Speeches, and Writings. Boston, 1854. 8°. 5930
    Miscellaneous Orations, Reports, &c. Boston, 1832. 8°. . . 646
Raphael; or, Life at Twenty. A. Lamartine. New York, 1849. 12°. . 3344
Raphael's Cartoons, Book of. R. Cattermole. London, 1845. 8°. . . 5095

Rappers, The; or, Absurdities of Spirit-Rapping. New York, 1854. 12°. 5883
Raspail, F. V. Domestic Medicine. London, 1853. 12°. 6123
Rasselas. S. Johnson. Boston, 1811. 12°. 291
The same. New York, 1843. Roy. 8°. 1984, 1
Ratlin the Reefer. E. Howard. London, 1851. 12°. 5667
Raumer, F. von. America and the American People. N. Y. 1846. 8°. . 2633
England in 16th, 17th, and 18th Centuries. Lond. 1837. 2 v. 8°. 2842
Ravenscliffe. Mrs. Marsh. New York, 1852. 8°. 414
Rawle, W. View of the Constitution of United States. Phil. 1829. 8°. 2688
Rawson, J. Dictionary of Synonymical Terms. Philadelphia, 1850. 12°. 3577
Ray, I. Medical Jurisprudence of Insanity. Boston, 1853. 8°. . . 5386
Ray, J. Wisdom of God in Creation. London, 1722. 12°. . . . 5559
Rayner, B. L. Life of Thomas Jefferson. Boston, 1834. 8°. . . . 2630
Reach, A. B. Claret and Olives. New York, 1852. 12°. . . . 830
Readers and Students, Handbook for. A. Potter. New York, 1843. 12°. 2197
The same. (H. F. L.) New York, 1848. 12°. . 3683, 165
Reading, Course of English. J. Kent. New York, 1853. 12°. . . 5203
Course of English. J. Pycroft. New York, 1845. 12°. . . 2297
Readings for Every Day in Lent. Jeremy Taylor. New York, 1851. 12°. 3815
for the Young, from Writings of Sir W. Scott. Phil. 1848. 2 v. 12°. 3119
Rebel, and other Tales. E. L. Bulwer. New York, 1835. 12° . . 1147
Rebelliad; a Poem of Harvard. C. Stetson. Boston, 1842. 12°. . . 1694
Rebellion & Civil Wars in Eng., Hist. of. Earl Clarendon. Ox. 1826. 8 v. 8°. 2256
Rebels; or, Boston before the Revolu. Mrs. L. M. Child. Bost. 1850. 12°. 3869
Rebels and Tories; or, Blood of the Mohawk. L. Labree. N. Y. 1851. 8°. 4337
Receipts, Cyclopædia of 6000. A. J. Cooley. New York, 1846. 8°. . 3537
Recollections of a Chaperon. Lady Dacre. London, 1852. 12°. . . 5685
of a Housekeeper. C. Gilman. New York, 1842. 16°. . . 1861
of a Literary Life. Mary R. Mitford. New York, 1852. 12°. . 3752
of a Policeman. T. Waters. New York, 1852. 12°. . . . 4770
of the United States Army. Boston, 1845. 16°. 2432
Records of Bubbleton Parish. Boston, 1854. 12°. 6151
of my Life. John Taylor. New York, 1833. 8°. 1394
Recreations of a Merchant. W. A. Brewer. Boston, 1836. 12°. . . 280
Rector of St. Bardolph's. F. W. Shelton. New York, 1853. 12°. . 5079
Rectory Guest; a Novel. Mrs. Grey. New York, 1849. 8°. . . 6005
Rectory of Valehead. R. W. Evans. Philadelphia, 1832. 12°. . . 1501
Redburn; his First Voyage. H. Melville. New York, 1849. 12°. . . 3450
Redemption, History of. J. Edwards. New York, n. d. 12°. . . 430
Redfield, J. W. Comparative Physiognomy. New York, 1852. 8°. . 4947
Redgauntlet. Sir W. Scott. 1848. 2 v. 12°. 999, 33, 34
The same. Edinburgh, 1849. 2 v. 12°. . . . 4100, 35, 36
The same. Edinburgh, 1850. Roy. 8°. 4531, 9
The same. Exeter, 1824. 2 v. 24°. 91
Red Hand of Ulster. Mrs. J. Sadlier. Boston, 1850. 18°. . . . 3755
Red Race of America. H. R. Schoolcraft. New York, 1847. 8°. . . 2832
Red Rover. J. F. Cooper. New York, 1845. 2 v. 12°. . . . 412
Redskins; Conclusion of Littlepage MSS. J.F.Cooper. N.Y. 1846. 2 v. 12°. 2604

Redwood; a Tale. Catherine M. Sedgwick. New York, 1850. 12°. . 3627
Reed, H. Life of Joseph Reed. Boston, 1848. 12°. . . . 1076, 18
Reed, J. Life and Correspondence. W. B. Reed. Phil. 1847. 2 v. 8°. 2794
Reed, W. B. Life and Corres. of Joseph Reed. Phil. 1847. 2 v. 8°. . 2794
Reef Rovings in South Seas. E. T. Perkins. New York, 1854. 8°. . 5972
Reel in a Bottle. G. B. Cheever. New York, 1852. 12°. . . . 3753
Rees, J. Mysteries of City Life. Philadelphia, 1849. 12°. . . . 3291
Reese, D. M. Humbugs of New York. New York, 1838. 12°. . . 960
Letters to Wm. Jay on Slavery. New York, 1835. 12°. . . 2600
Reese, J. J. American Medical Formulary. Philadelphia, 1850. 12°. . 3671
Reeve, J. History of the Old and New Testament. Boston, 1849. 12°. 3681
Reflections on the Works of God. C. C. Sturm. London, 1808. 2 v. 24°. 1495
Reformation of the 16th Cen. J. H. M. D'Aubigné. N.Y. 1843–53. 5 v. 12°. 1717
in England and Ireland. W. Cobbett. Philadelphia, n. d. 12°. . 1777
of the Church of England. G. Burnet. Lond. 1841. 2 v. roy. 8°. 3993
The same. New York, 1843. 3 v. 8°. 2057
Memorial of the. B. Bennet. Edinburgh, 1748. 8°. . . . 476
Reforms, Hints towards. H. Greeley. New York, 1850. 12°. . . 3856
and Reformers, Sketches of. H. B. Stanton. New York, 1850. 12°. 3440
Regent's Daughter. A. Dumas. New York, 1845. 8°. 2229
Reginald Dalton. J. G. Lockhart. New York, 1823. 2 v. 12°. . . 339
Reginald Hastings. E. Warburton. New York, 1850. 8°. . . . 3989
Reginald Lyle. Miss Pardoe. Mew York, 1853. 12°. 6140
Register of Arts. T. G. Fessenden. Philadelphia, 1808. 8°. . . . 738
Reichenbach, C. von. Dynamics of Magnetisms, Heat, &c. Lond. 1851. 8°. 4159
Reid, Capt. M. Boy Hunters. Boston, 1853. 12°. 5082
Desert Home. Boston, 1852. 12°. 926
Rifle Rangers. New York, 1852. 8°. 4558
Scalp Hunters; or, Adven. in Northern Mexico. Lond. 1853. 12°. 4510
Young Voyageurs. Boston, 1854. 12°. 5621
Reid, S. C. M'Culloch's Texas Rangers. Philadelphia, 1847. 12°. . 3085
Reid, T. Essays on the Intellectual Powers. Cambridge, 1850. 12°. . 3571
Inquiry into the Human Mind. New York, 1824. 16°. . . 88
Works; with Life by D. Stewart. Charlestown, 1813. 4 v. 8°. . 4609

Vol. 1. Life and Writings of Dr. Reid; Account of Aristotle's Logic, with Remarks; Inquiry into the Human Mind.
2. Essays on the Intellectual Powers of Man.
3. The same, concluded; Essays on the Active Powers of the Human Mind.
4. The same, concluded.

Reid, T. Treatise on Clock and Watch Making. Phil. 1832. Roy. 8°. . 1646
Rejected Addresses. H. and J. Smith. Boston, 1851. 12°. . . . 1565
Relic of the Revolution. C. Herbert. Boston, 1847. 12°. . . . 3049
Religion, Analogy of. J. Butler. New York, 1843. 12°. . . . 1779
History of the Revival of, 1740. J. Tracy. Boston, 1842. 8°. . 1959
Influence of, upon Health. A. Brigham. Boston, 1835. 12°. . 1773
of Geology. E. Hitchcock. Boston, 1851. 12°. 4207
of Nature Delineated. London, 1731. 4°. 5117
Philosophy of. T. Dick. Philadelphia, 1845. 12°. . . 2357, 3
Pleasures of Personal. J. Newton. Boston, 1839. 12°. . . 1486

Religion, Thoughts on. B. Pascal. London, 1836. 12°. 1860
Religions, Book of. J. Hayward. Boston, 1842. 12°. 2095
of the World. F. D. Maurice. Boston, 1854. 12°. 5605
Religious Affections, Treatise on. J. Edwards. New York, n. d. 12°. . 311
Religious Experience, Thoughts on. A. Alexander. New York, 1851. 12°. 4743
Religious Knowledge, Encyclopædia of. Brattleboro', 1850. Roy. 8°. . 4729
Religious Liberty, Struggles & Triumphs of. E. B. Underhill. N.Y. 1851. 12°. 4194
Religious Magazine. Vol. 3. 1836. 8°. 952
Religious Maxims. T. C. Upham. Philadelphia, 1854. 18°. . . 6253
Religious Progress, Discourses on. W. R. Williams. Boston, 1851. 12°. 4408
Religious System, Practical View of. W. Wilberforce. Bost. 1815. 12°. 213
Religious Thoughts and Opinions. W. von Humboldt. Bost. 1851. 12°. 5757
Reliques of Ancient English Poetry. T. Percy. London, 1847. 3 v. 12°. 1279
Remarkable Characters. J. Caulfield. London, 1819. 8°. 5897
Remarkable Places, Visits to. W. Howitt. Philadelphia, 1842. 8°. . 1764
Reminiscences of an Old Traveller in Europe. Edinburgh, 1833. 12°. . 1574
of Congress. C. W. March. New York, 1850. 12°. 3919
of the Rhine, Switzerland, and Italy. Philadelphia, 1835. 2 v. 12°. 279
of Sixty-five Years. E. S. Thomas. Hartford, 1840. 2 v. 12°. . 2301
of Thought and Feeling. Boston, 1853. 12°. 5046
Rena; or, the Snow-Bird. Caroline L. Hentz. Philadelphia, 1851. 12°. 4428
Rennie, J. Natural History of Birds. (H. F. L.) N.Y. 1846. 12°. 3683, 98
Renwick, H. B. Life of John Jay. New York, 1841. 12°. 183
Renwick, J. Life of De Witt Clinton. New York, 1840. 12°. . . 1470
The same. (H. F. L.) New York, 1846. 12°. . . 3683, 125
Life of Robert Fulton. Boston, 1844. 12°. 1076, 10
Life of Alexander Hamilton. New York, 1841. 12°. . . . 183
Life of Count Rumford. Boston, 1848. 12°. . . . 1076, 15
Life of David Rittenhouse. Boston, 1844. 12°. . . . 1076, 7
Lives of J. Jay and A. Hamilton. (H. F. L.) N.Y. 1846. 12°. 3683, 129
Repealers, The. Lady Blessington. Philadelphia, 1833. 2 v. 12°. . . 534
Reports of the University of the State of New York. Albany, 1843–48. 8°. 2852
Representative Men. R. W. Emerson. Boston, 1850. 12°. . . . 3484
Reptiles of Massachusetts. D. H. Storer. Boston, 1839. 8°. . . . 722
Republican Christianity. E. L. Magoon. Boston, 1849. 12°. . . 3354
Reresby, Sir J. Memoirs and Travels. London, 1813. 8°. . . . 4945
Rescued Nun. Baron St. Leger. New York, 1844. 8°. . . 2167, 2
Resignation; an American Novel. Boston, 1825. 12°. 1047
Resurrection of the Body. G. Bush. New York, 1845. 12°. . . 2522
Retribution; or, Vale of Shadows. Mrs. E. D. E. N. Southworth. N.Y. 1853. 8°. 5431
Retrospect; or, Review of Providential Mercies. Boston, 1822. 12°. . 1039
Retrospective Review. Vols. 1–16. London, 1820–28. 8°. . . . 5487
Reuben Medlicott; or, the Coming Man. M. W. Savage. N.Y. 1852. 12°. 4931
Revere, J. W. Tour of Duty in California. New York, 1849. 12°. . 3345
Reveries of a Bachelor. D. G. Mitchell. New York, 1850. 12°. . . 4086
Revised Statutes of Massachusetts. Boston, 1836. Roy. 8°. . . . 1351
Supplement to the same. Boston, 1849. Roy. 8°. . . 1351, 2
Revival of Religion, 1740, History of. J. Tracy. Boston, 1842. 8°. . 1959

Revolutionary Incidents of Queen's Co. H. Onderdonk, jun. N.Y. 1846. 12°. 3824
Revolutionary Orders of Gen. Washington. J. Whiting. N.Y. 1844. 8°. 2236
Revolutionary War. — See *American Revolution.*
Reynolds, E. W. Our Campaign; or, Thoughts of Life. Bost. 1851. 12°. 4455
Reynolds, G. W. M. Angela Wildon. New York, 1852. 8°. . . 645
Gipsy Chief. New York, 1851. 8°. 4500
Kenneth; a Romance of the Highlands. New York, 1852. 8°. . 4696
Pickwick Abroad in France. New York, 1851. 8°. . . . 4313
Pope Joan; or, the Female Pontiff. New York, 1851. 8°. . . 3805
Reynolds, Sir J. Discourses at Royal Academy. Boston, 1821. 12°. . 2449
Life. J. Northcote. London, 1818. 2 v. 8°. 2542
Literary Works; with Memoir. London, 1835. 2 v. 12°. . . 2586
Reynolds, J. Recollections of Windsor Prison. Boston, 1834. 12°. . 536
Reynolds, J. N. Voyage of the Potomac, 1831–34. New York, 1835. 8°. 1980
Rhetoric and Belles Lettres, Lectures on. H. Blair. Phil. 1848. 8°. . 635
and Oratory, Lectures on J. Q. Adams. Cambridge, 1810. 2 v. 8°. 1945
Aristotle's Treatise on. Trans. by T. Buckley. Lond. 1850. Post 8°. 4381
Art of; or, Elements of Oratory. J. Holmes. Phil. 1849. 12°. . 3305
Elements of. R. Whately. Boston, 1845. 12°. 1804
Philosophy of. G. Campbell. New York, 1844. 12°. . . 2304
Rhind, W. Studies in Natural History. Edinburgh, 1830. 12°. . . 2132
Rhine, The. V. Hugo. New York, 1845. 12°. 2508
Rhine, Switzerland, and Italy, Reminiscences of. Phil. 1835. 2 v. 12°. 279
Rhoades, J. A. Cruise in a Whale Boat. New York, 1848. 8°. . . 3206
Rhode Island Bar, Memoirs of. W. Updike. Boston, 1842. 8°. . . 2680
Book. Anne C. Lynch. Providence, 1841. 12°. 1728
Spirit of '76 in. B. Cowell. Boston, 1850. 8°. 3646
Rhone, Darro, and Guadalquivir. Mrs. Romer. London, 1843. 2 v. 8°. 4648
Rhyming, Spelling, & Pronouncing Dictionary. J. Walker. Phil. 1852. 8°. 500
Ribault, J. Life. J. Sparks. Boston, 1848. 12°. 1076, 17
Rice, J. H. and B. H. Memoir of J. Brainerd Taylor. New York, 1833. 12°. 336
Rich, A. Companion of Latin Dictionary. London, 1849. 12°. . . 5645
Richard Cœur-de-Lion, Life of. G. P. R. James. N.Y. 1842. 2 v. 12°. 1877
Richard, M. Histoire du Tonquin. Paris, 1778. 2 v. 12°. . . . 376
Richard Edney, and Governor's Family. S. Judd, jun. Bost. 1850. 12°. 4073
Richard of York; or, the White Rose of England. New York, 1851. 8°. 3826
Richard Savage. C. Whitehead. London, 1853. 12°. 5729
Richard III. Caroline A. Halsted. Philadelphia, 1844. 8°. . . . 2266
History of. Sir T. More. Cambridge, 1834. 12°. . . . 383, 9
Richards, Mrs. A. M. Memories of a Grandmother. Boston, 1854. 12°. 6280
Richards, W. C. Day in the Crystal Palace. New York, 1853. 12°. . 5618
*Richardson, C. Dictionary of the English Language. Phil. 1851. 2 v. 4°. 4902
Richardson, Sir J. Arctic Searching Expedition. New York, 1852. 12°. 318
Richardson, S. Clarissa Harlowe. London, 1764. 8 v. 12°. . . . 1832
Pamela; or, Virtue Rewarded. London, 1801. 4 v. 12°. . . 1833
Richardson, Major. Ecarté; or, the Salons of Paris. N.Y. 1851. 8°. . 4556
Matilda Montgomerie. New York, 1851. 8°. 4521
Wacousta; or, the Prophecy. New York, 1851. 8°. 4036

Richardson, Maj. Wau-nan-gee; or, Massacre at Chicago. N.Y. 1852. 8°. 4810
Richelieu, Oxenstein, & others, Lives of. G. P. R. James. Phil. 1836. 12°. 247
Richelieu; a Tale. G. P. R. James. New York, 1847. 2 v. 12°. . . 2305
Richelieu in Love; an Historical Comedy. New York, 1844. 8°. . . 2171
Riches Have Wings. T. S. Authur. New York, 1847. 12°. . . 2441
Richest Men of Massachusetts, Catalogue of. Boston, 1851. 8°. . . 4533
Richter, J. P. F. Flower, Fruit, and Thorn Pieces. Bost. 1845. 2 v. 12°. 2321
Life and Autobiography. Boston, 1842. 2 v. 12°. . . . 2340
Walt and Vult; or, the Twins. Boston, 1846. 2 v. 12°. . . 2552
Rickards, R. India, and its Native Inhabitants. London, 1829. 2 v. 8°. 3955
Ride on Horseback to Florence, through France. London, 1842. 2 v. 8°. 2691
Ridner, J. P. Artist's Chronomatic Handbook. New York, 1850. 12°. 4059
Rienzi; a Tale. E. L. Bulwer. New York, 1836. 2 v. 12°. . . . 1119
The same. Philadelphia, 1836. 8°. 2228, 1
Rifle Rangers; or, Advent. in South Mexico. M. Reid. N.Y. 1852. 8°. 4558
Riggs, S. R. Gram. and Dict. of Dakota Language. Wash. 1852. 4°. 1756, 4
Right and Wrong in Boston in 1836. Boston, 1836–37. 3 v. 16°. . . 1513
Right of Visitation and Search. H. Wheaton. Philadelphia, 1842. 8°. 2833
Rimini, and other Poems. L. Hunt. Boston, 1844. 12°. . . . 2410
Rinaldo Rinaldini. Boston, 1824. 2 v. 12°. 1103
Ringelbergius, J. F. Treatise on Study. Philadelphia, 1847. 12°. . . 3769
Ringan Gilhaize. J. Galt. New York, 1823. 2 v. 12°. 1902
Ripa, Father, Memoirs of. F. Prandi. New York, 1846. 12°. . . 2511
Ripley, G. (Editor.) Specimens of Foreign Standard Literature. — See *Specimens.*
and B. Taylor. Handbook of Literature, &c. N. Y. 1852. 12°. . 4488
Rise of Iskander. B. Disraeli. Philadelphia, 1845. 8°. . . . 2689
Ritchie, L. Game of Life. Philadelphia, 1833. 8°. . . . 1357, 1
The same. New York, 1844. 8°. 2167, 3
Russia and the Russians. Philadelphia, 1836. 12°. . . . 234
The same. Philadelphia, 1836. 8°. 2228, 2
Robber of the Rhine. Philadelphia, 1833. 12°. 2704
Rittenhouse, D. Life. J. Renwick. Boston, 1844. 12°. . . 1076, 7
Rival Beauties; a Novel. Miss Pardoe. New York, 1848. 8°. . . 3234
River of the Water of Life. G. B. Cheever. New York, 1849. 12°. . 3432
Road-Making, Principles and Practice of. W. M. Gillespie. N.Y. 1847. 8°. 3076
Roads and Railroad Vehicles, and Modes of Travelling. Lond. 1839. 12°. 3135
Treatise on Common. H. Law. London, 1850. 12°. . . . 6068
Rob of the Bowl. J. P. Kennedy. New York, 1854. 12°. . . . 1104
Rob Roy. Sir W. Scott. Boston, 1848. 2 v. 12°. . . . 999, 7, 8
The same. Edinburgh, 1849. 2 v. 12°. . . . 4100, 7, 8
The same. Edinburgh, 1850. Roy. 8°. . . . 4531, 3
Robber; a Novel. G. P. R. James. New York, 1835. 2 v. 12°. . . 1111
Robber of the Rhine. L. Ritchie. Philadelphia, 1833. 12°. . . . 2704
Roberts, E. Embassy to Cochin-China, Siam, and Muscat. N. Y. 1837. 8°. 945
Roberts, Emma. Scenes & Characteristics of Hindostan. Phil. 1836. 2 v. 12°. 1123
The same. Philadelphia, 1836. 8°. 2228, 1
Roberts, W. History of Letter-Writing. London, 1843. 8°. . . 4530
Robertson, I. L. Sketches of Public Characters. New York, 1830. 12°. 562

Robertson, J. P. and W. P. Francia's Reign of Terror. Phil. 1839. 2 v. 12°. 979
Robertson, W. Historical Disquisition on India. Phil. 1812. 8°. . . 1295
The same. London, 1804. 12°. 535
History of America. London, 1803. 4 v. 8°. 1213
The same, abridged. (H. F. L.) New York, 1848. 12°. 3683, 185
History of Greece. Edinburgh, 1793. 8°. 724
History of the Reign of Charles V. Philadelphia, 1812. 3 v. 8°. . 1294
The same. New York, 1829. 8°. 1392
The same, abridged. (H. F. L.) New York, 1848. 12°. 3683, 186
History of Scotland. New York, 1844. 8°. 953
Works. London, 1809. 12 v. 8°. 4670

Vols. 1–4. History of America.
5–8. History of the Reign of Charles V.
9. Historical Disquisition on India.
10–12. History of Scotland.

Robespierre, M. Life. G. H. Lewes. Philadelphia, 1849. 12°. . . 3077
Robin Day, Adventures of. R. M. Bird. Philadelphia, 1839. 2 v. 12°. . 990
Robin Hood and Capt. Kidd. W. W. Campbell. New York, 1853. 12°. 5284
Garlands and Ballads. Ed. by J. W. Gutch. Lond. 1853. 2 v. 8°. 5471
Robinson, A. Life in California. New York, 1846. 12°. . . . 2549
Robinson, E. Biblical Researches in Palestine. Boston, 1841. 3 v. 8°. . 1985
(Editor.) Calmet's Dictionary of the Bible. Bost. 1843. Roy. 8°. 1439
Greek Lexicon of the New Testament. New York, 1850. Roy. 8°. 4349
Robinson, Mrs. [Talvi]. The Exiles. New York, 1853. 12°. . . 5513
Heloise; or, the Unrevealed Secret. New York, 1850. 12°. . 3870
Life's Discipline; a Tale of Hungary. New York, 1851. 12°. . 4030
Robinson, F. California and the Gold Regions. New York, 1849. 12°. 3335
Mexico and her Military Chieftains. Philadelphia, 1847. 12°. . 3033
Organization of the Army of the United States. Phil. 1848. 2 v. 12°. 3087
Robinson, G. Travels in Palestine and Syria. Paris, 1837. 2 v. 12°. . 2122
Robinson, J. H. Silver Knife. Boston, 1854. 12°. 5820
Robinson, P. F. Designs for Gate-Cottages, Lodges, &c. Lond. 1837. 4°. 2890
Designs for Village Architecture. London, 1837. 4°. 5977
Robinson Suisse. M. Wyss. Traduit par Elise Voiart. Paris, 1843. 8°. 4548
Robinson Crusoe, Life and Adventures of. D. De Foe. N. Y. 1853. 8°. 2848
The same. London, 1841. 8°. 2654, 2
The same. New York, n. d. 8°. 48
Robinson Crusoe, The Real. X. B. de Saintaine. Boston, 1851. 12°. . 4184
Roche, R. M. Children of the Abbey. Philadelphia, n. d. 3 v. in 1. 24°. 25
Roche-Blanche. Anna M. Porter. Boston, 1822. 2 v. 12°. 382
Rochefoucauld, F. Moral Reflections, Sentences, &c. N. Y. 1851. 12°. 404
Rockwell, C. Sketches of Foreign Travel. Boston, 1842. 2 v. 8°. . 1684
Rocky Mountains and Mexico, Adv. in. G. F. Ruxton. N. Y. 1848. 12°. 3097
Bonneville's Journal. Ed. by W. Irving. Phil. 1837. 2 v. 12°. . 510
The same. New York, 1849. 12°. 3366
Expedition to. J. C. Frémont. Buffalo, 1851. 12°. 2639
Lewis and Clarke's Expedition to. New York, 1843. 2 v. 12°. . 1745
The same. (H. F. L.) New York, 1848. 2 v. 12°. 3683, 154–5
Scenes in. R. B. Sage. Philadelphia, 1846. 12°. . . . 2922

Rocky Mountains, Tour beyond. S. Parker. Auburn, 1846. 12°. . . 3028
Travels over, 1845-46. P. J. De Smet. New York, 1847. 12°. . 3061
Roderick Random. T. Smollett. New York, 1840. 8°. 270
The same. Philadelphia, 1851. 8°. 801, 2
Rodman, Ella. Grandmother's Recollections. New York, 1851. 12°. . 4188
Rodolphos; a Franconia Story. J. Abbott. New York, 1850. 12°. . . 5294
Roe, A. S. James Montjoy; or, I've Been Thinking. N. Y. 1850. 12°. 3501
Time and Tide; or, Strive and Win. New York, 1852. 12°. . 4869
To Love and To be Loved. New York, 1851. 12°. 4096
Roger of Wendover. Flowers of History. London, 1849. 2 v. post 8°. 4366
Rogers, E. C. Philosophy of Mysterious Agents. Boston, 1853. 12°. . 5279
Rogers, H. Eclipse of Faith. Boston, 1852. 12°. 4915
Defence of the Eclipse of Faith. Boston, 1854. 12°. 5840
Essays, contributed to the Edinburgh Review. Lond. 1850. 2 v. 8°. 4329

Vol. 1. Life and Writings of Thomas Fuller; Andrew Marvell; Luther's Correspondence and Character; Life and Genius of Leibnitz; Genius and Writings of Pascal; Plato and Socrates; Structure of the English Language; Sacred Eloquence — British Pulpit; Vanity and Glory of Literature.

2. Right of Private Judgment; Anglicanism, or Oxford Tractarianism; Recent Developments of Tractarianism; Reason and Faith, their Claims and Conflicts; Revolution and Reform; Treatment of Criminals; Prevention of Crime.

Reason and Faith, and other Miscellanies. Boston, 1853. 12°. . 5280

Life and Writings of Thomas Fuller; Andrew Marvell; Luther's Correspondence and Character; Genius and Writings of Pascal; Sacred Eloquence — British Pulpit; Vanity and Glory of Literature; Right of Private Judgment; Reason and Faith, their Claims and Conflicts.

Rogers, N. P. Newspaper Writings. Concord, 1847. 12°. 3051
Rogers, S. Poetical Works. Philadelphia, 1836. 8°. 580
Poetical Works. Edited by E. Sargent. Boston, 1854. 12°. . 5866
Roget, P. M. Thesaurus of English Words. Boston, 1854. 12°. . . 5781
Rokeby; a Poem. Sir W. Scott. Philadelphia, 1839. 12°. . . 860, 4
and Don Roderick. Sir W. Scott. Edinburgh, 1848. 12°. . 4102, 9
Roland, Mde., Biography of. Mrs. L. M. Child. Boston, 1832. 12°. . 2153
History of. J. S. C. Abbott. New York, 1850. 12°. . . . 4418
Roland Cashel. C. Lever. New York, 1850. 8°. 3521
Rolandsitten; or, the Deed of Entail. C. F. W. Hoffman. N.Y. 8°. 2167, 1
Rollin, C. Ancient History. New York, 1845. 2 v. roy. 8°. . . 704
et M. Crevier. Histoire Romaine. Paris, 1782. 16 v. 12°. . 2239
History of Alexander's Successors. Hartford, 1823. 2 v. 12°. . 454
Rollo on the Atlantic. J. Abbott. Boston, 1854. 12°. 5622
in Paris. J. Abbott. Boston, 1854. 12°. 5782
in Switzerland. J. Abbott. Boston, 1854. 12°. 6207
Roman Antiquities. A. Adam. New York, 1819. 8°. 626
and Ancient Mythology. C. K. Dillaway. Boston, 1831. 12°. . 155
Roman Catholic Doctrines, Acknowledged. S. Capper. Lond. 1850. 8°. 5412
Roman Church and Modern Society. E. Quinet. New York, 1845. 12°. 2512
Roman Emperors, History of. C. A. Elton. London, 1825. 12°. . . 3341
Roman Empire, Decline and Fall of. E. Gibbon. Boston, 1850. 6 v. 12°. 3872
The same. New York, 1826. 6 v. 8°. 775

Roman Empire, Fall of. J. C. L. de Sismondi. London, 1834. 2 v. 12°. 2381
Roman History. J. Warburton. London, 1792. 12°. 312
Roman Republic, Captains of. H. W. Herbert. New York, 1854. 12°. 6215
History of. J. Michelet. New York, 1847. 12°. 2969
of 1849. Theo. Dwight. New York, 1851. 12°. 4262
Roman Tablets; or, Facts, Anecdotes, &c., of Rome. London, 1826. 12°. 6324
Roman Traitor. H. W. Herbert. New York, 1843. 12°. 5516
Romanism at Rome; Letters to R. B. Taney. N. Murray. N.Y. 1852. 12°. 1095
Controversy with. C. H. Wharton. New York, 1817. 8°. . . 3636
Essays on the Errors of. R. Whately. London, 1845. 8°. . . 2651
History of. J. Dowling. New York, 1845. Roy. 8°. . . . 2619
Lectures on. J. Cumming. Boston, 1854. 12°. 6155
Letters to Bishop Hughes on. N. Murray. New York, 1849. 12°. 3666
Protestant Lectures on. London, 1851. 12°. 4611
Romance and Reality. Letitia E. Landon. Philadelphia, 1847. 8°. 1343, 1
The same. London, 1852. 12°. 5684
Romance Dust from the Historic Placer. W. S. Mayo. N.Y. 1851. 12°. 4163
Romance of Abelard and Heloïse. O. W. Wight. New York, 1853. 12°. 5367
of Adventure. Boston, 1852. 12°. 4795
of American History. J. Banvard. Boston, 1852. 12°. . . 4924
of the Harem. Miss Pardoe. Philadelphia, 1839. 2 v. 12°. . 1049
of History; Italy. C. Macfarlane. New York, 1832. 2 v. 12°. 1549
of the History of Louisiana. C. Gayarré. New York, 1848. 12°. 3107
of Natural History. C. W. Webber. Philadelphia, 1852. 8°. . 4814
of Student Life Abroad. R. B. Kimball. New York, 1853. 12°. 5055
of Travel. N. P. Willis. New York, 1840. 12°. 2335
of Yachting. J. C. Hart. New York, 1848. 12°. 3185
Romances, Early English Metrical. G. Ellis. London, 1848. Post 8°. . 4370
of Real Life. New York, 1829. 2 v. 12°. 582
Romans, Epistle to, Notes on. A. Barnes. New York, 1851. 12°. . 4732
with a Commentary. A. A. Livermore. Boston, 1854. 12°. . 6265
Lectures on. T. Chalmers. New York, 1850. 8°. . . 3539, 2
Romans in Greece; an Ancient Tale. Boston, 1799. 12°. 472
under the Empire, History of. C. Merivale. Lond. 1852. 3 v. 8°. 5133
Romaunt, C. (Editor.) Island Home. Boston, 1852. 12°. 4639
Rome and Naples, Journey to, in 1817. New York, 1818. 12°. . . . 320
*and the Surrounding Scenery. W. B. Cooke. London, 1840. 4°. 5455
as Seen by a New Yorker. W. M. Gillespie. N.Y. 1845. 12°. . 2311
Child's First History of. E. M. Sewell. New York, 1849. 12°. . 3310
Emperors, Augustus to Constantine. Mrs. H. Gray. Lon. 1850. 12°. 4282
History of. T. Arnold. New York, 1851. 8°. 5115
History of, abridged. A. Ferguson. (H. F. L.) N.Y. 1848. 12°. 3683, 187
History of. O. Goldsmith. London, 1812. 2 v. 8°. 4983
The same. Philadelphia, 1818. 12°. 290
History of. T. Keightley. New York, 1851. 12°. 1768
History of. T. Livy. Tr. by Spillan & Edmonds. Lon. 1849. 4 v. 8°. 4379
The same. Trans. by G. Baker. Philadelphia, 1836. 8°. . 803
The same. New York, 1842. 5 v. 12°. . 1854, 24–28

Rome, History of. B. G. Niebuhr. Philadelphia, 1844. 5 v. 8°. . . 2235
Lectures on History of. B. G. Niebuhr. London, 1849. 3 v. 8°. 3600
History of. (Lardner's Cab. Cyclop.) London, 1842. 2 v. 12°. . 2380
History of. Rollin and Crevier (in French). Paris, 1782. 16 v. 12°. 2239
History of. L. Schmitz. Andover, 1847. 12°. 3020
Liberty of. S. Eliot. New York, 1849. 2 v. 8°. 3419
The same. Boston, 1853. 2 v. 12°. 5238
Romer, Mrs. Rhone, Darro, and Guadalquivir. London, 1843. 2 v. 8°. 4648
Temples and Tombs of Egypt, &c. London, 1846. 2 v. 8°. . . 4647
Romish Church, Blots on. Ed. by Miss Christmas. London, 1851. 12°. 4613
Romulus, History of. J. Abbott. New York, 1852. 12°. 5023
Rookwood; a Novel. W. H. Ainsworth. London, 1853. 12°. . . 5712
*Roorbach, O. A. Bibliotheca Americana. New York, 1852. 8°. . . 5993
Rördansz, C. W. European Commerce. Boston, 1819. 8°. . . . 639
Rory O'More. S. Lover. New York, 1851. 8°. 919
Roscoe, H. Lives of Eminent British Lawyers. Phil. 1841. 2 v. 12°. . 2162
Life of Wm. Roscoe. Boston, 1853. 2 v. 12°. 1055
Roscoe, W. Life of Lorenzo de' Medici. London, 1836. 12°. . . 1742
Life and Pontificate of Leo X. London, 1846. 2 v. post 8°. . 2930
*Rose, H. J. Biographical Dictionary. London, 1850. 12 v. 8°. . . 5488
Rose d'Albret; or, Troublous Times. G. P. R. James. N. Y. 1844. 8°. 2068
Rose Douglas; an Autobiog. of a Minister's Daughter. N.Y. 1851. 12°. 3830
Rose of the Parsonage. R. Giseke. Philadelphia, 1854. 12°. . . 6307
Rose of Tistelon. Emilie F. Carlen. New York, 1844. 8°. . . . 2743
Rosenberg, C. G. Jenny Lind in America. New York, 1851. 12°. . 4409
Rosenstein, I. G. Theory and Practice of Homœopathy. Louisv. 1840. 12°. 1892
Ross, Sir J. Last Voyage of, 1829–33. London, 1836. 8°. . . . 1496
Memoirs of Admiral de Saumarez. London, 1838. 2 v. 8°. . . 3638
*Second Voyage to the Arctic Regions. London, 1835. 4°. . . 5895
Roth, M. Gymnastic Free Exercises. Boston, 1853. 12°. . . . 6139
Rothelan; a Romance of English Histories. J. Galt. N. Y. 1825. 2 v. 12°. 1929
Roué, The. Philadelphia, 1836. 2 v. 12°. 253
Roughing it in the Bush. Mrs. S. Moodie. New York, 1852. 12°. . 4874
Round Table; a Collection of Essays. W. Hazlitt. London, 1841. 12°. 1872
Rowbotham, J. French Grammar. Boston, 1841. 12°. 283
Rowland, H. A. Common Maxims of Infidelity. New York, 1850. 12°. 3493
Rowson, Mrs. History of Charlotte Temple. New York, 1814. 12°. . 1864
Rowton, F. The Debater. London, 1846. 12°. 4055
Roxobel. Mrs. Sherwood. New York, 1831. 3 v. 18°. 92
Royal Preacher. J. Hamilton. New York, 1851. 12°. 4297
Royal Progress in Scotland. Sir T. D. Lauder. Edinburgh, 1843. 4°. . 4954
Royal Sisters; a Romance. Agnes Strickland. Boston, 1845. 16°. . 2190
Royalists and Roundheads; or, Days of Charles I. Lond, 1850. 3 v. 12°. 4250
Royle, J. F. Culture and Commerce of Cotton in India. Lon. 1851. 2 v. 8°. 4327
Royston Gower. T. Miller. Philadelphia, 1838. 2 v. 12°. . . . 970
Rubens, P. P., Life and Genius of. Dr. Waagen. London, 1840. 12°. . 3070
Ruffini, G. Lorenzo Benoni; or, Life of an Italian. N. Y. 1853. 12°. . 5512
Ruffner, H. Fathers of the Desert. New York, 1850. 2 v. 12°. . . 4062

Ruins, The. C. F. C. Volney. New York, 1828. 12°. 344
of Ancient Cities. C. Bucke. (H.F.L.) N. Y. 1846. 2 v. 12°. 3683, 134-5
of Athens, and other Poems. G. Hill. Boston, 1839. 8°. . . 1255
Rules in Deliberative Assemblies. L. S. Cushing. Boston, 1850. 12°. . 13
in Deliberative Assemblies. B. Matthias. Philadelphia, 1851. 18°. 4761
Rumford, Count, Essays. Boston, 1798. 2 v. 8°. 570
Life. J. Renwick. Boston, 1846. 12°. 1076, 15
Rural and Domestic Life of Germany. W. Howitt. N. York, 1842. 8°. 1719
Rural Essays. A. J. Downing. New York, 1853. 8°. 5175
Rural Homes; or, Sketches of Country Houses. G. Wheeler. N.Y.1851. 12°. 4495
Rural Hours. Susan F. Cooper. New York, 1850. 12°. . . . 3896
Rural Letters. N. P. Willis. New York, 1849. 12°. 3278
Rural Life of England. W. Howitt. Philadelphia, 1841. 8°. . . 2061
Rural Records; or, Village Life. Jas. Smith. London, 1845. 12°. . 3137
Ruschenberger, W. S. W. Elements of Natural History. Phil. 1850. 2 v. 12°. 4299
Rush, B. Diseases of the Mind. Philadelphia, 1830. 8°. . . . 2164
Rush, J. Philosophy of the Human Voice. Philadelphia, 1845. 8°. . 5086
Rush, R. Residence at the Court of London. Philadelphia, 1845. 8°. . 2646
Ruskin, J. Lectures on Architecture and Painting. Phil. 1854. 12°. . 6170
Modern Painters. New York, 1847. 3 v. 12°. 3018
Seven Lamps of Architecture. New York, 1849. 12°. . . . 2910
Stones of Venice. New York, 1851. 8°. 4119
Russell; a Tale of Reign of Charles II. G. P. R. James. N. Y. 1847. 8°. 2797
Russell, J. Tour in Germany, 1820-22. Boston, 1825. 8°. . . . 631
Russell, Lady Rachael. Letters. Boston, 1820. 12°. 9
The same. Philadelphia, 1854. 12°. 6187
and Madame Guyon. Lives. L. M. Child. Boston, 1832. 12°. . 2376
Russell, M. History of the Barbary States. (H. F. L.) N. Y. 1846. 12°. 3683, 73
History of Egypt. (H. F. L.) New York, 1846. 12°. . 3683, 23
History of Nubia and Abyssinia. (H. F. L.) N. Y. 1848. 12°. 3683, 61
History of Palestine. (H. F. L.) New York, 1846. 12°. . 3683, 27
History of Polynesia. (H. F. L.) New York, 1848. 12°. . 3683, 158
Life of Cromwell. (H. F. L.) New York, 1848. 2 v. 12°. 3683, 62, 63
Russell, W. American Elocutionist. Boston, 1844. 12°. . . . 2142
Exercises in Elocution. Boston, 1841. 12°. 2128
Lessons in Enunciation. Boston, 1843. 12°. 1889
Rudiments of Gesture. Boston, 1838. 12°. 1899
Extraordinary Men. London, 1853. 12°. 5343
Russell, W. History of Ancient Europe. Philadelphia, 1801. 2 v. 8°. . 1966
History of Modern Europe to 1763. Philadelphia, 1822. 4 v. 8°. . 1998
The same, abridged. Hanover, 1810. 12°. 1023
The same, cont. to 1815. C. Coote. Phil. 1822. 2 v. 8°. 1998, 5, 6
Russell, W. S. Guide to Plymouth. Boston, 1846. 12°. . . . 2974
Russia. Marquis de Custine. New York, 1854. 12°. 6146
Age of Peter the Great. B. Kamenski. London, 1851. 12°. . 4615
and the Eastern Question. R. Cobden. Boston, 1854. 12°. . 5794
and Emperor Nicholas. London, 1846. 3 v. 12°. 4422
and Poland, Travels in. R. Johnston. New York, 1816. 8°. . 1397

Russia and the Russians. L. Ritchie. Philadelphia, 1836. 12°. . . 234
and the Russians in 1842. J. G. Kohl. Phil. 1843. 2 v. in 1. 8°. 2684
and Turkey; Czar and the Sultan. A. Gilson. N. Y. 1853. 12°. 5571
as it Is. Count A. de Gurowski. New York, 1854. 12°. . . 5919
Czar, his Court and People. J. S. Maxwell. N. York, 1848. 12°. 3115
History of. W. K. Kelly. London, 1854. 2 v. post 8°. . . 6196
Military and Political Power of. New York, 1817. 8°. . . 1331
Progress of. D. Urquhart. London, 1853. 12°. 5544
Secret History of the Court of. J. H. Schnitzler. Lond. 1847. 2 v. 8°. 4658
Secret Memoirs of the Court of. London, 1800. 2 v. 8°. . . 3647
The same. Philadelphia, 1802. 8°. 611
under Nicholas I. Trans. by A. C. Sterling. London, 1841. 12°. 3136
Russian Literature, History of. F. Otto. Oxford, 1839. 8°. . . . 3789
Russian Poets, Specimens of. J. Bowring. Boston, 1822. 12°. . . 1928
Russian Shores of the Black Sea. L. Oliphant. New York, 1854. 12°. 5791
Russians and the Knout. G. de Lagny. New York, 1854. 12°. . . 5857
Russo-Turkish Campaigns. F. R. Chesney. New York, 1854. 12°. . 5830
Ruth; a Novel. Mrs. Gaskell. Boston, 1853. 12°. 5223
Ruth Emsley; the Betrothed Maiden. W. H. Carpenter. Phil. 1850. 12°. 3891
Ruxton, G. F. Adventures in Mexico and Rocky Mount. N.Y. 1848. 12°. 3097
Life in the Far West. New York, 1849. 12°. 3438
Ryan, M. Medical Jurisprudence. Philadelphia, 1832. 8°. . . . 4553
Ryan, W. R. Personal Adv. in California, 1848–49. Lond. 1850. 2 v. 12°. 4232
Ryle, J. C. Wheat or Chaff? New York, 1852. 12°. 927

S.

Sabbath; a Poem. New York, 1805. 12°. 849
Sabbath, The Christian, in its Various Aspects. Edinburgh, 1850. 12°. . 4225
Sabbath Morning Readings: Genesis. J. Cumming. Boston, 1854. 12°. 5872
Exodus. J. Cumming. Boston, 1854. 12°. 6239
Sabin, E. R. Life and Reflections of Charles Observator. Bost. 1816. 12°. 214
Sabine, L. American Loyalists. Boston, 1847. 8°. 2789
Life of Edward Preble. Boston, 1848. 12°. 1076, 22
Sacred Biography. H. Hunter. Philadelphia, 1832. 8°. 1288
Sacred History of the World. S. Turner. New York, 1832. 12°. . . 115
The same. (H. F. L.) New York, 1846. 3 v. 12°. 3683, 32, 72, 84
Sacred Mountains. J. T. Headley. New York, 1847. 12°. . . . 2989
Sacred Poets of England and America. R. W. Griswold. N.Y. 1850. 8°. 4700
Sacred Scenes and Characters. J. T. Headley. New York, 1850. 12°. . 3833
Sacred Streams; or Rivers of the Bible. P. H. Gosse. N. Y. 1852. 12°. 4482
Sad Tales and Glad Tales. Boston, 1828. 12°. 514
Sadlier, Mrs. J. Red Hand of Ulster. Boston, 1850. 18°. . . . 3755
Sage, J. Works; with Memoir. Edinburgh, 1844. 3 v. 8°. 4686

Vol. 1. Memoir of Life and Times of John Sage; Editor's Preface; Fundamental Charter of the Presbytery in Scotland.
2, 3. Principles of the Cyprianic Age with regard to Episcopal Power and Jurisdiction.

Safford, W. H. Life of H. Blennerhassett. Cincinnati, 1853. 12°. . 5815
Sailor, Life of a. F. Chamier. London, 1852. 12°. 5689
Sailor's Horn-Book. H. Piddington. New York, 1848. 8°. . . . 3241
Sailors' Life and Sailors' Yarns. New York, 1847. 12°. . . . 2938
Sailors and Saints; or, Matrimonial Manœuvres. N. York, 1829. 2 v. 12°. 1170
St. Botolph's Church, Boston (Eng.). Boston (Eng.), 1842. 8°. . . 5396
St. Domingo, Description of Spanish. Philadelphia, 1796. . . . 3787
History and Condition of. J. Brown. Philadelphia, 1839. 2 v. 12°. 3510
St. George; or, Canadian League. W. C. McKinnon. Halifax, 1852. 2 v. 12°. 189
St. Giles and St. James. D. Jerrold. London, 1851. 12°. . . 6234, 1
St. John, B. Adventures in the Libyan Desert. New York, 1849. 12°. 3287
Purple Tints of Paris. New York, 1854. 12°. 5808
Village Life in Egypt. Boston, 1853. 2 v. 12°. 4998
St. John, J. A. Lives of Celebrated Travellers. N.Y. 1846. 3 v. 12°. 3683, 38–40
St. John, P. B. French Revolution in 1848. New York, 1848. 12°. . 2454
St. John, S. Elements of Geology. New York, 1851. 12°. . . . 4438
Saint Leger; or, Threads of Life. R. B. Kimball. N. York, 1850. 12°. 3474
St. Leon; a Novel. W. Godwin. London, 1850. 12°. . . . 5647
St. Petersburg, Pictures from. E. Jerrmann. New York, 1852. 12°. . 5062
St. Pierre, J. H. B. de. Paul and Virginia. Philadelphia, 1849. 18°. . 4461
Studies of Nature. London, 1801. 4°. 708
St. Real, Abbé. Conspiracy of the Spaniards, 1618. Boston, 1838. 12°. 1484
St. Ronan's Well. Sir W. Scott. Boston, 1848. 2 v. 12°. . . 999, 31, 32
The same. Edinburgh, 1849. 2 v. 12°. . . 4100, 33, 34
The same. Edinburgh, 1850. Roy. 8°. . . . 4531, 8
St. Valentine's Day. Sir W. Scott. Boston, 1848. 2 v. 12°. . . 999, 41, 42
The same. Edinburgh, 1849. 2 v. 12°. . . 4100, 42, 43
The same. Edinburgh, 1850. Roy. 8°. . . . 4531, 11
Saints, Lives of the. A. Butler. New York, 1845. 8°. 5996
Saints' Everlasting Rest. R. Baxter. Boston, 1850. 12°. . . . 1017
Santine, X. B. de. Picciola. Philadelphia, 1849. 12°. 3838
The Real Robinson Crusoe. Boston, 1851. 12°. 4184
Woman's Whims; or, the Female Barometer. N. Y. 1850. 12°. . 3676
Salad for the Solitary. New York, 1853. 12°. 5383
Salander and the Dragon. F. W. Shelton. New York, 1852. 16°. . 4398
Salathiel. G. Croly. Cincinnati, 1847. 2 v. 12°. 3149
Salem, Mass., Annals of. J. B. Felt. Salem, 1845–49. 2 v. 12°. . . 2521
Salem Witchcraft, Account of. J. Thacher. Boston, 1831. 12°. . . 839
History of. C. W. Upham. Boston, 1831. 12°. 886
Salle, R. de la. Life. J. Sparks. Boston, 1844. 12°. . . . 1076, 11
Sallust, C. C. Works. Trans. by W. Rose. New York, 1842. 12°. 1854, 5
Salmagundi. W. Irving and J. K. Paulding. New York, 1835. 2 v. 12°. 1813
Salmonia; or, Days of Fly-Fishing. Sir H. Davy. London, 1844. 12°. 6276
Salt Water Bubbles. J. S. Sleeper. Boston, 1854. 12°. . . . 6213
Salverte, E. Philosophy of Magic. London, 1846. 2 v. 8°. 4683
Sam Slick, the Clockmaker. T. C. Haliburton. Philadelphia, 1849. 12°. 3348
Sampson, M. B. Rationale of Crime, and its Treatment. N.Y. 1846. 12°. 2933
Sand, George. — See *Dudevant, Mde.*

Sandboys at the Great Exhibition. H. Mayhew. New York, 1852. 8°. 4807
Sandeau, J. Hunting the Romantic. New York, 1852. 12°. . . . 4878
Sands, R. C. Writings in Prose and Verse. New York, 1834. 2 v. 8°. . 1233
Sandwich Islands, History of. J. J. Jarves. Boston, 1844. 8°. . . . 1748
Life in. H. T. Cheever. New York, 1851. 12°. 4453
Notes. New York, 1844. 12°. 6162
Residence in. C. S. Stewart. Boston, 1839. 12°. . . . 53
Scenes and Scenery in. J. J. Jarves. Boston, 1843. 12°. . . 2298
Sanitary Condition of Cities, Report on. Philadelphia, 1849. 8°. . . 3987
Sanitary Report of Massachusetts. Boston, 1850. 8°. 3791
Santa Fé Expedition. G. W. Kendall. New York, 1850. 2 v. 12°. . 1765
Santa Fé, Exped. from, to Navajo Country. J. H. Simpson. Phil. 1852. 8°. 3586
Santarem, Viscount. Americus Vespucius & his Voyages. Bost. 1850. 12°. 4018
Santo Sebastiano; or, the Young Protector. Boston, 1833. 3 v. 12°. . 2471
Saracen; or, Matilda and Malek Adhel. Mde. Cottin. N.Y. 1810. 2 v. 12°. 855
Saracens, History of. S. Ockley. London, 1847. Post 8°. . . . 3556
Sarawak; its Inhabitants and Productions. H. Low. London, 1848. 8°. 4671
Sargent, E. First-Class Standard Reader. Boston, 1854. 12°. . . . 5816
(Editor.) Poetical Works of Thomas Campbell. Bost. 1854. 12°. 5743
(Editor.) Poetical Works of Samuel Rogers. Boston, 1854. 12°. 5866
(Editor.) Select Works of Benj. Franklin. Boston, 1853. 12°. . 5637
Standard Speaker. Philadelphia, 1852. 8°. 614
Sargent, J. Memoir of Henry Martyn. New York, n. d. 12°. . . . 447
Sargent, L. M. Hubert and Ellen, and other Poems. Boston, 1815. 18°. 33
Temperance Tales. Boston, 1852. 12°. 4622
Sartain's Magazine. Vols. 5–10. Philadelphia, 1849–52. 8°. . . . 3531
Satanstoe; or, the Littlepage MSS. J. F. Cooper. N.Y. 1845. 2 v. 12°. 2472
Sartor Resartus. T. Carlyle. Boston, 1837. 12°. 346
Saturday Evening. I. Taylor. Boston, 1833. 12°. 2355
Saul; a Poem. W. Sotheby. Boston, 1808. 12°. 846
Saulcy, F. de. Dead Sea and Bible Lands. Philadelphia, 1854. 2 v. 12°. 6306
Saumarez, Admiral de. Memoirs and Corres. J. Ross. Lond. 1838. 2 v. 8°. 3638
Saunders, F. Memories of the Great Metropolis. New York, 1852. 12°. 4756
Saurin, J. Sermons. New York, 1847. 2 v. 8°. 4717
Savage, The. Philadelphia, 1810. 12°. 411
Savage, M. W. Bachelor of the Albany. New York, 1848. 12°. . . 2878
Falcon Family; or, Young Ireland. Boston, 1848. 12°. . . . 2898
Reuben Medlicott; or, the Coming Man. New York, 1852. 12°. 4931
Savage, W. Dictionary of the Art of Printing. London, 1841. 8°. . 5088
Savarin, B. Physiology of Taste. Philadelphia, 1854. 12°. . . . 5598
Sawyer, L. Biography of John Randolph. New York, 1844. 8°. . . 2724
Sawyer, L. A. Dissertation on Servitude. New Haven, 1837. 12°. . 1536
Organic Christianity. Boston, 1854. 12°. 6249
Sawyer, F. W. Plea for Amusements. New York, 1847. 12°. . . 3060
Saxe, J. G. Poems. Boston, 1850. 12°. 3318
Poems. Boston, 1851. 12°. 4499
Saxe-Weimar, Duke of. — See *Bernhard*.
Saxon in Ireland. London, 1851. 12°. 4230

Saxton, L. C. Fall of Poland. New York, 1851. 2 v. 12°. . . . 4604
Say, J. B. Treatise on Political Economy. Philadelphia, 1836. 8°. . 1794
Saymore, S. E. Hearts Unveiled. New York, 1852. 12°. . . . 816
Scalp Hunters; or, Advent. in Northern Mexico. M. Reid. Lond. 1853. 12°. 4510
Scandinavia, History of. A. Crichton. New York, 1844. 2 v. 12°. . 1859
in 1850. W. Hurton. London, 1851. 2 v. 12°. 4257
Scandinavians, Ancient. M. Mallet. London, 1847. Post 8°. . . 3561
Scarlet Letter; a Romance. N. Hawthorne. Boston, 1850. 12°. . . 3653
*Scenery of Massachusetts. Northampton, 1842. 4°. 3795
Scenes and Songs of Social Life. I. F. Shephard. Boston, 1846. 12°. . 2929
at Washington; a Story. New York, 1848. 12°. 3101
in my Native Land. Mrs. L. H. Sigourney. Boston, 1845. 12°. . 2299
in our Parish. New York, 1833. 12°. 156
in the Rocky Mountains, Oregon, California, &c. Phil. 1846. 12°. 2922
where the Tempter has Triumphed. New York, 1849. 12°. . 3402
Schaff, P. History of the Apostolic Church. New York, 1853. 8°. . 5448
Schefer, L. Artist's Married Life. Boston, 1849. 12°. 3333
Schelling, F. W. J. Philosophy of Art. London, 1845. 12°. . . 2394
Schiller, F. von, Characters of. Mrs. E. F. Ellet. Boston, 1839. 12°. . 988
Æsthetic Letters, Essays, &c. Trans. by J. Weiss. Bost. 1845. 12°. 2345
Early Dramas and Romances. London, 1849. Post 8°. . . 3560

The Robbers; Fiesco; Love and Intrigue; Demetrius; The Ghost-Seer; The Sport of Destiny.

Ghost-Seer. London, 1853. 2 v. 12°. 5698, 5699
Historical Dramas. London, 1847. Post 8°. 3555
History of the Revolt in Netherlands. New York, 1847. 12°. . 2953
History of the Thirty Years' War. New York, 1846. 12°. . . 2954
Life. Boston, 1833. 12°. 427
Life. T. Carlyle. New York, 1846. 12°. 2498
Maid of Orleans. London, n. d. 12°. 2979
Poems and Ballads. Trans. by E. L. Bulwer. N. York, 1844. 12°. 2140
and Goethe, Correspondence of. New York, 1845. 2 v. 12°. . 2341
and Körner, Correspondence of. London, 1849. 3 v. 12°. . . 4585
Schlegel, A. W. von. Lectures on Dramatic Art and Liter. Phil. 1833. 8°. 1958
Schlegel, F. von. Æsthetic and Miscellaneous Works. Lon. 1849. Post 8°. 4373

Letters on Christian Art; Essays on Gothic Architecture; Romance-Poetry of the Middle Ages; Study of Romantic Poetry and Genius; Limits of the Beautiful; Language and Wisdom of the Indians.

Lectures on the History of Literature. New York, 1844. 12°. . 2344
Lectures on Modern History. London, 1849. Post 8°. . . 4375
Philosophy of History. London, 1846. Post 8°. 2343
Philosophy of Life and Language. London, 1847. Post 8°. . . 3080
Schleiden, M. J. Poetry of the Vegetable World. Cincinnati, 1853. 12°. 5316
Schlesier, —. Life of Wm. von Humboldt. New York, 1853. 12°. . 5243
Schlosser, F. C. History of the Eighteenth Century. Lond. 1843. 8 v. 8°. 5148
Schmitz, L. History of Rome. Andover, 1847. 12°. 3020
Schnitzler, J.H. Secret Hist. of Court and Gov. of Russia. Lon. 1847. 2 v. 8°. 4658
Schoedler, F. Book of Nature; an Introduc. to the Sciences. Phil. 1853. 8°. 5441

Schomburgk, R. H. Fishes of Guiana. Edinburgh, 1843. 2 v. 12°. 4901, 39, 40
School and Schoolmaster. A. Potter and G. B. Emerson. N.Y. 1844. 12°. 5074
School Architecture. H. Barnard. New York, 1854. 8°. . . . 5959
School for Fathers. T. Gwynne. New York, 1852. 12°. . . . 4923
School Returns of Massachusetts, 1838–39. Boston, 1839. 8°. . . 1616
Schoolmaster; Essays on Practical Education. London, 1836. 2 v. 12°. . 5041
For contents, see *Education.*
Schools, The Bible in our Public. G. B. Cheever. New York, 1854. 12°. 5749
Schoolcraft, H. R. Adventures in Ozark Mountains. Phil. 1853. 8°. . 5393
Expedition to Itasca Lake, 1832. New York, 1834. 8°. . . 3235
Indian Tales and Legends. New York, 1839. 2 v. 12°. . . 240
*Indian Tribes of North America. Washington, 1851–54. 4 v. 4°. 1723
Lead Mines of Missouri. New York, 1819. 8°. 1369
Notes on the Iroquois. Albany, 1847. 8°. 2841
Red Race of America. New York, 1847. 8°. 2832
Thirty Years' Residence with Indian Tribes. Phil. 1851. 8°. . 4544
Travels through the Northwest. Albany, 1821. 8°. . . . 771
Schubert, G. H. Mirror of Nature. Philadelphia, 1849. 12°. . . 3343
Schwarz, J. Descriptive Geog. and Sketch of Palestine. Phil. 1850. 8°. 3985
Science and Art, Lectures on. D. Lardner. New York, 1846. 2 v. 8°. . 2677
and Arts, Quarterly Journal of. — See *Quarterly.*
Literature and Art, Dictionary of. W.T. Brande. N.Y. 1848. Roy.8°. 2641
Martyrs of. Sir D. Brewster. (H. F. L.) New York, 1846. 12°. 3683, 130
Pleasures of. W. M. Rogers. Boston, 1836. 12°. . . . 898
Poetry of. R. Hunt. Boston, 1850. 12°. 4082
Sciences, History of the Inductive. W. Whewell. London, 1837. 3 v. 8°. 2273
Philosophy of. A. Comte. Ed. by G. H. Lewes. Lon. 1853. Post 8°. 5936
Philosophy of the Inductive. W. Whewell. Lond. 1840. 2 v. 8°. 2692
Scientific and Literary Journal. Boston, 1837. 8°. 951
Scientific and Literary Treasury. S. Maunder. London, 1848. 12°. . 4109
Scientific Dialogues. J. Joyce. London, 1846. Post 8°. . . . 4363
Scientific Knowledge, Cream of. London, 1841. 16°. 2400
Scientific Tracts. Conducted by J. V. C. Smith. Vol. 2. Bost. 1834. 12°. 859
Scientific Tracts for the Diffusion of Useful Knowledge. Bost. 1836. 12°. 898

Thacher, B. B. Self Education.
Park, R. Outline of Philosophy.
Alcott, W. A. Early Rising.
Howard, D. H. May-Flowers.
Jackson, C. T. Nat. Hist. of Water.
Rogers, W. M. Pleasures of Science.
Ladd, W. History of Peace Societies.
Graham, S. Science of Human Life.
Parker, J. R. History of Telegraphs.
Coffin, R. A. Combustion.
Fish, S. Granite Rock.
Fish, S. Theory of the Earth.

Scituate, Mass., History of. S. Deane. Boston, 1831. 8°. . . . 1446
Scotland. J. G. Kohl. Philadelphia, 1844. 8°. 2684
and the Scotch. Catherine Sinclair. New York, 1840. 12°. . 2414
Border Antiquities of. Sir W. Scott. Edinburgh, 1834. 12°. 4101, 7
Gazetteer of. J. P. Lawson. Edinburgh, n. d. 12°. . . . 5037
Genius of. R. Turnbull. New York, 1847. 12°. . . . 3017
History of. Sir W. Scott. Cambridge, 1830. 2 v. 12°. . . 380
History of. W. Robertson. New York, 1844. 8°. . . . 953
Queens of. Agnes Strickland. New York, 1851–53. 4 v. 8°. . 4028
Scenes and Legends of North of. H. Miller. Boston, 1851. 12°. 4464

Scotland, Summer in. J. Abbott. New York, 1848. 12°. 3110
Scots Worthies. J. Howie. Glasgow, 1839. 2 v. 8°. 2059
The same. New York, 1853. 8°. 4938
Scott, C. R. Rambles in Egypt and Candia. London, 1837. 2 v. 8°. . 3195
Scott, David. Memoir. W. B. Scott. Edinburgh, 1850. 8°. . . 5142
Scott, John. Paris Revisited in 1815. Boston, 1816. 12°. . . . 174
Scott, Jos. Geographical Dictionary of the U. States. Phil. 1805. 8°. . 1269
Scott, R., and O. Byrne. Practical Cotton Spinner. Phil. 1851. 8°. . 4539
Scott, R. B. Strategematicon; or, Ancient Military Policy. Lond. 1811. 8°. 1315
Scott, T. Treatises on Theological Subjects. Middletown, 1817. 6 v. 12°. 397
Scott, Sir W. Autobiography. Philadelphia, 1831. 12°. 1024
Critical and Miscellaneous Essays. Philadelphia, 1841. 3 v. 12°. 1772
Doom of Devorgoil; a Melo-Drama. New York, 1830. 12°. . 537
History of Scotland. Cambridge, 1830. 2 v. 12°. 380
Lay of the Last Minstrel. Boston, 1845. 12°. 69
Letters on Demonology and Witchcraft. New York, 1830. 16°. . 817
The same. (H. F. L.) New York, 1843. 12°. . . 3683, 11
Life. J. G. Lockhart. Philadelphia, 1837. 2 v. 8°. . . . 1259
The same. Edinburgh, 1848. 10 v. 12°. 4103
Life. D. MacLeod. New York, 1852. 12°. 5053
Life of Napoleon. Philadelphia, 1827. 3 v. 8°. 1612
Lives of the Novelists. Boston, 1826. 2 v. 12°. 1151
Paul's Letters to his Kinsfolk. Edinburgh, 1816. 8°. . . . 632
Tales of the Crusaders. New York, 1835. 8°. 1361
Tales of a Grandfather. Philadelphia, 1828. 2 v. 16°. . . . 108
Readings for the Young, from the Writings of. Phil. 1848. 2 v. 12°. 3119
Redgauntlet. Exeter, 1824. 2 v. 24°. 91
Poetical Works. Edinburgh, 1848. 12 v. 12°. 4102

Vols. 1-4. Scottish Border Minstrelsy.
5. Sir Tristrem.
6. Lay of the Last Minstrel.
7. Marmion.
8. Lady of the Lake.
Vol. 9. Rokeby; Don Roderick.
10. Lord of the Isles.
11. Bridal of Triermain, &c.
12. Dramas.

The same. Philadelphia, 1839. 6 v. 12°. 860

Vol. 1. Lay of the Last Minstrel; Ballads, Songs, &c.
2. Marmion; and Occasional Pieces.
3. Lady of the Lake; Vision of Don Roderick.
4. Rokeby; Bridal of Triermain.
5. Lord of the Isles; Field of Waterloo; Miscellanies.
6. Harold the Dauntless; Dramatic Pieces.

Prose Works. Boston, 1829. 6 v. 12°. 399

Vol. 1. Life of John Dryden.
2. Life of Jonathan Swift.
3, 4. Biographical Memoirs.
5. Paul's Letters to his Kinsfolk.
6. Chivalry, Romance, and the Drama.

The same. Edinburgh, 1834. 28 v. 12°. 4101

Vol. 1. Life of John Dryden.
2. Memoirs of Jonathan Swift.
3, 4. Memoirs of Eminent Novelists.
5. Paul's Letters to his Kinsfolk.
6. Chivalry, Romance, and the Drama.
7. Essay on Border Antiquities.
8-16. Life of Napoleon.
17-21. Periodical Criticism.
22-26. Tales of a Grandfather: Scotland.
27, 28. Tales of a Grandfather: France.

Scott, Sir W. Waverley Novels. Boston, 1848. 54 v. in 27. 12°. . 999

Vols. 1, 2. Waverley.
3, 4. Guy Mannering.
5, 6. Antiquary.
7, 8. Rob Roy.
9, 10. Black Dwarf; Old Mortality.
11, 12. Heart of Mid-Lothian.
13, 14. Bride of Lammermoor; Legend of Montrose. } Tales of My Landlord.
15, 16. Ivanhoe.
17, 18. Monastery.
19, 20. Abbot.
21, 22. Kenilworth.
23, 24. Pirate.
25, 26. Fortunes of Nigel.
27, 28. Peveril of the Peak.
29, 30. Quentin Durward.
31, 32. St. Ronan's Well.
33, 34. Red Gauntlet.
35, 36. Tales of the Crusaders: Betrothed; Talisman.
37, 38. Woodstock.
39, 40. Highland Widow; Two Drovers; Surgeon's Daughter.
41, 42. Saint Valentine's Day. } Chronicles of the Canongate.
43, 44. Anne of Geierstein.
45, 46. Count Robert of Paris.
47, 48. Castle Dangerous.
49–52. Stories from Scottish History.
53, 54. Stories from French History. } Tales of a Grandfather.

The same. Edinburgh, 1849. 48 v. 12°. 4100

Vols. 1, 2. Waverley.
3, 4. Guy Mannering.
5, 6. Antiquary.
7, 8. Rob Roy.
9. Black Dwarf; Old Mortality.
10. Old Mortality.
11. Old Mortality; Heart of Mid-Lothian.
12. Heart of Mid-Lothian.
13. Heart of Mid-Lothian; Bride of Lammermoor.
14. Bride of Lammermoor.
15. Legend of Montrose. } Tales of My Landlord.
16, 17. Ivanhoe.
18, 19. Monastery.
20, 21. Abbot.
22, 23. Kenilworth.
24, 25. The Pirate.
26, 27. Fortunes of Nigel.
28–30. Peveril of the Peak.
31, 32. Quentin Durward.
33, 34. St. Ronan's Well.
35, 36. Red Gauntlet.
37. Betrothed.
38. Talisman. } Tales of the Crusaders.
39, 40. Woodstock.
41. The Highland Widow; Two Drovers; My Aunt Margaret's Mirror; Tapestried Chamber; Laird's Jock.
42, 43. Fair Maid of Perth.
44, 45. Anne of Geierstein.
46, 47. Count Robert of Paris; Castle Dangerous.
48. Castle Dangerous; Surgeon's Daughter; Glossary for the Entire Work.

The same. (Abbotsford Ed.) Edinb. 1850. 12 v. roy. 8°. 4531

Vol. 1. Waverley; Guy Mannering.
2. Antiquary; Black Dwarf; Old Mortality.
3. Rob Roy; Heart of Mid-Lothian.
4. Bride of Lammermoor; Ivanhoe; Legend of Montrose.
5. Monastery; Abbot.
6. Kenilworth; Pirate.
7. Fortunes of Nigel; Peveril of the Peak.
8. Quentin Durward; St. Ronan's Well.
9. Red Gauntlet; Tales of the Crusaders.
10. Woodstock; Chronicles of Canongate.
11. Fair Maid of Perth; Anne of Geierstein.
12. Count Robert of Paris; Castle Dangerous, &c.

Scott, Gen. Winfield. Life. E. D. Mansfield. New York, 1846. 12° . 2598
and A. Jackson. Lives. J. T. Headley. New York, 1852. 12°. 4985

Scott, William. Lessons in Elocution. Boston, 1814. 12°. 957
Scott, Wm. B. Memoir of David Scott. Edinburgh, 1850. 8°. . . . 5142
Scottish Adventurers. (No titlepage.) 12°. 509
Scottish Bards. New York, 1854. 8°. 5436
Scottish Biography, Popular. W. Anderson. Edinburgh, 1842. 12°. . 3601
Scottish Chiefs. Jane Porter. Philadelphia, 1850. 3 v. in 1. 24°. . 29
The same. London, 1853. 2 v. 12°. 5697
Scottish Female Characters. J. Anderson. New York, 1851. 12°. . 4471
Scottish History, Stories from. Sir W. Scott. Boston, 1848. 4 v. 12°. 999, 49–52
The same. Edinburgh, 1849. 5 v. 12°. . . . 4101, 22–26
Scottish Language, Dictionary of. J. Jamieson. Edinburgh, 1846. 8°. . 5137
Scottish Life, Lights and Shadows of. J. Wilson. New York, 1849. 12°. 394
Scottish Poets, Lives of; with portraits. London, 1821. 3 v. 16°. . . 78
Scottish Writers, Lives of. D. Irving. Edinburgh, 1850. 2 v. 12°. . 6269
Scourge of the Ocean. Philadelphia, 1851. 8°. 906
Scout; or, Black Riders of Congaree. W. G. Simms. N.Y. 1854. 12°. 6226
Scouting Expeditions of Texas Rangers. S. C. Reid. Phil. 1847. 12°. . 3085
Screw Propellers and their Steam Engines. J. W. Nystrom. Phil. 1852. 8°. 5085
Scriptural Heroes; Sketches of the Puritans. J. Stoughton. N.Y. 1848. 12°. 3171
Scripture Lands; with 24 Maps. J. Kitto. London, 1850. Post 8°. . 4391
Scripture, Typology of. P. Fairbairn. Philadelphia, 1852. 2 v. 8°. . 4710
Scriptures, Authenticity and Inspiration of. A. Alexander. Phil. 1850. 12°. 4744
Scriptures, Coincidences in. J. J. Blunt. New York, 1851. 8°. . . 4704
Scrivener, I.W. Laconia; or, Legends of White Mount. Boston, 1854. 12°. 6238
Sculpture and the Plastic Art. Boston, 1850. 12°. 3480
and Sculptors, Sketches of. Mrs. H. F. Lee. Bost. 1854. 2 v. 12°. 5590
Painting, and Architecture, Hist. of. J. S. Memes. Bos. 1834. 12°. 1003
Sea and the Sailor; Notes on France & Italy. W. Colton. N. Y. 1851. 12°. 4439
Sea King; a Nautical Romance. Philadelphia, 1851. 8°. 4132
Sea Lions; or, the Lost Sealers. J. F. Cooper. New York, 1849. 12° . 3350
Sealsfield, C. Cabin Book. London, 1852. 12°. 2088
Seaman, E. C. Progress of Nations. New York, 1852. 12°. . . . 4984
Seaman's Friend; Sea Terms, &c. R. H. Dana, jun. Boston, 1851. 12°. 4254
Sears, R. (Editor.) Pictorial Library. New York, 1847. 8°. . . . 4800
Pictorial Family Magazine. Vols. 3–5. New York, 1846–49. 8°. 4950
Seaside and Fireside. H. W. Longfellow. Boston, 1850. 12°. . . 3482
Seasons, The. J. Thomson. Boston, 1810. 16°. 47
Book of. W. Howitt. Philadelphia, 1831. 16°. 1048
Pictorial Calendar of. Mary Howitt. London, 1854. Post 8°. . 5920
Second Love. Martha Martell. New York, 1851. 12°. 4157
Secret Belt of the Invisibles. A. Dumas. New York, 1848. 8°. . . 3534
Secret Church of Paris in 16th Century. M. A. S. Barber. Lon. 1851. 12°. 4608
Secret Foe. Ellen Pickering. Philadelphia, 1841. 2 v. 12°. . . . 2708
Secret History of the Court and Cabinet of St. Cloud. Phil. 1806. 8°. . 349
Secret Journals of Congress of the Confederation. Boston, 1820. 2 v. 8°. 1274
Secret Memoirs of the Court of Petersburg. Philadelphia, 1802. 8°. . 611
The same. London, 1800. 2 v. 8°. 3647
Secret Passion. F. Williams. New York, 1848. 8°. 2806

Secret Proceedings in the Convention at Philadelphia, 1787. Rich. 1839. 12°. 587
Sedgwick, Catherine M. Clarence. New York, 1849. 12°. 3423
Biog. and Poetical Remains of L. M. Davidson. N. Y. 1851. 12°. 1613
Home. Boston, 1841. 18°. 2196
Hope Leslie. New York, 1842. 2 v. 12°. 188
Letters from Abroad. New York, 1841. 2 v. 12°. . . . 1626
Life of Lucretia M. Davidson. Boston, 1844. 12°. . . 1076, 7
Linwoods. New York, 1835. 2 v. 12°. 1086
Live and Let Live. New York, 1837. 12°. 918
Means and Ends; or, Self-Training. Boston, 1839. 12°. . . 17
New England Tale, and Miscellanies. New York, 1852. 12°. . 4986
Poor Rich Man and Rich Poor Man. New York, 1836. 12°. . 103
Redwood. New York, 1850. 12°. 3627
Tales and Sketches. Second Series. New York, 1844. 16°. . . 809
Sedgwick, Mrs. Alida; or, Town and Country. New York, 1844. 8°. 2086
Allen Prescott. New York, 1834. 2 v. 12°. 466
Sedgwick, T. Discourse on the American Citizen. N. York, 1847. 8°. 3197
Public and Private Economy. New York, 1836–38. 2 v. 12°. . 1125
Seer, The. L. Hunt. London, 1841. Roy. 8°. 2614
Sega, J. True Civilization. Boston, 1830. 12°. 3371
Ségur, P. de. Expedition of Napoleon to Russia. N. Y. 1845. 2 v. 12°. 325
The same. (H. F. L.) New York, 1847. 2 v. 12°. 3683, 141, 142
History of Charles VIII. Philadelphia, 1842. 2 v. 12°. . . 3081
Selden, J. Table Talk. Cambridge, 1831. 12°. 383, 2
Select British Eloquence. C. A. Goodrich. New York, 1852. Roy. 8°. . 5083
Select Circulating Library, Waldie's. Philadelphia, 1835–38. 4 v. 4°. . 2034

1835. Roscoe, T. Fall of Granada.
Sharp, R. Letters and Essays.
Burnes, A. Travels into Bokhara.
Pilcher, Mde. Siege of Vienna.
Barham. R. H. My Cousin Nicholas.
Memes, J. S. Life of Wm. Cowper.
Opie, Mrs. A. Tale of Trials.
Alexander, J. E. Sketches of Portugal.
1836. Groly, G. Tales of the St. Bernard.
Marryat, F. Naval Annual.
Campbell, T. Letters from the South.
Keightley, T. The Crusaders.
Baillie, Joanna. New Dramas.
Boys, E. Captivity in France & Flanders.
Flint, T. Journal in Louisiana, 1835.
Murray, Lady. Lives of G. & Lady Baillie.
Barrow, G. Visit to Iceland, 1834.
Raumer, F. von. England in 1835.
Johnstone, Mrs. Clan Albin.
Warren, S. Diary of a Physician.
Madrid in 1835.
Hall, B. Schloss Hainfeld.
Wraxall, Sir N. W. Posthumous Memoirs of his own Time.
West, Mrs. Gossip's Story.
1837. Cottin, Mde. The Saracen.
Wraxall, Sir N. W. Historical Memoirs.
Marmaduke Paull.
Mexican Antiquities.
Gurney Papers.
Dickinson, T. Wreck of the Thetis.
Prior, J. Life of Goldsmith.
Guillemard, R. Advent. of Fr. Sergeant.
Ainsworth, W. H. Crichton.
Carne, J. Letters from the East.
Dutens, M. Memoirs of a Traveller.
Warren, S. Diary of a Physician.
Edom of the Prophecies.
Pardoe, Miss. City of the Sultan.
Revolt of the Tartars.
Ritter C. Researches in Island of Hayti.
Stickney, Sarah. Pretension.
Respectability, a Tale.
Ward, R. P. St. Lawrence.
1838. Ward, R. P. Fielding; or, Society.
Gurney Papers.
Johnson, W. R. Lecture on Schools of Art.
Matthews, H. Diary of an Invalid.
Landon, L. E. Ethel Churchill.
Household Wreck, a Tale.
Hogarth, G. Musical Hist. and Biography.
Reed, H. Lect. on Literary Opportunities.
Hopkinson, J. Lecture on Common Sense.
Genlis, Mde. de. Memoirs of Marchioness de Bonchamps.
Saintine, X. B. Picciola.
Pardoe, Miss. River and the Desert.
Brougham, H. George IV. & Queen Caroline.
Inglis, H. D. Rambles in Spain.
Kuzzilbash, a Tale of Khorasan.
Bethune, G. W. Lecture on Socrates.
Herve, F. Residence in Greece and Turkey.
Gurney Papers.
Mitchell, J. Life of Wallenstein.
Tyson, J. R. Lecture on Am. Revolution.
Scoresby, Rev. Mr. Case of Capt. Stewart.
Lamb, Miss. Mrs. Leicester's School.
Downing, C. T. Fan-Qui in China.
Mulgrave, Lord. Yes and No.
Young, A. Memoir of N. Bowditch.

Selborne, Natural History of. G. White. London, 1851. Post 8°. . 4178
The same. London, 1853. 12°. 2192
The same. (H. F. L.) New York, 1848. 12°. . . 3683, 147
Selby, P. J. Pigeons and Parrots. Edinburgh, 1843. 2 v. 12°. 4901, 9, 10
Select Passages from Great Authors. London, 1852. 12°. . . . 6273
Selections from Taylor, Latimer, Hall, &c. B. Montagu. N. Y. 1845. 12°. 2493
Self-Control; a Novel. Mary Brunton. Boston, 1848. 12°. . . . 3128
The same. London, 1850. 12°. 5650
Self-Culture of Women. Maria G. Grey and Sister. Boston, 1851. 12°. 4195
Self-Deception; or, Hist. of a Human Heart. Mrs. Ellis. N.Y. 1851. 3v. 8°. 4014
Self-Education; or, Means of Moral Prog. Baron Degerando. Bost. 1832. 12°. 2255
Philosophy of. B. B. Thatcher. Boston, 1836. 12°. . . . 898
Self-Formation; or, the History of an Individual Mind. Bost. 1846. 12°. 2557
Self-Made Men of America. J. Frost. New York, 1848. 12°. . . 3176
Selkirk, J. Recollections of Ceylon. London, 1844. 8°. . . . 4650
Semmes, R. Service Afloat and Ashore. Cincinnati, 1851. 12°. . . 4319
Senator's Son; or, the Maine Law. M. V. Fuller. Cleveland, 1853. 12°. 5324
Sense and Sensibility. Jane Austen. London, 1853. 12°. . . . 5690
The same. Philadelphia, 1838. 8°. 1585, 2
Seraphim, and other Poems. Elizabeth B. Barrett. London, 1838. 12°. 2475
Sergeant, J. Select Speeches. Philadelphia, 1832. 8°. 1409
Serious Call to a Holy and Devout Life. W. Law. Boston, 1818. 12°. . 329
Sermons to Asses, &c. J. Murray. London, 1819. 8°. 1364
Serpent Symbol. E. G. Squier. New York, 1851. 8°. 4118
Servia, History of. L. Ranke. London, 1853. Post 8°. 5921
Service Afloat; Narrative of a British Naval Officer. Phil. 1833. 8°. 1357, 2
Service Afloat and Ashore during Mex. War. R. Semmes. Cin. 1851. 12°. 4319
Servitude, Dissertation on. L. A. Sawyer. New Haven, 1837. 12°. . 1536
Seven Brothers of Wyoming. New York, 1852. 8°. 629
Seven Capital Sins. E. Sue. New York, 1849. 8°. 2896
Pride; Avarice; Anger; Envy; Voluptuous.
Seven Lamps of Architecture. J. Ruskin. New York, 1849. 12°. . . 2910
1776; or, the War of Independence. B. J. Lossing. New York, 1847. 8°. 2818
Sévigné, Mde. de, and her Contemporaries. Philadelphia, 1842. 2 v. 12°. 1680
Sewall, J. M. Miscellaneous Poems. Portsmouth, 1801. 12°. . . 97
Sewall, J. Massachusettensis; a Political Essay. Boston, 1819. 8°. . 781
Sewall, T. Examination of Phrenology. Washington, 1837. 8°. . . 1647
Seward, Anna, Memoirs of. E. Darwin. Philadelphia, 1804. 8°. . . 712
Seward, W. H. Life and Public Services of J. Q. Adams. Aub. 1849. 12°. 2908
Works. Edited by G. E. Baker. New York, 1853. 3 v. . . . 5388

Vol. 1. Biographical Memoir; Speeches in New York Senate; Speeches in the United States Senate; Debates in the United States Senate; Forensic Arguments.
2. Notes on New York; State Papers; Official Correspondence; Pardon Papers.
3. Orations and Discourses; Occasional Speeches and Addresses; Executive Speeches; Political Writings; General Correspondence; Letters from Europe; Speeches in the United States Senate.

Sewel, W. History of the Quakers. New York, 1844. 2 v. 8°. . . . 3217
Sewell, E. M. Amy Herbert. New York, 1853. 12°. 6225

Sewell, E. M. Child's First History of Rome. New York, 1849. 12°. . 3310
Earl's Daughter. New York, 1850. 12°. 3886
Experience of Life. New York, 1853. 12°. 5196
First History of Greece. New York, 1853. 16°. 5201
Gertrude. New York, 1845. 12°. 2481
Katharine Ashton. New York, 1854. 2 v. 12°. 6167
Laneton Parsonage. New York, 1846. 2 v. 12°. 2912
Sewell, J. Steam and Locomotion. London, 1852. 12°. . . . 6086
Seybert, A. Statistical Annals of the United States. Phil. 1818. 4°. . 2032
Seymour, E. S. Sketches of Minnesota. New York, 1850. 12°. . . 3512
Seymour, M. H. Mornings among the Jesuits at Rome. N.Y. 1849. 12°. 3401
Sforzosi, L. History of Italy. (H. F. L.) New York, 1846. 12°. 3683, 79
Sganzin, M. I. Civil Engineering. Boston, 1827. 8°. 2877
Shabby Genteel Story. W. M. Thackeray. New York, 1852. 12°. . 5019
Shady Side; or, Life in a Parsonage. Mary S. Hubbell. Bost. 1853. 12°. 5252
Shakers, Lines in Verse about. New York, 1846. 8°. 3197
Testimony of Christ's Second Appearing. Union Village, 1823. 12°. 3052
Two Years among the. D. R. Lamson. West Boylston, 1848. 12°. 2456
Shakspeare, W., and the Dramatists. S. T. Coleridge. N.Y. 1853. 12°. 5561, 4
and his Friends. R. F. Williams. Paris, 1838. 8°. 1059
and his Times. M. Guizot. New York, 1852. 12°. 5194
and his Times. N. Drake. Paris, 1838. 8°. 4513
Beauties of. W. Dodd. London, n. d. 18°. 2207
Biography. C. Knight. London, 1851. 8°. 5463
Birth-Town of. G. May. Evesham, 1847. 12°. 4026
Characters of his Plays. W. Hazlitt. Boston, 1818. 12°. . . 2154
Commentaries of the Hist. Plays. T.P.Courtenay. Lon.1840. 2 v. 12°. 1112
Concordance to. Mary Cowden Clarke. Boston, 1854. Roy. 8°. . 5973
Dramatic Art of. H. Ulrici. London, 1846. 8°. 3956
Dramatic Works. Boston, 1836. 7 v. roy. 8°. 2770

Vol. 1. Tempest; Two Gentlemen of Verona; Merry Wives of Windsor; Twelfth Night; Measure for Measure; Much Ado about Nothing.
2. Midsummer Night's Dream; Love's Labor Lost; Merchant of Venice; As You Like It; All's Well that End's Well; Taming the Shrew.
3. Winter's Tale; Comedy of Errors; Macbeth; King John; King Richard II.; King Henry IV., Part First.
4. King Henry IV., Part Second; King Henry V.; King Henry VI.
5. King Richard III.; King Henry VIII.; Troilus and Cressida; Timon of Athens; Coriolanus.
6. Julius Cæsar; Anthony and Cleopatra; Cymbeline; Titus Andronicus; Pericles.
7. King Lear; Romeo and Juliet; Hamlet; Othello.

The same. Cheswick, 1826. 10 v. 12°. 1836

Vol. 1. Tempest; Two Gentlemen of Verona; Merry Wives of Windsor; Twelfth Night.
2. Measure for Measure; Much Ado about Nothing; Midsummer Night's Dream; Love's Labor Lost.
3. Merchant of Venice; As You Like It; All's Well that Ends Well; Taming the Shrew.
4. Winter's Tale; Comedy of Errors; Macbeth; King John.
5. King Richard II.; King Henry IV.; King Henry V.
6. King Henry VI.
7. King Richard III.; King Henry VIII.; Troilus and Cressida.
8. Timon of Athens; Coriolanus; Julius Cæsar; Anthony and Cleopatra.
9. Cymbeline; Titus Andronicus; Pericles; King Lear.
10. Romeo and Juliet; Hamlet; Othello.

Shakspeare, W. Dramatic Works. New York, 1846. 6 v. 12°. . . 1845

Vol. 1. Life of Author; Tempest; Two Gentlemen of Verona; Merry Wives of Windsor; Measure for Measure; Comedy of Errors; Merchant of Venice.
2. As You Like It; Midsummer Night's Dream; Much Ado about Nothing; Love's Labor Lost; Taming the Shrew; All's Well that Ends Well; Twelfth Night.
3. Winter's Tale; Macbeth; King John; King Richard II.; King Henry IV.
4. King Henry V.; King Henry VI.; King Richard III.; King Henry VIII.
5. Coriolanus; Julius Cæsar; Anthony and Cleopatra; Timon of Athens; Titus Andronicus; Troilus and Cressida.
6. Cymbeline; King Lear; Romeo and Juliet; Hamlet; Othello; Pericles.

The same. New York, 1825. 10 v. 12°. 938

Vol. 1. Life; Tempest; Two Gentlemen of Verona; Merry Wives of Windsor.
2. Measure for Measure; Comedy of Errors; Merchant of Venice; As You Like It.
3. Midsummer Night's Dream; Much Ado about Nothing; Love's Labor Lost; Taming the Shrew.
4. (Missing.)
5. King John; Richard II.; Henry IV.
6. Henry V.; Henry VI.
7. Richard III.; Henry VIII.; Coriolanus.
8. Julius Cæsar; Anthony and Cleopatra; Timon of Athens; Titus Andronicus.
9. Troilus and Cressida; Cymbeline; King Lear; Romeo and Juliet.
10. Hamlet; Othello; Pericles.

Heroines, Girlhood of. Mary C. Clarke. New York, 1852. 2 v. 12°. 4450
*Illustrations of. London, 1826–29. 4°. 1576
Lectures on. H. N. Hudson. New York, 1848. 2 v. 12°. . . 3112
Library. Collected by J. P. Collier. London, 1843. 2 v. 8°. . 4656
Life and Beauties of. W. Dodd. Boston, 1850. 12°. . . . 880
Notes and Emendations on. J. P. Collier. New York, 1853. 12°. 5286
Outline Illustrations of. F. Howard. London, 1833. 5 v. 8°. . 5480
Quotations, Dictionary of. Philadelphia, 1851. 12°. . . . 4454
Remarks on Collier's and Knight's. A. Dyce. Lond. 1844. 8°. . 1115
Scholar. R. G. White. New York, 1854. 8°. 5989
Studies of. C. Knight. London, 1851. 8°. 5464
Supplement to the Plays. New York, 1848. Roy. 8°. . . . 2886
Vindicated from Collier's Corrections. S. W. Singer. Lond. 1852. 8°. 5490
Wisdom and Genius of. T. Price. Philadelphia, 1839. 8°. . 2458
Works, complete in one vol. London, 1850. 8°. 1965
Works. Edited by J. P. Collier. New York, 1853. Roy. 8°. . 5432
Works. Ed. by N. H. Hudson. Bost. 1851. 11 v. [only 6 pub.] 12°. 4421

Vol. 1. Tempest; Two Gentlemen of Verona; Merry Wives of Windsor; Twelfth Night.
2. Measure for Measure; Much Ado About Nothing; Midsummer Night's Dream; Love's Labor Lost.
3. Merchant of Venice; As You Like It; All's Well that Ends Well; Taming the Shrew.
4. Winter's Tale; Comedy of Errors; Macbeth; King John.
5. King Richard II.; King Henry IV.
6. King Henry VI.

Youth of. F. Williams. New York, 1847. 8°. 2807

Shakspeare Society's Publications. London, 1853. 18 v. 8°. . . . 6020

Vol. 1. Papers of the Shakspeare Society.
2. Illustrations of the Fairy Mythology of Midsummer Night's Dream. Edited by J. O. Halliwell.
3. Collier, J. P. Lives of the Original Actors of Shakspeare's Plays.
4. Eight Novels employed by English Dramatic Poets in the Reign o Elizabeth.

Shakspeare Society's Publications *continued.*

5. Thynn's Debate between Pride and Lowliness; Ghost of Richard III.; Tracts by John Ford.
6. Simrock, M. K. Remarks on the Plots of Shakspeare's Plays; Shakspeare's Henry IV.
7. Diary of Philip Henslowe, from 1591 to 1609.
8. Memoirs of Edward Alleyn.
9. Chester Plays, a Collection of Mysteries.
10. Coventry Mysteries; Marriage of Wit and Wisdom; Moral Play of Wit and Science.
11. Ralph Roister Doister; Gorboduc; Timon; Sir Thomas More; Patient Grissil.
12. Taming of a Shrew; First Sketch of the Merry Wives of Windsor; First Sketches of Second and Third Parts of Henry VI.; True Tragedy of Richard III.
13. Dramatic Works of Thomas Heywood, viz.: Edward IV; Fair Maid of the Exchange; Fortune by Land and Sea; Fair Maid of the West.
14. Heywood's Dramatic Works (continued): Royal King and Loyal Subject; A Woman Killed with Kindness; If You Know not Me, You Know Nobody; The Golden Age; The Silver Age.
15. Extracts from the Registers of the Stationers' Company, from 1557 to 1587.
16. Life of Inigo Jones, by Peter Cunningham; Ben Jonson's Conversations with Drummond of Hawthornden.
17. Revels at Court; Tarlton's Jests and Tarleton's News out of Purgatory.
18. Early Treatises on the Stage, viz.: Northbrooke's Treatise against Dicing, Dancing, Plays, and Interludes; Gosson School of Abuse; Heywood's Defence of Stage Plays.

Shannondale. Mrs. E. D. E. N. Southworth. New York, 1851. 8°. . 4013
Sharp, D. Tribute to J. Q. Adams. Boston, 1848. 8°. 3533
Sharp, G., Memoir of. C. Stuart. New York, 1836. 12°. 1534
Sharpe, S. History of Egypt under the Ptolemies. London, 1838. 4°. . 3611
Sharpe's London Journal. Vols. 9–13. London, 1849–53. 8°. . . 4009
Shattuck, L. Census Report of Boston, 1845. Boston, 1846. 8°. . . 2736
History of Concord, Mass. Boston, 1835. 8°. 2811
Shaw, C. Description of Boston. Boston, 1817. 12°. 848
Shaw, S. Journals; with Life by J. Quincy. Boston, 1847. 8°. . . 2810
Shaw, T. B. Outlines of English Literature. Philadelphia, 1849. 12°. . 3277
Shay's Rebellion in Massachusetts, 1786. G. R. Minot. Boston, 1810. 8°. 1336
Shea, J. G. Discovery and Exploration of Mississippi Valley. N.Y. 1852. 8°. 4953
Sheep, The; with Illustrations. London, n. d. Roy. 8°. . . . 3635, 2
Sheil, R. L. Sketches of the Irish Bar. New York, 1854. 2 v. 12°. . 5755
Shelley, B. P. Essays, Letters from Abroad, &c. Phil. 1840. 2 v. 12°. 1540
Poetical Works. Philadelphia, 1844. 8°. 581
Poetical Works. Edited by Mrs. Shelley. London, 1839. 4 v. 12°. 2385
Shelley, Mrs. M. W. Frankenstein. London, 1853. 12°. 5698
The same. Philadelphia, 1833. 2 v. 12°. 2333
Lives of Eminent French Writers. Philadelphia, 1840. 2 v. 12°. 1140
and others. Literary Men of Italy. Philadelphia, 1841. 2 v. 12°. 2135
Shells, Recent and Fossil. S. P. Woodward. London, 1851. 12°. . 6083
Shelton, F. W. Crystalline. New York, 1854. 12°. 5813
Rector of St. Bardolph's. New York, 1853. 12°. 5079
Salander and the Dragon. New York, 1852. 16°. 4398
Up the River. New York, 1853. 12°. 5595
Shenstone, W. Essays on Men and Manners. Philadelphia, 1804. 12°. 2336
Shepard, I. F. Scenes and Songs of Social Life. Boston, 1846. 12°. . 2929
Sheppard Lee. New York, 1836. 2 v. 12°. 231
Sherburne, J. H. Life and Character of J. Paul Jones. Wash. 1825. 8°. 679

Sherburne, J. H. Life and Character of J. Paul Jones. N. Y. 1851. 8°. 4316
Pencillings in England and on the Continent. Phil. 1847. 12°. . 2978
Sheridan, R. B. Life and Dramatic Works. London, 1852. Post 8°. . 2660
The same. London, 1848. Post 8°. 4377
Memoirs of. T. Moore. New York, 1853. 2 v. 12°. . . . 1372
Selection of Speeches. London, 1853. Roy. 8°. 5482
Speeches. London, 1842. 3 v. 8°. 3589
Sheridan, T. Lectures on Elocution. London, 1798. 8°. . . . 5012
Sherman, J. Memoir of Wm. Allen. London, 1851. 12°. . . . 4284
Sherwood, Mrs. Roxobel. New York, 1831. 3 v. 12°. 92
Shetland and the Shetlanders. Catherine Sinclair. New York, 1840. 12°. 1896
Shillaber, B. P. Life and Sayings of Mrs. Partington. N.Y. 1854. 12°. 5925
Rhymes with Reasons and Without. Boston, 1853. 12°. . . 5323
Ship and Shore. W. Colton. New York, 1835. 12°. 1084
Ship-Building. J. Peake. London, 1850. 2 v. 12°. 6071
Shipmaster's Assistant. London, 1808. 8°. 644
Shipmaster's Assistant. J. Blunt. New York, 1848. 8°. . . . 3242
Ships, Masting, Mast-making, and Rigging of. R. Kipping. Lon. 1854. 12°. 6072
and Boats, Forms of. W. Bland. London, 1853. 12°. . . 6094
Shipwreck by Lightning. R. B. Forbes. Boston, 1853. 8°. . . . 5404
of the Ship Oswego. J. Paddock. New York, 1818. 8°. . . 1297
Shipp, J., Military Career of. New York, 1829. 2 v. 12°. . . . 528
Shirley; a Tale. Caroline Bronte. New York, 1850. 8°. . . . 2865
Shoemakers, Lives of Distinguished. Portland, 1849. 12°. . . . 3280
Shooting, Hints to Sportsmen on. E. J. Lewis. Phil. 1851. 12°. . . 4167
and Guns. P. Hawker. Philadelphia, 1853. 8°. . . . 5933
Short, T. V. History of the Church of England. Philadelphia, 1843. 8°. 3606
Shortland, E. Southern Districts of New Zealand. Lond. 1851. 12°. . 4463
Shoulder-Knot. B. F. Tefft. New York, 1850. 12°. 3876
Shrewsbury, Mass., History of. A. H. Ward. Boston, 1847. 8°. . . 2844
Siam, Residence in. F. A. Neale. London, 1852. 12°. . . . 5261
and Cochin-China, Embassy to. J. Crawfurd. Lond. 1830. 2 v. 8°. 4816
Siamese Twins. E. L. Bulwer. New York, 1831. 12°. 549
Siberia, Exile into. A. von Kotzebue. New York, 1802. 12°. . . 871
Travels in. A. Erman. Philadelphia, 1850. 2 v. 12°. . . 3853
Sibley, J. L. History of Union, Maine. Boston, 1851. 12°. . . . 4434
Siborne, W. War in France and Belgium, 1815. Phil. 1845. 8°. . . 2711
Sichel, J. Spectacles; their Uses and Abuses. Boston, 1850. 8°. . . 3967
Sicily; a Pilgrimage. H. T. Tuckerman. New York, 1852. 12°. . . 4911
and Malta, Tour through. P. Brydone. London, 1775. 2 v. 8°. . 681
Sicilian Vespers, War of the. M. Amari. London, 1850. 3 v. 12°. . 4587
Sickness and Health of the People of Bleaburn. Boston, 1853. 12°. . 5236
Siddons, Mrs. Life. T. Campbell. New York, 1834. 12°. . . . 1165
Sidereal Heavens. T. Dick. Philadelphia, 1845. 12°. . . . 2357, 8
The same. (H. F. L.) New York, 1846. 12°. . . 3683, 99
Sidmouth, Lord, Life and Corres. of. G. Pellew. London, 1847. 3 v. 8°. 4133
Sidney, Alger. Discourses on Government. New York, 1805. 3 v. 8°. 793
Life. G. Van Santvoord. New York, 1851. 12°. . . . 4177

Sidney, E. Life of Rowland Hill. New York, 1834. 12°. . . . 2919
Sidney, H. Diary of the Times of Charles II. London, 1843. 2 v. 8°. . 4673
Sidney, Sir P. Defence of Poesy. Cambridge, 1831. 12°. . . . 383, 2
and H. Languet, Corres. of. Ed. by S. A. Pears. Lond. 1845. 8°. 2667
Sidney, S. Three Colonies of Australia. London, 1853. 8°. . . . 5153
Siebold, C. T. von. Anatomy of the Invertebrata. Boston, 1854. 8°. . 5891
Siege of Gibraltar, History of. Philadelphia, 1789. 12°. . . . 98
Sieges in Spain & Portugal under Wellington. Sir J.T.Jones. Lon.1846. 3v.8°. 5132
Sierra Leone and Gambia, Life in. T. E. Poole. London, 1850. 2 v. 12°. 4583
Sights and Sounds; the Mystery of the Day. H. Spicer. Lond. 1853. 12°. 5255
Signers of Dec. of Independence, Lives of. B. J. Lossing. N.Y. 1848. 12°. 1778
The same. C. A. Goodrich. Hartford, 1840. 12°. . . 3069
Sigourney, Mrs. L. H. Examples of Life and Death. N.Y. 1852. 12°. . 4748
Letters to my Pupils. New York, 1851. 12°. 4424
Myrtis, with other Prose Writings. New York, 1846. 12°. . . 2932
Olive Leaves. New York, 1852. 12°. 4479
Pleasant Memories of Pleasant Lands. Boston, 1844. 12°. . . 1837
Select Poems. Philadelphia, 1848. 12°. 3328
Scenes in my Native Land. Boston, 1845. 12°. 2299
Water-Drops. New York, 1848. 12°. 3062
Silk Culturist's Manual. J. D'Homergue. Philadelphia, 1839. 12°. . 1625
Silk, Third Massachusetts Report on. H. Colman. Boston, 1840. 8°. . 1607
Silliman, B. Travels in Europe in 1805–6. New Haven, 1820. 3 v. 12°. 378
(Ed.) American Journal of Science. N. Haven, 1836–54. 39 v. 8°. 921
Visit to Europe in 1851. New York, 1853. 2 v. 12°. . . . 5519
Silliman, B., jun. First Principles of Chemistry. Philadelphia, 1849. 12°. 3015
Silver Cup of Sparkling Drops. Ed. by Miss C. B. Porter. Buff. 1852. 12°. 4449
Silver-Knife. J. H. Robinson. Boston, 1854. 12°. 5820
Simcoe, J. G. Military Journal during the Am. Revolution. N.Y. 1844. 8°. 1983
Simms, J. R. Trappers of New York. Albany, 1851. 12°. . . . 4484
Simms, W. G. Beauchampe; or, the Kentucky Tragedy. Phil. 1842. 2 v.12°. 1678
Border Beagles; a Tale of Mississippi. Philadelphia, 1840. 2 v. 12°. 1465
Count Julian; or, Last Days of the Goth. Baltimore, 1845. 8°. . 2738
Damsel of Darien. Philadelphia, 1839. 2 v. 12°. . . . 1181
Egeria; or, Voices of Thought and Counsel. Phil. 1853. 12°. . 5527
Katherine Walton. New York, 1854. 12°. 5877
The same. Philadelphia, 1851. 8°. 4514
Kinsman; or, Black Riders of Congaree. Phil. 1841. 2 v. 12°. . 1598
Life of Chevalier Bayard. New York, 1847. 12°. . . . 3098
Life of Gen. Nath. Green. New York, 1849. 12°. . . . 3665
Life of Francis Marion. New York, 1844. 12°. 2182
Life of Capt. John Smith. New York, 1846. 12°. . . . 2983
Lily and the Totem. New York, 1850. 12°. 3921
Marie de Bernière. Philadelphia, 1853. 12°. 5301
Martin Faber, and other Tales. Philadelphia, 1846. 2 v. 12°. . 207
Melichampe; a Legend of the Santee. New York, 1854. 12°. . 269
Norman Maurice; a Drama. Philadelphia, 1853. 12°. . . 5366
Partisan; a Tale of the Revolution. New York, 1854. 12°. . 1099

Simms, W. G. Pelayo; a Story of the Goth. New York, 1838. 2 v. 12°. 1144
Poems. New York, 1853. 2 v. 12°. 5762

Vol. 1. Norman Maurice, a Tragedy; Atlantis, a Tale of the Sea; Tales and Traditions of the South; City of the Silent.
2. Southern Passages and Pictures; Historical and Dramatic Sketches; Scripture Legends; Francesca da Rimini.

Scout; or, Black Riders of Congaree. New York, 1854. 12°. . 6226
Sword and the Distaff. Philadelphia, 1853. 12°. 5341
Views and Reviews in American Literature. N. York, 1845. 12°. 2582
Wigwam and the Cabin. Philadelphia, 1853. 12°. 2486
Woodcraft; or, Hawks about the Dovecote. New York, 1854. 12°. 6248
Yemassee; a Romance of Carolina. New York, 1854. 12°. . 1142
Simond, L. Tour in Great Britain, 1810–11. Edinburgh, 1817. 2 v. 8°. 677
Tour and Residence in Switzerland, 1817–19. Bost. 1822. 2 v. 8°. 702
Simmons, P. L. Colonial Magazine. Vols. 1–6. London, 1845–46. 8°. 3218
Sir John Franklin and Arctic Regions. Buffalo, 1852. 12° . . 968
Simonds, W. Clinton; a Book for Boys. Boston, 1854. 12°. . . 5620
Simple Story. Mrs. Eliza Inchbald. London, 1851. 12°. . . . 5655
Simpson, J. H. Exped. from Santa Fé to Navajo Country. Phil. 1852. 8°. 3586
Simpson, R. Traditions of the Covenanters. Edinburgh, 1850. 12°. . 4265
Simpson, S. Workingman's Manual. Philadelphia, 1831. 8°. . . 4020
Simpson, T. Discoveries on the North Coast of America. Lon. 1843. 8°. 4344
Life and Travels of. A. Simpson. London, 1845. 8°. . . 4684
Sinclair, Catherine. Beatrice; or, Unknown Relatives. N. Y. 1853. 12°. 5257
Country Hospitalities. Philadelphia, 1851. 12°. 4016
Jane Bouverie. New York, 1851. 12°. 3798
Kaleidoscope of Anecdotes and Aphorisms. London, 1851. 12°. . 4400
Modern Accomplishments; or, March of Intellect. N. Y. 1849. 12°. 3426
Modern Flirtations. New York, 1853. 12°. 5335
Modern Society (Sequel to Modern Accomp.). N. Y. 1849. 12°. . 3425
Scotland and the Scotch. New York, 1840. 12°. 2414
Shetland and the Shetlanders. New York, 1840. 12°. . . . 1896
Sir Edward Graham. New York, 1850. 8°. 3972
Sinclair, Sir J. Code of Health and Longevity. London, 1844. 8°. . 4944
Singer, S. W. Shakspeare vindicated from Collier's Correc. Lon. 1853. 12°. 5490
Single Blessedness. New York, 1852. 12°. 4854
Singleton Fontenoy. J. Hannay. New York, 1851. 8°. . . . 4006
Sir Edward Graham. Catherine Sinclair. New York, 1850. 8°. . . 3972
Sir Jasper Carew, Knt. C. Lever. New York, 1854. 8°. . . . 5965
Sir Ralph Esher. L. Hunt. London, 1853. 12°. 5737
Sir Roger de Coverley. From the Spectator. Boston, 1852. 12°. . . 4493
Sir Tristrem; a Musical Romance. Sir W. Scott. Edinburgh, 1848. 12°. 4102, 5
Sir Theodore Broughton; or, Laurel Water. G. P. R. James. N.Y. 1848. 8°. 2887
Sirr, H. C. China and the Chinese. London, 1849. 2 v. 8°. . . 4822
Sierra Leone, Visit to, 1834. F. H. Rankin. Philadelphia, 1836. 8°. 2228, 2
Sismondi, J. C. L. de. Fall of the Roman Empire. Lond. 1834. 2 v. 12°. 2381
History of the Italian Republics. London, 1832. 12°. . . 2382
Literature of the South of Europe. London, 1823. 4 v. 8°. . . 2233
Sister Agnes; or, the Captive Nun. New York, 1854. 12°. . . . 6201

Sisters; or, England and France. New York, 1846. 8°. . . . 2746
Sisters; or, the Fatal Marriages. H. Cockton. New York, 1851. 8°. . 4151
Six Months in Italy. G. S. Hillard. Boston, 1853. 2 v. 12°. . . 5505
Six Years Later. A. Dumas. Philadelphia, 1853. 8°. 5407
Sketch Book. W. Irving. New York, 1849. 12°. 1206
The same. New York, 1850. 12°. 3370
Sketches and Rambles. J. T. Headley. New York, 1850. 12°. . . 3655
and Recollections. J. Poole. Philadelphia, 1835. 2 v. 12°. . . 1098
and Stories from Life. Mrs. H. F. Lee. Boston, 1850. 12°. . 3490
by a Traveller. Boston, 1830. 12°. 359
from Life. L. Blanchard. New York, 1846. 12°. 2548
from a Student's Window. S. L. Goodrich. Boston, 1841. 12°. 2302
in France. A. Dumas. Philadelphia, 1852. 8°. 4693
in Ireland. W. M. Thackeray. Philadelphia, 1843. 8°. . . 1750
of American Character. S. J. Hale. Boston, 1829. 18°. . . 176
of American Society, by Seatsfield. New York, 1844. 8°. . . 2081
of Every-Day Life. Fredrika Bremer. New York, 1848. 8°. . 2072
of Every-Day Life. C. Dickens. Philadelphia, 1849. 8°. . . 843
of Irish Character. Mrs. S. C. Hall. New York, 1829. 12°. . 2105
of Life and Character. T. S. Arthur. Philadelphia, 1850. 8°. . 3634
of Married Life. Mrs. E. L. Follen. Boston, 1841. 12°. . . 1866
of Paris, by an American. Philadelphia, 1838. 12°. . . . 370
of Public Characters. I. L. Robinson. New York, 1830. 12°. . 562
of a Seaport Town. H. F. Chorley. Phil. 1836. 2 v. 12°. . 436
Skin and the Hair, Treatise on. E. Wilson. Philadelphia, 1854. 12°. . 6177
Skinner, J. S. (Editor). Plough, Loom, and Anvil. Vol. 1. Phil. 1848. 8°. 3409
Skinner, Major. Overland Journey to India. Philadelphia, 1837. 12°. 913
Slack, H. J. Ministry of the Beautiful. Philadelphia, 1850. 12°. . . 4068
Slade, A. Turkey and the Turks. New York, 1854. 12°. 5807
Slater, S., Memoir of. G. S. White. Philadelphia, 1836. 8°. . . 1237
Slave Trade, African. T. F. Buxton. Philadelphia, 1839. 12°. . . 1527
History of the Abolition of. T. Clarkson. N. York, 1836. 3 v. 12°. 1548
Slaver, Twenty Years of an African. Ed. by B. Mayer. N. Y. 1854. 12°. 6199
Slavery. W. E. Channing. Boston, 1835. 12°. 1118
and Abolitionists. Catherine E. Beecher. Phil. 1837. 12°. . . 1509
Arguments for. Harper, Hammond, and others. Phil. 1853. 12°. 5361
as it Is; Testimony of 1000 Witnesses. New York, 1839. 8°. . 1443
Character and Relations of. L. A. Sawyer. N. Haven, 1837. 12°. 1536
Federal Government in behalf of. W. Jay. N. Y. 1839. 12°. . 1547
Illustrated in its Effects upon Woman. Boston, 1837. 12°. . . 1519
in the United States. J. K. Paulding. New York, 1836. 12°. . 242
in the United States, Picture of. G. Bourne. Boston, 1838. 12°. 1524
Letters on. Angelina E. Grimké. Boston, 1838. 12°. . . 1531
Letters on American. J. Rankin. Boston, 1838. 12°. . . 1546
Letters on, to Wm. Jay. D. M. Reese. New York, 1835. 12°. . 2600
Letters and Speeches on. H. Mann. Boston, 1851. 4623
Miscellaneous Writings on. W. Jay. Boston, 1853. 12°. . . 5333
Question. E. P. Barrows, jun. New York, 1836. 16°. . . 1505

Slavery, Testimony of God against. La R. Sunderland. N.Y. 1839. 16°. 1511
Treatise on the Law of. J. D. Wheeler. N. York, 1837. Roy. 8°. 1352
Unconstitutionality of. G. W. F. Mellen. Boston, 1841. 12°. . 2094
Sleep Psychologically Considered. B. Fosgate. New York, 1850. 12°. . 3894
Sleeper, J. S. Salt Water Bubbles. Boston, 1854. 12°. 6213
Smalley, E. Worcester Pulpit. Boston, 1851. 12°. 4211
Smeaton, A. C. Builder's Pocket Companion. Philadelphia, 1852. 12°. 5003
Smedley, E. Sketches of Venetian Hist. (H.F.L.) N.Y. 1846. 2 v. 12°. 3683, 43, 44
Smedley, F. Colville Family. New York, 1853. 12°. 5517
Frank Fairlegh. New York, 1850. 8°. 3997
Harry Coverdale's Courtship. New York, 1853. 12°. . . . 5363
Lewis Arundel; or, Railroad of Life. New York, 1851. 8°. . 4518
Smee, A. Elements of Electro-Metallurgy. New York, 1852. 12°. . 985
Smellie, W. Philosophy of Natural History. Boston, 1829. 8°. . . 1414
Smith, Adam. Life. London, 1833. 8°. 602
Wealth of Nations; with Life. London, 1850. 8°. 676
Smith, Albert. Adventures of Christopher Tadpole. N. York, 1848. 8°. 2897
Adventures of Mr. Ledbury. London, 1853. 12°. 5734
Marchioness of Brinvilliers. London, 1852. 12°. 5680
Month at Constantinople. Boston, 1852. 12°. 391
Pottleton Legacy. London, 1850. 12°. 5031
Story of Mont Blanc. New York, 1853. 12°. 5515
Smith, Alexander. Poems. Boston, 1853. 12°. 5321
Smith, Capt. Alexander. Life, by Himself. Boston, 1819. 12°. . . 1042
Smith, C. B. Life in Earnest. Hartford, 1848. 12°. 3172
Smith, C. H. Dogs. Edinburgh, 1843. 2 v. 12°. 4901, 18, 19
Horses, Asses, &c. Edinburgh, 1843. 12°. 4901, 20
Introduction to Mammalia. Edinburgh, 1843. 12°. . . 4901, 15
Natural History of the Human Species. Boston, 1851. 12°. . 4476
Smith, E. Character of Jesus Christ. Boston, 1814. 12°. 310
Smith, Elizabeth E. Three Eras of Woman's Life. New York, 1836. 12°. 230
Smith, Elizabeth O. Bertha and Lily. New York, 1854. 12°. . . 6172
Smith, E. P. Manual of Political Economy. New York, 1853. 12°. . 5337
Smith, F. G. Domestic Medicine and Surgery. Philadelphia, 1851. 12°. 474
Smith, G. Consular Cities of China. London, 1847. 8°. 4960
Smith, Horace. Arthur Arundel. New York, 1844. 12°. 2212
Adam Brown, the Merchant. New York, 1843. 8°. 2762
Gaieties and Gravities. New York, 1852. 12°. 1011
Gale Middleton. Philadelphia, 1834. 2 v. 12°. 606
Love and Mesmerism. New York, 1846. 8°. 2647
New Forest. New York, 1829. 2 v. 12°. 515
Tales of the Early Ages. New York, 1832. 2 v. 12°. . . . 3578
Tor Hill. New York, 1837. 12°. 494
and James. Horace in London. Boston, 1813. 18°. 162
and James. Rejected Addresses. Boston, 1841. 12°. . . . 1565
Smith, Horatio. Festivals, Games, &c. (H. F. L.) N.Y. 1846. 12°. 3683, 25
Smith, James. Memoirs, Letters, and Comic Miscel. Phil. 1841. 2 v. 12°. 1137
Rural Records; or, Glimpses of Village Life. London, 1845. 12°. 3137

Smith, Jeremiah. Life. J. H. Morison. Boston, 1845. 12°. . . . 2353
Smith, Captain John. Life. G. S. Hillard. Boston, 1838. 12°. . 1076, 2
Life. W. G. Simms. New York, 1846. 12°. 2983
Smith, J. F. Amy Lawrence, the Freemason's Daughter. N.Y. 1852. 8°. 4695
Fred Arden; or, the Jesuit's Revenge. New York, 1854. 8°. . 6028
Harry Ashton. New York, 1853. 8°. 5465
Stanfield Hall. New York, 1851. 8°. 3804
Woman and her Master. New York, 1854. 8°. 5932
*Smith, J. J. Designs for Monuments and Mural Tablets. N.Y. 1846. 4°. 4857
Smith, J. S. Mirabeau; a Life History. Philadelphia, 1848. 12°. . 3152
Smith, J. T. Antiquarian Ramble in London. London, 1846. 2 v. 8°. . 4343
Smith, J. V. C. Pilgrimage to Egypt. Boston, 1852. 12°. . . . 254
Pilgrimage to Palestine. Boston, 1853. 12°. 5184
Scientific Tracts and Family Lyceum. Vol. 2. Boston, 1834. 12°. 859
Turkey and the Turks. Boston, 1854. 12°. 5850
Smith, J. W. Compendium of Mercantile Law. New York, 1850. 8°. 4305
Smith, M. Geographical View of Upper Canada. Phil. 1813. 12°. . 484
Smith, R. A. Philadelphia as it Is in 1852. Philadelphia, 1852. 12°. . 4788
Smith, S. Louisa P. Poems. Providence, 1829. 12°. 438
Smith, Thomas, Journals of, 1720–1788. Portland, 1821. 12°. . . 497
and S. Deane, Journals of. Ed. by W. Willis. Portland, 1849. 8°. 3605
Smith, Seba. Powhatan; a Metrical Romance. New York, 1841. 12°. . 157
Sinless Child, and other Poems. New York, 1843. 12°. . . 2370
Smith, Sydney. Essays, Speeches, and other Writings. Phil. 1848. 8°. 3418, 3
Miscellaneous Sermons. Philadelphia, 1846. 12°. . . . 3284
Sketches of Moral Philosophy. New York, 1850. 12°. . . 3899
Works. Philadelphia, 1844. 2 v. 12°. 2165
Smith, W. Classical Dictionary. Ed. by C. Anthon. N.Y. 1851. Roy. 8°. 4347
*Dictionary of Greek and Roman Antiquities. London, 1849. 8°. 3958
*Dict. of Greek and Roman Biog. & Mythol. London, 1849. 3 v. 8°. 3957
History of Greece. Boston, 1854. 12°. 5763
Smith, William. Memoir of Johann G. Fichte. Boston, 1846. 12°. . 2905
Smith, William. History of New York. Albany, 1814. 8°. . . . 670
Smith, Sir W. Sidney. Life and Corres. J. Barrow. Lond. 1848. 2 v. 8°. 5146
Smith, W. L. G. Uncle Tom's Cabin as it Is. Buffalo, 1852. 12°. . 4904
Smithsonian Contributions to Knowledge. Wash. 1848–54. 6 v. 4°. . 1756

Vol. 1. Squier, E. G. and E. H. Davis. Ancient Monuments of the Mississippi Valley.
2. Walker, S. C. Planet Neptune.
Lieber, F. Vocal Sounds of Laura Bridgeman.
Bailey, J. W. Microscopical Examination of Soundings.
Ellet, C. Physical Geography of the United States.
Gibbes, R. W. Mosasaurus and Three Allied New Genera.
Agassiz, L. Classification of Insects from Embryological Data.
Hare, R. Explosiveness of Nitre.
Bailey, J. W. Microscopical Observations.
Squier, E. G. Aboriginal Monuments of New York.
Walker, S. C. Ephemeris of Neptune.
Downes, J. Occultations visible in United States in 1851.
3. Locke, J. Observations on Terrestrial Magnetism.
Secchi, A. Researches on Electrical Rheometry.
Girard, C. Fresh Water Fishes of North America.
Harvey, W. H. Marine Algæ of North America.
Gray, A. Plantæ Wrightianæ Texano-Neo-Mexicanæ.
Davis, C. H. Law of Deposit of the Flood Tide.

Smithsonian Contributions to Knowledge *continued.*

Whittlesey, C. Ancient Works in Ohio.
Walker, S. C. Ephemeris of Neptune for 1852.
Downes, J. Occultations visible in United States in 1852.
4. Riggs, S. R. Grammar and Dictionary of the Dakota Language.
5. Leidy, J. A Flora and Fauna within Living Animals.
Leidy, J. Extinct Species of Fossil Ox.
Wyman, J. Anatomy of the Nervous System of Rana Pipiens.
Harvey, W. H. Marine Algæ of North America, Part II.
Gray, A. Plantæ Wrightianæ Texano-Neo-Mexicanæ.
6. Torrey, J. Plantæ Fremontianæ.
Torrey, J. Batis Maritima of Linnæus.
Torrey, J. Darlingtonia Californica.
Stimpson, W. Marine Invertebrata of Grand Manan.
Coffin, J. H. Winds of the Northern Hemisphere.
Leidy, J. Ancient Fauna of Nebraska.
Downes, J. Occultations of Planets and Stars by the Moon, 1853.

Smollett, T. History of England, 1688–1760. Phil. 1832. 2 v. 8°. . 730
The same. Philadelphia, 1846. 8°. 705, 3
Humphrey Clinker. New York, 1835. 12°. 396
Roderick Random. New York, 1840. 8°. 270
Select Works. Philadelphia, 1851. 2 v. 8°. 801

Vol. 1. Peregrine Pickle; Ferdinand Count Fathom.
2. Roderick Random; Sir Launcelot Greaves; Humphrey Clinker; Adventures of an Atom; Poems.

Travels through France and Italy. London, 1778. 2 v. 12°. . 866
Works; with Memoir by T. Roscoe. London, 1845. 8°. . . 2862
Smuggler, The. J. Banim. New York, 1832. 2 v. 12°. 403
The same. London, 1851. 12°. 5656
Smuggler; a Tale. G. P. R. James. New York, 1847. 8°. . . . 2616
Smuggler's Son, and other Tales. Philadelphia, 1842. 12°. . . . 1755
Smyth, T. Unity of the Human Races. New York, 1850. 12°. . . 3857
Smyth, W. Lectures on Modern History. Cambridge, 1841. 2 v. 8°. . 1677
Smyth, W. H. Cycle of Celestial Objects. London, 1844. 2 v. 8°. . 5466
Smyth, W. W. Year with the Turks. New York, 1854. 12°. . . 5810
Snarleyyow; or, Dog-Fiend. F. Marryat. Philadelphia, 1837. 2 v. 12°. 902
The same. Philadelphia, 1847. 8°. 1766, 2
The same. London, 1853. 12°. 5733
Snelling, W. J. Polar Regions of Western Continent. Boston, 1831. 8°. 2671
Snow, C. H. History of Boston. Boston, 1825. 8°. 1971
Snow Image, and other Tales. N. Hawthorne. Boston, 1852. 12°. . 4598
Snowdon; a Novel. T. E. Hook. New York, 1845. 8°. 2665
Soaps, Art of Manufacturing. P. Kurten. Philadelphia, 1854. 12°. . 5761
Social Destiny of Man; or, Association. A. Brisbane. Phil. 1840. 12°. 2136
Social Life amid the Alps. J. H. D. Zschokke. New York, 1844. 12°. 3006
Social Statics; or, Condit. of Human Happiness. H. Spencer. Lon. 1851. 8°. 4153
Society, Essay on the History of Civil. A. Ferguson. Boston, 1809. 8°. 3259
Natural History of. W. C. Taylor. New York, 1841. 2 v. 12°. . 1849
in America. H. Martineau. New York, 1837. 2 v. 12°. . . 367
Society of Friends; a Domestic Narrative. Mrs. J. R. Greer. N.Y. 1853. 12°. 5248
Socrates (the Advocate). Ecclesiastical History. London, 1853. Post 8°. 5747
Solar System. J. R. Hind. New York, 1852. 12°. 4880
Phenomena and Order of. J. P. Nichol. New York, 1843. 12°. 2308
Soldier of Lyons. Mrs. C. Gore. London, 1852. 12°. 5675

Soldier's Faithful Friend. London, 1766. 2 v. 12°. 1451
Solitary Hours. Caroline Southey. New York, 1846. 12°. . . . 2926
Solitude, Advantages of. J. G. Zimmermann. London, 1808. 2 v. 12°. 1865
Sweetened. J. Meikle. Pittsburg, 1818. 12°. 405
Somers, Lord. Life. London, 1833. 8°. 602
Somerset, Earl of, Trial for Poisoning Sir Thos. Overbury. Lond. 1846. 8°. 4644
Somervile, W. The Chase; a Poem. Baltimore, 1814. 18°. . . . 32
Somerville, Mary. Connection of the Physical Sciences. Lond. 1842. 12°. 2540
Physical Geography. Philadelphia, 1848. 12°. 3168
Somnolism and Psycheism. J. W. Haddock. London, 1851. 12°. . 4286
Songs of England and Scotland. London, 1835. 2 v. 12°. 3132
Sophocles. Tragedies. Oxford Translation. London, 1849. Post 8°. . 4383
Translated by T. Francklin. New York, 1840. 12°. . . 1854, 14
Sorcery and Magic, Narratives of. T. Wright. New York, 1852. 12°. . 4768
Sotheby, W. Saul; a Poem. Boston, 1808. 12°. 846
Soul; or, Scriptural Psychology. G. Bush. New York, 1845. 12°. . 3610
Power of, over the Body. G. Moore. New York, 1847. 12°. . 3012
Soule, Caroline A. Home Life. Boston, 1854. 12°. 6317
Soule, R., jun. Mem. of the Sprague Family; a Poem. Bost. 1847. 12°. 3064
Soulié, F. Mysteries of the Heaths. New York, 1844. 8°. . . 2167, 1
Soult, Marshal, Extract from the Journal of. Newburyport, 1817. 12°. . 1172
Sound, Philosophy of, and Hist. of Music. W. M. Higgins. Lond. 1838. 12°. 6325
Transmission of, Report on. W. S. Inman. London, 1836. 8°. . 4554
South, J. F. Household Surgery. London, 1851. 18°. 4774
South, Letters from the. J. K. Paulding. New York, 1835. 2 v. 12°. . 1093
South Africa. — See *Africa.*
South America, Miranda's Attempt to Revolutionize. Boston, 1808. 12°. 1063
Travels in. A. von Humboldt. London, 1852. 3 v. post 8°. . 5384
United Provinces of. V. Pazos. New York, 1819. 8°. . . 1324
Voyage to. G. Juan and A. de Ulloa. Lond. 1758. 2 v. 8°. . 5909
and Mexico, View of. Montreal, 1827. 12°. 200
South Carolina, View of. J. Drayton. Charlestown, 1802. 8°. . . 1379
South-West. J. H. Ingraham. New York, 1835. 2 v. 12°. . . . 1100
Southern Medical Student. G. M. Wharton. Philadelphia, 1851. 12°. . 4038
Southennan. J. Galt. New York, 1830. 2 v. 12°. 1930
Southworth, Mrs. E. D. E. N. Curse of Clifton. Phil. 1853. 12°. . 5229
Deserted Wife. New York, 1850. 8°. 3970
Discarded Daughter. Philadelphia, 1852. 2 v. 12°. . . . 4851
Lost Heiress. New York, 1854. 8°. 5985
Mother-in-Law. New York, 1851. 8°. 4122
Retribution; or, Vale of Shadows. New York, 1853. 8°. . . 5431
Shannondale. New York, 1851. 8°. 4013
Virginia and Magdalene. New York, 1854. 8°. 5981
Southey, Caroline. Chapters on Churchyards. New York, 1842. 12°. . 3014
Early Called. New York, 1842. 12°. 1045
Solitary Hours. New York, 1846. 12°. 2926
Southey, R. Book of the Church. Boston, 1825. 2 v. 8°. . . . 3612
(Translator.) Chronicle of the Cid. Lowell, 1846. 8°. . . 2672

Southey, R. Common-Place Book. New York, 1849. 8°. 3389
The Doctor. New York, 1836. 2 v. 12°. 1082
Life of Henry Kirke White. New York, 1849. 8°. . . . 3421
Life of Lord Nelson. New York, 1835. 12°. 154
The same. (H. F. L.) New York, 1843. 12°. . . 3683, 6
Life of John Wesley, and Hist. of Methodism. N.Y. 1847. 2 v. 12°. 3005
Life of William Cowper. Boston, 1839. 2 v. 12°. . . . 1204
Madoc. Boston, 1821. 2 v. 8°. 745
Poetical Works. New York, 1842. 8°. 1424
Poet's Pilgrimage to Waterloo. Boston, 1816. 12°. . . . 890
Tale of Paraguay. Boston, 1827. 16°. 814
Soyer, A. Pantropheon; or, History of Food. Boston, 1853. 8°. . . 5460
Spaewife; a Tale of Scottish Chronicles. J. Galt. Phil. 1824. 2 v. 12°. 1932
Spain, Arabs in. J. A. Condé. Tr. by Mrs. J. Foster. Lond. 1854. 3 v. 8°. 5939
and Morocco, Travels in, 1848. D. Urquhart. N.Y. 1850. 2 v. 12°. 3854
The same. London, 1850. 2 v. 8°. 4653
Glimpses of, in 1847. S. T. Wallis. New York, 1849. 12°. . 3448
History of the Reign of Philip II. R. Watson. N.Y. 1818. 8°. 638
her Institutions, Politics, &c. S. T. Wallis. Boston, 1853. 12°. . 5212
Memoirs of, from 1621 to 1700. J. Dunlop. Edinb. 1834. 2 v. 8°. 4545
Moors in. M. Florian. (H. F. L.) New York, 1848. 12°. 3683, 177
Notes of an Attaché in. J. E. Warren. London, 1851. 8°. . 4323
The same. New York, 1851. 12°. 4451
*Picturesque Antiquities of. N. A. Wells. London, 1846. 8°. . 2042
Queens of. Anita George. New York, 1850. 12°. . . . 3505
Reminiscences of. C. Cushing. Boston, 1833. 2 v. 12°. . . 2134
Wanderings in. T. Gautier. London, 1853. 12°. . . . 5638
Wanderings in, in 1843. M. Haverty. London, 1844. 2 v. 12°. . 4630
Year in. A. S. Mackenzie. New York, 1836. 3 v. 12°. . . 1193
Spalding, W. History of English Literature. New York, 1853. 12°. . 5265
Italy and the Italian Islands. Edinburgh, 1841. 3 v. 16°. . . 4589
The same. (H. F. L.) New York, 1848. 3v. 12°. 3683, 151–3
Spanglers and Tinglers; or, the Rival Belles. J. B. Jones. Bost. 1850. 8°. 372
Spaniards and their Country. R. Ford. New York, 1847. 2 v. 12°. . 2993
Spanish America. R. H. Bonnycastle. Philadelphia, 1819. 8°. . . 764
Spanish Ballads, Ancient. J. G. Lockhart. New York, 1842. 8°. . . 2349
*Spanish Dictionary. M. Velazquez. New York, 1852. Roy. 8°. . . 4844
Spanish Grammar. A. Elwes. London, 1852. 12°. 6120
Spanish Inquisition, Letters on. T. J. O'Flaherty. New York, 1842. 12°. 3679
Spanish Life, Pictures of. H. D. Wolff. London, 1851. 8°. . . . 5413
Spanish Literature, History of. G. Ticknor. New York, 1849. 3 v. 8°. 3515
Spanish Student; a Play. H. W. Longfellow. Cambridge, 1843. 12°. . 2126
Sparing to Spend. T. S. Arthur. New York, 1853. 12°. 5539
Sparks, J. (Ed.) Corres. of the Amer. Revolution. Boston, 1853. 4 v. 8°. 5389
(Ed.) Diplomatic Corres. of the Am. Revolution. Bost. 1829. 12 v. 8°. 3613
Life of Ethan Allen. Boston, 1834. 12°. 1076, 1
Life of Benedict Arnold. Boston, 1838. 12°. 1076, 3
Life of Benjamin Franklin. Boston, 1840. 8°. 1792, 1

Sparks, J. Life of John Ledyard. Boston, 1848. 12°. 1076, 24
(Editor.) Essays and Tracts in Theology. Boston, 1823. 2 v. 12°. 368

Vol. 1. Turretin, J. A. Fundamentals in Religion.
Abauzit, F. Essays.
Blackburne, F. Confessions of Faith.
Hoadly, B., Selections from.
2. Whitby, D. Last Thoughts.
Hare, F. Study of the Scriptures.
Newton, I. Account of Two Corruptions of Scripture.
Butler, C. Historical Outline.

(Ed.) Library of Amer. Biography. 1st & 2d s. Bos. 1834–48. 25 v. 12°. 1076

Vol. 1. Stark, John, by E. Everett.
Brown, Chas. B., by W. H. Prescott.
Montgomery, R., by J. Armstrong.
Allen, Ethan, by J. Sparks.
2. Wilson, Alex., by W. B. O. Peabody.
Smith, Capt. John, by G. S. Hillard.
3. Arnold, Benedict, by J. Sparks.
4. Wayne, Anthony, by J. Armstrong.
Vane, Sir Henry, by C. W. Upham.
5. Eliot, John, by C. Francis.
6. Pinkney, Wm., by H. Wheaton.
Ellery, Wm., by E. T. Channing.
Mather, Cotton, by W. B. O. Peabody.
7. Phips, Sir Wm., by F. Bowen.
Putnam, Israel, by O. W. B. Peabody.
Davidson, L. Maria, by C. M. Sedgwick.
Rittenhouse, David, by J. Renwick.
8. Edwards, Jonathan, by S. Miller.
Brainerd, David, by W. B. O. Peabody.
9. Steuben, Baron, by F. Bowen.
Cabot, Sebastian, by C. Hayward, jun.
Eaton, Wm., by C. C. Felton.
10. Fulton, Robert, by J. Renwick.
Hudson, Henry, by H. R. Cleveland.
Warren, Joseph, by A. H. Everett.
Marquette, by J. Sparks.
11. Salle, R. de la, by J. Sparks.
Henry, Patrick, by A. H. Everett.
12. Otis, James, by F. Bowen.
Oglethorpe, Jas., by W. B. O. Peabody.
Vol. 13. Sullivan, John, by O. W. B. Peabody.
Leisler, Jacob, by C. F. Hoffman.
Bacon, Nathaniel, by W. Ware.
Mason, John, by G. E. Ellis.
14. Williams, Roger, by W. Gammell.
Dwight, Timothy, by W. B. Sprague.
Pulaski, Count, by J. Sparks.
15. Rumford, Count, by J. Renwick.
Pike, Z. M., by H. Whiting.
Gorton, Samuel, by J. M. Mackie.
16. Stiles, Ezra, by J. L. Kingsley.
Fitch, John, by C. Whittlesey.
Hutchinson, Anne, by G. E. Ellis.
17. Ribault, John, by J. Sparks.
Rale, Sebastian, by C. Francis.
Palfrey, Wm., by J. G. Palfrey.
18. Lee, Charles, by J. Sparks.
Reed, Joseph, by H. Reed.
19. Calvert, Leonard, by G. W. Burnap.
Ward, Samuel, by W. Gammell.
Posey, Thomas, by J. Hall.
20. Greene, Nathaniel, by G. W. Greene.
21. Decatur, Stephen, by A. S. Mackenzie.
22. Preble, Edward, by L. Sabine.
Penn, Wm., by G. E. Ellis.
23. Boone, Daniel, by J. M. Peck.
Lincoln, Benj., by F. Bowen.
24. Ledyard, John, by J. Sparks.
25. Davie, W. R., by F. M. Hubbard.
Kirkland, Samuel, by S. K. Lothrop.

Life of Charles Lee. Boston, 1848. 12°. 1076, 18
Life of Father Marquette. Boston, 1844. 12°. . . . 1076, 10
Life of Gouverneur Morris. Boston, 1832. 3 v. 8°. 1947
Life of Count Pulaski. Boston, 1847. 12°. 1076, 14
Life of John Ribault. Boston, 1848. 12°. 1076, 17
Life of R. de la Salle. Boston, 1844. 12°. 1076, 11
Life of George Washington. Boston, 1837. 12 v. 8°. . . 1430, 1
Reply to Lord Mahon. Cambridge, 1852. 8°. 4838
Second Reply to Lord Mahon. Boston, 1852. 8°. 5123
Speaker, Academical. B. D. Emerson. Philadelphia, 1835. 12°. . . 1807
American. J. Frost. Philadelphia, 1844. 12°. 1806
New American. T. Hughs. Philadelphia, 1835. 12°. . . 2158
New American. J. C. Zachos. New York, 1852. 8°. . . 3587
Standard. E. Sargent. Philadelphia, 1852. 12°. 614
Speakers of the House of Com., Lives of. J. A. Manning. Lon. 1851. Roy. 8°. 5147
Spear, C. (Editor.) Prisoner's Friend. Vols. 1–4. Boston, 1848–52. 8°. 5945
Punishment of Death. Boston, 1844. 12°. 1938
Spear, Mrs. Chloe, Memoir of. Boston, 1832. 16°. 1510
Specimens of American Poetry. S. Kettell. Boston, 1829. 3 v. 12°. . 1184
of the British Critics. J. Wilson. Philadelphia, 1846. 12°. . 2559

Specimens of British Poets. T. Campbell. Philadelphia, 1853. Roy. 8°. 5443
of the Early English Poets. G. Ellis. London, 1845. 3 v. 12°. . 5043
of Early English Metrical Romances. G. Ellis. Lond. 1848. Post 8°. 4370
of For. Standard Literature. Ed. by G. Ripley. Bost. 1838–42. 14 v. 12°. 962

Vol. 1. Cousin, V., and T. Jouffroy. Philosophical Miscellanies. Translated by G. Ripley.
2. Jouffroy, T., and B. Constant. Philosophical Miscellanies. Translated by G. Ripley.
3. Goethe, J. W. von, and F. Schiller. Select Minor Poems. Translated by J. S. Dwight.
4. Eckermann, J. P. Conversations with Goethe. Translated by S. M. Fuller.
5, 6. Jouffroy, T. Introduction to Ethics. Translated by W. H. Channing.
7–9. Menzel, W. German Literature. Translated by C. C. Felton.
10, 11. De Wette, W. M. L. Theodore; or, the Sceptic's Conversion. Translated by J. F. Clarke.
12, 13. De Wette, W. M. L. Human Life, or Practical Ethics. Translated by S. Osgood.
14. Uhland, Körner, &c. Songs and Ballads. Translated by C. T. Brooks.

of the Russian Poets. J. Bowring. Boston, 1822. 12°. . . . 1928
Spectacles; their Uses and Abuses. J. Sichel. Boston, 1850. 8°. . . 3967
Spectator, The. J. Addison and R. Steele. New York, 1854. 6 v. 8°. . 5898
The same. New York, 1842. 2 v. 8°. 792
The same. New York, 1853. 2 v. 12°. . . . 5562, 4, 5
The same. London, 1743. 4 v. 12°. 832
Selections from the. (H. F. L.) New York, 1848. 2 v. 12°. 3683, 181–2
Spectator, The. Vols. 22, 23. London, 1849–50. 4°. 3730
Speculative Philosophy, Critical Essays on. F. Bowen. Bost. 1842. 12°. 2093
of Europe in 19th Century. J. D. Morell. New York, 1851. 8°. 3422
Speeches, British Cicero, a Selection of. T. Browne. Phil. 1810. 3 v. 8°. 2175
of Chatham, Sheridan, Erskine, and Burke. Lond. 1853. Roy. 8°. 5482
of Governors of Mass., from 1765 to 1775. Boston, 1818. 8°. . 576
Spencer, C. C. Treatise on Music. London, 1854. 12°. 6081
Treatise on Playing the Piano-Forte. London, 1853. 12°. . . 6082
Spencer, H. Social Statics; or, Cond. of Human Happiness. Lon. 1851. 8°. 4153
Spencer, H. L. Poems. Boston, 1850. 12°. 3845
Spencer, J. A. Travels in Egypt and the Holy Land. N. Y. 1850. 8°. . 3546
Spencer, J. C. Defence of Dr. E. Nott. Albany, 1854. 8°. 5953
Spencer, I. S. Pastor's Sketches. New York, 1853. 12°. 5502
Spenser, E., and the Fairy Queen. J. S. Hart. Philadelphia, 1854. 12°. 6223
Poetical Works. Ed. by G. S. Hillard. Boston, 1839. 5 v. 12°. . 1920
Spherical Trigonometry. J. Hann. London, 1849. 12°. 6100
Sphinx Incruenta; or, Enigmas and Charades. Edinburgh, 1835. 12°. . 6321
Spicer, H. Sights and Sounds; the Mystery of the Day. Lond. 1853. 12°. 5255
*Spiers, A. French and English Dictionary. New York, 1852. Roy. 8°. 4935
Spindler, C. Invalide; or, Pictures of the French Revol. N. Y. 1844. 8°. 2726
The Jew. New York, 1844. 8°. 2751
Spineto, Marquis. Hieroglyphics and Egyptian Antiq. Lond. 1845. 8°. 4667
Spirit Manifestations in America. H. Spicer. London, 1853. 12°. . . 5255
Spirit Rapper. O. A. Brownson. Boston, 1854. 12°. 6246
Spirit Rapping Unveiled. H. Mattison. New York, 1853. 12°. . . 5281
Spirit of Laws. Baron C. Montesquieu. London, 1823. 2 v. 8°. . . 1799
The same. Worcester, 1802. 2 v. 8°. 796

Spirit of the Age; or, Contemporary Portraits. London, 1825. 12°. . 2288
Spirits, Apparitions, &c., Philosophy of. A. Calmet. Phil. 1850. 12°. . 3883
Philosophy of. C. M. Burnett. London, 1850. 8°. 5410
Spiritual Manifestations, Phenomena of. E. C. Rogers. Bost. 1853. 12°. 5279
Spiritual Medium; or, "To Daimonion." Boston, 1852. 12°. . . 5033
Spiritual Vamperism. C. W. Webber. Philadelphia, 1853. 12°. . . 5302
Spiritualism. J. W. Edmonds and G. T. Dexter. New York, 1853. 8°. 5447
Spooner, L. Trial by Jury. Boston, 1852. 8°. 5170
Spooner, S. Anecdotes of Painters, Engravers, &c. N. Y. 1853. 3 v. 12°. 5750
Sports, Pastimes, &c., Boy's Treasury of. Philadelphia, 1847. 12°. . 2442
Sportsman and his Dog. London, 1850. 12°. 5045
Sportsman's Vade Mecum. Ed. by H. W. Herbert. N. York, 1850. 12°. 4070
Sportsmen, Hints to. E. J. Lewis. Philadelphia, 1851. 12°. . . 4167
Sprague, C. Boston Theatre Prize Poem. Boston, 1824. 12°. . . 490
Poems and Prose Writings. Boston, 1850. 12°. 1609
Sprague, J. T. History of the Florida War. New York, 1848. 8°. . 2873
Sprague, W. B. The Excellent Woman, in Proverbs. Boston, 1852. 12°. 4637
Life of Timothy Dwight. Boston, 1844. 12°. 1076, 14
Sprague Family, Memorial of; a Poem. R. Soule, jun. Bost. 1847. 12°. 3064
Spratt, T. A. B., and E. Forbes. Travels in Lycia. Lond. 1847. 2 v. 8°. 4662
Spring, G. First Things; a Series of Lectures. N. York, 1851. 2 v. 8°. 4117
Glory of Christ. New York, 1852. 2 v. 8°. 1002
Spring, S. Giafar al Barmeki. New York, 1836. 2 v. 12°. . . . 294
Monk's Revenge; or, the Secret Enemy. New York, 1847. 8°. . 2791
Springer, J. S. Forest Life and Forest Trees. New York, 1851. 12°. . 4459
Springfield, R. Horse and his Rider. London, 1847. 12°. . . . 5835
Spring-Tide; or, the Angler and his Friends. J.Y.Akerman. Lon. 1850. 12°. 4278
Spurzheim, J. G. Elementary Principles of Education. Bost. 1836. 12°. 146
Examination of Objections, &c. Boston, 1833. 12°. . . . 2556
Life and Philosophy of. A. Carmichael. Boston, 1833. 12°. . 564
Phrenology. Boston, 1832. 2 v. 8°. 1417
Phrenology in Connection with Physiognomy. Boston, 1833. 8°. 2085
Spy, The. J. F. Cooper. New York, 1852. 12°. 421
Spy Unmasked; or, Memoirs of E. Crosby. H. L. Barnum. N.Y. 1828. 8°. 1363
Squanders of Castle Squander. W. Carleton. London, 1852. 2 v. 12°. . 5030
Squier, E. G. Nicaragua; its People, Scenery, &c. N.Y. 1852. 2 v. 8°. 4560
Serpent Symbol. New York, 1851. 8°. 4118
*and E. H. Davis. Monuments of Miss. Valley. Wash. 1848. 4°. 1756, 1
Squire, The. Ellen Pickering. New York, 1845. 8°. 2741
Staël. Mde. de. Biography. Mrs. L. M. Child. Boston, 1832. 12°. . 2153
Corinne; or, Italy. New York, 1847. 12°. 895
The same. London, 1853. 12°. 5700
The same (in French). New York, 1851. 12°. . . . 2099
Germany. London, 1814. 3 v. 8°. 2607
Ten Years' Exile. New York, 1821. 12°. 309
Stage, The, Before and Behind the Curtain. A. Bunn. Phil. 1840. 2 v. 12°. 419
History of the English. T. Betterton. Boston, 1814. 8°. . . 2074
Personal Recollections of. W. B. Wood. Phil. 1854. 12°. . . 6313

Stage, Record of the Boston. W. W. Clapp, jun. Boston, 1853. 12°. . 5523
View of the English. W. Hazlitt. London, 1818. 8°. . . . 2289
Standard Drama. — See *Drama.*
Standard Library Cyclopædia. London, 1848. 4 v. post 8°. 4390
Standard Speaker. E. Sargent. Philadelphia, 1852. 8°. 614
Standish, the Puritan; a Tale. E. Grayson. New York, 1850. 12°. . 3848
Stanfield Hall. J. F. Smith. New York, 1851. 8°. 3804
Stanford, Jane K. Lady's Gift. Philadelphia, 1836. 12°. 896
Stanley; or, Recollections of a Man of the World. Phil. 1838. 2 v. 12°. 1138
Stanley, A. P. Life and Correspondence of Thomas Arnold. N.Y. 1845. 12°. 2350
The same. New York, 1846. 8°. 3536
Stanley Buxton; or, the Schoolfellows. J. Galt. Phil. 1833. 2 v. 12°. . 1925
Stanley Thorn. H. Cockton. New York, 1852. 8°. 1638
Stansbury, H. Valley of Great Salt Lake of Utah. Wash. 1853. 8°. . 4939
Stanton, H. B. Sketches of Reforms and Reformers. N.Y. 1850. 12°. . 3440
Star Chamber. W. H. Ainsworth. New York, 1854. 8°. . . . 5948
Stark, J. Life. E. Everett. Boston, 1838. 12°. 1076, 1
Starling, Elizabeth. Noble Deeds of Woman. Boston, 1850. 12°. . 3673
State Papers and Pub. Docs. of the U.S., 1789–1818. Bost. 1815–19. 12 v. 8°. 1944
State Trials, Modern. W. C. Townsend. London, 1850. 2 v. 8°. . . 5483
of the United States. F. Wharton. Philadelphia, 1849. 8°. . 2669
State Triumvirate; a Political Tale. New York, 1819. 12°. . . . 93
Statesman's Manual. S. T. Coleridge. New York, 1853. 12°. . 5561, 1
Statesmen of America in 1846. Sarah M. Maury. Phil. 1847. 12°. . 4469
of the Time of George III. Lord Brougham. Phil. 1854. 2 v. 12°. 6186
The same. 2d and 3d series. New York, 1839–44. 2 v. 12°. 983
Statics and Dynamics. T. Baker. London, 1851. 12°. 6105
Staunton, Sir G. Embassy to the Emperor of China. Phil. 1799. 2 v. 8°. 1270
The same. London, 1797. 8°. 716
Staunton, H. Chess-Player's Companion. London, 1849. Post 8°. . 3567
Chess-Player's Handbook. London, 1847. Post 8°. . . . 3566
Staunton, W. Dictionary of the Episcopal Church. New York, 1839. 12°. 2447
Steam and Locomotion. J. Sewell. London, 1852. 12°. 6086
and the Steam Engine. W. Templeton. Philadelphia, 1854. 12°. 5573
Steam Boilers, Treatise on. R. Armstrong. London, 1850. 12°. . . 6075
Steam Engine, Popular Lectures on. D. Lardner. New York, 1828. 12°. 1176
Treatise on. D. Lardner. London, 1853. 12°. 6057
Steam Marine Engines. R. Murray. London, 1852. 12°. 6088
Steam Navigation and Propellers. R. Macfarlane. New York, 1851. 12°. 4058
Steamboat; a Tale. J. Galt. New York, 1823. 12°. 1907
Steamboat Disasters and Railroad Accidents. Worcester, 1846. 12°. . 2103
Stedman, C. History of the American Revolution. Dublin, 1794. 2 v. 8°. 1917
Steel, Manufacture of. F. Overman. Philadelphia, 1851. 12°. . . 4203
Steele, R., and J. Addison. Guardian and Tatler. N.Y. 1852. Roy. 8°. 4840
The same. New York, 1853. 12°. 5562, 3
The Spectator. New York, 1854. 6 v. 8°. 5898
The same. New York, 1842. 2 v. 8°. 792
Steele, Mrs. Heroines of Sacred History. New York, 1850. 12°. . . 4045

Steinmetz, A. History of the Jesuits. Philadelphia, 1848. 2 v. 8°. . 3165
Jesuit in the Family. London, 1847. 12°. 1110
Novitiate; or, Year among the English Jesuits. N.Y. 1846. 12°. 2945
Step-Mother. G. P. R. James. New York, 1846. 2 v. 8°. . . . 2678
Stephen, Sir J. Critical and Miscellaneous Essays. Phil. 1843. 12°. . 1741

Life of Wm. Wilberforce; Lives of Whitfield and Froude; D'Aubigné's History of the Reformation; Life and Times of Richard Baxter; Taylor's Physical Theory of Another Life; Port-Royalists; Ignatius Loyola and his Associates; Taylor's Edwin the Fair.

The same. Philadelphia, 1848. 8°. 3418, 7
Lectures on History of France. New York, 1852. 8°. . . 4697
Stephen, T. Book of the English Constitution. Glasgow, n. d. 8°. . 2859
Stephens, Mrs. Ann S. Fashion and Famine. New York, 1854. 12°. . 6157
Stephens, Mrs. H. M. Home Scenes and Home Sounds. Bost. 1854. 12°. 5627
Stephens, A. J. Rise and Prog. of the Eng. Constitution. Lon. 1838. 2 v. 8°. 5474
Stephens, J. L. Travels in Central America. New York, 1848. 2 v. 8°. 1635
Travels in Egypt, Arabia Petræa, &c. New York, 1837. 2 v. 12°. 1054
Travels in Greece, Turkey, Russia, &c. New York, 1843. 2 v. 12°. 879
Travels in Yucatan. New York, 1843. 2 v. 8°. 1721
Stephenson, R. M. Treatise on Railways. London, 1850. 12°. . . 6077
Sterling, J. Life. T. Carlyle. Boston, 1851. 12°. 4486
Poetical Works. Philadelphia, 1842. 12°. 2337
Sterne, L., Beauties of. Boston, 1807. 16°. 73
Works; with Life. Philadelphia, 1831. 8°. 2080

Tristram Shandy; Sentimental Journey through France and Italy; Letters.

Stetson, Genealogical Sketch of the Family of. J. S. Barry. Bost. 1847. 8°. 3046
Stetson, C. Rebelliad; a Poem of Harvard. Boston, 1842. 12°. . . 1694
Steuben, Baron. Life. F. Bowen. Boston, 1844. 12°. . . 1076, 9
Stevens, A. Introd. of Methodism into Eastern States. Bost. 1848. 12°. . 3048
Stevens, R. Essay on Average. Boston, 1833. 8°. 2060
Stevens, W. B. History of Georgia. Vol. 1. New York, 1847. 8°. . 2858
Stevenson, A. Treatise on Lighthouses. London, 1850. 12°. . . 6069
Steward; a Romance of Real Life. H. Cockton. New York, 1852. 8°. 4549
Stewart, C. S. Residence in the Sandwich Islands. Boston, 1839. 12°. 53
Society in Great Britain and Ireland. Phil. 1834. 2 v. 12°. . . 1033
Stewart, D. Philosophy of the Human Mind. Boston, 1836. 2 v. 8°. . 1370
Philosophy of the Active and Moral Powers of Man. Cam. 1849. 12°. 3427
Stewart, K. J. Freemason's Manual. Philadelphia, 1851. 12°. . . 4191
Stewart, V. A., History and Adventure of. H. R. Howard. N.Y. 1836. 12°. 233
Stickney, Sarah. Poetry of Life. Philadelphia, 1835. 2 v. 12°. . . 1102
Pretension. Philadelphia, 1837. 2 v. 12°. 942
See also *Ellis, Mrs. S.*
Stiles, Ezra. Life. A. Holmes. Boston, 1798. 8°. 714
Life. J. L. Kingsley. Boston, 1846. 12°. 1076, 16
Stiles, W. H. Austria in 1848-49. New York, 1852. 2 v. 8°. . . 4833
Stilling, H., Autobiography of. New York, 1845. 8°. 2737
Theobald; or, the Fanatic. Philadelphia, 1846. 12°. . . . 2514
Stimson, A. L. Easy Nat; or, the Three Apprentices. N. Y. 1854. 12°. 6173
Stirling, Earl of. Life. W. A. Duer. New York, 1847. 8°. . . 2800

Stirling, W. Cloister Life of Charles V. Boston, 1853. 12°. . . 5359
Stock Exchange, Chronicles and Characters of. J. Francis. Bost. 1850. 8°. 3949
Stöckhardt, J. A. Principles of Chemistry. Cambridge, 1850. 12°. . 3927
Stoddard, R. H. Adventures in Fairy Land. Boston, 1853. 12°. . . 5234
Poems. Boston, 1852. 12°. 4492
Stone-Blasting and Quarrying. Sir J. Burgoyne. London, 1852. 12°. . 6058
Stone, E. M. History of Beverly, Mass. Boston, 1843. 12°. . . 3072
Stone, W. L. Life of Joseph Brant. New York, 1838. 2 v. 8°. . . 1946
Border Wars of the Revol. (H. F. L.) N.Y. 1848. 2 v. 12°. 3683, 167–8
Poetry and History of Wyoming. New York, 1841. 12°. . . 2966
Stones of Venice. J. Ruskin. New York, 1851. 8°. 4119
Storer, D. H. Fishes and Reptiles of Massachusetts. Boston, 1839. 8°. 722
Stories about Animals. F. C. Woodworth. New York, 1850. 12°. . 3311
The same. Boston, 1851. 12°. 3937
about Birds. F. C. Woodworth. Boston, 1851. 12°. . . . 3938
from Blackwood. New York, 1852. 12°. 4929
from English History. Agnes Strickland. New York, 1854. 12°. 5630
from History. Agnes Strickland. New York, 1854. 12°. . . 5629
from History. Mrs. S. C. Hall and Mrs. J. Foster. N. Y. 1852. 12°. 4996
from History of the Jews. New York, 1853. 12°. . . . 5628
from the Italian Poets. L. Hunt. New York, 1846. 12°. . . 2564
of English and Foreign Life. W. and M. Howitt. Lon. 1853. Post 8°. 5944
of Waterloo. W. H. Maxwell. London, 1851. 12°. . . . 5657
Storms, Philosophy of. J. P. Espy. Boston, 1841. 8°. 1981
Story, J., Beauties of, with Sketch of Life. Boston, 1839. 24°. . . 1498
Commentaries on Constitution of the U. States. Bost. 1833. 3 v. 8°. 1796
The same. Boston, 1851. 2 v. roy. 8°. 4312
Commentaries on the Law of Bills of Exchange. Bost. 1847. 8°. 3594
Commentaries on the Law of Partnership. Boston, 1846. 8°. . 3595
Commentaries on the Law of Promissory Notes. Boston, 1847. 8°. 3593
Life and Letters. Edited by W. W. Story. Boston, 1851. 2 v. 8°. 4559
Miscellaneous Writings. Boston, 1835. 8°. 2063
The same. Edited by W. W. Story. Boston, 1852. 8°. . 4698
Story, W. W. Law of Contracts not under Seal. Boston, 1847. 8°. . 2219
Law of Sales of Personal Property. Boston, 1847. 8°. . . 3792
Poems. Boston, 1847. 12°. 2950
Story of a Family. Boston, 1850. 8°. 3644
of a Feather. D. Jerrold. London, 1851. 12°. . . . 6234, 3
of a Royal Favorite. Mrs. C. Gore. New York, 1846. 8°. . . 2664
without a Name. G. P. R. James. New York, 1852. 8°. . . 375
Stoughton, J. Life and Labors of Philip Doddridge. Boston, 1853. 12°. 5075
Scriptural Heroes; or, Sketches of the Puritans. N. Y. 1848. 12°. 3171
Stowe, Mrs. H. B. Sunny Memories in Foreign Lands. Bost. 1854. 2 v. 12°. 6156
Key to Uncle Tom's Cabin. Boston, 1853. 8°. 5174
Uncle Tom's Cabin. Boston, 1852. 2 v. 12°. 3109
Strabo, Geography of. Tr. by Hamilton & Falconer. Lond. 1854. 3 v. 8°. 6194
Strafford, Earl of. Life. J. Forster. London, 1831. 12°. . . 1831, 2
Straith, H. Treatise on Fortification and Artillery. London, 1850. 2 v. 8°. 4823

Strauss, G. L. German Reader. London, 1852. 12°. 6118
Grammar of the French Language. London, 1853. 12°. . . 6116
Grammar of the German Language. London, 1852. 12°. . . 6117
Strategematicon; or, Ancient Military Policy. R. B. Scott. Lon. 1811. 8°. 1315
Stratford-upon-Avon and Vicinity. G. May. Evesham, 1847. 12°. . 4026
Strawberry, Cultivation of. R. G. Pardee. New York, 1854. 12°. . 6268
Stray Subjects Arrested and Bound Over. Philadelphia, 1848. 12°. . 3181
Stray Yankee in Texas. P. Paxton. New York, 1853. 12°. . . . 5258
Street, A. B. Frontenac; a Metrical Romance. New York, 1849. 12°. 3413
Strickland, Agnes. Lives of the Queens of England. Phil. 1848. 12 v. 12°. 3524
The same. Philadelphia, 1843. 11 v. 12°. 1911

Vol. 1. Matilda of Flanders; Matilda of Scotland; Adelicia of Louvaine; Matilda of Boulogne; Eleanora of Aquitaine.
2. Berengaria of Navarre; Isabella of Angouleme; Eleanor of Provence; Eleanora of Castille; Marguerite of France; Isabella of France; Philippa of Hainault; Anne of Bohemia.
3. Isabella of Valois; Joanna of Navarre; Katherine of Valois; Margaret of Anjou; Elizabeth Woodville; Anne of Warwick.
4. Elizabeth of York; Katherine of Aragon; Anne Boleyn; Jane Seymour; Anne Cleves; Katherine Howard.
5. Katherine Parr; Mary, First Queen Regent.
6. Elizabeth, Second Queen Regent.
7. Elizabeth, concluded; Anne of Denmark.
8. Henrietta Maria; Catharine of Braganza.
9. Mary Beatrice of Modena.
10. Mary Beatrice, concluded; Mary II., Queen Regent.
11. Mary II., concluded; Anne, Queen Regent.
12. Anne, concluded.

Lives of the Queens of Scotland. New York, 1851–53. 4 v. 12°. 4028

Vol. 1. Margaret Tudor; Magdalene of France; Mary of Lorraine.
2. Mary of Lorraine, continued; Margaret Douglas.
3, 4. Mary Stuart (Mary, Queen of Scots).

Pilgrims of Walsingham. New York, 1854. 12°. 6147
Royal Sisters; a Romance. Boston, 1845. 16°. 2190
Stories from English History. New York, 1854. 12°. . . . 5630
Stories from History. New York, 1854. 12°. 5629
Strickland, W. P. History of American Bible Society. N.Y. 1849. 8°. 3388
Strive and Thrive; a Tale. Mary Howitt. Boston, 1841. 18°. . . 2161
Strong, A. B. Illustrated Natural History. New York, 1848. 2 v. 8°. . 4512
Struenzée, Count; the Skeptic and the Christian. Boston, 1853. 12°. . 5253
Struggles for Life; Autobiog. of a Dissenting Minister. Phil. 1854. 12°. 5827
Stuart, C. Memoir of Granville Sharp. New York, 1836. 12°. . . 1534
Stuart, H. W. V. Eve of the Deluge. London, 1851. 12°. . . . 4256
Stuart, J. Three Years in North America. New York, 1833. 2 v. 12°. . 1171
Stuart, M. Hist. and Defence of the Old Test. Canon. And. 1845. 12°. 4749
Stuart of Dunleath. Mrs. C. E. S. Norton. London, 1851. 3 v. 12°. . 4238
Stubbs's Calendar; or, the Fatal Boots. W. M. Thackeray. N.Y. 1850. 18°. 3763
Student-Life Abroad, Romance of. R. B. Kimball. N. York, 1853. 12°. 5055
Student-Life of Germany. W. Howitt. Philadelphia, 1842. 8°. . . 2075
Student's Manual. J. Todd. Northampton, 1835. 12°. 885
Studies of Nature. J. H. B. de St. Pierre. London, 1801. 4°. . . 708
Study, Treatise on. J. F. Ringelbergius. Philadelphia, 1847. 12°. . 3769
Sturge, J. Visit to the United States, 1841. Boston, 1842. 12°. . . 1909
Sturm, C. C. Reflections on the Works of God. Lond. 1808. 2 v. 24°. 1495

Stuyvesant; a Franconia Story. J. Abbott. New York, 1854. 12°. . 5295
Subaltern in America. Philadelphia, 1853. 12°. 298
Subaltern's Furlough. E. T. Coke. New York, 1833. 2 v. 12°. . . 1195
Sublime and Beautiful, Essay on the. E. Burke. New York, 1846. 12°. 299
The same. Boston, 1839. 8°. 1588, 1
The same. New York, 1835. 8°. 446, 1
Substance and Shadows. Emma Wilmont. Boston, 1854. 12°. . . 5962
Success in Life; The Lawyer. Mrs. L. C. Tuthill. N.Y. 1850. 12°. . 3677
The Mechanic. Mrs. L. C. Tuthill. N. York, 1850. 12°. . 4052
The Merchant. Mrs. L. C. Tuthill. N. York, 1850. 12°. . 3137
Successful Merchant. W. Arthur. New York, 1852. 12°. 1056
Suddards, W. British Pulpit. New York, 1845. 2 v. 8°. . . . 6019
Sue, E. Anger; or, the Firebrand. New York, 1849. 8°. . . . 3255
Children of Love. New York, 1850. 8°. 3966
Commander of Malta. New York, 1849. 8°. 3299
De Rohan; or, Court Conspirator. New York, 1845. 8°. . . 2838
Envy. New York, 1848. 8°. 3214
Latreaumont; or, the Court Conspirator. Philadelphia, 1849. 8°. 3300
Marquis de Letorière. New York, 1844. 8°. 2167, 2
Matilda. New York, 1843. 8°. 2173
Mysteries of Paris. New York, 1843. 8°. 1749
Pride. New York, 1847. 8°. 2785
Seven Capital Sins. New York, 1849. 8°. 2896
Pride; Avarice; Anger; Envy; Voluptuousness.
The Temptation. New York, 1845. 8°. 2748
Wandering Jew. New York, 1846. 2 v. roy. 8°. 2622
*The same (in Spanish and Illus.). Paris, 1846. 4 v. roy. 8°. 6029
Sullivan, F. S. Lectures on Const. and Laws of Eng. Port. 1805. 2 v. 12°. 3584
Sullivan, Jas. Hist. of Land Titles in Massachusetts. Boston, 1801. 8°. 747
History of the District of Maine. Boston, 1795. 8°. . . . 577
Sullivan, John. Life. O. W. B. Peabody. Boston, 1844. 12°. . 1076, 13
Sullivan, W. Moral Class Book. Boston, 1831. 12°. 422
Historical Causes and Effects from 476 to 1517. Bost. 1838. 12°. . 922
Public Characters and Events, 1783–1815. Boston, 1834. 12°. . 1228
Public Men of the Revolution. Philadelphia, 1847. 8°. . . . 2809
Sully, Duke of, Memoirs of. Trans. by C. Lennox. Phil. 1817. 5 v. 8°. 1300
Summer and Winter in the Pyrenees. Mrs. S. Ellis. Lond. 1841. 12°. 4571
Cruise in the Mediterranean. N. P. Willis. N. York, 1853. 12°. 5273
Day Book. New York, 1842. 12°. 1888
Tours; or, Notes of a Traveller. Theo. Dwight. N.Y. 1847. 12°. 3037
in Scotland. J. Abbott. New York, 1848. 12°. 3110
on the Lakes. S. Margaret Fuller. Boston, 1844. 12°. . . . 2104
Time in the Country. R. A. Willmott. New York, 1852. 12°. . 4908
Summerfield; or, Life on a Farm. D. K. Lee. Auburn, 1852. 12°. . 4796
Sumner, C. Orations and Speeches. Boston, 1850. 2 v. 12°. . . 4079
Phi-Beta-Kappa Oration. Boston, 1846. 8°. 3197
White Slavery in Barbary States. Boston, 1853. 12°. . . . 5249
Sunbeams and Shadows. Georgie A. Hulse. New York, 1851. 12°. . 4429

Sunderland, La Roy. Anti-Slavery Manual. New York, 1839. 16°. . 1506
Testimony of God against Slavery. New York, 1839. 16°. . . 1511
Sunny Memories of Foreign Lands. Mrs. H. B. Stowe. Bost. 1854. 2 v. 12°. 6156
Sunny Side; or, Country Minister's Wife. Mrs.E.S.Phelps. Phil. 1851. 18°. 4397
Sunshine in the Palace and Cottage. L. B. Urbino. Boston, 1854. 12°. 5792
Sunshine of Greystone. E. J. May. New York, 1854. 12°. . . . 5785
Supernatural, Glimpses of the. C. W. Elliott. New York, 1852. 12°. . 4895
Supernatural Illusions. P. I. Begbie. London, 1851. 2 v. 12°. . . 4197
Supernaturalism in New England. J. G. Whittier. N.Y. 1847. 12°. . 2963
Superstitions, Truths in Popular. H. Mayo. Edinburgh, 1851. 12°. . 4221
Surenne, G. French Pronouncing Dictionary. New York, 1851. 12°. . 4873
Surgeon's Daughter. Sir W. Scott. Boston, 1848. 12°. . . 999, 40
The same. Edinburgh, 1849. 12°. 4100, 48
The same. Edinburgh, 1850. Roy. 8°. . . . 4531, 10
Surgery, Household. J. F. South. London, 1851. 18°. 4774
Modern. R. Druitt. Philadelphia, 1851. 8°. 5991
Surr, T. S. George Barnwell. New York, 1845. 12°. 18
Surveying, Land and Engineering. T. Baker. London, 1850. 12°. . 6076
Theory and Practice of. R. Gibson. New York, 1821. 8°. . 810
Sutherland, A. Achievements of the Knights of Malta. Phil. 1846. 2 v. 12°. 2996
Sutton, H. M. (Editor.) Papers of Lord Lexington. London, 1851. 8°. 4300
Swainson, W. Birds of Western Africa. Edinburgh, 4843. 2 v. 12°. 4901, 11, 12
Fly-Catchers. Edinburgh, 1843. 2 v. 12°. 4901, 13
Swallow Barn. J. P. Kennedy. Philadelphia, 1832. 2 v. 12°. . . 1207
Swamp Steed; a Novel. New York, 1852. 8°. 381
Sweden, General View of. M. Catteau. London, 1790. 8°. . . . 653
and Gothland, Rambles in. London, 1847. 8°. 4146
History of. A. Fryxell. London, 1844. 2 v. 12°. 4578
Travels in. Countess Hahn-Hahn. London, 1845. 24°. . . 2419
Swedenborg, E. Apocalypse Revealed. Boston, 1836. 3 v. 12°. . . 903
Athanasian Creed. Boston, 1828. 16°. 58
Christian Religion. Boston, 1833. 8°. 797
Compendium and Life of. Boston, 1853. Roy. 8°. 5995
Delights of Wisdom concerning Conjugial Love. Bost. 1833. 8°. 798
Divine Love and Divine Wisdom. Boston, 1828. 16°. . . . 57
Doctrine of New Jerusalem. Boston, 1829. 16°. 59
Earths in our Solar System. Boston, 1828. 12°. 14
Examination of the Claims of. New York, 1852. 12°. . . . 4891
Heavenly Arcana. Boston, 1837. 3 v. 8°. 668
Intercourse of the Soul and Body. Boston, 1828. 16°. . . . 79
Treatise on the Last Judgment. Boston, 1828. 12°. . . . 8
Worship and Love of God. Boston, 1832. 12°. 904
Swedenborgianism, Essays on. T. Parsons. Boston, 1845. 12°. . . 2346
Sweethearts and Wives. T. S. Arthur. New York, 1844. 12°. . . 2195
Sweetser, W. Dyspepsia and Digestion. Boston, 1837. 12°. . . 1090
Mental Hygiene; or, Intellect and the Passions. N.Y. 1850. 12°. 4050
Swett, J. A. Diseases of the Chest. New York, 1852. 8°. . . . 4804
Swett, S. Battle of Bunker Hill. Boston, 1818. 12°. 190

Swift, J. Gulliver's Travels. New York, 1847. 12°. 2982
Memoirs. Sir W. Scott. Boston, 1829. 12°. . . . 399, 2
The same. Edinbugh, 1834. 12°. 4101, 2
Tale of a Tub. London, 1837. 24°. 847
Works; with Memoir by T. Roscoe. London, 1843. 2 v. roy. 8°. 2861

Vol. 1. Life; Gulliver's Travels; Tale of a Tub; Battle of the Books; Journal to Stella, &c.; Tracts, Political and Historical; Miscellanies in Prose.
2. Drapier's Letters, &c.; Tracts, Religious and Miscellaneous; Miscellaneous Papers — Tatler, Spectator, &c.; Miscellanies in Prose, by Swift and Sheridan.

Works; edited by T. Sheridan. New York, 1812. 24 v. 12°. . 6333

Vols. 1, 2. Life of Jonathan Swift, by T. Sheridan.
3. Tale of a Tub; Battle of the Books; Miscellaneous.
4. Short Political Articles.
5. The Examiner; October Club; Conduct of the Allies.
6. Short Political Articles.
7. History of the Four last Years of the Queen; History of England.
8. Miscellaneous and Periodical Papers.
9. (Missing.)
10, 11. Poems.
12–14. Miscellaneous.
15–20. Letters.
21. Journal to Stella.
22. Journal to Stella; Polite Conversation.
23. Martinus Scriblerus: Key to the Lock; Memoirs of P. P.; History of John Bull; Miscellaneous.
24. Miscellanies in Verse and Prose; Index to the 24 vols.

Arbuthnot, Pope, and Gay; Miscellanies. London, 1847. 10 v. 12°. 287
Swindell, J. G. Well-Digging, Boring, &c. London, 1854. 12°. . . 6055
Swiss Family Robinson. New York, 1852. 12°. 3312
The same (in French). Paris, 1843. 8°. 4548
Switzerland, *W. Beattie. Illust. by W. H. Bartlett. Lond. 1834. 4°. 3744
and Italy, Tour through, 1801–2. Philadelphia, 1805. 2 v. 8°. . 684
in 1847. T. Mügge. London, 1848. 2 v. 12°. 4588
Letters from. J. W. von Goethe. London, 1849. Post 8°. . . 4376
Sketches of. J. F. Cooper. Philadelphia, 1836. 4 v. 12°. . . 229
Tour in. Hellen M. Williams. Dublin, 1798. 2 v. 12°. . . 873
Sword and the Distaff. W. G. Simms. Philadelphia, 1853. 12°. . . 5341
Sybil; or, the Two Nations. B. Disraeli. New York, 1845. 8°. . . 2283
Sybil Lennard; a Novel. Mrs. Grey. Philadelphia, 1848. 8°. . . 6002
Sydenham, Sequel to Alice Paulet. Philadelphia, 1833. 2 v. 12°. . . 529
Sydney Clifton. New York, 1839. 2 v. 12°. 186
Sylvester Sound, the Somnambulist. H. Cockton. New York, 1849. 8°. 2216
Sympathies of the Continent. J. B. von Hirscher. Oxford, 1852. 12°. 5237
Synonymes, English. G. Crabbe. Boston, 1819. 8°. 1292
English. G. F. Graham. New York, 1847. 12°. . . . 3004
Dictionary of. J. Rawson. Philadelphia, 1850. 12°. . . . 3577
of the New Testament. R. C. Trench. New York, 1854. 12°. . 6295
Syria, Howadji in. G. W. Curtis. New York, 1852. 12°. . . . 4799
and the Holy Land. W. K. Kelly. London, 1844. 8°. . . 3190
Palestine and Asia Minor. F. A. Neale. London, 1851. 2 v. 12°. 4446
State and Prospects of. C. G. Addison. Phil. 1838. 2 v. 12°. . 835
War in. Sir C. Napier. London, 1842. 2 v. 12°. . . . 3058

T.

Table Talk. S. T. Coleridge. New York, 1835. 2 v. 12°. 1249
W. Hazlitt. New York, 1845. 2 v. 12°. 2372
The same. London, 1824. 2 v. 8°. 2290
L. Hunt. London, 1851. 12°. 6274
J. Selden. Cambridge, 1831. 12°. 383, 2
of Books, Men, and Manners. Ed. by C. Evelyn. N. Y. 1853. 12°. 5032
or, Selections from the Ana. Edinburgh, 1827. 16°. . . . 1862
Tacitus, C. Works. Translated by A. Murphy. Philadelphia, 1840. 8°. 1997
Les Six Premiers Livres des Annales. Paris, 1768. 3 v. 12°. . 407
Works. Oxford Translation. London, 1854. 2 v. post 8°. . . 5935

Vol. 1. The Annals.
2. The History; Germany; Agricola; Dialogue on Orators.

Talbot, G. H. Philosophy of French Pronunciation. N. Y. 1854. 12°. 6282
Talbot and Vernon; a Novel. J. L. McConnell. New York, 1850. 12°. 3847
Tale of a Tub. J. Swift. London, 1837. 24°. 847
Tale of Paraguay. R. Southey. Boston, 1827. 16°. 814
Tales. J. H. D. Zschökke. Trans. by P. Godwin. N. Y. 1845. 2 v. 12°. 2477
and Sketches. Cath. M. Sedgwick. New York, 1844. 16°. . 809
and Sketches. Tr. from Italian, &c. by N. Greene. Bost. 1843. 12°. 1657
and Souvenirs of a Residence in Europe. Philadelphia, 1842. 12°. 1659
and Traditions of Hungary. Ther. Pulszky. Lond. 1851. 3 v. 12°. 4240
from the German. Trans. by N. Greene. Boston, 1837. 2 v. 12°. 917
from the Gesta Romanorum. New York, 1845. 12°. . . . 2375
German Popular. Bros. Grimm. New York, 1853. 2 v. 12°. . 5608
of the Borders and of Scotland. J. M. Wilson. N. Y. 1848. 2 v. 8°. 2889
of the Crusaders. Sir W. Scott. Boston, 1848. 2 v. 12°. . 999, 35, 36
The same. Edinburgh, 1849. 2 v. 12°. . . 4100, 37, 38
The same. Edinburgh, 1850. Roy. 8°. 4531, 9
The same. New York, 1835. 8°. 1361
of the Early Ages. Horace Smith. New York, 1832. 2 v. 12°. . 3578
of Fashion and Reality. Misses Beauclerk. Phil. 1836. 12°. . 236
of Glauber-Spa. C. M. Sedgwick and others. N. Y. 1832. 2 v. 12°. 433
of a Grandfather: Scottish Hist. Sir W. Scott. Phil. 1828. 2 v. 12°. 108
The same. Edinburgh, 1849. 5 v. 12°. . . 4101, 22–26
The same. Boston, 1848. 4 v. 12°. 999, 49–52
of a Grandfather: French History. Boston, 1848. 2 v. 12°. 999, 53, 54
The same. Edinburgh, 1849. 2 v. 12°. . . 4101, 27, 28
of the Grotesque and Arabesque. E. A. Poe. Phil. 1840. 2 v. 12°. 2310
of the Hall; Poems. G. Crabbe. London, 1819. 2 v. 8°. . . 683
of Humor and Romance. Trans. by R. Holcroft. N. Y. 1840. . 511
of Many Lands. M. F. Tytler. Edinburgh, 1846. 12°. . . 4268
of my Neighborhood. G. Griffin. Philadelphia, 1836. 2 v. 12°. . 2183
of Passion. New York, 1829. 2 v. 12°. 561
of the Peerage and Peasantry. Lady Dacre. N. Y. 1835. 2 v. 12°. 239

Tales of the Peerage and Peasantry. Lady Dacre. London, 1852. 12°. 5687
of a Physician. W. H. Harrison. Philadelphia, 1853. 2 v. 12°. . 856
of the Southern Border. C. W. Webber. Philadelphia, 1853. 12°. 5322
of a Traveller. W. Irving. New York, 1851. 12°. 3364
of Woman. New York, 1829. 12°. 1161
of the Woods and Fields. Mrs. Marsh. New York, 1836. 12°. . 238
Talfourd, T. N. Critical and Miscellaneous Writings. Phil. 1842. 12°. . 1701
The same. Philadelphia, 1848. 8°. 3418, 7

British Novels and Romances; Mackenzie; Sir W. Scott; Godwin; Maturin; Rymer on Tragedy; Cibber's Apology; John Dennis's Works; Modern Periodical Literature; Wordsworth; Lord Guilford; Hazlitt on the Drama; Wallace's Prospects; Pulpit Oratory; Lisbon; Lloyd's Poems; Modern Improvements; Chapter on Time; Profession of the Bar; Wine Cellar; Hazlitt; Brief Miscellanies.

Final Memorials of Charles Lamb. London, 1848. 2 v. 12°. . 6326
Literary Sketches and Letters of C. Lamb. New York, 1848. 12°. 3213
Tragedies, Sonnets, and Verses. New York, 1846. 12°. . . 2403
Talleyrand, Prince. Life. Philadelphia, 1834. 8°. 2091
*Tallis's Illustrated Atlas. Ed. by R. M. Martin. London, 1851. 4°. . 4948
Tancred; or, the New Crusade. B. Disraeli. New York, 1848. 8°. . 2778
Tanglewood Tales. N. Hawthorne. Boston, 1853. 12°. . . . 5506
Tanning, Currying, and Leather-Dressing. C. Morfit. Phil. 1852. 8°. . 4951
Tappan, H. P. Step from the New World to the Old. N.Y. 1852. 2 v. 12°. 4872
Tartary, Thibet, and China, Jour. to, 1844–46. M. Huc. N.Y. 1852. 2 v.12°. 946
Tasistro, L. F. Random Shots and Southern Breezes. N.Y. 1842. 2 v. 12°. 1656
Tasso, T. Jerusalem Delivered. Trans. by J. H. Wiffen. N. Y. 1850. 12°. 16
The same. Trans. by E. Fairfax. London, 1844. 2 v. 12°. 16
The same. Trans. by J. Hoole. Newburyport, 1810. 2 v. 8°. 748
Love, Madness, and Imprisonment of. R.H. Wilde. N.Y.1842. 2 v. 12°. 2127
Taste, Physiology of. B. Savarin. Philadelphia, 1854. 12°. . . . 5598
Tatler, The. Addison, Steele, and others. New York, 1809. 5 v. 12°. . 894
and Guardian. Addison, Steele, and others. N. Y. 1852. Roy. 8°. 4840
The same. New York, 1853. 12°. 5562, 3
The same. New York, 1842. 8°. 792, 3
Tayler, C. B. Earnestness; or, Life of an English Bishop. N.Y. 1850. 12°. 3913
May You Like it. Philadelphia, 1851. 12°. 4190
Tayler, W. E. Popery; its Character and its Crimes. Lond. 1851. 12°. 4441
Taylor, Bayard. Journey to Central Africa. New York, 1854. 12°. . 6185
Eldorado; or, Adventures in California. N. York, 1850. 2 v. 12°. 3835
Poems of the Orient. Boston, 1855. 12°. 6231
Rhymes of Travel, Ballads and Poems. New York, 1849. 12°. . 3334
Romances, Lyrics, and Songs. Boston, 1852. 12°. 4478
Views A-Foot; or, Europe seen with Knapsack. N. Y. 1852. 12°. 2940
Taylor, B. F. January and June. New York, 1854. 12°. . . . 5633
Taylor, G. Indications of the Creator. New York, 1851. 12°. . . 4456
Taylor, H. Edwin the Fair, and Isaac Comnenus. London, 1845. 24°. 2412
Notes from Life, in Seven Essays. Boston, 1853. 12°. . . . 5285

Money; Humility and Independence; Wisdom; Choice in Marriage; Children; The Life Poetic; Ways of the Rich and the Great.

Philip Van Artevelde. Cambridge, 1835. 12°. 2322

Taylor, F. W. Broad Pennant; or, Cruise of U. S. Flag Ship. N.Y. 1848. 12°. 3082
Flag Ship; or, Voyage round the World. N. Y. 1840. 2 v. 12°. . 2116
Taylor, I. Advice to the Teens. Boston, 1838. 16°. 87
Fanaticism. New York, 1834. 12°. 1848
Home Education. New York, 1838. 12°. 2356
Natural History of Enthusiasm. Boston, 1830. 12°. 1923
The same. New York, 1849. 12°. 3609
Process of Historical Proof. London, 1828. 8°. 2287
Saturday Evening. Boston, 1833. 12°. 2355
Wesley and Methodism. New York, 1852. 12°. 3906
Taylor, J. B. Memoir. J. H. and B. H. Rice. New York, n. d. 12°. . 336
Taylor, J. S. Selections from Writings. London, 1843. 8°. 4546
Taylor, Jane. Contributions of Q. Q. Boston, 1831. 2 v. 12°. . . 862
The same. New York, 1850. 2 v. 12°. 3664
Taylor, Jeffreys. Young Islanders. New York, 1842. 16°. . . . 2096
Taylor, Jeremy. Holy Living and Dying. Philadelphia, 1843. 12°. . 2406
Readings for Lent. New York, 1851. 12°. 3815
Selection from. Cambridge, 1831. 12°. 383, 8
Whole Works. [Vol. 1 wanting.] London, 1844. 3 v. roy. 8°. . 2279
Taylor, John. Identity of Junius. New York, 1818. 8°. 1326
Records of my Life. New York, 1833. 8°. 1394
Taylor, R. C. Statistics of Coal. Philadelphia, 1848. 8°. 3240
Taylor, Tom. (Editor.) Autobiog. of B. R. Haydon. N.Y. 1853. 2 v. 12°. 5591
Taylor, Thomas. Life of William Cowper. Philadelphia, 1834. 12°. . 423
Taylor, W. Historic Survey of German Poetry. London, 1830. 3 v. 8°. 5467
Taylor, W. B. S. Fine Arts in Great Britain. London, 1841. 2 v. 12°. 4628
History of the University of Dublin. London, 1845. 8°. . . . 4663
Taylor, W. C. History of Ireland. (H. F. L.) N.Y. 1848. 2 v. 12°. 3683, 51, 52
Life and Times of Sir Robert Peel. London, n. d. 2 v. 8°. . . 3632
Manual of Ancient and Modern History. New York, 1845. 8°. . 2253
Memoirs of the House of Orleans. Philadelphia, 1850. 2 v. 12°. 3837
Natural History of Society. New York, 1841. 2 v. 12°. . . . 1849
Tea and the Tea Trade. G. Nye, jun. New York, 1850. 8°. . . . 3942
Teacher and the Parent. C. Northend. New York, 1853. 12°. . . . 5358
Technology, Chemical. F. Knapp. London, 1848. 2 v. 8°. 4137
Popular. E. Hazen. (H. F. L.) N.Y. 1848. 2 v. 12°. 3683, 149, 150
Teeth, Essay on. H. Wells. Hartford, 1838. 12°. 3583
Preservation of. D. K. Hitchcock. Boston, 1840. 24°. . . . 1499
Structure and Diseases of. H. and J. Burdell. N.Y. 1838. 8°. . 4042
Tefft, B. F. Hungary and Kossuth. Philadelphia, 1852. 12°. . . . 4626
Shoulder-Knot. New York, 1850. 12°. 3876
Tehuantepec, Isthmus of. J. J. Williams. New York, 1852. 2 v. 8°. . 4843
Teignmouth, Lord. Life of Sir William Jones. London, 1804. 8°. . 762
The same. London, 1807. 8°. 1974
Telegraph, Electric, Anecdotes of. London, n. d. 24°. 5047
Electric, Historical Sketch of. A. Jones. New York, 1852. 8°. . 4845
Electric, Treatise on. E. Highton. London, 1852. 12°. . . . 6059
Telegraphs, History of. J. R. Parker. Boston, 1836. 12°. . . . 898

Telemachus, Adventures of. S. de la M. Fénélon. N.Y. 1847. 2 v. 12°. 2238
The same. Trans. by G. Bagnall. Dublin, 1792. 2 v. 12°. 170
Tell-Tale; or, Home Secrets. Mrs. E. S. Phelps. Boston, 1853. 18°. . 5188
Temperance Tales. L. M. Sargent. Boston, 1852. 12°. 4622
Edited by Miss C. B. Porter. Buffalo, 1852. 12°. 4449
and Sketches. T. W. Brown. Auburn, 1853. 12°. 5331
Temperance Tracts of the American Tract Society. New York, n. d. 12°. 545
Tempest and Sunshine; or, Life in Ky. Mary J. Holmes. N.Y. 1854. 12°. 5804
Temple, E. Travels in Peru. Philadelphia, 1833. 2 v. 12°. . . . 1205
Temples and Tombs of Egypt, Nubia, &c. Mrs. Romer. Lond. 1846. 2 v. 8°. 4647
Templeton, W. Steam and the Steam Engine. Philadelphia, 1854. 12°. 5573
Temptation. E. Sue. New York, 1845. 8°. 2748
Ten Nights in a Bar-Room. T. S. Arthur. Philadelphia, 1854. 12°. . 6169
Ten Thousand a Year. S. Warren. Philadelphia, 1841. 6 v. 12°. . 966
Tenant of Wildfell Hall. Miss Bronte. New York, 1848. 12°. . . 3155
Tencin, Mde. de. Œuvres. Amsterdam, 1786. 7 v. 12°. 10
Tennent, Sir J. E. Belgium. London, 1841. 2 v. 12°. 4572
History of Modern Greece. London, 1845. 2 v. 8°. 5138
Tennant, W. East Indian Recreations. London, 1804. 2 v. 8°. . . 969
Tennessee, History of. W. H. Carpenter & T. S. Arthur. Phil. 1854. 12°. 6288
Tennessean Abroad. R. W. MacGavock. New York, 1854. 12°. . . 6279
Tennessean's Story. Philadelphia, 1852. 12°. 3470
Tent and the Altar. J. Cumming. Boston, 1854. 12°. 5873
Tennyson, A. In Memoriam. Boston, 1850. 12°. 3888
Poems. Boston, 1849. 2 v. 12°. 1704
The Princess; a Medley. Boston, 1848. 12°. 3100
Terrible Tractoration; and other Poems. T. G. Fessenden. Bost. 1836. 12°. 736
Testimony of Christ's Second Appearing. Union Village (O.), 1823. 12°. 3052
Texan Expedition against Mier. T. J. Green. New York, 1845. 8°. . 2623
Texan Santa Fé Expedition. G. W. Kendall. New York, 1850. 2 v. 12°. 1765
Texas and Gulf of Mexico. Mrs. Houstoun. Philadelphia, 1845. 16°. . 2189
and New Mexico, Explorations in. J.R.Bartlett. N.Y. 1854. 2 v. 8°. 5950
Emigrant's Guide to. D. Woodman, jun. Boston, 1835. 12°. . 1466
History of. D. B. Edward. Cincinnati, 1836. 12°. 304
Visit to, 1831. New York, 1834. 12°. 3779
Visit to, with a Sketch of the War. New York, 1836. 16°. . . 84
Thacher, J. Demonology, Ghosts, and Apparitions. Boston, 1831. 12°. 839
Military Journal of the American Revolution. Boston, 1823. 8°.. 637
Thacher, P. O. (Judge), Criminal Cases tried before. Boston, 1845. 8°. . 2774
Thackeray, W. M. Book of Snobs. New York, 1852. 12°. . . . 4884
Confessions of Fitz-Boodle, &c. New York, 1852. 12°. . . 5060
English Humorists of the 18th Century. New York, 1853. 12°. . 5342
Great Hoggarty Diamond. New York, 1848. 8°. 3244
History of Henry Esmond. New York, 1852. 8°. 5111
History of Pendennis. New York, 1850. 2 v. 8°. 4034
Irish Sketch Book. New York, 1846. 8°. 2171
Jeames's Diary, Legend of the Rhine, &c. New York, 1853. 12°. 5277
Journey from Cornhill to Grand Cairo. New York, 1846. 12°. . 2561

Thackeray, W. M. Kickleburys on the Rhine. New York, 1851. 12°. . 3812
Luck of Barry Lyndon. New York, 1853. 2 v. 12°. 5181
Men's Wives. New York, 1852. 12°. 5001
Mr. Brown's Letters to a Young Man. New York, 1853. 12°. . 5235
Paris Sketch Book. New York, 1852. 2 v. 12°. 2166
Punch's Prize Novelists, &c. New York, 1853. 12°. 5266
Shabby Genteel Story. New York, 1852. 12°. 5019
Sketches in Ireland. Philadelphia, 1843. 8°. 1750
Stubb's Calendar; or, the Fatal Boots. New York, 1850. 18°. . 3763
Vanity Fair; a Novel without a Hero. New York, 1848. 8°. . 3219
Yellowplush Papers. New York, 1852. 12°. 1058
Thaddeus of Warsaw. Jane Porter. London, 1853. 12°. 5696
The same. Hartford, 1848. 24°. 20
Thalatta. Ed. by S. Longfellow and T. W. Higginson. Bost. 1853. 12°. 5306
Thames, Picturesque Tour of. J. F. Murray. London, 1849. 8°. . . 4659
Thatcher, B. B. The Boston Book. Boston, 1836, '37, '41. 3 v. 12°. . 248
Indian Biography. New York, 1843. 2 v. 12°. 2427
The same. (H. F. L.) New York, 1846. 2 v. 12°. 3683, 45, 46
Thayer, Mrs. J. Passion, and other Tales. Boston, 1846. 12°. . . . 2569
Théâtre Français au Moyen-Age. Monmerqué et Michel. Par. 1839. Roy. 8°. 3548
Theatre, History of the American. W. Dunlop. New York, 1832. 8°. . 1993
of the Greeks. Cambridge (Eng.), 1827. 8°. 5910
Theatrical Apprenticeship of Sol Smith. Philadelphia, 1846. 16°. . . 2362
Theatrical Dictionary. London, 1792. 12°. 3123
Theatrical Illustrations. J. Cumberland. London, n. d. 16°. . . . 2981
Theism, Atheism, &c., Sermons of. Theo. Parker. Boston, 1853. 12°. . 6316
Theobald; or, the Fanatic. H. Stilling. Tr. by S. Schæffer. Phil. 1846. 12°. 2514
Theodore. W. M. L. De Wette. Boston, 1841. 2 v. 12°. . . . 962, 10, 11
Theological Essays. F. D. Maurice. New York, 1854. 12°. 5772
Theological Essays. T. De Quincey. Boston, 1854. 2 v. 12°. . . . 5828
Theological Repository. Vol. 1. New York, 1812. 8°. 783
Theology, Explained and Defended. Timo. Dwight. N. Y. 1854. 4 v. 8°. 5999
Essays and Tracts on. Edited by J. Sparks. Bost. 1823. 2 v. 12°. 368
History of Doctrines. K. R. Hagenbach. Edinburgh, 1850. 2 v. 8°. 5151
Institutes of. T. Chalmers. New York, 1849. 2 v. 12°. . . . 3415
Lectures on Christian. G. C. Knapp. New York, 1850. 8°. . 4709
Natural. — See *Natural.*
Treatise on. T. Scott. Middletown. 1817. 6 v. 12°. 397
Theory of Human Progression. Boston, 1851. 12°. 4433
Theller, E. A. Canada in 1837-38. Philadelphia, 1841. 2 v. 12°. . 3130
Thesaurus of English Words. P. M. Roget. Boston, 1854. 12°. . . 5781
Thessalonians, Timo., Titus, and Phil., Notes on. A. Barnes. N.Y. 1849. 12°. 4736
Thierry, A. Historical Essays. Philadelphia, 1845. 8°. 2635
Thiers, A. Consulate and Empire. New York, 1852. 2 v. 8°. . . . 2754
History of the French Revolution. Philadelphia, 1842. 4 v. 8°. . 1724
Thiodolf, the Icelander. F. de la M. Fouqué. New York, 1845. 12°. . 2581
Thirlwall, C. History of Greece. London, 1843. 7 v. 12°. 1879
Thirty Years among the Players. J. Cowell. New York, 1845. 8°. . 1821

Thirty Years from Home. S. Leech. Boston, 1843. 16°. 1744
Since; or, the Ruined Family. G. P. R. James. N. Y. 1848. 8°. 3239
View of the U. S. Government. T. H. Benton. N. York, 1854. 8°. 5931
War in Germany, History of. F. Schiller. New York, 1846. 12°. 2954
This, That, and the Other. Ellen L. Chandler. Boston, 1854. 12°. . 5841
Tholuck, F. A. G. Guido and Julius. Boston, 1854. 12°. . . . 6221
Thomas, Caroline. Farmingdale. New York, 1854. 12°. . . . 5868
Thomas, E. S. Reminiscences of Sixty-five Years. Hart. 1840. 2 v. 12°. 2301
Thomas, Isaiah. History of Printing in America. Worc. 1810. 2 v. 8°. 1376
Thomas, F. W. Beechen Tree; a Tale in Rhyme. New York, 1844. 12°. 2097
Clinton Bradshaw. Philadelphia, 1835. 2 v. 12°. 1101
East and West. Philadelphia, 1836. 2 v. 12°. 271
Thomas, J. Travels in Egypt and Palestine. Philadelphia, 1853. 12°. . 5304
Thomas, J. J. American Fruit Culturist. Auburn, 1852. 12°. . . 5078
Farm Implements. New York, 1854. 12°. 5884
Thome, J. A., & J. H. Kimball. Emancipation in W. Indies. N.Y. 1838. 8°. 699
Thompson, A. C. Better Land; or, the Believer's Journey. Bost. 1854. 12°. 6193
Thompson, D. P. Green Mountain Boys. Boston, 1854. 12°. . . 3117
Locke Amsden; or, the Schoolmaster. Boston, 1850. 12°. . . 3041
Lucy Hosmer. Burlington, 1848. 8°. 3205
May Martin, and other Tales. Boston, 1852. 12°. . . . 1064
Rangers; or, the Tory's Daughter. Boston, 1851. 2 v. 12°. . . 4104
Thompson, G. Lectures in England. Boston, 1836. 12°. . . . 1553
Letters and Addresses of, in United States. Boston, 1837. 12°. . 1537
Reception in England. Boston, 1836. 12°. 1507
Thompson, H. Life of Hannah More. Philadelphia, 1838. 2 v. 12°. . 1052
Thompson, J. P. Memoir of David Hale. New York, 1850. 12°. . 3452
Photographic Views of Egypt. New York, 1854. 12°. . . 5869
Thompson, W. Recollections of Mexico. New York, 1846. 8°. . . 2713
Thompson, Mrs. (Editor.) Lady of Milan. New York, 1846. 8°. . . 2644
Thomson, J. The Seasons. Boston, 1810. 16°. 47
Thomson, Mrs. History of the Jacobites. London, 1845. 3 v. 8°. . . 4672
Thomson, A. T. Materia Medica and Therapeutics. London, 1843. 8°. 4692
(Editor.) Philosophy of Magic. London, 1846. 2 v. 8°. . . 4683
Thomson, Mrs. A. T. Life of Sir Walter Raleigh. Phil. 1831. 12°. . 410
Thoreau, H. D. Walden; or, Life in the Woods. Boston, 1854. 12°. . 6166
Week on the Concord and Merrimack Rivers. Boston, 1849. 12°. 3374
Thoresby, R., Diary of, 1677–1724. London, 1830. 4 v. 8°. . . . 5478
*Thorne, A. Irish Almanac and Directory for 1851. Dublin, 1851. 8°. 11
Thorburn, G. Fifty Years' Reminiscences of New York. N.Y. 1845. 18°. 2421
Forty Years in America. Boston, 1834. 12°. 1934
Men and Manners in Britain. New York, 1834. 12°. . . . 2150
Thornton, H. Paper Credit in Great Britain. Philadelphia, 1807. 8°. . 656
Thornton, J. Preciousness of Christ. Boston, 1834. 12°. . . . 1480
Thornton, J. Q. Oregon and California in 1848. N. York, 1849. 2 v. 12°. 3279
Thorpe; a Quiet English Town. W. Mountford. Boston, 1852. 12°. . 877
Thought, Growth of. W. Withington. Boston, 1851. 12°. . . . 6244
Thoughts in Prison. W. Dodd. Boston, n. d. 12°. 463

Three Courses and a Desert. Illust. by G. Cruikshank. Lond. 1850. Post 8°. 4392
Three Eras of Woman's Life. E. E. Smith. New York, 1836. 2 v. 12°. 230
Three Guardsmen. A. Dumas. New York, 1846. 8°. 2686
Three Histories. Maria J. Jewsbury. Boston, 1831. 12°. 542
The same. Philadelphia, 1833. 8°. 1357, 3
Three Sisters and Three Fortunes. G. H. Lewes. New York, 1848. 8°. 3230
Three Years in the Pacific. Philadelphia, 1834. 8°. 1415
Throop, G. H. Lynde Weiss; an Autobiography. Phil. 1852. 12°. . 140
Thrope, T. Catalogue of Books. London, 1842. 8°. 5894
Thrope, T. B. Hive of the Bee-Hunter. New York, 1854. 12°. . . 5867
Thucydides. Peloponnesian War. Tr. by H. Dale. Lond. 1849. 2 v. post 8°. 4389
Translated by W. Smith. New York, 1842. 2 v. 12°. 1854, 22, 23
Tibet, Tartary, and Mongolia. H. T. Prinsep. London, 1851. 12°. . 5369
Ticknor, C. Philosophy of Living. (H. F. L.) New York, 1846. 12°. 3683, 77
Ticknor, G. History of Spanish Literature. New York, 1849. 3 v. 8°. 3515
Ticonderoga; or, the Black Eagle. G. P. R. James. N.Y. 1854. 8°. . 5975
Tieck, L. Elves, and other Tales. Trans. by T. Carlyle. N.Y. 1846. 8°. 2679
Tim Bobbin's Lancashire Dialect. London, 1828. 12°. 1293
Timbuctoo, Account of. J. G. Jackson. Philadelphia, 1810. 12°. . 284
Time and Tide; or, Strive and Win. A. S. Roe. New York, 1852. 12°. 4869
Time the Avenger. Mrs. Marsh. New York, 1851. 8°. 3809
Timpson, T. Memoirs of British Female Missionaries. Lond. 1841. 12°. 2446
Tin Trumpet; or, Heads and Tales. Philadelphia, 1836. 2 v. 12°. . . 228
The same. Philadelphia, 1836. 8°. 2228, 2
Tip-Top; or, the Noble Aim. Mrs. L. C. Tuthill. New York, 1853. 12°. 5546
Titian. Life. J. Northcote. London, 1830. 2 v. 8°. 2292
To Daimonion; or, the Spiritual Medium. Boston, 1852. 12°. . . 5033
To Love and To be Loved. A. S. Roe. New York, 1851. 12°. . . 4096
Tobacco Using, Beauties and Deformities of. L. B. Coles. Bost. 1851. 12°. 4477
Tocqueville, A. de. Am. Institutions and their Influence. N.Y. 1851. 12°. 3829
Democracy in America. New York, 1839. 2 v. 8°. 948
To-Day; a Literary Journal. Edited by C. Hale. Boston, 1852. 2 v. 8°. 5418
Todd, J. Daughter at School. Northampton, 1854. 12°. . . . 5535
Student's Manual. Northampton, 1835. 12°. 885
Token; a Christmas Present. Ed. by N. P. Willis. Boston, 1829. 12°. 842
Toliver, E. Our Folks at Home. Philadelphia, 1855. 12°. . . . 6191
Tom Burke of "Ours." C. Lever. Philadelphia, 1846. 8°. . . . 2177
Tom Cringle's Log. F. Chamier. New York, 1845. 8°. . . . 1091
Tom Jones, History of. H. Fielding. London, 1831. 2 v. 12°. . . 4253
The same. Philadelphia, 1843. 8°. 1232, 1
The same. London, 1808. 3 v. 16°. 6334
Tom Racquet and his Three Maiden Aunts. New York, 1851. 12°. . 4112
Tomline, G. Life of William Pitt. Philadelphia, 1821. 2 v. 8°. . . 1978
Tomlinson, C. Treatise on Locks. London, 1853. 12°. . . . 6093
Treatise on Mechanics. London, 1854. 12°. 6040
Treatise on Natural Philosophy. London, 1853. 12°. 6037
Treatise on Pneumatics. London, 1852. 12°. 6043
Warming and Ventilation. London, 1850. 12°. 6074

Tonga Islands, Account of the Natives of. W. Mariner. Bost. 1820. 8°. 751
Tonna, Mrs. [Charlotte Elizabeth]. Poems. New York, 1845. 16°. . 2955
Works. New York, 1849. 2 v. 8°. 3541

Vol. 1. Personal Recollections; Osric, a Poem; Rockite; Hellen Fleetwood; Siege of Derby; Letters from Ireland; Miscellaneous Poems; Flower Garden.
2. Judea Capta; Deserter; Falsehood and Truth; Judah's Lion; Conformity; Wrongs of Women; Passing Thoughts; Izram, a Mexican Tale; Principalities and Powers; Second Causes; Poems.

Tooke, A. Pantheon of the Heathen Gods. New York, 1816. 12°. . 159
Tor Hill. Horace Smith. New York, 1837. 12°. 494
Torrey, Mary I. City and Country Life. Boston, 1853. 12°. . . 5329
Totemwell. E. Payson. New York, 1854. 12°. 6312
Tour in Zealand, 1802. London, 1805. 12°. 603
Tourist's Guide in Europe. J. H. Sherburne. Philadelphia, 1847. 12°. 2978
Tower Menagerie, Natural History of. London, 1829. 12°. . . . 6311
Tower of London. W. H. Ainsworth. London, 1845. 8°. . . . 1977
Townsend, G. Old Testament in Hist. & Chron. Order. Bost. 1839. Roy. 8°. 4727
New Testament in Hist. and Chron. Order. Bost. 1840. Roy. 8°. 4728
Townsend, W. C. Modern State Trials. London, 1850. 2 v. 8°. . . 5483
Tracts of the American Unitarian Association. Bost. 1827–40. 13 v. 12°. 1640
For contents, see vol. 13.
Tracy, E. C. Life of Jeremiah Evarts. Boston, 1845. 8°. . . . 4714
Tracy, J. History of the Revival of Religion, 1740. Boston, 1842. 8°. . 1959
Trade, Colonial and Lake, Report on. I. D. Andrews. Wash. 1852. 8°. 2747
Tradesman; or, Commercial Magazine. London, 1808–12. 8°. . . 719
Trafton, M. Rambles in Europe. Boston, 1852. 12°. 4591
Traits and Trials of Early Life. L. E. Landon. Philadelphia, 1847. 8°. 1343, 1
of the Aborigines of America; a Poem. Cambridge, 1822. 12°. . 507
of the Tea Party; Memoir of G. R. T. Hewes. N. Y. 1835. 12°. 1471
of Travel. T. C. Grattan. Boston, 1829. 12°. 292
Transylvania, Pesth, and Vienna, 1850. A. A. Paton. London, 1851. 8°. 4325
Trap to Catch a Sunbeam, &c. Matilda Planché. Boston, 1852. 12°. . 6293
Trappers of New York. J. R. Simms. Albany, 1851. 12°. . . . 4484
Traveller, Sketches by a. Boston, 1830. 12°. 359
Travellers, Lives of Celebrated. J. A. St. John. N. Y. 1846. 3 v. 12°. 3683, 38–40
Travelling, Modes of; Roads and Vehicles. London, 1839. 12°. . . 3135
Travels of a Philosopher. M. le Poivre. Baltimore, 1818. 12°. . . 1029
of Rolando; or, a Tour round the World. New York, 1852. 12°. 5016
round the World. M. de Pagés. London, 1793. 3 v. 8°. . . 572
Treadwell, S. B. American Liberties and Am. Slavery. N.Y. 1838. 12°. 1555
Treasure Trove; or, £, *s. d.* S. Lover. London, 1846. 12°. . . . 1816
Treasury, Biographical. S. Maunder. London, 1851. 12°. . . . 4470
of History. S. Maunder. London, 1850. 12°. 4107
of Knowledge. S. Maunder. London, 1848. 12°. 4106
of Natural History. S. Maunder. London, 1849. 12°. . . 4108
Scientific and Literary. S. Maunder. London, 1849. 12°. . . 4109
Trees and Shrubs, Encyclopædia of. J. C. Loudon. London, 1842. 8°. . 5893
and Shrubs of Britain. J. C. Loudon. London, 1844. 8 v. 8°. . 1514
For contents, see *Loudon, J. C.*

Trees and Shrubs of Mass., Report on. G. B. Emerson. Bost. 1846. 8°. 2803
Timber and Fruits. Boston, 1830. 12°. 868
Trelawney, Capt. Adventures of a Younger Son. London, 1851. 12°. . 5664
Trench, R. C. Lessons in Proverbs. New York, 1853. 12°. . . 5206
Notes on the Miracles of our Lord. New York, 1852. 8°. . . 4712
Notes on the Parables of our Lord. New York, 1851. 8°. . . 4713
Study of Words. New York, 1852. 12°. 4785
Synonymes of the New Testament. New York, 1854. 12°. . . 6295
Trenton Falls Illustrated. Ed. by N. P. Willis. New York, 1851. 12°. 4271
Trevelyan. London, 1851. 12°. 5666
Trial by Jury, Essay on. L. Spooner. Boston, 1852. 8°. . . . 5170
of the Amistad Prisoners, 1839. New York, 1839. 8°. . . 1444
of Earl of Somerset for Poisoning Sir T. Overbury. Lond. 1846. 8°. 4644
of Matt. F. Ward for Murder. New York, 1854. 8°. . . . 5982
of J. W. Webster for Murder. G. Bemis's Report. Bost. 1850. 8°. 4315
The same. J. W. Stone's Report. Boston, 1850. 8°. . 3952
Trials; a Tale. Philadelphia, 1824. 2 v. 12°. 364
American Criminal. P. W. Chandler. Boston, 1841–44. 2 v. 12°. 1921
and Confessions of an American Housekeeper. Phil. 1854. 12°. . 5812
Celebrated, of the Aristocracy. P. Burke. London, 1849. 8°. . 4522
Modern State. W. C. Townsend. London, 1850. 2 v. 8°. . . 5483
of a Mind in Progress to Catholicism. L. S. Ives. Bost. 1854. 12°. 5839
Remarkable Criminal. P. J. A. von Feuerbach. N.Y. 1846. 12°. 2584
State, of the United States. F. Wharton. Philadelphia, 1849. 8°. 2669
Trignometry, Plane. J. Hann. London, 1854. 12°. 6101
Spherical. J. Hann. Lond. 1849. 12°. 6100
Trinitarianism, Reasons for not Believing in. A. Norton. Camb. 1833. 12°. 1774
Tripp, A. Crests from the Ocean World. Boston, 1853. 12°. . . 5239
Trippings in Author Land. Emily Chubbuck. New York, 1846. 12°. . 2506
Tristram Shandy. L. Sterne. Philadelphia, 1831. 8°. 2080
Troil, U. von. Letters on Iceland. Dublin, 1780. 8°. 596
Trollope, A. La Vendée; an Historical Novel. London, 1850. 3 v. 12°. 4281
Trollope, Frances. Charles Chesterfield. New York, 1851. 8°. . . 4524
Domestic Manners of the Americans. New York, 1832. 8°. . 2078
Paris and the Parisians in 1835. New York, 1836. 8°. . . 607
Petticoat Government. London, 1850. 3 v. 12°. 3980
Vicar of Wrexhill. London, 1852. 12°. 5672
Widow Barnaby. London, 1852. 12°. 5674
Trollope, T. A. Travels in Italy, Switzerland, France, &c. Lond. 1850. 12°. 4224
Trollope, W. Analecta Theologica; Commen. on N. Test. Lon. 1842. 2 v. 8°. 4934
Belgium since the Revolution of 1830. London, 1842. 12°. . 4629
Trowbridge, J. T. Hearts and Faces; or, Home Life. Boston, 1853. 12°. 5532
True, the Beautiful, and the Good. V. Cousin. New York, 1854. 12°. 6153
True American. J. Coe. Concord, 1840. 12°. 3116
Trumbull, H. Discovery of America, Indian Wars, &c. Bost. 1841. 8°. 759
The same. Boston, 1833. 8°. 1334
Trumbull, J. M'Fingal; an Epic Poem. Hallowell, 1813. 16°. . . 1462
Autobiography, Reminiscences, &c., 1756–1841. N.Y. 1841. 8°. 1649

Truth, Essays on the Pursuit of. S. Bailey. Philadelphia, 1831. 12°. . 2156
The same. Boston, 1854. 12°. 5855
Stranger than Fiction. Cath. E. Beecher. New York, 1850. 12°. 3881
Truths in Popular Superstitions. H. Mayo. Edinburgh, 1851. 12°. . 4221
Truxton, T. Treatise on Latitude, Longitude, &c. Philadelphia, 1794. 4°. 2009
Tschudi, J. J. von. Travels in Peru, 1838-42. New York, 1847. 12°. . 2967
Tucker, A. Light of Nature Pursued. Cambridge, 1831. 4 v. 8°. . 2226
Tucker, B. Sacred and Profane History. Richmond, 1806. 12°. . . 324
Tucker, G. Life of Thomas Jefferson. Philadelphia, 1837. 2 v. 8°. . 1432
Tucker, J. M. Life and Naval Memoirs of Lord Nelson. Lond. 1848. 8°. 3467
Tucker, S. Rainbow of the North. London, 1851. 12°. 4270
Tuckerman, H. T. Characteristics of Literature. Philadelphia, 1849. 12°. 3377
Artist Life; or, Sketches of American Painters. N. Y. 1847. 12°. 3057
Italian Sketch Book. New York, 1848. 12°. 3121
Memorial of Horatio Greenough. New York, 1853. 12°. . . 5377
Month in England. New York, 1853. 12°. 5748
The Optimist. New York, 1850. 12°. 3658
Poems. Boston, 1851. 12°. 3819
Rambles and Reveries. New York, 1841. 12°. 1633
Sicily; a Pilgrimage. New York, 1852. 12°. 4911
Thoughts on the Poets. New York, 1846. 12°. 2589
Tudor H. Tour in North America, 1831-32. London, 1835. 2 v. 12°. . 1231
Tudor, W. Life of James Otis. Boston, 1823. 8°. 599
Tuggs's at Ramsgate, and other Sketches. C. Dickens. Phil. 1837. 12°. 911
Tupper, M. F. Author's Mind; Book of Titlepages. Phil. 1847. 12°. . 2972
Ballads for the Times. Philadelphia, 1851. 12°. 4192
Crock of Gold. New York, 1849. 12°. 2480
Geraldine; a Sequel to Coleridge's Christabel. Boston, 1846. 12°. 2510
Hactenus. Boston, 1848. 12°. 2448
Poetical Works. Boston, 1849. 12°. 1621
Proverbial Philosophy. Philadelphia, 1846. 12°. 2146
Thousand Lines. Philadelphia, 1846. 12°. 2568
Twins. New York, 1849. 12°. 2494
Turkey and Greece, Picturesque Sketches of. A. de Vere. Phil. 1850. 12°. 3909
*and Italy, Character and Costume in. T. Allom. Lond. n. d. 4°. 2050
and its Destiny. C. MacFarlane. Philadelphia, 1850. 2 v. 12°. 3868
and the Turks. A. Slade. New York, 1854. 12°. . . . 5807
and the Turks. J. V. C. Smith. Boston, 1854. 12°. . . . 5850
Christianity Revived in. H. G. O. Dwight. New York, 1850. 12°. 3936
Stories of Travels in. London, 1830. 12°. 3652
Visit to. W. Colton. New York, 1851. 12°. 4219
Turkish Evening Entertainments. Tr. by J. P. Brown. N.Y. 1850. 12°. 3500
Turkish Empire, History of. E. Upham. Philadelphia, 1833. 8°. 1357, 2
Turks, Year with the. W. W. Smyth. New York, 1854. 12°. . . 5810
Turle, J., and E. Taylor. People's Music Book. Part 2. Lond. 1844. Roy. 8°. 6011
Turnbull, D. Cuba, Porto Rico, and the Slave Trade. London, 1840. 8°. 4680
Turnbull, L. Railroad Accidents Prevented. Philadelphia, 1854. 12°. . 6224
Turnbull, R. Christ in History. Boston, 1854. 12°. 5603

Turnbull, R. Genius of Italy. New York 1849. 12°. 3301
Genius of Scotland. New York, 1847. 12°. 3017
Turner, E. Elements of Chemistry. Philadelphia, 1835. 12°. . . . 3507
Turner, J. Easy Guide to Vocal Music. Boston, 1836. 12°. 1474
Turner, S. History of the Anglo-Saxons. Philadelphia, 1841. 2 v. 8°. · 1953
Sacred History of the World. New York, 1832. 12°. 115
The same. (H. F. L.) New York, 1846. 3 v. 12°. 3683, 32, 72, 84
Turnley, J. Popery in Power. London, 1850. 8°. 4301
Turnover; a Tale of New Hampshire. Boston, 1853. 12°. 5352
Turretin, J. A. Fundamentals in Religion. Boston, 1823. 12°. . . 368, 1
Tuthill, Mrs. L. C. Beautiful Bertha. New York, 1854. 16°. . . . 6216
Nursery Book for Young Mothers. New York, 1849. 16°. . . 3307
Success in Life; The Lawyer. New York, 1850. 12°. . . . 3677
Success in Life; The Mechanic. New York, 1850. 12°. . . . 4052
Success in Life; The Merchant. New York, 1850. 12°. . . . 3437
Tip-Top; or, the Noble Aim. New York, 1853. 12°. 5546
Tutor's Ward; a Novel. New York, 1852. 8°. 4557
Tutti Frutti. Prince Pückler Muskau. New York, 1834. 12°. . . . 2602
Tweedie, W. K. Lamp to the Path. Boston, 1844. 12°. 5824
Seed-Time and Harvest. Boston, 1854. 12°. 5864
Twelvemonth's Campaign. C. F. Henningsen. Philadelphia, 1836. 12°. 224
Twelve Years' Military Adventure. London, 1840. 2 v. 8°. 4649
Twenty Years After. A. Dumas. New York, 1846. 8°. 2687
Twice-Told Tales. N. Hawthorne. Boston, 1851. 12°. 418
Twins and Heart. M. F. Tupper. New York, 1849. 12°. 2494
Twiss, H. Public and Private Life of Lord Eldon. Phil. 1844. 2 v. 8°. 2089
Two Admirals; a Tale. J. F. Cooper. New York, 1851. 12°. . . . 1683
Two Brides. T. S. Arthur. Philadelphia, 1850. 8°. 672
Two Brothers; a Novel. Philadelphia, 1850. 8°. 3998
Two Generations; a Novel. Earl of Belfast. London, 1851. 2 v. 12°. . 4237
Two Lives; or, To Seem and To Be. Maria J. McIntosh. N.Y. 1851. 12°. 4868
Two Lives; or, Eros and Anteros. New York, 1849. 8°. 3464
Two Old Men's Tales. Mrs. Marsh. New York, 1848. 8°. 3154
The same. London, 1853. 12°. 5728
Two Roads. J. Knorr. Philadelphia, 1854. 12°. 5811
Two Sisters. Lady C. Bury. New York, 1849. 8°. 3463
Two Sisters; or, Life's Changes. Philadelphia, 1844. 8°. 2138
Two Wives; or, Lost and Won. T. S. Arthur. Philadelphia, 1851. 16°. 4202
Two Years before the Mast. R. H. Dana, jun. New York, 1840. 12°. . 1491
The same. (H. F. L.) New York, 1846. 12°. . . . 3683, 106
Tyerman, D., and G. Bennet, Journal of Travels. Boston, 1832. 3 v. 12°. 1567
Tyler, S. Robert Burns; as a Poet and as a Man. New York, 1848. 12°. 3177
Tyndale, W. Doctrinal Treatises. Cambridge (Eng.), 1848. 8°. . . 5913
Tylney Hall; a Novel. T. Hood. Philadelphia, 1844. 8°. 2798
The same. London, 1852. 12°. 5673
Typee; a Peep at Polynesian Life. H. Melville. New York, 1848. 12°. 2571
Types of Mankind. S.G.Morton. Ed. by Nott & Gliddon. Phil. 1854. Roy.8°. 5928
Typology of Scripture. P. Fairbairn. Philadelphia, 1852. 2 v. 8°. . 4710

Tytler, A. F. Elements of General History. New York, 1818. 8°. . 566
Universal History. Boston, 1850. 2 v. 8°. 692
and E. Nares. Universal Hist. (H.F.L.) N.Y. 1846. 6 v. 12°. 3683, 86–91
Tytler, Ann F. Leila; or, the Island. New York, 1853. 12°. . . . 5318
Tytler, P. F. Disc. on North Coasts of Am. (H.F.L.) N.Y. 1848. 12°. 3683, 53
Life of Sir Walter Raleigh. Philadelphia, 1833. 8°. . . 1357, 3
Tytler, M. F. Tales of Many Lands. Edinburgh, 1846. 12°. . . . 4268

U.

Ugly Effie, and other Tales. Caroline L. Hentz. Philadelphia, 1853. 8°. 5157
Uhland, L. Songs and Ballads. Boston, 1842. 12°. 962, 14
Ulrici, H. Shakspeare's Dramatic Art. London, 1846. 8°. 3956
Uncle Tom's Cabin. Mrs. H. B. Stowe. Boston, 1852. 2 v. 12°. . . 3109
Uncle Tom's Cabin as it Is. W. L. G. Smith. Buffalo, 1852. 12°. . 4904
Uncle Tom's Cabin in Ruins. Boston, 1853. 12°. 5182
Uncle Tom's Cabin, Key to. Mrs. H. B. Stowe. Boston, 1853. 8°. . 5174
Uncle Sam's Farm Fence. A. D. Milne. New York, 1854. 12°. . . 5825
Uncle Sam's Palace. Emma Wellmont. Boston, 1853. 12°. . . . 5520
Underground Railroad. Philadelphia, 1853. 12°. 5551
Underhill, E. B. Struggles & Triumphs of Religious Liberty. N.Y. 1851. 12°. 4194
Understanding, Conduct of. J. Locke. (H. F. L.) N. Y. 1848. 12°. 3683, 171
Essay on the Human. J. Locke. Philadelphia, 1845. 8°. . . 872
Undine; a Romance. F. de la M. Fouqué. New York, 1839. 12°. . 1560
The same. New York, 1845. 12°. 2332
Undying One, and other Poems. Mrs. C. E. S. Norton. N. Y. 1854. 12°. 5879
Unfortunate Man. F. Chamier. New York, 1835. 2 v. 12°. . . . 406
Ungewitter, F. H. Europe, Past and Present. New York, 1850. 12°. . 3897
Union, Maine, History of. J. L. Sibley. Boston, 1851. 12°. . . . 4434
Unitarian Tracts. — See *Tracts.*
Unitarianism, Discourses in Defence of. O. Dewey. Bost. 1840. 3 v. 12°. 1556
United Irishmen, Lives and Times of. R. R. Madden. Phil. 1842. 2 v. 12°. 1936
United States, Appeal respecting. R. Walsh, jun. Phil. 1819. 8°. . 693
and Canada, Excursion through, 1822–23. London, 1824. 8°. . 1429
Census of 1840, Compendium of. Washington, 1842. Folio. . 2033
Census of, 1850. Washington, 1853. 4°. 5890
Constitution of. Edited by W. Hickey. Philadelphia, 1848. 12°. 4098
The same. Philadelphia, 1847. 12°. 3075
Constitution of, and of the Several States. Charlestown, 1812. 12°. 316
*The same. New York, 1852. 8°. 5902
Constitution of, Commentaries on. J. Story. Bost. 1833. 3 v. 8°. 1796
The same. Boston, 1851. 2 v. roy. 8°. 4312
Constitution of, View of. W. Rawle. Philadelphia, 1829. 8°. . 2688
Constitution of, Writings on. J. Marshall. Boston, 1839. 8°. . 2054
Defence of Const. and Gov. of. J. Adams. London, 1787. 3 v. 8°. 701
Diplomatic Correspondence. Washington, 1833. 7 v. 8°. . . 3615
Exploring Expedition, 1838–42. C. Wilkes. Phil. 1845. 5 v. roy. 8°. 2244

United States Exploring Expeditions. J. S. Jenkins. Auburn, 1850. 8°. 3620
*Gazetteer of. T. Baldwin and J. Thomas. Philadelphia, 1854. 8°. 5494
*Gazetteer of. J. Hayward. Hartford, 1853. 8°. 5402
Geographical Dictionary of. J. Scott. Philadelphia, 1805. 8°. . 1269
Glimpse of. A. Cunnynghame. London, 1851. 8°. 5411
History of. G. Bancroft. Boston, 1853. 6 v. 8°. 954
History of. C. A. Goodrich. Hartford, 1826. 12°. . . . 68
History of. W. Grimshaw. Philadelphia, 1821. 12°. . . 331
History of. J. Grahame. London, 1833. 2 v. 8°. . . . 1617
History of. S. Hale. (H. F. L.) N.Y. 1846. 2 v. 12°. 3683, 119, 120
History of. R. Hildreth. New York, 1849–51. 6 v. 8°. . . 2851
History of. N. Webster. Cincinnati, 1835. 12°. . . . 1504
History and Topography of. J. H. Hinton. Boston, 1834. 2 v. 4°. 2028
History of the Independence of. W. Gordon. Lond. 1788. 4 v. 8°. 578
Laws of. Philadelphia, 1796–1801. 5 v. 8°. 1214
National and State Governments of. C. Mason. Bost. 1842. 12°. 2155
Notes on. G. Combe. Philadelphia, 1841. 2 v. 12°. . . . 1603
Origin and Progress of. W. M'Cartney. Philadelphia, 1847. 12°. 3043
Pictorial History of. J. Frost. Philadelphia, 1846. 4 v. roy. 8°. 2777
Pictorial History of. H. Murray. Boston, 1851. 8°. . . . 4007
Power and Progress of. G. T. Poussin. Philadelphia, 1851. 8°. 4320
Presidents' Addresses and Messages. New York, 1842. 8°. . . 1782
Presidents' Messages, 1789–1846. E. Williams. N.Y. 1846. 2 v. 8°. 2781
Public Statutes at Large. Ed. by R. Peters. Bost. 1845. 8 v. roy. 8°. 3243
Society in. F. and T. Pulszky. New York, 1853. 2 v. 12°. . 5245
Society and Manners in. M. Chevalier. Boston, 1839. 8°. . . 691
Speaker. J. E. Lovell. New Haven, 1839. 12°. . . . 1155
State Papers and Public Docs., 1789–1818. Bost. 1815–19. 12 v. 8°. 1944
Statistical Account of. D. B. Warden. Edinburgh, 1819. 3 v. 8°. 2257
Statistical Annals of. A. Seybert. Philadelphia, 1818. 4°. . 2032
Statistical View of. F. Pithin. New York, 1817. 8°. . . 3974
Travels in. A. Bunn. Philadelphia, 1853. 12°. . . . 5594
Travels in, 1807–8. E. A. Kendall. New York, 1809. 3 v. 8°. . 571
Travels in, 1841–42. C. Lyell. New York, 1845. 2 v. 12°. . 2479
Travels in, 1806–11. J. Melish. Philadelphia, 1812. 2 v. 8°. . 1321
Travels in. J. Palmer. London, 1818. 8°. 770
Travels in. Lady E. S. Wortley. London, 1851. 3 v. 12°. . 4285
Second Visit to. Sir C. Lyell. New York, 1849. 2 v. 12°. . 3396
Visit to, 1841. J. Sturge. Boston, 1842. 12°. 1909
Weakness and Inefficiency of the Government of. ——, 1845. 12°. 2906
*Universal Cambist and Commercial Inst. P. Kelly. Lond. 1821. 2 v. 4°. 6027
Universal Prayer, Death, &c. R. Montgomery. Boston, 1829. 12°. . 498
Universalist, The Anti- J. Priest. Albany, 1839. 8°. 3786
University of Dublin, History of. W. B. S. Taylor. London, 1845. 8°. 4663
Updike, W. Memoirs of the Rhode Island Bar. Boston, 1842. 12°. . 2680
Upham, C. W. Life of Sir Henry Vane. Boston, 1840. 12°. . 1076, 4
Oration before the New England Society. Boston, 1847. 8°. . 3197
Witchcraft, and the Delusion at Salem, 1692. Boston, 1831. 12°. 886

Upham, E. History of the Turkish Empire. Philadelphia, 1833. 8°. 1357, 2
Upham, T. C. Imperfect Mental Action. (H. F. L.) N.Y. 1846. 12°. 3683, 100
Manual of Peace. New York, 1836. 8°. 6014
On the Will. Portland, 1834. 8°. 3790
Religious Maxims. Philadelphia, 1854. 18°. 6253
Up Country Letters. —. Mansfield. New York, 1852. 12°. . . . 4893
Up the Rhine. T. Hood. New York, 1852. 12°. 4875
Up the River. F. W. Shelton. New York, 1853. 12°. 5595
Upper Ten Thousand. C. A. Bristed. New York, 1852. 12°. . . 4852
Urbino, L. B. Sunshine in the Palace and Cottage. Boston, 1854. 12°. 5792
Ure, A. Dictionary of Arts, Manufactures, and Mines. N.Y. 1849. 8°. 1687
*The same. New York, 1853. 2 v. 8°. 1687
Urquhart, D. Pillars of Hercules; or, Spain & Morocco. Lond. 1850. 2 v. 8°. 4653
The same. New York, 1850. 2 v. 12°. 3854
Progress of Russia. London, 1853. 12°. 5544
Usborne, T. H. Magician Priest of Avignon. London, 1851. 2 v. 12°. 4607
Use of Sunshine. New York, 1852. 12°. 295
Useful Arts; with Applications of Science. J. Bigelow. Bost. 1840. 2 v. 12°. 2923
their Birth and Development. S. Martin. London, 1851. 12°. . 4214
Handbook of. T. Antisell. New York, 1852. 12°. . . . 4603
Usury, Funds, and Banks. J. O'Callaghan. Burlington, 1834. 12°. . 3661
Utah and the Mormons. B. G. Ferris. New York, 1854. 12°. . . 6150
and Valley of Great Salt Lake. H. Stansbury. Wash. 1853. 8°. 4939
Utopia, and Richard III. Sir T. More. Cambridge, 1831. 12°. . . 383, 9
Utterance; a Collection of Poems. Caroline A. Briggs. Bost. 1852. 12°. 4620

V.

Vagamundo; or, the Attaché in Spain. J. E. Warren. N.Y. 1851. 12°. 4451
The same. London, 1851. 8°. 4323
Vala; a Mythological Tale. P. Godwin. New York, 1851. 8°. . . 4803
Valentine, D. T. History of the City of New York. N.Y. 1853. 8°. . 5479
Valentine, Dr. W. Budget of Wit and Humor. New York, 1849. 12°. 3282
and Yankee Hill's Metamorphoses. New York, 1852. 12°. . . 5231
Valentine McClutchy, the Irish Agent. W. Carleton. N. Y. 1846. 12°. 2927
Valentine Vox, the Ventriloquist. H. Cockton. Philadelphia, 1848. 8°. 1650
Value, Nature, Measures and Causes of. S. Bailey. London, 1825. 8°.. 6010
Van Amringe, W. F. Theories of the Nat. Hist. of Man. N.Y. 1848. 8°. 4354
Vanbrugh, Sir J. Dramatic Works. Ed. by L. Hunt. Lond. 1851. Roy. 8°. 4527
Van Buren, M., Life and Opinions of. W. M. Holland. Hart. 1836. 12°. 1847
Vancouver, G. Voyage round the World, 1790–95. Lond. 1798. 3 v. 4°. 2008
Vandenhoff, G. Art of Elocution. London, 1846. 12°. 2352
Van Doren, W. H. Mercantile Morals. New York, 1852. 12°. . . 5020
Vane, C. W. Story of the Peninsular War. New York, 1848. 12°. . 3161
War in Germany and France, 1813–14. Philadelphia, 1831. 12°. 305
Van Egmont, J. E., and J. Heyman. Travels. London, 1759. 2 v. 8°. . 1211
Van Halen, J. Imprisonment by the Inquisition. New York, 1828. 8°. 741

Vane, Sir H. Life. C. W. Upham. Boston, 1840. 12°. . . 1076, 4
Life. J. Forster. London, 1831. 12°. 1831, 4
Van-Ess, W. L. Life of Napoleon. Philadelphia, 1809. 4 v. 8°. . . 1628
Vanity Fair; a Novel without a Hero. W. M. Thackeray. N.Y. 1848. 8°. 3219
Van Santvoord, G. Life of Algernon Sidney. New York, 1851. 12°. . 4177
Van Schaack, P. Life and Corres. H. C. Van Schaack. N.Y. 1842. 8°. 4958
Vara; or, the Child of Adoption. New York, 1854. 12°. . . . 5798
Varley, D. Treatise on Mineralogy. London, 1853. 12°. 6039
Vassa, G., an African. Life, by himself. Boston, 1837. 12°. . . 1539
Vasari, G. Lives of Painters, Sculptors, and Architects. Lond. 1851. Post 8°. 4185
Vasey, G. Delineations of the Ox Tribe. London, 1851. 8°. . . . 4322
Vathek; an Arabian Tale. W. Beckford. London, 1853. 12°. . . . 5702
Vattel, E. de. Law of Nations. Dublin, 1792. 8°. 601
Vegetable Substances as Food. (H. F. L.) New York, 1848. 12°. 3683, 169
Description and History of. Boston, 1830. 12°. 868
Vegetable World. C. Williams. Boston, 1833. 12°. 56
Poetry of. M. J. Schleiden. Cincinnati, 1853. 12°. . . . 5316
Velazquez, M. Spanish Dictionary. New York, 1852. Roy. 8°. . . 4844
Venetia. B. Disraeli. Philadelphia, 1837. 2 v. 12°. 565
The same. Philadelphia, 1845. 8°. 2689
Venetian History, Sketches of. E. Smedley. New York, 1834. 2 v. 12°. 114
The same. (H. F. L.) New York, 1846. 2 v. 12°. 3683, 43, 44
Venice; the City of the Sea. E. Flagg. New York, 1853. 2 v. 12°. . 5518
Stones of. J. Ruskin. New York, 1851. 8°. 4119
Ventilation and Warming. C. Tomlinson. London, 1850. 12°. . . 6074
Theory and Practice of. London, 1825. 8°. 4017
Warming, and Sound. W. S. Inman. London, 1836. 8°. . . 4554
Ventriloquism Explained, and Juggler's Tricks. Amherst, 1834. 16°. . 2970
Verdicts; a Poem. London, 1852. 12°. 5300
Vericour, L. R. de. Modern Literature of France. Boston, 1848. 12°. . 3158
Vermont, Gazetteer of. J. Hayward. Boston, 1849. 12°. 5556
History of. W. H. Carpenter and T. S. Arthur. Phil. 1854. 12°. 6289
History of. S. Williams. Burlington, 1809. 2 v. 8°. . . . 1215
Verplanck, G. C. Discourses and Addresses. New York, 1833. 12°. . 1850
Very, J. Essays and Poems. Boston, 1839. 12°. 3581
Versification, System of English. Erastus Everett. New York, 1848. 12°. 3108
Vespucius, Americus, and his Voyages. Viscount Santarem. Bost. 1850. 12°. 4018
Life and Voyages. C. E. Lester. New York, 1846. 8°. . . 2712
Vestal, The; a Tale of Pompeii. T. Gray, jun. Boston, 1830. 12°. . 483
Vestiges of the Natural History of Creation, and Sequel. N.Y. 1845. 12°. 2316
The same. New York, 1850. 16°. 4066
Vicar of Wakefield. O. Goldsmith. New York, 1845. 12°. . . . 2
The same. Edinburgh, 1833. 12°. 1835, 2
The same. New York, 1850. 12°. 3454, 3
Vicar of Wrexhill. Mrs. F. Trollope. London, 1852. 12°. . . . 5672
Victim of Excitement. Mrs. C. L. Hentz. Philadelphia, 1854. 12°. . 5767
Victims of Society. Countess of Blessington. Philadelphia, 1846. 2 v. 12°. 360
Victories of the British Armies. W. H. Maxwell. London, 1847. 12°. . 3133

Vidocq, E. T. Autobiography. Philadelphia, 1834. 8°. 2223
Views of Society and Manners in America. New York, 1821. 8°. . . 1276
Vigny, A. de. Cinq-Mars; or, Conspiracy under Louis XIII. N.Y. 1847. 8°. 2773
Village Architecture. P. F. Robinson. London, 1837. 4°. . . . 5977
Village Choir, Memoirs of a New England. Boston, 1829. 12°. . . 1525
Village Life in Egypt. B. St. John. Boston, 1853. 2 v. 12°. . . . 4998
Village Notary; a Hungarian Romance. Baron Eötvös. N. Y. 1850. 8°. 3643
Village of Mariendorpt. Anna M. Porter. Boston, 1821. 4 v. 12°. . 302
Village Sayings and Doings. Philadelphia, 1836. 8°. . . . 2228, 2
Villette. Caroline Bronte. New York, 1853. 8°. 5158
Vince, S. Elements of Astronomy. Philadelphia, 1811. 8°. . . . 616
Vinet, A. Homiletics; or, Theory of Preaching. New York, 1854. 12°. 5742
Virgil, M. P. Æneid. Trans. by J. Dryden. New York, 1844. 12°. 1854, 12
Eclogues and Georgics. Tr. by Wragham & Sotheby. N.Y.1844. 12°. 1854, 11
Works, Latin Text and Translation. New York, 1811. 2 v. 8°. . 6447
Works. Translated by Davidson. London, 1850. Post 8°. . . 4382
Works. Translated by J. Dryden. New York, 1825. 16°. . . 4
Virginia, First Settlers of. New York, 1806. 12°. 442
Historical Collections of. H. Howe. Charleston, 1845. 8°. . . 2719
History of. T. S. Arthur and W. H. Carpenter. Phil. 1852. 12°. 4865
Virginia and Magdalene. Mrs. E. D. E. N. Southworth. N. Y. 1854. 8°. 5981
Virginia Comedians. C. Effingham. New York, 1854. 12°. . . 6210
Vision of Sir Launfal. J. R. Lowell. Cambridge, 1848. 12°. . . 3330
of Don Roderick. Sir W. Scott. Philadelphia, 1839. 12°. . . 860, 3
Visions of Quevedo. Trans. by W. Elliot. Philadelphia, 1832. 16°. . 41
of the Times of Old. R. Bigsby. London, 1848. 3 v. 8°. . . 4820
Visits and Sketches at Home and Abroad. Mrs. Jameson. N.Y. 1834. 2 v.12°. 2369
to Remarkable Places. W. Howitt. Philadelphia, 1842. 8°. . 1764
Vivian Gray. B. Disraeli. Baltimore, 1833. 2 v. 12°. 1149
The same. Philadelphia, 1845. 8°. 2689
Vocabalaire des Termes de Commerce. J. Peuchet. Paris, 1801. 8°. . 1248
Voice from the Main Deck. Boston, 1843. 16°. 1744
from the Parsonage. H. G. Park. Boston, 1854. 12°. . . 5856
Philosophy of the Human. J. Rush. Philadelphia, 1845. 8°. · 5086
Voices of the Dead. J. Cumming. Boston, 1854. 12°. 5823
of the Night. H. W. Longfellow. Cambridge, 1839. 12°. . . 94
of Nature to the Soul of Man. Ed. by H. T. Cheever. N.Y. 1852. 12°. 4918
Volney, C. F. C. The Ruins; Meditation on the Revolutions. N.Y.1828. 12°. 344
Les Ruines; Méditation sur les Revolutions. Paris, 1827. 8°. . 344
Voltaire, F. M. A. de, and his Times. L. Bungener. Boston, 1855. 12°. 6220
History of Charles XII. New York, 1851. 16°. 5183
La Pucelle d'Orleans. Paris, 1816. 16°. 82
Life. Lord Brougham. Philadelphia, 1845. 12°. 2524
Works, translated. London, 1780. 5 v. 8°. 1915
Vose, J. System of Astronomy. Concord, 1827. 8°. 634
Voyage autour du Monde, 1785–88. G. Dixon. Paris, 1789. 2 v. 8°. . 1245
for a N. W. Passage, 1819–20. Sir W. E. Parry. Phil. 1821. 8°. 1316
The same; Second Voyage. New York, 1824. 8°. . . 1272

Voyage of Governor Phillip to Botany Bay. Dublin, 1790. 8°. . . 523
of the Jamestown. R. B. Forbes. Boston, 1847. 8°. 2799
of the Margaret Oakley. T. J. Jacobs. New York, 1844. 12°. . 2170
of the Potomac, 1831–34. J. N. Reynolds. New York, 1835. 8°. 1980
of the Potomac, 1831–34. F. Warriner. New York, 1835. 12°. 1256
round the World, 1836–42. Sir E. Belcher. Lond. 1843. 2 v. 8°. 2853
round the World. T. Gerstæcker. New York, 1853. 12°. . . 5372
round the World. A. J. von Krusenstern. London, 1813. 2 v. 4°. 2016
round the World. M. de la Peyrouse. Boston, 1801. 16°. . . 876
round the World. Ida Pfeiffer. New York, 1852. 12°. . . 4596
round the World, 1790–95. G. Vancouver. Lond. 1798. 3 v. 4°. 2008
to N. W. Coast of America. G. Franchere. New York, 1854. 12°. 5818
to the S. Atlantic Ocean, 1829–31. Abby J. Morrell. N.Y. 1833. 12°. 2805
to the Southern Hemisphere. J. Hawkesworth. Perth, 1789. 4 v. 12°. 169
to West Coast of Africa. J. A. Carnes. Boston, 1852. 12°. . 4798
Voyages and Commercial Enterprises. R. J. Cleveland. Cam. 1842. 2 v. 12°. 897
and Travels. A. Delano. Boston, 1817. 8°. 640
and Travels, Fragments of. Capt. B. Hall. London, 1842. 8°. . 2610
and Travels, General Collection of. J. Pinkerton. Phil. 1810. 6 v. 4°. 2000
For contents, see *Pinkerton, J.*
and Travels, History and Collec. of. R. Kerr. Edin. 1824. 18 v. 8°. 5489
and Travels. D. Tyerman and G. Bennet. Boston, 1832. 3 v. 12°. 1567
autour du Monde. A. Montémont. Paris, 1853. Roy. 8°. . . 5976
aux Montagnes D'Ecosse. Vol. 1. Geneva, 1785. 8°. . . 806
from 1799 to 1844. G. Coggeshall. New York, 1851. 8°. . . 4303
Mariner's Library of Popular. Boston, 1833. 12°. 1169
of Discovery. Sir W. E. Parry. (H.F.L.) N.Y. 1846. 2 v. 12°. 3683, 107–8
round the World. (H. F. L.) New York, 1848. 12°. . 3683, 172
round the World. London, 1850. 16°. 4582
round the World. J. Cook. London, 1853. 2 v. roy. 8°. . . 5457
The same, abridged. Philadelphia, n. d. 2 v. 16°. . . 3
*Vyse, H. Pyramids of Gizeh. London, 1840. 3 v. 4°. 3794

W.

Wagen, Dr. Life and Genius of Peter Paul Rubens. London, 1840. 12°. 3070
Wacousta; or, the Prophecy. Major Richardson. New York, 1851. 8°. 4036
Wade, Mrs. D. B. L. Burman Slave Girl. Boston, n. d. 16°. . . 1508
Wade, J. History of the Middle and Working Classes. Lond. 1835. 12°. 2109
Letters of Junius, & Evidence of Authorship. Lond. 1850. 2 v. post 8°. 4374
Waif; a Collec. of Poems. Ed. by H. W. Longfellow. Cam. 1845. 12°. 2188
Wainwright, J. M. Pathways of our Lord. New York, 1851. Roy. 8°. 4008
Wakefield, P. Beauties and Wonders of Nature and Art. Phil. 1819. 12°. 435
Wakeman, J. Mysterious Parchment. Boston, 1853. 12°. . . . 5522
Wakondah, the Master of Life; a Poem. New York, 1841. 8°. . . 1671
Waldenses, History of the Persecution of. A. Muston. Lond. 1852. 12°. 5260
*The. W. Beattie. Illust. by Bartlett & Brockedon. Lond. 1836. 4°. 3746

Walden; or, Life in the Woods. H. D. Thoreau. Boston, 1854. 12°. . 6166
Waldo, S. P. American Naval Heroes. Hartford, 1823. 8°. . . 651
Tour of James Monroe, and Life. Hartford, 1818. 12°. . . 315
Wales, Falls, Lakes, & Mountains of North. L. S. Costellow. Lon. 1845. 12°. 2388
Pedestrian's Guide through North. G. J. Bennett. Lond. 1840. 8°. 4665
Walker, A. Beauty in Woman. Hartford, 1848. 12°. 1753
Walker, C. V. Electrotype Manipulation. Philadelphia, 1852. 12°. . 5005
Walker, D. British Manly Exercises. Philadelphia, 1850. 12°. . . 2200
Walker, J. Dictionary of the English Language. Phil. 1811. 8°. . . 1287
English Pronouncing Dictionary. New York, 1823. 8°. . . 660
Rhyming, Spelling, and Pronouncing Dictionary. Phil. 1852. 8°. 500
Walks & Talks of an Amer. Farmer in Eng. F. L. Olmsted. N.Y. 1852. 12°. 147
Wallace; a Franconia Story. J. Abbott. New York, 1850. 12°. . . 3813
Wallace, Sir W., History of. New York, 1820. 12°. 387
Wallenstein (Duke of Friedland). Life. J. Mitchell. Lond. 1840. 12°. 4567
Wallis, Mrs. M. D. Life in Feejee. Boston, 1851. 12°. 4160
Wallis, S. T. Glimpses of Spain in 1847. New York, 1849. 12°. . 3448
Spain, her Institutions, Politics, &c. Boston, 1853. 12°. . . 5212
Walpole, B. C. Life of Charles James Fox. New York, 1807. 12°. . 468
Walpole, H. Castle of Otranto. London, 1853. 12°. 5702
Letters, 1735–48. Philadelphia, 1842. 4 v. 8°. 1963
Letters to Sir H. Mann. Ed. by Lord Dover. N.Y. 1833. 2 v. 12°. 1230
Memoirs of the Reign of George III. Philadelphia, 1845. 2 v. 8°. 2617
and Contemporaries, Memoirs of. E. Warburton. Lond. 1851. 2 v. 8°. 4147
Walsh, R. Brazil in 1828–29. Boston, 1831. 2 v. 12°. 2106
Walsh, R., jun. Appeal respecting the United States. Phil. 1819. 8°. . 693
Walsh, R. M. Sketches of Living Characters in France. Phil. 1841. 12°. 2296
Walt and Vult; or, the Twins. J. P. Richter. Boston, 1846. 2 v. 12°. 2552
Walter, H. History of England. London, n. d. 7 v. 8°. 6021
Walter, T. U., and J. J. Smith. 200 Designs for Cottages. Phil. 1847. 4°. 2980
Walton, I. Life of Richard Hooker. Oxford, 1843. 8°. . . 1961, 1
Lives of Donne, Wotton, Hooker, &c. New York, 1846. 12°. . 2942
The same. Cambridge, 1831. 12°. 383, 5–6
and C. Colton. Complete Angler. New York, 1848. 12°. . . 1869
Wandering Jew. E. Sue. New York, 1846. 2 v. roy. 8°. 2622
The same (in Spanish, and Illust.). Paris, 1845. 4 v. roy. 8°. 6029
War, and the Principles of Christianity. J. Dymond. Phil. 1834. 12°. 2129
Art of. N. Machiavelli. Albany, 1815. 8°. 1330
Art of (in French). G. R. Faesch. Leipzig, 1771. 2 v. 8°. . 710
in France and Belgium, 1815. W. Siborne. Phil. 1845. 8°. . 2711
Germany and France in 1813–14. C. W. Vane. Phil. 1831. 12°. 305
in Syria. Sir Charles Napier. London, 1842. 2 v. 12°. . . 3058
of 1812, History of. New York, 1815. 12°. 132
of 1812, History of. J. T. Headley. New York, 1853. 2 v. 12°. 5533
of 1812, History of. C. J. Ingersoll. Philadelphia, 1852. 3 v. 8°. 5177
of 1812, in the Western Country. Lexington, 1816. 8°. . . 546
of 1812, Sketches of. Rutland, Vt., 1815. 8°. 2073
of the Sicilian Vespers. M. Amari. London, 1850. 3 v. 12°. . 4587

Waraga; or, the Charms of the Nile. W. Furness. New York, 1850. 12°. 3485
Warburton, E. Conquest of Canada. New York, 1850. 2 v. 12°. . 3839
Crescent and the Cross; or, Eastern Travel. N.Y. 1845. 2 v. 12°. 2377
Darien; or, the Merchant Prince. New York, 1852. 8°. . . . 3324
Hochelaga; or, England in the New World. N.Y. 1846. 2 v. 12°. 2914
Memoirs of Horace Walpole. London, 1851. 2 v. 8°. . . . 4147
Reginald Hastings. New York, 1850. 8°. 3989
Warburton, J. Roman History. London, 1792. 12°. 312
Ward, A. H. History of Shrewsbury, Mass. Boston, 1847. 8°. . . 2844
Ward, F. De W. India and the Hindoos. New York, 1850. 12°. . 3935
Ward, J. Adolphe Renouard. London, 1852. 12°. 5641
Ward, Matt. F. English Items. New York, 1853. 12°. 5211
Trial for Murder. New York, 1854. 8°. 5982
Ward, N. Simple Cobler of Aggawam, 1645. Reprint, Boston, 1843. 12°. 1939
Ward, R. P. De Vere. New York, 1831. 2 v. 12°. 350
Fielding; or, Society. Philadelphia, 1837. 3 v. 12°. 907
The same. (Select Cir. Lib.) Philadelphia, 1837. 4°. 2034, 1838
Illustrations of Human Life. London, 1843. 3 v. 12°. . . . 4564
Vol. 1. Atticus, or the Retired Statesman; St. Lawrence.
2, 3. Fielding, or Society.

Ward, S. Life. William Gammell. Boston, 1848. 12°. . . . 1076, 19
Warden, D. B. Statistical Account of United States. Edinb. 1819. 3 v. 8°. 2257
Warden, W. Letters on Napoleon at St. Helena. Boston, 1817. 16°. . 815
Wardlaw, R. National Church Establishments. London, 1839. 8°. . 1419
Ware, H., jun. Hints on Extemporaneous Preaching. Bost. 1831. 12°. 1882
Memoir. J. Ware. Boston, 1846. 12°. 2537
Works. Boston, 1846. 4 v. 12°. 2934
Ware, J. Memoir of Henry Ware, jun. Boston, 1846. 12°. . . . 2537
Ware, Mary L. Memoir. E. B. Hall. Boston, 1853. 12°. . . . 5076
Ware, W. Julian; or, Scenes in Judea. New York, 1841. 2 v. 12°. . 1631
Lectures on Works and Genius of Wash. Allston. Bost. 1852. 12°. 4913
Life of Nathaniel Bacon. Boston, 1844. 12°. 1076, 13
Probus; or, Rome in the Third Century. N. York, 1838. 2 v. 12°. 1109
Sketches of European Capitals. Boston, 1851. 12°. 4426
Zenobia. New York, 1838. 2 v. 12°. 482
Warkworth Castle; a Historical Romance. London, 1851. 3 v. 12°. . 4245
Warming and Ventilation. C. Tomlinson. London, 1850. 12°. . . 6074
Theory and Practice of. London, 1825. 8°. 4017
Ventilation, and Sound, Report on. W. S. Inman. Lond. 1836. 8°. 4554
Warner, Anna. Carl Krinken. New York, 1854. 12°. 5626
Law and the Testimony. New York, 1853. Roy. 8°. 5424
Queechy. New York, 1852. 2 v. 12°. 1050
Mr. Rutherford's Children. New York, 1853. 12°. 5547
Wide, Wide World. New York, 1851. 12°. 4083
Warner, H. W. Liberties of America. New York, 1853. 12°. . . . 5356
Warren, Maine, Annals of. C. Eaton. Hallowell, 1851. 12°. . . . 959
Warren, I. Mud Cabin. New York, 1853. 12°. 5526
Warren, Jos. Life. A. H. Everett. Boston, 1844. 12°. . . . 1076, 10

Warren, J. C. Address before Boston Soc. of Nat. Hist. Bost. 1853. 8°. 5406
*Description of a Skeleton of the Mastodon. Boston, 1852. 4°. . 4937
Preservation of Health. Boston, 1854. 12°. 5797
Warren, J. E. Notes of an Attaché in Spain. London, 1851. 8°. . . 4323
The same. New York, 1851. 12°. 4451
Para; or, Adventures on the Amazon. New York, 1851. 12°. . 4258
Warren, S. Confessions of an Attorney. New York, 1852. 12°. . . 4772
Diary of a Late Physician. New York, 1838. 3 v. 12°. . . 2191
Experiences of a Barrister. New York, 1852. 12°. . . . 4771
Lily and the Bee. New York, 1851. 12°. 4468
Merchant's Clerk. New York, 1836. 12°. 457
Moral and Professional Duties of Attorneys. N. York, 1849. 12°. 2464
Now and Then. New York, 1848. 12°. 3096
Ten Thousand a Year. Philadelphia, 1841. 6 v. 12°. . . . 966
Warreniana. Boston, 1851. 12°. 3818
Warriner, F. Cruise of the Potomac, 1831–34. New York, 1835. 12°. 1256
Warton, T. History of English Poetry. London, 1840. 3 v. 8°. . . 5476
Warwick, E. Classification of Noses. London, 1848. 12°. . . . 4969
Warwick Woodlands. H. W. Herbert. New York, 1851. 12°. . . 3842
Washburn, E. Judicial History of Massachusetts. Boston, 1840. 8°. . 2090
Washington, G., and his Generals. J. T. Headley. N. Y. 1847. 2 v. 12°. 2975
and his Generals. G. Lippard. Philadelphia, 1847. 8°. . . 2831
and the Generals of the Revolution. Philadelphia, 1847. 2 v. 12°. 3047
Essay on. M. Guizot. Boston, 1840. 12°. 66
Life. J. Marshall. Phil. 1805–7. 5 v. 8°. 1267
Life. J. K. Paulding. (H. F. L.) New York, 1846. 2 v. 12°. 3683, 75, 76
Memory of. N. Hervey. Boston, 1852. 16°. 4595
Mother and Wife of. Marg. C. Conkling. Auburn, 1850. 12°. . 3849
Political Legacies. Boston, 1800. 12°. 558
Revolutionary Orders of. J. Whiting. New York, 1844. 8°. . 2236
Writings, with Life. J. Sparks. Boston, 1837. 12 v. 8°. . . 1430

Vol. 1. Life by Jared Sparks.
2. Official Letters relating to the French War, and Private Letters before the American Revolution.
3–8. Correspondence and Miscellaneous Papers relating to Am. Revolution.
9. Correspondence from his Resignation as Commander-in-Chief to his Inauguration as President.
10, 11. Correspondence from the Beginning of his Presidency to the End of his Life.
12. Speeches and Messages to Congress; Proclamations and Addresses.

and Adams, Administrations of. G. Gibbs. N. York, 1846. 2 v. 8°. 2728
Water, Cold, Tepid, and Friction Cure. R. T. Claridge. N. Y. 1849. 12°. 3404
Natural History of. C. T. Jackson. Boston, 1836, 12°. . . 898
Treatise on the Power of. J. Glynn. London, 1853. 12°. . . 6090
Wisdom of God displayed in. J. K. Mitchell. Phil. 1833. 8°. 1357, 3
Water-Cure, Life at; or, Month at Malvern. R. J. Lane. Lond. 1846. 12°. 4964
Water Drops. L. H. Sigourney. New York, 1848. 12°. . . . 3062
Water Treatment. E. L. Bulwer and J. Forbes. New York, 1849. 12°. 3392
Water Witch. J. F. Cooper. Philadelphia, 1838. 2 v. 12°. . . . 1168
Waterloo, Stories of. W. H. Maxwell. London, 1850. 12°. . . . 5657
Story of the Battle of. G. R. Gleig. New York, 1847. 12°. . 3023

Waterhouse, G. R. Marsupialia. Edinburgh, 1843. 12°. . . 4901, 24
Waters, T. Recollections of a Policeman. New York, 1852. 12°. . . 4770
Waterston, R. C. Discourse on J. Q. Adams. Boston, 1848. . . . 3533
Moral and Spiritual Culture. Boston, 1844. 12°. . . . 2130
Waterston, W. Cyclopædia of Commerce. London. 1846. 8°. . . 3544
*The same. London, 1846. 8°. 3996
Watson, H. C. Camp-Fires of the Revolution. Philadelphia, 1850. 8°. 3828
Nights in a Block House. Philadelphia, 1852. 12°. . . . 1198
Old Bell of Independence. Philadelphia, 1852. 12°. 142
Watson, Robt. History of the Reign of Philip II. New York, 1818. 8°. 638
Watson, Rich. Life of J. Wesley. New York, 1831. 12°. . . . 1904
Watson, Rich. Reply to Gibbon. New York, n. d. 12°. 504
Reply to Paine. New York, n. d. 12°. 504
Watts, I. Improvement of the Mind. Boston, 1833. 12°. . . . 1483
Wau-nan-gee; or, Massacre of Chicago. Maj. Richardson. N.Y. 1852. 8°. 4810
Waverley Garland. Boston, 1853. Roy. 8°. 5110
Waverley; or,'Tis Sixty Years Since. Sir W. Scott. Bost. 1848. 2 v. 12°. 999, 1, 2
The same. Edinburgh, 1849. 2 v. 12°. 4100, 1, 2
The same. Edinburgh, 1850. Roy. 8°. 4531, 1
Way to Do Good. J. Abbott. New York, 1852. 12°. 6206
Wayfaring Sketches among the Greeks and Turks. London, 1849. 12°. . 4967
Wayland, F. Elements of Intellectual Philosophy. Boston, 1854. 12°. . 6319
Elements of Moral Science. Boston, 1839. 12°. 1448
Elements of Political Economy. New York, 1837. 8°. . . 799
Memoir of Adoniram Judson. Boston, 1853. 2 v. 12°. . . 5536
University Sermons. Boston, 1849. 12°. 3189
Wayne, A. Life. J. Armstrong. Boston, 1840. 12°. . . . 1076, 4
Ways of the Hour. J. F. Cooper. New York, 1850. 12°. . . . 3674
Weale, J. Dictionary of Terms of Art, &c. London, 1850. 12°. . . 6061
London and its Vicinity in 1851. London, 1851. 12°. . . . 4406
Wealth of Nations. Adam Smith. London, 1850. 8°. 676
Weaver, G. S. Hopes and Helps for the Young. New York, 1853. 12°. 5269
Webb, J. W. Altowan; or, the Rocky Mountains. N.Y. 1846. 2 v. 12°. 2924
Webber, C. W. Hunter Naturalist. Philadelphia, 1851. Roy. 8°. . 1340
Old Hicks, the Guide. New York, 1848. 12°. 3160
Romance of Natural History. Philadelphia, 1852. 8°. . . . 4814
Spiritual Vampirism. Philadelphia, 1853. 12°. 5302
Tales of the Southern Border. Philadelphia, 1853. 12°. . . 5322
Outlines of Universal History. Boston, 1853. 8°. . . . 5165
Webster, D. Diplomatic and Official Papers. New York, 1848. 8°. . 3207
Life. (No titlepage.) 1174
Life. C. W. March. New York, 1850. 12°. 3919
Life and Memorials of. S. P. Lyman. New York, 1853. 2 v. 12°. 5069
Memorial of, from City of Boston. Boston, 1853. 8°. . . . 5114
Obituary Addresses in Congress on. Washington, 1853. 8°. . 5420
Private Life. C. Lanman. New York, 1852. 12°. . . . 5052
Speeches and Forensic Arguments. Boston, 1848. 3 v. 8°. . . 788
Works; with Biography by E. Everett. Boston, 1851. 6 v. 8°. . 1648

Webster, D., the American Statesman. J. Banvard. Boston, 1853. 12°. 5554
Webster, J. W. Trial for Murder: G. Bemis's Report. Boston, 1850. 8°. 4315
The same: J. W. Stone's Report. Boston, 1850. 8°. . . 3952
Webster, N. Dictionary of Eng. Language. Springfield, 1845. 2 v. roy. 8°. 2231
*Dictionary of the English Language. Springfield, 1849. 4°. . 2040
History of the United States. Cincinnati, 1835. 12°. . . . 1504
Papers, Political, Literary, and Moral. New York, 1843. 8°. . 1994
Week's Delight; or, Games and Stories. New York, 1854. 12°. . . 5613
Weems, M. L. Life of Benjamin Franklin. Philadelphia, 1829. 12°. . 1019
Weights and Measures, Dictionary of. J. H. Alexander. Balt. 1850. 8°. 3978
and Measures, Report on. J. Q. Adams. Washington, 1821. 8°. 1254
Weir, J. Winter Lodge; or, Vow Fulfilled. Philadelphia, 1854. 12°. . 5801
Weiss, C. History of the French Protestants. N. York, 1854. 2 v. 12°. 5799
Welby, Amelia B. Poems. New York, 1846. 12°. 2988
Well-Digging, Boring, &c. J. G. Swindell. London, 1854. 12°. . . 6055
Weldron Family; or, Vicissitudes of Fortune. Providence, 1848. 12°. . 3227
Wellesley, R. (Marq.) Memoirs & Corres. R. R. Pearce. Lond. 1846. 3v. 8°. 4661
Weld, H. H. Autobiog. and Life of Benjamin Franklin. N.Y. 1848. 8°. 3265
Corrected Proofs. Boston, 1836. 12°. 2151
Wellington, Duke of. Life. F. L. Clarke and W. Dunlap. N.Y. 1814. 8°. 615
Life. W. K. Kelley. London, 1853. 12°. 6272
Life. W. H. Maxwell. London, 1845. 3 v. 8°. 5092
Sieges of, in Spain. Sir J. T. Jones. London, 1846. 3 v. 8°. . 5132
and Sir R. Peel. Lives. New York, 1852. 12°. 4992
Wellmont, Emma. Substance and Shadows. Boston, 1854. 12°. . . 5962
Uncle Sam's Palace. Boston, 1853. 12°. 5520
Wells, H. Essay on Teeth. Hartford, 1838. 12°. 3583
*Wells, N. A. Picturesque Antiquities of Spain. London, 1846. 8°. . 2042
Wells, T. Letters on Palestine. Boston, 1846. 12°. 2555
Wemyss, F. C. Life of an Actor and Manager. N. York, 1847. 2 v. 12°. 2968
Wensley; a Story without a Moral. E. Quincy. Boston, 1854. 12°. . 5860
Wentworth, T. (Earl of Strafford.) Life. J. Foster. London, 1831. 12°. 1831, 2
Wept of Wish-ton-Wish. J. F. Cooper. Philadelphia, 1833. 2 v. 12°. . 850
Werne, F. Expedition to the White Nile. London, 1849. 2 v. 12°. . 4019
Wesley, J., and Methodism. I. Taylor. New York, 1852. 12°. . . 3906
Life. R. Watson. New York, 1831. 12°. 1904
Life, and History of Methodism. R. Southey. N.Y. 1847. 2 v. 12°. 3005
West, Annals of the. J. H. Perkins. Cincinnati, 1846. 8°. . . . 3247
Letters from the. G. W. Ogden. New Bedford, 1823. 12°. . 1175
Life in the Far. G. F. Ruxton. New York, 1849. 12°. . . 3438
West, Mrs. Letters to a Young Man. Charlestown, 1803. 2 v. 12°. . 286
West, Benjamin, Life and Studies of. J. Galt. Philadelphia, 1816. 8°. 1327
West, G. Evidence of the Resurrection of Jesus Christ. Bost. 1834. 12°. 1478
West Indies and America. London, 1845. 8°. 3198
and N. America, Impressions in, 1849. R. Baird. Phil. 1850. 12°. 3873
Domestic Manners at. Mrs. Carmichael. Phil. 1833. 8°. . 1357, 2
Emancipation in. J. A. Thome & J. H. Kimball. N.Y. 1838. 8°. 699
A Winter in the. J. J. Gurney. New York, 1840. 8°. . . . 1286

West Indies, Residence in. R. R. Madden. Philadelphia, 1835. 2 v. 12°. 1077
History of British Colonies in. B. Edwards. Lond. 1794. 2 v. 4°. 2004
Tour through the British. D. McKinnen. London, 1804. 12°. . 196
Western Characters. J. L. McConnel. New York, 1853. 12°. . . 5563
Western Clearings. C. M. Kirkland. New York, 1845. 12°. . . 2525
Western Country, War of 1812 in. Lexington, 1816. 8°. . . . 546
Western Gazetteer. S. R. Brown. Auburn, 1817. 8°. 757
Western Islands of Scot., Journey to. S. Johnson. N.Y. 1843. Roy. 8°. 1984, 2
Western States and Territories, Annals of. J. H. Perkins. Cin. 1846. 8°. 3247
Guide for Emigrants. J. M. Peck. Boston, 1831. 12°. . . 1493
Western Travel. H. Martineau. New York, 1838. 2 v. 12°. . . 1117
Westminster, Description of. London, 1836. 24°. 2117
Westminster Review. Vols. 21–61 [continued]. N.Y. 1834–54. Roy. 8°. 2825
Westward Ho! J. K. Paulding. New York, 1832. 2 v. 12°. . . 431
Whale and his Captors. H. T. Cheever. New York, 1850. 12°. . . 3317
Whale Fishery, Northern. New York, 1831. 16°. 818
The same. New York, 1848. 16°. 3683, 14
Whales, Natural History of. R. Hamilton. Edinburgh, 1843. 12°. 4901, 26
Whaling Cruise, Etchings of. J. R. Browne. New York, 1850. 8°. . 2753
Wharton, C. H. Controversy with Romanism. New York, 1817. 8°. . 3636
Wharton, F. State Trials of the United States. Phil. 1849. 8°. . . 2669
Wharton, G. M. Southern Medical Student. Philadelphia, 1851. 12°. 4038
What to Observe in Medical Cases. Philadelphia, 1853. 12°. . . 5754
Whately, R. Elements of Logic. New York, 1839. 12°. . . . 1805
Elements of Rhetoric. Boston, 1845. 12°. 1804
Essays on the Dangers to Christian Faith. London, 1839. 8°. . 2652
Essays on the Difficulties in St. Paul's Writings. Lond. 1845. 8°. 2650
Essays on the Errors of Romanism. London, 1845. 8°. . . 2651
Historic Doubts relative to Napoleon. New York, 1853. 12°. . 6203
Kingdom of Christ, in Two Essays. London, 1845. 8°. . . . 2653
Wheat and Silk, Third Mass. Report on. H. Colman. Boston, 1840. 8°. 1607
Wheat or Chaff? J. C. Ryle. New York, 1852. 12°. 927
Wheatly, C. Illust. of the Book of Common Prayer. Lond. 1849. Post 8°. 4394
Wheaton, H. Discourse on Germany. Boston, 1847. 8°. 3197
Elements of International Law. Philadelphia, 1846. 8°. . . 3538
History of the Northmen. Philadelphia, 1831. 8°. . . . 2174
Life of William Pinkney. Boston, 1840. 12°. 1076, 6
Right of Visitation and Search. Philadelphia, 1842. 8°. . . 2833
Wheaton, R. Memoir and Selections from Writings. Boston, 1854. 12°. 5610
Wheeler, G. Rural Homes; or, Houses for the Country. N.Y. 1851. 12°. 4495
Wheeler, H. G. History of Congress. New York, 1848. 2 v. 8°. . 3200
Wheeler, J. D. Treatise on the Law of Slavery. N.Y. 1837. Roy. 8°. . 1352
Whelpley, S. Compend of History. New York, 1844. 12°. . . 333
Whewell, W. Elements of Morality and Polity. N.Y. 1845. 2 v. 12°. 2490
History of the Inductive Sciences. London, 1837. 3 v. 8°. . . 2273
Indications of a Creator. Philadelphia, 1845. 12°. . . . 2359
Philosophy of the Inductive Sciences. London, 1840. 2 v. 8°. . 2692
Plurality of Worlds. Boston, 1854. 12°. 5817

Whig Review. — See *American Whig Review.*
Whim, and its Consequences. G. P. R. James. New York, 1848. 8°. . 3220
Whims and Oddities, in Prose and Verse. T. Hood. N.Y. 1852. 12°. . 4990
Whimsical Woman. Emilie F. Carlen. New York, 1854. 12°. . . 5814
Whimsicalities. T. Hood. New York, 1852. 12°. 4759
Whipple, E. P. Essays and Reviews. New York, 1848. 2 v. 12°. . 3184

Vol. 1. T. B. Macaulay; Poets and Poetry of America; T. N. Talfourd; Words; James's Novels; Sydney Smith; Daniel Webster; Neal's History of the Puritans; Wm. Wordsworth; Lord Byron; English Poets of Nineteenth Century; Vagaries of Volition.
2. Old English Dramatists; Dr. South's Sermons; Romance of Rascality; Croakers of Society and Literature; British Critics; Rufus Choate; Coleridge as a Philosophical Critic; Prescott's Histories; Prescott's Conquest of Peru; Shakspeare's Critics; Richard Brinsley Sheridan; Appendix.

Lectures on Literature and Life. Boston, 1850. 12°. . . . 3435

Authors in their Relations to Life; Novels and Novelists; Charles Dickens; Wit and Humor; Ludicrous Side of Life; Genius; Intellectual Health and Disease.

Whitby, D. Last Thoughts. Boston, 1823. 12°. 368, 2
White, C. Essays in Literature and Ethics. Boston, 1853. 12°. . . 5254
White, G. Natural History of Selborne. London, 1851. Post 8°. . 4178
The same. London, 1853. 12°. 2192
The same. (H. F. L.) New York, 1848. 12°. . . 3683, 147
White, G. S. Samuel Slater, and History of Cotton Manufac. Phil. 1836. 8°. 1237
White, H. K., Beauties of, in Poetry and Prose. Boston, 1827. 12°. . 307
Complete Works, with Life. R. Southey. New York, 1849. 8°. 3421
Poetical Works. Philadelphia, 1836. 8°. 580
Remains. Boston, 1815. 2 v. 16°. 50
White, J. B. Autobiography. Ed. by J. H. Thom. Lond. 1845. 3 v. 12°. 2503
White, J. E. Letters on England. Philadelphia, 1816. 2 v. 8°. . . 1375
White, R. G. Shakspeare's Scholar. New York, 1854. 8°. . . . 5989
White-Jacket; or, World in a Man-of-War. H. Melville. N.Y. 1850. 12°. 3654
White Mountains, Legends of. I. W. Scrivener. Boston, 1854. 12°. . 6238
*Scenery of. W. Oakes. Boston, 1848. 4°. 3747
White Slave; or, Memoirs of a Fugitive. R. Hildreth. Bost. 1852. 12°. 4882
White Slave; or, Russian Peasant Girl. New York, 1845. 8°. . . 2750
White Slavery; New Emancipation Cause. W. Burton. Worc. 1839. 12°. 1489
in Barbary States. C. Sumner. Boston, 1853. 12°. . . . 5249
White Slaves of England. Auburn, 1853. 8°. 5385
Whiteboy; a Story of Ireland. Mrs. S. C. Hall. New York, 1845. 8°. 2640
Whitefield, G., Memoirs of. J. Gillies. Boston, 1813. 12°. . . . 208
Whitehead, C. Richard Savage. London, 1853. 12°. 5729
Whiting, J. Revolutionary Orders of Gen. Washington. N.Y. 1844. 8°. 2236
Whiting, H. Life of Z. M. Pike. Boston, 1846. 12°. . . . 1076, 15
Whiting, W. Argument in a Patent Case. Boston, 1853. 8°. . . 5437
Argument on Case of Mystic River Flats. Boston, 1851. 8°. . 4143
Whitman, Z. G. History of the Anc. & Hon. Artillery Co. Bost. 1820. 8°. 750
Whitney, J. D. Metallic Wealth of the U. States. Philadelphia, 1854. 8°. 5990
Whittier, J. G. Chapel of the Hermits, &c. Boston, 1853. 12°. . . 5207
Lays of my Home, and other Poems. Boston, 1843. 12°. . . 1893

Whittier, J. G. Old Portraits and Modern Sketches. Boston, 1850. 12°. 3479
Literary Recreations and Miscellanies. Boston, 1854. 12°. . . 6222
Poems. Boston, 1849. 8°. 1559
Songs of Labor, and other Poems. Boston, 1850. 12°. . . 3922
Stranger in Lowell. Boston, 1845. 12°. 2478
Supernaturalism in New England. New York, 1847. 12°. . . 2963
Whittingham, Maj. Ten Months' Residence in Berlin. London, 1846. 8°. 1129
Whittlesey, C. Life of James Fitch. Boston, 1846. 12°. . . 1076, 16
Who shall be Heir? Ellen Pickering. Philadelphia, 1847. 8°. . . 2706
Wide, Wide World. Anna Warner. New York, 1851. 12°. . . 4083
Widow and the Marquis. T. E. Hook. London, 1842. 12°. . . . 5678
Widow Barnaby. Mrs. F. Trollope. London, 1850. 12°. . . . 5674
Widow Rugby's Husband, &c. J. H. Hooper. Philadelphia, 1851. 12°. 4173
Wieland; or, the Transformation. C. B. Brown. New York, 1846. 8°. 2715
Wife Hunter. Caroline Pichler. New York, 1844. 8°. . . . 2167, 1
Wife's Sister; or, Forbidden Marriage. Mrs. Hubback. N. Y. 1851. 8°. 4131
Wiggins, J. Embanking Lands from the Sea. London, 1852. 12°. . 6089
Wight, O. W. Romance of Abelard and Heloïse. N. Y. 1853. 12°. . 5367
(Editor.) Philosophy of Sir W. Hamilton. New York, 1853. 12°. 5371
Wigwam and the Cabin. W. G. Simms. Philadelphia, 1853. 12°. . 2486
Wikoff, H. Sketches of Louis Napoleon. New York, 1849. 12°. . . 3352
Wilberforce, S. Journal and Letters of Henry Martyn. N. Y. 1851. 12°. 4168
Wilberforce, W. Correspondence. Ed. by his Sons. Phil. 1841. 2 v. 12°. 1771
Devotions at Home. Boston, 1838. 12°. 1485
Life. R. I. and S. Wilberforce. Philadelphia, 1841. 2 v. 12°. . 1770
Practical View of the Religious System. Boston, 1815. 12°. . 213
Wild Irish Boy. D. J. Murphy. New York, 1808. 2 v. 12°. . . 306
Wild Jack; or; the Stolen Child. Mrs. C. L. Hentz. Phil. 1854. 12°. . 5768
Wild Scenes and Wild Hunters. C. W. Webber. Phil. 1851. Roy. 8°. 1340
in a Hunter's Life. Compiled by J. Frost. Auburn, 1851. 12°. . 4216
of the Forest and Prairie. C. F. Hoffman. N. Y. 1843. 2 v. 12°. 1727
Wild Sports of the West. W. H. Maxwell. Phil. 1851. 8°. . . . 4125
The same. Philadelphia, 1846. 8°. 2663
Wilde, R.H. Love, Madness, and Imprisonment of Tasso. N.Y. 1842. 2 v. 12°. 2127
Wilderness and the War Path. J. Hall. New York, 1846. 12°. . . 2580
Wilhelm Meister's Apprenticeship. J. W. von Goethe. Bost. 1851. 2 v. 12°. 1802
Wilkes, C. California and Oregon, with Maps. Philadelphia, 1849. 8°. 3296
U. S. Exploring Expedition, 1838–42. Phil. 1845. 5 v. roy. 8°. . 2244
Wilkes, G. Europe in a Hurry. New York, 1852. 12°. . . . 5021
Wilkinson, G. Handbook for Travellers in Egypt. London, 1847. 12°. 60
Wilkinson, Sir J. G. Ancient Egyptians. London, 1837. 3 v. 8°. . 2656
Popular Account of Ancient Egyptians. London, 1854. 2 v. 12°. 5752
Wilkinson, J. J. G. Human Body, and Man. Philadelphia, 1851. 12°. 4487
Will, The, Inquiry respecting. J. Day. New Haven, 1838. 12°. . . 2986
Treatise on. T. C. Upham. Portland, 1834. 8°. . . . 3790
Will Watch; from Autobiog. of a British Officer. Phil. 1855. 3 v. 12°. 1085
Willard, Emma. History of Mexican War and California. N. Y. 1849. 12°. 3286
Letters from France and Great Britain. Troy, 1833. 12°. . . 3760

Willard, J. Address at 200th Anniversary of Lancaster, Ms. Bost. 1853. 8°. 5456
William of Malmesbury. Chronicle of English Kings. Lond. 1847. Post 8°. 3563
William the Conqueror, History of. J. Abbott. New York, 1850. 12°. . 3575
Williams, C. Vegetable World. Boston, 1833. 12°. 56
Williams, Mrs. C. R. Biog. of W. Barton and S. Olney. Prov. 1839 12°. 1571
Williams, E. Memoirs of the Presidents of the U. States. N.Y. 1849. 8°. 2067
(Editor.) Presidents' Messages, 1789–1846. N. York, 1846. 2 v. 8°. 2781
Williams, F. S. Our Iron Roads. London, 1852. 8°. 5084
Williams, G. Jerusalem. London, 1849. 2 v. 8°. 4655
Williams, Helen M. Letters from France. New York, 1794. 4 v. 12°. . 1043
Tour in Switzerland. Dublin, 1798. 2 v. 12°. 873
Williams, J., an American Slave, Narrative of. New York, 1838. 16°. . 1515
Williams, J. Life of Alexander the Great. (H. F. L.) N.Y. 1843. 12°. 3683, 7
Williams, J. J. Isthmus of Tehuantepec. New York, 1852. 2 v. 8°. . 4843
Williams, Roger. Life. W. Gammell. Boston, 1844. 12°. . . 1076, 14
Memoir. J. D. Knowles. Boston, 1834. 12°. 563
Spirit of. L. D. Johnson. Boston, 1839. 12°. 49
Williams, R. F. Luttrells; or, the Two Marriages. N. York, 1851. 8°. 4005
Secret Passion. New York, 1848. 8°. 2806
Shakspeare and his Friends. Paris, 1838. 8°. 1059
Youth of Shakspeare. New York, 1847. 8°. 2807
Williams, S. History of Vermont. Burlington, 1809. 2 v. 8°. . . 1215
Williams, W. R. Discourses on Religious Progress. Boston, 1851. 12°. 4408
Lectures on the Lord's Prayer. Boston, 1851. 12°. 4407
Williams, S. W. Middle Kingdom; or, China. N.Y. 1848. 2 v. 12°. . 3102
Williamson, H. Climate in America. New York, 1811. 8°. . . . 662
History of North Carolina. Philadelphia, 1812. 2 v. 8°. . . 680
Williamson, W. D. History of Maine. Hallowell, 1832. 2 v. 8°. . 569
Willis, N. P. A l'Abri; or, the Tent Pitched. New York, 1839. 12°. . 987
Dashes at Life. New York, 1845. Roy. 8°. 2638
Famous Persons and Places. New York, 1854. 12°. 6184
Fun-Jottings; or, Laughs I have taken a Pen to. N.Y. 1853. 12°. 5534
Health Trip to the Tropics. New York, 1853. 12°. 5577
Hurry-Graphs. New York, 1851. 12°. 4162
Inklings of Adventure. New York, 1836. 2 v. 12°. 223
Life, Here and There. New York, 1850. 12°. 3924
Memoranda of the Life of Jenny Lind. Philadelphia, 1851. 12°. 4097
Pencillings by the Way. New York, 1852. 12°. 1130
People I have Met. New York, 1850. 12°. 3483
Poems. New York, 1849. 8°. 1942
Prose Works. Philadelphia, 1850. Roy. 8°. 5164
Romance of Travel. New York, 1840. 12°. 2335
Rural Letters. New York, 1849. 12°. 3278
Summer Cruise in the Mediterranean. New York, 1853. 12°. . 5273
(Editor.) The Token. Boston, 1829. 12°. 842
(Editor.) Trenton Falls Illustrated. New York, 1851. 12°. . 4271
Willis, W. Hist. of Portland, and Jours. of Smith & Deane. Port. 1849. 8°. 3605
Williston, E. B. Eloquence of the U. S. Middletown, 1827. 5 v. 8°. . 6030

Wilmot, Mrs. Blue-Stocking Hall. New York, 1828. 2 v. 12°. . . 550
Wilmott, R. A. Gems of Epistolary Correspondence. London, 1836. 12°. 4569
Summer Time in the Country. New York, 1852. 12°. . . 4908
Willoughby, Lady, Diary of. Mrs. Rathbone. New York, 1845. 12°. . 2328
Wills, J. Lives of Illustrious Irishmen. Dublin, 1839. 6 v. 8°. . . 3591
Wilson, A. American Ornithology. Ed. by T. M. Brewer. N.Y. 1852. 8°. 5924
Life. W. B. O. Peabody. Boston, 1838. 12°. . . . 1076, 2
Wilson, D. Evidences of Christianity. Boston, 1845. 2 v. 12°. . . 4745
Wilson, E. Treatise on the Skin and Hair. Philadelphia, 1854. 12°. . 6177
(Editor.) Hufeland's Art of Prolonging Life. Boston, 1854. 12°. 5589
Wilson, F. A. Britain Redeemed and Canada Preserved. Lond. 1850. 8°. 5414
Wilson, John. Treatise on English Punctuation. Boston, 1855. 16°. . 3858
Wilson, Prof. John. Critical and Miscellaneous Essays. Phil. 1848. 8°. 3418, 4
The same. Philadelphia, 1842. 3 v. 12°. 1662
Dies Boreales; or, Christopher under Canvass. Phil. 1850. 12°. . 3879
Genius and Character of Robert Burns. Philadelphia, 1854. 12°. 5760
The same. Philadelphia, 1851. 12°. 2484
Lights and Shadows of Scottish Life. New York, 1849. 12°. . 394
The Foresters. Boston, 1845. 12°. 1469
Noctes Ambrosianæ. Philadelphia, 1843. 4 v. 12°. . . . 1801
The same. Ed. by S. Mackenzie. New York, 1854. 5 v. 12°. 6235
Specimens of the British Critics. Philadelphia, 1846. 12°. . . 2559
Wilson, J. M., & J. P. Lawson. Gazetteer of Ireland. Dub. n. d. 2 v. 12°. 5038
Wilson, J. Mackay. Tales of the Borders. New York, 1848. 2 v. 8°. . 2889
Wilson, J. P. Essay on Grammar. Philadelphia, 1817. 12°. . . 586
Windham, W., and W. Huskisson, Select Speeches of. Phil. 1837. 8°. . 1817
Windle, Mary J. Legend of the Waldenses, & other Tales. Phil. 1852. 12°. 4605
Wines, E. C. Laws of the Ancient Hebrews. New York, 1853. 8°. . 5390
System of Popular Education. Philadelphia, 1838. 12°. . . 1452
Wines, Handbook of. T. McMullen. New York, 1852. 12°. . . 4777
Wing and Wing; a Tale. J. F. Cooper. Philadelphia, 1842. 2 v. 12°. 1703
Winslow, H. Young Man's Aid. Boston, 1837. 12°. 2994
Winslow, O. Midnight Harmonies. New York, 1851. 12°. . . . 4187
Winsor, J. History of Duxbury. Boston, 1849. 8°. 2579
Winsor Prison, Recollections of. J. Reynolds. Boston, 1834. 12°. . 536
Winter, Amalie. Michaelo and the Twins. Bath, n. d. 12°. . . . 5640
Winter, C., Memoirs of. W. Jay. New York, 1811. 12°. . . . 1018
Winter Evening Book. New York, 1842. 12°. 1881
Winter Evening Tales. J. Hogg. Hartford, 1847. 2 v. 12°. . . . 1461
Winter Lodge; or, Vow Fulfilled. J. Weir. Philadelphia, 1854. 12°. . 5801
Winter Studies and Summer Rambles. Mrs. Jameson. N.Y. 1839. 2 v. 12°. 1060
Winthrop, John. Hist. of New England from 1630–49. Bost. 1853. 2 v. 8°. 1784
Winthrop, Prof. John. Lectures on Comets; with Life. Bost. 1811. 12°. 875
Winthrop, R. C. Addresses and Speeches. Boston, 1852. 8°. . . 4836
*Wisconsin, Iowa, &c., Geological Survey of. R. D. Owen. Phil. 1852. 4°. 5167
Wise, Lieut. Los Gringos; or, View of Mexico & California. N.Y. 1849. 12°. 3429
Wise, D. Young Man's Counsellor. Boston, 1851. 12°. . . . 4090
Wise, J. System of Æronautics. Philadelphia, 1850. 8°. . . . 4148

Wisner, W. Incidents in the Life of a Pastor. New York, 1851. 12°. . 4436
Wirt, W. Letters of the British Spy. New York, 1836. 12°. . . 2133
Life and Character of Patrick Henry. Hartford, 1852. 8°. . . 594
Memoirs. J. P. Kennedy. Philadelphia, 1850. 2 v. 12°. . . 3443
Wit and Humor; selected from Eng. Poets. L. Hunt. N.Y. 1846. 12°. 2587
Witchcraft, Lectures on the Salem, 1692. C. W. Upham. Bost. 1831. 12°. 886
Withington, L. The Puritan. Boston, 1836. 2 v. 12°. 400
Withington, W. Growth of Thought. Boston, 1851. 12°. . . . 6244
Wives of England. Mrs. Sarah Ellis. New York, 1843. 8°. . . 1826
Woehler, F. Analytical Chemist's Assistant. Philadelphia, 1852. 12°. . 5024
Wolff, H. D. Madrilenia; or, Spanish Life. London, 1851. 8°. . . 5413
Wolff, J. Narrative of a Mission to Bokhara, 1843-45. N.Y. 1845. 8°. 2626
Wolsey, T. (Cardinal). Life. London, 1833. 8°. 602
The same. London, 1831. 12°. 1831, 1
Woman and her Master. J. F. Smith. New York, 1854. 8°. . . 5932
in America. Mrs. A. J. Graves. (H. F. L.) N.Y. 1848. 12°. 3683, 166
in America. Maria J. McIntosh. New York, 1850. 12°. . . 3629
Excellent, described in Proverbs. W. B. Sprague. Bost. 1852. 12°. 4637
in France in the 18th Century. Julia Kavanagh. Phil. 1850. 12°. 3855
in the 19th Century. S. Margaret Fuller. New York, 1845. 12°. 2313
Noble Deeds of. Elizabeth Starling. Boston, 1850. 12°. . . 3673
Remedy for the Wrongs of. Cath. E. Beecher. Boston, 1851. 12°. 4415
Woman's Friendship. Grace Aguilar. New York, 1851. 12°. . . 3650
Woman's Influence and Woman's Mission. Philadelphia, 1854. 12°. . 5843
Woman's Record. Mrs. S. J. Hale. New York, 1853. Roy. 8°. . . 5104
Woman's Whims; or, Female Barometer. X. B. Saintine. N.Y. 1850. 12°. 3676
Women, Characteristics of. Mrs. A. Jameson. Boston, 1846. 8°. . . 266
Duties of Young. E. H. Chapin. Boston, 1850. 12°. . . 2451
Heroic, of the West. J. Frost. Philadelphia, 1854. 12°. . . 5765
History of the Condition of. L. M. Child. Bost. 1838. 2 v. 12°. 1880
Lectures to Young. W. G. Eliot. Boston, 1853. 12°. . . 5553
Legal Rights and Duties of. E. D. Mansfield. Salem, 1845. 12°. 2574
Lives of Celebrated. S. G. Goodrich. Boston, 1849. 12°. . 4900, 6
Memorable. Mrs. N. Crosland. Boston, 1854. 12°. . . . 6229
Memoirs of Celebrated. Mde. Junot. Phil. 1835. 2 v. 12°. . 1030
Noble Deeds of American. Edited by J. Clement. Buf. 1851. 12°. 4217
of the American Revolution. Mrs. E. F. Ellet. N.Y. 1848. 3 v. 12°. 3170
of the Bible. P. C. Headley. Auburn, 1850. 12°. . . . 3846
of Christianity. Julia Kavanagh. New York, 1852. 12°. . . 4762
of England. Mrs. Sarah Ellis. New York, 1843. 8°. . . . 1826
of Israel. Grace Aguilar. New York, 1851. 2 v. 12°. . . 4029
of the West, Pioneer. Mrs. E. F. Ellet. New York, 1852. 12°. . 4919
Thoughts to, on Self-Culture. Maria G. Grey. Bost. 1851. 12°. 4195
Wonder-Book for Girls and Boys. N. Hawthorne. Boston, 1852. 12°. 4601
Wonderful Museum, Kirby's. London, 1850. 5 v. 8°. 4669
Wonders of Creation. D. R. Preston. Boston, 1807. 2 v. 12°. . . 206
Wonders of the Universe. New York, 1831. 8°. 579
Wondrous Tale of Alroy. B. Disraeli. Philadelphia, 1845. 8°. . . 2689

Wondrous Tale of Alroy. B. Disraeli. Philadelphia, 1833. 2 v. 12°. . 1179
Wood, G. Peter Schlemihl in America. Philadelphia, 1848. 12°. . 4928
Wood, J. G. Illustrated Natural History. New York, 1853. 12°. . 5609
Wood, N. Practical Treatise on Railroads. London, 1838. 8°. . . 4340
Wood, T. Mosaic History of Creation. New York, 1831. 8°. . . 4015
Wood, W. B. Personal Recollections of the Stage. Phil. 1854. 12°. . 6313
Wood, W. M. Wandering Sketches of People and Things. Phil. 1849. 12°. 3465
Wood Leighton. Mary Howitt. Philadelphia, 1837. 3 v. 12°. . . 965
Woodbury, L. Writings, Political, Judicial, &c. Boston, 1852. 3 v. 8°. 5091
Woodcraft; or, Hawks about the Dovecote. W. G. Simms. N.Y. 1854. 12°. 6248
Woodman, D., jun. Guide to Texas Emigrants. Boston, 1835. 12°. . 1466
Woodman; a Romance. G. P. R. James. New York, 1847. 8°. . . 2802
Woodreve Manor; or, Six Months in Town. A. H. Dorsey. Phil. 1852. 12°. 4879
Woodrooffe, Anne. Shades of Character. New York, 1852. 2 v. 12°. . 4848
Woods, D. B. Sixteen Months in the Gold Diggings. N. York, 1851. 12°. 4597
Woodstock. Sir W. Scott. Boston, 1848. 2 v. 12°. 999, 37, 38
The same. Edinburgh, 1849. 2 v. 12°. . . 4100, 39, 40
The same. Edinburgh, 1850. Roy. 8°. 4531, 10
Woodward, S. P. Recent and Fossil Shells. London, 1851. 12°. . . 6083
Woodworth, F. C. Miscellany of Entertaining Knowl. Bost. 1853. 12°. 5187
Stories about Animals. New York, 1850. 12°. 3311
The same. Boston, 1851. 12°. 3937
Stories about Birds. Boston, 1851. 12°. 3938
World as it Is: England and Wales. Philadelphia, 1854. 16°. . 6308
The same: Scotland and Ireland. Philadelphia, 1854. 16°. 6309
Woolhouse, W. S. B. Differential Calculus. London, 1854. 12°. . 6108
Woolrych, H. W. Life of Judge Jeffreys. Philadelphia, 1852. 12°. . 4862
Worcester, Mass., History of. W. Lincoln. Worcester, 1837. 8°. . . 3201
Worcester Pulpit. E. Smalley. Boston, 1851. 12°. 4211
Worcester, J. E. Dictionary of the English Language. Bost. 1848. Roy. 8°. 2888
Elements of Ancient and Modern Geography. Boston, 1844. 12°. 3867
Worcester, S., Life and Labors of. S. M. Worcester. Bost. 1852. 2 v. 12°. 994
Words, Handbook of Anglo-Saxon Derivatives. New York, 1854. 12°. . 6329
Handbook of Anglo-Saxon Root. New York, 1854. 12°. . . 6330
Meaning of. A. B. Johnson. New York, 1854. 12°. . . . 6331
Study of. R. C. Trench. New York, 1852. 12°. . . . 4785
Thesaurus of English. P. M. Roget. Boston, 1854. 12°. . . 5781
Wordsworth, W. Complete Poetical Works. Phil. 1851. Roy. 8°. . 1433
The Excursion; a Poem. New York, 1849. 12°. . . . 3436
Memoirs. C. Wordsworth. Boston, 1851. 2 v. 12°. . . . 4205
Prelude; a Poem. New York, 1850. 12°. 3904
Working and Middle Classes, History of. J. Wade. London, 1835. 12°. 2109
Working-Man, The. C. Quill. Philadelphia, 1839. 12°. . . . 1520
Workingman's Manual. S. Simpson. Philadelphia, 1831. 8°. . . 4020
World, The. London, 1794. 4 v. 12°. 166
and its Inhabitants. S. G. Goodrich. Boston, 1849. 12°. . 4900, 20
as it Is: England and Wales. F. C. Woodworth. Phil. 1854. 16°. 6308
as it Is: Scotland and Ireland. F. C. Woodworth. Phil. 1854. 16°. 6309

World as it Moves; a Periodical. Vol. 2. 1849. (No titlepage.) . . 3407
Here and There; from "Household Words." N. York, 1852. 12°. 4396
*of Science, Art, & Industry. Ed. by B. Silliman, jun. N.Y. 1854. 12°. 5946
World's Laconics. E. Berkeley. New York, 1853. 12°. . . . 5029
World's Progress; a Dict. of Dates. Ed. by G. P. Putnam. N.Y. 1852. 12°. 2041
Worlds, More than One. Sir D. Brewster. New York, 1854. 12°. . 6299
Wormeley, Elizabeth. Amabel; a Family History. N. York, 1853. 12°. 5240
Wortley, Lady E. S. Travels in the United States. Lond. 1851. 3 v. 12°. 4285
Wotton, Sir H., Sir W. Raleigh, and others. Poems. London, 1845. 12°. 2505
Wrangell, F. von. Polar Sea Expedition, 1820–23. London, 1844. 12°. 5002
The same. (H. F. L.) New York, 1848. 12°. . . 3683, 148
Wraxall, N. W. Historical Memoirs. Philadelphia, 1837. 8°. . . 727
The same. (Selec. Cir. Lib.) Phil. 1837. 4°. . . 2034, 1837
Posthumous Memoirs of his own Time. Philadelphia, 1836. 8°. . 1325
The same. (Selec. Cir. Lib.) Philadelphia, 1836. 4°. 2034, 1836
Wreath; a Collection of Poems. Hartford, 1827. 18°. 34
The same. Hartford, 1836. 16°. 940
Wreck of the Glide. W. G. Dix. Boston, 1846. 12°. 2917
Wren, Sir Christopher. Life. London, 1833. 8°. 602
Wright, G. Gentleman's Miscellany. Exeter, 1797. 12°. . . . 828
Wright, H. C. Human Life Illustrated by my Experience. Bost. 1849. 12°. 3289
Wright, Silas. Life. J. S. Jenkins. Auburn, 1847. 12°. . . . 3178
Wright, T. England under the House of Hanover. Lond. 1848. 2 v. 8°. 5159
(Editor.) Early Travels in Palestine. London, 1848. Post 8°. . 3562
Narratives of Sorcery and Magic. New York, 1852. 12°. . . 4768
Wuthering Heights; a Novel. Miss Bronte. New York, 1848. 12°. . 3106
Wyandotte; or, the Hutted Knoll. J. F. Cooper. N. York, 1843. 2 v. 12°. 1734
Wycherley, W. Dramatic Works. Ed. by L. Hunt. Lond. 1851. Roy. 8°. 4527
Wynne, J. Lives of Literary and Scientific Men. New York, 1850. 12°. 3920
Wyoming, Poetry and History of. W. L. Stone. New York, 1841. 12°. 2966
Wyss, M. Swiss Family Robinson. New York, 1852. 12°. . . . 3312
The same (in French). Paris, 1843. 8°. 4548

X.

Xenophon. The Anabasis. Trans. by E. Spelman. N. York, 1831. 12°. 141, 1
The same. New York, 1844. 12°. 1854, 1
The Cyropædia. Trans. by M. A. Cooper. N. York, 1831. 12°. 141, 2
The same. New York, 1844. 12°. 1854, 2
Works. Trans. by J. S. Watson. London, 1854. Post 8°. . . 6327

The Anabasis; Expedition of Cyrus; Memorabilia of Socrates.

Xerxes, History of. J. Abbott. New York, 1850. 12°. 4490

Y.

Yachting, Romance of. J. C. Hart. New York, 1848. 12°. 3185
Yankee, The. Edited by J. Neal. Vol. 1. Portland, 1828. 4°. . . . 2015
Yankee Notions; a Medley. Boston, 1838. 12°. 956
Yankee Stories. T. C. Haliburton. Philadelphia, 1849. 12°. . . . 3348
Yankee Yarns and Yankee Letters. T. C. Haliburton. Phil. 1852. 12°. 1573
Yates, W. H. Modern History and Condition of Egypt. Lond. 1843. 8°. 3994
Year-Book of the American Congregational Union. New York, 1854. 8°. 5491
Year-Book; or, Manual of Reference. Ed. by B. B. Edwards. Phil. 1838. 12°. 2125
Year of Consolation. Frances K. Butler. New York, 1847. 2 v. 12°. . 3002
Yeast; a Problem. C. Kingsley, jun. New York, 1851. 12°. . . 4218
Yellowplush Papers. W. M. Thackeray. New York, 1852. 12°. . . 1058
Yemassee; a Romance of Carolina. W. G. Simms. New York, 1854. 12°. 1142
York, Mrs. Sarah E. Memoir. Mrs. R. B. Medbery. Bost. 1853. 12°. 5035
Youatt, W. The Dog. Philadelphia, 1847. 8°. 2764
Structure and Diseases of the Horse. New York, 1852. 12°. . 5077
Youmans, E. L. Alcohol and the Constitution of Man. N.Y. 1854. 12°. 6158
Young, Alex. Chronicles of the Pilgrim Fathers. Boston, 1844. 8°. . 1957
Chronicles of Colony of Massachusetts Bay. Boston, 1846. 8°. . 2733
Discourses on Kirkland and Bowditch. Boston, 1838–40. 8°. . 2225
Young, Arthur. Travels in France, 1787–89. Dublin, 1793. 2 v. 8°. . 605
The same. London, 1792. 4°. 2007
Young, E. Night Thoughts. London, 1802. 8°. 31
The same. Philadelphia, 1820. 2 v. 24°. 31
The same. New York, 1851. 12°. 4592
Works. Charlestown, 1811. 3 v. 12°. 52
Young, J. R. Arithmetic and Key. London, 1854. 2 v. 12°. . . 6095
Young Americans Abroad. Edited by J. O. Choules. Boston, 1852. 12°. 4638
Young Artist; or, Dream of Italy. T. S. Arthur. New York, 1850. 12°. 3768
Young Christian. J. Abbott. New York, 1851. 12°. 633
Young Duke. B. Disraeli. New York, 1831. 2 v. 12°. 426
The same. Philadelphia, 1845. 8°. 2689
Young Emigrants, and other Tales. New York, 1851. 12°. 4473
Young Governess; or, the Education of Circumstances. N.Y. 1851. 12°. 4200
Young, Hopes and Helps for the. G. S. Weaver. New York, 1853. 12°. 5269
Young Husband's Book. Philadelphia, 1836. 24°. 2201
Young Islanders. Jefferys Taylor. New York, 1842. 16°. . . . 2096
Young Kate; or, the Rescue. New York, 1846. 2 v. 12°. . . . 2199
Young Ladies, Advice to. T. S. Arthur. Boston, 1848. 12°. . . 3059
Young Lady's Friend. Boston, 1836. 12°. 296
Young Lady's Offering. L. H. Sigourney and others. Boston, 1851. 12°. 3079
Young Maiden. A. B. Muzzey. Boston, 1841. 12°. 1578
Young Man's Aid. H. Winslow. Boston, 1837. 12°. 2994
Young Man's Counsellor. D. Wise. Boston, 1851. 12°. 4090
Young Man's Own Book. Philadelphia, 1836. 24°. 2202

Young Marooners on the Florida Coast. F. R. Goulding. Phil. 1852. 16°. 5185
Young Men, Advice to. W. Cobbett. New York, 1844. 12°. . . 26
Advice to. T. S. Arthur. Boston, 1847. 16°. 2434
Duties of. E. H. Chapin. Boston, 1840. 12°. 1463
Lecture to, on Chastity. S. Graham. Boston, 1837. 12°. . . 1733
Lectures to. H. W. Beecher. Indianapolis, 1844. 12°. . . 2181
Lectures to. R. W. Clarke. Boston, 1853. 12°. 5543
Lectures to. W. G. Eliot, jun. Boston, 1854. 12°. . . . 5639
Lectures to. C. B. Smith. Hartford, 1848. 12°. . . . 3172
Young Men's Chris. Assoc., Twelve Lectures before. Lond. 1850. 2 v. 12°. 4204
Young Muscovite; or, Poles in Russia. F. Chamier. N. Y. 1834. 2 v. 12°. 1106
Young Patroon; or, Christmas in 1690. P. H. Myers. N.Y. 1849. 12°. 3326
Young Pilgrim. Mrs. Hofland. New York, 1828. 12°. . . . 353
Young Voyageurs. M. Reid. Boston, 1854. 12°. 5621
Young Wife. W. A. Alcott. Boston, 1837. 12°. 912
Young Women, Duties of. E. H. Chapin. Boston, 1850. 12°. . . 2451
Lectures to. W. G. Eliot, jun. Boston, 1853. 12°. . . . 5553
Youth, Golden Steps for. J. M. Austin. Auburn, 1850. 12°. . . 3860
Youth of Jefferson; or, College Scrapes. New York, 1854. 12°. . . 6181
Youth of Shakspeare. R. F. Williams. New York, 1847. 8°. . . 2807
Youth's Handbook of Entertaining Knowledge. London, 1844. 2 v. 12°. 4261
Yucatan, Incidents of Travel in. J. L. Stephens. N.Y. 1843. 2 v. 8°. . 1721
Yusef; or, the Journey of the Frangi. J. R. Browne. N. Y. 1853. 12°. 5292

Z.

Zachos, J. C. New American Speaker. New York, 1852. 8°. . . 3587
Zanoni. E. L. Bulwer. New York, 1842. 2 v. 12°. 1681
Zealand, Tour in, 1802. London, 1805. 12°. 603
Zenobia; or, Fall of Palmyra. W. Ware. New York, 1838. 2 v. 12°. 482
Zimmermann, J. G. On Solitude. London, 1808. 2 v. 12°. . . 1865
Zincali; or, Gypsies of Spain. G. Borrow. Philadelphia, 1844. 8°. . 2124
Zohrab. J. Morier. London, 1837. 12°. 5708
Zoölogical Recreations. W. J. Broderip. Philadelphia, 1845. 12°. . 4411
Zoölogy, Principles of. L. Agassiz and A. A. Gould. Bost. 1848. 12°. 3141
Zschökke, J. H. D. Incidents of Social Life amid the Alps. N.Y. 1844. 12°. 3006
Tales. Trans. by P. Godwin. New York, 1845. 2 v. 12°. . . 2477
Zwingle, U. Life. J. G. Hess. London, 1812. 8°. 2295

ADDENDA.

Abrantes, Duchess d'. Memoirs of Napoleon. N. York, 1854. 2 v. 12°. 6448
Accum, F. Adulterations of Food and Culinary Poisons. Phil. 1820. 18°. 2428
Acts of the Apostles; with Commentary. A. A. Livermore. Bost. 1853. 12°. 6264
Afraja; a Norwegian and Lapland Tale. T. Mügge. Phil. 1854. 12°. . 6301
African Crusoes. Mrs. R. Lee. Philadelphia, 1854. 12°. . . . 6262
Alice Seymour; a Home Tale. Mrs. Grey. Philadelphia, 1854. 8°. . 6001
Allan Breck; a Novel. G. R. Gleig. Philadelphia, 1835. 2 v. 12°. . 4044
Allen, Ethan, and Green Mount. Heroes. H.W. De Puy. Bost. 1853. 12°. 6310
Allen, T. History of London. London, 1830. 4 v. 8°. 6035
American, The True. J. Coe. Concord, 1840. 12°. 3116
Anglo-Saxon Derivatives, Handbook of. New York, 1854. 12°. . . 6329
Anglo-Saxon Root-Words, Handbook of. New York, 1854. 12°. . . 6330
Atlas Historique. A. Le Sage. Paris, n. d. Folio. 3711
*Atlas, New American. H. S. Tanner. Philadelphia, 1823. Folio. . 3704
Astronomy, Letters on. D. Olmsted. New York, 1847. 8°. . . . 3226
Australian Wanderers. Mrs. R. Lee. Philadelphia, 1854. 12°. . . 6263

Bacon, J. Life and Times of Francis I. London, 1830. 2 v. 8°. . . 6444
Bailey, S. Nature, Measures, and Causes of Value. London, 1825. 8°. 6010
Questions for Literary Societies. London, 1823. 8°. . . . 6009
Baines, E. History of the French Revolution of 1789. Phil. 1835. 2 v. 8°. 6436
Barnum, P. T. Autobiography. New York, 1855. 12°. . . . 6355
Bartlett, D. W. Life of Joan of Arc. Auburn, 1854. 12°. . . . 6277
*Bartlett, W. H. Pilgrim Fathers of New England. London, 1853. 8°. 6007
Bayley, J. Confessions of a Converted Infidel. New York, 1854. 12°. . 6302
Bayley, Sir J. Law of Bills of Exchange. Boston, 1826. 8°. . . 6024
Beckett, G. A. à. Comic Blackstone. Philadelphia, 1844. 12°. . . 6323
Beecher, E. Papal Conspiracy Exposed. Boston, 1855. 12°. . . 6351
Bills of Exchange, Law of. Sir J. Bayley. Boston, 1826. 8°. . . 6024
Blue Laws of Connecticut, Code of 1650. Hartford, 1822. 12°. . . 6341
Boaden, J. Life of John Philip Kemble. Philadelphia, 1825. 8°. . . 6437

Bolingbroke, Lord. Works. Philadelphia, 1841. 4 v. 8°. 6031
*Book of Family Crests. London, 1854. 2 v. 12°. 6275
Boston, Description of. C. Shaw. Boston, 1817. 12°. 848
Brewster, Sir D. More Worlds than One. New York, 1854. 12°. . 6299
Popular Treatise on Magnetism. Edinburgh, 1851. 12°. . . 6271
British Pulpit. W. Suddards. New York, 1845. 2 v. 8°. 6019
Brown, J. History and Condition of St. Domingo. Phil. 1837. 2 v. 12°. 3510
Burdell, H. and J. Structure and Diseases of the Teeth. N. Y. 1838. 8°. 4042
*Burke, J. and J. E. General Armory of Heraldry. London, 1853. 8°. 6006
Burlamaqui, J. J. Natural and Political Law. Cambridge, 1807. 2 v. 8°. 6025
Burr, Aaron. Life. S. L. Knapp. New York, 1835. 12°. 6340

Cabin Boy's Story; a Nautical Romance. New York, 1854. 12°. . . 6267
Caldwell, C. Unity of the Human Race. New York, 1830. 12°. . . 925
Carpenter, W. H., and T. S. Arthur. History of Illinois. Phil. 1854. 12°. 6283
History of New Jersey. Philadelphia, 1854. 12°. . . 6284
History of New York. Philadelphia, 1854. 12°. . . 6285
History of Ohio. Philadelphia, 1854. 12°. . . . 6286
History of Pennsylvania. Philadelphia, 1854. 12°. . . 6287
History of Tennessee. Philadelphia, 1854. 12°. . . 6288
History of Vermont. Philadelphia, 1854. 12°. . . . 6289
Catel, C. S. Treatise on Musical Harmony. Boston, 1832. 12°. . . 6338
Caulincourt, A. A. de. Recollections of Napoleon. Lond. 1838. 2 v. 12°. 6339
Chess, Lessons in. W. Lewis. London, 1831. 8°. 6445
Churchyards, Chapters on. Caroline Southey. New York, 1842. 12°. . 3014
City Side; or, Passages from a Pastor's Portfolio. Boston, 1854. . . 6304
Civil Engineering. M. I. Sganzin. Boston, 1827. 8°. 2877
Civilization, What is True. J. Sega. Boston, 1830. 12°. 3371
Coe, J. True American. Concord, 1840. 12°. 3116
Coggeshall, W. T. Easy Warren and his Contemporaries. N. Y. 1854. 12°. 6320
Comic Blackstone. G. A. à Beckett. Philadelphia, 1844. 12°. . . 6323
Congress of Nations, Prize Essays on. Boston, 1840. 8°. 6017
Connecticut, Code of 1650, and the Blue Laws. Hartford, 1822. 12°. . 6351
Constitution of the United States, View of. W. Rawle. Phil. 1829. 8°. 2688
Creation, Mosaic History of. T. Wood. New York, 1831. 8°. . . 4015
Cruikshank, G. Illustrations of Smollett, &c. London, 1832. 12°. . 6344
Cumberland, J. Theatrical Illustrations. London, n. d. 16°. . . 2981
Curtis, Laura J. Now-a-Days. New York, 1854. 12°. 6250

Davy, Sir H. Life. J. A. Paris. London, 1831. 2 v. 8°. 6443
Salmonia; or, Days of Fly-Fishing. London, 1854. 12°. . . 6276
Day, J. On the Will. New Haven, 1838. 12°. 2986
Dead Sea and Bible Lands. F. de Saulcy. Philadelphia, 1854. 2 v. 12°. 6306
De Foe, D. History of the Plague. London, n. d. 24°. 28
De Puy, H. W. Ethan Allen and Green Mount. Heroes. Bost. 1853. 12°. 6310
Drake, S. G. Book of the Indians. Boston, 1836. 8°. 6446

Drake, S. G. Indian Captivities. Boston, 1839. 12°. 6442
Dumont, E. Recollections of Mirabeau. Philadelphia, 1833. 8°. . . 6438
Dunsford, H. Practical Advantages of Homœopathy. Phil. 1842. 12°. 6441
Dwight, Timo. Travels in N. England and N. York. N.Y. 1821. 4 v. 8°. 6034

Easy Warren and his Contemporaries. W. T. Coggeshall. N.Y.1854. 12°. 6320
*Edinburgh Encyclopædia. Phil. 1832. 18 v. text, and 9 v. plates. 4°. . 6450
Ellen de Vere; Sequel to Harry Ashton. J. F. Smith. N. Y. 1854. 8°. 6452
Eloquence of the United States. E. B. Williston. Middlet. 1827. 5 v. 8°. 6030
Elton, C. A. History of the Roman Emperors. London, 1825. 12°. . 3341
Enfield, W. Institutes of Natural Philosophy. Boston, 1811. 4°. . 6026
England, History of. H. Walter. London, n. d. 7 v. 12°. . . . 6021
English Grammar, Elementary. R. G. Latham. New York, 1854. 12°. 6297
English Language, Handbook of. R. G. Latham. New York, 1854. 12°. 6296
Enigmas and Charades. Edinburgh, 1835. 12°. 6321

Fables for the Holy Alliance. T. Moore. London, 1823. 12°. . . . 6342
Faggots for the Fireside. S. G. Goodrich. New York, 1855. 12°. . . 6350
*Family Crests, Book of. London, 1854. 2 v. 12°. 6275
Farrington, Mrs. Sarah P. Ruth Hall. New York, 1855. 12°. . . 6357
Ferguson, A. History of Civil Society. Boston, 1809. 3259
Fielding, H. History of Tom Jones. London, 1831. 2 v. 12°. . . 4253
Works; with Life by A. Murphy. London, 1808. 14 v. 12°. . 6335

Vol. 1. Life; Plays.
2–5. Plays.
6. History of Joseph Andrews.
7–9. History of Tom Jones.
10–11. Amelia.
12. History of Jonathan Wild; Charge to Grand Jury; Causes of the late Increase of Robbers.
13. Journey from this World to the Next; Journal of a Voyage to Lisbon; The True Patriot; The Jacobite's Journal.
14. Covent-Garden Journal; Miscellanies; Index.

Fish Breeding, Artificial. Trans. by W. H. Fry. New York, 1854. 12°. 6328
Fossil Spirit; a Dream of Geology. J. Mill. New York, 1854. 16°. . 6303
Frances I, Life and Times of. J. Bacon. London, 1830. 2 v. 8°. . . 6444
Fred Arden; or, the Jesuit's Revenge. J. F. Smith. New York, 1854. 8°. 6028
French Pronunciation, Philosophy of. G. H. Talbot. N. Y. 1854. 12°. 6282
French Revolution of 1798, History of. E. Baines. Phil. 1835. 2 v. 8°. 6436
Fry, W. H. (Trans.) Artificial Fish Breeding. New York, 1854. 12°. . 6328

Garrick, D. Life. A. Murphy. London, 1801. 2 v. 8°. 6440
Gaskell, Mrs. Moorland Cottage. New York, 1851. 12°. 3799
Gay, J. Poetical Works. London, 1812. 24°. 1467
Geldart, Mrs. T. May Dundas; or, Passages in Young Life. N.Y.1855. 12°. 6318
Gibson, R. Theory and Practice of Surveying. New York, 1821. 8°. . 810
Gil Blas, Histoire de. A. R. Le Sage. Paris, 1818. 4 v. 16°. . . . 6336
Giseke, R. Rose of the Parsonage. Philadelphia, 1854. 12°. . . . 6307

Gleig, G. R. Allan Breck. Philadelphia, 1835. 2 v. 12°. 4044
Goodrich, S. G. Faggots for the Fireside. New York, 1855. 12°. . . 6350
Graham, S. Lecture to Young Men on Chastity. Boston, 1837. 12°. . 1733

Handbook of Anglo-Saxon Derivatives. New York, 1854. 12°. . . . 6329
of Anglo-Saxon Root-Words. New York, 1854. 12°. 6330
Hansard, T. C. Art of Printing. Edinburgh, 1851. 12°. 6270
Heber, R. (Bishop). Life, by his Widow. New York, 1830. 2 v. 8°. . 6032
Higgins, W. M. Philosophy of Sound and Hist. of Music. Lon. 1838. 12°. 6325
Hill, Rowland. Life. E. Sidney. New York, 1834. 12°. 2919
Home Life; a Peep across the Threshold. Mrs. C. A. Soule. Bos. 1854. 12°. 6317
Homœopathy, Practical Advantages of. H. Dunsford. Phil. 1842. 12°. 6441
House on the Rock. Matilda Planché. Boston, 1852. 12°. 6291

Ida May. Mary Langdon. Boston, 1855. 12°. 6352
Ida Norman; or, Trials and their Uses. Mrs. L. Phelps. N.Y. 1854. 12°. 6300
Indian Captivities. S. G. Drake. Boston, 1839. 12°. 6442
Indians, Book of the. S. G. Drake. Boston, 1836. 8°. 6446
Inebriate's Hut. Mrs. S. A. Southworth. Boston, 1855. 12°. . . 6349
Infidel, Confessions of a Converted. J. Bayley. New York, 1854. 12°. . 6302
Inman, W. S. Report on Ventilation, Warming, &c. London, 1836. 8°. 4554
Insurance, Treatise on the Law of. W. Phillips. Boston, 1823. 8°. . 6023
Intellectual Philosophy, Elements of. F. Wayland. Boston, 1854. 12°. 6319

John Bull in America. J. K. Paulding. New York, 1825. 12°. . . 255
Johnson, A. B. Meaning of Words. New York, 1854. 12°. . . 6331

*Kelly, P. Universal Cambist. London, 1821. 2 v. 4°. 6027
Kemble, J. P. Life. J. Boaden. Philadelphia, 1825. 8°. . . . 6437
Knapp, S. L. Life of Aaron Burr. New York, 1835. 12°. 6340
Kœppen, A. L. The World in the Middle Ages. N. Y. 1854. 2 v. 12°. 6305
Koningsmarke. J. K. Paulding. New York, 1823. 2 v. 12°. . . 260

Lamb, C., Final Memorials of. T. N. Talfourd. London, 1848. 2 v. 12°. 6326
Langdon, Mary. Ida May. Boston, 1855. 12°. 6352
Langon, Baron. Napoleon Memoirs. Philadelphia, 1838. 2 v. 12°. . 6337
Last of his Name. E. Perce. New York, 1854. 12°. 6315
Law, Natural and Political. J. Burlamaqui. Cambridge, 1807. 2 v. 8°. 6025
of Bills of Exchange. Sir J. Bayley. Boston, 1826. 8°. . . 6024
of Insurance. W. Phillips. Boston, 1823. 8°. 6023
Leaves from the Tree Igdrasyl. Martha Russell. Boston, 1854. 12°. . 6346
Le Sage, A. Atlas Historique. Paris, n. d. Folio. 3711
Le Sage, A. R. Histoire de Gil Blas. Paris, 1818. 4 v. 16°. . . 6336

Lewis, W. Lessons in Chess. London, 1831. 8°. 6445
London, History of. T. Allen. London, 1830. 4 v. 8°. . . . 6035
Police and Crimes of. London, 1829. 8°. 6018
Louis Philippe, Rise and Fall of. B. P. Poore. Boston, 1848. 12°. . 2422

Martin Merivale. J. T. Trowbridge. Boston, 1855. 12°. . . . 6356
Matilda. E. Sue. New York, 1843. 8°. 2173
May Dundas; a Tale. Mrs. T. Geldart. New York, 1855. 12°. . . 6318
Medical Jurisprudence. M. Ryan. Philadelphia, 1832. 8°. . . . 4553
Memoirs of Celebrated Characters. A. Lamartine. N. Y. 1854. 2 v. 12°. 6314
M'Fingal; an Epic Poem. J. Trumbull. Hallowell, 1813. 16°. . . 1462
Middle and Working Classes, History of. J. Wade. London, 1835. 12°. 2109
Mirabeau, Recollections of. E. Dumont. Philadelphia, 1833. 8°. . . 6438
Moore, T. Fables for the Holy Alliance. London, 1823. 12°. . . 6342
Mosaic History of the Creation. T. Wood. New York, 1831. 8°. . . 4015
Murphy, A. Life of David Garrick. London, 1801. 2 v. 8°. . . 6440
Music, History of, and Philos. of Sound. W. M. Higgins. Lond. 1838. 12°. 6325
Singer's Companion. New York, 1854. 12°. 6345
Treatise on Harmony. C. S. Catel. Boston, 1832. 12°. . . 6338

Napoleon, Memoirs. London, n. d. 2 v. 8°. 6439
Memoirs. Baron Langon. Philadelphia, 1838. 2 v. 12°. . . 6337
Memoirs. Duchess d'Abrantes. New York, 1854. 2 v. 12°. . 6448
Recollections of. A. A. de Caulincourt. London, 1838. 2 v. 12°. 6339
Natural Philosophy, Institutes of. W. Enfield. Boston, 1811. 4°. . 6026
New England and New York, Travels in. T. Dwight. N.Y. 1821. 4 v. 8°. 6034
New York Review. Vols. 1-10. New York, 1837-42. 8°. . . . 6033
News Boy. New York, 1855. 12°. 6353
Newspapers, Bound. —
Advertiser, Daily, 1813-14. Boston.
Advertiser, Tri-Weekly, 1829-30. Boston.
Advertiser, Semi-Weekly, 1845. Boston.
Advertiser, Daily, 1852-53. Boston.
Christian Register, 1823-39. Boston.
Christian Watchman, 1833. Boston.
Christian World, 1843-46. Boston.
Columbian Centinel, 1811. Boston.
Courier, Semi-Weekly, 1845. Boston.
Evening Gazette, 1823-27. Boston.
Globe, Semi-Weekly, 1835-45. Washington.
National Intelligencer, 1812-15. Washington.
New England Galaxy, 1824-27. Boston.
Post, Daily, 1852-53. Boston.
Recorder, 1833. Boston.
Repertory, 1809-11, 1813-14, 1820-27. Boston.
The Times, 1840, 1849. London.

Newspapers, *continued.*
Transcript, 1852–53. Boston.
Tribune, Daily, 1852–53. New York.
Niagara Falls, Guide to. S. De Veaux. Buffalo, 1839. 12°. . . 6343
Nuts to Crack; or, Quips, &c., of Oxford and Cambridge. Phil. 1835. 12°. 6322

Pamphleteer, The. Vols. 1–6. London, 1813–15. 8°. 6022
Papal Conspiracy Exposed. E. Beecher. Boston, 1855. 12°. . . . 6351
Paris, J. A. Life of Sir Humphry Davy. London, 1831. 2 v. 8°. . . 6443
Parlor Magic. Boston, 1838. 16°. 6335
Phillips, W. Treatise on the Law of Insurance. Boston, 1823. 8°. . 6023
Pitkin, T. Statistical View of the United States. New York, 1817. 8°. 3974
Plague, History of the. D. De Foe. London, n. d. 24°. 28
Poetry of Woman; a Collection of Tales. Boston, 1841. 12°. . . 1897
*Portraits of Political Reformers. J. Saunders. London, 1840. Folio. . 6451

Russell, Martha. Leaves from the Tree Igdrasyl. Boston, 1854. 12°. . 6346
Ruth Hall. Mrs. Sarah P. Farrington. New York, 1855. 12°. . . 6357

*Saunders, J. Portraits of Political Reformers. London, 1840. Folio. . 6451
Sigourney, Lydia H. Western Home, and other Poems. Phil. 1854. 12°. 6348
Singer's Companion. New York, 1854. 12°. 6345
Smith, J. F. Ellen de Vere; Sequel to Harry Ashton. N. Y. 1854. 8°. 6452
Southworth, Mrs. S. A. Inebriate's Hut. Boston, 1855. 12°. . . 6349
Swell Life at Sea; or, Fun, Frigates, and Yachting. N. York, 1854. 12°. 6347

*Tanner, H. S. New American Atlas. Philadelphia, 1823. Folio. . 3704
Tefft, B. F. Webster and his Masterpieces. New York, 1855. 2 v. 12°. 6354
Triumphs of Perseverance and Enterprise. New York, 1854. 12°. . . 6332
Trowbridge, J. T. Martin Merivale. Boston, 1855. 12°. . . . 6356

Webster, D., and his Masterpieces. B. F. Tefft. N. York, 1855. 2 v. 12°. 6354
Western Home, and other Poems. Mrs. L. H. Sigourney. Phil. 1854. 12°. 6348

www.ingramcontent.com/pod-product-compliance
Lightning Source LLC
LaVergne TN
LVHW020224110826
845151LV00003B/816

* 9 7 8 1 4 2 5 5 3 2 4 0 6 *